S0-AAE-836

GOLF FOREVER

Edited by Jack Sheehan

Book Design by Edward Horcharik
Copy Editing by Laura Brundige

Cataloguing-in-Publication Data Available

ISBN 1-932173-06-4

06 05 04 03 4 3 2 1

Printed in Hong Kong

A Stephens Media Group Company
PO Box 1600, Las Vegas, Nevada 89125-1600
702-387-5260 / 702-387-2997 Fax

GOLF FOREVER

The Spine and More • A Health Guide to Playing The Game

Jackson T. Stephens & T. Glenn Pait, M.D.

Dedication

I dedicate *Golf Forever* to my dear friend Clifford Roberts. In his lifetime there was no greater patron and supporter of the game of golf.

Also, to my family and my friends and all the men and women who play this wonderful game.

And certainly to the young people in our country–that they might grow up learning to appreciate and love this game for a lifetime. It is our hope that this book will help them learn how to play forever.

Jack Stephens

I wish to express my love and gratitude to my family–my wife Carol and daughters Allyson, Kelly and Kathleen-for their endless support and tolerance of the duties involved with writing this book in addition to a busy surgical clinical practice.

T. Glenn Pait, M.D.

CONTENTS

ACKNOWLEDGEMENTS

Undertaking a project such as writing a book is a task that can never be accomplished by one individual. A multitude of individuals is needed to take an idea through all the stages that ultimately result in a book. Encouragement and support is needed, particularly during difficult moments when the authors find themselves struggling.

Every book needs an individual who truly takes a project, nurses it, and keeps it focused and on track: an individual who brings the team together. It is Craig Campbell to whom the authors are greatly indebted for bringing this team together and keeping them focused. It is Craig who helped put the "brand on this steer."

We are very thankful to Tim Finchem, Commissioner of USGA, for his support in the writing of this book.

There are numerous professional and non-professional golfers whom the authors must acknowledge: Ben Crenshaw, Ken Venturi, Jerry Pate, Curtis Strange, Fred Couples, Davis Love III, Greg Norman, David Duval, Retief Goosen, Hall Sutton, Bernhard Langer, Arnold Palmer, Fuzzy Zoeller, Tom Watson, Kristi Albers, JoAnn Carner, Judy Rankin and Raymond Floyd. We would also like to recognize Larry Mize, PGA, for his contributions and demonstrating conditioning exercises for the spine in Tom Boers' chapter on "Rehabilitation of the Spine." We are also indebted to Sidney L. Matthew, noted golf historian, for his advice, guidance and assistance. We also wish to thank Rand Jerris and Ms. Maxine Vigliota of the United States Golf Association (USGA) Museum and Archives for their assistance in providing hard-to-find photographs.

The authors are greatly indebted to President George H. W. Bush (41st President of the United States), who was kind enough to give his support to this book. We also thank President Bill Clinton for sharing his own golf/back advice.

We are also greatly indebted to our dear friend Don Knotts, known and loved by millions throughout the world for his ability to entertain us all, who is also a good golfer and a lover of the sport.

To the late Sam Snead, we are indebted, as is the world, for his contributions to the sport and for making golf exciting for all of us. He will always be remembered and forever missed.

We are very thankful to Medtronic Sofamor Danek for numerous contributions and encouragement for this project. Medtronic Sofamor Danek developed *Basic Anatomy & Pathology of the Spine,* which is a training book for their sales representatives. Their book on anatomy and pathology was brought to the attention of the authors. This core curriculum for basic spinal training is an excellent textbook. The illustrations by John Marston are outstanding. It became readily apparent that these illustrations would be a great addition to *Golf Forever.* Discussions with Medtronic Sofamor Danek representatives resulted in their permission to use numerous figures in *Golf Forever.* We wish to thank James J. Bindseil, Patient Counsel; Jeri Province, of the Legal Department; Cristie Manuel, eBusiness Marketing; Julio Gallego, M.D.; Anthony T. Schnuerer, P.A.; Laura D. Woods, Graphic Artist, International Marketing; Jennifer June, Administration Assistant, Marketing Communications; and John Thomas and William E. Gaston, Spine Specialists. Medtronic Sofamor Danek is a medical and spinal company, leader in research and development of numerous innovative medical devices, including spinal reconstructive implants (www.medtronic.com.)

We wish to thank DePuy AcroMed, Johnson & Johnson for their contributions of educational illustrations. They are leaders in medical products, research and spinal devices and implants. Their websites, www.allaboutbackpain.com and www.depuyacromed.com, are excellent sources of information for all individuals who have an interest in spinal topics, diagnosis and treatment of spinal diseases. We are particularly thankful to Kristy Davis, Director of eBusiness Strategy; Heather Mickool, Administrative Business Analyst of eBusiness Strategy; Catherine W. Smith, Vice President, Law, DePuy AcroMed, Inc., and Office of General Counsel, Johnson & Johnson Law Department; Hollybeth Normandin; James Cady and Roger Purifoy, Spine Specialists. Many of the outstanding illustrations of DePuy AcroMed, Johnson & Johnson are from the talents of Kevin Marks, MMAA, BA (hons), Creative Director of MARKS *Creative* (www.markscreative.com), Wallington, Surrey, England. Mr. Marks was so kind to provide illustrations for this book, which truly help show individuals the normal spine, as well as the abnormal spine.

One of the most often visited sites on the internet for disorders of the spine is SpineUniverse.com (www.spineuniverse.com). SpineUniverse.com provides educational avenues for all individuals who wish to know more about afflictions of the spine. This is truly an outstanding educational site on the Internet for all golfers, whether they have a spinal problem or not. It became evident that SpineUniverse and their dedicated, educational spine illustrations would highlight *Golf Forever.* After we discussed the golf book project with individuals at SpineUniverse, they were gracious to allow us to share some of their illustrations, which can only benefit and increase the reader's knowledge of spinal diseases. We are very grateful to Tracy Clark, Chief Operating Office; Susan Spinasanta, Manager, Content Development; Mary Clare Walsh, Director, Professional Content Development; the entire Editorial Board; and to the Physicians and the Staff of SpineUniverse.com.

Many individuals from the University of Arkansas for Medical Sciences, Little Rock, Arkansas, provided their talents, guidance, wisdom and encouragement throughout this book project. We are grateful to Chancellor I. Dodd Wilson for his support and encouragement throughout this project. We wish to thank Richard Pierson, Hospital Director, for his permission to use many of the images of radiological equipment. The authors are very grateful to Rudy L. Van Hemert, Jr., M.D., Assistant Professor of Radiology, who provided endless radiological images, MRIs, and CT scans for this book. In addition, we wish to thank Dr. Ernie Ferris, Professor and Chairman of Radiology; Dr. Edgardo J.C. Angtuaco, Professor and Chief of Neuroradiology; Eren Erdem, M.D., Assistant Professor of Radiology; Gary L. Purnell, M.D., Associate Professor of Radiology and Nuclear Medicine Services; Ronald C. Walker, M.D., Assistant Professor of Radiology and Medical Director of PET Center; and James E. McDonald, M.D., Radiology; Leta N. Peterson, R.N., Division Nurse; Arch L. Bullock, Jr., R.T.; Thomas E. Myrick, R.T., Barbara Jo Varnon, R.T., R.T.(N.), C.N.M.T., Operating Room Radiology; Dianne N. Daughhetee, R.T.; Phillip Taylor, P.A.C.S.; and to Patty L. White, for her assistance in Bone Densitometry.

Dr. Hugo E.R. Jason, Director, Rheumatology & Immunology Division, provided many pictures of arthritic disorders; we thank him. We also wish to recognize Dr. Stavros Manolagas, Director, Immunology & Metabolism Division, for his contributions to the Osteoporosis chapter; R. Lee Archer, M.D., Neurology, and Arlyn Howard, R.N., Clinical Neurosurgery, for their physical examination demonstration. We are also grateful to E. Brian Russell, M.D., Sports Dermatology, for his contributions. We wish to thank Dr. Mike Griffey, Orthopaedic Surgery; Amy Theriac, Medical Photographer; Tracy Turner and Diana McCray, Photographer; Deborah Fewell, L.P.N., EMG Tech; and Heather Hanley, R.T., EEG, for their assistance. We also wish to recognize Drs. Kenan Arnautovic and Victor G. Williams for their help.

For the Physical Medicine & Rehabilitation department, we are especially grateful to William C. Rogers, P.T., C.W.F., Manager, Outpatient Rehab Therapy, who provided guidance and photographs, and to the staff, including Iain J. Cameron, P.T., Felantra Frazier and Betty L. Stephens. We also wish to thank Paul Creel, Hand Therapist, and his staff for their help with hand therapy and rehabilitation.

We wish to thank Hitachi Medical Systems America, Inc. for their contributions of open MRI photographs. We wish to recognize Sheldon Schaffer, Vice President & General Manager, Magnetic Resonance, and Vicki Lock, Marketing Communications Specialist, for their assistance.

We are grateful to Kyphon, Inc., (www.kyphon.com) for their photographic contributions to the Osteoporosis chapter. We wish to recognize Ben Murdock for his assistance.

Many individuals from the Augusta National Golf Club contributed encouragement and advice. We especially wish to thank William W. "Hootie"Johnson, David Spencer and Bob Kletock, Professionals at Augusta, and Barbara Spencer, Archivist.

Other individuals who should be noted and thanked include Scott Chiarizzio, Spine Specialist, AESCULAP.; Lynn McCullough, R.N., Arkansas Spine Center, P.A.; Teresa Jones, Orthopaedic Specialist; and Joan Gatewood, Administrative Assistant, Human Performance & Rehabilitation Center, Columbus, Georgia; as well as James Terry, Carlos Arrington, and Barry Daniels, who were always around and provided services beyond the call of duty. We are also very thankful to Bobby Partee and Porter Puckett for their typing skills and to Cecilia Hallman for her dedication and assistance with this book. We would also like to thank Bernice Ramsey for her encouragement.

We recognize the individuals who work with one of the authors (TGP) on a daily basis. To Kim M. Vognet, R.N., Neurosurgery and Spine, we are thankful for her administrative support and data gathering throughout this project. And special thanks go to Betty J. Patterson, the individual who spent as many hours as the authors in putting this book to final completion, for without her, the project could never have moved along in such a smooth fashion. We only hope that her sanity has survived this book.

The authors are also greatly indebted to Thomas Mitchell, Editor-in-Chief, *Las Vegas Review-Journal,* Stephens Media Group, who, upon hearing of this project, gave advice and guidance and agreed that this project was worth publishing. We wish to thank our publisher, Carolyn Hayes Uber, President, Stephens Press, LLC, for her advice, work, encouragement and contributions. We also wish to thank Laura Brundige, Copy Editor and Phillip Hayes, Production Manager, Stephens Press, for their involvement and hours of work on the book.

Our thanks to Jack Sheehan for his dedication, encouragement, and always available advice throughout the writing of this book. We greatly appreciate his editorship and productive criticism. He is to be commended for his enduring ability to deal with the unpredictable schedules of the authors.

And finally, all of the authors wish to thank their families and the many friends, too numerous to name, for their encouragement and daily inquiries about the book.

INTRODUCTION

Jack Stephens

While golf is an honorable and ancient sport, and its traditions are cherished by all of us who love the game, we must also accept that the sport is rapidly evolving. Golf has become so popular, and the monetary rewards for its champions so pronounced, that science and technology are playing an ever-increasing role in the way the game is played.

Debate rages on about the limits that should be imposed on club and ball manufacturers, and golf course architects today face concerns about their finest work's becoming outdated. While I'm confident that common sense and respect for the history of the game will dictate these matters, I am concerned that there is not enough focus on what the human body and mind can achieve. This book is designed to help golfers of all ability levels: beginners, weekend duffers, club champions, and beyond, to appreciate that their very best chance of enjoying this great game for a lifetime is to have a deeper understanding of their own bodies and how they work in the game of golf.

In my 40 years as a member of Augusta National, and my eight years presiding over the presentation of the Masters green jacket in the Butler Cabin, I have been privileged to watch the game played at its highest level and by its greatest champions. I have the utmost admiration for the rare combinations of skills required to claim the title of Masters champion: the strength, the touch, the ability to harness emotion and control nerves. These are traits that all champions have in common. But I have also noticed through the years how the body shapes of golf's greatest players have changed.

Today's top golfers are a leaner, hungrier lot than champions of years past. They pay far more attention nowadays to diet, conditioning, and general off-course activities than some of our colorful champions of the past.

Jackie Burke Jr., our Masters champion in 1956, remarked not long ago: "These kids today all have golf psychologists. Well, Jimmy Demaret and I had our own psychologist that we met after nearly every round. He was always waiting for us in the 19th hole, and his name was Jack Daniels."

Not only will you not find today's great young players like Tiger Woods, Sergio Garcia, and Charles Howell III in the bar after a round, they have in fact redefined the so-called 19th hole. They recognize that the first 30 minutes after a competitive round is far better spent cooling down, letting the body and mind relax after the rigors of a four-hour physical and mental workout. You would more likely find the new wave of champions in the fitness trailer, or sharpening their skills on the practice green, or on the driving range tweaking something in their technique that they felt needed more work before the next day's round. And the fluid these young men put in their bodies is far more likely to be water or a replacement sport drink than something that requires proof of age.

It is no secret that Tiger's influence on the game has been immense since he started breaking records as a teenager. He has alluded often to the greatness of Jack Nicklaus and how Jack's 18 major championships are the benchmark that drives him forward. Tiger's work with Butch Harmon and a personal trainer from Las Vegas, Dr. Keith Kleven, has a twofold purpose: to keep him swinging the golf club with maximum efficiency and effectiveness, and to keep his body conditioned to create peak performance with minimum risk of injury. Each year Tiger sets not only golfing goals, but physical strength and flexibility and agility goals—how much weight he can bench press or push on a leg machine, or how high he can jump. Tiger understands that to approach or pass Nicklaus' records, he must keep his body—his machine—operating at peak performance.

And that is a lesson that can be learned by all of us who play golf, regardless of our age or physical limitations. Our most important accessory in playing our best golf is not the newest high compression golf ball, or the latest large-headed driver with the most technologically advanced materials in its shaft. It's our own body.

It is critical that we understand what we can do with our own bodies, and to acknowledge our limitations. While we all may envy John Daly's ability to fly a golf ball over 300 yards with a swing that covers a nearly 360-degree arch, he is unique in his ability to do that. Nor can most of us make the full-shoulder turn of a Freddie Couples without ending up wearing a back brace. But we can make certain that our body weight is more carefully watched and controlled, we can do some simple stretching exercises before we go to the driving range or golf course, and we can prevent unnecessary injuries by being careful how we lift our golf bags out of our car trunks.

We have endeavored in *Golf Forever* to provide a wealth of practical information and medical advice pertinent to the game so that all my wonderful friends who share a common passion for golf can enjoy this game throughout their lives.

Jack Stephens

AN OVERVIEW OF GOLF INJURIES

CHAPTER 1

T. Glenn Pait, M.D., F.A.C.S.

I've been very fortunate so far in my career because I've not had a situation where a back problem has prevented me from playing. But as one grows older the care and maintenance of muscles surrounding the spine must be looked at, especially the lower back.

Ben Crenshaw

Golf is usually not considered to be a strenuous and physically demanding sport. In fact, it was once thought to be more of a game than a true sport. Many golfers still may not appreciate the fact that golf is indeed a truly demanding sport. It may take a while for them to feel the wear and tear on their bodies, but eventually the aches and pains associated with playing a sport will announce themselves.

Golf is not entirely a benign or safe sport. Over the years there have been some unusual injuries brought about by playing golf. One case involved a very excited gentleman who threw his putter into the air, hitting his partner in the head, knocking him out and causing a closed head injury. Another situation was one of a woman who was *so* excited about making a very long putt that she jumped up and down, throwing her arms up in the air. Unaware of where her golf bag was located, she fell over the bag and broke both of her wrists. In another situation, a disgruntled golfer was upset with his playing ability on a particular day. What he didn't realize was that it would be his last day ever to play golf. He threw his club against a tree, causing the shaft to break. The shaft then hit another tree and rebounded into the path of the golfer. The broken shaft plunged into his body, causing his death. Finally, there was a situation where the golfer missed a shot. He swung his club in anger, unfortunately killing his caddie. He was convicted of involuntary manslaughter. These are just a few unusual examples to demonstrate that golf *can* be a hazardous sport. These frivolous examples notwithstanding, golf can be a rigorous sport. The demands that golf places on an individual's body must be taken seriously. A golf swing involves a significant rotatory torque of the body with a wide range of motion at very high speeds. Doing this over and over again can lead to problems, particularly if the golfer is unprepared.

Touring golf professionals sustain an average of two injuries per year. While playing this highly competitive sport, a professional is constantly practicing, refining, and modifying his or her techniques, all of which can cause injuries. In fact, repetitive practice swings are the most common mechanisms of injury among professionals, amateurs, and weekend golfers. Golf is a demanding sport that takes great skill to play well. Such skill is achieved by practicing on a frequent basis. It's the prolonged practice sessions that may cause injuries to the musculoskeletal system due to poor conditioning, not exercising regularly, and a poor swing technique. These are all things that any golfer can remedy. They can improve golfing skills and decrease chances of injury. Professional male golfers suffer most commonly from lower back problems. The next most common injury for professional golfers involves the wrist and shoulder. Female professional golfers, on the other hand, are more likely to suffer from wrist problems and then back problems (Table 1). It is the lead arm that is most commonly involved in injuries (for the right-handed golfer that would be the left arm), while the incidents of injuries to the non-leading arm are quite low.

Table 1 Professional Golfer Injury Site

Men	Women
Low Back	Wrist
Wrist	Low Back
Shoulder	Shoulder
Elbow	Elbow
Knees	Knees

Table | 2 Amateur Golfer Injury Site

Men	Women
Low Back	Elbow
Elbow	Low Back
Wrist	Shoulder
Shoulder	Wrist
Knees	Knees

Not surprisingly, for the male amateur and weekend golfer the lower back is the site most often involved in injury. The next most common problems involve the elbow, then the wrist, the shoulder, and finally the knees. For the amateur lady golfer it is the elbow, followed by her low back, shoulders, wrists, and finally the knees (Table 2). Again, these injuries are most often the result of a poor swinging mechanism. Most of the injuries occur at or near the time of impact. As the club nears its target, it may be traveling at speeds in excess of 100 miles per hour (161 km per hour). The sudden hitting of the ball will cause a sudden deceleration that brings about a great deal of stress on the body. Such stress is being felt by millions of people playing golf, and more players are entering the sport each year. Some 75% of players will sustain at least one injury from golf. Individuals between the ages of 30 to 50 years will experience an injury about every three years. The maturing (aging) process increases the injury rate significantly. For the 50 year-old golfer, and up, the injury rate is an astounding 65%. Golfers less than 50 years of age have about a 58% injury rate. These statistics demonstrate that an awful lot of golfers are simply not ready to play the game. Unfortunately, the unprepared injury victim will lose about 5–6 weeks of playing time per year due to injuries. If golfers want to play better and more golf, they must get in shape, stay in good condition and learn better techniques. Their spines and bodies will thank them.

Physical inactivity is often associated with a loss of strength of the neck, upper back, and low back muscles. If a golfer is not adequately physically conditioned, he or she has an increased chance of developing neck and low back problems, which will have a negative impact on his or her game. The outcome will be seen on the scorecard. Individuals who frequently play sports are at risk of experiencing an overuse syndrome, brought about by strenuous muscle movements. Sports-related neck and back pain account for many of the referrals to physicians and healthcare providers caring for spine problems. If a golfer has a history of spinal problems such as back pain and performs only a short warm-up, the attempt to prepare the muscles for play may not be adequate. In fact, just performing a short warm-up for 6–8 minutes will not help prevent the reoccurrence of a back problem. All golfers must have an adequate warm-up. If an individual has a history of spine problems, it is a fairly good predictor that he or she may have recurrent back problems in the future. If a golfer has such a history, it is important that measures be taken to prevent the occurrence of pain. For newcomers the chance of golf related back problems is between 5%–8%.

To be fair, golf may not be the cause of all spine problems on the course. Players may need to take a close look at themselves when not on the golf course. What are they doing when they're not playing golf? A golfer should evaluate his or her activities, movements and posture at work and at home. Golf may aggravate problems that began elsewhere. Recurrent pain while golfing is strongly influenced by the type of previous spine or back disorder. The more frequent and severe the previous pain, the greater the chance of recurring troubles. If a golfer is playing another type of sport, such as tennis, he or she will have a higher lifetime incidence of spinal problems, particularly low back problems. If he or she stops playing the other sport, the chances for spinal problems decrease as compared to those who continue to engage in multiple sporting activities. Golfers who engage in other sporting activities increase their chances of having sports-related discomfort or pain when compared to those players who play only golf. Other sports involving strenuous activities, strange postures and funny movements have the potential to cause problems, including spinal problems. If a golfer is serious about golf forever, he or she may want to rethink playing the other sports. Eventually the golfer will have to choose.

Once a golfer has decided to golf forever, he should strongly consider joining a local fitness center. The center should have trainers who understand the physical demands of golf and can start a golfer on a golf-conditioning program. Golfers who exercise on a regular basis and are physically prepared for the challenges of the game have fewer risks of sustaining an injury. Another benefit of a golf-conditioning program is that golfers who exercise improve their handicaps faster than those who do not exercise. Golfers who are dedicated to playing golf forever must recognize the importance of a conditioning and exercise program. They must not only practice their golf techniques, but their exercises as well. There is an appropriate exercise program for golfers of all ages and with different medical and spinal problems. They need to discuss their golfing desires with their doctors or health providers, physical therapists, trainers and golf professionals. It's never too late for an active golfer to start a beneficial health-improving exercise problem.

An often overlooked aspect of golfing is the need for adequate sleep the night before playing. Good sleep helps an individual stay healthy and improves mental skills, which every golfer needs on the course. No one knows for sure why we sleep or need sleep. Sleep patterns vary significantly between individuals. Sleep amounts and needs change throughout our lives. Newborns sleep the most. Babies sleep between 17 and 18 hours a day. They just don't sleep when their parents want them to sleep. By age 4 or 5, children sleep approximately 10 to 12 hours a day. Near age 10, the average sleep time falls to around 10 hours a night. The average young adults need some 8 hours of sleep a night to function well throughout the day. Some may get by with less sleep and others will need more. As we mature, we require less sleep than in young adulthood. Most adults need 7 to 9 hours of sleep a night to function optimally during their waking hours. Mature (elderly) individuals tend to sleep less and their sleep is often more easily interrupted. Most golfers probably know how much sleep they need in an average night to feel their best. However many mature golfers complain about sleep problems, not realizing that their behavior is usually quite normal for their life stage. They should not get into a vicious cycle of worrying about a lack of sleep. If an individual's brain and body needs sleep, he or she will grab the needed sleep. An individual should not immediately turn to sleeping pills as the answer. If sleep becomes a problem and the lack of it interferes with daily activities, a physician should be consulted. There are numerous types of sleep disorders, and further medical evaluation and testing will be needed to help find and treat the cause. Playing a round of golf half-awake increases the risk of injuries and certainly takes the pleasure out of the game. It's also a quick way to lose playing partners, and marshals tend to be less tolerant of sleeping players. The bottom line is: always get "your" amount of sleep before playing.

BODY CHANGES THAT OCCUR WITH MATURING

CHAPTER 2

Jackson T. Stephens and T. Glenn Pait, M.D.

I could go into a long dissertation about my back. In 1961 I was in an automobile accident. I was a passenger and was hit broadside and went into the worse slump you could imagine. Because of contract obligations I tried to play and my game got worse and I hit rock bottom. It took me two years to come out of that slump, but it was worth it because 1964 was a wonderful year.

But there's a story from that year that I always recall whenever the subject of bad backs comes up. I had won the U.S. Open and Hartford Open already that year, and I was leading the American Golf Classic going into the last round. I was paired with Bill Collins and on the practice tee he threw out his back. So here I was leading the tournament, and it was the only time I can ever remember playing and having to pick two balls out of the cup on every hole. Bill couldn't even bend over, so he would make his putt, I'd pick it out of the hole, hand it to him, and ask him to step aside while I made mine. Somehow I went on to win, but I think my own back was sore by the end of the day from all that bending over.

Ken Venturi

We are all maturing. That's a polite way of saying that we are all aging (perhaps some more gracefully than others). Our aging population is perhaps the single most important demographic change that will have a major effect on society. In fact the over-85 age group is the fastest growing segment of the population in the industrialized world. Today in the United States there are 76 million people age 50 or older. They make up about 28% of the total population. In only a decade there will be 96 million people in the over-50 age group (32% of the population).

The life expectancy for men and women has risen over the last 100 years. This is due to advancements in medicine and surgery, better nutrition, environmental improvements at home and work, increased educational opportunities, and more leisure time. In 1900, individuals could only expect to live to be about 45. Today, at age 65, men can anticipate to live another 14 or more years. Women can look forward to 18 more years of life. Even 85 year-old men and women will have some 7 to 9 years of living ahead of them. What we want is to have our retirement years filled with good health. There is no single formula to ensure that we will indeed have our good health when we retire. However, there are good health habits that we are never too old to begin.

One important habit is to make sure that you see your doctor or healthcare provider on a regular basis. Preventive medicine is a major key for good health. Development of new diagnostic tests and medications will allow early treatments of health-compromising diseases. Refinements of surgical techniques and earlier physical therapy and rehabilitation treatments will provide avenues to return to normal daily activities and golfing sooner. The ability to quickly communicate the latest updates in medical health information through radio, television and the internet will provide better educational opportunities to understand our bodies in times of good and bad health. Better understanding of health problems is an important way to prevent them.

Today, women are assuming a greater importance in the older population than ever before. The answer to this is quite simple; there are more women than men. Among those between the ages of 50–54, there are 95 men for every 100 women. As we move into our seventh and eighth decades, there are only 41 men for 100 women. As we mature, we all value our freedom. In fact, among people 80 years of age or older, some 52% now live alone. This number will only increase.

One of the biggest factors that will allow the aging population to continue to grow is improvement in educational levels. Among people over 75 years of age, approximately 62% completed high school. 86% of individuals between the ages of 50 to 54 years have high school diplomas. Higher levels of education will allow many individuals to pursue other areas of satisfaction after retirement. Some will continue to work either in paid occupations or volunteer positions. They will look for leisure activities, such as golf. There is no doubt that the aging populations, particularly the Baby Boomers, are better educated and more materialistic than were their parents.

This new maturing population, known as the Baby Boomers, is the first generation to be influenced by mass marketing and advertising campaigns. They are the first generation to travel frequently for job advancements. They have left hometowns and sought their fortunes elsewhere. They have developed important skills that have made them a wealthier generation. This new, maturing Baby Boomer generation is the first generation to truly challenge aging. Remaining youthful is a major concern of this generation. The Baby Boomers intend to stay around for a long time. They want to work and play longer than their forefathers. It has been projected by the U.S. Census Bureau that by the year 2010 more than half of all Americans will be older than 35, and 25% of the population will be over 55 years of age.

A great deal of medical research is directed towards preventing aging and allowing an individual to live a longer, more productive, and satisfying life. In one study after another, it has been shown that exercise is the key to reducing premature mortality from such diseases as strokes, hypertension, diabetes mellitus, and coronary artery disease. Exercise can significantly slow down age-associated declines in vasometabolic rate and can enhance maximal aerobic capacity in middle-aged individuals and older adults. Exercising can benefit numerous organ systems in our bodies. Sadly, there is only a 30% chance that an average individual will exercise regularly. Some 300,000 deaths could be prevented annually with regular exercise (three times a week). Exercise is an important factor for better health and a longer golf life.

The musculoskeletal system will benefit greatly from a regular exercise program by reduction in age-related bone loss. Exercise will help to maintain and increase muscle mass, which will improve overall muscle strength as well as neuromuscular coordination. There is no single pharmacologic agent that can hold greater promise of bringing about better health and promoting sought-after personal independence than regular exercise. Exercises should be incorporated into all golfers' daily activities, especially before and after play. The 19th hole should entail exercises and water replacement.

Good muscle health plays an important part in the game of golf. Muscle strength peaks at about the age of 30 and begins to decline shortly after the age of 50. It is alarming to realize that muscle mass and muscle strength, without some type of exercise, will decline approximately 15% per decade between the ages of 50 and 70. It will continue to decline by some 30% after the age of 70. If we are not using and exercising muscles, atrophy will start, which is visible by a reduction of muscle size. As we continue to age and do not exercise, there is progressive loss of muscle and tendon flexibility. When both of these decline, it will lead to a restriction of joint motion, and when joints lose their movements, they become more susceptible to injury.

As we age and lose musculoskeletal function, we will become weaker. We will develop more pains with movements and immobility will bring about changes in soft tissues. These changes will particularly be felt in joints, tendons, and ligaments.

Somewhere in middle age, most of us will notice a progressive loss of strength. Between the ages of 30 and 80, the strength of muscle groups in the arms, the back and the legs will decrease as much as 60%. This loss of muscle mass results from a decrease in the number and size of individual muscle cells. Such muscle cell loss starts at about age 25. At this age, the skeletal muscle mass begins to decline at an average of 4% per decade until the age of 50. After the age of 50, muscle mass decreases at about 10% per decade. Any golfer is concerned about muscle strength and power, all of which is provided by muscles. As we mature, muscles lose their elasticity and power. Fibrous tissue in the muscles increases. This tissue merely fills in, almost like scar tissue, and therein decreases the muscle fibers. With a decrease in muscle fibers comes a decrease in muscular contractions, which translates into less muscle power.

These changes start gradually in our late 20s and increase at a faster pace after the age of 50. With continued aging, the muscle is further replaced by fat. So what does all this mean? Simply that with aging, we have a more difficult time maintaining how we work, play and look.

Our body shapes all change. Mature golfers don't look the same as they did at 16. Our physical stamina is reduced and our athletic ability decreases. We often joke about how our derrieres become less firm and develop a suburban spread. Our waistlines expand and soon our bellies develop a bulge. Our arms, legs, and necks begin to get a little wrinkly, but this is no reason to despair. The phenomenon of aging happens to all of us and it's merely that wonderful process of maturing. It is a natural process that the passing years will take away much of our muscular prowess and our form. Most of us will accept the fact that we cannot expect at 60 to be in the same physical and psychological shape as when we were 20. What we need to do as we age is readjust our thermostats. This means that our activities, particularly golf, must be modified to fit our years. But you can keep your body in good shape for your age. Just don't try to be 20 when you're 60; you don't have the physiological reserves to do so. So think of yourself as being in good shape for your age. And this can be validated when we do something about our conditioning.

Many individuals live a far more sedentary lifestyle than nature intended. This inactivity promotes an acceleration of the aging process. Soon they're overweight, frumpy, and very deconditioned. A key element to staying in good shape and maintaining the body's thermostat at the appropriate age is to become physically active. It's important to developement a regular exercise plan and a sensible but not extreme diet. The bottom line is that any individual is never too old to be in better shape.

An individual should not try to make up for inactivity with only weekend athleticism. He or she needs to consult a doctor or healthcare provider about beginning an exercise program. It's important that the program is tailored to match an individual's ability and health history. There are two types of aging: one is chronological (the number of birthdays); the other is biological (more a reflection of how well we've maintained our bodies). Some individuals may be 45 years old, but their organs resemble the organs of much older individuals. There are some 50 year-old individuals who look like they're 70; on the other hand, there are golfers in their 70's who look like 50 year-old players. Why? No doubt genetic inheritance plays a part in the aging process; however, lifestyles influence the process. Some 70 year-olds, after a one-year age-specific exercise program, have the biological age of individuals much younger than 70. In fact, they nearly have a biological age of 40.

There is no question that aging will increase body fat. It doesn't matter what condition you're in, even if you exercise every day, fat will replace muscle. However, much of that middle age spread has very little to do with biological aging. Most of it deals with overindulgence, a sedentary lifestyle, and just ignoring the need to exercise. This battle of the bulge usually starts in middle age. When we were young, we played, ran, jumped, and enjoyed the great outdoors much more than is possible as working individuals. But here's something to think about. As we grow older, our caloric needs also diminish. When we're younger, between 18 and 35 years of age, we require some 2000 calories per day; however, between 35 and 55, our demands will drop to about 1850 a day, and after 55 down to 1700 calories a day. Therefore, if you're over 55 and still eat as if you were 25 and haven't changed your physical activity, you probably have some unwanted pounds.

The best way to deal with the battle of the bulge and unwanted pounds is prevention. Reign in your appetite, don't overindulge, and avoid snacking and nibbling. And implement exercising. Even at work there are simple ways to think about exercising. For instance, you may want to avoid taking the elevator up and down. A nice slow walk in the stairwell might be preferable for toning the legs and providing aerobic benefit. Another consideration could be parking your car a little farther away from your destination. It's like the "new car" principle. Anyone who has bought a new car will park "miles" from the store in a large parking lot. Anything to avoid that first ding in the door or chip in the paint. Continuing the "new car" principle provides some degree of physical activity. It's important to never underestimate the importance of exercise in slowing the aging process. A sedentary lifestyle and unwanted excess pounds can mount up to health problems in the future. Being overweight increases the risks of heart disease, diabetes, spinal problems, kidney and liver diseases, stroke and other ailments. Being out of shape will make you more prone to accidents, and all these problems will affect, if not cripple, your golf game. And remember, eating in a responsible fashion will literally add years to your life, and years to your golfing life. Eating between 5 and 6 servings daily of fresh fruits and vegetables will promote good health and extend your lifespan.

Our cardiopulmonary system, the heart and lungs, also changes as we age. Our maximum oxygen utilization declines by about 5–15% per decade after the age of 25. An exercise program can help reduce the rate of oxygen decline by almost 50%. Regular exercise will increase maximum oxygen uptake, which can continue well into our 70s.

An active lifestyle is extremely important for the preservation of healthy body functions. The ability to continue to play "golf forever" is the goal of every golfer. Understanding some of the aging changes occurring within our bodies may allow us to influence how rapidly some of them occur.

SPINE CHANGES WITH AGING

Aging changes in the spine are referred to as degenerative changes. Often, a radiologist, after reading an X-ray, will report the findings as degenerative changes. These are not necessarily abnormal or pathological changes. If they are not causing problems, these degenerative changes are considered to be part of the normal maturing or aging processes of the spine. These changes are due to biochemical and biomechanical changes in our bodies. The exact reasons these changes come about are not totally understood. However, there are theories to explain them. The first theory is called the **developmental theory.** We age because the embryonic or cellular tissue just fails. As with anything, it gives out, all occurring at the cellular level. The second theory is **genetics**. Genes that are responsible for maintaining a cellular steady state energy level just get tired. They fail to do their jobs. When this happens, we age. The final theory is the **vascular theory**. If nutrient and oxygen-laden blood does not travel to an organ, its cellular structures change. The changes cause aging. The bottom line is that probably all the above theories are responsible to some degree for aging changes.

FIRST DECADE OF LIFE

In the first ten years of life, the elements in the spine look good. The intervertebral discs are normal height. They are filled with adequate water and proteins. Discs are able to do their jobs, which is to produce a hydrostatic load-bearing structure that is able to withstand all kinds of stresses and strains. During the first ten years of life, we put our spines through an awful lot of wear and tear. In fact, we rarely think about any type of spine care or hygiene in the first ten years of life. Good spine care is the furthest thing from our minds at that age. The discs are able to convert axial loads, the pressure of

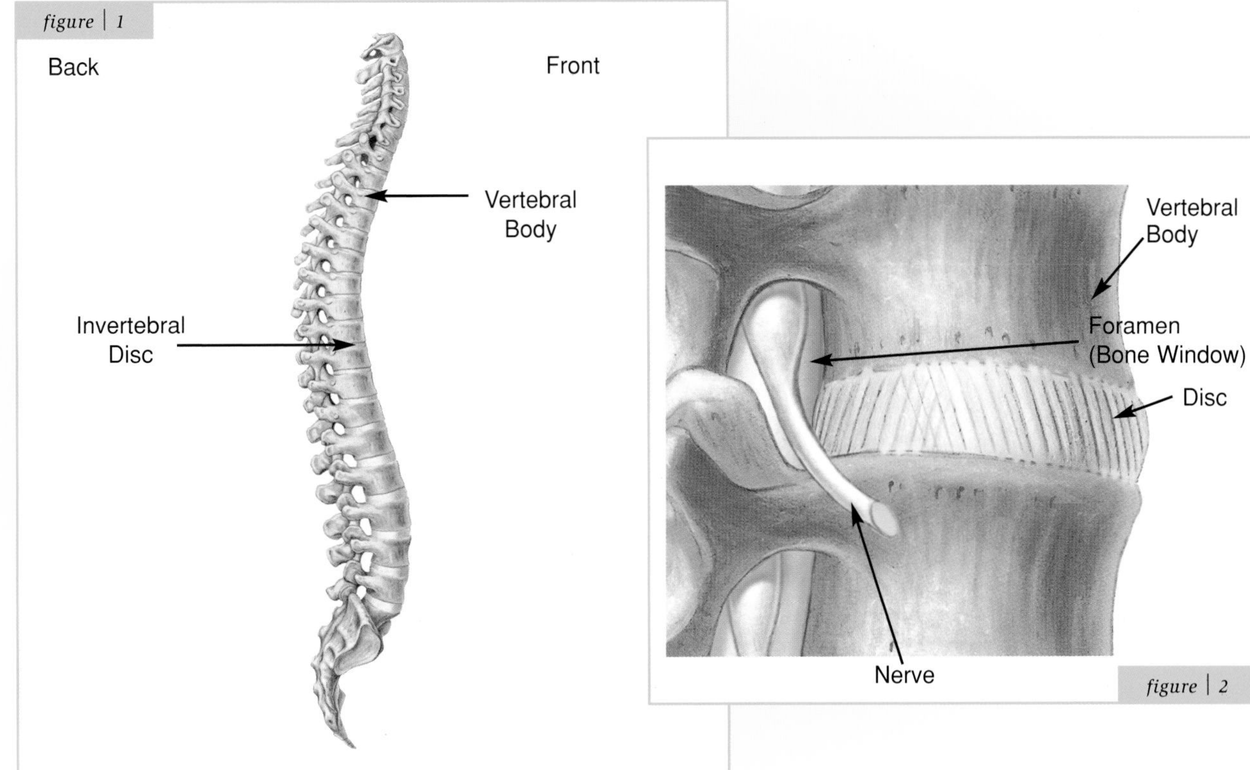

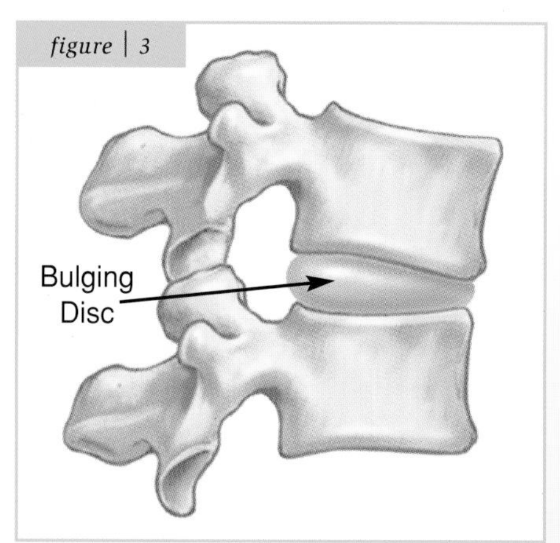

figure | 3

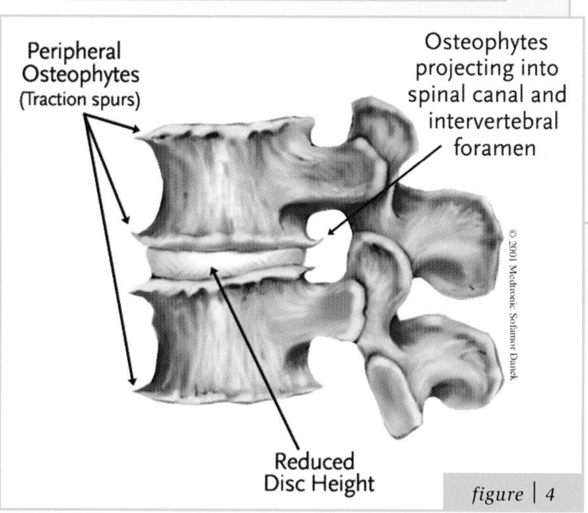

figure | 4

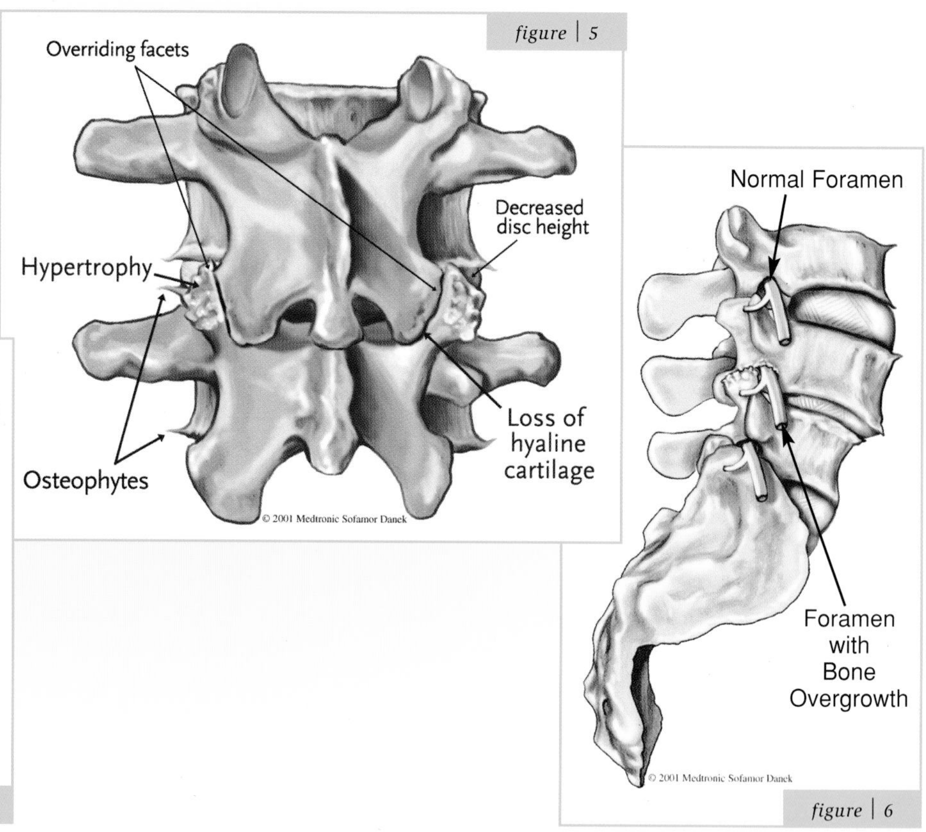

figure | 5

figure | 6

standing, into tensile strain that is transferred to the annular fibers and the vertebral body endplates. The individual vertebral bodies in the spine are almost all nearly square and strong (Fig. 1). The joints are all filled with healthy fluid. The intervertebral foramen, bone windows, are without impediments as nerves course through them (Fig. 2). There is ample space inside the spinal canal for the spinal chord. All is well with the spine.

SECOND DECADE

In the second decade of life, spine changes begin to occur. The discs begin to take on another appearance. They may begin to bulge or protrude (Fig. 3). A good way to think about disc changes is to think of a balloon. When the balloon is filled with water, it begins to sag. In fact, in the second decade of life, many of us begin to sag in places we would prefer not to. The joints that we used with abandon in that carefree first decade begin to demonstrate wear and tear, becoming asymmetric, which means that they are not alike on both sides. They take on different configurations and begin to enlarge from all of the wear and tear. Changes are evident in x-rays, but in most cases do not produce any major problems. We continue to do what we would normally do. Trauma and repetitive activity accelerate the aging process and, for some, trauma and repetitive activity may include golf. That's why it is important for golfers to get regular medical check-ups and undergo good spine evaluations, even if they're not having any problems. Smoking and use of tobacco products can add 7–10 years to a golfer's general medical and spine health. Good spine health includes reducing and finally stopping the use of all tobacco products, both smoke and smokeless.

THIRD TO FIFTH DECADES OF LIFE

The changes in the third through fifth decades of life are now much more pronounced. The vertebral bodies begin to lose height; they are not as tall as they used to be. The intervertebral disc height has also decreased. Due to the decrease in disc height, adjacent bones begin to approach each other. The loss of bone height results in less room in the foraminae, bone windows, for exiting nerve roots. Such loss may bring about the formation of bone spurs or osteophytes (Fig. 4). The joints, too, have changed. The joint capsules are no longer filled with healthy synovial fluid, and the joints begin to thicken with bony overgrowth. These joint and bone changes are called osteoarthritis. The overgrowth of bone in the joints will reduce the room in the foramen (Fig. 5). With continued bone growth the nerve can become squeezed or pinched as it is exiting the bone window of the spinal canal. A pinched nerve causes pain. Finally, the ligamentum flava, a thick spinal ligament, gets thicker. These changes of aging are most pronounced in the cervical (neck) and the lumbar (lower) spine. We often think that the loss of height as we age is due to a loss of the discs and their water content. Surprisingly, that's not the case. It's actually loss of height of the vertebral bodies. All of these changes to the discs and bones are associated with fewer movements in the spine segments. The joints and bones are just not able to move the way they used to. As the discs age, they are less able to do their jobs. In fact, they often become incompetent. If they are unable to do their jobs, this may cause a slippage or a sliding of one bone or vertebra onto another. This is referred to as degenerative **spondylolisthesis**. The slippage is an abnormal type of movement, which will lead to bone spur formation. These bone spurs are often called traction spurs and are frequently associated with encroachment on exiting nerves (Fig. 6). Such encroachment, over a period of time, may cause symptoms, which often include pain and numbness or tingling in the arms or legs.

POSTURAL CHANGES OF A MATURING SPINE

Physiological changes of the aging spine will cause postural alterations. Such alterations will bring about changes in the normal alignment of the spine. The normal spinal curvatures are the way the spine is able to unload some of the pressures from the joints. We can see this happening to our spines when we stand in a more flexed (bent forward) posture, rather than a more extended one. When we are flexed over, there is more room for all of our neural elements exiting from the foramina. If we extend our back, leaning backwards, the foraminae (bone windows) are closed or narrowed, which may cause discomfort in some individuals. Many of the changes associated with maturing or aging are best appreciated in the neck and low back. For the most part, the changes occur in the neck at C5–C6, C6–C7. In the lumbar spine (low back), the changes occur at the L4–L5 space, the L3–L4 space and the L5–S1 space, respectively.

BIOCHEMICAL CHANGES OF A MATURING SPINE

Biochemical changes occur throughout the spine. The earliest changes occur in the intervertebral discs. In a young adult, the nucleus pulposus (inside gel of the disc) contains about 85% water and the annulus fibrosus (outside disc layer) has about 78% water content. With age, the water content falls to about 70%; this will lead to a decrease in the pressure inside the discs (Fig. 7). These changes gradually occur between the ages of 30 and 80. Discs lose the ability to imbibe water. During sleep, discs take up nutrients and water; therefore when you wake up in the morning, you are actually taller, sometimes by as much as one inch (2.5 cm.) (Fig. 8). In fact, if you eliminate gravity all together, as in outer space, astronauts are actually two inches taller than when they are on earth. Another way to note that you are actually taller is by driving away from home. Did you ever notice that when you get into your car in the early morning hours one of the first things that you do, after you adjust the seat belts, of course, is to adjust the rear view mirror. Why? When you come home in the evening, after adjusting the seat belt, you again adjust that rear view mirror. What's happening? It must be a rear view mirror gremlin. The answer is that the gremlin is actually in the discs of the spine. You wake up in the morning and the discs are rehydrated and taller. As you go through the day, the pressures of walking, standing and bending placed on the spine cause loss of disc height. As we grow older, our discs lose their ability to imbibe water. When this happens, the discs cannot evenly distribute pressures or loads placed upon them. In addition to water loss, the discs lose important proteins, proteoglycans and collagen.

With aging, there is no longer a clear distinction between the annulus (outside) and nucleus pulposus (inside). In fact, the inside and the outside of the discs begin to look an awful lot alike. There's a gradual loss of the protein and collagen content in the discs. This means that the discs have a lessened ability to imbibe or to take up nutrients. This is due, in part, to the loss of special proteins in the discs. The discs are not what they used to be. There is also a decrease in the number of cells per unit of tissue in the annulus. We just don't have as many cells as we used to. In addition to the changes to the disc itself, there are also changes in the endplates. The endplates are located between the bony vertebral bodies and the discs (Fig. 9). Changes in the endplates cause a decrease of nutrient transfer to the discs. The endplates begin to calcify. An alteration of blood delivery to the discs is thought to initiate part of the aging process itself. Disc changes cause nearby structures such as joints and facets to change as well. These

figure | 7

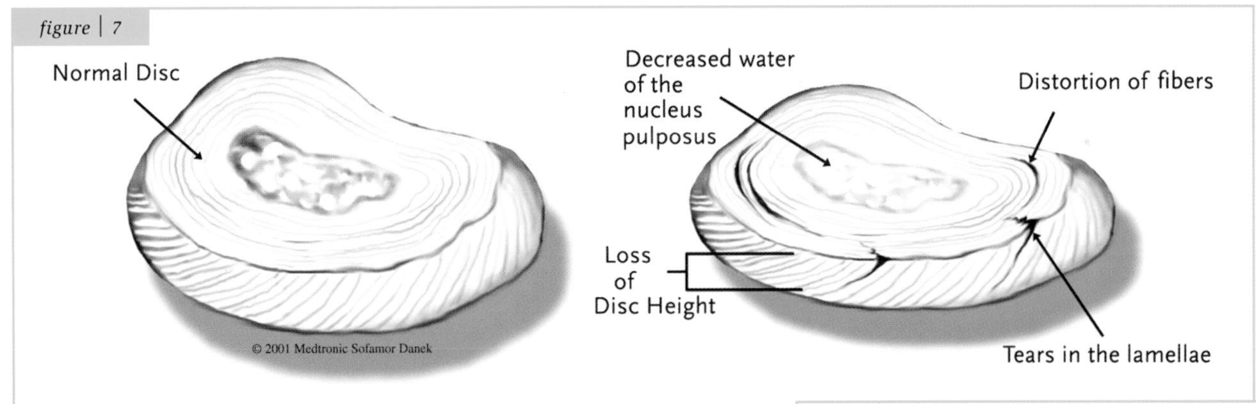

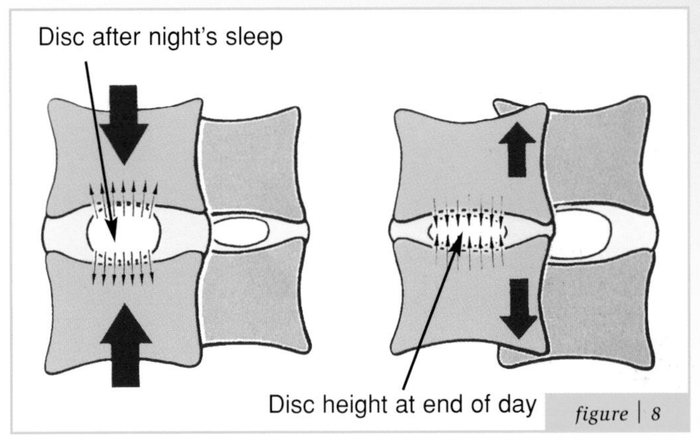

figure | 8

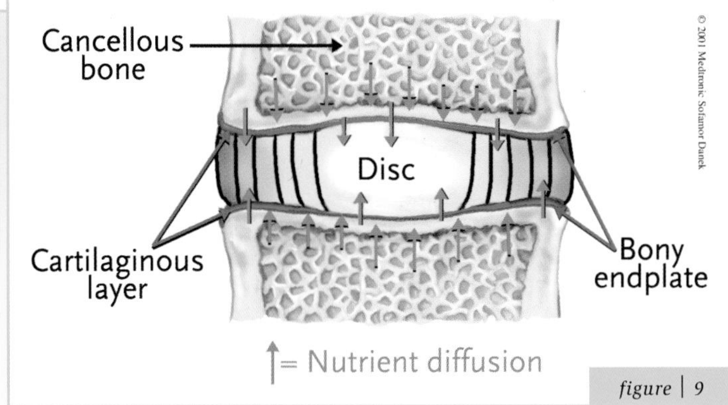

figure | 9

nearby structures must help to compensate and distribute spine loads. The discs are changing, but the loads that are placed upon them are the same; we're still standing upright.

Biomechanical and biochemical changes bring about a decreased ability of the spine, particularly the discs, to tolerate certain activities. This decreased capacity to handle pressures and loads brings about altered mechanics. These altered mechanics promote changes in nearby structures. Changes in nearby structures associated with disc changes cause segmental instability, which translates into spinal changes of aging.

SEQUELAE TO AGING

For most of us, changes of aging occur very gradually. They usually come about without any major alterations in our lives. For some people with smaller than normal bones in their backs, this may become a problem. For other individuals, spinal changes appear faster than normal. And when changes come about faster than normal, problems are more likely to develop. These problems usually announce themselves with pain.

DISC HERNIATION

With aging, the annulus (outer layer) of the disc weakens. Fissures or tears in the outer layer produce this weakening (Fig. 10). This causes a decreased resistance to stress and pressure loads. The disc may not be able to resist and deal effectively with all the stresses placed on it; therefore, it has an increased risk of rupturing. There are several types of disc herniations. One is the acute type of disc herniation. Think of a jelly donut. Squeeze it really quickly. All the jelly comes shooting out. Just like a jelly donut, when the disc has great pressure placed upon it, the material inside is forced out. The disc gel that's forced out becomes a space occupying mass. When the gel shoots out of the disc, it will then pinch or compress exiting nerves: this is called a **soft** acute disc herniation (Fig. 11). Another type of disc herniation is called a bulging disc, or a protrusion of the disc. This occurs when the disc loses its height with aging. A loss of height will cause a weakening of the outer annulus itself. The disc decreases in height. These changes allow some degree of movement at this level. The body does not like such movement and will attempt to prevent or to remedy this abnormal motion. It does this by developing calcification. This calcification can turn into a bone spur (Fig. 12). It, too, can become a space occupying mass. Because it's made of bone, it is called a **hard** disc. The rupture can occur at several different locations, front, back, or along the sides. An acute, sudden disc herniation is more common in middle age. Many golfers often engage in activities that perhaps they shouldn't, such as lifting loads more than they should. Acute disc herniations are less often seen with advancing age. One of the reasons is that as we grow older, water is lost from the disc; therefore, the disc is less likely to herniate. The best time for a disc to herniate is between the ages of 30 and 50 years of age. Again, this is a time when we are most active and the disc is still in relatively good shape.

STENOSIS

Alterations of the disc, brought about by aging changes or degeneration, cause loss of hydrostatic mechanisms between the bones in the spine. With the passing of time, the anterior portions of the vertebrae become closer together. They are subjected to more pressures, which promote bone spurs (osteophytes) in front. Loss of height in front causes a stretching of the joints or facets in back. This will create a continuous stretching mode on those joints and their capsules. Continuous stretching causes a thickening of the joint capsules and ligaments. Over time, the thickening of the ligaments and joint capsules will bring about hypertrophic

figure | 10

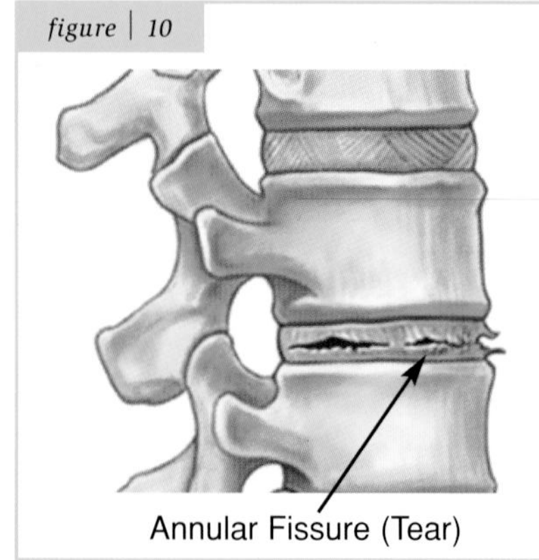

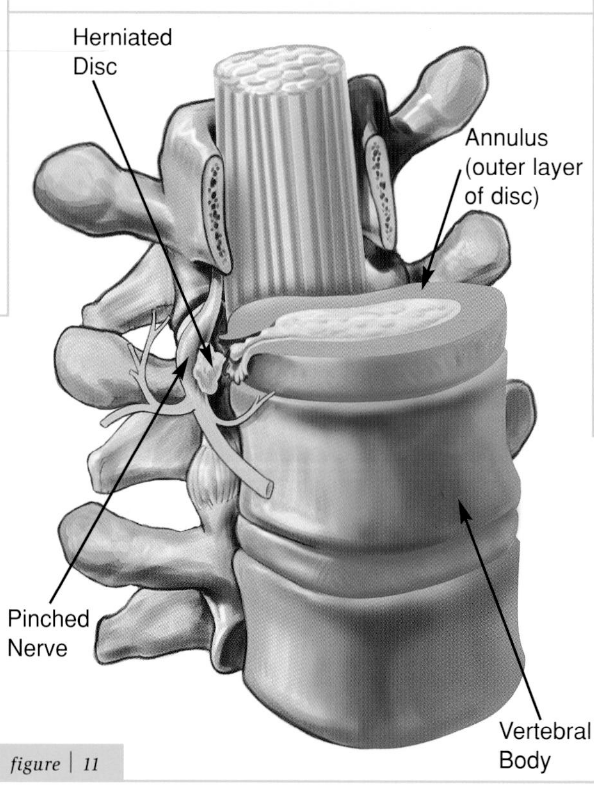

figure | 11

figure | 12

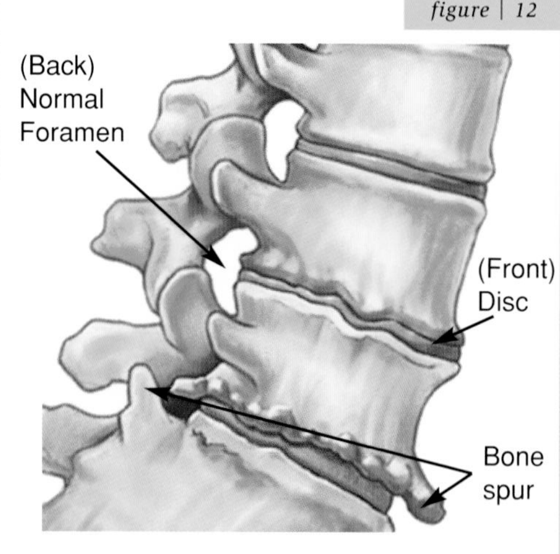

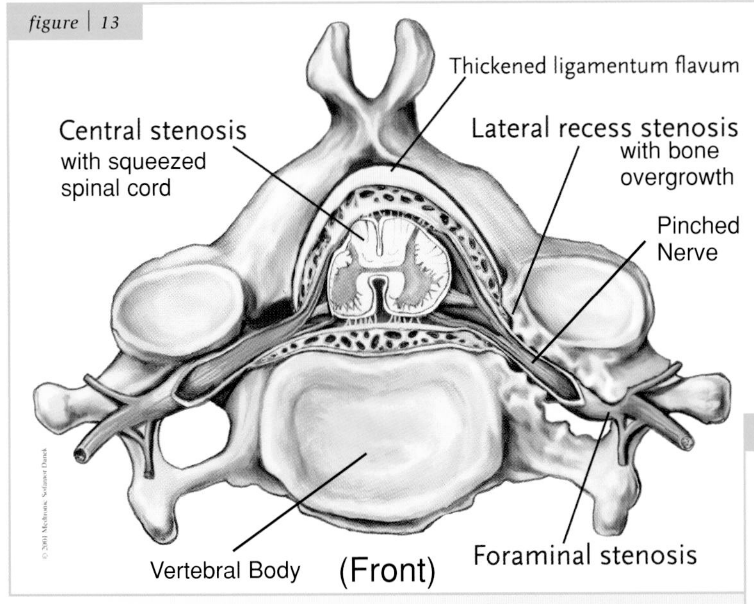

figure | 13

figure | 14

© 2001 Medtronic Sofamor Danek

bony changes or overgrowth of bone called osteophytes. This often occurs at the site in which the nerves in the spine are exiting the foramen. Bone spurs may encroach upon either the spinal cord or nerve roots. Such pressure on important nerve structures may bring about different types of pain. All of these changes cause a narrowing of the central spinal canal and nerve foramen (bone windows). This is called **early stenosis**. It's like trying to put a size 10 foot into a size 8 shoe. With time, the size 10 foot may now be placed into a size 5 or 3 shoe. The foot becomes very uncomfortable and walking becomes a problem. The same thing happens with a tight spinal canal. All sorts of problems can occur. A narrowed spinal canal of the cervical (neck) spine can cause pain, numbness, and tingling in an arm as well as walking difficulties (Fig. 13). Many people with stenosis of the lumbar spine or low back area find that walking bent over slightly will reduce their discomfort while walking. In fact, many patients report that, if they use a cart at the market or grocery store, they're better able to shop (Fig. 14). The so-called "grocery store syndrome" is an indication of spinal stenosis.

SPINE INSTABILITY

Spine instability means that there are abnormal movements of certain structures in the spine. Such movements can eventually cause problems. Spine specialists refer to spine instability as a state in which movement occurs beyond the physiologic constraints of the spine. This means that spine structures are moving beyond their abilities. The causes of these abnormal movements may be congenital abnormalities (present at birth), trauma, and/or aging. The second major problem of spinal instability is trauma. Trauma such as an automobile accident or a fall can bring about instability or abnormal movements due to injuries to the ligaments and bones. Finally, normal aging may bring about instability. Disc changes, joint changes (arthritis), and just a laxity of the ligaments due to wear and tear can lead to abnormal spine movements. When the movements are too great, nearby structures, such as the spinal cord and nerves, may be irritated, causing pain, or may be placed into harm's way, requiring surgical therapies.

Aging is a universal human experience. There is no way to hide from it. In our youth, we watched as our elders grappled with the effects of aging. We never envisioned that we, too, were under the influence of the aging process. In fact, we welcomed the process. To be 16 and then 21, to drive and legally taste the fruit of the vine, was truly what aging was all about. With the passing of the years, however, we soon no longer welcome the addition of years to our age. The effects of the inevitable process of aging begin to be seen in us, in our generation. One of the most serious and feared consequences of the aging process is the loss of the recuperative power to recover quickly from various illnesses. Fortunately, scientific research is beginning to unravel some of the mysteries of the aging process. The field of medicine and science devoted to studying aging is gerontology. Through such research a new perception of aging is emerging. Getting older does not mean losing one's health, quality of life and freedom. Medical advances are discovering ways to slow down and reduce many of the affections of age. However, we must all take responsibility for our health and practice lifestyles that extend good health, which is the first step to golf forever. An inscription on a tombstone in New England graveyard reads: "As you are today, so once was I. As I am today, soon you will be." The writing is true, but the outcome should be delayed as long as possible.

SOME BASIC FACTS ABOUT SPINE AND SPINAL CORD ANATOMY

CHAPTER 3

T. Glenn Pait, M.D.

I began the game of golf at age six, but did not suffer my first serious golf injury until age 28. While hitting low one-iron shots in Pensacola, preparing for the 1982 British Open at Troon, I felt a sudden pop, then a deep burn in my left shoulder joint upon striking the ball. After several years of severe pain, numerous orthopedic examinations diagnosed a torn cartilage. In 1985, the cartilage was removed through arthroscopy. The next year the rotator cuff was repaired. Joint reconstruction and a capsular shift followed in 1987. Still a young man in my early thirties, my golfing days were limited without relief other than surgery. The pain continued.

While reviewing slow-motion video, it was discovered that my swing mechanics did not allow the left arm to properly release, thus producing stress on my shoulder at impact. A person must understand the relationship of body mechanics and their dynamics to repetitively strike a golf ball properly. Once I understood the anatomical relationship between my muscles, skeleton, and joints, I began swinging the club with increased body and arm rotation without pain.

Only a few great swings in golf have avoided serious injury. Prior to the 1970s most golf instruction was communicated verbally, in writing, or by simply visualizing other golfers. Today, high-speed video photography and biomechanical technology implement golf instruction and support the importance of physical conditioning and body mechanics. The golf swing is a geometric progression. As technology and learning advance, I am thankful to say the struggles of injury found in almost every serious golf competitor should be greatly reduced.

Jerry Pate

The spine is a very complex structure, one of the most intricate mechanisms in our body. It's always moving, even when we are asleep. It's never without some type of demand being placed upon it. There are 33 vertebrae (back bones) in our spines. Our spines have been divided into five sections, which make it easier to understand. Our neck is called the **cervical spine**, which has 7 vertebrae. The next level is the upper back or the **thoracic spine**; it has 12 vertebrae. The upper low back is called the **lumbar spine** and has 5, sometimes 6, vertebrae. The sacrum is the buttock area, where the vertebrae have fused or grown together. There aren't any spaces between them. The final section is called the **coccyx**. This is truly the tailbone and has 4 to 5 different sections that are also fused (Fig. 1).

The vertebrae can be divided into two sections: the anterior arch (front) or **vertebral body**, and the posterior arch (back) called the **posterior elements** (Figs. 2A, 2B). The posterior elements are made up of two pedicles that form the sidewalls of the **vertebrae**, and the **laminae** (the 'rooftops' of the backbones) (Fig. 3). The vertebral body up front and the posterior elements in back enclose a special area called the vertebral foramen (canal) (Fig. 3). Through this canal course the spinal cord and nerves. Attached to the lamina is another bone that's called the **spinous process**. This is a bony element that projects backwards like the dorsal fin of a shark. This fin is located in the middle of each rooftop (lamina) (Fig. 3). On each side of the vertebral body are two sets of bony wings called the **transverse processes** (Fig. 3). A good way to envision the spine vertebral anatomy is to think of a house. The foundation of the house is the vertebral body. It provides a strong foundation on which everything else rests. The walls of the house are the pedicles. They connect the foundation and rooftops. The rooftop (lamina) has a steeple called **a spinous process**. On each side of the house there are two projections extending from the walls, the **transverse processes**. Through the middle of the spine house is where the spinal cord and nerves course. The posterior elements are joined together by joints called **facet joints** (Fig. 4).

When something is on top of something else, it's said to be in the superior position; when something is underneath something else, it is said to be in the inferior position (Fig. 5). A projection of bone called the **superior articular process** projects upward and sits on top of the **inferior articular process** (Fig. 4). The inferior articular process projects downward and joins the superior articular process to form a **facet joint** (Fig. 4). This joint is a junction between the bones in the skeleton that allows for movement. In the spine this special joint is called **a synovial joint** (Fig. 6). Synovial means that there is a transparent viscous fluid inside the joint that is much like the white of an egg. A membrane on the surface of the bone secretes the material. With age, these membranes secrete less "egg white," and thus the joints age.

Intervertebral foraminae are bone windows, or small canals through which nerves from the spinal cord travel (Fig. 7). Under normal situations, there is enough room in the foramen to allow nerves connected to the arms and legs to travel unobstructed. Go back to the house diagram. The window of the house is the intervertebral foramina. Let's take a garden hose, a nerve, and move it from the inside to the outside through the window. Now, put an

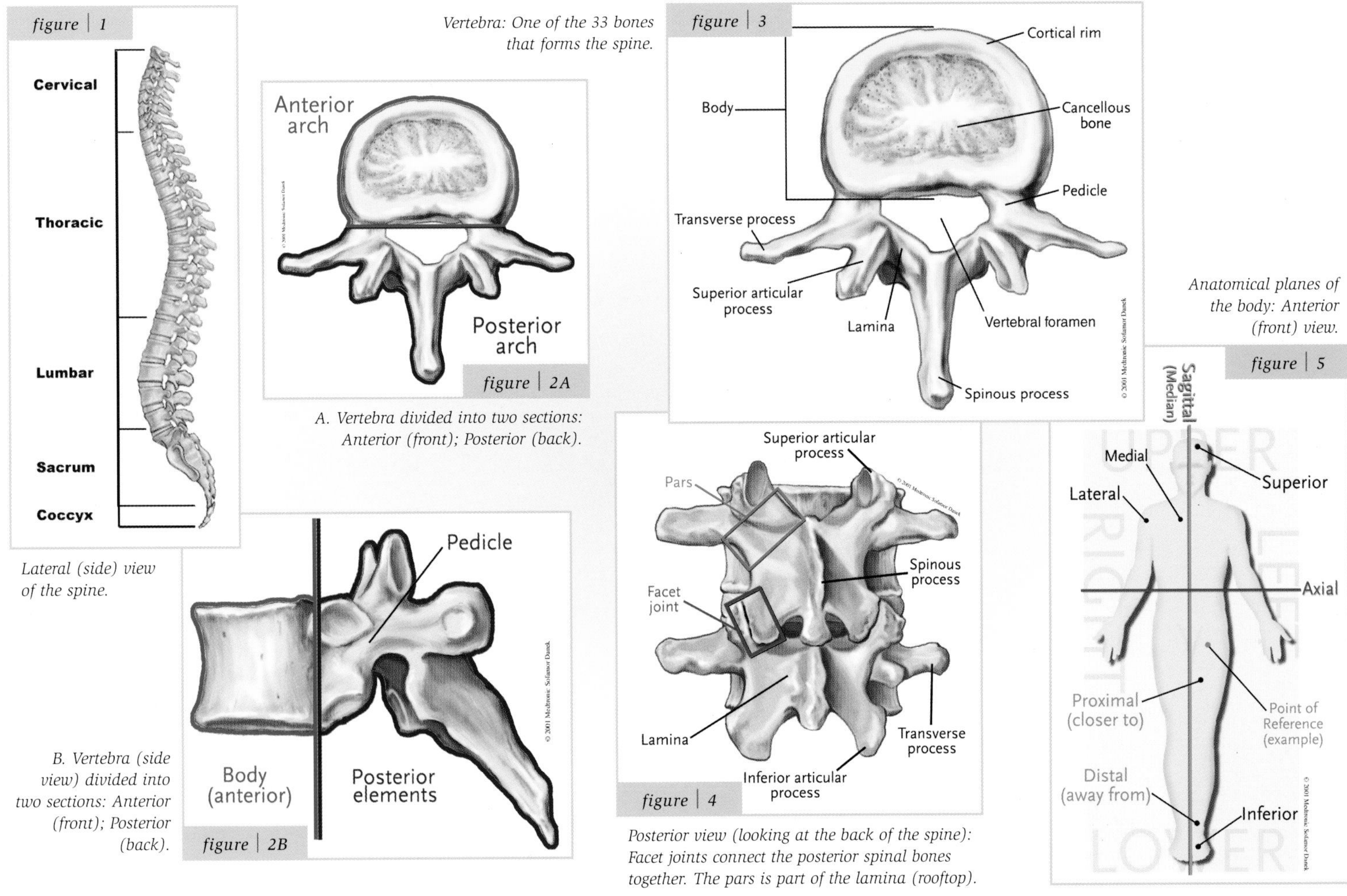

Lateral (side) view of the spine.

Vertebra: One of the 33 bones that forms the spine.

A. Vertebra divided into two sections: Anterior (front); Posterior (back).

B. Vertebra (side view) divided into two sections: Anterior (front); Posterior (back).

Posterior view (looking at the back of the spine): Facet joints connect the posterior spinal bones together. The pars is part of the lamina (rooftop).

Anatomical planes of the body: Anterior (front) view.

air-conditioner in the window; the hose needs to move over a bit. It's no longer quite as free as it used to be. Now put a flower on top of the air conditioner. There is even less room, and if enough items are placed into the window, the garden hose will be squeezed. With time, bone spurs develop in these windows, the foraminae. Bone spurs are just like the air-conditioner, in that they take up space and may "squeeze the garden hose." When this happens, it causes pain, and the pain radiates down into the arm or legs. This type of pain is called a radicular type of pain, meaning that it radiates down an extremity. The cause of the pain depends on what's in the window.

The intervertebral discs are like shock absorbers or jelly donuts that are situated between the vertebrae in the spine (Fig. 8). Discs are unique in regard to body structure. They are situated between vertebrae and allow movement between the bones. They permit movements such as bending (flexion), extension and rotation. They are the largest structures in the body with a blood supply. They start to lose their blood supply by the second and third decades of life. After that, the discs are essentially **avascular**, which means they have no significant blood supply going to them. If there is no blood going to a part of the body, it degenerates, or ages. For most of us, this will be the site of a great deal of our discomfort and will cause many a lost day of playing golf. If we have a better understanding of what makes up the disc, then we can give it more respect. If we don't, it'll certainly let us know.

If you put all of those discs together they make up about one-quarter of the length of our entire spinal column. (Fig. 1) Discs are the thickest in the cervical (neck) and the lumbar (low back) areas. They are largest here because that's where the movements of the spinal column or vertebral column are the greatest. These discs are located throughout the cervical spine, except at the very top of the neck, at the atlas (C1) and the axis (C2), and at the very lower part of the spinal column, the sacrum and coccyx. Each disc is held between the bony vertebrae by a cartilaginous layer called the **endplate**. It is this cartilaginous layer that actually anchors the disc space into place (Fig. 9). The endplates do more than just keep the discs from sliding out of place: they are important in maintaining the health of the discs. Discs need to be kept healthy and need nutrients. With aging, the disc spaces are no longer provided an adequate blood supply; the nutrients are provided by the endplates (Fig. 10). The intervertebral discs are the spine's shock-absorbing system that actually changes throughout the day. At night when you're flat in bed, you actually grow taller. There is no pressure on the discs and the discs begin to swell (Fig. 11B). As you get up in the morning and go about your daily activities, you actually shrink (Fig. 11A). At night, the entire process starts all over again. If we didn't have gravity, we wouldn't have this problem. In fact, space travelers actually grow because there is no gravity in space. Some astronauts have been known to grow at least two inches in space. When they return and gravity once again influences their spines, they shrink back to normal.

Now, let's take a little closer look at the intervertebral discs. The outside, or the peripheral, part of the doughnut is called the **annulus fibrosus**. (Fig. 12) The annulus fibrosus can be thought of as a strong outside ring of fibers, or a radial tire. It is made up of fibro-cartilaginous tissue and various proteins. The layers (laminated) are arranged in concentric layers (Fig. 13). The fibers in the layers slant in alternative directions and cross each other at right angles (Fig. 8). This configuration is very important. It allows the annulus to absorb stress by

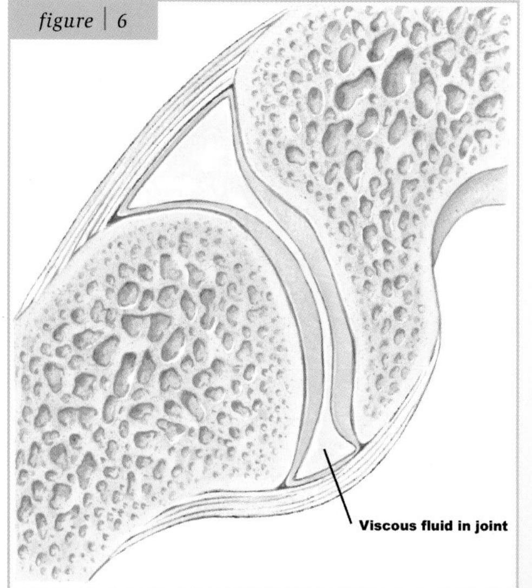

Synovial joint with viscous fluid between bones.

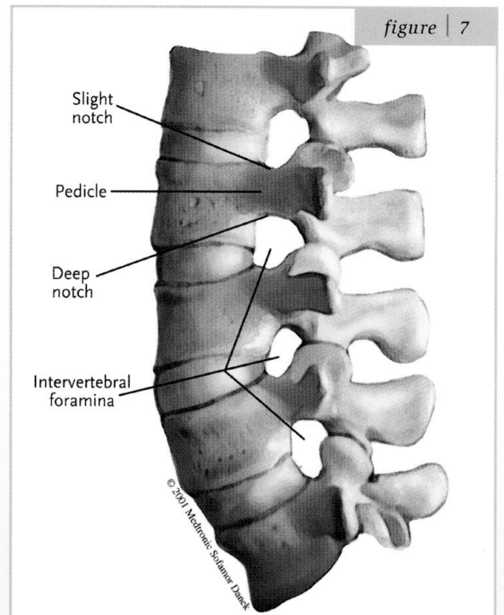

Lateral (side) view of the spine: Slight notch and deep notch are parts of the pedicle around which nerves travel when exiting the spinal canal.

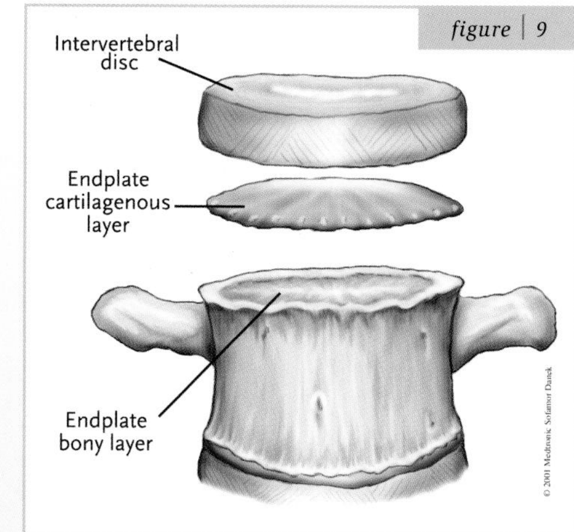

The endplate is situated between the intervertebral disc and the bone of the vertebra.

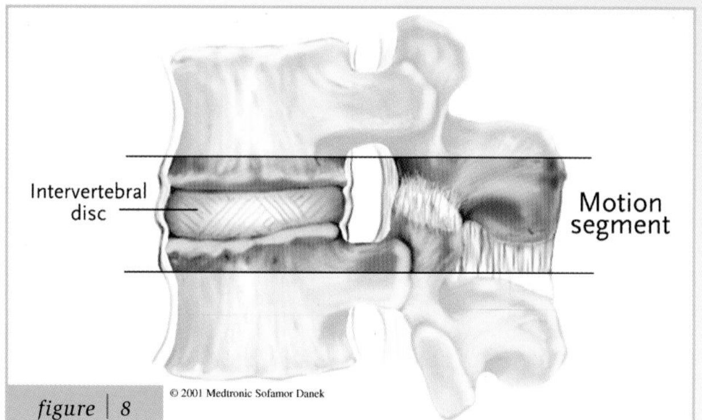

Lateral (side) view of a spine section. The intervertebral discs are shock absorbers between the bones (vertebrae) in the spine. The intervertebral disc is part of the elements in the spine that allow movement (motion segment).

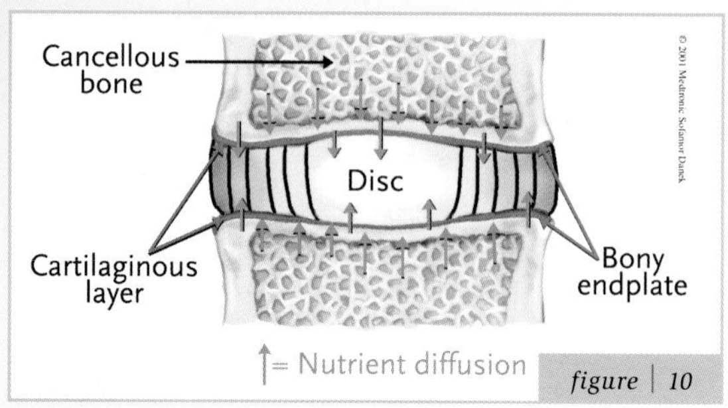

The intervertebral discs are Avascular; they receive nutrients by diffusion through the endplates.

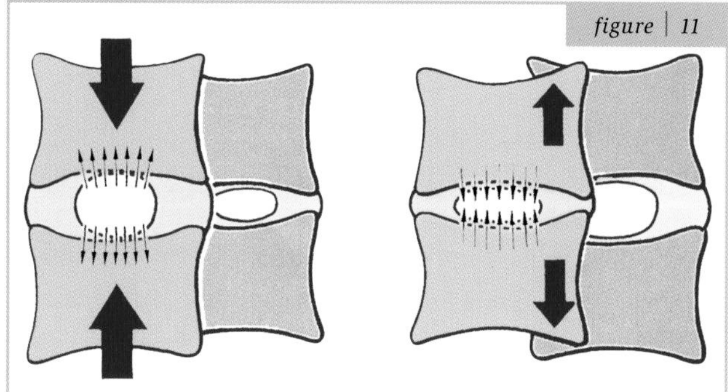

A. Intervertebral disc loses height during the day due to compression when standing.

B. Intervertebral disc regains height at night when lying flat (horizontal) in bed.

expanding and contracting (Fig. 13). You stand up; you move; you pull. The annulus is always working. The annulus has the help of ligaments, and the ligaments help to strengthen the outer portion of the annulus. There is a ligament in front called the **anterior longitudinal ligament,** and a ligament in back called the **posterior longitudinal ligament** (Fig. 14). Contained within the annulus fibrosus is a gel material called the **nucleus pulposus**. As we age, the layers of the annulus change. They mature and go through degenerative changes. Degenerative changes are a normal part of living. Aging changes develop in the annulus. Fissures develop and breaks form all along the surfaces (Fig. 15). When the annulus ages, it decreases or loses its elasticity and the capacity to keep the nucleus pulposus (gel) inside when the forces on the annulus become too great. When this occurs, the nucleus pulposus can move to the surface or pop out of the annulus, like squeezing a jelly donut. If you squeeze the jelly donut just a little bit, you can see some of the jelly inside coming to the surface of the doughnut; it bulges outward. That is what happens with a bulging disc (Fig. 15). If you were to squeeze the donut all the way down, the jelly would actually come out. This occurs when there is a split in the annulus and the gel (nucleus) is forced out of the disc. This is called a **disc herniation** (Fig. 15).

The nucleus pulposus of the disc (the inside) is made up of water, collagen, and proteoglycans (PGS). Proteoglycans are very special molecules because they are the molecules that pull in and retain water. Attracting water into the disc makes the disc stronger. The water in the gel-like disc center provides an increased ability to resist compression forces when we stand up. The gelatinous makeup of the nucleus pulposus allows it to change shape and permits the vertebrae to rock forward and backward on one another, thus facilitating flexion and extension movements of the spine (Fig. 16).

As the day progresses, the amount of water in our disc also changes. Any sudden increase in the compression loads on the spine, such as jumping up and down, causes the gel to flatten. The resistance of the surrounding annulus fibrosus accommodates the outward thrust of the disc. If you have a faulty annulus, like a bad tire, you may have a blowout, or a shot shock. The disc changes with age. As we get older the water content of the disc diminishes and is replaced by fibrocartilage. Due to the decreased water and gel, the discs shrink, become thin, and lose their elasticity (Fig. 14). Such changes happen to all of us.

THE SPINAL CORD

The spinal cord is a network of nerves and nerve pathways that are contained in a tube-like structure. This cylindrical tube is about the size of one's little finger and has the consistency of something like toothpaste. It is located in the central canal of the bony spine (Fig. 17). Many times individuals will confuse the spine and the spinal cord. The spine is the bone and the spinal cord is soft tissue. The spinal cord is wrapped in a lining, or a strong fibrous membrane called the **dura mater** (Fig. 18). Inside the dura mater is the **cerebrospinal fluid**, also referred to as spinal fluid. The fluid is contained in a compartment called the subarachnoid space. The fluid bathes the spinal cord. The spinal fluid itself is actually made within the brain and circulates around the brain and downward around the spinal cord. The spinal fluid provides a medium that surrounds the spinal cord and offers some degree of protection. The spinal fluid also provides nutrients to the spinal cord and is involved in removing waste products associated with the spinal cord. The normal spinal fluid looks like water; if it is discolored, yellow or cloudy, this may indicate that a disease process is present, such as a spinal cord tumor or infection. Spinal fluid contains various proteins, glucose (sugar), sodium, chloride, and blood cells; all of which can be evaluated in a laboratory to determine whether the levels are abnormal or normal.

The spinal cord begins at the base of the skull called the **foramen magnum** (the large hole in the skull). It is continuous with the brain. Together, the spinal cord and brain make up the central nervous system (Fig. 19).

Just like the bony spine, the spinal cord is divided into the cervical (neck), thoracic (mid-spine), and lumbosacral (lower spine) regions. Cervical spinal nerves are the nerves leaving the spinal cord at the cervical region (neck). These nerves (8 pairs) supply the back of the head, the neck, the shoulders, the arms, the hands, and the diaphragm. Thoracic spinal nerves are located in the thoracic region of the spinal cord. There are 12 thoracic nerves, which supply the chest, some muscles of the back, and parts of the abdomen. The lumbar spinal nerves originate from the lower end of the spinal cord. They supply the lower parts of the abdomen, the back, the buttocks, and some parts of the external genital organs and parts of the legs. The last nerves are the sacral spinal nerves. These nerves, of which there are five, supply the thighs and lower parts of the legs, the feet, most

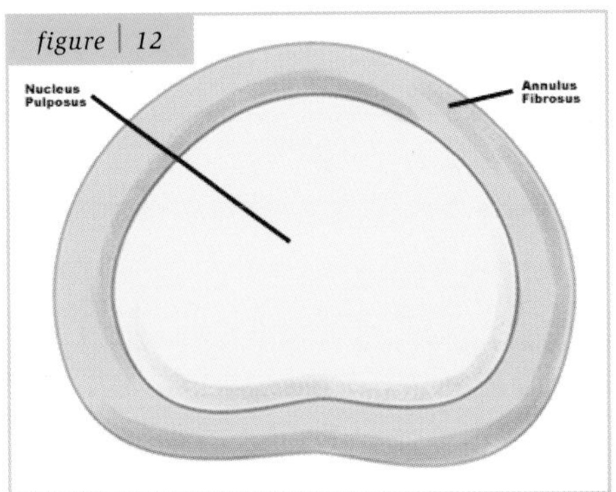

The Intervertebral Disc: Annulus fibrosus (outer fiber ring); Nucleus pulposus (inner gel).

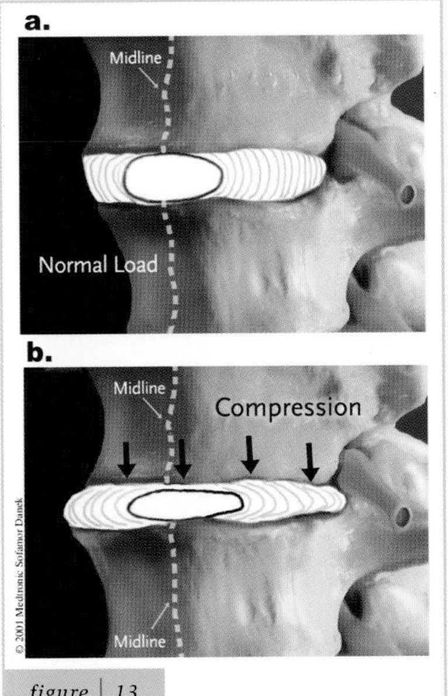

figure | 13

The annulus fibrosus (outer layer of the disc) is laminated to absorb stress forces by expanding and compressing. Annulus layers are expanded. Annulus layers are compressed.

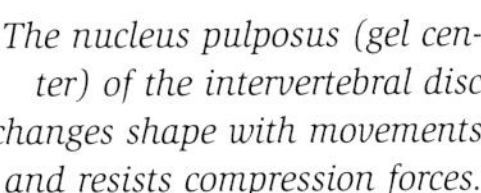

The nucleus pulposus (gel center) of the intervertebral disc changes shape with movements and resists compression forces.

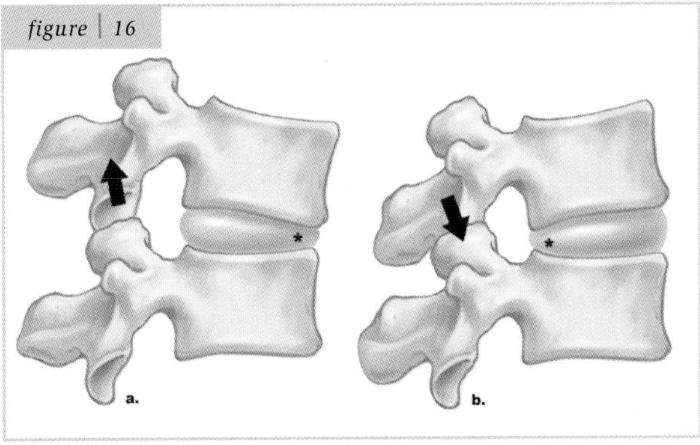

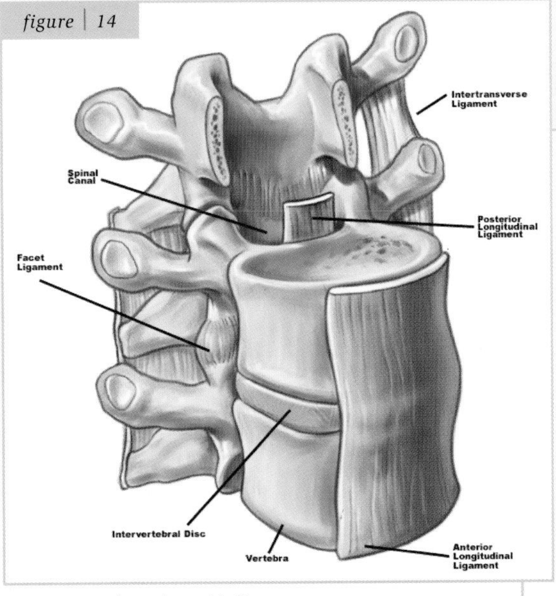

Front view of vertebra with ligaments.

The aging intervertebral disc.

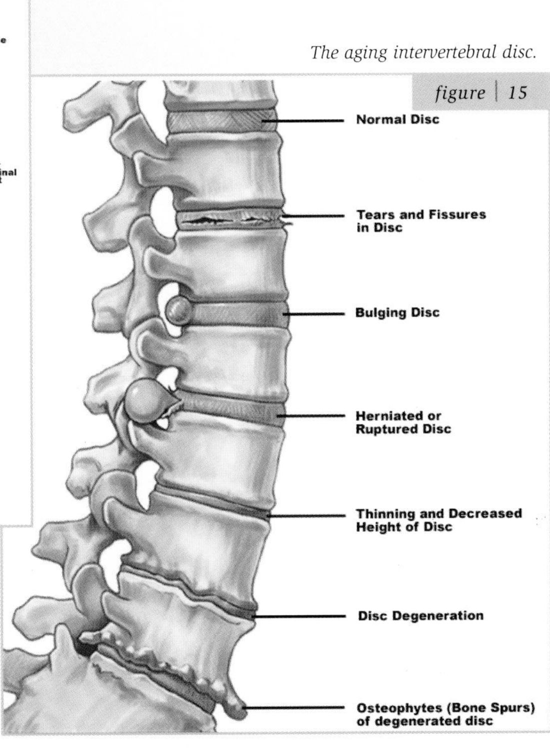

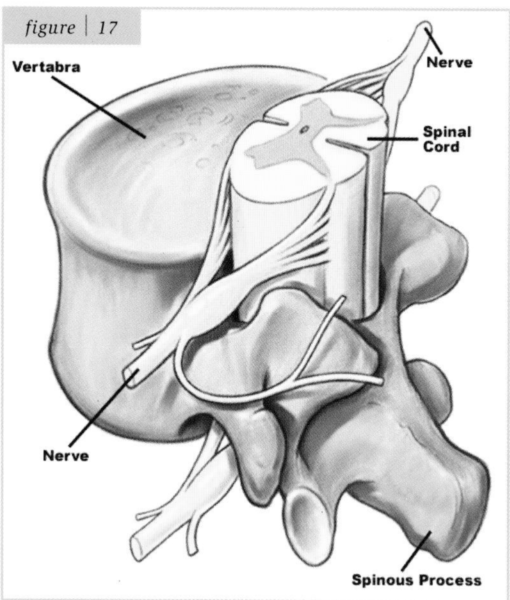

The spinal cord is a cylindrical tube located in the spinal foramen, or central cord.

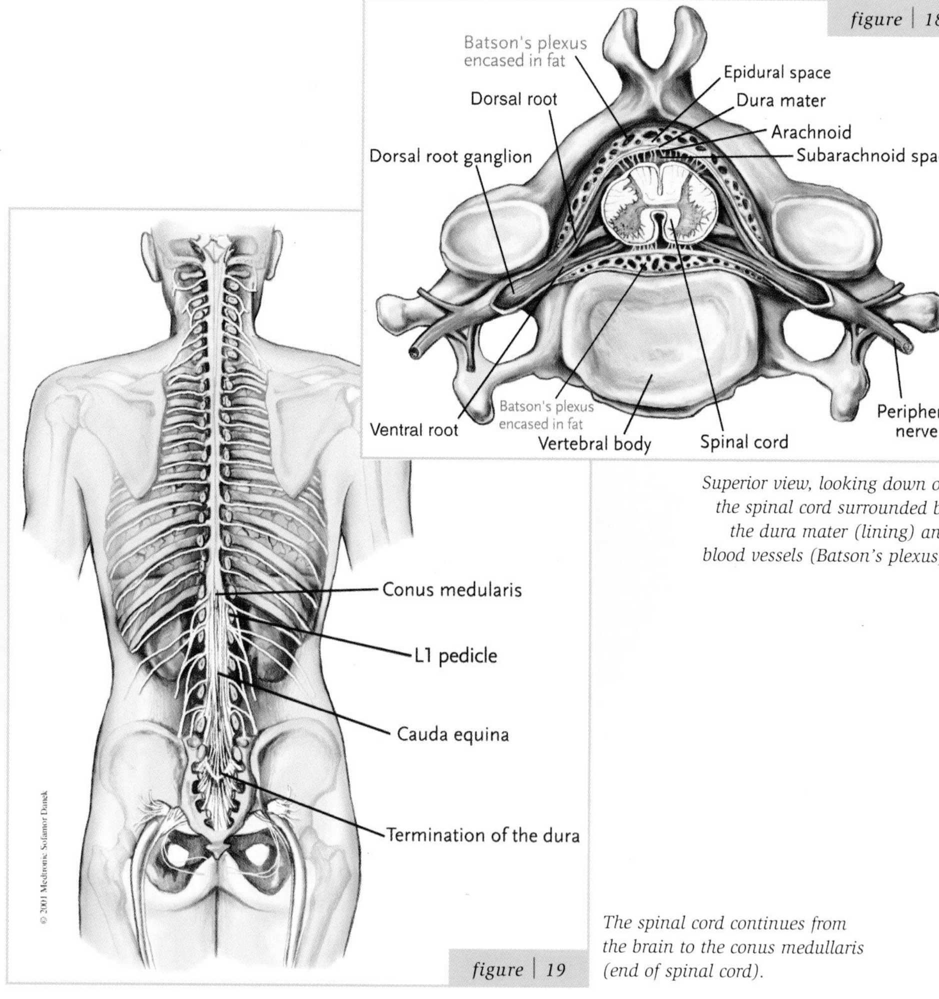

Superior view, looking down on the spinal cord surrounded by the dura mater (lining) and blood vessels (Batson's plexus).

The spinal cord continues from the brain to the conus medullaris (end of spinal cord).

of the external genital organs, and the area around the anus (Fig. 20).

The spinal cord ends, in the adult, at about the level of the lower first lumbar vertebra, the waist level. In an adult male, the spinal cord is about 18 inches long (45cm), and in the female, it is about 17 inches (43cm). It is much shorter than the length of the bony spine. The spinal cord tapers off into a special part called the **conus medullaris** (Figs. 19, 20). Along the whole length of the spinal cord are attached some 31 pairs of spinal nerves. The nerves leave the spinal cord and travel through the intervertebral foramen (windows of the spine). Once the leaving the foramen, the nerves travel throughout the body to organs, muscles, skin, blood vessels, in fact, all body structures. The nerves at the end of the spinal cord form a collection of nerves called the **cauda equina** that descend to the lower lumbar and sacral spinal levels. Their appearance resembles the tail of a horse; thus the name cauda (tail) and equina (Figs. 19, 20, 21).

The spinal cord is the network of nerves that carry all messages to and from the brain to the rest of the body. The nerves of the spinal cord are divided into **upper motor neurons** (UMNs) and **lower motor neurons** (LMNs). The upper motor neurons are the inside nerves; the nerves located within the spinal cord itself. Their function is to carry messages back and forth from the brain to nerves. The lower motor neurons are those nerves that branch out from the spinal cord and course through other parts of the body.

Our nervous system, constituted by the brain, spinal cord and nerves, is divided into different parts. In fact, there are three. The brain and spinal cord constitute the **central nervous system** (CNS). Nerves that are outside the brain and the spinal cord constitute the **peripheral nervous system** (PNS). The final type of nervous system is the **sympathetic and parasympathetic nervous system**. This part of the nervous system is a rather diffuse system of nerves that control involuntary functions such as blood pressure and temperature regulation.

When we want to move an arm, we merely think "arm, move," and it does so. Desire to move is initiated in the brain; that message is carried into the various divisions of the spinal cord and eventually is transmitted to nerves, causing our muscles to contract, which brings about the movement; it is a truly remarkable system. A structure about the size of our little finger and made up of a very special type of tissue allows us to move, appreciate sensations, control bowel, bladder, sexual functions, and blood pressure! However, the spinal cord is a very unforgiving structure. If it is injured or damaged or becomes diseased, it cannot regenerate itself. It is just like the brain: if it is injured, it is very difficult, if not impossible, to recover all the functions from the damaged site.

More and more individuals are living with spinal cord injuries than ever before. There are about 10,000 new cases of spinal cord injuries every year. The majority of these injuries occurs in the male population between the ages of 14 and 30. Most of these injuries are traumatic; they result from motor vehicle accidents, violence, or falls. The precise nature of a spinal cord injury varies from individual to individual, but usually it is due to pressure being placed upon the spinal cord. When a toothpaste tube is squeezed, it doesn't readily pop back into shape. The same occurs with the spinal cord. During a traumatic event, a great amount of force is placed onto the body and is transmitted to the bony spinal column. If the force is too great for the protecting spinal column to handle, the bones may dislocate or move in an abnormal direction, or may fracture. The fracturing of spinal bones or their abnormal movement can cause injury to the spinal cord. Such injury can apply mechanical pressure to the spinal cord, causing irreversible damage (Fig. 22). The outcome of injury to the spinal cord depends upon the level of the injury and the type of injury to the spinal cord. Spinal cord injuries are divided into two types, complete and incomplete injuries. A **complete spinal cord injury** means that the spinal cord has been totally injured; there is no function below the level of the injury. This means that there is no appreciation of sensation and no ability to voluntarily move the limbs below the site of the injury. In a complete spinal cord injury, both sides of the body are equally affected. The second type of spinal cord injury is referred to as an **incomplete spinal cord injury**, which means that some degree of functioning below the level of injury may be present. An individual with an incomplete spinal cord injury may be able to feel a leg, but is unable to move the leg. Such an injury may allow an individual to function more on one side than on the other, which means that one arm may be stronger than the other arm. The level of the injury determines which body functions are preserved and which functions are lost. Overall, individuals with incomplete spinal cord injuries tend to do better than those with complete spinal cord injuries.

Injuries to the cervical spine, or neck, usually result in loss of the use of both arms and legs. This is referred to as **quadriplegia**. Injuries above the C4 level (cervical vertebra #4) usually require a breathing machine, or ventilator, to keep the individual alive. Individuals with such injuries are not able to breathe by themselves. Individuals with an injury at the C5 level (cervical vertebra #5) will often be able to move their shoulders and their biceps; however, they will have no movement of their hands or fingers. Wrist functioning is lost. One level below, at C6 (cervical vertebra #6), the wrist level is preserved; however, the individual cannot move his or her hands: the hands have no functions. Patients with a C7 (cervical vertebra #7) and a T1 (thoracic vertebra #1) injury can move the arms to some degree, but will have dexterity problems in the hands and fingers. Therefore, the lower the injury to the spinal cord, the more function is preserved. Injuries to the thoracic spinal cord (thoracic spine) will usually result in preservation of arm movement; however, leg functions are usually lost. The inability to move the legs is referred to as **paraplegia**. High thoracic lesions, which means between T1 (thoracic vertebra #1) and T8 (thoracic vertebra #8), will preserve functions of the hands, but there is often poor control of the trunk because of loss of abdominal muscles. Lower thoracic spinal cord injuries, T9 (thoracic vertebra #9) to T12 (thoracic vertebra #12), will preserve trunk and most abdominal muscle control. Sitting is usually not a major problem. Injuries in the lumbar and the sacral spine will bring about loss of movement of the hips and legs (Table 1).

Loss of movement of the arms and legs is one of many problems experienced by a quadriplegic or paraplegic patient. Other body functions will be greatly affected or influenced by the spinal cord injury. Spinal cord injury

Table 1 Professional Golfer Injury Site

Men	Women
Low Back	Wrist
Wrist	Low Back
Shoulder	Shoulder
Elbow	Elbow
Knees	Knees

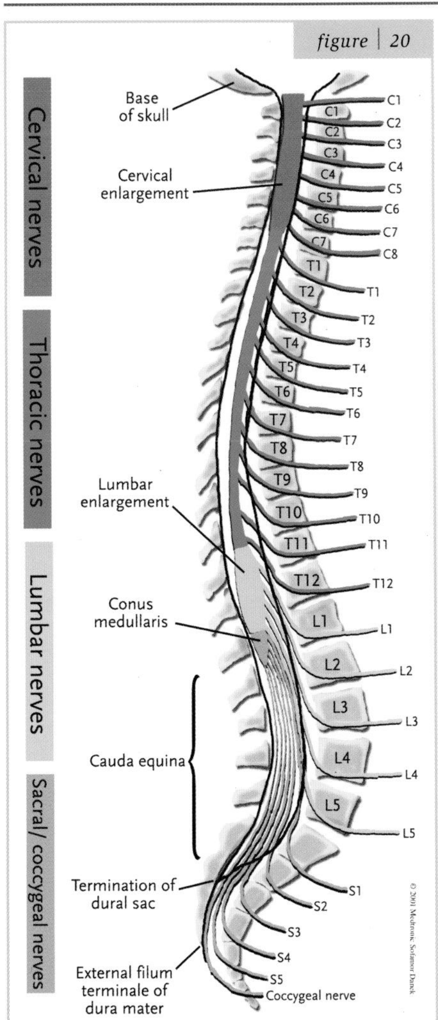

figure 20 *Spinal cord segments.*

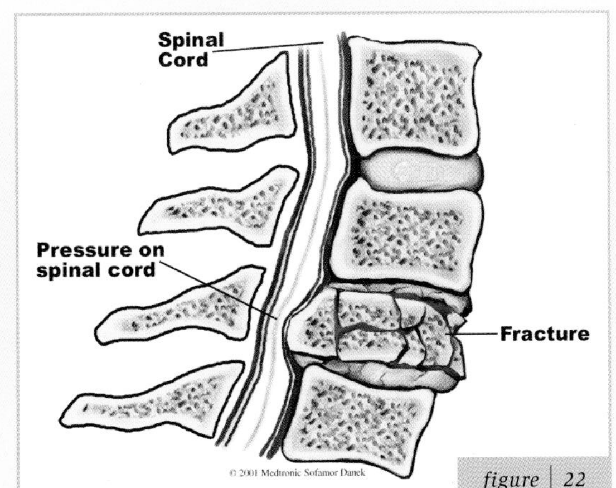

figure 22

Vertebra fracture compressing the spinal cord.

31 pairs of nerves are attached to the spinal cord.

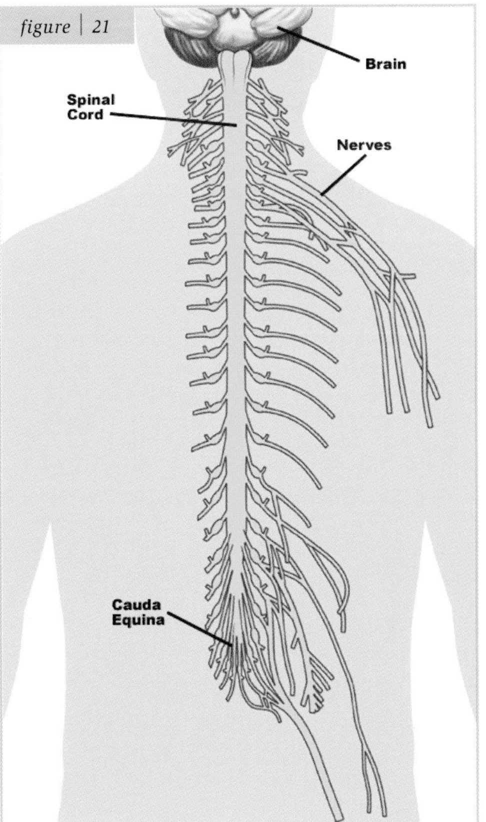

figure 21

patients may experience loss or dysfunction of bowel, bladder and sexual functions. In men with spinal cord injuries, sexual functioning is a major problem and may result in infertility. Women, on the other hand, will not have a fertility problem; however, they may experience other problems during pregnancy. Other effects of spinal cord injuries include the inability to regulate blood pressure, control of body temperature, and an inability to sweat below the level of the injury. Another devastating result of a spinal cord injury is chronic pain. The pain is often very difficult to control and may not allow the individual to live a productive, effective life. Individuals with spinal cord injuries will undergo numerous challenges throughout their lives. They need the support of loved ones, family, physicians, physical therapists and other healthcare providers.

There are teams of dedicated scientists and researchers throughout the world trying to find a cure for paralysis due to spinal cord injuries. For many individuals who are disabled due to a spinal cord injury, golfing is a possibility. There are national organizations dedicated to allowing disabled golfers to continue to enjoy the sport. With specialized equipment and training, these individuals can still participate.

THE MUSCLES OF THE GOLF SWING

CHAPTER 4

Bruce Mendelson, M.S., P.T., PhD.

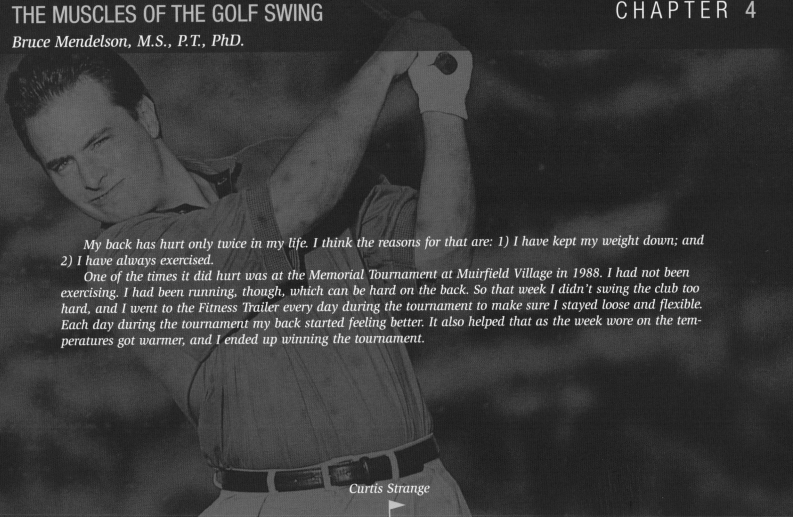

My back has hurt only twice in my life. I think the reasons for that are: 1) I have kept my weight down; and 2) I have always exercised.

One of the times it did hurt was at the Memorial Tournament at Muirfield Village in 1988. I had not been exercising. I had been running, though, which can be hard on the back. So that week I didn't swing the club too hard, and I went to the Fitness Trailer every day during the tournament to make sure I stayed loose and flexible. Each day during the tournament my back started feeling better. It also helped that as the week wore on the temperatures got warmer, and I ended up winning the tournament.

Curtis Strange

Golf is a relatively unique sport in that it can be enjoyed and played throughout one's lifetime. However, to get the most out of each golf experience, and to play in a pain-free manner, one must have a healthy musculoskeletal system. Most golfers are more than willing to make a commitment to the game in order to enhance performance. One of the beauties of this type of dedication to the sport is that one is also making a commitment to good spinal function and good overall health.

The golf swing is a complex athletic maneuver. For most shots, one must generate explosive power in a controlled manner. This dynamic action involves essentially every major muscle group in the body. The golf swing is repeated many times during a typical round or practice session, which puts considerable stress on the musculoskeletal system. On a typical 18-hole course, a ten-handicap golfer will make at least 50 full golf swings, a number of practice swings, and walk between 5 and 6 1/2 miles. The golfer will expend roughly 600–1000 kcal (equivalent to two bowls of cereal). Therefore, there is also an element of cardiovascular conditioning necessary to enjoy a typical round of golf. This chapter will discuss the major muscles involved in playing a round of golf and will outline a number of exercises that should be included in the overall fitness program of any golfer.

Most golf enthusiasts realize that physical fitness is important for a healthy lifestyle and can positively influence all aspects of golf participation. Essentially all successful professional golfers spend many hours per week participating in strenuous fitness programs in order to sharpen their games and to prevent injury. In fact, a large percentage of tour professionals employ physical therapists and personal trainers to ensure that the exercise programs target the necessary musculoskeletal structures. These programs are designed to increase strength, flexibility, and endurance. The benefits of a good fitness program are enormous. One will have a stronger and more consistent swing, will be less likely to suffer a musculoskeletal injury, will be less likely to become fatigued during a round, and will be therefore enabled to concentrate on the game, and, most importantly, to exhibit better overall health.

A good overall fitness program will consist of aerobic exercise, strength and flexibility training combined with a healthy diet. Aerobic means the consumption of oxygen. During exercise the heart rate goes up as the body needs more oxygen to meet the demands of the body during the activity. Oxygen-rich blood travels from the heart and lungs to the demanding muscles. When the heart rate reaches 60% of its maximum, the individual is working aerobically. The exercising golfer is now utilizing oxygen and burning fat as the primary fuel source. Aerobic exercise should be performed 3–5 times per week for 20–60 minutes at each session. Performing aerobic exercises will greatly benefit the golfer, as well as others, in terms of burning off unwanted calories and fat. The increased cerebral (brain) blood flow will benefit the golfer at work and on the course. In fact, the whole body will reap the rewards from exercising. All of which means better golf forever. Examples of good aerobic exercises are: bicycling, running, using a stair-stepping machine, and swimming. The activity should be performed at a level that brings the heart rate to 60–90% of the maximum heart rate. Two widely accepted methods of calculating maximum heart rate are:

Max. Heart Rate = 220 – Age *(low estimate)*
Max. Heart Rate = 210 – (0.5 × Age) *(high estimate)*

Many of the machines used for aerobic exercise come equipped with a heart rate monitor. Or, one can simply take a pulse for 15 seconds and then multiply by 4. Using the information above, one can calculate that a 45 year-old should attempt to keep the heart rate between 114 and 169 beats per minute during exercise. One should start at the low end of the range during the first few weeks of the program and gradually work towards a higher rate as the perceived exertion during exercise decreases.

Strength training should consist of resisted exercises, such as weight lifting, targeted towards major muscle groups. A good starting program should consist of 10–12 exercises that work the major muscles of the arms, legs, and trunk. Each exercise should be performed at 1 set of 8–12 repetitions, 2–3 times per week.

A regular stretching program as well as an efficient warm-up and cool-down routine are also vital components of an overall fitness program. Stretches should be held for about 30 seconds and should be performed 1–2 times per day. Before a workout or a round of golf, it is important to warm up for 5–10 minutes. The warm-up can consist of a series of stretches coupled with breathing and relaxation exercises followed by some mild to moderate aerobic activities, such as walking or jogging. These activities serve to increase blood flow and temperature in the muscles, which will increase performance and decrease the risk of injury. A cool-down period is also important. One should try to avoid getting into an air-conditioned vehicle or clubhouse right after a round of golf or any workout. One should instead try to walk and/or stretch for 5–10 minutes to allow muscles and joints to relax gradually. This will allow the muscles to get rid of the byproducts of exercise, such as lactic acid, and will decrease the chance of post-exercise muscle soreness.

Proper nutrition is also important for good overall health and can increase performance on the golf course. For efficient muscular performance, one should eat a diet low in fat, high in vitamins, and rich in fiber. Proper hydration is also necessary. Most people have heard that one should drink about 64 ounces of water per day, at several intervals throughout the day. A better estimate of water intake for an athlete can be calculated by dividing the weight of the athlete by 2. The result of this calculation is the number of ounces of water that should be consumed per day (90 ounces for a 180 lb. golfer). In addition, one should also replace any water lost in perspiration during a workout or during a round of golf. This amount can be estimated by weighing oneself before and after the activity. The number of pounds lost should be multiplied by 16 to determine the number of ounces of water that should be replaced following a workout. A golfer should drink at least one 8 ounce glass of water before teeing off and drink during the round at a rate of about one 8 ounce serving for each hour of golf played.

Table 1 The golf swing can be divided into 5 distinct phases:

Setup/address	The starting position or set-up posture.
Take away/backswing	The time from ball address to the top of the backswing.
Transition	The time from the end of the backswing until the arms return to horizontal.
Acceleration	From the time the arms are horizontal until contact is made with the ball.
Follow-through	From the time of ball contact until the end of the golf swing.

MUSCLES OF THE NECK AND UPPER BACK

The musculature of the neck and upper back is extremely important for the control of posture and for smooth motion of the shoulders and arms. It is obvious to most golfers that proper posture is essential for a comfortable and strong set-up position. However, one may not realize that good posture also plays a critical role in the power generation and the consistency of the golf swing. The phases of the golf swing are outlined in Table 1. Maintenance of good posture during a dynamic action such as the golf swing requires a balance of stability and mobility. One must have enough strength to control the stability of the head and arms during the forceful motions of the golf swing, and enough endurance to allow the swing to remain consistent and stable throughout the round or practice session. Muscles in front are called the anterior group, and those of the back are referred to as the posterior group (Table 2). Muscles are attached to bone by strong fibrous bands called tendons.

Mobility of the musculoskeletal system is also essential. Flexibility of the muscles and joints is important for the production of a full swing and for other small details like keeping one's eye on the ball during trunk rotation. The muscles of the neck and upper back also play a vital role in controlling motion of the shoulder blade. The shoulder blade should move freely over the body wall during all functional motions of the head, neck, and arms. These muscles also must stabilize the shoulder blade during force-generating motions of the arms, such as the ball-striking portion of the golf swing. Any imbalance in the strength or flexibility of the musculature of the neck and upper back can adversely affect the function of the arms and cervical spine.

In ideal postural alignment of the head and upper back, the head should be centered over the neck and trunk (Fig. 1A). When a person is viewed from the back, the height of the two shoulders should be relatively symmetrical. However, it is common for the shoulder blade and shoulder musculature to be positioned about 1/2 an inch lower on the dominant side compared to the non-dominant side (lower on the right for a right-handed person). When observed from the side, the earlobe should be positioned directly above the shoulder, and the mid-back should have a gentle curve with a small hump towards the back. (Fig. 1A) The most common upper body postural problem is to have the head be positioned too far forward. (Fig.1B) The earlobe becomes located in front of the shoulder. This is often accompanied by an increase in the curve of the mid-back and a forward rounding of the shoulders. This "forward-head" posture is very common in people with desk-jobs who lean forward to look at material on their desk, such as a computer screen. These postural imbalances are often also observed in people who lift weights and in physical laborers. These folks tend to build the muscles located in the front of the chest and to neglect the muscles of the upper back. These postural deviations tend to limit motion of the shoulder complex, which can lead to dramatic decreases in power generation of the golf swing.

With ideal posture, the muscles located in the front and the back of the neck equally support the weight of the head. In individuals with "forward-head" posture,

Table 2 Major Muscles of the Neck and Upper Back

Front of Neck	Sternocleidomastoid, scalenes, longus colli, and longus capitus
Back of Neck	Cervical paraspinals, Levator scapulae, and upper trapezius
Upper Back	Middle and lower trapezius, Rhomboids, and serratus anterior

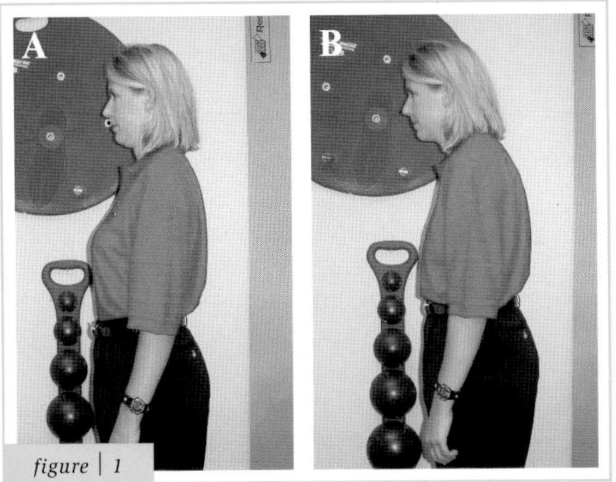

figure | 1

A: Ideal posture, B: Forward head posture

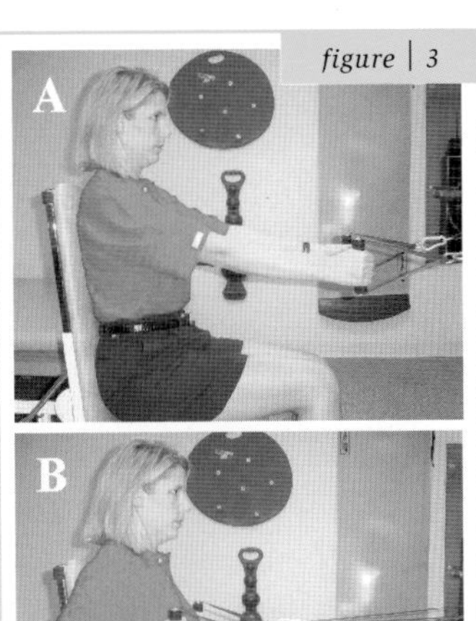

figure | 3

A: Seated rows: From a starting position with elbows straight, shown in figure A, pull the handles backward and concentrate on pulling your shoulder blades together as shown in figure B.

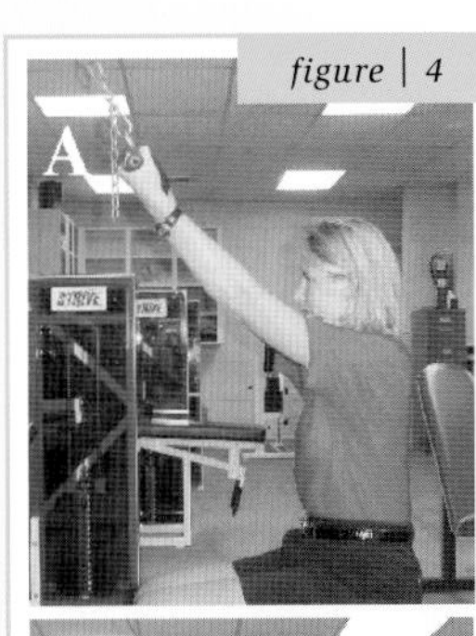

figure | 4

Latissimus pull downs: From a strating position with elbows straight and arms over your head, shown in figure A, pull the bar down to the mid chest area. Keep your back straight and don't lean backward, shown in figure B.

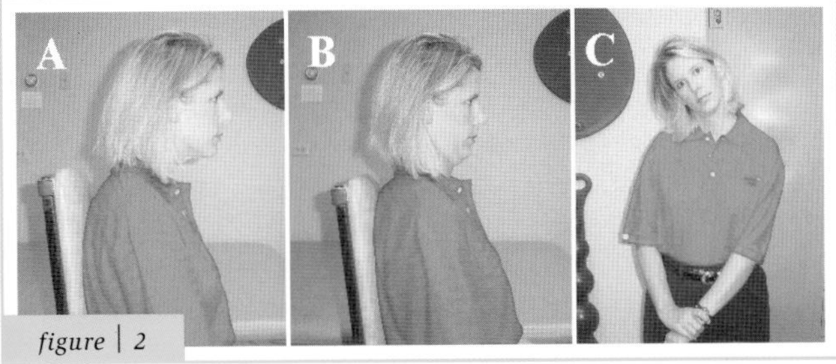

figure | 2

Neck Retraction: To perform, sit in a comfortable position as shown in figure A, then pull your head straight back keeping your eyes and jaw level, as shown in figure B. Hold 5 seconds.

C: Lateral Neck Stretch: To perform, grab your left wrist with your right hand and pull down and to the right. At the same time, tilt your head to the right. Hold this stretch for 10–20 seconds. It is generally a good idea to perform 3–5 of these stretches in both directions, twice a day

the weight of the head is supported primarily by the muscles located in the back of the neck. The workload of these muscles is therefore increased, which can subsequently produce muscle spasms in the back of the neck, significant headaches, and restrictions in neck range of motion. The rounding of the shoulders tends to over-stretch and weaken muscles that control the motion of the shoulder blade. These muscular imbalances can lead to alterations and inconsistencies in all portions of the golf swing.

The key to optimal function of the upper back and neck is to obtain sufficient range of motion of the neck and to build enough strength in the musculature of the upper back to maintain good postural alignment during all portions of the golf swing. The muscles of the neck should be stretched daily. Figure 2 shows two effective stretches that can be done either while sitting at your desk, or just before walking up to the first tee. A modification of the stretch shown in Figure 2C can be performed in a golf cart during a round (Fig. 17B). Additionally, one should add at least one mid-back strengthening exercise to his or her fitness program. Figures 3 and 4 show two exercises that will strength the muscles that are located between the shoulder blades. Building appropriate muscular balance in this region will allow the shoulder blades to be located in the optimal position, about 2–3 inches from the spine, and the head to be located in a stable position above the trunk. These simple exercises should not only improve the golf swing, they should also help alleviate headache and stress at work, therefore increasing productivity and allowing the golfer more time out on the course.

MUSCLES OF THE CHEST, SHOULDER AND UPPER EXTREMITY

The musculature of the chest, shoulder and upper extremity is of obvious importance to all aspects of the golf swing. The small muscles of the forearm and hand play vital roles in the fine control of the position of the clubface. The large muscles of the arm, chest, and shoulder must be flexible in order to complete a full swing and strong in order to generate power during the acceleration phase. All of these muscles also provide stability during ball contact. There have been a number of elegant studies that have defined which muscles are active during each particular phase of the golf swing. For example, the muscles that contract to rotate the arm away from the midline are active during the extremes of shoulder range of motion during the back-swing and follow-through phases of the swing. Whereas the muscles that function to rotate the arm toward the midline are preferentially activated during the acceleration phase of the swing (Table 3).

The muscles of the chest are active during all phases of the golf swing, but are most active during the acceleration

Table | 3 Major Muscles of the Chest, Shoulder, and Upper Extremity

Chest	Pectoralis major and minor
Shoulder	Deltoids
Rotator Cuff	Supraspinatus, Infraspinatus, teres minor and subscapularis
Front of arm	Biceps and Brachialis
Back of arm	Triceps
Front of forearm	Wrist flexors and forearm rotators (pronators)
Back of forearm	Wrist extensors and forearm rotators (supinators)

phase. These muscles are very powerful and function to aid in most lifting tasks. Individuals who lift weights or have physically demanding occupations often preferentially strengthen the chest muscles, while tending to neglect the upper back muscles. This pattern can cause and/or exacerbate the "forward-head" posture. To counteract this common detrimental postural problem, one must not only strengthen the upper back muscles, but also stretch the chest musculature. Figure 5 shows a simple doorway stretch that has proven to be effective in stretching the chest musculature and alleviating "forward-head" posture. It is also a good idea to stretch the chest muscles periodically during a round of golf (Fig. 17A). Improving postural alignment will allow a greater range of motion during the golf swing. This will, in turn, produce greater club-head speed and increased ball flight.

The rotator cuff muscles are also active during all phases of the golf swing. These muscles act primarily to rotate the arm and to stabilize the shoulder joint. The rotator cuff is stressed in any activity where the hands are raised above the level of the shoulders. A round of golf that normally consists of more than 50 full swings repetitively stresses the rotator cuff and the shoulder. The shoulder and rotator cuff represent the 4th most injured anatomical site in golfers.

About 10% of golf injuries in professional and recreational golfers occur in the shoulder region. These injuries are associated with decreased strength and flexibility in the muscles of the rotator cuff. Shoulder injuries also increase in frequency with increased age. There are some relatively simple exercises that can be performed to stretch and strengthen the rotator cuff muscles. These will help prevent injury to the region and will promote a fuller and more powerful swing. The stretches shown in Figure 6 can be easily be performed anywhere and are good exercises to do as part of a warm-up routine. To warm up, one can replace the wand shown in Figure 6 with a golf club and do the stretch while standing (Fig. 17C and D). The exercises shown in Figures 7 and 8 will strength the rotator cuff. One or two sets of 10–12 repetitions of these exercises performed at least twice a week will decrease the likelihood of a shoulder injury and will help increase the power-generating capacity of your swing.

The elbow is another area that is commonly injured in golfers. The term "golfer's elbow" refers to an injury of the front of the elbow. The site of injury is usually located where a number of muscles that act to flex the wrist attach to the bone. This is obviously a common injury observed in golfers. However, injury to the back of the elbow, where the muscles that extend the wrist attach, is also relatively common. The muscles of the front and back of the forearm help to stabilize the wrist during contact with the ball. Research has shown that the wrist flexors (muscles in the front) exhibit a burst of activity at ball contact while the wrist extensors (muscles in the back) are continually active throughout the transition and acceleration phases. The regions where these muscles attach to bone are subject to repetitive minor trauma with every ball strike. It is therefore essential that these muscles be flexible and well conditioned so that the repetitive trauma does not lead to tissue damage. Injury to the front of the elbow tends to occur more often in the right arm of a right-handed golfer. This appears to be due to the high amount of tension that is generated in the area when there is simultaneous contraction of the muscles and ball contact. Injury can be due to overuse of muscles that are not well conditioned or to an inordinate amount of tension created in a single swing. This latter situation can occur when a shot is hit "fat" and there is excessive contact with the ground. Single-swing trauma can also occur when the club encounters a hard object such as a rock or tree root. Injury to the back of the elbow tends to occur in the lead arm (the left arm in a right-handed golfer). This injury tends to be caused by overuse of the wrist extensor muscles. The chance of occurrence is increased

figure | 5

Doorway Stretch: To perform, stand in a doorway with your feet about 1.5 feet from the door and your hands at shoulder height on the door frame. Slowly lean into the door. You should feel a stretch in the chest area. Hold this position for about 10 seconds. Repeat 5-10 times, once or twice a day.

figure | 6

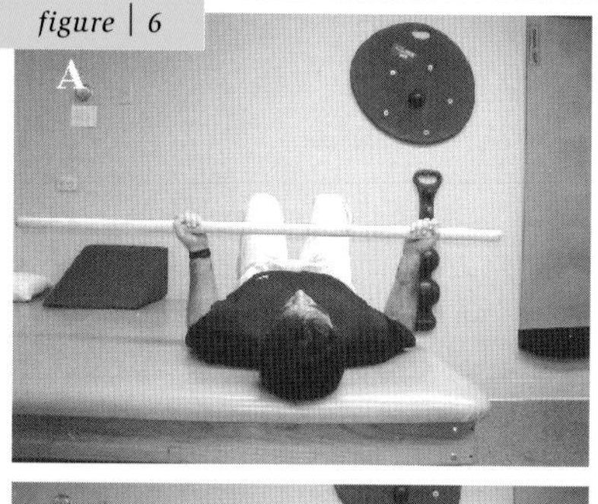

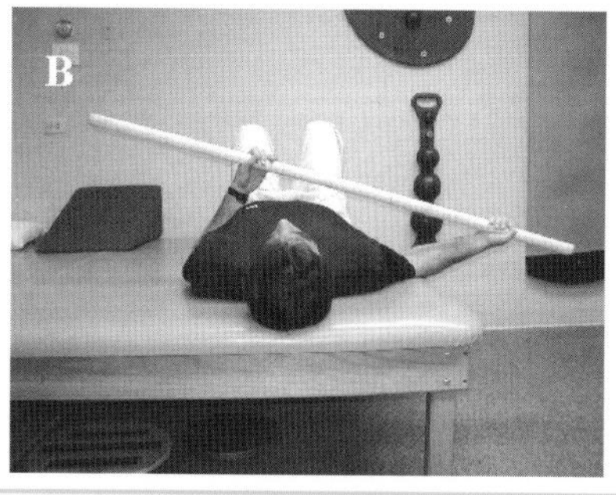

Shoulder Rotation Stretch: Hold a long dowel, or broom with palms up. Keep your elbows at your sides. First push to the right until you feel a stretch (shown in figure B). Hold this stretch for 10–20 seconds. Then push to the left and hold for the same amount of time. Perform 3–5 stretches on each side.

figure | 7

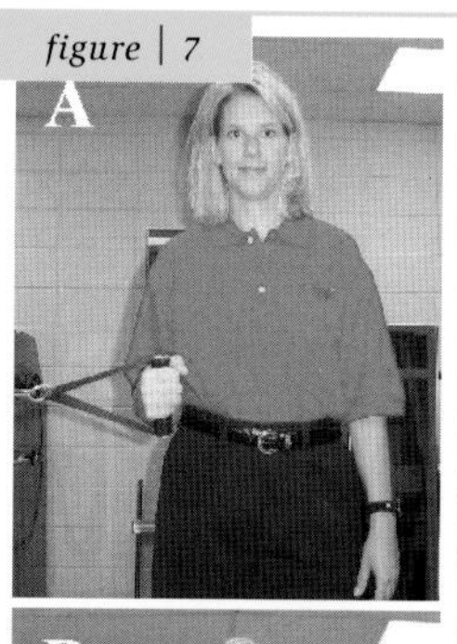

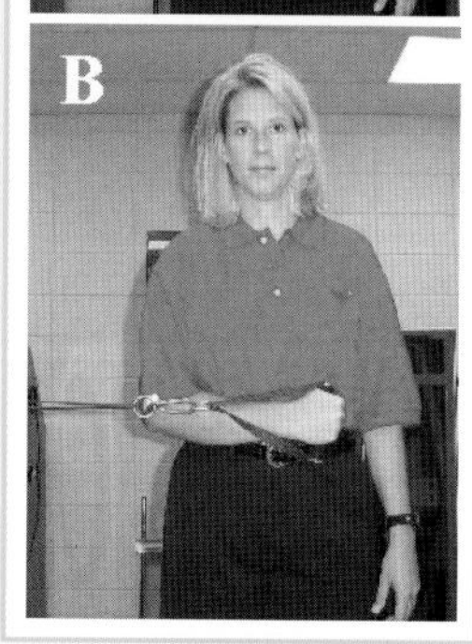

Shoulder internal rotation to strengthen your rotator cuff. Grasp the handle with your elbow bent at 90° and your hand in front of your body (figure A). While keeping your elbow at your side, pull the handle across your body (figure B).

figure | 8

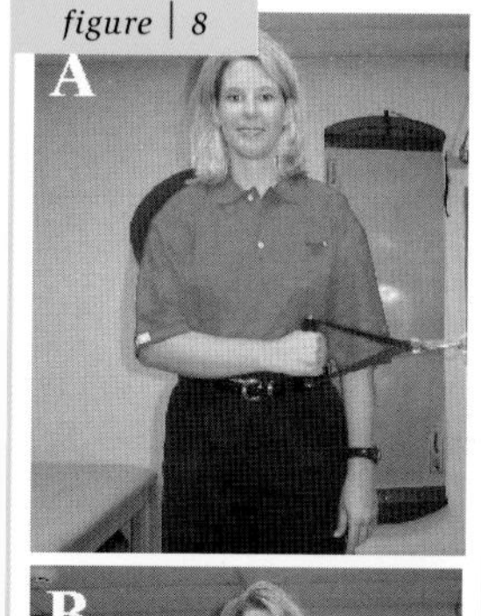

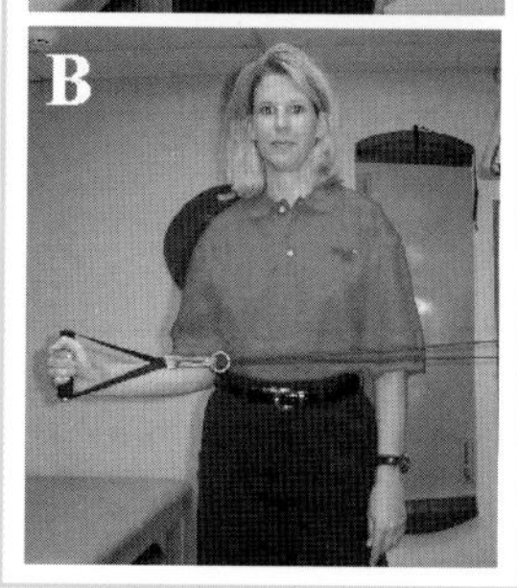

Shoulder external rotation to strengthen your rotator cuff. Grasp the handle with your elbow bent at 90° and your hand in against the front of your body (figure A). While keeping your elbow at your side, pull the handle away from the midline of your body (figure B).

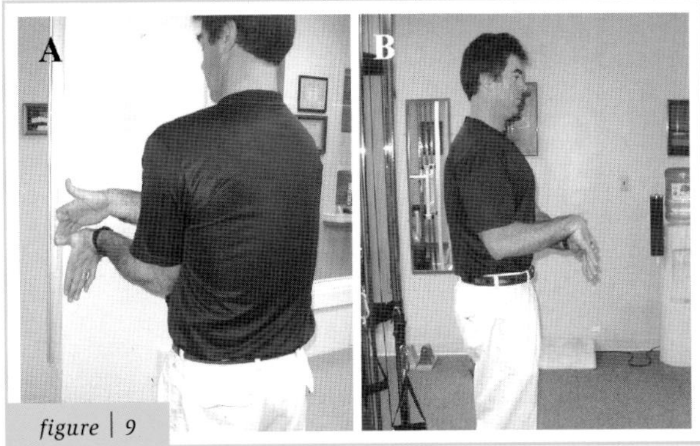

figure | 9

Wrist Stretches:
A: To stretch your wrist flexors, stand with your palm against a wall and try to flatten your palm against the wall. Then, pull your thumb backward, gently. This is also a good carpal tunnel stretch.

B: To stretch your wrist extensors, put gradual pressure against the back of your hand and bend your wrist until a stretch is felt. Both stretches should be held for 10–20 seconds.

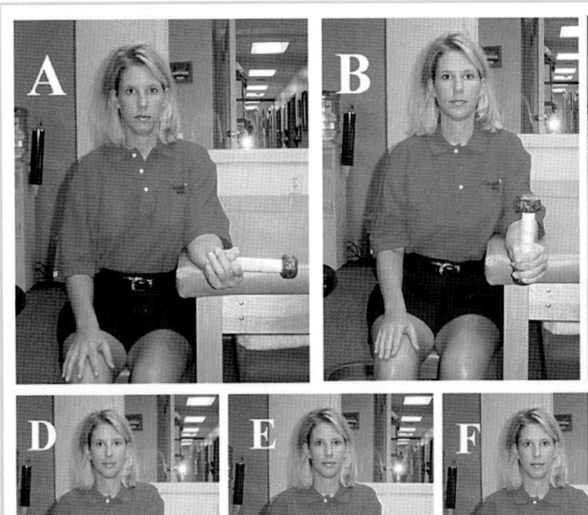

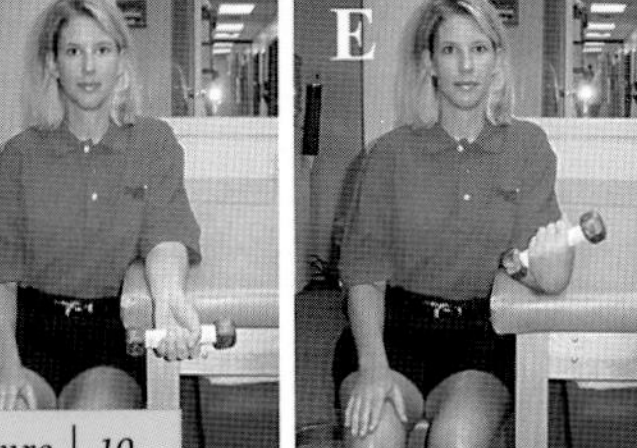

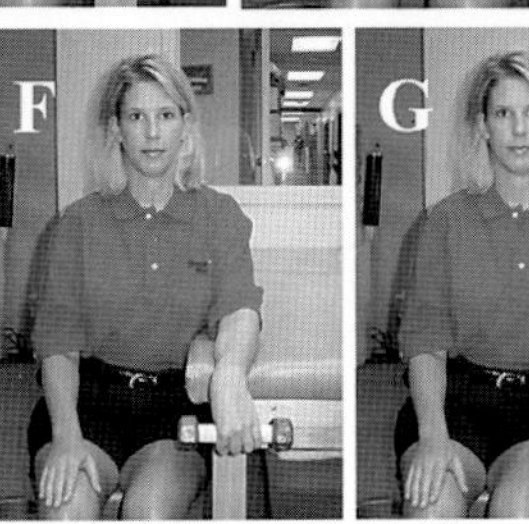

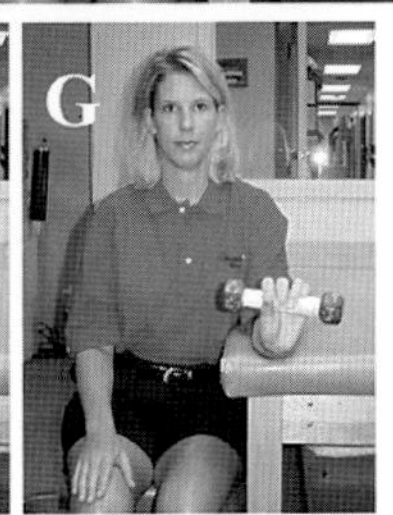

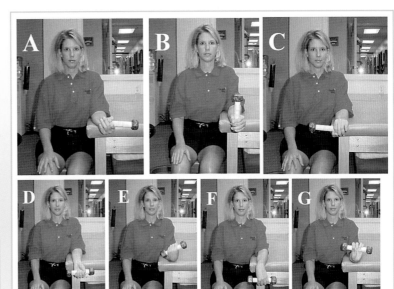

figure | 10

Wrist strengthening:
A-C: Thor's hammer wrist rotation: While holding a dumbbell at one end, rotate the wrist from one side to the other as far as possible. Repeat on the other wrist.

D-F: Wrist curl: While holding a dumbbell in your hand, palm up, bend your wrist up toward your body.

F-G: Reverse wrist curl: While holding a dumbbell in your hand with your palm facing down, bend your wrist up toward your body.

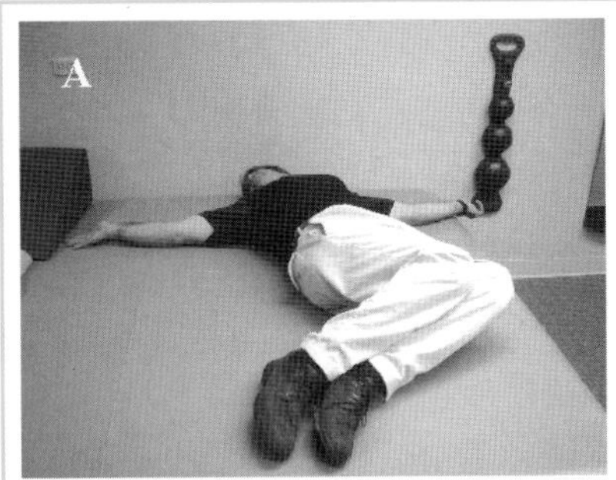

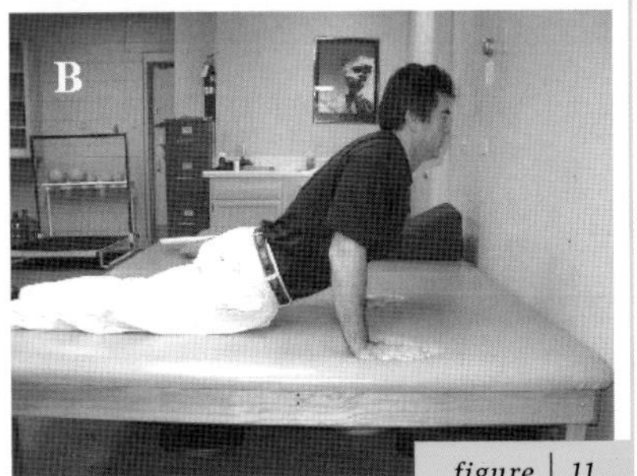

figure | 11

A: Lower Trunk Stretch: Start lying on your back with your knees bent. Bring both knees down to one side while you look to the opposite side. Hold this position for 10–20 seconds.

B: Press up: Start lying on your stomach with your hands under your shoulders. Press up, and attempt to straighten your elbows while keeping your hips in contact with the exercise mat. Keep your lower back and buttocks relaxed. Hold this position for 2 seconds. Repeat 10 times.

with a tight grip or by excessive wrist motion during the acceleration and follow-through phases.

To decrease the probability of elbow injury the muscles of the forearm should be well conditioned and flexible. The stretches shown in Figure 9 should be performed at least every other day and should be part of the warm-up session. The forearm muscles are often neglected in a general strengthening program. Figure 10 outlines some exercises to strengthen the major muscles of the forearm. These exercises should be performed 2–3 times per week. Injury to the elbow can cause sharp pain at the instant of ball contact, which will adversely affect the outcome of the swing. Recovery from this type of elbow injury can be prolonged and detrimentally affect a whole season. Therefore, the key should be injury prevention.

MUSCLES OF THE TRUNK

The muscles of the trunk provide stability, mobility, and power during all aspects of the golf swing (Table 4). Flexibility of the trunk musculature allows for trunk rotation and the transfer of force from the lower body to the upper body during the swing. Studies have shown that the most noticeable difference in the golf swings of professional versus amateur golfers is the amount of trunk rotation. More skilled players were found to have about twice as much trunk rotation compared to players of lesser caliber. Increased trunk flexibility leads to a larger arc of the golf swing, which produces more club head speed and greater distance of ball travel. Players with deficits in trunk flexibility that result in decreased trunk rotation are found to use muscular substitution patterns in order to attempt to generate sufficient club-head speed. These substitution patterns tend to be less efficient, which results in decreased ball flight and increased stress and strain on the musculoskeletal system. Therefore, mobility through the trunk region is necessary for a smooth powerful swing that does not overstress the spine or other elements of the mid-body.

It is important to perform trunk stretch exercises 3–5 times per week. The stretches shown in Figure 11 are easy and feel pleasant to perform. The back-lying trunk twist described in Figure 11A is a good general low-back stretch and can be done in bed before getting up in the morning. The press-up exercise shown in Figure 11B not only stretches out the abdominal musculature, but it also helps to nourish the joints of the lower spine and assists in maintaining the correct position of the disks that serve as cushions between adjacent vertebrae. It is also a good practice to stretch the muscles and

Table | 4 Major Muscles of the Trunk

Low Back	Erector spinae, Transversospinalis and quadratus lumborum
Abdominal region	Rectus abdominus and abdominal oblique

joints of the trunk multiple times during a round of golf (Fig. 16C, 18A, and 18B).

Trunk strength is important in the generation of power and the maintenance of the correct spine angle throughout the golf swing. The golf swing also can induce a tremendous amount of stress on the spine. The proper sequencing of trunk muscle activation helps to maintain the spine angle during the swing and helps prevent spinal injury. The muscles of the low back and the abdomen are highly active throughout the golf swing. The back muscles appear to be active primarily to stabilize the region while the abdominal muscles act to rotate and flex the trunk. Both muscle groups tend to be active on the right and left sides simultaneously, which helps to control posture and to maintain trunk stability during rotation. The high level of trunk muscle activity necessary to produce an effective swing can lead to fatigue of these muscles at late stages of a round or practice session. Muscular fatigue can lead to swing deviations, producing shots that go off line and swing alterations that can stress muscles and joints. The exercises in Figure 12 will help to strengthen the muscular cylinder of the trunk. The prone (leg facing down) leg raise is a very efficient exercise to strengthen the muscles of the low back while the side-lying pelvic raise more specifically targets the quadratus lumborum (Fig. 12A). The quadratus lumborum is important for stabilization of the low back during all movements of the trunk. The bent knee crunch is a good exercise to strengthen the abdominal muscles. These exercises should be part of any fitness program for golfers and are often also used during rehabilitation following trunk injury.

MUSCLES OF THE LOWER EXTREMITY

The muscles of the lower extremities provide the base of support for the golf swing (Table 5). There is also important power generation that begins in the lower extremities and is transferred through the trunk and upper extremities to the club and ball. All major muscles of the body have been classified into two groups by the Finnish physician Vladimir Janda. There are muscles that are very important for postural control that are prone to tightness. The other set of muscles is more involved with movement, and these muscles are prone to weakness. Most golfers who routinely walk 18 holes have relatively good strength in the muscles of the legs. Most general fitness programs include many good exercises to strengthen the major muscles of the lower extremities. However, most individuals have tight muscles associated with the lower extremities. This type of muscle imbalance can easily go unnoticed, but can have detrimental affects on the low back, can make walking painful, and can adversely influence the golf swing.

The hamstrings, located in the back of the thigh, and the hip flexors, located in the front of the hip, are postural muscles that often exhibit tightness. The hamstrings normally act to bend the knee. However, if the hamstrings are tight, they

Table | 5 Major Muscle Groups of the Lower Extremity

Buttocks	Gluteal muscles, piriformis and quadratus femoris
Front of hip	Hip flexors
Outer thigh	Tensor fascia latae
Inner thigh	Adductors
Front of thigh	Quadriceps and sartorius
Back of thigh	Hamstrings
Back of leg	Ankle plantar flexors
Front of leg	Ankle dorsiflexors

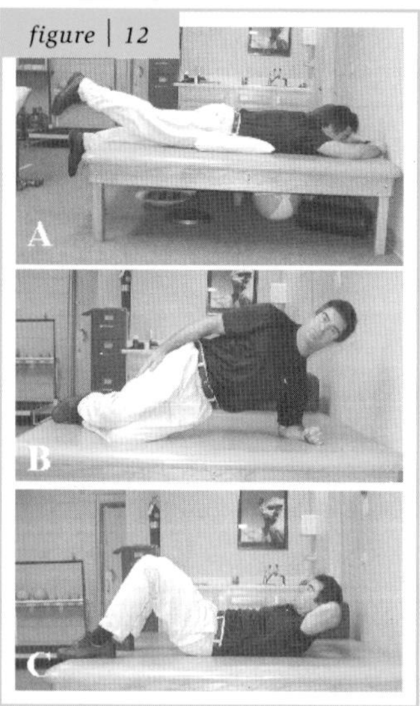

figure | 12

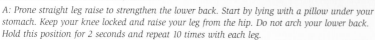

A: Prone straight leg raise to strengthen the lower back. Start by lying with a pillow under your stomach. Keep your knee locked and raise your leg from the hip. Do not arch your lower back. Hold this position for 2 seconds and repeat 10 times with each leg.

B: Sidelying pelvic raise to strengthen your lower back. Start by lying on your side propped up on an elbow. Your other hand should rest on your thigh. Raise your hips until your spine forms a straight line (figure B). Hold this position for 2–4 seconds. Repeat 8–15 times on each side.

C: Curl up: Start lying on your back with your hands clasped behind your neck. Flatten your low back against the exercise mat. Use your abdominal muscles to raise your head and shoulders so that your shoulder blades come off of the exercise mat. Repeat 10–50 times.

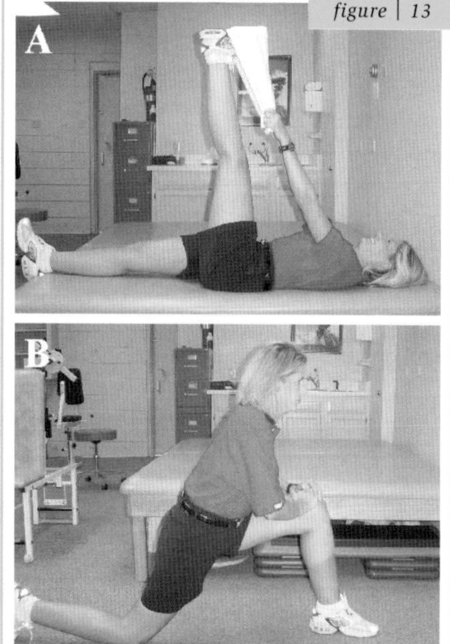

figure | 13

A: Hamstring stretch: While lying on your back, loop a towel under your foot. Use the towel to help raise your leg to a vertical position while keeping your knee straight. You should feel a stretch in the back of your thigh. Hold the stretch for 10–20 seconds. Perform 3–5 repetitions on each leg.

B: Hip flexor stretch: With one leg behind you, as shown, slowly push the pelvis downward slightly arching your back. A stretch should be felt in the front of your hip. Hold the stretch for 10–20 seconds. Perform 3–5 repetitions on each leg.

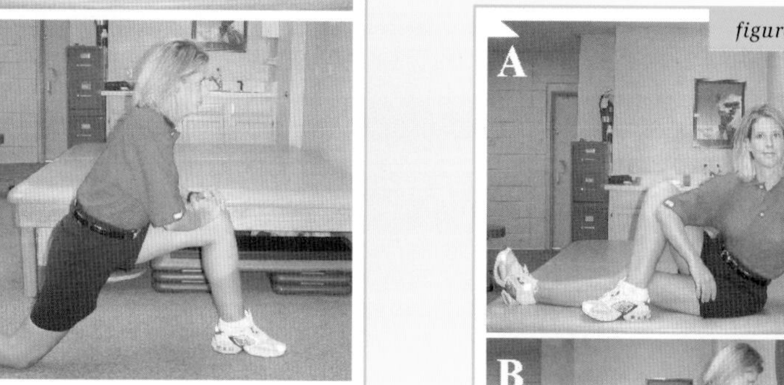

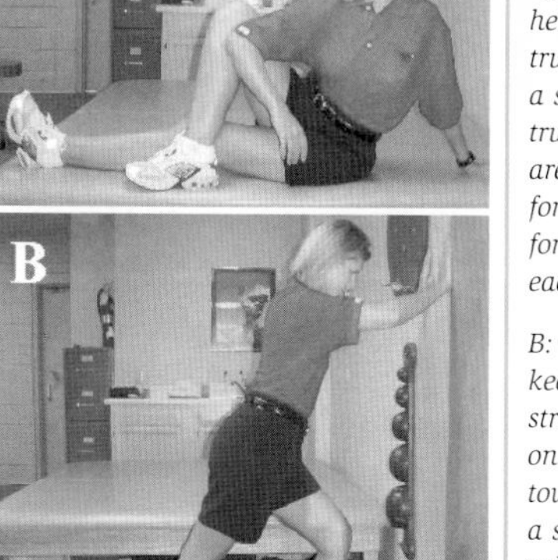

figure | 14

A: Low back/gluteal stretch: While in a sitting position, cross on leg over the other. Push your elbow against your knee to help you rotate your trunk. You should feel a stretch in the lower trunk and gluteal area. Hold the stretch for 10–20 seconds. Perform 3–5 repetitions in each direction.

B: Calf stretch: While keeping the back leg straight, with the heel on the floor, lean toward the wall until a stretch is felt in the calf. Hold the stretch for 10–20 seconds. Perform 3–5 repetitions on each leg.

figure | 15

Before the round it is important to stretch the legs. A hamstring stretch for the back of the thigh is shown in figure A. A stretch for the quadriceps, located in the front of thigh is shown in figure B and figure C shows a stretch for the calf. Each of the stretches should be held for 10–20 seconds.

figure | 16

It is also important to stretch the muscles of the hips and thighs before starting your round. A good, general low back and gluteal region stretch is shown in figure A. Figure B shows a stretch for the hip flexors, located in the front of the thigh and figure C shows a good stretch for the left side of the trunk and outside of the left thigh. All stretches should be held for 10–20 seconds and be performed on both sides of the body.

figure | 17

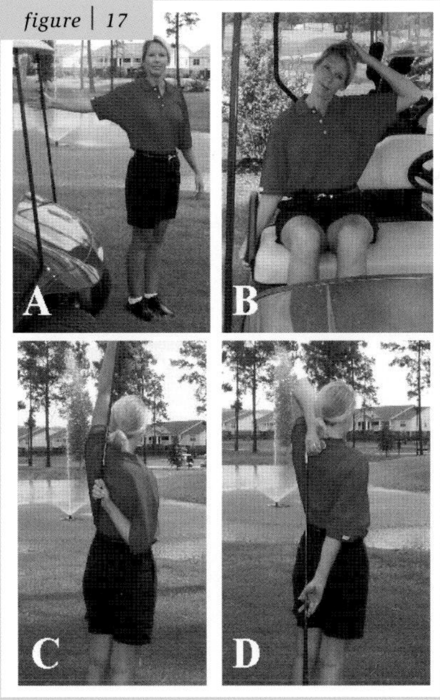

Upper body stretches should also be performed before a round. A chest stretch is shown in figure A. Figure B shows a good general neck stretch. It is important to anchor the shoulder by holding on to the seat with one hand, while using the other hand to pull the neck into a stretched position. Figures C and D show how one can use a golf club to stretch the rotator cuff muscles of the shoulder.

figure | 18

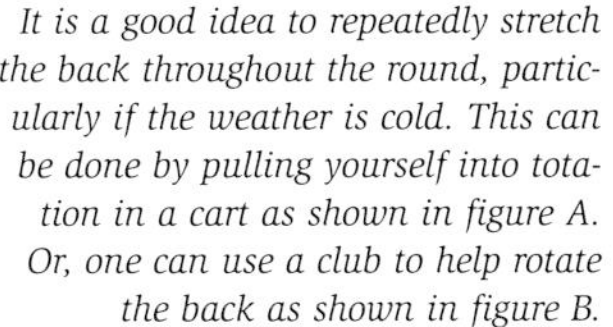

It is a good idea to repeatedly stretch the back throughout the round, particularly if the weather is cold. This can be done by pulling yourself into rotation in a cart as shown in figure A. Or, one can use a club to help rotate the back as shown in figure B.

tend to flatten the low back. This can lead to low back pain and decreased trunk motion. To test hamstring flexibility, one can simply bend at the waist and attempt to touch the floor. If you can't touch the top of your toes, your hamstrings are tight. The stretching technique in Figure 13A should be performed at least every other day if you have tight hamstrings. A modified hamstring stretch is an essential part of both the warm up and cool down activities that should bracket your round of golf (Fig. 15A). The muscle bellies of the major hip flexors are located next to the spine, behind the abdominal organs. Some of these muscles run from the vertebrae of the low back to the bones in the front of the thigh. Many individuals have extremely tight hip flexors. This tightness tends to accentuate the normal curve found in the low back and increases the apparent size of the buttock by making that region stick out. This postural abnormality leads to compression of the joints of the low back and often to significant back pain. The hip flexor stretches in Figures 13B and 16B can be performed anywhere, should be part of a warm-up routine, and will help prevent low back injury.

There are a number of muscles in the region of the buttocks that are involved in rotating the thigh. Thigh rotation is an integral part of the back-swing and follow-through portions of the golf swing. The majority of patients who come to a physical therapy clinic complaining of low back or hip pain exhibit tightness in the muscles that rotate the thigh outward. This tightness can lead to "duck feet" type alterations in stance and gait, where the feet point out. Tight external rotators also can put pressure on one of the major nerves of the lower extremity, the sciatic nerve. This can lead to shooting pain down the back of the leg that can extend to the foot. Tight external rotators will also cause shortening of the back-swing and follow-through leading to decreased power generation. Figures 14A and 16A describe an exercise that will stretch the major external rotators of the hip, which are located in the buttock region.

The muscles located in the back of the calf are also particularly prone to tightness. These are postural muscles that are continuously active to help control posture. These muscles are also highly active during walking and running. Decreased flexibility in the muscles in the back of the calf can lead to altered walking with subsequent fatigue and cramping of muscles of the leg. Tightness in these muscles can also lead to injury of the Achilles tendon and to foot problems. The calf stretches demonstrated in Figures 14B and 15C should be part of both warm-up and cool-down programs.

CONCLUSION

A healthy musculoskeletal system is essential for lifelong health and for enjoyment of the game of golf. Golfers of all skill levels and of all ages benefit from a good overall fitness program. The general trend toward increased levels of fitness in professional golfers has led to a general increase in level of play, with a decrease in the rate of injury. The exercises outlined in this chapter are designed to supplement a good overall fitness program. These additions should help add to the stability, mobility and strength of the muscles important to the golf swing. Participation in golf adds to both physical and mental fitness and can be enjoyed by individuals of all ages. Taking care of the muscles important in golf will result in a higher level of play and a more enjoyable forever golf experience.

MEDICAL RADIOLOGY

CHAPTER 5

T. Glenn Pait, M.D.

Back trouble is probably the main reason I got into golf. I have always loved sports, and during my high school years I played them all-football, basketball, baseball, and track. In my senior year I injured my back during football season. I had been named All-American and had been offered several college scholarships. My coach suggested that I rest my back for six months and then make a decision about my future in college sports. That summer after my senior year I really started working on my golf game seriously for the first time in my life. I loved the game, and it was easier on my back than the other sports. I have played golf daily ever since.

I have always appreciated the importance of a daily exercise routine and a healthy diet. I never smoked and I stayed away from alcohol. I was working out before working out was "cool." I would do exercises such as sit-ups and push-ups in my hotel room at night when on Tour. Swimming is the only thing that would really make my back hurt, so I stayed away from the pool. Now that I am 89, I am having a few aches and pains in my back. My doctor told me while looking at my x-ray in the fall of 2001 that my spine looked like a "nightmare." Oh well, I just keep moving-working in my yard and hitting golf balls every day that the sun shines. Golf is truly a game for life. (Sam died on May 23, 2002, not long after sharing this story with us –Ed.)

Sam Snead

Medical radiology is a discipline of medical science that is dedicated to the visualization and imaging of the human body for the diagnosis and treatment of diseases and injury. Advancements in technology have allowed the development of new machines and techniques to view and investigate the body's internal organs and their functions. The ability to view internal organs provides the opportunity to evaluate the anatomy of the organ to confirm a diagnosis without an exploratory operation. It also creates avenues of treatment in which a physician can carry out a procedure while watching the organ. Imaging is the technique of creating pictures on film and computers of body structures. Imaging was born in a physics laboratory at the University of Würzburg in Würzburg, Germany. On November 8, 1895, Dr. Wilhelm Conrad Röntgen (sometimes spelled Roentgen) was studying the properties of the cathode ray tube. During his experiments he noted a strange luminescence which created shadow pictures. With further studies, he discovered an invisible ray that he concluded was entirely new and called them "X," for X the unknown. His discovery was published on December 28, 1895. Within weeks Röntgen's work was replicated throughout the scientific world. Soon X-rays were everywhere. The first prize from Alfred Nobel's endowment for outstanding scientific accomplishments was awarded to Wilhelm Conrad Röntgen in physics in 1901. The discovery of X-Rays changed the practice of medicine forever and has saved countless lives.

Medical radiology is divided into three divisions: diagnostic, therapeutic and interventional. Diagnostic radiology involves the imaging of body organs and tissues and their functions. Ionizing radiation in diagnostic radiology provides a window to view normal and abnormal anatomy. Changes in organs caused by disease and injury can often be detected. In addition, the results of medical and surgical therapies for diseases and trauma can be evaluated and their outcomes recorded. Therapeutic radiology is better known as radiation oncology. It is the branch of medicine that uses ionizing radiation in the treatment of cancer and tumors. Hopefully, the dose of radiation will be sufficient to destroy the cancerous cells with only temporary injury to neighboring normal cells. If the cancer does not shrink after the radiation treatments, it may be radioresistant and require other therapies. Radiation therapy may be the only treatment for certain diseases, and is intended to effect a cure. It is sometimes used in combination with other cancer-treatment drugs (combined modality therapy). In some cases radiation is palliative therapy that is applied for the relief of symptoms such as pain. It is often given either before or after surgical removal of certain tumors that could not be totally excised or to prevent the tumor's recurrence. A growing field of radiology and surgery is interventional radiology. It is the nonsurgical treatment of certain diseases using imaging techniques to navigate small catheters, balloons, filters, and micro-instruments through blood vessels and into organs. A common interventional radiology procedure is balloon angioplasty in which a small balloon catheter is guided into a blocked or narrowed artery and inflated to open it to renewed blood flow. This is often the procedure for coronary (heart) artery disease. Other indications for interventional radiology include: chemoembolization, the delivery of anticancer drugs directly into a tumor; cerebral

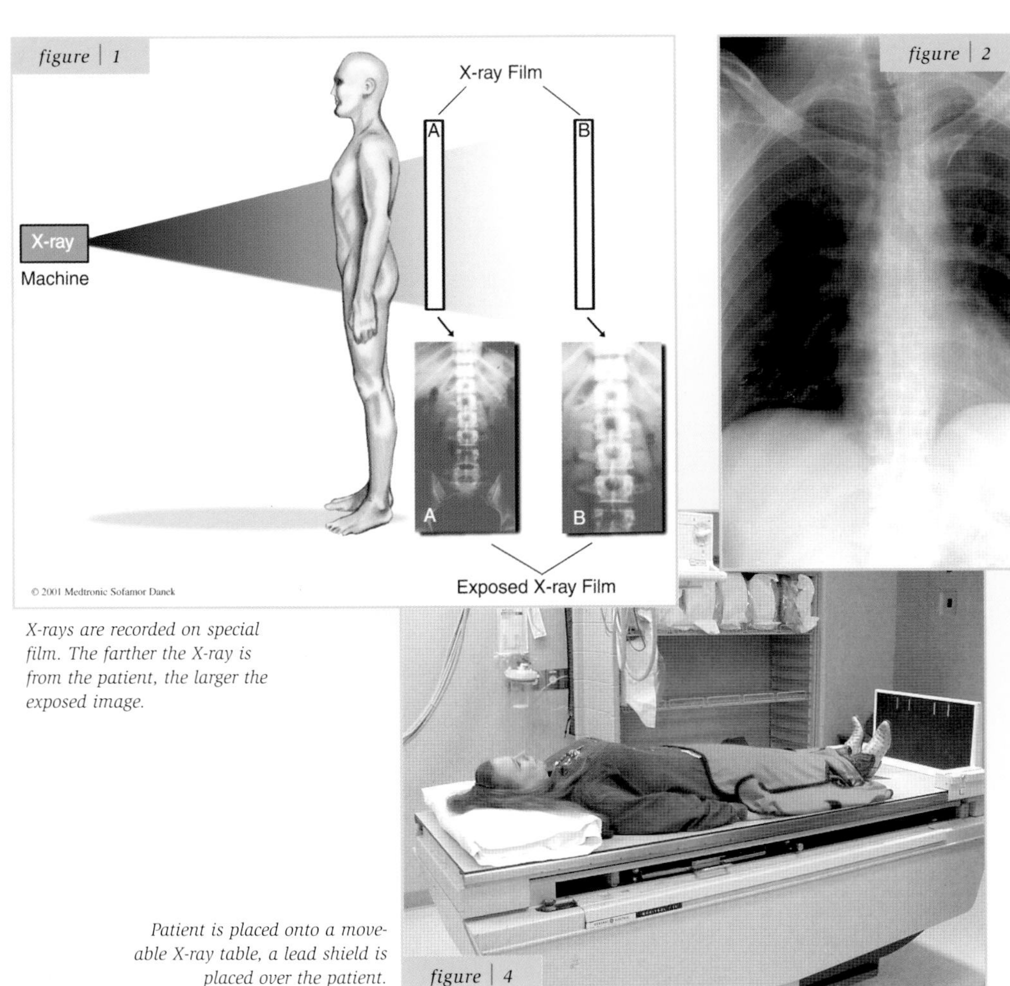

X-rays are recorded on special film. The farther the X-ray is from the patient, the larger the exposed image.

Plain X-ray of the chest.

Patient is placed onto a moveable X-ray table, a lead shield is placed over the patient.

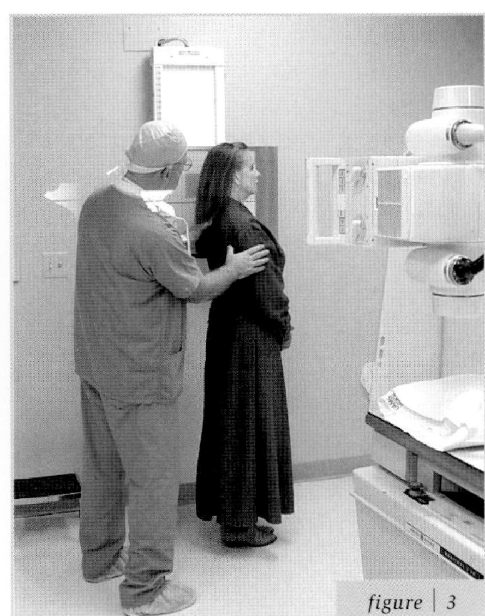

Patient is positioned standing by an X-ray technologist.

angioplasty, inflation of a balloon into a brain aneurysm (blood blister) to seal off the aneurysm and prevent rupture and catastrophic hemorrhage; thrombolysis, delivery of blood clot dissolving drugs into blood vessels; vertebroplasty; and fallopian tube catherization, opening of closed fallopian tubes in women experiencing infertility problems. Interventional radiology is a growing field with expanding indications.

X-RAYS (RADIOGRAPHS/ROENTGENOGRAMS)

X-rays or radiographs are often referred to as plain X-rays or plain films. X-rays are still commonly used despite the development of other more sophisticated computer-assisted tests such as the CAT scan or the MRI. Almost every medical and dental clinic has X-rays. These machines are very busy. This is because they are quick and easy to obtain; the films can be developed without much delay; and are relatively inexpensive. Plain X-rays are very useful in evaluating structures such as bone, teeth, and certain soft tissues like the breast. They can be helpful locating lost metal or shrapnel in the body. Unfortunately, they are not very good for evaluating most organ systems other than to detect size, i.e. an enlarged heart. They give very little insight into the true evaluation of blood vessels. In certain situations they may be able to detect air near or in organs if there is a large enough amount of air present.

X-rays are a type of radiation that is similar to light waves, but at a much higher energy level. This high energy level is needed in order to pass through body tissues. The ability of the X-rays to penetrate structures of the body depends on the density of the tissue. X-rays will pass very easily through soft tissues but will have a somewhat more difficult task passing through a denser tissue such as bone. X-rays are recorded on photographic film that turns black when hit by the X-ray. The farther the X-ray film is from the patient, the greater the magnification of the final exposed X-ray image (Fig. 1). When focused onto a part of the body, such as the chest to evaluate the lungs, the parts that allow the X-ray to pass through without any impedance, such as air in the lung, will appear black on the film. Soft tissues such as skin, fat, and muscle will show up as shades of gray. Very dense substances such as bone, will be seen as white. There is a gradation on X-rays; a black view shows air, gray-white abnormalities are soft tissues, and very white structures represent calcification or bone (Fig. 2). When an individual has an X-ray taken, he or she is either placed onto a moveable table or asked to stand up (Fig. 3). It is important not to move while on the X-ray table or standing. Any movement will effect the quality of the X-ray. During the actual X-ray procedure, the areas not being filmed may be shielded (Fig. 4). Women are always asked if they are pregnant before having an X-ray because the radiation may cause abnormalities during the early stages of pregnancy. Patients are only exposed to the X-ray beam for just a fraction of a second, the whole procedure taking only a few minutes. The technician will tell a patient to "Hold still, take a deep breath, and don't move." They will then hear a high-pitched noise. That's all there is to it. X-rays produce a two-dimensional image, so more X-rays may be taken from different views and angles to provide more information.

The different patient positions describe the part of the patient first exposed to the X-ray beams and the direction the beams are traveling through the patient. For instance, the posterior to anterior (P-A) view means that the radiation is passed from the patient's back (posterior) to the front (anterior) (Fig. 5). The anterior to posterior (A-P) view occurs when the X-ray beam travels through the patient from the front (anterior) to the back (posterior) (Fig. 6). Lateral X-rays describe the radiation beam passing through the patient's side, either the right or left (Fig. 7).

X-rays can produce very clear images of bone. They are often the first radiologic study performed when there is a broken bone; this applies to the spine. X-rays are used to evaluate for loss of bone density, particularly when dealing with osteoporosis. X-rays can detect loss of height of the vertebral bodies of the spine that will be consistent with a fracture (Fig. 8). Findings on X-rays can often prompt the need for further radiologic study, such as a CAT scan or MRI. The final analysis: X-rays are an excellent choice for evaluation for bony abnormalities of the spine.

MAGNETIC RESONANCE IMAGING (MRI)

Magnetic Resonance Imaging is commonly referred to as an MRI or just MR. It is an imaging procedure that does not use ionizing radiation to produce pictures of the body. MRI utilizes a computer to process images of the body's tissues such as the intervertebral discs, spinal cord, nerves, bone marrow, tendons, arteries, breasts, brain, and other soft tissue structures including tumors. In fact, it is one of the most often used tests to image the spine, spinal cord and nerves (Fig. 9). The MRI has been around since the 1970s. Most hospitals and many medical clinics now have MRI units. Often, the first imaging test obtained for many types of back or spinal problems will be an MRI. It is often obtained before plain X-rays. It is not an inexpensive test, and it takes longer than many other radiology tests. The MRI is a technological advancement that allows a better understanding of the spinal cord and discs. It provides highly detailed images of soft tissue components such as the discs, spinal cord and nerves. With a good quality MRI the annulus (outer disc layer) and ligaments can also be visualized. The MRI pictures are very similar to those of a CAT scan; however, the MRI and the CAT scan are not the same type of radiological examinations. They often supplement each other and provide anatomy details that help physicians and radiologists when the images are compared. The MRI is better for viewing soft tissues and can distinguish abnormal tissue such as tumors and changes in the discs. CAT scan (computer axial tomography) is better for studying bony elements (Fig. 10). The MRI and CAT scan are both computer-assisted machines. The MRI does not involve the use of radiation; instead, it uses strong electromagnets and special radio waves. A CAT scan, on the other hand, uses radiation or X-ray beams to produce a picture of the body tissue.

If an individual needs to undergo an MRI there are a couple of important items he or she must take into consideration before having this study. If the patient has any metal at all in his or her body, the radiologist or the radiology assistants must be informed. This could adversely affect the outcome of the study. In fact, any metal at all in the body may cancel the study if it is the wrong type of metal. The MRI is a magnet, and any metal items will be subject to the magnetic fields and will be drawn to the magnet. There have been instances of a metal object traveling through the air into the MRI machine. Also, if an individual has had any experience around metalworking, it is important that they tell their doctor or radiologist. During the years of exposure to this type of metal work, tiny slivers of metal so small that an individual may have no idea that they are in their eyes may become a major problem in the MRI. Those little metal slivers will be influenced by the strong magnetic fields and could become little razor blades circling around in the eyes, possibly causing blindness. Therefore, prior to exposure to the MRI, a CAT

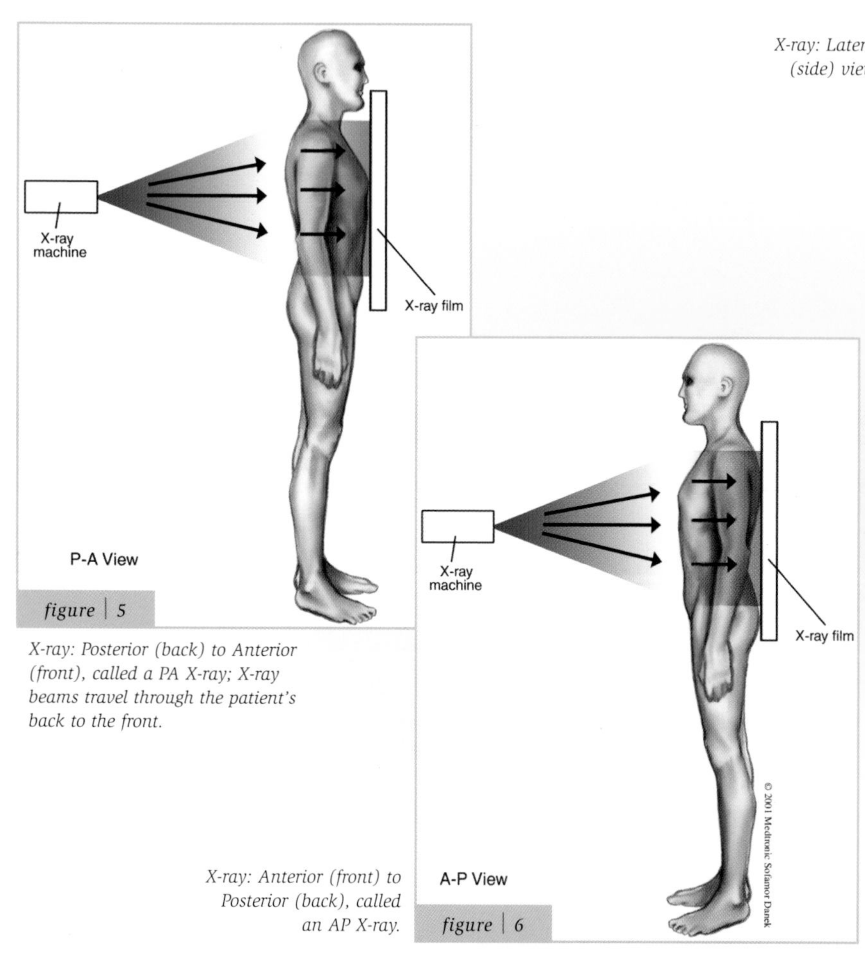

figure | 5

X-ray: Posterior (back) to Anterior (front), called a PA X-ray; X-ray beams travel through the patient's back to the front.

figure | 6

X-ray: Anterior (front) to Posterior (back), called an AP X-ray.

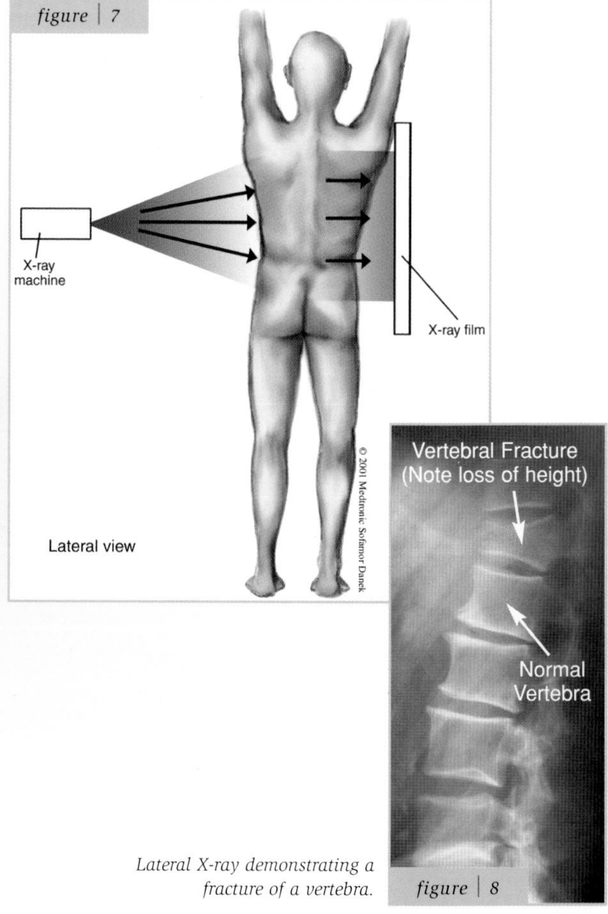

figure | 7

X-ray: Lateral (side) view.

figure | 8

Lateral X-ray demonstrating a fracture of a vertebra.

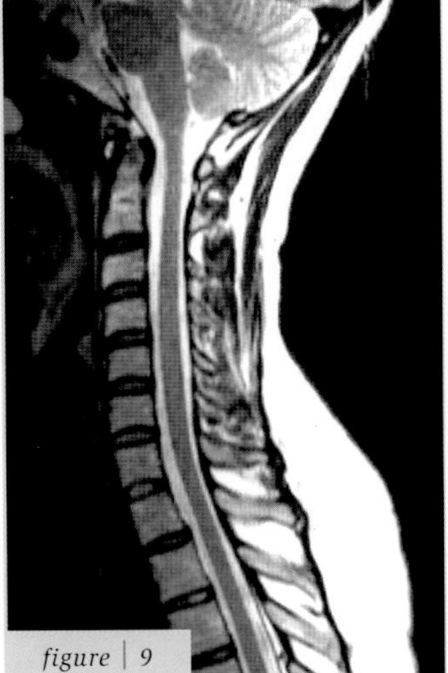

figure | 9

Normal MRI of the cervical (neck) spine showing the spinal cord, spine and discs.

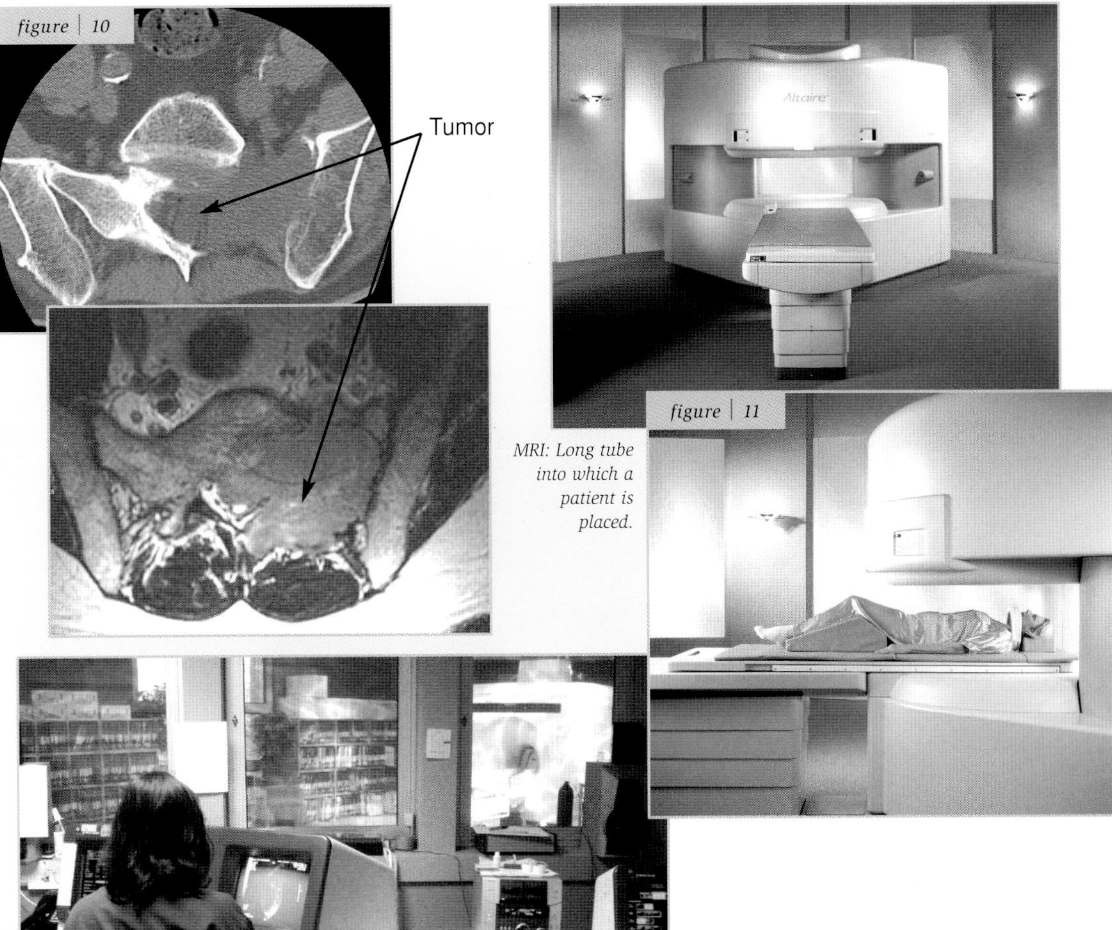

figure | 10

A. A (CAT) CT scan of sacral tumor. Bone structures are well-appreciated, bone destroyed by the tumor.

B. MRI of same sacral tumor. Soft tissue is better visualized, bone destruction is less well seen as compared to the CAT (CT) scan.

figure | 11

MRI: Long tube into which a patient is placed.

figure | 12

MRI technician checks on the patient throughout the study.

scan may be needed to detect whether or not there are any metal fragments in the eyes. When undergoing a MRI, metal items can not be taken into the MRI scanning room. Also the patient will need to remove any important credit cards from their body. The magnet will erase the credit cards and the next time the patient drives up to an ATM bank machine the card will not work. If individuals have fears of being enclosed in close spaces, i.e. claustrophobia, they may not be able to tolerate the closed MRI. The MRI is a long tube in which they will be placed (Fig. 11). There are two types of MRI; one is closed and the other is open. It is best for any patient with a history of claustrophobia to tell the MRI providers; it would be a waste of time to make an appointment and wait only to learn that they cannot have the examination. Open MRIs are intended for those people who have a fear of enclosed spaces. Some people feel that the quality of an open MRI isn't as good as a closed MRI, but it all depends on the MRI itself. All MRIs are not equal. There are MRIs that are on the cutting edge with the latest software and then there are MRIs that are not up to par. If an individual needs to undergo the study, they should make sure they get a good quality study. More powerful MRIs are now becoming available that will demonstrate even more information about the body's internal environment.

When a patient undergoes an MRI, he or she is placed onto a hard, motorized bed. Patient and bed are slowly moved into the tunnel, long tube, of the scanner. Once inside the MRI, the scans or images are taken. The patient will be asked to be very still while inside the imaging machine. Any type of movement will bring about artifacts that may prevent a complete and accurate examination. The complete procedure will take anywhere between 15 to 60 minutes, depending upon the type of MRI or MRIs requested for a given suspected problem. If the individual becomes anxious, there is an intercom which can be used to call for assistance. Intermittently throughout the examination, the MRI technicians will check on the patient to see how he or she is doing (Fig. 12). If patients develop any sort of anxiety, they should ask for help. The test may need to be discontinued. In such a situation completion of a good quality MRI may not be possible. A pre-MRI sedative may help an anxious or claustrophobic patient to get through the test. In fact, if a patient has problems being in tight places, the referring physician may prescribe a medication to be taken before going into the MRI tunnel. It is best to go to the tests with a family member or friend. A patient may become very anxious about the examination, and if given a sedative, can not be allowed to drive. After the examination, patients may have some increased fear about what may be found, so it may be best to have someone drive them home.

The MRI is a marvelous machine and a technological wonder. That's why the technology involved in its development has won Nobel Prizes. The MRI activates very powerful electromagnets that can create a magnetic field up to 30,000 times stronger than the earth's magnetic field. The strong magnetic field changes the alignment of protons in hydrogen atoms in the body. When the atoms in the body are exposed to a very strong magnetic field, they line up parallel to each other. Short pulses of radio wave lengths from a radio frequency magnet will knock the atoms out of alignment. A patient can tell that the atoms are about to be knocked out of alignment when they hear the radio frequency pulses; these are loud booms during the examination. The atoms do not like to be out of alignment and therefore quickly re-align. When the atoms re-align they emit very tiny signals that are detected by a receiving magnet. These tiny signals are passed on to a computer. The computer evaluates these signals and then creates an image based on the strength and the origin of the signals. The computer creates a picture of where the atoms live and the organ system being studied.

Sometimes the computer will need some assistance to better visualize an organ or to detect abnormalities such as scar or a tumor. This enhancement is provided by a contrast medium. The contrast medium is an iodine-based substance called **Gadolinium** that is injected through a vein. The contrast agent will enhance visualization of a particular structure. Some types of tumors will soak up the injected dye very quickly and will light up on the MRI images. This is an excellent method to see certain tumors of the spine and spinal cord (Fig. 13A and B). This contrast dye is also very good at detecting scar tissue. If an individual has had previous spine surgery, there may be a great deal of scar at the operation site. The body heals by scar. However, too much scar tissue, particularly in the wrong place, can cause problems. If a scar grows around a nerve, it can squeeze it and cause pain. The MRI is an excellent tool to detect scarring around nerves (Fig. 6). If, however, an individual has a sensitivity to iodine or seafood, in particular shellfish, he or she needs to tell the doctor. The patient may not be able to tolerate the dye. An iodine allergy could cause a reaction that could be life threatening.

Magnetic Resonance Imaging is a rapidly growing scientific and medical field. There are many new advances in this field of imaging. There are special MRI examinations that allow radiologists, physicians, and scientists to visualize joints, muscles, organs, blood vessels and brain functions.

The MRI is an excellent test to evaluate abnormalities of the spine and surrounding tissues. Millions of people have safely undergone an MRI. Patients with severe spinal pain, however, may not be able to lie comfortably on the hard MRI bed. If they move during the test, the results may not be adequate and may not allow the images to be read by the radiologist. They will need medication to decrease the pain to enable them to tolerate this examination. Women who are pregnant *must* consult their physician first. Risks to a developing fetus and long term effects are not known.

Patient's Checklist before the MRI

1. Metal history (shrapnel, occupational history, surgical implants, body piercing)
2. Allergies (iodine and/or seafood)
3. Severe pain (cannot lie still)
4. Claustrophobia (needs sedative?)
5. Insurance (will they pay for this test? part or all?)

COMPUTERIZED AXIAL TOMOGRAPHY (CAT SCAN)

Computerized axial tomography is commonly referred to as a CAT scan or CT scan. Development of this type of imaging has been a major advance in medical imaging and medical science. In 1973, Sir Godfrey Hounsfeld and Allen Cormack received the Nobel Prize in medicine for their work on the CAT scan. The introduction of the CAT scan, just like plain X-rays, changed medicine forever. It has saved countless lives with the early detection of disease. It also paved the road for easier acceptance of other medical imaging and radiology tests such as magnetic resonance imaging (MRI).

A computer-assisted tomography (CAT scan) is a machine that produces and detects X-rays in conjunction with a computer. A CAT scanner uses X-rays in a different way from an ordinary X-ray machine. The X-rays produced by a CAT scanner show hundreds of different layers of density in body tissues. An ordinary X-ray can demonstrate only a few levels of density. A plain X-ray can only show dense tissue, like bone, or soft tissue, such as swelling of muscles, and can

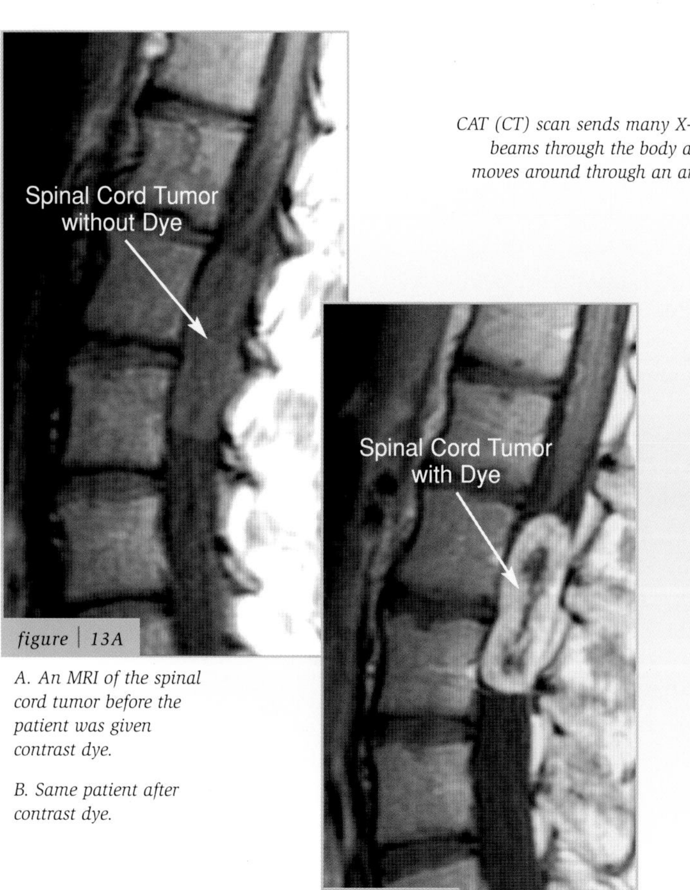

figure | 13A

A. An MRI of the spinal cord tumor before the patient was given contrast dye.

B. Same patient after contrast dye.

figure | 13B

CAT (CT) scan sends many X-ray beams through the body as it moves around through an arch.

figure | 14

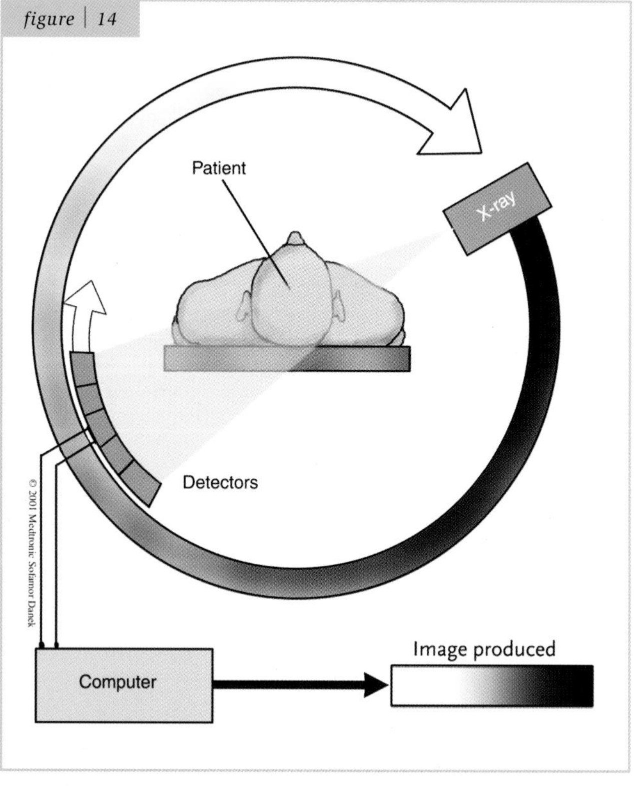

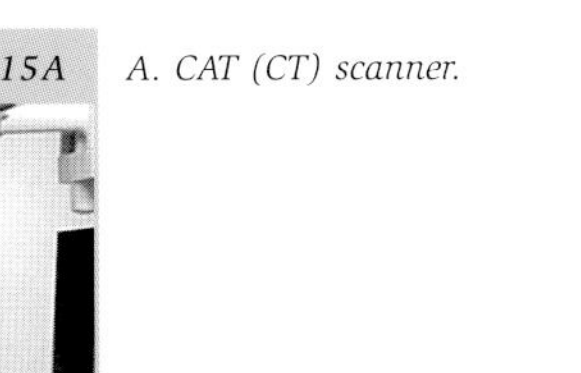

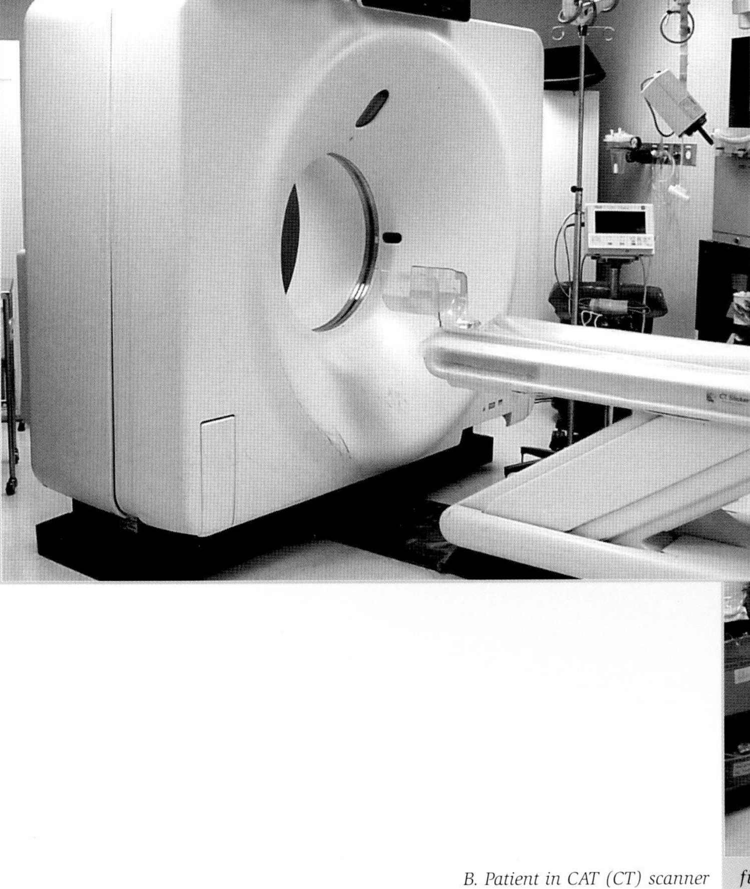

figure | 15A A. CAT (CT) scanner.

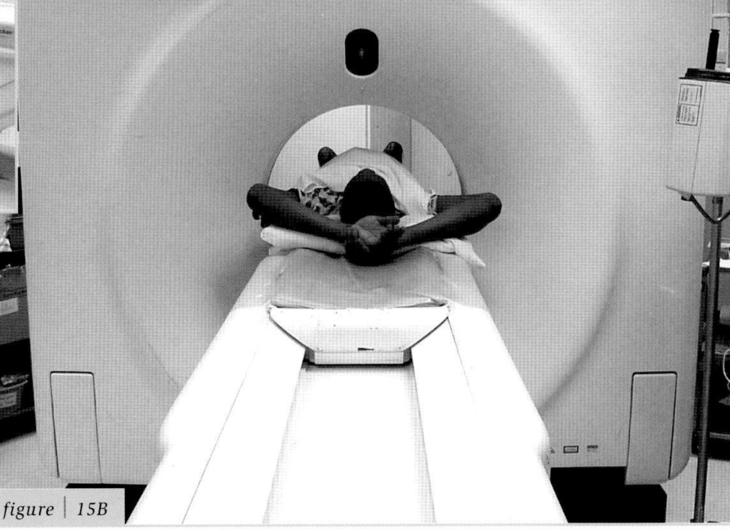

B. Patient in CAT (CT) scanner figure | 15B

detect air, but, a CAT scan can produce details of body anatomy in the spine and other organs that would be impossible with an ordinary X-ray. Instead of sending just one beam of radiation through the body, a CAT scan radiation source will send a succession of many narrow beams through the body as it moves around through an arch (Fig.14). The radiation source and detectors are always opposite each other. A good way to envision a CAT scanner is that it is composed of many baseball pitchers. The pitchers all have their catchers. The pitchers are the radiation sources and the catchers are the detectors. With the plain X-ray machine there is only one baseball pitcher and only one catcher, and they all stay in the same place. With the CAT scanner there are multiple baseball pitchers and catchers moving around in a circle. The baseball is the X-ray or radiation beam. The X-rays are thrown from the X-ray source, just as the pitcher throws the ball, and the X-rays pass through the body and are caught by the catcher. The information from the catcher or detector is then sent to the computer. The computer will use the data sent by the catcher and build up a cross-sectional picture of the body that is seen on a monitor.

Since its development, the CAT scanner has undergone numerous changes and advancements in not only hardware but in software as well. The CAT scan is a very rapid exam that can take only several minutes, depending on the information needed (Fig. 15A and B). Now there are CAT scanners that can provide three-dimensional images. The 3-D image can often provide even more information about the bones of the spine, skull, arms and legs.

The CAT is quicker to perform than an MRI. This is especially important after a serious traumatic event or accident. In a trauma situation there may be many metal items around the patient that cannot be put into an MRI scanner. A CAT scan is a very useful and safe method to guide needles into the spine and other organs to obtain biopsies from abnormal areas. In certain situations, the CAT scan may need to be enhanced by iodine contrast-enhancing dyes. Such dyes are helpful to better visualize tumors or abnormal blood vessels. Another indication for contrast dye, particularly in a patient with a history of spine surgery is to help evaluate for the presence of another intervertebral disc herniation or scar formation at the operation site. The use of a contrast agent allows the scar to be better appreciated by the radiologist. The scar is a natural process involved in healing. Sometimes, however, the scar can grow around nerve roots and cause pain like the pre-operative pain.

Overall, the CAT scan is an excellent machine to evaluate abnormalities of the spine, especially the bony elements. Radiation exposure during the CAT scan is generally quite low. Claustrophobia is usually not a problem and metal implants are not as great a concern with the CAT scan as with an MRI. However, a problem encountered with the use of a CAT scan is with individuals who have undergone placement of a metal implant, i.e. back rods or screws. These metal devices may produce artifacts that could interfere with visualizing the targeted area. Today, in order to lessen such artifacts, new types of metals have been introduced for implants. Most implants today are made of titanium and some devices are made of carbon. These devices certainly lessen the degree of artifact produced as compared to the stainless steel implants.

The CAT scan and MRI do not do exactly the same job. They are excellent tests to compliment each other, all depending upon why the test is being obtained. If the question to be answered involves soft tissue abnormalities, then the MRI may be the study of choice. On the other hand, if it is a bony abnormality, a CAT scan may be used to inspect the spine. The final decision of determining which test to obtain is ultimately the decision of the patient, physician, radiologist, or health care provider.

RADIONUCLIDE SCANNING

Radionuclide scanning is a radiology technique that provides images from radiation sources emitted from a substance in the body. You may ask "how does the body get a radioactive substance?" The doctor puts it there. The radioactive substance is injected into the bloodstream through a needle placed into a vein. The radioactive substance is carried through the bloodstream to the tissues targeted for the study. Different tissues take up different types of radioactive substances. A special radiation counter, a type of Geiger counter, is positioned outside the body. The device is called a Gamma counter. The radioactive substances produce gamma rays, which are very similar to X-rays and are detected by the Gamma counter. This data is then sent to a computer for analysis. The computer interprets this data and converts it into an image or picture that is displayed on a monitor. The image is built up dot by dot. Each dot represents a certain amount of radiation emitted from the radiation source. Areas of intense activity are referred to as hot spots, meaning that there is a great deal of uptake of the radionuclide; with increased activity going on in the area. Areas of less intense color are referred to as cold spots, meaning that there is little uptake of the radionuclide material (Fig. 16).

A radionuclide study is an excellent examination to evaluate the image and function of certain structures. When patients undergo this type of scan, they are placed on a special adjustable bed that can move forward or backward (Fig. 17). Before the machine is turned on the patient will have been injected with the radioactive material. He or she will be asked to lie quietly during the examination. Radiation being emitted from the target area inside the patient's body is detected by the gamma camera. This procedure will last between 30–60 minutes.

Radionuclide scans can be important studies to evaluate the activities of organs and bones. They will provide information about how the organs or targeted body parts are functioning. This technique will be helpful in detecting abnormal levels of activity of organs. In regards to the spine, it is used to detect any unusual or increased activity of the bone that may be abnormal (Fig. 18). Abnormal physiological functioning of the bone or other tissues can develop before any anatomical or structural changes occur. A good way to think about what a radionuclide study is actually doing is to compare it to detecting termites in a wall. The termites may be in the wall and have been busy eating away at the wall for a long time before the wall comes tumbling down. The wall is full of termites long before they are detected. The radionuclide scan is detecting the activity of the termites. Increased activity or hot spots may represent abnormal activity in the organ or bone being studied. Radionuclide studies of the bone can detect infection in the bone weeks before it can be detected on ordinary X-rays. They are also an excellent resource in monitoring tumor activity in the bone as well as determining how well certain treatments have worked. Radionuclides are always administered in very small amounts, so there is little concern for over-exposure to radiation-containing substances. They break down quickly in the body and should not pose any other problems. These studies are very helpful in evaluating broken bones. When there is some concern as to the severity or age of a fracture, this study can be very helpful. In the early stages of a broken bone, there is activity going on

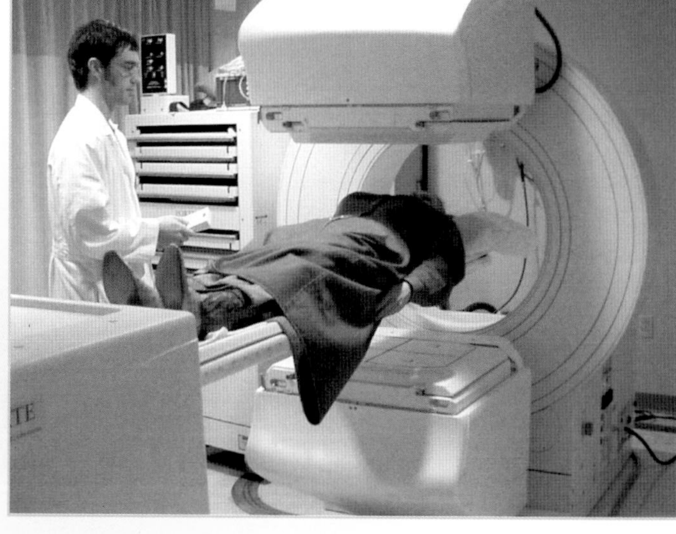

figure | 17 *Patient positioned onto a moveable table for a radionuclide scan.*

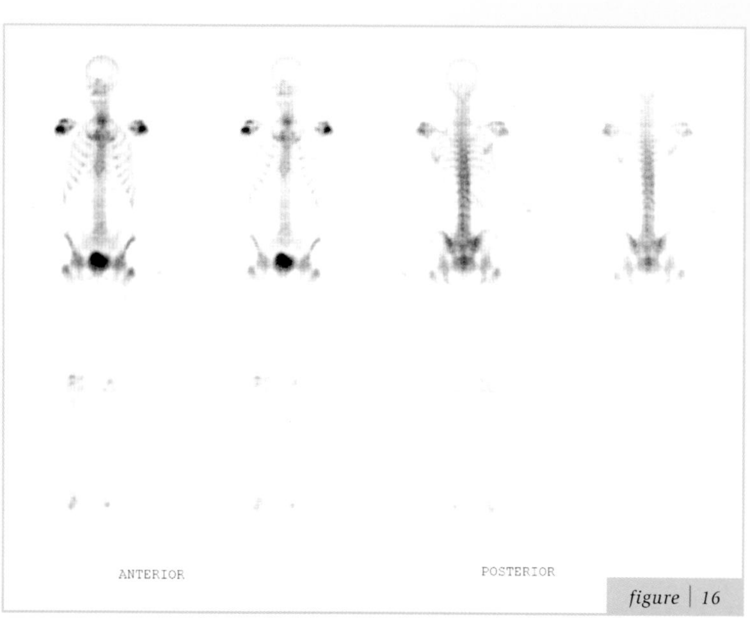

figure | 16 *Radionuclide scan*

Radionuclide scan with abnormal "hot spots" consistent with metastatic cancer.

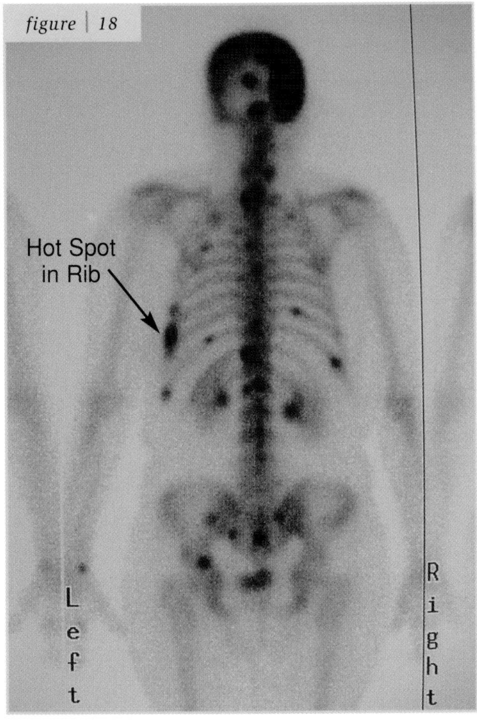

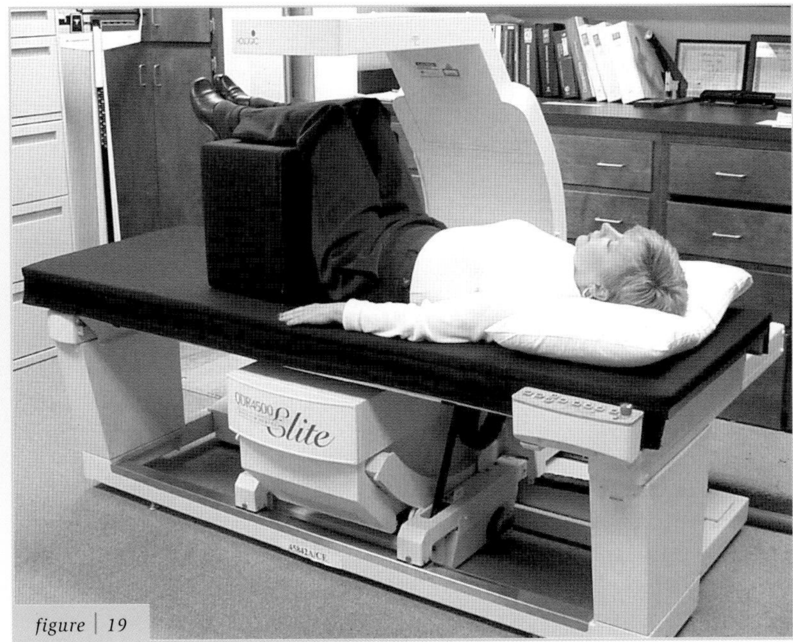

Patient undergoing bone densitometry test.

to repair the broken bone, which will produce a hot spot. As time goes by, the healing process is completed and therefore there is decreased activity at the fracture site.

BONE DENSITOMETRY

Bone Densitometry is a test using low doses of X-rays to measure the bone mass or bone density in the body. A simple way to think of bone mass is that it is the weight of the skeleton. The sites to measure bone mass are in the spine, hips and arms. These are the sites that are most likely to fracture when the bone mass is low. These are the are weight-bearing structures of the skeleton. The amount of bone mass determines the skeleton's strength and how much force or work that it can withstand before it fractures. Forces like playing golf when the skeleton becomes weak can lead to problems. There are cases of spine fractures sustained during golfing.

There are several methods for measuring bone mass. The most commonly used method is Dual Energy X-ray Absorptiometry (DEXA). Bone densitometry is a test to screen for and diagnose osteoporosis. Osteoporosis is a loss of bone tissue or mass that causes bones to become brittle and therefore more susceptible to fractures. Bone densitometry can also help diagnose other bone diseases, including cancers that arise from within the bone (primary tumors) or metastatic cancers. It also helps with the diagnosis of other metabolic bone diseases, *e.g.* thyroid diseases.

A bone densitometry test is performed by placing a person on a padded table while the X-ray passes over the whole body or over a selected site like the hip or the spine (Fig. 19). During the examination the person is asked to lie very still. Any movement may distort the study and prevent an accurate assessment of the skeleton being examined. The machine is shaped like a big "C." The low dose X-ray generating device is located below the table and the X-ray detecting grid is located above, so the X-rays pass from below upwards. The "C" arm of the machine will move along the length of the spine or to the site being examined. The average test will last between 20–30 minutes. As the X-rays pass through the body the varying absorption of the rays is picked up by the detecting arm and passed on to a computer. The computer will then convert the information into an image of the skeleton, hip or spine and analyze the quantity of bone at the site being studied. The computer will calculate the average density of the bone and compare it with the normal range for a person's age and sex. The results of the tests are reported as **bone mineral density (BMD)**, which is the amount of bone per unit of skeletal area.

When the spine is being evaluated the person's lower legs will be placed onto a foam pad for a better imaging position. If the arm is a problem, the patient may be asked to sit in a chair beside the machine and the arm will be placed into a holding device while the test is performed. In some situations total body skeleton measurement may be needed. This will provide individual measurements of the legs, the pelvis, trunk, ribs, arms, skull and spine. It is very important not to move during the procedure. If patients are having any type of pain and cannot lie still, they may want to come back another day or ask the doctor for medication to help them make it through the examination. Any movement during the examination will lead to inaccurate diagnosis and could mean that they may need to repeat the test.

Bone densitometry, as in any radiological study, must be correlated with a person's history, physical examination and laboratory tests. Bone densitometry may provide insight into skeletal fragility in certain situations, and can assess abnormal skeletal bone development in children and help determine whether these bones are likely to fracture. Long-term steroid use may lead to bone density problems and possible spine fractures. Bone densitometry testing is an excellent method to help determine whether bone replacement treatments are being effective, particularly treatment for osteoporosis. If an individual has a history of osteoporosis and wish to play golf, he or she may want to discuss this with the doctor and consider bone densitometry testing. There are treatments available for osteoporosis, and this is one test that will help determine when and if they should return to golf.

Bone densitometry is a safe, painless procedure that's an open machine as opposed to a usually closed MRI examination. It does not involve the use of needles, intravenous injections or taking other medications to help enhance the image. Radiation exposure is very small and it is estimated that the amount of the exposure to radiation is the equivalent to flying across the United States in a jet, or less than 10% of the radiation that a patient would receive from a plain X-ray. Densitometry can be performed as a measure of bone density in children. In comparison to other radiologic studies it is a relatively inexpensive test. However, there may be a waiting list for the study.

POSITRON EMISSION TOMOGRAPHY SCANNING (PET)

Positron emission tomography is a special type of radionuclide scanning (Fig. 20). It has been used as a research tool since the 1970s. It is a costly piece of equipment and is expensive to maintain. In addition, until recently insurance companies considered it to be an experimental study and did not cover the cost of the scan. However, it is now being used more often for clinical work. Physicians such as oncologists (cancer specialists), neurologists (medical brain specialists), neurosurgeons (brain surgeons, spine surgeons), orthopedic surgeons (bone and spine surgeons), cardiologists (heart doctors), and psychiatrists are utilizing PET scans more often for a growing lists of indications. PET differs from the CAT scan and the MRI by imaging metabolic activity of tissues (the way cells function) rather than the anatomic structures of organs. In other words, the PET scan is able to detect disease on a cellular level before there are visible structural changes that are better appreciated on a CAT scan or MRI. This is the major reason that the PET scan is becoming more important in clinical medicine. It can trace the metabolic functions and changes in tissues and organs. The PET scan detects and images the normal and abnormal metabolic activities of body tissues and organs. It can be very helpful in evaluating the behavior of certain types of cancers, *i.e.* whether the cancer cells are active or dormant. PET is very useful in diagnosing and staging cancers such as lung, breast, gastrointestinal, brain, ovary, and musculoskeletal (Fig. 21 A, B, C, D, and E). It is becoming more important in detecting bony abnormalities and tumors such as multiple myeloma. Cancer cells demonstrate certain metabolic patterns. Cancers often have increased rates of blood flow, DNA synthesis, protein synthesis, amino acid transport, and glucose (sugar) breakdown. In brief, cancer cells use up lots of glucose. The PET scan measures the way the cells burn glucose. The PET scan is able to detect the increased metabolic activities by using radioactive tracers that are injected into the bloodstream. The tracers concentrate in the tissues or organs that are using more glucose. Therefore, it can help guide treatments and provide follow-up for the evaluation of disease or tumor recurrence. PET studies are often effective in tracking the results of surgery, chemotherapy, and radiation therapies.

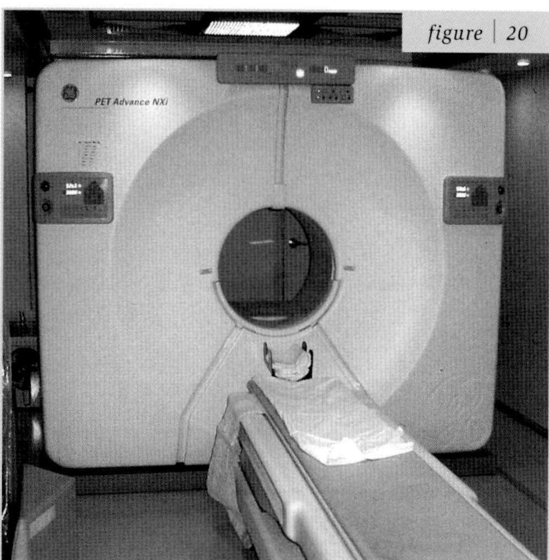

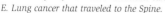

figure | 20 *Positron Emission Tomography Scan (PET)*

Positron emission tomography scan (PET).
A. Normal (front view) of whole body text.
B. Metastatic cancer in organs and spine.
C. Normal lateral (side) view of the body.
D. Lateral (side) view with metastatic cancer.
E. Lung cancer that traveled to the Spine.

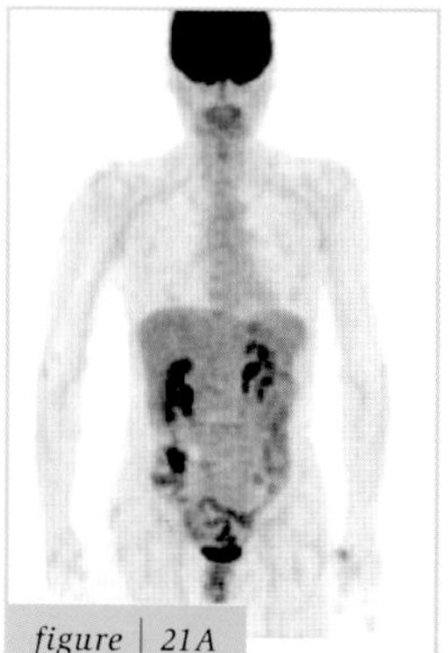

figure | 21A

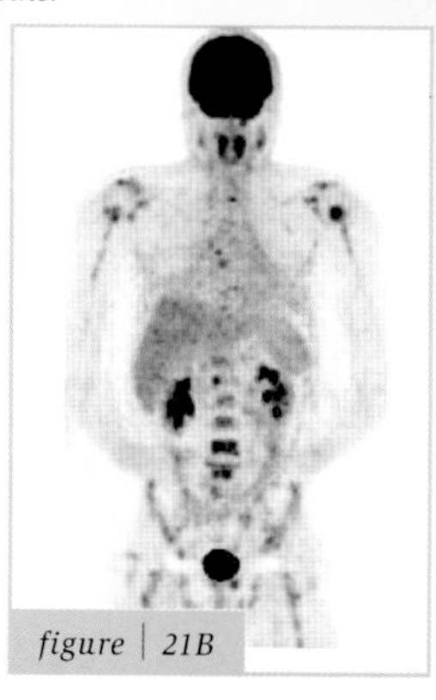

figure | 21B

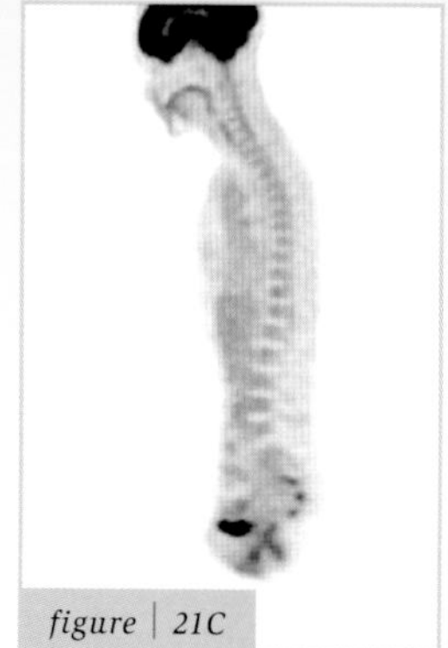

figure | 21C

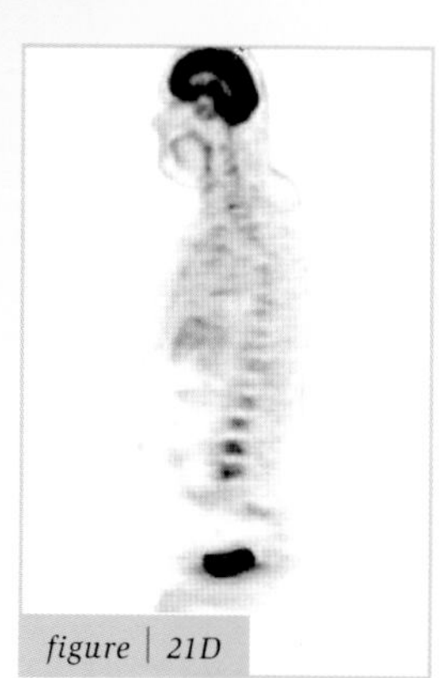

figure | 21D

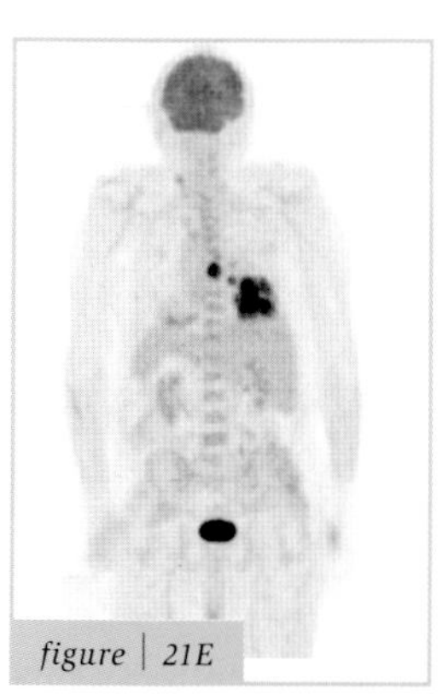

figure | 21E

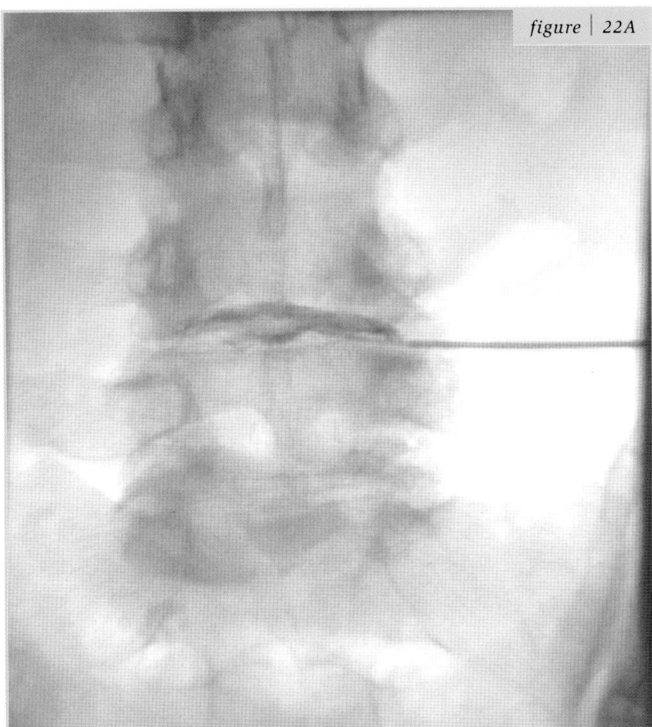

figure | 22A A. Discogram needle placed in a lumbar disc (front view X-ray).

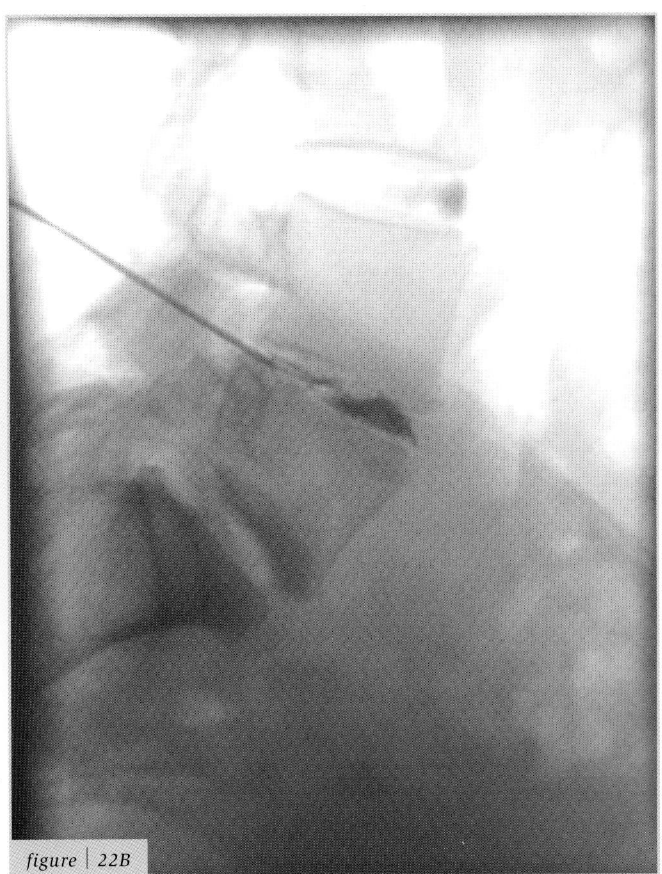

figure | 22B B. Lateral (side) view of discogram. Needle into the disc space between L4 and L5 (L-lumbar spine).

PET scans are used in cardiology to identify heart muscle that is weakened or damaged. Such patients may benefit from heart procedures such as angioplasty or heart (coronary) artery bypass surgery. These scans are proving to be valuable in brain imaging. They may diagnose brain tumors and the tumors' metabolic activities. They can also help locate the origins of epileptic (seizures) sites in the brain. The PET scans are able to reveal brain blood flow problems that will cause or have caused a stroke. Psychiatrists and mental health care providers are using PET scans to examine and assess patients, brain function in schizophrenia, manic-depressive disorders, dementia, and other mental health illnesses. Finally, PET scans are allowing new insights into brain functions such as speech, reading, dreaming, and memory.

Women who are pregnant are not able to undergo a PET scan because of the radioactive isotopes. However, for most patients, the test is safe. Risks are minimal. One common risk is an allergic reaction to the chemical isotope. Patients with a history of sensitivities to contrast dyes or other substances should always ask their doctor if this risk applies to them. Before the procedure the patient is seated in a quiet waiting room. A small amount of radioactive substance is injected into a patient's vein. After the injection the patient relaxes in the room while the material circulates throughout the body and adequately localizes in the tissues. The study itself lasts about 30 minutes. The isotope tracer is quickly broken down and eliminated by the body, usually within 12 hours. PET scans are assuming an increased role in the diagnosis and management of many illnesses and diseases. More diagnostic medical facilities are now providing PET scans.

A new breed of PET is emerging on the scene. It is the PET Fusion Imaging. This is a very innovative tool in diagnostic radiology. It is a hybrid machine. It combines Positron Emission Tomography (PET) with a CAT (CT) scanner, providing two tests in one. The results of the two types of scanner are fused together. The CAT scanner provides the anatomical details and the PET scanner the functional (cellular) activities of tissues and organs. The combined technology may provide even more exciting diagnostic avenues to evaluate disease processes. For physicians and radiologists the combined (fused) image may provide more information in less time. The Fused scanner produces images that detect the presence of a tumor, its size and its metabolic activities. Today, some radiologists believe that the combined images still do not produce as good an image as the two separate studies obtained on two different machines. As with any technology, PET Fusion Imaging will improve.

DISCOGRAM

A discogram is an invasive test that involves inserting a needle into a disc that is suspected as the source of certain types of back pain. This test is called a provocative test. The test will try to provoke or bring about pain; a pain not unlike the pain causing discomfort. It is often performed when other tests do not adequately support a diagnosis. The most common reason for performing this test is for discogenic pain, or degenerative disc disease, that is coming from the disc. Degenerative disc disease is a term used by spine specialists to mean changes consistent with aging. Sometimes a discogram will be used to aid spine specialists in the pre-operative planning, particularly when a bone graft or fusion is anticipated.

This examination is usually performed in a radiology suite. The patient is placed on the stomach or side. A special X-ray machine called a fluoroscope is used to help guide the surgeon or radiologist performing the test. The skin is cleaned with a scrubbing solution and a sterile drape is placed at an anticipated site of needle placement. A numbing medication is injected at the site of needle entry. It's important for patients to inform their doctors if they are sensitive to any medications before the procedure. The numbing medication, usually lidocaine, will cause a burning sensation as it is injected. It compares to a dentist's numbing the gums before any dental work. The needle is very carefully inserted into the skin and under a special X-ray machine is slowly advanced into a disc that is thought to be a pain source. The disc that is to be tested or provoked is often identified on an MRI as a bad disc After the needle has been inserted into the disc various X-ray views of the disc will be obtained to be sure the needle has been inserted correctly. Once the needle is in the correct position a radiographic dye is injected into the disc. This injection will sometimes cause pain. If the pain is like that which prompted the patient to see a doctor, it is called **concordant pain**. Concordant pain proves that this specific disc is the problem disc and supports the fact that this disc may not be able to do the job that it is called upon to do while standing, moving or other activities. If the pain does not reproduce pain, it is called **discordant pain**, and it can be assumed that this particular disc is not the source of the patient's pain.

This test is painful and is intended to provoke the pain that has been causing problems. The patient needs to be awake in order to tell the doctor what kind of pain is produced during the injecting phase of the test. Sometimes at the conclusion of the test the radiologist or physician may inject some type of pain medication at the injection site. Often this is a steroid medication that is an anti-inflammation medication intended to help alleviate the discomfort.

In some situations, a CAT scan or MRI follows the discogram. The dye that is injected into the disc will show up well on a CAT scan or MRI. The radiologist will evaluate the disc carefully. If any of the dye escapes outside the confines of the disc this may indicate an abnormal disc (Fig. 23A, B, C). A good way to think about a discogram is to envision taking a large balloon and placing part of the balloon under water while the opening is above water. Next, fill the balloon with red ink. If the red ink leaks out of the balloon it will be seen as a stream of ink coming out of the hole in the balloon. This is what happens with a discogram. There are risks with the discogram as with any invasive procedure. The infection rate is low and infection after the study is rare, less than 0.1%.

There is always a slight risk of nerve damage. The needle can be inserted into the disc space and even under close guidance, the inserted needle can cause pain, like an electrical sensation or numbness in the leg. There is also a slight chance of a discogram headache. If the needle goes in too close to the site of spinal fluid, the spinal fluid could leak out and cause a headache. In most cases this is quite rare and with bed rest the headache will disappear. A discogram is a controversial test and is not used by all surgical and non-surgical spine specialists; however, it depends on the experience of the physician, radiologist and surgeon. Patients should always ask their doctors if they use this test and whether they find it helpful. If a patient trusts his or her physician and surgeon, and the doctors trust this examination and feel that it is an important part of evaluations for a particular kind of spine or disc disorder, the discogram may benefit the patient.

MYELOGRAM

A myelogram is an invasive study in which a needle is usually inserted into the lumbar spine, low back area. It is inserted at a site below the spinal cord. The needle

A. Normal MRI after a discogram.
B. Abnormal MRI after a discogram.
C. Axial MRI (looking from top down): Tear of annulus (outer disc layer) with migration of the dye out of the disc.

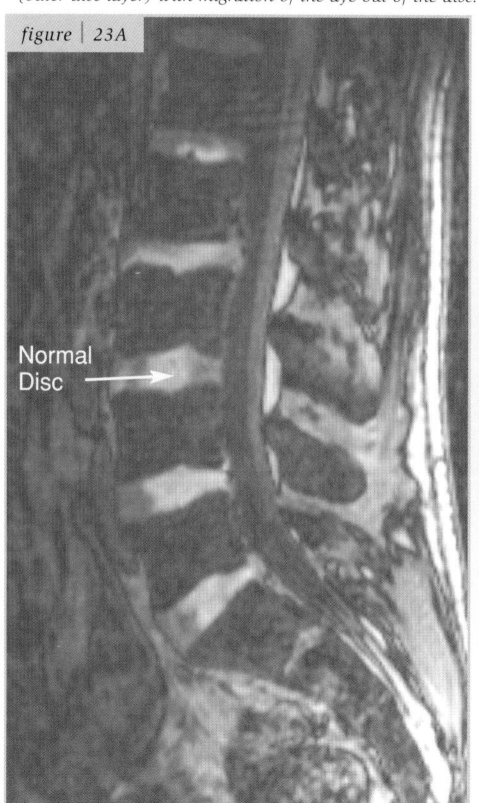

figure | 23A

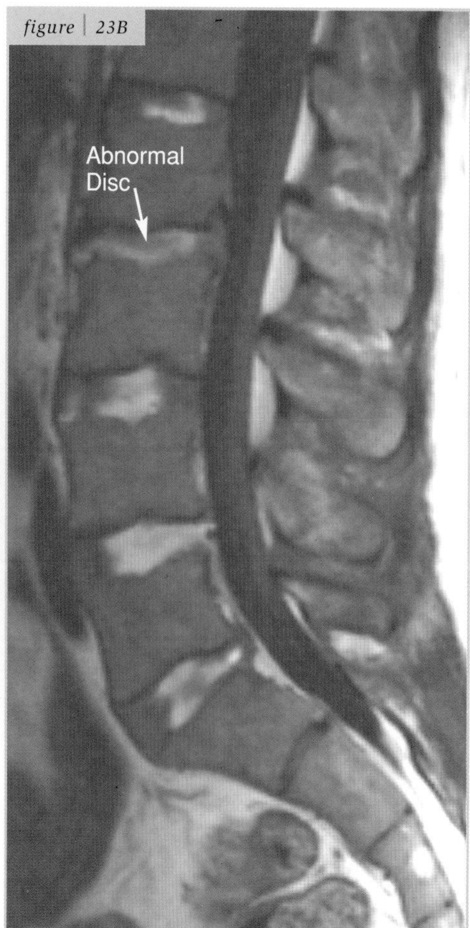

figure | 23B

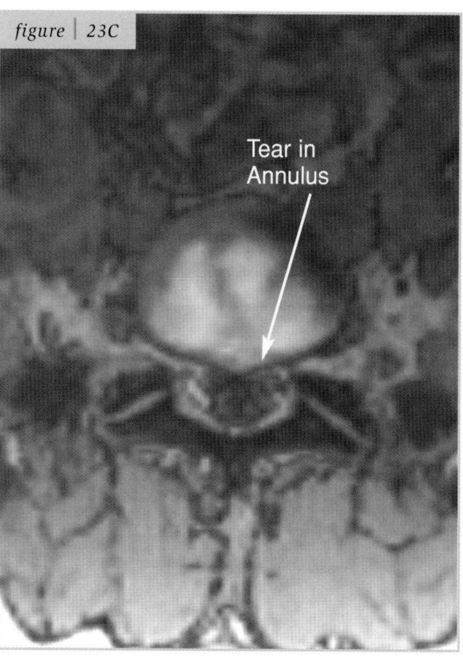

figure | 23C

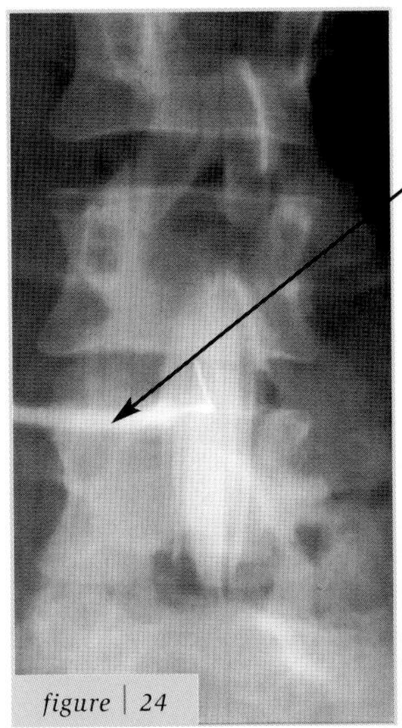

figure | 24

Myelogram needle placed into the spinal fluid sac (thecal sac).

A. Normal myelogram: the contrast dye flows unobstructed in the spinal canal.

B. Abnormal myelogram: The radiographic contrast dye is blocked.

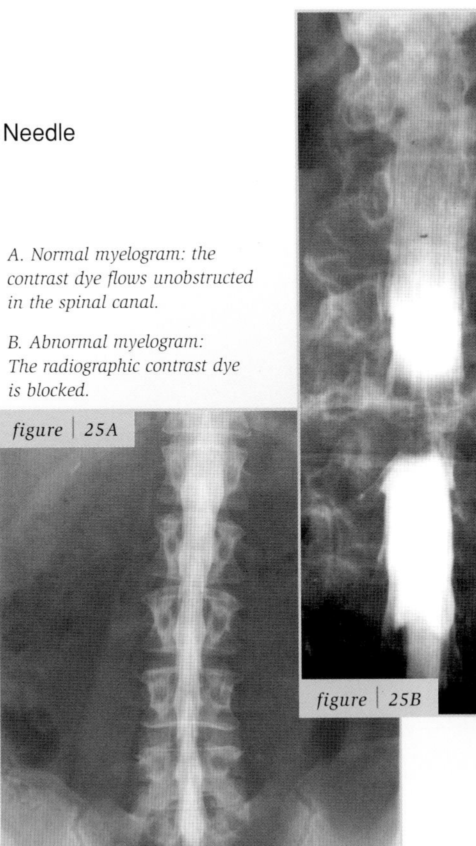

figure | 25A

figure | 25B

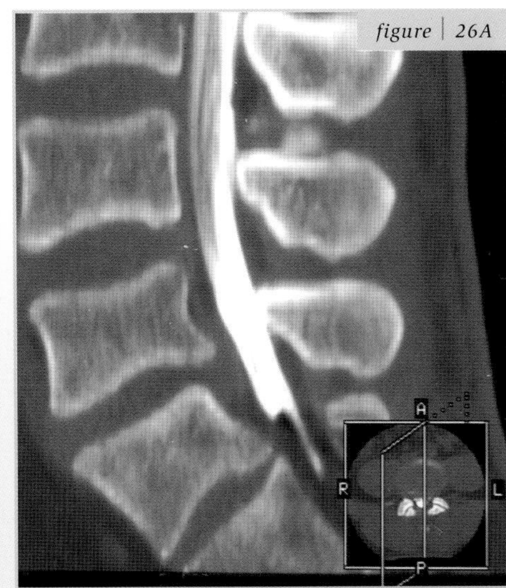

figure | 26A

A. Lateral CAT (CT) scan after myelogram: Normal test, the dye flows freely in the spinal canal.

B. Normal axial CAT (CT) scan after a myelogram. Plenty of room in the central spinal canal for the nerves.

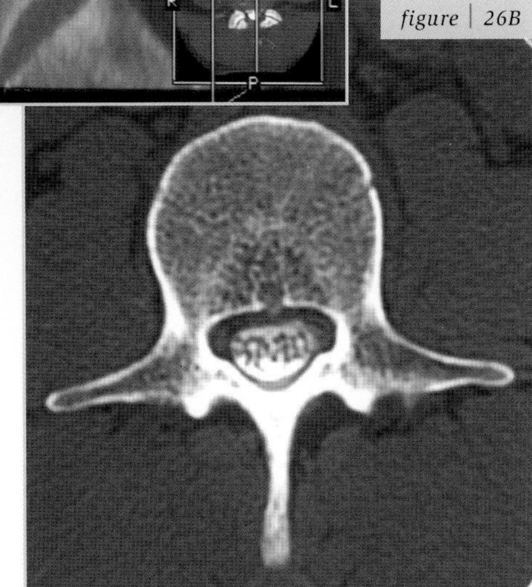

figure | 26B

is placed into the thecal sac. This is the sac that surrounds the spinal cord and nerves. In the thecal sac is spinal fluid. Envision a small syringe filled with a colored dye that is injected into a balloon. If the dye is a contrast material, the dye will show up on the X-ray. This is what happens in a myelogram. Sometimes the myelogram cannot be performed in the low part of the back, and it would then be performed on the upper part of the neck. Myelograms are performed at one end of the spine or the other.

A myelogram is used to help diagnose disorders of the spine, spinal cord and nerves. It isn't used today as often as it was in years past because of the availability of magnetic resonance imaging (MRIs). Such technological advancements have helped to reduce invasive tests such as myelograms. There are certain situations, however, where a physician and surgeon may need to see the relationship of a nerve to its bony housing; the myelogram may help. This test is done on an outpatient basis, usually at a hospital or other diagnostic center, and is performed by a radiologist or a surgeon. The patient is asked to come to the medical center with someone who can drive him or her home. The test takes from between 30–60 minutes depending on the information that is needed. Following the examination, the patient is taken to an observation area or a recovery room and placed on his or her back, with the head slightly elevated, for several hours. If there are no complications the patient will be allowed to go home. Once at home, one is advised to rest and avoid bending, pulling, lifting or sexual activity for at least 24 hours in order to allow the needle insertion site to heal. The patient is also advised to drink plenty of water and juice including caffeine drinks. If a headache develops, it usually means that the hole through which the needle coursed during the examination has not healed up. The patient will be advised to lie flat in bed until the headache is gone.

During the examination, the patient is placed on the stomach on a padded X-ray table. The needle site will be cleaned with a cleaning solution. The area is then draped in a sterile fashion and the skin is numbed with medication. A special X-ray machine is brought around the table, a fluoroscopy machine. Under the X-ray machine the needle is guided into the thecal sac filled with spinal fluid (Fig.24). After the dye is injected, the table is moved up and down allowing the dye to flow to the top and then to the bottom of the patient's spine. X-ray pictures are obtained as the dye is injected (Fig. 25A and B). After completion of the injection of the contrast dye, a CAT scan may be obtained to allow the physician to appreciate the dye inside the thecal sac and the relationship to the bone surrounding spinal nerves (Fig. 26A and B).

As with any invasive testing, there are some down sides. One of the most important is allergies or sensitivity to the contrast dye. If patients are allergic to seafood or shellfish, they must report this to the doctor. Several adverse reactions to contrast dye have been noted, including hives, swelling and difficulty breathing. In some situations the difficulty breathing can be very serious and can prompt emergency medical treatment including the placement of a tube down the patient's throat in order to allow adequate passage of air into the lungs. This type of allergy can be controlled or lessened by pre-medication given in the form of steroids. However, if the reaction is severe the myelogram may not be the best choice to study the spine. There are rare cases of seizures occurring after the insertion of the dye. The dye is water-soluble and will be absorbed and passed out of the body. Any history of kidney problems should be discussed with a physician or radiologist prior to a myelogram. The kidneys are the organs that will process and eliminate the contrast dye. If the kidneys are not working well, the contrast dye may worsen the kidney problem. If a patient is a diabetic, he or she will need to discuss this before undergoing the test. The physician will want to be sure that blood sugar levels are under control prior to a myelogram. Individuals taking blood-thinning medications will need to discontinue the medications prior to the examination and a blood test to monitor blood clotting factors will need to be obtained. A myelogram is an invasive test and the needle will pass into the body. If the patient's blood is thinned this may cause unwanted bleeding. Finally, if patients have any problems lying on their stomachs they may not be able to undergo myelograms.

Usually there are not many problems associated with a myelogram; however, as with any type of invasive procedure, complications and problems can arise. The most common problem after a myelogram is something called **myelogram headache**. The headache is caused when the spinal fluid leaks out of the needle entrance hole after the needle has been removed. This headache can become quite severe and bring about nausea, vomiting, and dizziness. Lying flat and drinking a lot of fluids will usually help the headaches improve. If the headaches are severe, the patient should call the physician or the radiologist who performed the examination. If, after 24 hours, the headache returns and is just as bad as before, a doctor should be consulted. Usually in this situation, the patient will need a **blood patch**. A blood patch is usually placed by a radiologist or an anesthesiologist. This is a technique that seals the little hole in the thecal sac by using clotted blood. The physician performing the examination will take a small amount of blood from an arm vein and then will inject it into the site of the myelogram. This will seal the tiny hole and within several hours the leaking will stop.

A myelogram is a test that has been used for a long time by spine specialists. It is not used today as often as it was in the past due to the advent of the MRI. With further improvements of the MRI this test will be utilized even less. The use of the myelogram is dependent upon the experience of the physician, surgeon, or radiologist who has requested the study. In certain situations, it is still a very useful examination.

NEUROLOGY DIAGNOSTIC TESTS

Nerve Conduction Study (NCS) and Electromyography (EMG)

In certain situations, the physiological activity of nerves and muscles may need to be evaluated to determine if they are working normally. This is done by performing a nerve conduction study (NCS) and electromyography (EMG). Nerve conduction studies determine if the nerves are conducting electrical impulses in a normal manner. EMG is helpful to differentiate between a muscle problem and a nerve problem.

After there has been pressure on a nerve for several weeks, usually more than 3 weeks, changes may occur in the muscle supplied by the damaged nerve. Compression or squeezing of the nerve will slow down the electrical activity or conduction along the nerve. Think of the nerve as a garden hose with water running through it: when it is squeezed less water comes out the end. Essentially, this is what happens when a nerve is pinched anywhere along the nerve path. Electrical studies try to locate where the nerve is being pinched. These studies can help determine the difference between nerve degeneration (nerve neuropathy) from nerve compression (radiculopathy). If the conduction studies are slower than normal, this may indicate nerve impairment or damage. Nerve conduction studies (NCS) are not painful tests. During this exam the patient is asked to sit or lie down and the arm or leg is supported on a pillow or foam cushion. The doctor or

figure | 27A

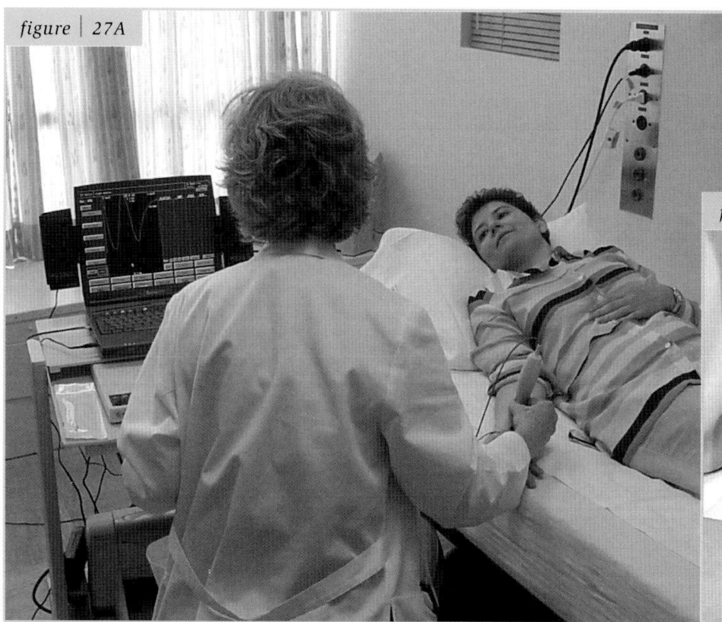

figure | 27B

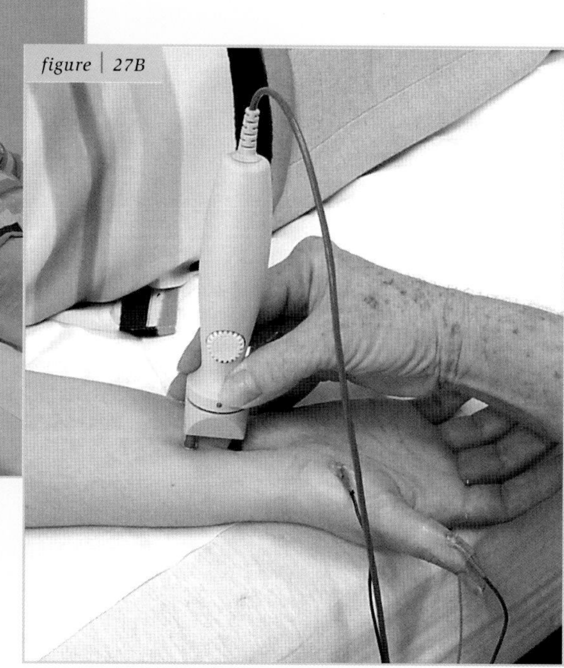

A. Technologist performing Nerve Conduction Study (NCS) on a patient.

B. Close-up of Nerve Conduction Study (NCS).

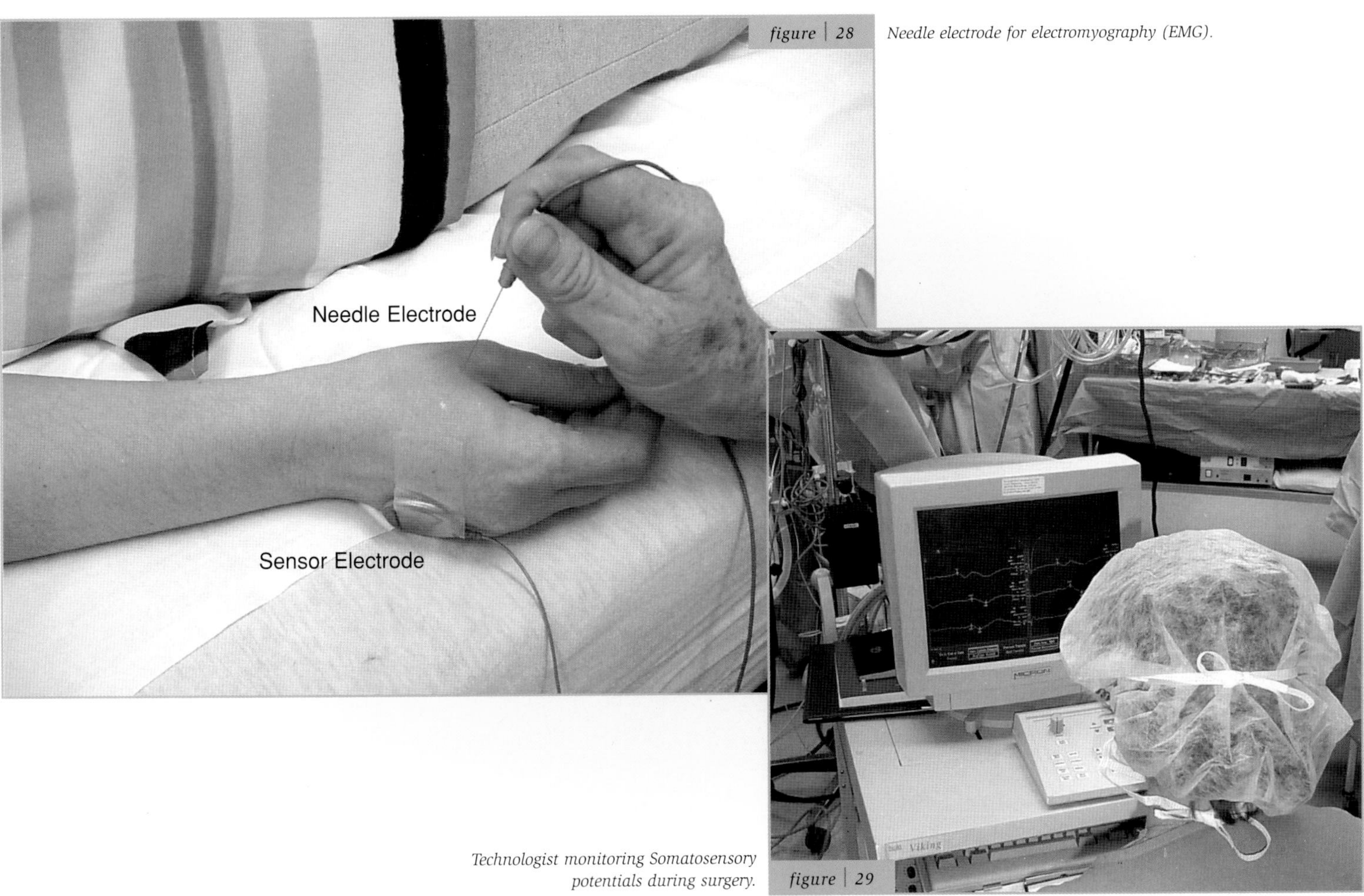

figure | 28 *Needle electrode for electromyography (EMG).*

Technologist monitoring Somatosensory potentials during surgery. figure | 29

the technician will hold a special probe against the skin above the nerve to be tested. The nerve is stimulated by the electrical impulse sent from the probe down the nerve to a recording electrode (Fig. 27). The response to the stimulation and the speed at which this response occurred will indicate whether or not the nerve has been damaged and how much the nerve has been damaged. The results are displayed on a monitor and recorded on tracing paper.

Electromyography (EMG) is not a painless examination. It is a physiological test that involves needles (Fig. 28). The EMG is used to distinguish between nerve and muscle disorders. During the examination a recording needle is placed into a muscle. The needle will record the electrical activity of the muscle when it is at rest and when moved to contract the muscle. The response of the muscle is recorded on a piece of tracing paper. This examination by itself does not give a total diagnosis of exactly what may be the problem, and may not accurately determine which nerve is being compressed. It simply helps to support what is suspected by the doctor to be the problem. The bottom line about electrical diagnostic tests is that they help to support the suspected diagnosis.

Somatosensory Evoked Potentials (SSEPs)

A Somatosensory evoked potentials (SSEP) is obtained to assess the speed of electrical conduction across the spinal cord itself. It is one of the electro-diagnostic tests used to assess physiological functioning. If the spinal cord is being compressed or is damaged the electrical signals traveling from the spinal cord to the arms and legs will be much slower. It is not always 100% correct. It is an examination to help guide and support a suspected diagnosis.

Somatosensory Evoked Potentials may also be used during spine surgery. After the patient is asleep, the technician places very small needles into the arms and legs During the operation the surgeon will ask the somatosensory technician about the status of the spinal cord and nerve functions (Fig. 29). If the surgeon is working near or around the spinal cord these tests may help the surgeon know when his/her work around the spinal cord is causing a disturbance to the electrical activity of the spinal cord. The surgeon may stop and/or come back to the site later in the operation. As with any electro-physiologic testing it is not always reliable, but is a means to help guide the doctor and surgeon in providing treatment.

Diagnostic Radiology Test

Advancements in radiology diagnostic imaging have improved remarkably in the last decade. The ability to visualize the organs and spine of the body is improving with technology. However, it is important to remember that imaging studies such as X-rays, CAT scans, MRIs and others are simply tools used by a physician to help confirm what is suspected based upon a medical history and a physical examination. A final diagnosis, particularly when dealing with the spine can often not be made based solely upon radiological studies. Even today a radiological study is still an image or picture of what ***may*** lie within the human body, and even under the best of situations may not provide an answer.

THE CERVICAL SPINE (NECK)

CHAPTER 6

T. Glenn Pait, M.D., F.A.C.S.

I am 77 now. I still love golf, but my game has gone south. I'd kill to break 100 these days on big courses. So I find that my back and also my hips provide excuses that my playing partners will accept. I do better throwing out to the younger players this fail-safe excuse: "I almost got all of that one, but my back tightened up." But if I use that excuse with older guys, they then persist in telling me about their own body-part problems. It ruins the game.

Some "back experts" have told me as I approach the first tee, "I find that if I lie on the ground and do the RAF exercises, my back will loosen up and permit a painless follow-through. Try it, George!"

I say, no way. At this stage of my life I need the excuse more than a pain-free back. Now let me tell you about my hips!

President George Bush (#41)

ANATOMY

The cervical spine has seven vertebrae and six intervertebral discs. The vertebrae in the cervical spine are numbered 1 though 7. The first one is C1 (the C stands for cervical). The second vertebra is called C2, then C3, C4, C5, C6, and C7 (Fig. 1A and B). The discs between the vertebrae are referred to as interspaces. When physicians or other healthcare providers refer to the disc between certain vertebrae, they use the number of the vertebra above and below the targeted discs. For instance, the space between the second cervical vertebra and the third cervical vertebra is called the C2–3 disc or interspace. The one between C3 and C4 is the C3–4 interspace, and so forth. The cervical spine has two very special bones located at the top of the spine. These bones are called the **atlas** and the **axis**. The atlas is C1 and the axis is C2. C1 has no vertebra. It is a ring of bone with joints on each side (Fig. 2). The second cervical vertebra, C2, has a peg-like structure that sticks up from its body. It resembles a tooth; so it's called the **odontoid,** or the **dens**. The tooth of C2 fits through the bony ring of C1 (Fig. 3). C1 and C2 act like a universal joint, in that they allow the head to rotate from side to side and move backwards and forwards. The other bones of the cervical spine are referred to as **subaxial**, which means below the axis. These bony elements allow us to move our heads forward (flexion) and backward (extension). In fact, the arrangement of the cervical spine allows movement in all planes, which means you can move your neck up, down, and sideways. At about the age of 15 years most of the flexion and extension movement in the neck is centered at the mid-cervical and lower cervical levels around C4–C5 or C5–C6, C6–C7. That's why so much neck pain in adults is located at these levels. We humans don't have powerful antigravity muscles like other animals. We don't have large teeth to protect ourselves and we don't have the speed to get away from predators. What we do have is a very mobile neck that allows us to look around and survey the environment. The arrangement of the bones of the cervical spine is quite unique. Unfortunately, it is a neglected part of our spines, particularly when it comes to exercises. While playing golf, one readily recognizes the importance of having a neck and cervical spine that moves, and moves without pain.

COMMON DISORDERS

The cervical spine is the most mobile portion of the spine. It has a remarkable degree of mobility and flexibility. For the neck to function normally it must be flexible enough to move without any discomfort. The neck and cervical spine moves approximately 600 times an hour, awake or asleep. A healthy neck can move in six different directions. Movements of the neck include **flexion (forward)** and **extension (backward).** The next kind of movement is called **rotation**, or turning the head to the left and the right, or moving the chin over the shoulder. The final movement involves **bending**, or moving the ears toward the shoulders. These six movements should be accomplished without any discomfort.

Neck pain and cervical spine discomfort is a very common problem for many adults. In fact, almost all adults sometime in their lives will have aches and pains in their necks. We often refer to neck pain as an unpleasant situation, for instance, "He's a pain in the neck!" or "It's a real pain in the neck now at

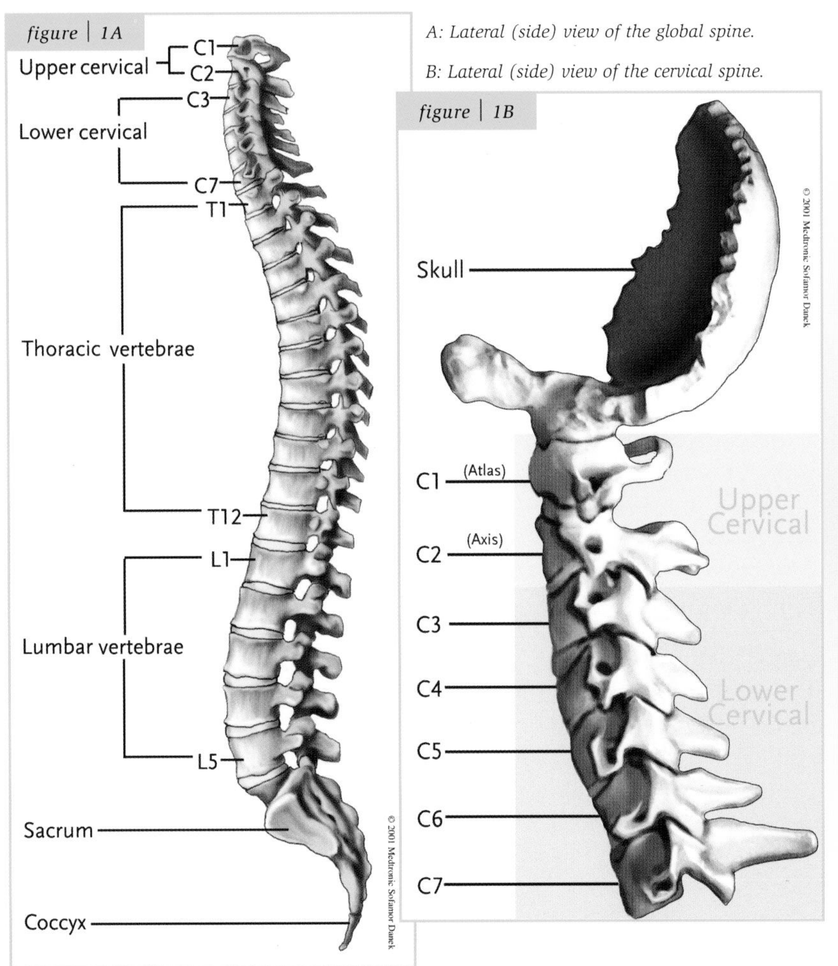

A: Lateral (side) view of the global spine.

B: Lateral (side) view of the cervical spine.

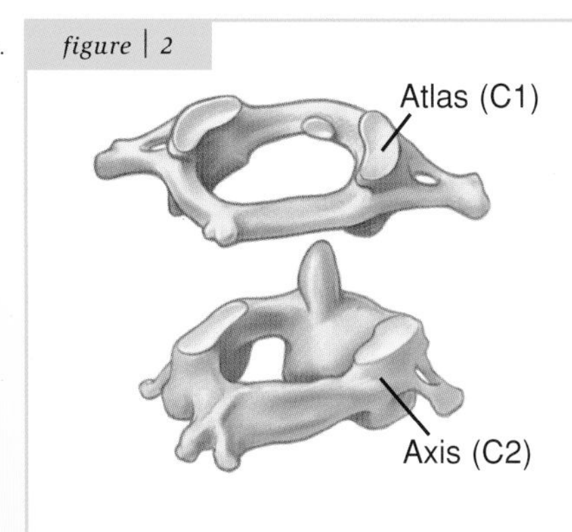

The atlas and the axis.

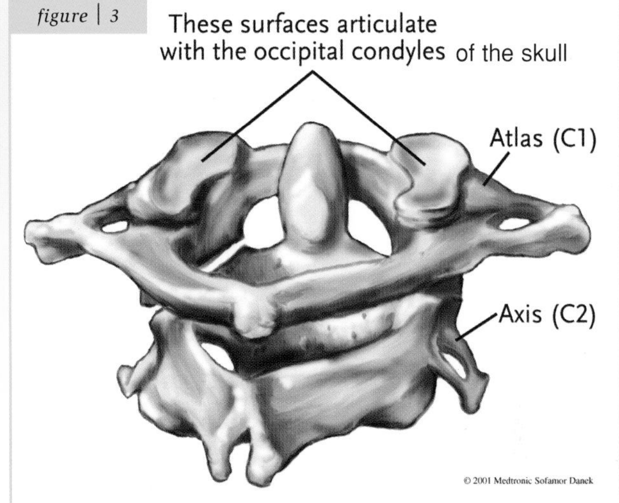

The odontoid or dens fitting through the atlas.

work!" or "That's a real pain in the neck to have to do that!" Just hearing any one of those expressions brings about some form of understanding, but when we say we *really* have pain in our neck and the pain is compromising activities of everyday living, it becomes another matter. When it interferes with the ability to play golf, something has to be done about it. A golfer needs a strong, healthy neck to continue to play the game. The spine changes with aging. These changes are often referred to as **degenerative changes**. These changes come about because of the everyday wear and tear on the neck. It's when the aging or degenerative changes cause pain that interferes with work and play that we take notice.

Cervical spine problems can be put into two basic categories. The first includes only the bones making up the cervical spine. Discomfort and pain brought about by bony disorders is often referred to as a **mechanical or spondylogenic** type of neck pain. This means that the bony structures of the neck may not be totally able to tolerate the demands of supporting the head and the constant neck movements. The inability to do so results in neck pain. The second category includes discomfort that deals with **soft tissues** of the neck. Soft tissue structures include intervertebral discs, muscles, ligaments, and tendons. Unless the neck hurts, an individual doesn't think much about the bones or soft tissue structures of the neck. The cervical spine is always in motion while supporting the head, which weighs as much as 15 pounds (6.80 kg). In fact, the cervical spine connects the head to the rest of the body. It's no wonder that the cervical spine is at risk for becoming the site for a great deal of pain. Everyday wear and tear, poor posture, tension, and accidents all can cause disorders of the neck or cervical spine. There are many different medical problems of the cervical spine. Often it's very difficult to determine exactly how or why the problems developed. The problems range from minor muscle aches and pains to more serious categories which could require surgical intervention and rehabilitation. However, in most situations, most neck problems are self-limiting.

Sometimes neck pain can originate from areas not related to the cervical spine, for instance, from the shoulder or the arm. When the pain comes from another source it is called **referred pain**. Referred pain is a well-known occurrence of discomfort in which the source of the problem is perceived as pain at a site away from its cause. There are several conditions that may cause neck pain with or without arm pain. The most common causes are cervical sprain or strain, disc herniation, spondylosis (aging changes), and arthritis. A less common, but unfortunately becoming more frequent, cause is cancer or tumors.

NECK SPRAIN OR NECK STRAIN

Two of the most common mischief-makers causing pain in the neck are due to overuse of the neck. Often a sprain and strain are used to mean the same problem; however, they are not exactly the same kind of injury. A sprain is an injury to a ligament or the strong tissue that holds bones together. When a ligament is stretched or torn it is called a **sprain**. This type of injury can happen to one or more ligaments. The severity of a sprain all depends on how badly the ligaments are injured. There are two types of sprain: a partial tear and complete tear. The worst sprain is one that involves **multiple ligament tears**, all of which are complete tears.

On the other hand, a strain is an injury to muscles or to the tendons connecting the muscles to their bony attachments caused by an over-stretching of a muscle or a tendon. A strain can also be partial or complete. The causes of a strain and a sprain are very similar. They both involve an injury to soft tissues of the neck. Sometimes the trauma or the events bringing about such an injury will be minor. It can be caused from twisting or a sudden movement that stretches a muscle or ligament beyond its stretching capability. It is like stretching a rubber band too far. The most common symptom caused by both strains and sprains is pain. Most of the time the pain is located only in the neck. The pain usually does not radiate into the arms. With minor sprains or strains there is usually localized tenderness and pain at the injury site. There may also be some loss of neck movement due to muscle stiffness. With more severe injury there are usually muscle spasms. Any movement will exacerbate the pain. When these symptoms occur, the head is sensed as being quite heavy, or heavier than normal. The neck begins to feel as if it is unable to support the head. A good way to think about it is that the head is like a golf ball sitting on a tee, the neck. The tee can certainly handle the golf ball, but if a bowling ball is placed onto the tee, the tee becomes incapable of holding up the ball. This is how an individual may feel about his head after sustaining a sprain or strain; the head is too heavy for the neck. The first treatment for a sprain or strain is to stop stressing the neck tissues. If you're playing golf, do not continue. The pain is telling you to stop. If you continue playing, you may turn a simple injury into a more complete injury, meaning a longer recuperation time and a longer period of time away from golf, possibly costing a season of golf. The first line of defense is to end the activity, go back to the clubhouse and rest. Once in the clubhouse, a cold pack, ice pack, or a plastic bag filled with crushed ice wrapped in a towel will be helpful in reducing the swelling in the neck. Keep the ice on the injury for *only* ***about*** 20 minutes. *Do not put the ice directly on the skin.* It can cause skin burns and injury. Apply the ice packs 3–4 times daily in the first 24 to 48 hours. The ultimate goal is to reduce the swelling. The cold treatments will help to reduce the swelling and prevent muscle spasms. The cold does this by reducing blood flow to the injured area. Another type of cold therapy is called **cold massage**. This is done by rubbing a piece of ice gently over the painful, inflamed neck muscles for two to five minutes, or until the skin becomes numb. The difference between a cold pack and a cold massage is that with the massage, the ice is constantly moving; therefore, not allowing it time to damage the underlying skin. An excellent way to apply a cold massage is to place water into a Styrofoam cup. The cup is then placed into a freezer to become ice. After the water has frozen solid in the Styrofoam container, peel about two inches (5 cm) off the cup exposing a layer of ice. The bottom of the cup now is the 'handle' and allows better control for the ice massage. Keeping a few ice message cups in the freezer may come in handy.

Often, over-the-counter pain medications, which can be purchased at any pharmacy or drug outlet store, can provide help in alleviating discomfort caused by a sprain or strain. One of the most often used class of medications for this type of cervical neck pain is the non-steroidal anti-inflammatory drugs **(NSAIDs)**. These medications work by blocking the pain-generating chemicals. They will help reduce both the inflammation and swelling, which will abate the pain. Before using these medications, it's advisable to discuss their use with a pharmacist or healthcare provider. Individuals who have histories of any stomach problems, particularly stomach ulcers or high blood pressure, should always discuss these medications with a physician or pharmacist before buying over-the-counter non-steroidal anti-inflammatory medications. All anti-inflammatory medications can be irritating to the stomach. The over-the-counter NSAIDs are the easiest to obtain; a doctor's prescription is not needed to purchase the medication. Certain prescription non-steroidal anti-inflammatory medications may be gentler to the stomach. They may be gentler to the stomach, but they're more harmful to your pocketbook—they cost more. Aspirin can also be taken to ease the pain. *Do not use aspirin or any non-steroidal anti-inflammatory medications if you have a sensitivity to these medications.* Acetaminophen may also be helpful with pain management, but will not reduce tissue swelling since it doesn't contain the anti-inflammatory agents that are contained in an aspirin or a NSAID. There are a variety of anti-inflammatory medications available at any pharmacy or mega-market. No single over-the-counter drug has been proven to be significantly better than any other NSAID. One thing an individual should never do is mix various medications. Never take one type of anti-inflammatory medicine and then 30 minutes later try another anti-inflammatory drug. This may cause significant problems in the stomach or gastrointestinal system, one of which is bleeding. Whenever anyone uses any over-the-counter medications, he or she should discuss their use with a pharmacist, read the insert, and follow the directions. Consumers need to ensure that they are able to safely take the medication. If individuals are currently taking other prescription medications or alternative medications, such as herbal supplements, they must discuss their medication situation with a pharmacist, a physician, or a healthcare provider. Herbal and other alternative medications are still medications, and they may have harmful interactions with non-steroidal anti-inflammatory medications. It's best to be safe when using different medications. NSAIDs should never be used for a prolonged period of time without consulting a healthcare provider or doctor.

After about 24 to 48 hours, the pain from a sprain or a strain should get better. Once the muscles start to feel normal, that's when you start to use **heat therapy**, usually after the first 48 hours. Heat therapy will help to relax those embarrassed soft tissues such as muscles, ligaments, and tendons. It will also increase the blood flow to the area to help in healing. Heat therapy is sometimes used in exercises or physical therapy to provide gentle stretching of the neck muscles. When you apply the heat therapy with gentle stretching exercises, the benefits may be greater. If a sprain or strain just doesn't get better after about two to three days, a physician or healthcare provider may be needed. They may recommend a day or two of rest and prescribe other stronger medications, including a muscle relaxant to help break up the muscle spasm. If the pain is truly intense, a narcotic may be given for just a few days to alleviate the pain during this acute period. Other therapies such as ultrasound (painless sound waves aimed at neck muscles), massage therapy, acupuncture, or chiropractic therapies may also help to relieve the inflammation in the neck and speed up the healing process. The good news about this type of injury is that the vast majority of individuals will respond to this therapy in the first three days, and by the end of the 10 days they should feel much better. While recuperating, patients need to avoid heavy lifting, bending or pulling activities, as well as sexual activity; it too puts strain on the neck. If they are not getting better or develop new symptoms, such as pain radiating down the arm, it's time to call a physician. The patient should try to recall the onset of the problem. Did it start while playing golf? Is the pain primarily located in the neck or does it radiate into one or both arms? The patient needs to inform the doctor totally about their pains. In most situations, the doctor will continue what is

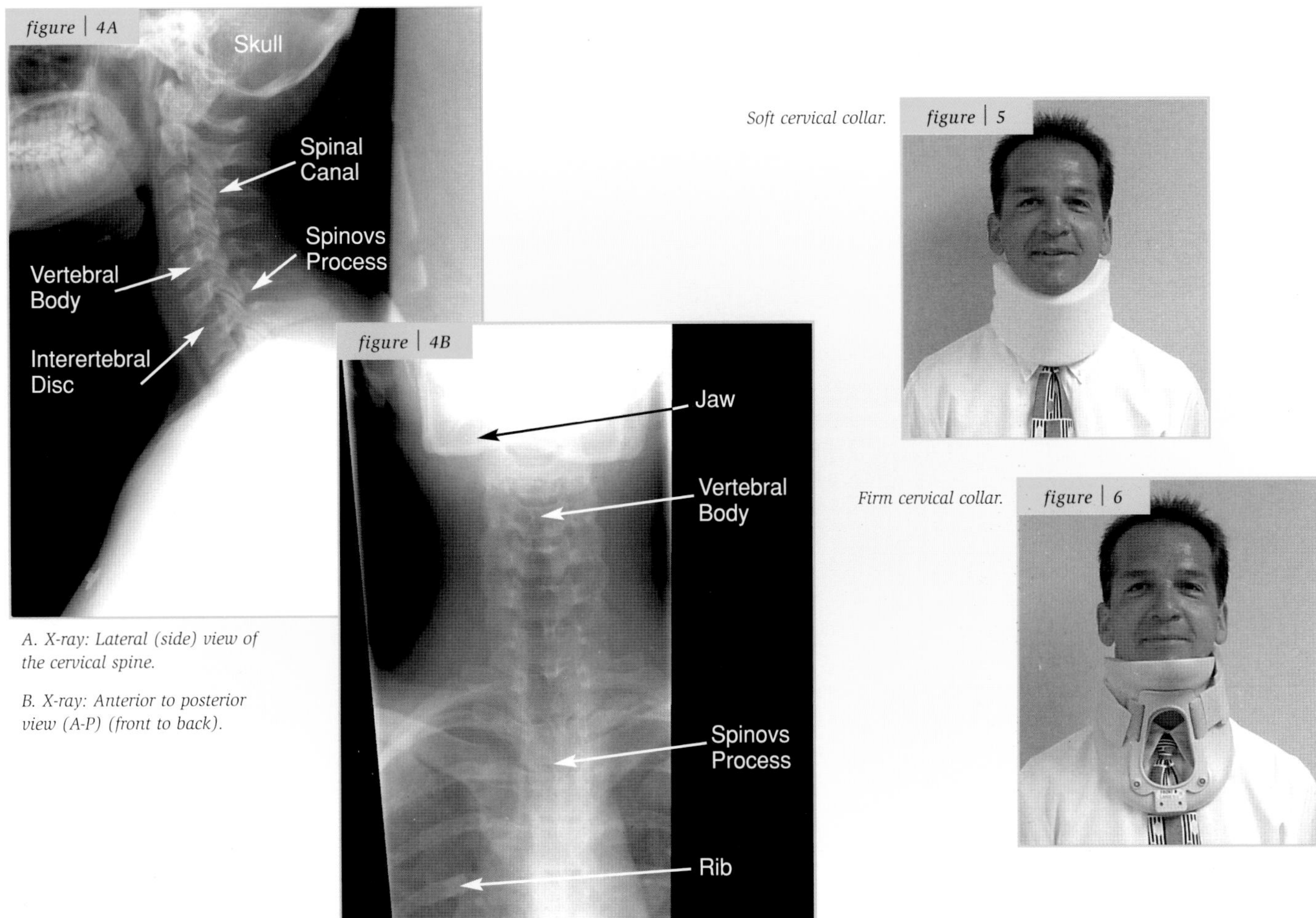

A. X-ray: Lateral (side) view of the cervical spine.

B. X-ray: Anterior to posterior view (A-P) (front to back).

Soft cervical collar.

Firm cervical collar.

called **conservative** or **non-aggressive therapy**. The physician may order plain X-rays of the neck. The physician will need to see all the bone of the cervical spine, from the top (the base of the skull at C1) down to the beginning of the thoracic spine (T1). A lateral (side) view and an anterior-posterior (front) view will be obtained (Fig. 4A and B). Also, a dynamic X-ray, an X-ray in which the patient will be asked to move the head forward and backward, will be obtained. These X-rays are obtained after a physician or healthcare provider has obtained complete medical history and performed a physical examination. Need for any further radiological testing will be based on the findings of the history and examination. In most situations, the physician will place the patient's neck into a collar; usually a soft collar will do just fine (Fig. 5). If it does not offer the comfort and support needed, a more rigid collar made of Styrofoam or plastic will be used (Fig. 6). This collar is initially worn 24 hours a day; therefore, a properly fitted and comfortable collar is important. If the collar isn't comfortable, more than likely the patient will not wear it. The anti-inflammatory medications (NSAIDs) are usually continued along with an anti-muscle spasm medication, if muscle spasms are present. If a patient is taking anti-muscle spasm medication, he or she should not engage in any dangerous activities, such as driving a car or using dangerous tools; these medications may cause drowsiness. If another week has passed and the golfer is still not feeling better, another call and/or return visit to the physician may be needed. A Magnetic Resonance Imaging (MRI) test may be needed. The MRI is a radiological machine used to visualize the soft tissues. In some situations, the degree of tearing in the ligaments or muscles can be seen. If there is no evidence of injury to other structures in the neck, a local or trigger point injection may be given at the area of maximum tenderness. Localized tender areas in the muscles around the bony structures of the neck are referred to as **trigger points**. In many cases, an individual can achieve marked relief from painful neck symptoms by infiltration of these trigger points with a combination of lidocaine (xylocaine) and a steroid preparation. The need for the steroid is to decrease the inflammation at a specific injury site. The more localized the trigger point, usually, the more effective this form of therapy.

When things start to get better in the neck, it is time to consider some type of rehabilitation therapy. Rehabilitation is needed to restore function of the neck. In most situations, this includes an exercise program to reduce stiffness, restore flexibility and increase the strength of the muscles. A physical therapist will evaluate the musculature of the cervical spine and a patient's posture. The therapist will provide treatments to improve and maintain good neck and cervical spine hygiene. This is very important for the golfer. The physical therapist will teach ways to position the neck during standing, sitting, lying down, and sleeping. The therapist will also perform exercises on the cervical spine and will guide the patient through these exercises so that they may be continued at home. As the neck begins to improve, having less pain and more flexibility, the exercises will increase. The final goal is to return the injured patient to daily activities, which include golf. It is very important that the golfer works closely with the therapists and relates to them not only the desire to return to daily activities such as driving and working, but also to golf. Strengthening exercises may be modified to accommodate golf. It is important to be honest with a therapist so that together the patient and the therapist can determine when the golfer safely can return to playing. The patient may be tempted to return to golf too early. It may be a beautiful springtime day with no pollen in the air and patients feel up to getting out on the golf course, but deep down they know that they are not ready. They shouldn't be tempted and say to themselves that they have only a little bit of soreness in the neck. "I won't play hard." They are just fooling themselves and may be setting themselves up for a setback in therapy. Returning to golf before attaining normal, pain-free function will increase the chance of re-injury and could lead to a more chronic problem. A moderate strain or sprain may require 3 to 6 weeks of therapy before returning to a full schedule of activities, including golf. Severe sprain or strain may take even longer, but remember—do not return to golf before it is time. After the sprain or strain is totally healed and the structures in the neck are ready to return to golf, it's time to take a few golf lessons. The returning golfer needs to talk to a golf professional about his or her neck problems, diagnosis and treatments. Lessons, training, and advice provided by a professional might help to prevent a repeat of the sprain or strain, which took the player away from the game of golf.

WHIPLASH

Whiplash is a **hyperextension injury** to the neck. Our necks are remarkable engineering feats, but sometimes they just can't handle certain situations. Whiplash is one of those situations. This occurs when the head is extended too far backward; the weight of the head exceeds the neck's ability to control it. Whiplash usually happens when the head is suddenly jerked backwards beyond its normal limits. This sudden throwing of the head backward and then recoiling forward causes overstretching, tearing and bleeding of the neck muscles and ligaments. It can even cause the intervertebral discs of the cervical spine to be subjected to significant forces. The discs can bulge, tear, and even rupture from this type of activity. However, most of the pain brought about after whiplash injury is due to **muscle damage**. Injured muscles quickly develop spasms. Muscle spasms can cause headaches, localized pain, or pain radiating into the arms and along the shoulder blades. Whiplash is a special type of sprain and strain. It is treated in much the same way as any sprain or strain, but it usually requires a longer period of time for recuperation. Dedication to a physical therapy and rehabilitation program is essential if a golfer is to return to playing. If the pain from a sprain and a strain does not improve within three to seven days, it's best to consult a physician.

INTERVERTEBRAL DISC

The intervertebral disc is a fibro-elastic soft tissue structure located between two vertebrae (Fig. 7). It acts like a shock absorber between the vertebrae. The cervical disc is made up of two components: the inside is called the **nucleus pulposus**; the outside is called the **annulus fibrosus**. A good way to envision a cervical intervertebral disc is to think about a jelly donut. A donut is made up of two components, just like a cervical disc. Inside the donut is the jelly, just like the nucleus pulposus of the disc. The outside of the donut is made up of pasta, which resembles the annulus fibrosus of the disc. The nucleus pulposus is made up of a gelatinous substance composed of proteins, collagen fibers, and water. Water makes up about 80–90% of the nucleus in youth. The water content gradually decreases to about 70% in the fifth decade of life. With age, the intervertebral discs lose height and becomes less able to deal with pressures and loading weights placed upon them (Fig. 8). A healthy intervertebral cervical disc is able to tolerate loading forces created by jumping, running, or hitting a golf ball. In a healthy state, the intervertebral disc is able to adjust to the demands of life. The nucleus of the intervertebral disc

figure | 7

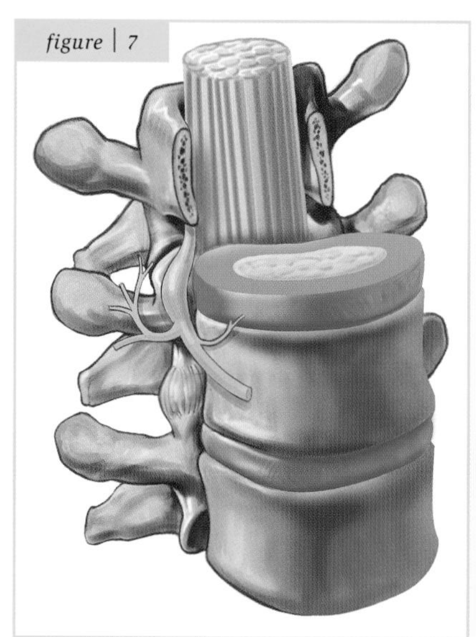

Normal intervertebral disc.

figure | 9

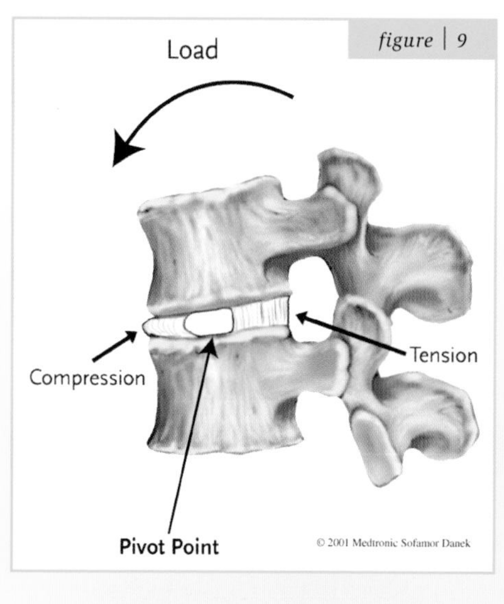

Intervertebral disc during motion.

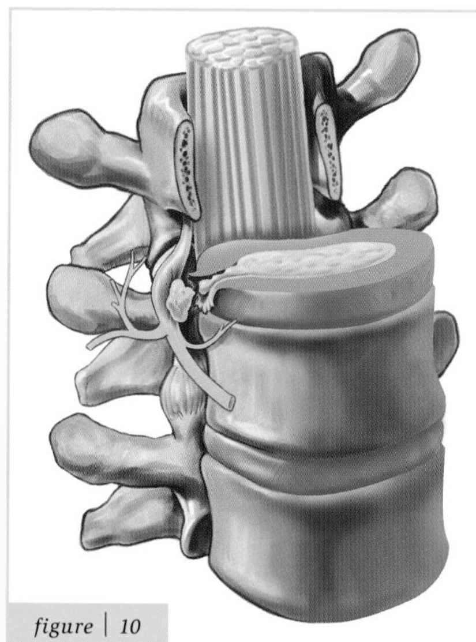

Disc herniation with pressure on the nerve.

figure | 10

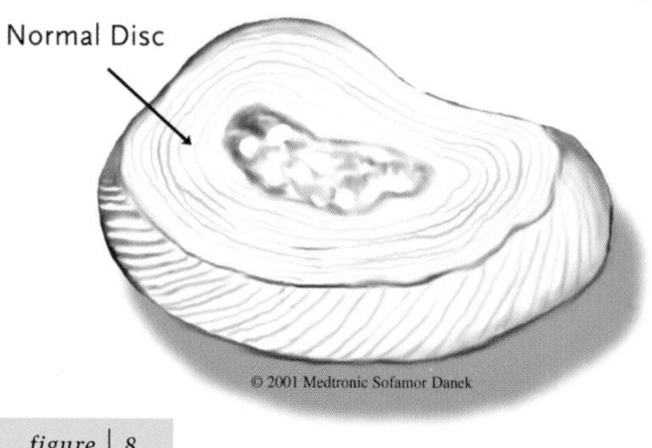

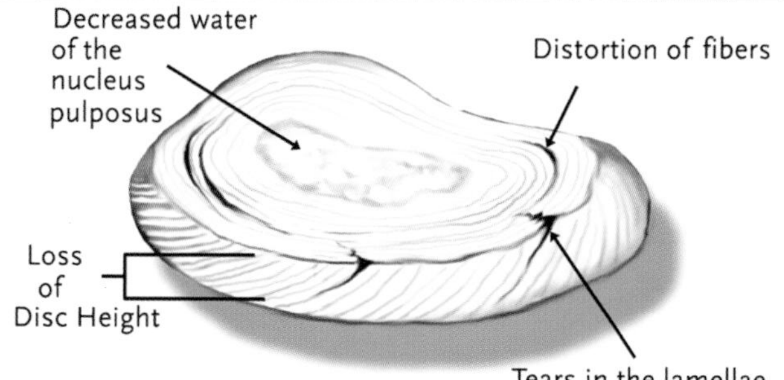

Normal disc and maturing/aging disc (degenerative disc).

figure | 8

Table | 1 The most common clinical manifestations of cervical disc herniation.

	Manifestations			
Level of Disc Herniation	C4–5	C5–6	C6–7	C7–T1
Root Compressed	C5	C6	C7	C8
Weakness	Deltoid	Biceps	Triceps, wrist extension	Hand intrinsics, wrist flexion
Sensory Loss	Lateral shoulder	Lateral arm & forearm, thumb & lateral aspect of index finger	Middle finger	Ring & little fingers
Reflex Involvement	Deltoid, Pectoralis	Biceps	Triceps	Finger flexion

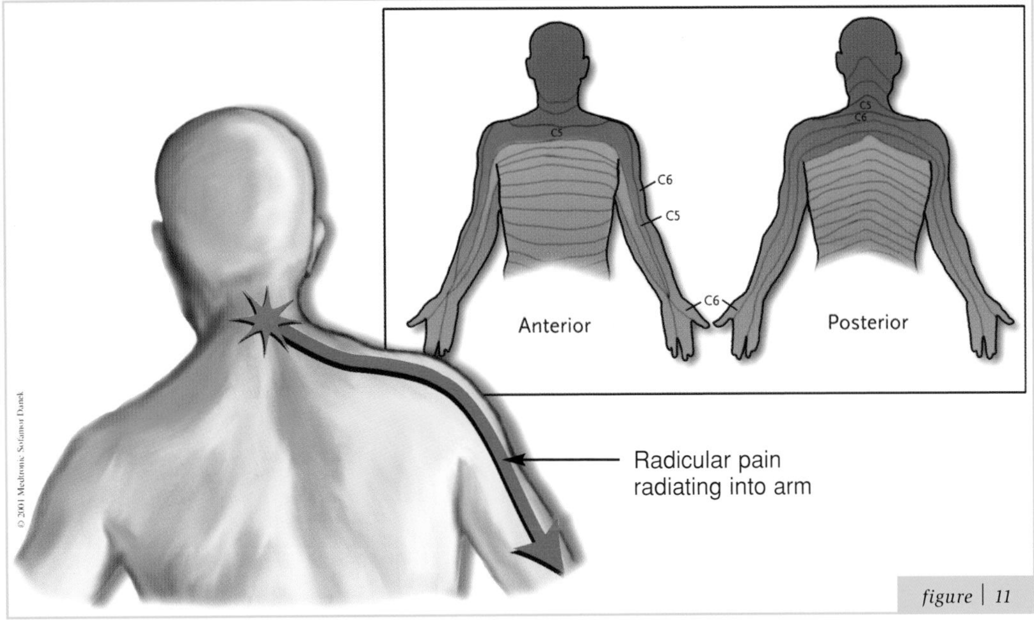

figure | 11
Radicular pain.

will act like a deformable hydrostatic ball. The outer annulus will expand to accommodate the changes of the nucleus. Moving the neck during a golf swing will increase the axial load on the intervertebral disc. The central nucleus will flatten out. The surrounding annulus fibrosus will accommodate the changes of the central nucleus by expanding outward. In a healthy disc, the annulus will be able to contain the central nucleus. During a golf swing, both the annulus fibrosus and the nucleus pulposus experience a multitude of forces simultaneously. When the golfer bends his or her head downward and rotates it from side to side, the concave side of the disc goes into compression while the convex side is in tension (Fig. 9). The compression side of the nucleus pulposus bulges and forces the annular fibers on that side to expand outward. The other side of the disc, the tension side, causes the fibers of the annulus fibrosus to become taut. Torsional forces during the golf swing are also transmitted to the annulus fibrosus and nucleus pulposus. In a healthy spine, the compression and stretching of the annulus fibrosus are well tolerated. The central nucleus pulposus deforms and then returns to a more normal configuration. If there is a defect in the outer annulus such as a tear, this may allow the central nucleus to be squeezed outward. Migration of the nucleus pulposus through the annulus is referred to as a **cervical disc herniation**. When a disc herniates, the gelatinous nucleus pulposus is usually squeezed backwards, which can put pressure on nerves and sometimes the spinal cord itself (Fig. 10).

CERVICAL DISC HERNIATION

Individuals with acute cervical disc herniations will experience severe pain to the degree that they are unable to continue their normal activities. When the term **acute cervical disc herniation** is used, it means that the disc has herniated rather suddenly. Some patients will be able to recall exactly when the disc ruptured. Many times, they were engaged in heavy lifting, bending, pulling activities, or playing golf. Other patients may be unable to recall when their neck problems began. An acute cervical disc herniation occurs rather suddenly: it has not been going on for weeks, but more likely days. An acute cervical disc herniation is usually called a **soft disc**. This means that the disc is not hard or calcified.

When an acute soft disc herniation occurs, it usually shoots out from the side of the disc. If the disc material bulges or extrudes along the side of the disc, there is a great chance that the material may impinge on exiting nerves (Fig. 10). Pressure on the nerves will cause pain. Pain is the most common complaint of patients with a cervical disc herniation. The neck pain will limit movement of the neck, particularly extension. With aging, bone spurs may be found along the side of the foramen, nerve windows. The disc will decrease the space in the foramen and, therefore, irritate the nerve even more. If the nerve is irritated, the patient will complain of discomfort radiating into an arm. The nerves in the neck exit from the spinal cord in a particular pattern. A doctor may be able to determine the site of the disc herniation based on the patient's physical examination, particularly the strength of the affected arm (Table 1). The patient with an acute disc herniation will often hold an arm above and behind the head. This maneuver will reduce the pinching or pressure on the nerve and decrease the pain. Most patients with an acute disc herniation will present with neck pain, without any evidence of a traumatic or precipitating event, and report pain radiating into the arm accompanied with numbness, tingling, or an arm that feels asleep (Fig. 11).

After a physician examines a patient who presents with what appears to be a cervical disc herniation, special radiological studies may be ordered. A plain X-ray of the cervical spine may be performed. The plain X-ray will not show the soft tissue disc herniation, but will allow the doctor to evaluate the bones of the neck. X-rays will allow the radiologist and doctor to determine whether there are bone spurs (osteophytes) or fractures of the cervical spine. Today, magnetic resonance imaging (MRI) is usually the study of choice to evaluate for a cervical disc herniation. (Fig. 12A and B). A patient with severe pain may not be able to tolerate the MRI without pain medication. A good quality MRI will demonstrate the discs to be evaluated. The MRI will also allow the radiologist to view other soft tissue structures, particularly the spinal cord and the nerve root (Fig.13A and B). For those patients who cannot tolerate a closed MRI, there are now open MRIs. In certain situations where the MRI cannot be obtained, *i.e.* patients with pacemakers or metal implants, a myelogram followed by computed axial tomography (CAT scan) may be recommended. A myelogram is performed by a radiologist or physician who passes a needle into the dural sac containing spinal fluid and injects contrast dye into the fluid (Fig. 14). The myelogram needle is usually placed into the lumbar spine below the level of the spinal cord; in certain special cases the needle can be inserted into a space between the atlas (C1) and the axis (C2). If the patient is sensitive to iodine, this study cannot be performed without special preparation using steroids. The myelogram/post-CAT scan is a much more invasive test than the MRI (Fig. 15). The patient usually comes to the hospital accompanied by a friend or relative; the myelogram will be performed, and in 6–8 hours the patient will be allowed to leave if there have not been any complications. The patient will not be allowed to drive himself or herself home. One of the most common problems after a myelogram is a **post-myelogram headache**. Usually with time, this problem will resolve. There are cases in which the headaches continue because of spinal fluid leakage from the needle hole in the dura. This is like sticking a small needle into a water filled balloon. After the needle is removed, the water may slowly leak out. When spinal fluid leaks out, it causes a severe headache. If this occurs, the patient is recommended to lie flat in bed and drink plenty of fluids. If it does not improve, they will need to return to the hospital for further evaluation.

Sometimes, a physician will order electrical diagnostic studies to evaluate the functions of nerves that travel into the arms, which include electromyograms (EMG) and nerve conduction studies (NCS) (Fig. 16A and B).

CONSERVATIVE TREATMENT

Generally, most patients with an acute cervical disc herniation will get better with time. Conservative therapy will often bring about resolution of the discomfort. Surgery is usually not required. The first line of treatment for an acute cervical disc herniation is rest. The nonsteroidal anti-inflammatory medications (NSAIDs) will help decrease not only the pain, but also nerve inflammation. In certain situations, the pain may be so great that an oral narcotic agent may be added for the severe pain. Use of narcotics is usually taken for a short period of time, less than two weeks. In most cases, 60%-80% of the severe symptoms will resolve in some 4–6 weeks. During this period of time, rest is important and the patient should not play golf. If the pain continues after approximately 10 to 14 days, other types of therapies may be needed. These include physical therapy, which will help strengthen the muscles of the neck. Cranial traction may be an option. This form of therapy involves placing a halter around the patient's head and neck, and gentle traction is applied

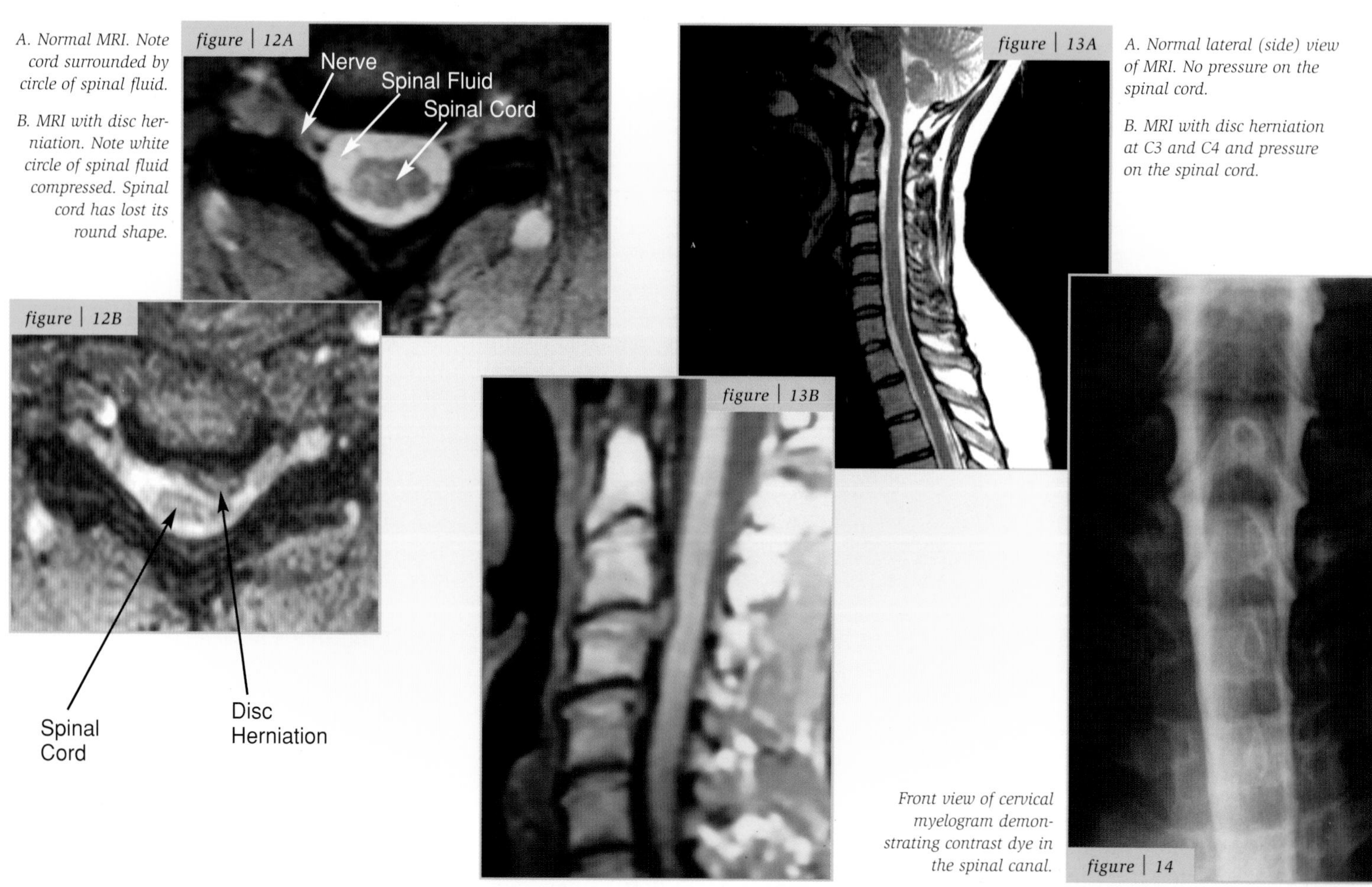

A. Normal MRI. Note cord surrounded by circle of spinal fluid.

B. MRI with disc herniation. Note white circle of spinal fluid compressed. Spinal cord has lost its round shape.

A. Normal lateral (side) view of MRI. No pressure on the spinal cord.

B. MRI with disc herniation at C3 and C4 and pressure on the spinal cord.

Front view of cervical myelogram demonstrating contrast dye in the spinal canal.

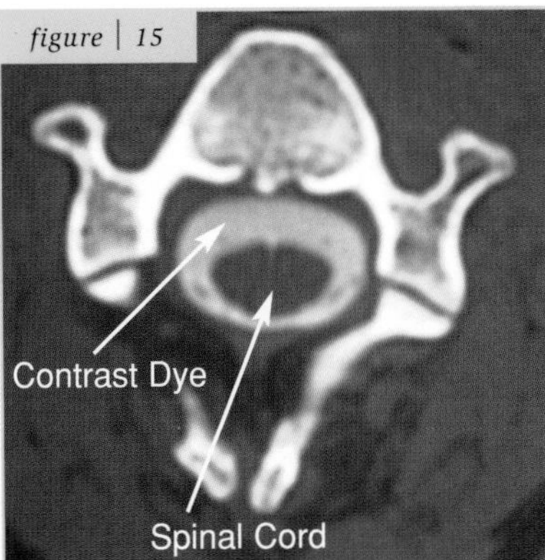

figure | 15

CAT (CT) scan after a myelogram (lateral/side view).

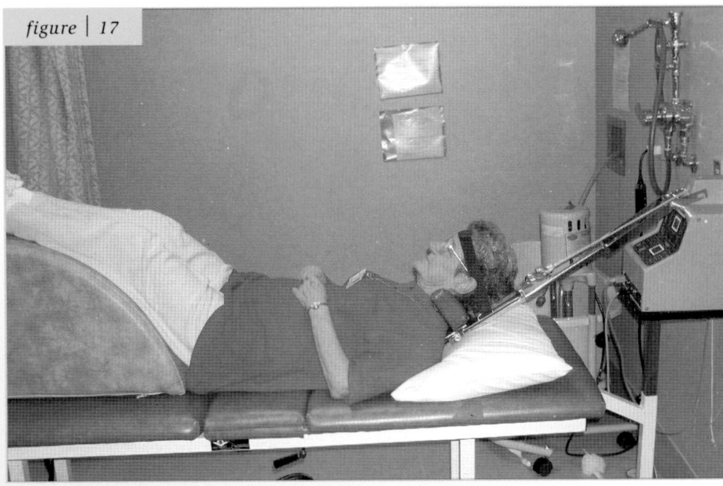

figure | 17

Patient in cervical traction.

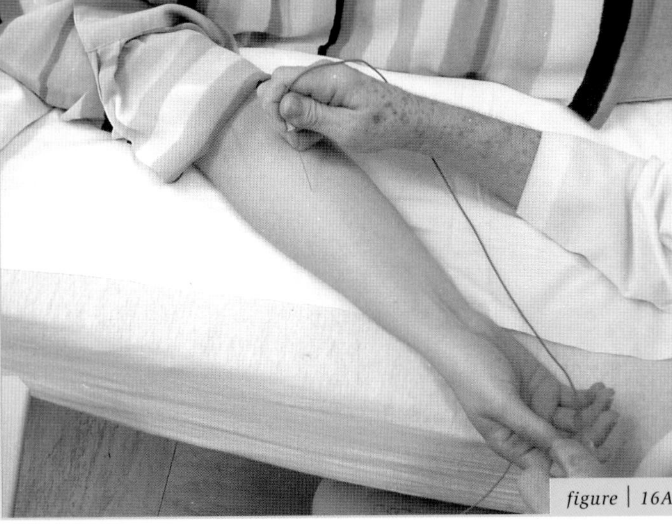

figure | 16A

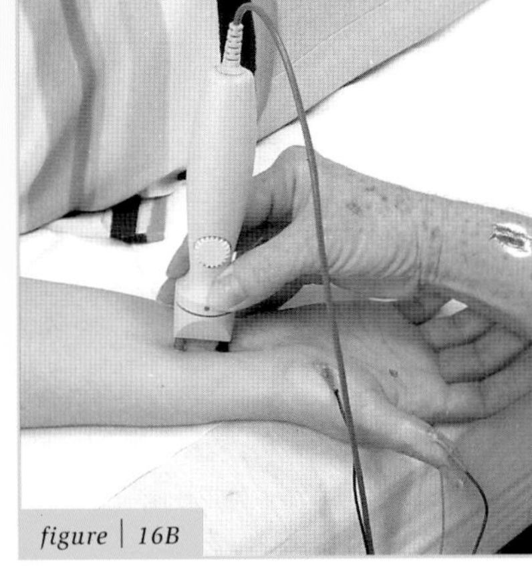

figure | 16B

A. Electromyogram (EMG)–placement of needle electrode into arm.

B. Nerve Conduction Study (NCS).

(Fig. 17). This will open up the foramen, bone window, through which the irritated nerve is coursing. Traction may be performed under the supervision of a physical therapist or self-administrated at home. It is best to begin traction under the observance and trained eye of a physical therapist. There are those patients who have used the traction incorrectly and further aggravated their pain and disc herniation. Other individuals may respond well to ultrasound and diathermy (heat therapy) (Fig. 18). Certain chiropractic therapies may help relieve pressure on exiting nerves. A physician trained in chiropractic medicine performs such therapies. Some individuals do not get better and will need more invasive therapy; therefore, when medical and physical treatments do not help alleviate the discomfort and surgery is not yet an option, epidural injections may be considered. These are usually performed by a pain physician. A spinal needle is place at the site of the nerve irritation for injection of pain-relieving medication or steroids. Some patients do very well with epidural steroid injections, others report that they experienced no long-lasting benefits. If epidural steroid injections do work, they may be repeated every two weeks, up to a total of three times within one year. If the patient improves with conservative therapy, he or she must remember that the neck is still injured. Before returning to the golf course, it is important that the patient discuss the desire to return to golf with his or her physician and physical therapist. It is also very helpful for the patient to be evaluated by a golf professional for analysis of his or her swing and golf equipment.

SURGICAL THERAPIES

If conservative therapy, including epidural steroid injections, fails to relieve the arm pain and neck discomfort, and the patient's quality of life is markedly reduced; surgical therapies become an option. Patients who do not benefit from conservative therapy and are continually plagued with compromised lifestyles beyond 6 to 8 weeks of conservative therapy become surgical candidates. Worsening pain is a relative indication for surgery on a disc abnormality. If there is evidence of progressive weakness in the arm muscles or sensory changes, indications for surgery become stronger. The patient is referred to a spine surgeon, either a neurological or orthopedic surgeon. The surgeon will evaluate the patient by taking a history and performing a physical examination. The surgeon will evaluate the radiological studies obtained by the referring physician or order further tests. If the patient's history, physical examination and radiological studies confirm that a herniated disc is compromising a nerve, then surgery becomes a strong option. The surgeon will discuss the patient's symptoms, any type of weakness (neurological deficit), and review the radiological studies.

The herniated disc may be removed either from surgery performed in front of the neck (anterior approach) or the posterior approach (back of the neck). The approach depends on the offending disc's location and constituency. If the disc is located to the far side, either the anterior or the posterior approach may be recommended. Many spine surgeons favor the anterior approach for cervical disc herniations.

The anterior (front) approach for a cervical disc herniation is accomplished with the patient in the supine position on the operating table. This means that the patient is looking up at the ceiling. The procedure is performed under a general anesthetic given by an anesthesiologist. The incision is usually made in a crease in the neck. The appropriate disc level is identified by using X-rays or a special type of X-ray machine called **fluoroscopy**

(Fig. 19). Identifying the abnormal level will allow the surgeon to choose the appropriate crease in the neck to make the incision. Using a crease means that the incision will course transversely across the patient's neck. In certain situations, this incision may not be possible and the surgeon will have to make a vertical incision. There is a natural plane in the muscles of the neck that allows the surgeon to dissect down to the cervical spine. Fluoroscopy or X-rays will help the surgeon identify the correct level. Sometimes, the patient will have more than one disc herniation and will need multiple discs removed. However, for those individuals presenting with neck pain for the first time, it is usually a single disc that has herniated. The most common site for a disc herniation is at the C6-C7 level (60–70%). The next level usually involved in a disc herniation is at the C5-C6 level (20%), then the C7-T1 level (10%), and at the C4-C5 level (2%). After the disc has been removed, the surgeon may place a bone graft. Use of the patient's own bone, autograft, usually requires the surgeon harvesting bone from the hip. Many patients would prefer not to have bone harvested from their hip and would choose bone from the bone bank, allograft. Some surgeons recommend taking the patient's own bone; however, many surgeons have excellent results using banked bone and, in fact, use of the patient's own bone versus banked bone often yields very similar results. If bone is harvested from the patient's hip, it may be best to harvest the bone from the left side. In the event the patient ever experiences appendicitis, there will be no scar on which to blame the underlying pain as coming from the site of the bone graft. Most physicians will be able to distinguish appendicitis from a previous bone graft harvest site, but why add to the confusion?

The advancement of metallurgy has brought forth a new generation of internal fixation devices (plates and screws), although for a single-level bone fusion use of a bone plate generates controversy among surgeons (Fig. 20A, B, and C). The use of an internal fixation device, such as a plate secured to the cervical bones with screws, may eliminate or reduce the need for a cervical collar after surgery. For the single-level disc fusion, there is probably very little difference between the outcome of surgery, which means good bone fusion, by using either an internal plate or a collar. The plate allows the patient more freedom after surgery and may eliminate or reduce the time or need for a cervical collar. If the patient undergoes more than one level of disc removal (discectomy), a bone plate may improve the surgical outcome (Fig. 21). Today, all anterior cervical plate and bone screw systems are made of titanium, which is MRI and airport compatible. The operation includes removal of the offending disc and placement of a bone graft. It is the bone graft that will grow and mature and provide long-lasting stability for the patient. The plates and screws act only as a neutralization device, like placing a broken arm into a cast. The cast allows the bony ends to stay apposed to each other and promotes bone healing. If all goes well, the patient may be allowed to go home the day of surgery, usually after an appropriate observation period or the next day. Immediately after surgery, the patient is encouraged to avoid heavy lifting, bending and pulling activities. The patient cannot drive. Returning to golf will be a decision made by the patient's surgeon, physician, therapist and the patient. If a cervical plate is used, the patient is a non-smoker and is not medically burdened, golf may be considered within approximately six weeks after surgery. It is important that the patient readjust his or her "thermostat," which means to avoid going out and trying to kill the ball. The patient will need to return to golf slowly under the watchful eyes of

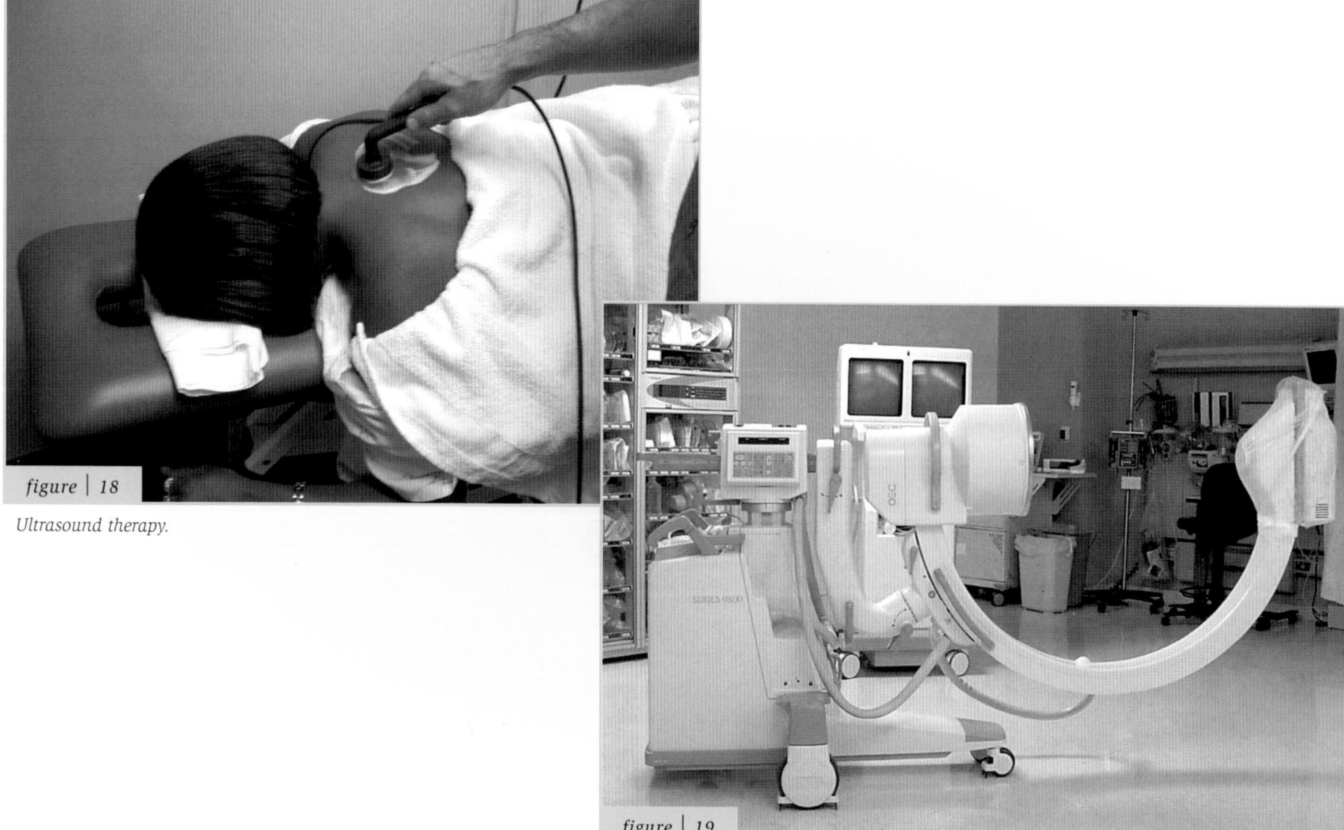

figure | 18

Ultrasound therapy.

figure | 19

Fluoroscopy X-ray machine with monitors.

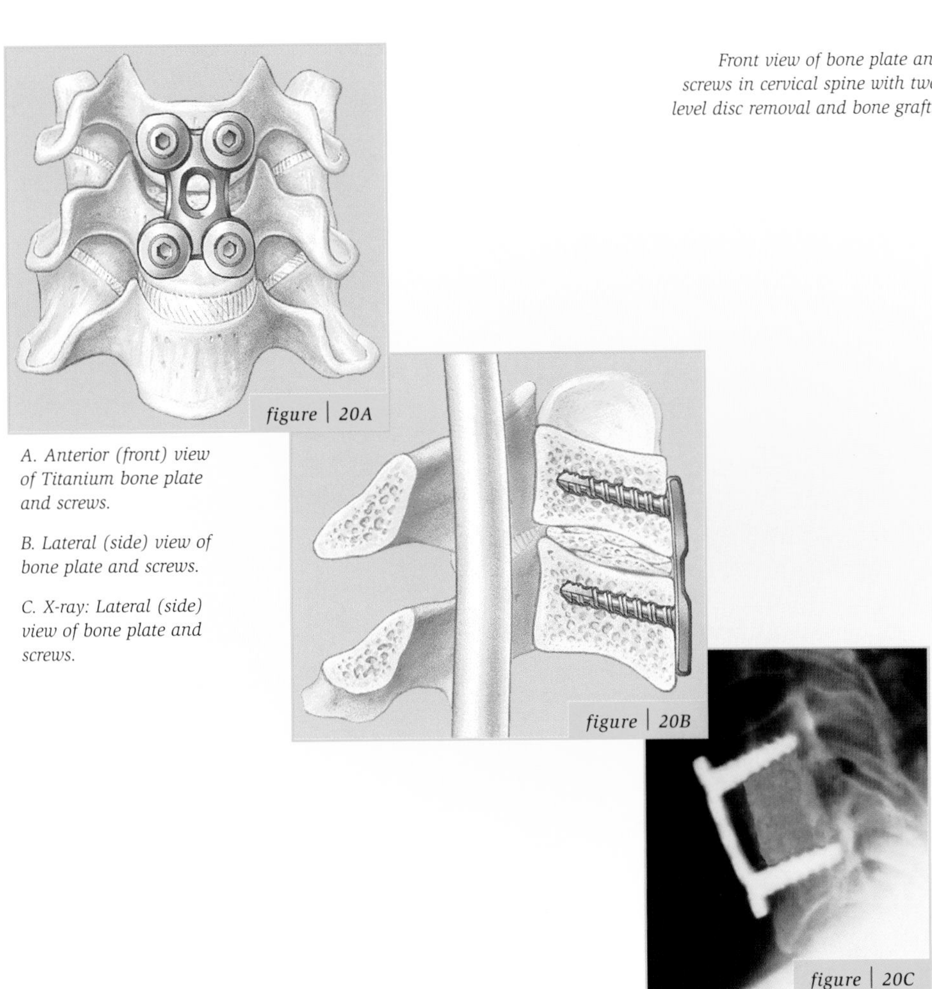

A. Anterior (front) view of Titanium bone plate and screws.

B. Lateral (side) view of bone plate and screws.

C. X-ray: Lateral (side) view of bone plate and screws.

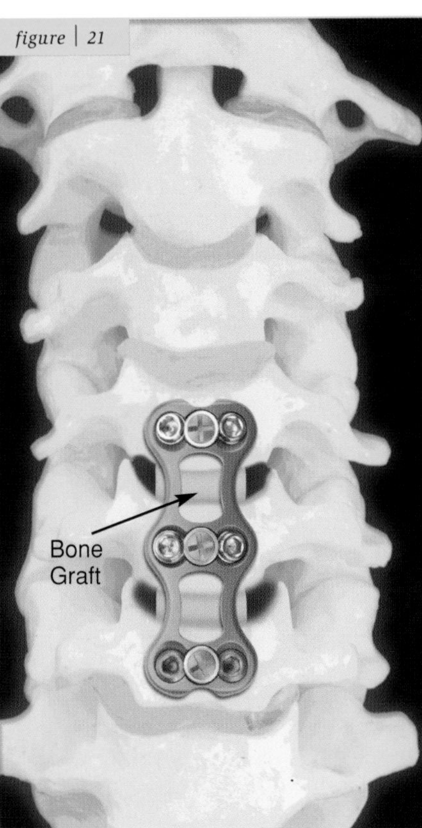

Front view of bone plate and screws in cervical spine with two-level disc removal and bone grafts.

healthcare providers and a golf professional. Learning exercises to maintain cervical muscle strength is important.

Advancements in medical technology continue to provide better treatment for patients with cervical disc disease. Artificial cervical disc replacement is quickly becoming a new option for patients. In Europe, results of total replacement of an injured cervical disc are promising. Patients undergoing disc replacement may be able to return to their work and other activities earlier than those undergoing bone graft and plate fixation procedures. Patients with disc replacement surgery do not have to wait for the bone graft, fusion, to heal before returning to their daily activities. This may mean an earlier return to playing golf.

For some individuals, the disc herniation may not occur along the side of the disc, but in the center. If the disc herniates to the side and causes arm pain, this is referred to as a **radiculopathy**, which means pain radiates into the arm and is a cervical nerve syndrome (Fig. 11). If the disc herniates into the center of the spinal canal and pushes on the spinal cord, it may cause a **myelopathy**. This is a very serious type of disc herniation. The patient may experience weakness in the hands and arms. Complaints are more generalized. Discomfort is throughout both arms and not confined to a single nerve, as noted with a radiculopathy. In addition, there may be leg weakness in which the patient will report feelings of heaviness in the legs and difficulty walking. Bowel and bladder problems may develop: the patient may experience retention or incontinence of urine. These symptoms may indicate that the patient has a great risk for a spinal cord injury. The patient's physical examination will be different from that of a patient who experiences a disc that has herniated to the side. The physician may find **pathological reflexes**, abnormal reflexes. The patient may have difficulty walking, a **spastic gait**. The reflexes will be hyperactive, which means that when the reflexes are tested using a hammer, the arms or the legs may jerk in a more profound fashion. Some patients will report a sudden electrical type of sensation radiating down their neck and back, which is triggered by movement of the neck. This is referred to as a **Lhermitte's sign** (named after the neurologist who first described this abnormal finding). There are other signs that can produce a clinical picture like an acute disc herniation and produce a Lhermitte's sign. Such conditions include multiple sclerosis, cervical spondylosis (stenosis), spinal cord tumor, blood vessel malformations of the spinal cord, Vitamin B deficiency and radiation myelopathy (radiation to the neck for cancer). The patient's situation is serious and the patient must see a doctor at once. The patient's evaluation will be the same as that of a patient with a lateral (side) disc herniation. If the abnormality is an acute disc herniation pushing on the spinal cord, the operation will usually be performed anteriorly or in front of the neck in the same manner as in an acute lateral disc herniation. The patient with a myelopathy may or may not return to playing golf as suddenly as a patient with an acute lateral disc herniation; it all depends upon the amount of compromise or damage to the spinal cord. In most cases a patient with a myelopathy will need a longer duration of therapy and will need more involved physical therapy to return to playing golf. A patient who experiences myelopathy should not give up the desire to return to playing golf. It is possible, but will require commitment, dedication and hard work. The rewards of returning to the game of golf will be well worth it.

For patients who have experienced a cervical disc herniation and have returned to playing golf, they must remember they have bad necks and, therefore, they have to take measures to reduce the chances of another disc herniation. For the patient who has undergone disc surgery, there is always a chance of herniation of another disc above or below the previous herniation site; thus, they must take measures to reduce the risks of another disc herniation. These measures include:

1. Exercises to strengthen the musculature of the cervical spine. This exercise program should include gentle stretching exercises.
2. Awareness of good posture while riding in a car, sitting at a desk or walking. Drooping of the shoulders results in hyperextension of the neck and cervical spine. The need to look up further extends the neck backwards. Bending down causes the head to move backwards. Poor posture can result in compensatory spinal changes, which can aggravate a cervical spine disorder.
3. Caution with certain daily activities that can cause prolonged extension or flexion of the cervical spine, which may give rise to problems. Computer use may cause over extension of the cervical spine. During use the computer should be at the appropriate height; the patient should not have to extend the head forward or backward to view the screen. If patients wear bifocals, they may wish to obtain glasses that will not require that they extend their head in order to see the monitor. The computer screen should be glare-free or flat. Activities that can promote prolonged neck flexion problems include reading in bed or low lounge chairs, writing, sewing, washing dishes, and putting practice. Such postural situations can produce nerve root irritation.
4. Correction of poor sleeping posture may help to prevent aggravation of neck syndromes. Many people sleep with more than one pillow that causes prolonged flexion of the neck, which may worsen neck pain. Sleeping without a pillow may also bring about pain. Other patients must rest in the prone position. This keeps the neck and cervical spine in a rotated and bent position, which is harmful. Finding the right pillow can be of great help. Neck pain patients should experiment with pillows. There are several commercially available cervical pillows. A good pillow to try is a rounded, contoured pillow that prevents rotation and neck bending.
5. When involved in arduous tasks such as heaving lifting, lift in a proper fashion by using the legs to do most of the work. In fact, if any patient has a history of neck problems or has undergone surgery, he or she should not engage in any arduous combat activities such as heavy lifting or bending.
6. And finally, if patients smoke, they should stop. Patients who smoke have a higher incidence of non-healing of bone grafts after surgery and, overall, just do not do as well. Smokers will have a more difficult time in rehabilitation and will need a more prolonged period of physical therapy before returning to playing golf.

CERVICAL SPONDYLOSIS

A common bony neck problem that physicians and spine specialists encounter is **cervical spondylosis**. Spondylosis is a catchall term that refers to the chronic degenerative changes that occur in the vertebrae, joints, ligaments, and intervertebral discs of the cervical spine. Degenerative refers to the normal loss of tissue structure and function as a result of the aging or maturing process. Normal aging brings about changes not only in the bony structures, but also in the intervertebral disc interspaces. Such changes of aging are gradual; in fact, degenerative or aging changes can be found in joints and bones throughout the body. Just because a process is undergoing degenerative changes, it does not always mean that there are clinical problems. We all have degenerative changes going on in our spines and continue to live normal, effective and productive lives. When these degenerative aging changes produce pain, they become medically important. Such changes usually occur at the joint sites in the cervical spine. The joints of the cervical spine make up walls of the **foramen** (holes through which nerves exit). Wear and tear of the joints causes inflammation. Inflammation of the joints will cause the joints to enlarge, or hypertrophy. Enlargement and inflammation of the

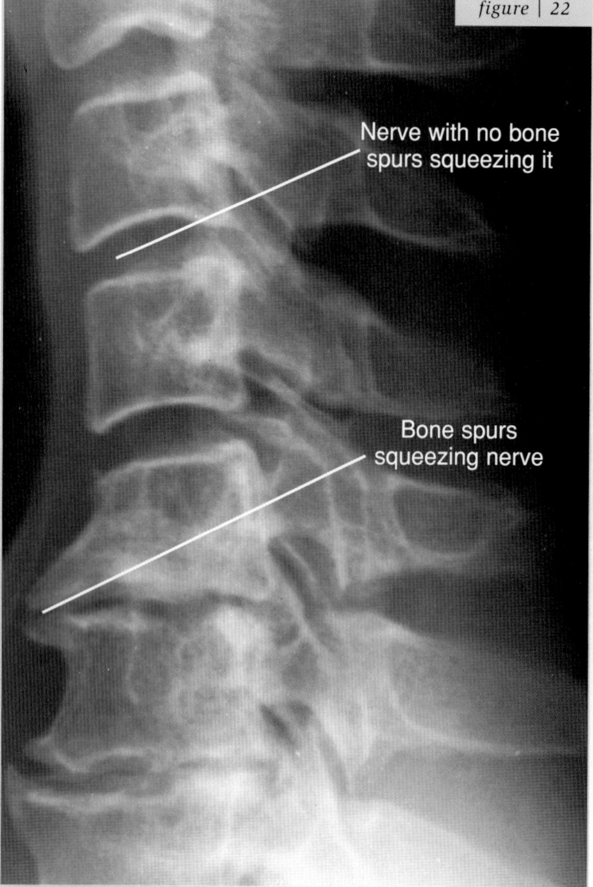

X-ray (lateral) demonstrating degenerative changes in the cervical spine.

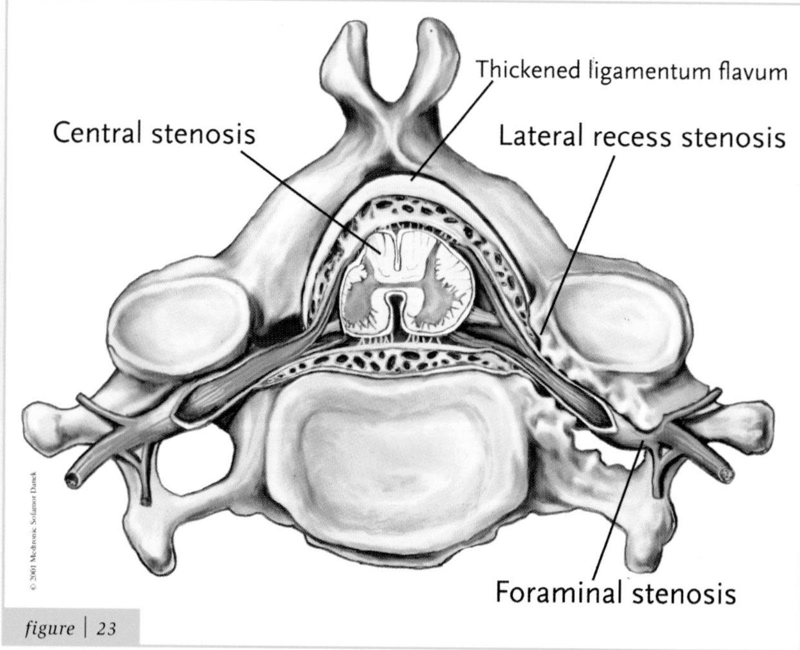

Bony overgrowth pinching the nerve as it courses through the neuroforamen (bone window).

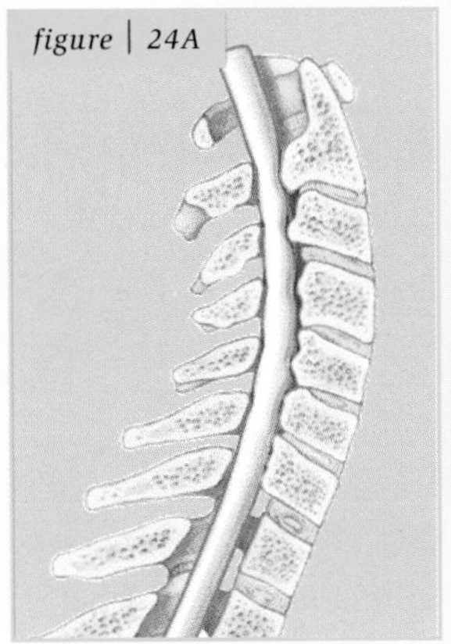

Stenosis:
A. Loss of central canal diameter due to bone spurs.

B. MRI (lateral view) demonstrating stenosis. Note decreased white spinal fluid and osteophyte sites.

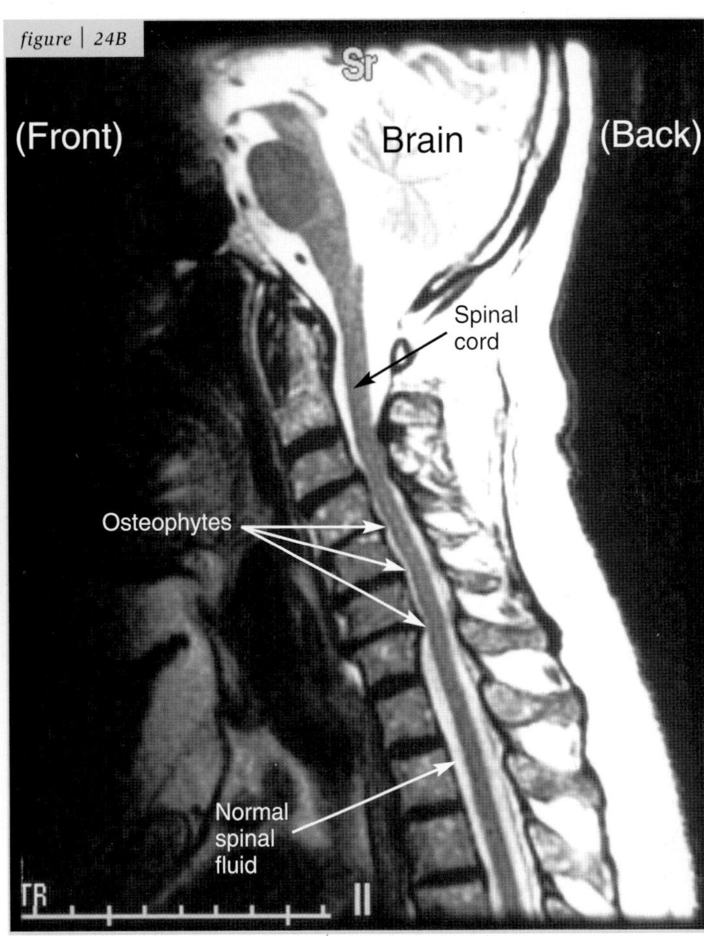

joints is referred to as **osteoarthritis**. Movement of an inflamed or irritated joint will elicit pain; therefore, just moving the neck can be very painful. In the early stages of osteoarthritis, the discomfort can be treated with over-the-counter medications such as non-steroidal anti-inflammatory medications (NSAIDs). Long-term use of this type of medication needs a physician's guidance and close observation. Side effects from long-term use of these medications include stomach problems, especially gastrointestinal bleeding.

Aging or degenerative changes of the cervical spine also affects the vertebrae and the intervertebral discs. As the intervertebral discs age, they lose water. Loss of water will cause the discs to shrink in height. A reduction in disc height will cause the formation of peripheral osteophytes. These bony structures are known as **bone spurs** (Fig. 22). Some physicians and surgeons refer to them as **traction spurs**. They are found near the cortical rim of the vertebra at the point of attachment to the annulus fibrosus of the intervertebral disc. The formation of bone spurs is nature's way of trying to stabilize the spine by preventing unwanted movements of the aging spine. However, in an attempt to bring about stabilization of the cervical spine, bone spurs may grow to a very large size. They may grow to a size that interferes with the diameter of the neuroforamen through which a nerve courses. The osteophytes can pinch the nerve as it's exiting the neuroforamen (Fig. 23). When this occurs, this produces pain like that produced by a disc herniation. Movement of the neck may aggravate the symptoms. In fact, many patients will find a certain position of the neck that is more comfortable than others. This is an attempt to try to enlarge the neuroforamen diameter by neck position. It is when the osteophytes project into the neuroforamen and produce pain that medical and sometimes surgical therapies are needed.

CERVICAL SPINE STENOSIS

Cervical spondylosis includes a problem called **cervical stenosis**. This condition occurs when the central spinal canal, the space for the spinal cord, becomes narrower, or smaller (Fig. 24A and B). A good way to think about cervical stenosis is that, if a foot is the spinal cord and a shoe is the bony spine, an individual with stenosis may be trying to put a size 10-foot into a size 5- shoe. The fit is not comfortable. Radiological studies show that 90% of men over the age of 50 and 90% of women over the age of 60 have evidence of degenerative changes in their cervical spines. No one's exactly sure how genetics or family histories will predispose an individual to cervical spondylosis and stenosis. It's fair to say that if an individual has a strong family history of neck problems, particularly spinal stenosis, he or she may have a predisposition for such problems. Wear and tear of daily activities promotes the development of bony ridges or bone spurs. The bone spurs develop from the **vertebrae**, calcifying ligaments, joints, and the discs. It takes years for bone spurs to develop. Physicians refer to bone spurs as a **chronic neck problem**. This is a progressive process. Fifty percent of the population over the age of 50 years will have signs of bone spurs and spinal canal narrowing. Individuals may have this problem and never know about it until experiencing some event, such as a fall, sudden neck movement, an automobile accident, or swinging a golf club. An individual may suffer from mild pain to severe shooting neck pains. The pains may initially be located in just the neck. If nerves are being squeezed as they exit the foraminae, pain shoots down into the arms. This pain can be made much worse with neck movements. Sometimes such pains can be like an electric shock. When this happens, the spinal cord may be irritated. The electric shock sensation is a symptom not to be ignored. Some individuals with such neck pain may have episodes where it gets better and then gets worse. Long periods of non-progressive symptoms are common. Any neck pain that doesn't get better is worrisome. A golfer should never continue playing with such symptoms. Pain means stop!

Another symptom of a tight, narrowed spinal canal is numbness or tingling sensation in the arms. Some people describe this sensation as "pins and needles" or "my arm's asleep," and others will describe it as a "burning sensation." Some develop hand clumsiness or weakness in the arms. For others, early signs of neck problems begin in the legs with weakness. When such leg symptoms occur, the neck may be the problem site. Headaches in the back of the head are not uncommon. Headaches caused by cervical spondylosis are called **cervicalgia**. If bowel or bladder problems occur, particularly episodes of incontinence, an urgent medical evaluation is needed. Another problem is sexual dysfunction. Things in this department change as we age, but if serious sexual problems associated with the above symptoms occur, a doctor's visit is warranted. Problems with walking, bowel or bladder difficulties, and weakness may indicate a serious consequence of cervical spondylosis or stenosis called **cervical myelopathy**. Myelopathy is caused by a very narrow central cervical spinal canal. The onset of myelopathy is usually insidious. Reversal of the symptoms depends on how long they have been present. The longer the symptoms have been going on, i.e., the longer the walking problems, the less likely that the symptoms will resolve, even with therapy. However, without treatment the problems could worsen. Untreated cervical spondylosis causing myelopathy could progress into total paralysis. Thus, cervical spine problems should never be ignored.

DOCTOR'S VISIT

When a physician or healthcare provider is consulted, many questions will be asked. Having the answers beforehand can save you and the doctor a lot of time and provide the doctor with important information. The first thing the physician will do is to take a medical history (ask a lot of questions). Next is the examination; the physician will look at the patient's head to make sure it's a normal looking head, with no evidence of trauma. The physician will examine the neck, the upper back and the lower back of the patient, and will ask the patient to move the neck in various directions, forward and backward and sideways (both right and left). It's very important that, if these maneuvers elicit or cause pain, the patient informs the doctor. The doctor will inspect the patient's arms and legs, making sure that the muscles aren't atrophied (wasted) or twitching. Strength is referred to as **motor function**. Sensory is the **tactile examination**. The sensory part of the examination will involve the use of a sharp pin to test the patient's ability to feel. Today disposable pins are used. Sometimes a doctor will use a vibrating fork to evaluate the individual's response to vibrations. At this particular time, the doctor may bring out the percussion hammer to evaluate reflexes (Fig. 25). The doctor may tweak the finger to see what happens with the thumb (Fig. 26). If the finger is tweaked and the thumb moves, this may demonstrate an abnormal sign. Abnormal signs may indicate that something is wrong. This sign is called a **Hoffman's sign**, which indicates that the spinal cord is being irritated. The next important sign that the physician will check for is called a **Babinski's sign**. This sign is tested by scraping the bottom of the foot (Fig. 27). If the big toe goes up, the Babinski's sign is positive. If the doctor takes the foot and moves it back and forth quickly and the foot continues

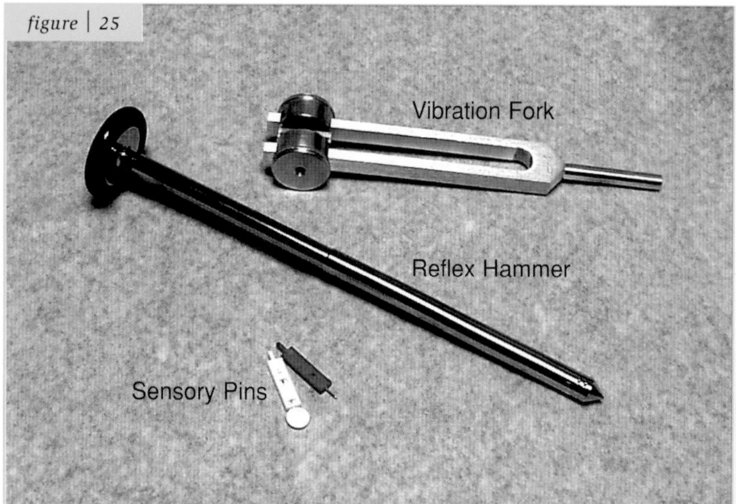

figure | 25

Vibration Fork; Reflex Hammer, Pins for Sensory Test (top to bottom).

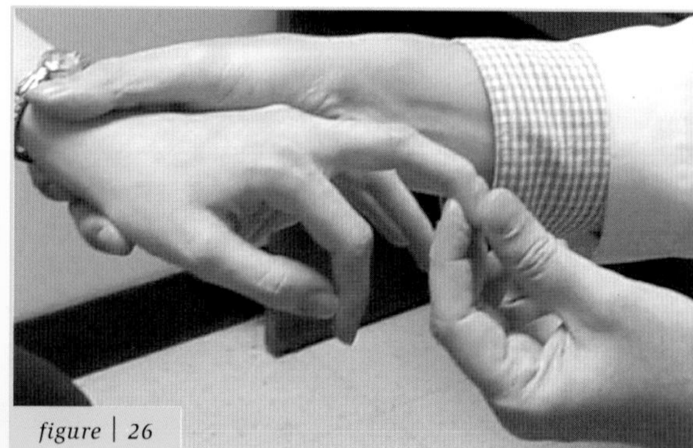
figure | 26

Hoffman's sign test.

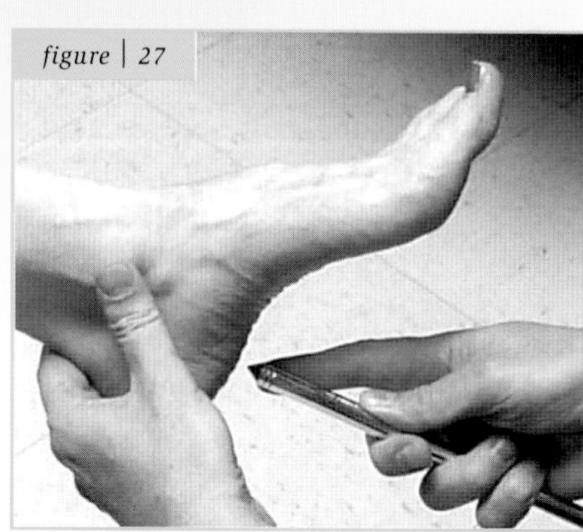
figure | 27

Babinski's sign test.

X-ray: Oblique view demonstrating foramen (bone windows) through which nerves travel.

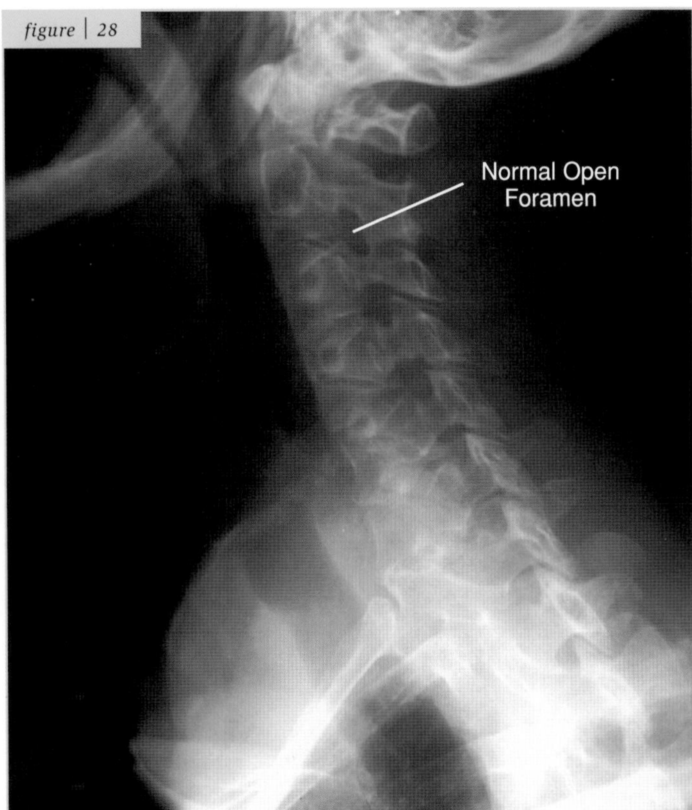

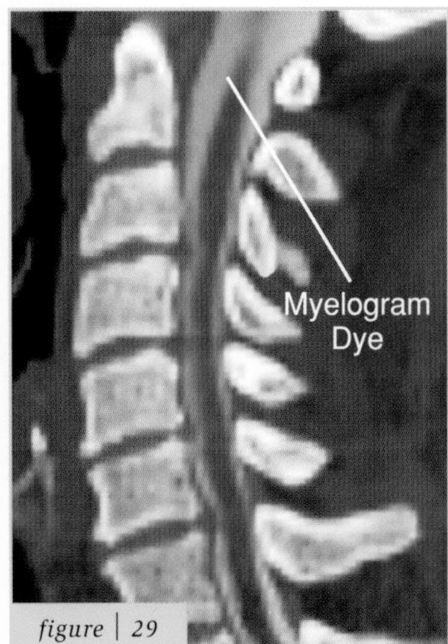

Lateral (side) view of CAT (CT) scan after myelogram demonstrating the contrast dye in the spinal canal.

to jerk, this is called **clonus**; it's another sign that maybe there's some nervous system irritation. The doctor will ask the patient to walk, to stand on tiptoes, on heels, and walk tandemly. Tandem walking is walking a line placing one foot in front of the other. If the patient can't tandem walk well, it's one of those things needing a closer look. The doctor may perform a rectal examination. A patient may ask, "A rectal examination because I'm having problems in my neck?" Yes! Not only should a patient be able to sense or feel this type of examination, a finger in the rectum, but sometimes the sphincter, the muscle that squeezes the anus tight, may be loose, and the patient may not feel the finger. A loose sphincter and the inability to feel the examiner's finger is certainly an indication that something may not be right. After the history taking and physical examination, other tests may be ordered.

RADIOLOGICAL IMAGING

A common radiological test a physician will often order to evaluate the cervical spine is an **X-ray**. The doctor may obtain a **lateral** X-ray (side view) and a front-to-back X-ray called an A/P (anterior-to-posterior) view (Fig. 4A and B). Other views include an **oblique** film, which allows visualization of the foraminae, the holes through which nerves exit (Fig. 28). On the lateral X-ray, the doctor will be able to study the bone structures and the spinal canal size. If the canal's diameter is less than 13mm, the physician may be concerned. If it is less than 11mm, this will warrant further evaluation in most situations. Less than 11mm diameter means that perhaps there is not enough space in the spinal canal for the spinal cord. This finding will usually prompt other more involved radiological studies.

A technique that is used to evaluate the bony structures in more detail is **computerized axial tomography (CAT scan)**. Sir Godfrey Newbold Hounsfield and Allan MacLeod Cormack developed Computerized Axial Tomography. In 1979, Drs. Hounsfield and Cormack were awarded the Nobel Prize. The CAT scan allows the radiologist to appreciate the bony structures in the cervical spine. Alone, the CAT scan may not tell the whole story; therefore, to evaluate the soft tissues, the discs, the spinal cord and nerves, a test called **magnetic resonance imaging (MRI)** may be needed. Today, this study does not entirely replace the CAT scan. The CAT scan shows the bone and the MRI demonstrates the soft tissue. By comparing the MRI and the CAT scan, the radiologist and physician will be able to better evaluate what type of neck problem is occurring. Sometimes, instead of a CAT scan or an MRI, the physician may feel more comfortable ordering a **myelogram** and then a CAT scan. Contrast dye is injected into the spinal fluid and allowed to float up towards the neck. X-rays will be obtained; this is the myelogram. After the myelogram, a CAT scan will usually be performed. The post-myelogram CAT scan, the CAT scan obtained after the myelogram, will demonstrate the dye column and if it's being compressed by any abnormal bony elements (Fig. 29). If there is compression and pressure on the spinal cord, surgery may be needed.

TREATMENT OPTIONS

After all the radiological studies, or images, have been obtained, the patient and the physician will meet again and discuss options regarding what's to be done next. The options may include the following:

- Continue non-aggressive or conservative therapy (medications, physical therapy or alternative therapies). Follow the patient's symptoms for worsening signs.
- Surgery.

It's very important that the patient have a good relationship with the physician or healthcare provider. The patient must be able to talk openly and honestly about his or her problems. The patient may be referred to a spine specialist. There are two types of spine specialists: one is a **non-surgical** spine specialist and the other is a **surgical** spine specialist. Non-surgical spine specialists include rheumatologists, physiatrists (rehabilitation/musculo-skeletal physicians), radiologists, pain specialists (anesthesiologists, neurosurgeons), chiropractic physicians, acupuncturists, physical therapists, and massage therapists. Surgical spine specialists are either neurosurgeons or orthopedic surgeons.

Usually a family physician or other healthcare provider will help guide the patient through this complex process of deciding whom to consult. It's important to have confidence in a physician and be able to talk to him or her about any problems. A golfer will need to ask how his or her neck problem affects the ability to play golf.

If the problem is symptomatic cervical spondylosis or stenosis, surgical options may be discussed. Surgery involves either going in front of the neck, an anterior approach, or going from the back of the neck, a posterior approach. When considering surgery, it's important to have a good feeling about the surgery. The patient must approach any type of surgical therapy with a positive attitude. Only the patient can ultimately decide to have the operation. Even though a patient's loved ones may be supportive, the patient is the one who will make the decision. The patient should sit down with the surgeon and talk about the surgical options. Does the surgeon feel that the particular problem is best addressed by anteriorly or posteriorly? It's important to ask questions. The patient needs to discuss with the doctor exactly what will happen after surgery. How long will they be out of work? Can they drive? Can they have sex and if no, when? When can they play golf? The patient must have realistic goals. The surgeon will talk to the patient about all the good things and bad things that can happen with surgery. It's like flying—the patient gets on the airplane in his or her hometown and safely flies away. In most cases, the individual arrives safely, but sometimes, the plane crashes. The patient will need to weigh the benefits and risks of surgery. The patient may want to talk to a loved one, or may want to call the family doctor and discuss the options. In most cases, the patient doesn't have to make a decision right then and there about surgery.

CERVICAL SPINE SPONDYLOSIS SURGERY

Anterior Surgery: An operation in front of the neck is referred to as an anterior operation. There are two ways in which the surgeon can remove bone spurs from in front. One is going through the disc space and then removing the bone spurs that have accumulated and anchored themselves near the disc. After removing these discs with special instruments, the surgeon will need to perform a bone graft or fusion (Fig. 30). The surgeon, in this situation, is a spine farmer; he or she is putting seeds (bone seeds) into the patient, the soil. Therefore, it is up to the patient to help heal and grow good solid bone. The bone can be taken either from the patient's own body (**autogenous graft**) or from the bone bank (allograft). It's up to the patient and the surgeon to decide which type of bone graft to use. If the bone spurs are too large, the patient may need the second type of anterior surgery, a **corpectomy**. A corpectomy means removal of the front of the vertebra in order to get to the bone spurs (Fig. 31). After the corpectomy has been performed and the offending bone spurs removed, a **bone graft is** needed. A long piece of bone graft is placed from the vertebral body above to the vertebral body below

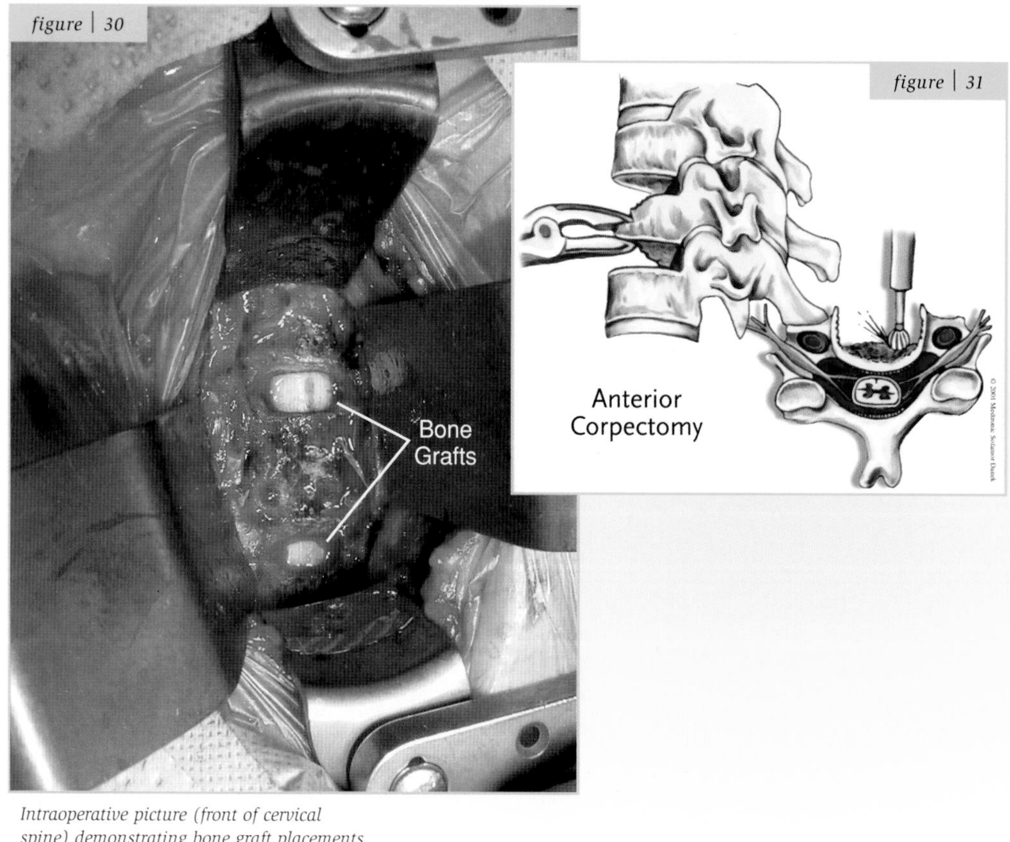

figure | 30

Intraoperative picture (front of cervical spine) demonstrating bone graft placements in the disc spaces.

figure | 31

Corpectomy.

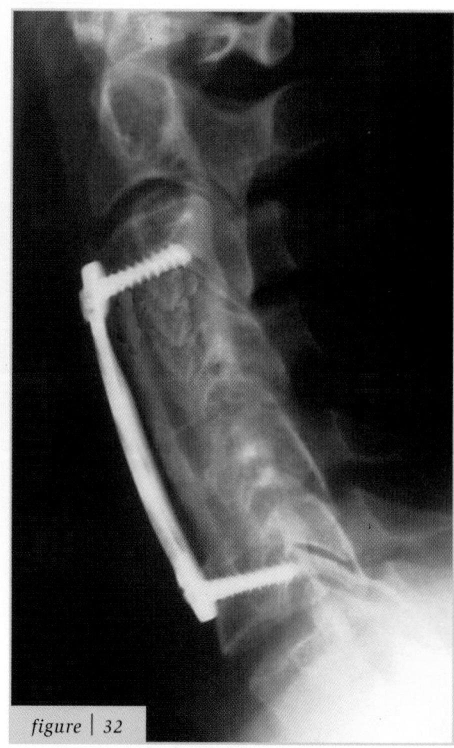

figure | 32

X-ray: Lateral (side) view with bone plate, screws and bone graft.

CAT (CT) scan: Lateral (side) view demonstrating bone mass behind vertebrae compromising the central spinal canal diameter.

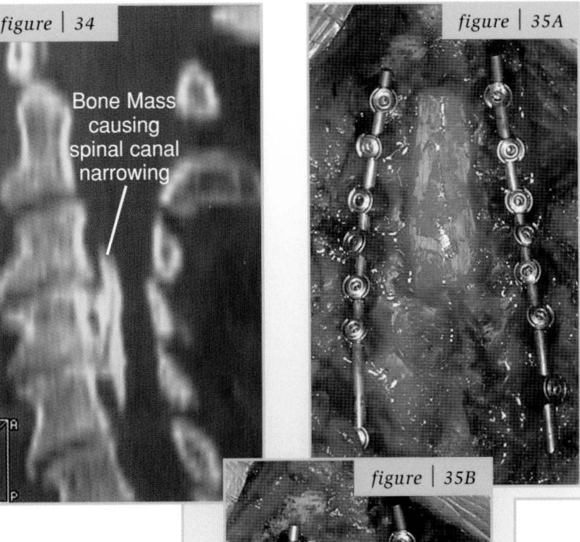

A. Titanium reconstruction rods and screws placed after a laminectomy.

B. Intraoperative photo demonstrating bone screws and rods with a crosslink.

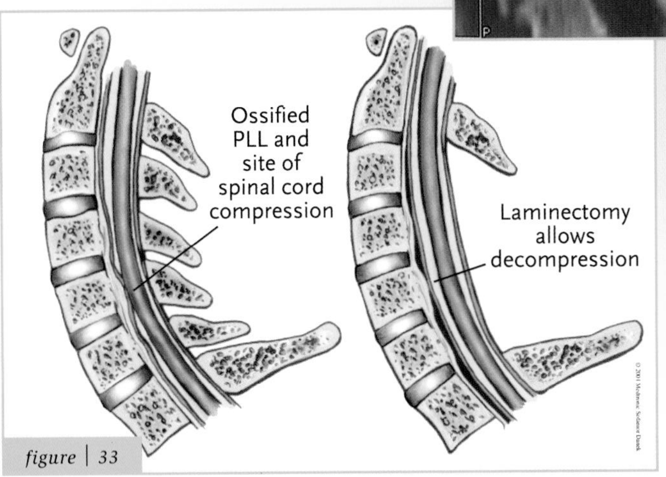

Laminectomy: Removal of spinous processes and lamina from back of neck.

figure | 35B

Laminoplasty.

figure | 36

Lamina cut

Lamina notched to form a hinge

(Fig. 32). In some situations, a metal **bone cage** is used. Bone is usually taken from the patient's hip, placed into the bone cage and the cage placed into the corpectomy site. After the corpectomy and, sometimes, after the **discectomy**, a metal **bone plate** will be placed onto the corpectomy site. A bone plate is made of a special metal called **titanium.** (Fig. 32) The patient need not worry; he can still go through an airport without setting off the alarm. In almost all cases, the bone plate will stay with the patient for the rest of his or her life. After the anterior surgery, the patient may or may not need to wear a brace or a cervical collar. It depends on the surgery performed. Sometimes after this type of surgery, the patient may experience mild swallowing difficulties that are usually short-lived, days to weeks. Some patients may even have hoarseness; in most cases, this resolves with time. Most patients are admitted to the hospital the same day as the surgery and go home later after a period of observation. In other situations, the patient may stay a few days in the hospital.

Posterior surgery: The operation in back of the neck is referred as a **posterior approach**. The posterior approach may involve removing the lamina, the rooftop of the neck bones. This operation is called a **laminectomy** (Fig. 33). In some cases, the bony spurs or the calcification extends too many cervical levels for an operation in front; therefore, the operation in back of the spine may be indicated (Fig. 34). In the **laminectomy** operation, taking away the lamina is like cutting off the top of a shoe in order to give the foot room. Sometimes the surgeon will remove only the rooftop. In other situations, there may be more to do than just take off the rooftops. The surgeon may need to remove more bone. If this happens, it's like taking more and more of the shoe away and leaving only the sole. The patient can't go walking around with only a sole. Thus, some type of fixation device will need to be placed along the remaining bony elements. It's like putting straps around a foot to hold it onto the sole of a shoe. The surgeon may need to stabilize the cervical spine with bone plates or rods with bone screws. These bone plates and rods are called **reconstruction plates** or **reconstruction rods**. The screws are placed into the far sides of the remaining bony elements and then attached to rods. In special cases surgery is needed for spinal stabilization of the cervical spine with bone plates in front and rods in the back (Fig. 35A, B).

If this type of operation is performed, it will decrease the range of motion of the neck. Another type of posterior operation is a **laminoplasty**. In this procedure, the surgeon will cut bone on one side of the lamina all the way through and then just cut partway down on the other side. The lamina, bony roof, is not removed as in the laminectomy, but is propped open, giving the spinal cord more room (Fig. 36). The laminae may be propped open by using bone from the patient's hip, ribs or the **spinous processes** (bony protuberances). Some surgeons may use bank bone. These bone grafts are placed along the side that has been opened, and are held in place by specially bent titanium reconstruction plates (Fig. 37 A and B). After the back of the neck surgery, the patient may or may not need to wear a brace. The surgeon will determine the duration for wearing the brace. The patient may or may not need rehabilitation after this type of surgery. Golfers need to ask before surgery how this will affect their game. In most situations, some type of reconditioning will be needed. The goal of surgery is to take away some of the pain, but more importantly, this type of surgery is performed to prevent any further damage to the spinal cord and nerves. The best way for the patient to get back to the golf course is to follow the instructions of the surgeon, physiatrist, physical therapist and family doctor. Patients will need to make modifications in their golf game. In most situations, golfers will be able to get báck to playing. It may take anywhere from six weeks to 3 to 6 months of reconditioning therapy before patients can think about reconditioning therapy to return to the golf course.

INFLAMMATORY DISORDERS

An inflammatory spinal disorder is an inflammation in the joints of the cervical spine. One of the most common inflammatory spinal disorders is **arthritis**. Some of the more common inflammatory disorders include **rheumatoid arthritis**, **juvenile rheumatoid arthritis (JRA)**, and **ankylosing spondylitis**. With these particular problems, it's not until an individual has a major problem that he or she seeks professional help; therefore, there's often a delay in diagnosis with these particular problems. These inflammatory disorders can cause significant problems. These are often crippling disorders and, in certain situations, can even be life threatening. Inflammation can start in any joint, and the cervical spine certainly has a lot of joints. Sometimes the inflammation can be quite extensive; this can involve numerous joints. Inflammatory problems can become chronic. This group of disorders needs to be treated immediately in order to prevent any permanent joint changes.

TUMORS

Tumors of the spine are those tumors that arise from the bones in the cervical spine. Primary spine tumors, fortunately, are usually rare. Primary means that they arise from the bones in the cervical spine. The other type of bone tumor, which is not as rare, is a **metastatic tumor**. Metastatic means that it's a cancer that has traveled from elsewhere; for instance, breast or lung cancer. The cancer develops in the lung or the breast and is carried by the blood to distant sites. The bone is an excellent place for these tumors to grow. Bones are filled with blood, which provides nutrients for the cancer cells. If a patient with a history of cancer develops neck pain, the diagnosis is cancer to the cervical spine until proven otherwise.

SYMPTOMS

The most common presenting symptom of a tumor in the cervical spine is pain. More than 80% of individuals will complain of pain in the neck. The pain will become persistent. It is aggravated by movement of the head and often awakens the patient from a night's rest, a sound sleep. The pain is relentless; it occurs whether they're lying flat or moving. No activity will usually make it better and no position will totally alleviate it. Pressure on the nerves exiting from the spinal cord by the tumor can cause pain in the arms and produce numbness and tingling sensations in the arms and legs. The patient may also notice weakness in the arms and legs. If the spinal cord is compressed, this may produce **spasticity** with legs that are jumpy and stiff. Another problem that warrants urgent evaluation is the loss of bowel or bladder control. If an individual can't walk anymore, he or she must seek medical attention. Usually by this time such patients are not playing golf, but should be in a physician's office or an emergency room. The other signs of cancer, problems that may be quite worrisome, are easy fatigability. The patient golfer used to be able to play without a sense of early fatigue. He or she used to play 18 holes vigorously, but now, after the third hole, is tired. Something may be wrong. Also, weight loss; partners on the links look at the patient and say "Hey! You're losing weight!" As time goes by the patient may hear the expression "Oh,

A. X-ray: Anterior (front) view of bone plates after laminoplasty.

B. X-ray: Lateral (side) view of bone plates and screws after laminoplasty.

figure | 37A

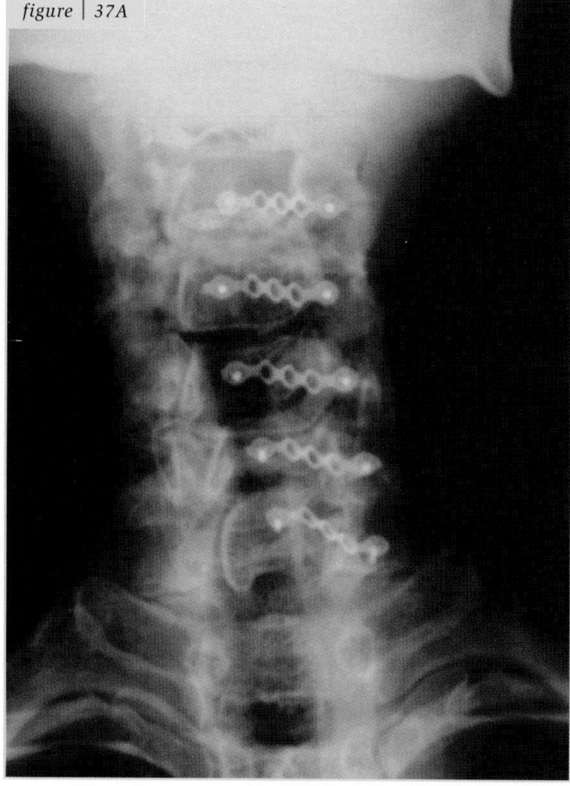

figure | 37B

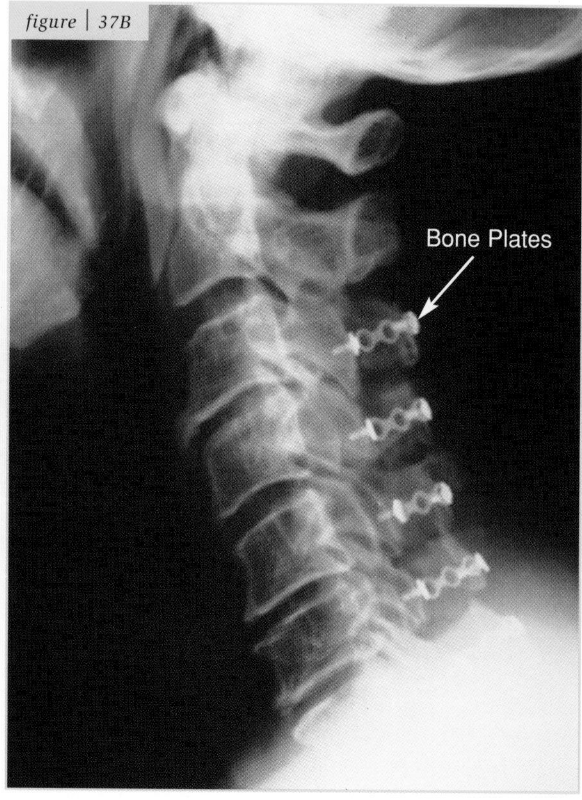

you're still losing weight." After a while, the loss of weight is not healthy. In some patients, cancer of the cervical spine will be the first sign that they have cancer. Other signs, such as lumps or bumps in the groin or under the arms, or a funny looking mole—a black, irregular shaped mole (melanoma)—on the skin, or a cough with shortness of breath, are serious symptoms and signs that shouldn't be ignored.

TREATMENT OPTIONS

If a spine tumor is causing pressure on the spinal cord or nerves, a primary care provider will refer the patient to a surgeon. Surgical options will be operating anteriorly or posteriorly. During surgery, the patient may or may not need to have internal fixation, stabilization, using plates, rods, or screws after a bone graft has been performed. Any therapy after surgery, i.e., chemotherapy or radiation therapy, will depend upon the type of tumor. The only way to truly know what type of tumor is causing the mischief is to obtain a biopsy of the tumor and send it to a pathologist, who will stain it by placing it in various baths of dye and then evaluate it under a microscope. Added therapies such as chemotherapy or radiation therapy will depend on the tumor type and classification. Having cancer in the cervical spine doesn't mean the end of golf. Returning to playing will take time, however. Rehabilitation and reconditioning exercises will play a major role for the returning golfer.

CONCLUSION

Any treatment of cervical spine problems must be individualized. A multidisciplinary approach to the disorder may offer the best chance for a long lasting resolution of the pain. Excellent results can often be obtained in many disorders of the cervical spine by conservative measures. After experiencing a cervical disorder, the individual may have some degree of residual disability. The involved soft tissues and bony elements will be less tolerable of unusual stresses, including golfing. Patients and golfers with neck problems need always to be mindful of the importance of proper usage, protection and conditioning of their necks to prevent recurrent attacks of pain and disability. Surgical therapies should be avoided unless there are strong and definitive indications for them; otherwise the operative outcomes will be disappointing and the preoperative symptoms may be worse than they were before surgery. Even with good spinal care the changes of aging are inevitable; however, early recognition and treatment of cervical spinal disorders are the best avenues toward golf forever.

THE THORACIC SPINE (MID-SPINE)

CHAPTER 7

T. Glenn Pait, M.D., F.A.C.S.

The most important thing is to figure out your own back, and how it works. As a professional golfer known to have a trick back, I bet I've received more than 100 letters with suggestions about my back: sit this way, roll over this way, put your knees to your chest. There's not enough hours in the day to do all that. Your back needs to be treated whichever way will make it feel better.

My big secret is that I found Tom Boers. I really don't let anyone else touch it. Tom's able to get my back to where I can play golf, which is all I ask. I would imagine that for the average player who doesn't have quite as rhythmic a swing, and doesn't have access to a guy like Tom, he's going to be in 10 times the trouble. For me I can't compete with the best players if my back isn't feeling good. Some weeks I seek out Tom and he works on it. But I'll tell you it's a very tough thing to figure out. I would suggest to amateurs that you find one person who understands your back and can work on it, and don't seek out the advice of several different people.

Fred Couples

The thoracic spine is the middle portion of the spine. It is the section of the spine that is situated between the cervical spine (neck) and the lumbar spine (lower back) (Fig. 1).The thoracic spine is made up of twelve vertebrae, and between each vertebral body is an intervertebral disc (Fig. 2). The thoracic spine is the true chest part of the spine. It is connected to the sternum (chest bone) by the ribs. The ribs provide a unique type of protection for the thoracic spine. The ribs connect the sternum and the thoracic spine to create a cage. The cage protects vital organs like the heart and the lungs (Fig. 3). The ribcage prevents many of the movements that are common in the cervical and lumbar areas. Thus in the thoracic spine, there are essentially no significant bending motions. Repetitive bending and extension/flexion activities cause many of the degenerative diseases that are found in the cervical (neck) and lumbar (low back) spine. The type of motion that occurs in the thoracic spine is mostly rotational; this is an important type of motion for the golfer (Fig. 4).

The thoracic spine, like the cervical spine, encases the spinal cord. The end of the spinal cord, the conus medullaris, is located in the lower segments of the thoracic spine (Fig. 5). The spinal cord in the cervical spine has more room than it does in the thoracic spine. Because there is less room for the spinal cord in the thoracic spine than in the cervical spine, smaller types of abnormalities produce compression on the thoracic spinal cord than if the same abnormalities occurred elsewhere.

Pain in the thoracic spine is a common presenting complaint for many golfers. Like most back problems such maladies are usually short-lived and resolve with patience and a little tender loving care. Pain occurring in the thoracic spine during or after a round of golf should be taken seriously. This means that the golfer should not continue playing until the discomfort has resolved.

Many conditions produce pain in or around the thoracic spine. In most cases, the pain generator originates from two sources. The first is from nearby organs. Physicians refer to such pain as **viscerogenic thoracic pain**. Visceral refers to a viscus, which is a large interior cavity in the body; therefore, such pain literally means that it is coming from an organ inside one of the body cavities. If it's the thoracic spine, it's the thoracic cavity. The second type of pain arises from the spine and spinal nerves; this type of pain is referred to as **spondylogenic**. Spondylo- is the medical term referring to the spine. Spondylogenic pain syndromes also include pain originating from the muscles.

There are many visceral conditions or diseases that can masquerade as spinal problems. Therefore, it is important that a physician consulted for treatment of spinal problems of the thoracic spine recognize a possible visceral or organ etiology for what seemingly appears to be either a muscle or a spinal condition. Organs in both the chest and the abdomen can simulate thoracic spine, spondylogenic pain.

The best-known organ to cause thoracic discomfort is the **heart**. Problems of the heart and blood vessels are referred to as **cardiovascular disorders**. The most common cardiovascular disorders include **angina pectoris** (chest pain), **myocardial infarction** (heart attack), **mitral valve prolapse** (heart valve insufficiency), **pericarditis** (heart lining inflammation), and **aortic aneurysm** (blood vessel blister). Angina pectoris literally means constricting pain in the chest. It is a common problem that indicates the presence

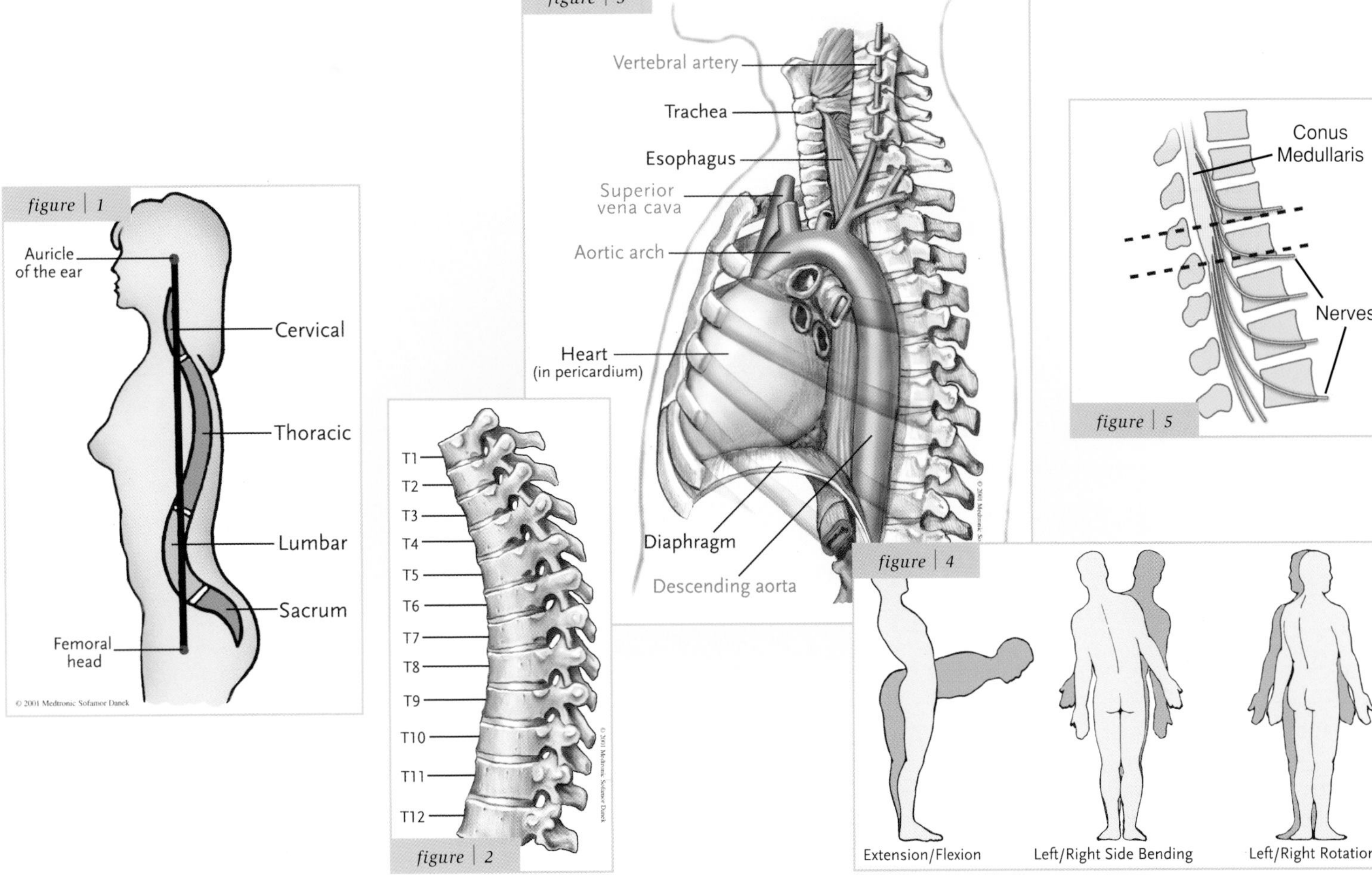

of an obstruction in one of the heart arteries (coronary arteries). The obstruction causes an insufficiency in the supply of blood to the heart. Usually, an artery with about 75% obstructed can transport enough blood to the heart and not cause any pain when the patient is at rest or is inactive. But anything that causes the heart to work more, such as exercise, golf, emotion and stress, will increase the need for more blood to travel to the heart. If the arteries of the heart cannot accommodate this heightened demand for more blood and oxygen, the result is angina. The obstruction to the blood vessels is the result of **atherosclerotic plaques**. Atherosclerosis is a process in which the wall of the artery develops local degeneration, which is referred to as **plaque**. The smooth inner lining of the small heart artery will become roughened and irregular as a substance called **cholesterol** is deposited in the wall of the artery. Soon, scar tissue is formed.

Blood clots may form on these plaques, making the artery less able to do its job of providing vital oxygen to the heart muscle. Over time, the heart artery may become completely blocked. When this occurs, the section of the heart muscle supplied by the artery is denied blood. When heart cells are deprived of blood and oxygen, they eventually die. Initially, there may not be any extremely painful sensation. The condition may be felt for one to several minutes as tightness or a vice-like sensation in the middle of the chest or across the whole front of the chest. The sensation may travel to the neck, the lower jaw, the shoulders, and into one or both arms. Therefore, if for any reason the golfer, at any time during play, experiences such a sensation, it means to stop and tell your partner that you're having some unusual chest tightness and symptoms. You should be transported immediately back to the clubhouse, and an ambulance should be called. Some patients may describe the chest pain as a "squeezing" or a "heaviness" in the chest. Others will describe it as a "choking, burning pressure." In some individuals the discomfort is noted to be present only on one side of the chest, usually the left side, and it is not uncommon for the pain to radiate into the back. Sometimes these episodes may be very brief. In fact, the pain may be stopped totally by resting. This occurs because the heart no longer has to work as hard as when there is a reduced demand for blood and oxygen. For instance, teeing off may cause angina. Sitting in the golf cart or on a bench for a few moments may cause the pain to subside totally. Here are some common activities that can precipitate or bring about angina:

- playing golf;
- becoming emotionally upset about one's performance on a given day;
- running to catch an airplane;
- walking in the cold or against the wind;
- after eating;
- walking along the course, pulling the golf cart; and
- sexual activities.

If an individual experiences pain during any of these activities, he or she should not ignore it, but rather seek medical attention. Anginal discomfort can be treated effectively with medications that can enhance the blood supply to the heart by dilating the heart blood vessels. Angina is a symptom to be taken very seriously; it does not mean that one has to give up golf. However, it does mean that the individual's lifestyle must change. Many golfers lead entirely normal lives working every day and continuing to play golf. The bottom line: an individual who has angina must readjust and modify his or her lifestyle. This includes changing the diet and exercising regularly as prescribed by a physician. Medications will help control the chest discomfort, the angina; however, they cannot totally cure the condition. If the attacks become more severe, more frequent, and last longer, other medical treatments will be needed. The individual with unstable angina will need a **coronary angioplasty** or even **coronary artery bypass surgery** to increase the blood supply and oxygen to the heart muscle. Coronary angioplasty is a procedure in which a physician will thread a long thin tube containing a deflated balloon into one of the arteries of the upper leg. Using a special video fluoroscopy X-ray machine, the tube is navigated up to the clogged coronary artery. After the clogged coronary artery is reached, the balloon is inflated. When the balloon inflates, it actually opens up the obstruction in the coronary artery so that more blood flow will travel through it. This process is called **revascularization**. The procedure is very helpful for many patients; however, a small percentage of individuals will relapse with return of their angina. It is these individuals who may need coronary artery bypass surgery. This surgery involves taking a vein from the leg to replace the clogged artery in the heart. In some situations, a medical laser is used to vaporize plaques in arteries or to help revascularize the heart. Each type of treatment depends on the individual patient and the approach recommended by the treating medical physician and coronary team.

A heart attack, or **myocardial infarction**, in contrast to the incomplete blockage of an artery caused by angina, involves total blockage of the coronary artery. It is the total blockage of the heart artery that causes the death of heart cells in the areas supplied by the affected artery. Heart attacks are usually caused by a small part of the atherosclerotic plaque that breaks off and is carried downstream along the coronary artery to a point where the artery narrows. Here, the plaque can go no farther and becomes lodged and totally blocks the flow of blood. A heart attack can also be caused by a blood clot forming on a plaque. The plaque will rupture, which causes the release of various substances that will increase the clotting of blood. The clot forms in the plaque and becomes so large that it can totally block off the flow of blood. It is not known exactly when a plaque will rupture and cause a clot.

If an individual is experiencing severe chest pain, taking an aspirin can significantly change the outcome of the heart attack. For some individuals, taking an aspirin as prescribed by their doctor may significantly reduce the incidence of heart attacks. In fact, it's a good idea when playing golf to have a bottle of aspirin handy. The pain from a heart attack will last considerably longer than pain felt with angina. The pain that is usually associated with angina will last only a few minutes, and will go away with rest. On the other hand, resting will not alleviate the pain from a heart attack. Heart attack pain can last for many minutes and up to several hours. The longer the pain lasts, the greater the risk for suffering heart muscle damage. The bottom line is that chest pain should not be ignored. For the golfer, having chest pain means stop playing and call for medical help.

There are several risk factors that increase the incidence of cardiovascular disease. It's important to note that not everybody at risk will necessarily get the disease, but it should be appreciated that the more risk factors an individual may have, the more likely they are to develop the disease. Here are a few of the risk factors that an individual cannot necessarily control:

- The most common is age; the older you are, the more likely you are to have heart problems.
- Both men and women have heart disease. In fact, just because a golfer is a woman doesn't mean that she cannot have a heart attack.
- A family history of heart disease will increase the chances of a given individual having heart problems.

Here are some of the factors that an individual can control:

- At the top of the list is **smoking**. If a golfer smokes a pack a day, the risk of having a heart attack is about twice that of a non-smoker. Smoking is a major cause of an individual's not being able to play golf forever. Golfers who smoke should have a goal of making their game smoke-free. If a golfer has tried to stop smoking and failed, he or she should not give up. Many golfers are able to make their game smoke-free on their second or third try. Today there are many avenues to help an individual stop smoking. Smoking cessation programs can be very helpful. There are tobacco substitutes such as nicotine gum and patches, which can also help the smoking golfer stop. It's also important for the smoking golfer to discuss a plan of quitting smoking with his or her physician in order to continue to play golf forever.
- Another controllable avenue to heart disease is **high blood cholesterol**. Cholesterol is a substance found in the blood, which contributes to atherosclerosis or hardening and narrowing of the heart arteries. High levels of blood cholesterol are linked to an increase in cardiovascular heart disease. There are two major types of cholesterol in the body. The **high-density lipoprotein (HDL) cholesterol** is the good cholesterol. This is actually the plaque-clearing cholesterol in the body. High levels of HDL cholesterol have been associated with a low risk of heart disease. The **low-density lipoprotein (LDL) cholesterol** is the bad cholesterol. This is cholesterol that has been associated with a higher risk for cardiovascular disease. If an individual has the bad type of cholesterol, it's very important to discuss its treatment with one's physician. There are many medications which can be helpful for controlling high cholesterol levels. Also, following instructions from a dietitian will be very beneficial.

High blood pressure, hypertension, makes the heart work harder. Blood pressure is the force that the blood flow exerts on the arteries. The pressure increases as the blood is forced through smaller and smaller arteries. High blood pressure will also contribute to the development of atherosclerosis. Having high blood pressure will increase the risk of having a heart attack as well as a stroke. It's important for all golfers to have their blood pressure checked on a regular basis. If the blood pressure is high, there are many ways in which a physician can help to lower it. Some will include a change in diet, exercise, and medications. Other causes that will increase the risk of a heart attack include obesity, stress, and diabetes mellitus (blood sugar problems). Being overweight causes the heart to work harder. An overweight golfer will have a more difficult time playing; therefore, if a golfer's overweight, he or she should ask the doctor or a dietitian for a program for weight loss. A healthy weight loss is gradual and is accomplished through improved eating habits and an exercise program. A golfer who has diabetes must always be under the care of a physician and should follow instructions very carefully. And finally, a lack of regular exercise is a contributing factor for heart disease. Exercise is critical for keeping the heart strong, controlling blood pressure, maintaining good cholesterol levels, and providing good blood circulation throughout the body. It's important for an individual to check with his or her doctor before beginning an exercise program, and for the program to begin very gradually. A regular exercise program will provide the golfer with an increased sense of well being, which will only improve his or her play.

Pericarditis is an inflammation of the membrane surrounding the heart. The membrane surrounding the heart is the pericardium. There are several disease processes, which can bring about such an inflammation. A heart attack can cause inflammation to the pericardium. Other causes include bacterial, viral, or fungal infections. Any injury to the peri-

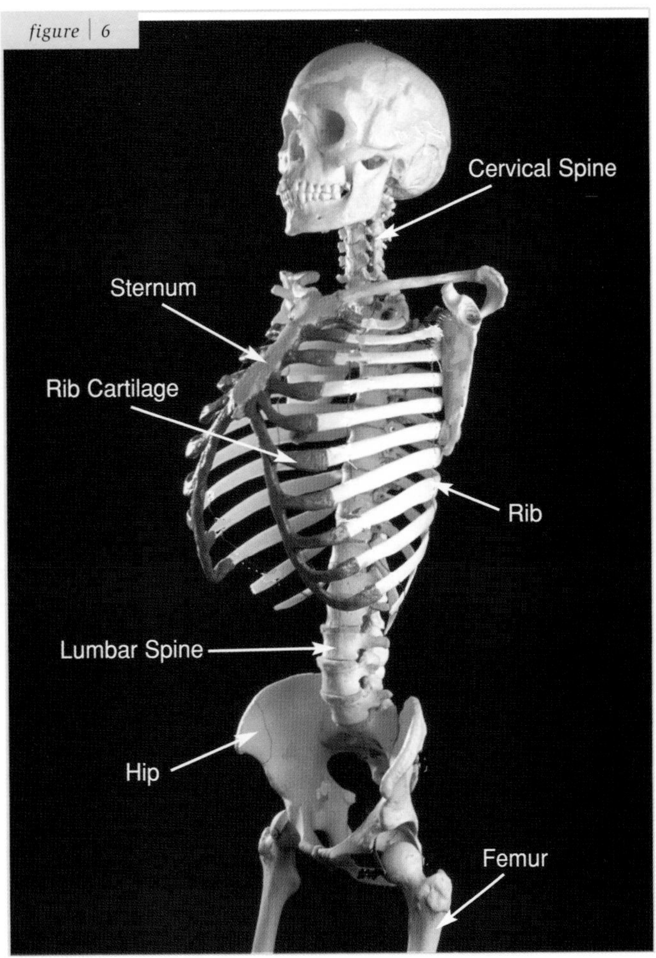

cardium, *i.e.*, trauma, can bring about inflammation. Sometimes tumor or cancer can spread from nearby lungs, breasts, or distant organs and create inflammation of the heart's membrane. Pericarditis is sometimes associated with rheumatoid arthritis, kidney problems, and systemic lupus erythematosus (SLE). In some patients, fluid will accumulate around the heart membrane; this is referred to as a pericardial effusion, fluid around the heart. If the fluid builds up, it may interfere with the hearts ability to work and to pump blood out to the body. The treatment for pericarditis depends upon its cause. The ability to return to playing golf after experiencing pericarditis can only be done so with the approval of a physician. There are many other causes that will cause chest pain and the list can be quite frightening. Causes may vary depending on the sex of the individual, their age, and a history of any other medical problems or burdens. The bottom line, when experiencing any severe type of chest pain, it's best to assume that the pain has something to do with the heart and seek emergency medical care immediately. If it turns out that the problem is caused by something else, the chest pain was actually a false alarm, and nothing is lost especially a life.

Another category that should be touched on for the golfer is **chest wall pain**. This is pain, which originates in tissues in the chest wall, rather than in organs or the heart. Chest wall pain is often associated with a muscle strain; this can occur in a golfer by being over zealous in addressing a ball. It can also occur after prolonged coughing episodes. In most cases, it can be treated with over-the-counter medications such as the non-steroidal anti-inflammatory medications, and usually in three to five days the chest pain should improve. It's important to rest the strained muscle, which means no more playing golf until the pain resolves. If the pain does not get better in about three to five days, it's time to call a physician.

Another cause of chest wall pain is **costochondritis,** an inflammation of the ribs or the cartilage where the ribs attach to the sternum (breastbone) (Fig. 6). This type of inflammation can cause severe chest pain. The inflammation can involve multiple sites, but is usually located only on one side. The exact cause of this type of inflammation is not known; however, there are some common causes, one of which is **trauma** or injury. If pushing on the sternum, the chest bone, causes pain, costochondritis may be the cause. Costochondritis can be aggravated by any activity, including golf; therefore, it's best not to play and to minimize activities that will cause stress on the chest wall. Taking an anti-inflammatory medication will often bring about a reduction not only in the pain, but also the inflammation. Usually, the pain will get better with rest within three to five days. If it does not, a physician should be consulted. Physical therapy may be helpful in reducing some of the inflammation. Other therapies include cortisone or steroid injections to the painful inflamed cartilage. The pain from costochondritis can sometimes be sharp and can be confused with heart pain. Therefore, if there's any doubt at all about the pain, a doctor should be consulted immediately. It's best not to take any chances.

Costochondritis can be an independent condition, meaning that it arises all by itself and has no relationship with any other diseases. On the other hand, it may indicate that there is a more widespread disorder causing mischief and is now announcing itself as chest wall pain. Some of the other illnesses that can be linked to costochondritis include certain types of arthritis and inflammatory bowel disease. Sometimes costochondritis is associated with another syndrome called

Tietze syndrome. They're not exactly the same condition; however, they do cause pain in the chest wall. Tietze syndrome is associated with a swelling in the front of the chest. Costochondritis usually does not cause swelling. Tietze syndrome, just like costochondritis, is an inflammation of the cartilage in the upper front of the chest. Patients with Tietze syndrome usually develop swelling over the ribs and breastbone (sternum). This localized swelling is the distinguishing finding of this syndrome. Swelling may be associated with redness and tenderness. The inflamed area may feel warm to touch. The pain is often quite sharp and it too can be confused with heart pain. Again, as with any sharp chest pain, it's best to assume that the underlying problem deals with the heart. Never take chances. Tietze syndrome can last from days to weeks. Needless to say, this type of discomfort will not allow a golfer to play. The treatment is the same as costochondritis. This includes use of anti-inflammatory medications and rest. Physical therapy and steroid injections may be needed if the discomfort from the inflamed cartilage continues. Sometimes icepacks applied to the site of local swelling may help to reduce pain and inflammation. It's best not to return to any golfing activities, even putting, until all the symptoms have resolved.

Common Causes of Chest Pain

- Angina
- Myocardial infarct (heart attack)
- Pleurisy (inflammation of the lung lining)
- Hyperventilation
- Gastric (stomach) ulcer
- Gallbladder inflammation (Cholescystitis)
- Gallstones (Cholelithiasis)
- Anxiety
- Pneumonia
- Costochondritis
- Cough (long-term)
- Herpes zoster
- Indigestion
- Gastroesophageal reflux disease (heartburn)
- Mitral valve prolapse
- Asthma
- Pulmonary embolism (blood clot to lungs)
- Aneurysm (blood blister)
- Trauma

SPONDYLOGENIC (SPINE) PAIN

Thoracic spine pain is referred to as **spondylogenic pain**. This means that the pain originates from a bony element near or around the spine. There are many different types of thoracic pain syndromes, and many times it's not as easy to find the exact etiology of the pain.

The Cyriax's Syndrome and the Davies-Colley's Syndrome both refer to the Rib-tip Syndrome. This is also called the Slipping Rib Syndrome or the Clicking Rib Syndrome. Drs. Cyriax and Davies-Colley were physicians practicing at the beginning of the last century. They were the first to describe and bring attention to this particular problem. The syndrome is of importance to golfers because it involves the ribs, and the ribs connect directly to the spine. Therefore, any type of rotation produced by swinging a golf club may cause pain. A rather severe discomfort is produced by any type of pressure placed on the nerves traveling in close association with an abnormal rib. Usually, the ribs that are involved in this syndrome are the last four to five ribs. Palpating or applying gentle pressure over the painful rib can usually reproduce the pain. Sneezing, coughing, taking a deep breath, or moving the arms can elicit the discomfort. In certain situations, the pain may be confused with angina or intra-abdominal disorders. It can also be confused with a disc herniation or symptomatic degeneration in the thoracic spine. If the syndrome involves the 12th, last rib, it is often referred to as the **12th Rib Syndrome**. The diagnosis of this particular problem requires a very careful physical examination. The physician may order other supporting studies such as a CAT scan, MRI, X-rays, or bone scan to ensure that there are no other pathological entities at work creating the pain. Use of non-steroidal anti-inflammatory medications can be quite helpful. Injections of a steroid medication may alleviate some of the pain, and in more severe cases, the rib itself may be surgically excised to bring about relief. This is usually not the first syndrome to be thought of by a doctor when a patient presents with a severe attack of pain in the thoracic region radiating from in front, around the flank, and then into the back. Nevertheless, it is one of those syndromes which should be considered when there aren't any other causes for the patient's discomfort or pain. One thing for certain, if a golfer has a Slipping Rib Syndrome, this most assuredly will compromise a round of play. The golfer should not continue to play until the pain has resolved totally.

Costovertebral Pain Syndromes is a set of syndromes just as complex as the name appears. But, let's look at it in a simpler way. Costo- is a medical anatomical term for the rib. Vertebral means the vertebrae. Thus, this is the site where the ribs attach to the vertebral bodies. This is the site of a joint or articulation of the rib to the thoracic spine (Fig. 7). There are several ligaments attaching the ribs to the vertebral bodies, and the rib's head makes up a joint that is fixed to the thoracic spine. Just as in any other part of the spine, osteoarthritis can involve the costovertebral joints. The first, 11th, and 12th ribs are more subject to arthritis than the other rib sites. Nevertheless, any site along the spine can be involved with osteoarthritis. Arthritic bony changes increase with age. After about the age of 40, almost 50–60% of the population will have spines with some type of osteoarthritis at these complex joints in the thoracic spine. Just as with any other joint, these joints can become inflamed and painful. The pain is often unilateral, either on one side or the other. The pain is described as an achy, sometimes a burning sensation, and may travel along a rib to and from the thoracic spine. During a physical examination, there's usually tenderness to palpation along the inflamed rib. And some patients report that coughing, sneezing, twisting, or playing golf will increase the pain. A history of trauma, such as falling or swinging clubs, may predispose an individual to changes in the costovertebral joints. Any movements, particularly rotation and twisting, will aggravate the discomfort at any site along the inflamed joints. A physical examination by a doctor will help determine the painful level. The doctor may order radiological studies such as X-rays, computer axial tomography (CAT scan), or magnetic resonance imaging (MRI). The CAT scan, however, may be the most helpful because of its ability to view bony architecture better than the MRI. After other possible causes of pain have been ruled out, treatment may include use of the non-steroidal anti-inflammatory medications, acetaminophen, and aspirin. In certain situations when the pain is very severe, stronger pain medications such as an opioid may be prescribed. In some situations, injections of a local anesthetic into the joint may be a helpful diagnostic test as well as providing some degree of pain relief. The local anesthetic or pain medication may be followed by use of a corticosteroid solution into the painful area. Golf is out of the question until this painful syndrome has resolved. Once it has resolved, it's important for the patient to remember that he or she has a costovertebral joint abnormality. Therefore, before returning to the course, the golfer must be released by a doctor to play again, and be evaluated by a physical therapist who has an interest in golf, to help strengthen the golf muscles. It's also

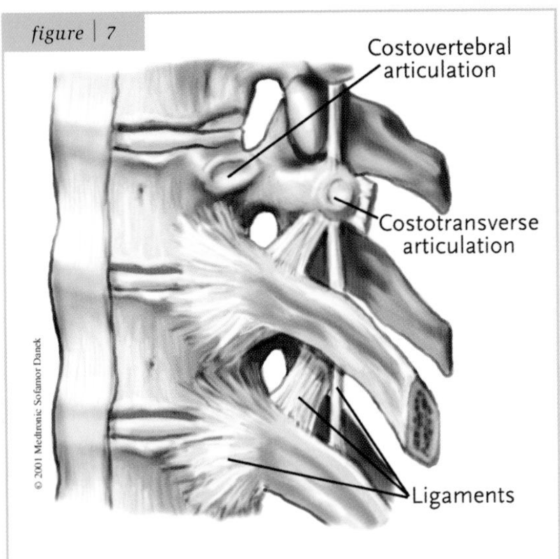

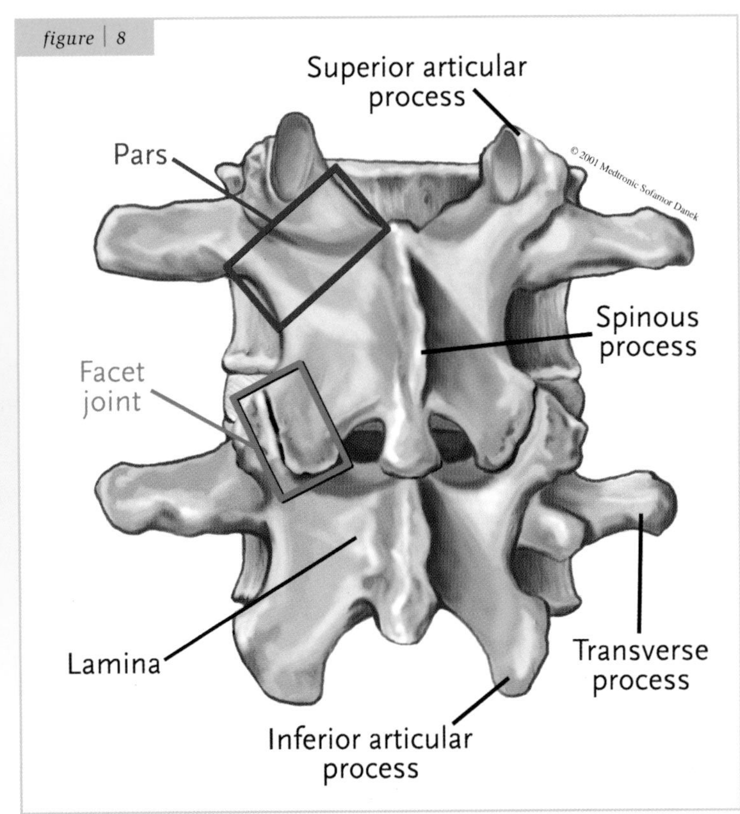

a good idea to discuss with a professional your problem and have your golf swing re-evaluated, so that it does not aggravate a pre-existing condition.

Golfing involves the torsion of the spine. The part of the spine most involved in such movement is the thoracic spine. Sometimes golfers will experience pain in the middle of the thoracic spine or the lower portion of the thoracic spine. Such pain is usually related to rotation of the spine. The pain usually occurs on the side of the lead arm. For a right-handed golfer, this occurs on the left side. This is because of the **lateral oblique muscle** (a major golf muscle). This large golfing muscle pulls on the spine and the rib and may cause damage. The repetitive golf swing will only compound the situation. Sometimes, the problem can become serious enough to cause severe discomfort and disability. Palpation at the site of injury may worsen the pain. X-rays will be needed to evaluate for rib fractures. Bone scans may reveal the rib stress fractures more clearly. Treatment involves use of non-steroidal anti-inflammatory medications or acetaminophen, rest, and in certain situations, selective nerve blocks. If the pain continues and is relentless, the physician will need to look for other causes for the pain, which will prompt the need for imaging such as magnetic resonance imaging (MRI) and computed axial tomography (CAT scan). After the discomfort has resolved, the golfer must be evaluated for his or her swing technique and will need to seek the advice of a professional before returning to play.

Any time golfers experience pain along the rib they should stop playing. Stress fractures of the ribs have been reported in golfers. Being somewhat overzealous during a swing can fracture a rib. Usually when this occurs, the golfer will stop playing immediately. A fractured or broken rib causes severe discomfort. In most cases, the fracture will be located on the posterolateral aspect of the rib. This means that the fracture occurs in the back and along the side. The more commonly fractured ribs are the 4th to 6th ribs. Some physicians and therapists believe that the reason a fracture occurs is because of weakness in one of the golf muscles. The muscle that is most often cited as being the mischief-making muscle is the **serratus anterior muscle**. It is thought that this muscle is either weak or easily fatigued, which places undue stress on the rib. After repetitive activity, the rib may fracture. The physical examination will demonstrate severe pain at the fracture site. Usually, an X-ray will demonstrate the fractured rib, and in certain situations a bone scan may be needed. Usually, a CAT scan is obtained to evaluate the spine to ensure that it too has not been involved in the fracture. Treatment is aimed at alleviating the pain. Non-steroidal anti-inflammatory medications may be very helpful. If stronger medications are needed, an opioid may be prescribed. Rest is imperative. A golfer should not return to playing golf until the rib has healed, physical therapy and rehabilitation have been undergone, his or her swing has been re-evaluated, and a doctor and therapist have released him or her to return to play.

The Facet Joint Syndrome is pain that results from wear and tear or degeneration of the facet joints. The facet joints are the joints at the back of each vertebra, which link the vertebra to together (Fig. 8). Wear and tear will eventually cause inflammation of the facet joints, which brings about pain. **Facet Arthropathy** refers to a painful degenerative spine joint. Spinal aging changes can occur anywhere along the cervical, lumbar, and the thoracic spine. It is not always an easy spine problem to diagnose. In fact, there is some debate among physicians over the diagnostic criteria, and it is often a difficult problem to treat. Facet arthropathy most often occurs in the lumbar spine; however, it does occur in the thoracic spine. Degenerative changes in the facet joints in the thoracic spine can occur anywhere along the thoracic spine. Facet arthropathy may come about because of repetitive overloading of the spine, especially when rotation is the repetitive activity, for instance, in golfing. Many times, the facet joints may demonstrate some degree of asymmetry, which means that one side is larger than the other side. Usually, pain is the symptom that prompts the golfer to seek medical attention. The pain may be made better or worse with rest. Many times, the patient reports that the pain is worse getting out of bed in the morning. Some individuals will also note that the pain is worse when they are less active. In many situations, the pain gets better as the day progresses. The physical examination, just as in any other medical problem, is very important. X-rays, CAT scan, and an MRI are usually the tests used to evaluate for a facet joint syndrome. The CAT scan may be more helpful because it demonstrates the bony architecture better than the MRI (Fig. 9A and B). The bone scan may be helpful to evaluate for any increased metabolic activity, which demonstrates the angry, inflamed joint. Therapy, unfortunately, involves not playing golf. The rotational activity in golf can only aggravate the inflamed, painful facet. Use of a non-steroidal anti-inflammatory medication or a mild analgesic may be very helpful in the initial phases of the discomfort. Physical therapy is a very important part of treatment; it will strengthen the muscles that will help to stabilize the facet joint. For those individuals in which the facet pain becomes intractable and cannot be managed with only medications, a facet block may be helpful. This is a procedure in which a trained physician or radiologist will place a needle, under radiological guidance, into the targeted painful joint. For many patients, this may be very helpful. In other situations, a procedure called a **facet rhizotomy** may be considered. This is a procedure involves destroying the nerves surrounding the joints. In selective cases, pain relief has been achieved. For some golfers other avenues of therapy may provide relief and allow them to return to playing golf. Such other forms of therapy include manipulation, chiropractic therapies, and massage therapy. Again, whatever form of therapy is used to treat a painful facet joint, it's important that the patient ask the physician about the doctor's experience in treating such a problem. Treatment of a facet joint syndrome may not be an easy matter. In most situations, the patient must be committed to getting better and follow the instructions of the physician and treating team. Returning to playing golf again should only be done after being released by the treating medical team. Returning to golf too soon with a facet syndrome will most assuredly compromise the golfer's game, and may even compromise the golfer's ability to continue to play forever. If medical management fails to alleviate the patient's pain, surgery may be a consideration. Surgery would depend upon the surgeon's experience. The operation involves removing the painful facet joint. After the joint has been removed, a bone graft procedure, bone fusion, is performed, and then subsequent use of internal fixation devices such as metal bone screws, rods, and hooks. Consideration for surgery should be the last option.

THORACIC DISC DISEASE

The thoracic spine has intervertebral discs, or shock absorbers, situated between the vertebral bodies (Fig. 2). They are smaller in size than the discs located in the cervical spine (neck) or the lumbar spine (low back area). The thoracic spine is unique in that it has ribs to

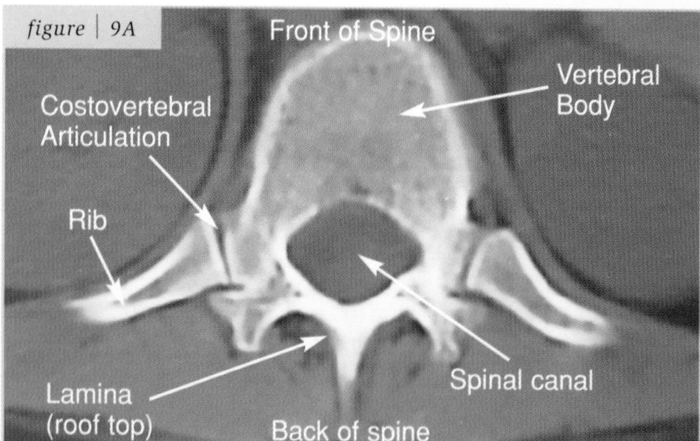

CAT (CT) scan axial view looking down into the spine -- demonstrates bony elements better than an MRI

MRI does not demonstrate bony structures as well as CAT scan

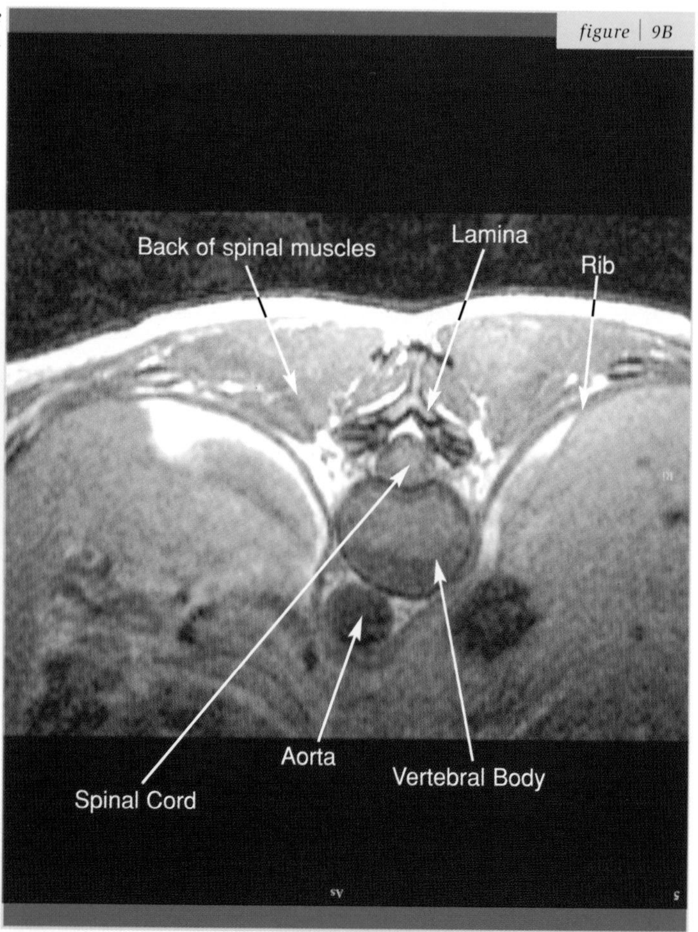

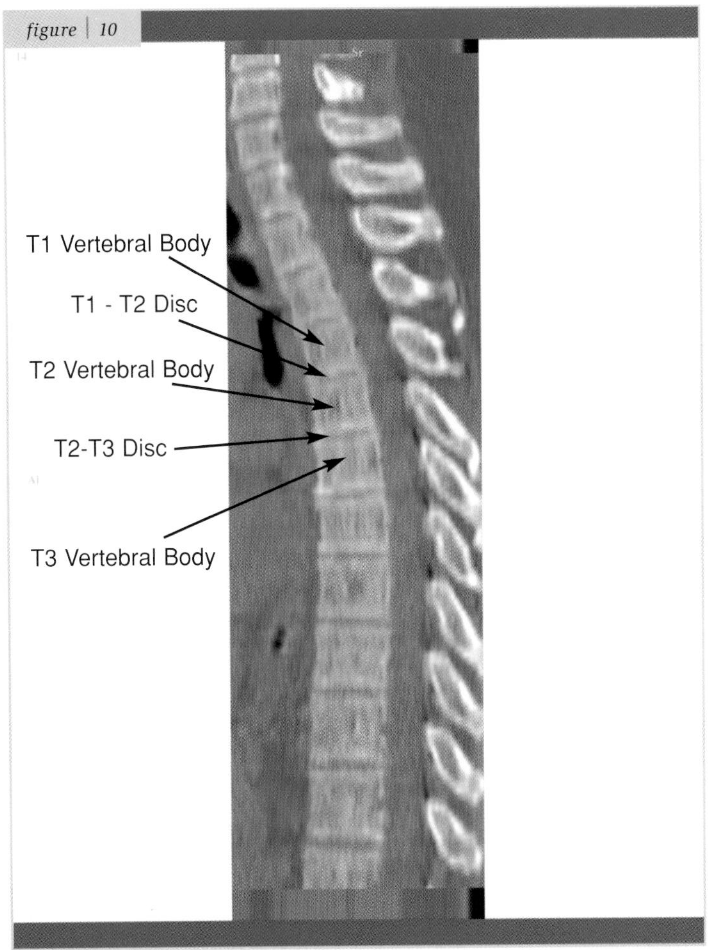

Figure 10
CAT (CT) Scan
Side view demonstrating thoracic vertebral bodies and disc numbering.

protect it from many movements, which can cause problems in the cervical spine (neck) and the lumbar spine (low back area). The lower incidence of disc problems of the thoracic spine, as compared to the cervical and lumbar areas, is attributed to the limited movement of the thoracic spine. Even though the intervertebral discs of the thoracic spine are smaller than those in the cervical and lumbar spine, it does not mean that thoracic discs cannot and do not cause problems. They can rupture and cause discomfort and pain just like discs in the cervical and lumbar spine. Unlike the cervical and lumbar spine, there is less room in the central canal. That means that a smaller disc herniation can cause bigger problems than if the same herniation occurred in the cervical or lumbar spine.

Thoracic disc herniations occur less often than in other parts of the spine. In fact, only about 1% to 2% of all the disc operations are due to thoracic disc herniations. Thoracic discs are labeled just as they are in the cervical and lumbar spine. The first thoracic vertebra is called T1; the second vertebra is called T2. The disc between the first and second thoracic vertebra is called the T1–T2 intervertebral disc. The next is seated between the T2 and T3 vertebra and is called the T2–T3 intervertebral disc, and so forth (Fig. 10). The most common sites for thoracic disc herniations occur from the levels T9 through T12. The least common sites for thoracic disc herniations to occur are those discs in the upper thoracic spine, from T1 through T5. Herniations in the thoracic spine are more likely to occur in the midline or the middle of the disc, as compared to a tendency for disc herniations in the neck and low back area to rupture along the sides.

Thoracic disc changes are due to the consequences of maturing and aging. The ribs may offer protection to the thoracic discs; however, they cannot prevent the degenerative changes of maturing. Increased pressures on the thoracic discs and weakening of the outside of the discs (annulus) are major factors in bringing about disc problems. Disc herniations in the thoracic spine may also occur due to trauma, in association with conditions such as scoliosis, and just the effects of wear and tear of ligaments and other soft tissues.

Most patients will give no history of a precipitating event's bringing about their discomfort. A few patients may associate their problems with some specific event such as swinging a golf club, working in the garden, weightlifting, or just walking. Symptoms vary from patient to patient.

The most common presenting symptom of a thoracic disc herniation is pain in the mid-back area. The pain may be unilateral (on one side) or bilateral (on both sides). The discomfort may be mild to severe. Some patients will note that any type of movement or activity will bring about pain, and many times in the physician's office the patient's movement will be markedly limited. The pain may radiate around from the back to the chest. Coughing, sneezing, taking a deep breath, and of course swinging a golf club may worsen the pain. Numbness is a common complaint among patients with thoracic disc herniations. The numbness, just like pain, may be on one side or on both sides, and may extend into the legs. Some patients report a girdle-like band of tightness or heaviness around their trunk where the numbness level begins. In more serious disc herniations, unsteadiness of walking or stiff legs are noted by the patient. Other patients will seek medical attention due to urinary problems, including incontinence, retention, or an increased need or frequency to urinate. Many times the patient will report that after urinating they feel that their bladder is not empty; therefore, they note that they have to attend to this matter more frequently. Other patients will be plagued with abnormal bowel functions, either not going or going too often. Men may report problems with potency; erections are difficult to obtain, and women may experience a decreased sensation during sex. Other symptoms of thoracic disc herniation may include the absence of sweating of the feet and, in some cases, small ulcerations or skin changes may occur in the lower extremities and the feet. In certain individuals, there is no pain or discomfort at all. However, they develop progressive weakness in their lower extremities. The weakness worsens over time and then they begin to experience urinary bladder and bowel problems. Disturbances in urinary bladder, bowel, and sexual functioning are late manifestations of disc herniations. All of these symptoms may simulate a disease such as multiple sclerosis; therefore, it's important that patients be evaluated not only for multiple sclerosis, but also for disc herniations. In some individuals, the thoracic disc herniation occurs very quickly. When this occurs, the disc material may push against the spinal cord to the extent that the individual cannot move or feel their legs. This is a medical emergency. The bottom line with all the above-mentioned symptoms is that they should not be ignored.

Pain in or around the thoracic spine, with or without radiations to the chest, can be caused by other medical problems. Due to the infrequency of thoracic disc herniations and the many symptoms produced by such herniations, there may be a delay in diagnosis or even a wrong diagnosis. Other spine diseases that can mimic or produce the same symptoms as a disc herniation include arthritis, spine tumors, infections, joint problems, and fractures (osteoporosis). Certain medical problems can also produce symptoms very similar to thoracic disc herniation symptoms. Such medical situations include ulcers, esophageal reflux (heartburn), pancreatitis, gall bladder disease, tumors in the abdomen, kidney problems (colic or stones), aortic aneurysms (blood vessel ballooning), and of course, heart disease. Sometimes Herpes can cause severe pain, not unlike a disc herniation. These are medical situations that a doctor will need to sort out and subsequently provide treatment.

The physician or healthcare provider will perform a physical examination. There is no one single finding for a thoracic disc herniation. There's usually, just like in other problems, a set of findings obtained by the physician. There will be limitation of movement, which is accompanied by muscle spasm. Patients may have numbness or tingling sensation, which is noted by the physician when they're asked whether or not they can feel a pinprick. The doctor will note the ability to detect pinprick, as well as vibration from a special tuning fork. Other patients may demonstrate weakness in their legs. Some patients will exhibit funny ways of walking, stiff-legged or spastic. They may report that they walk like a duck. The doctor will use a reflex hammer to test for the presence or absence of reflexes (Fig. 14). If the spinal cord is being irritated, the patient may have exaggerated or increased reflexes. A rectal examination will be needed to determine whether or not nerves leading to the bowels and rectum are being compromised.

After the physical examination, the doctor will order several studies. X-rays will be obtained to evaluate the bony structure and the alignment of the spine (Fig. 11A and B). Magnetic resonance imaging (MRI) has revolutionized the diagnosis of thoracic disc herniations, as well as other diseases affecting the thoracic spine and spinal cord. Thoracic disc disease that is squeezing or compressing a nerve usually causes pain radiating around into the chest. The MRI, in most cases, will clearly demonstrate the health of the thoracic discs. There are two types of thoracic disc herniations. One is the soft jelly type of disc herniation; this is the one that is best appreciated by the

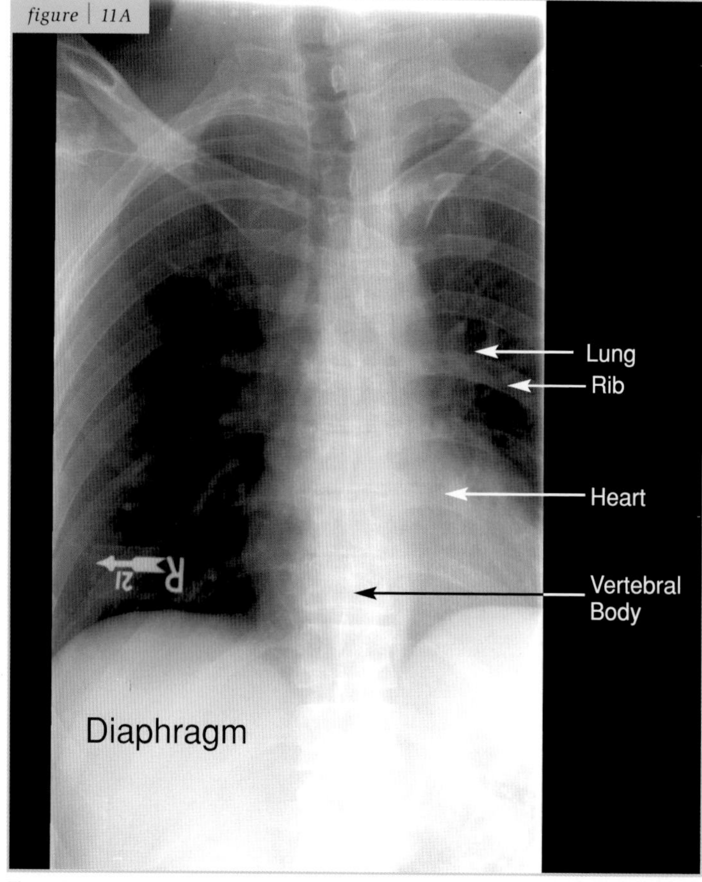

Figure 11A
AP (Front View/X-Ray of Thoracic Spine)

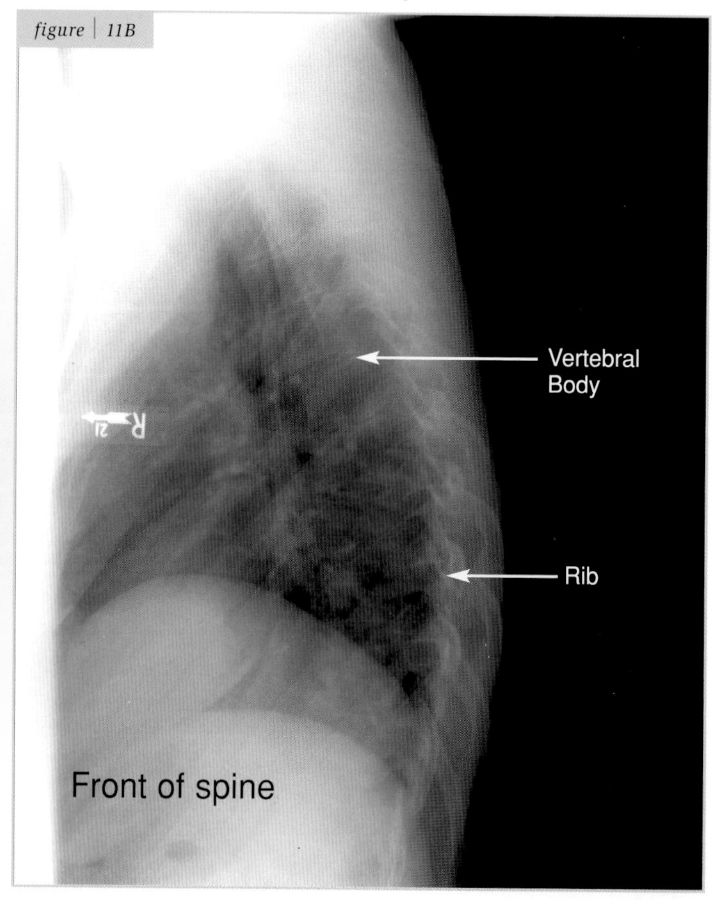

figure | 12A

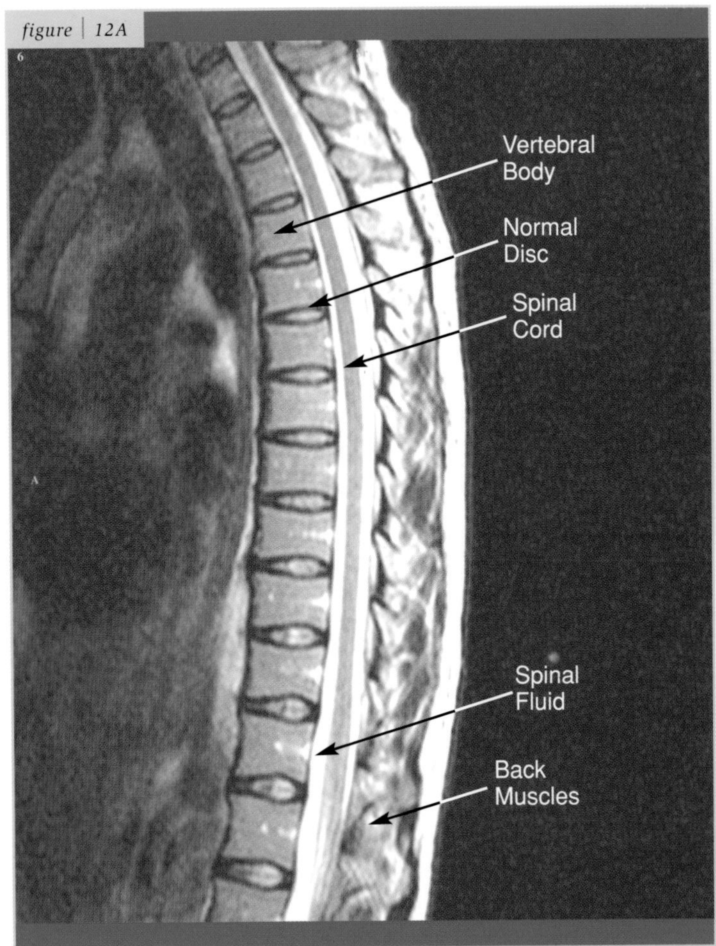

Normal MRI side view

figure | 12B

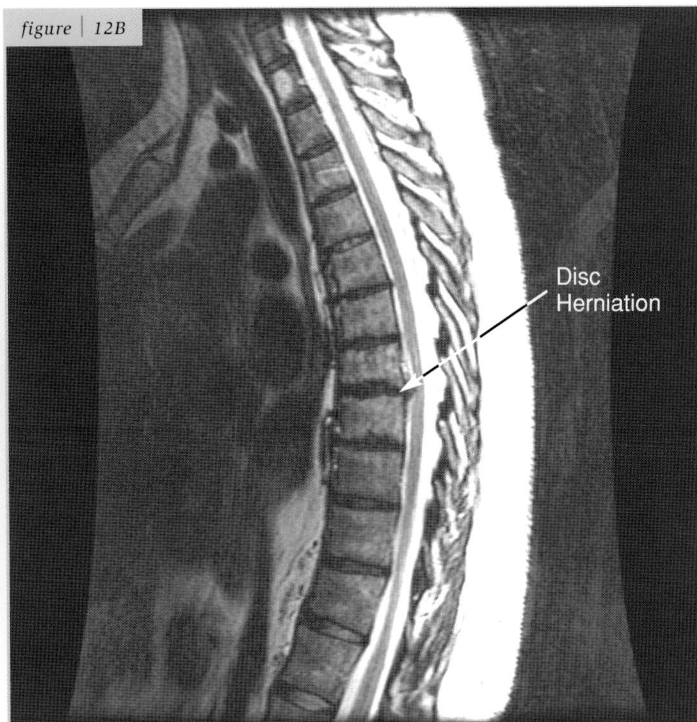

MRI with Disc Herniation: (Note loss of spinal fluid at Herniation site)

MRI (Fig. 12A and B). There's also a hard disc herniation, which is made up of calcium or bone. Calcification in a disc space is highly suggestive of a thoracic disc herniation. To better appreciate the degree of calcification, computed axial tomography (CAT scan) may be needed (Fig. 13A and B). In certain situations, a myelogram (putting a needle into the spine spaces and injecting dye into the spinal canal) is still used by many physicians and spine specialists. Usually after the myelogram, a CAT scan is obtained. Other tests may be ordered to evaluate for thoracic disc herniations. Usually, these tests help to clarify a clinical finding. Such tests include the electrophysiological test, electromyography, and spinal cord evoked potential studies.

The treatment of a thoracic disc herniation depends on the symptoms and the findings on the physical examination. One of the greatest fears of learning about a thoracic disc herniation is that many individuals will immediately think this means surgery. It does not necessarily mean surgery is imminent. Surgical avenues of care depend on whether the symptoms are getting worse, bowel/bladder problems are present, and progressive weakness is occurring. It the patient relates that he or she is actually getting better, surgery is not the immediate avenue to pursue. Medical or conservative treatment is often the form of therapy recommended for an individual with a disc herniation. The first line of therapy is to stop all the activities that may aggravate or worsen the symptoms or pain. This means that the golfer will have to put down the clubs. If the pain is severe, the patient may need to take a few days off from work and take it easy. Bed rest should only be for approximately two to three days; longer time in bed may actually aggravate the situation by causing unwanted muscle weakness. If, after a few days in bed, things appear to be getting better, the patient should get out of bed. A gentle-walking program, under the direction of a physician, may benefit the patient. Medications are given in the early course of a disc herniation. The most-used medications to help with the discomfort from a thoracic disc herniation are the anti-inflammatory medications or acetaminophen. The very strong anti-inflammatory medications are usually given to individuals who have no history of sensitivity to such medications and do not have a history of stomach problems. Anti-inflammatory medications can often aggravate or irritate the stomach, particularly in those with a history of such problems. The newer anti-inflammatory medications are less likely to do so; however, they can still cause stomach problems, *i.e.*, pain, burning, even stomach bleeding. It's important when patients are given medications that they follow directions on how to use the medication. For some patients, anti-inflammatory medications will not help with the pain; therefore, a stronger pain medication is needed, a narcotic. If narcotic pain medications are prescribed, they're usually not prescribed for long periods of time. Physical therapy and massage therapy may also benefit the patient who is improving. For those patients who do not improve with rest and medications, epidural steroid injections (ESI) may be considered. There is no guarantee that such injections will help. Some patients state that steroid injections actually aggravate their discomfort; others report benefit. In fact, only about half of the individuals with a disc herniation who are refractory to medications may benefit from steroid injections.

If the patient continues to be plagued with symptoms, particularly discomfort from a thoracic disc herniation, surgical therapy may be considered. Surgery is reserved for patients whose lifestyles are compromised and whose symptoms are persistent or worsening. Surgery for thoracic disc herniation depends upon several factors. One is the location of the disc herniation, the type of disc herniation (soft or hard calcification), and the experience and preference of the surgeon. The process of removing the herniated disc is referred as a **discectomy**. The surgeon will decide whether or not the procedure should be performed from in front, the side, or from the back of the spine. This depends upon the level where the disc is herniated. If the surgery is to be performed from the back, the patient is placed onto the operating table in the prone position, which means face down. An incision is made through the middle of the back or along the side over the area of the herniated disc. Once the incision is made through the skin, the muscles are then very gently moved to the side, allowing the surgeon to appreciate the bony elements of the thoracic spine. Fluoroscopy X-rays during surgery will allow the level and site of the disc herniation to be identified by the surgeon (Fig. 14). After the correct level has been identified, the surgeon may use a surgical drill or special instruments to remove a small section of the bony housing to reveal the underlying disc herniation.

A common procedure to remove the disc is referred to as a **costotransversectomy**. This surgical term describes which bones are being removed by the surgeon to reveal the disc herniation. The costo- is an anatomical term referring to the ribs, and the transverse refers to the transverse process, which is a bone of the thoracic spine. A surgical microscope or magnification surgical loupes may allow the surgeon to better see the disc herniation (Fig. 15A and B). The disc itself is removed by using small surgical instruments that fit inside the disc. Improvement of surgical tools and use of the microscope have allowed less bone to be removed to reveal the mischief, the pain-producing disc herniation. In other cases, surgery may be performed from the side or in front of the spine. This may require an open procedure, which is called a **thoracotomy**. The spine surgeon may work with a chest surgeon to expose the herniated disc. Again, just as with surgery from the back, a microscope or special magnifying surgical loupes may be used by the surgeon. In some situations, a different type of procedure may be performed. This is a closed surgical technique, which is called a **thorascopic microsurgical procedure**. This operation employs the use of an endoscope, which is a special surgical tool allowing the surgeon to work through a tube with special optics to allow visualization and subsequent removal of the herniated disc. The procedure for excision of a thoracic disc herniation varies from patient to patient, just like the presenting symptoms; therefore, the surgical procedure will have to match each patient in order to allow optimal outcome.

After the surgery, physical therapy is often needed. Strengthening exercises and reconditioning exercises will be provided by a physical therapist. Returning to one's everyday activities depends upon the condition the patient was in before the surgery. For golfers, it's important that they discuss with their doctor their desire to return to golf. Thus the doctor will be better able to recommend a physical therapist with a special interest in rehabilitation for the golfer. A golfer should never return to playing golf without the permission of the doctor and therapist. It's also important, before returning to golf, that players be evaluated by a professional to determine whether or not their swings may aggravate their muscles and spine after undergoing thoracic disc surgery. As with any surgery, returning to golf depends upon the type of surgery, the patient's overall condition after surgery, and his or her dedication and motivation to return to playing golf. And in most cases, the golfer will be able to return, but must

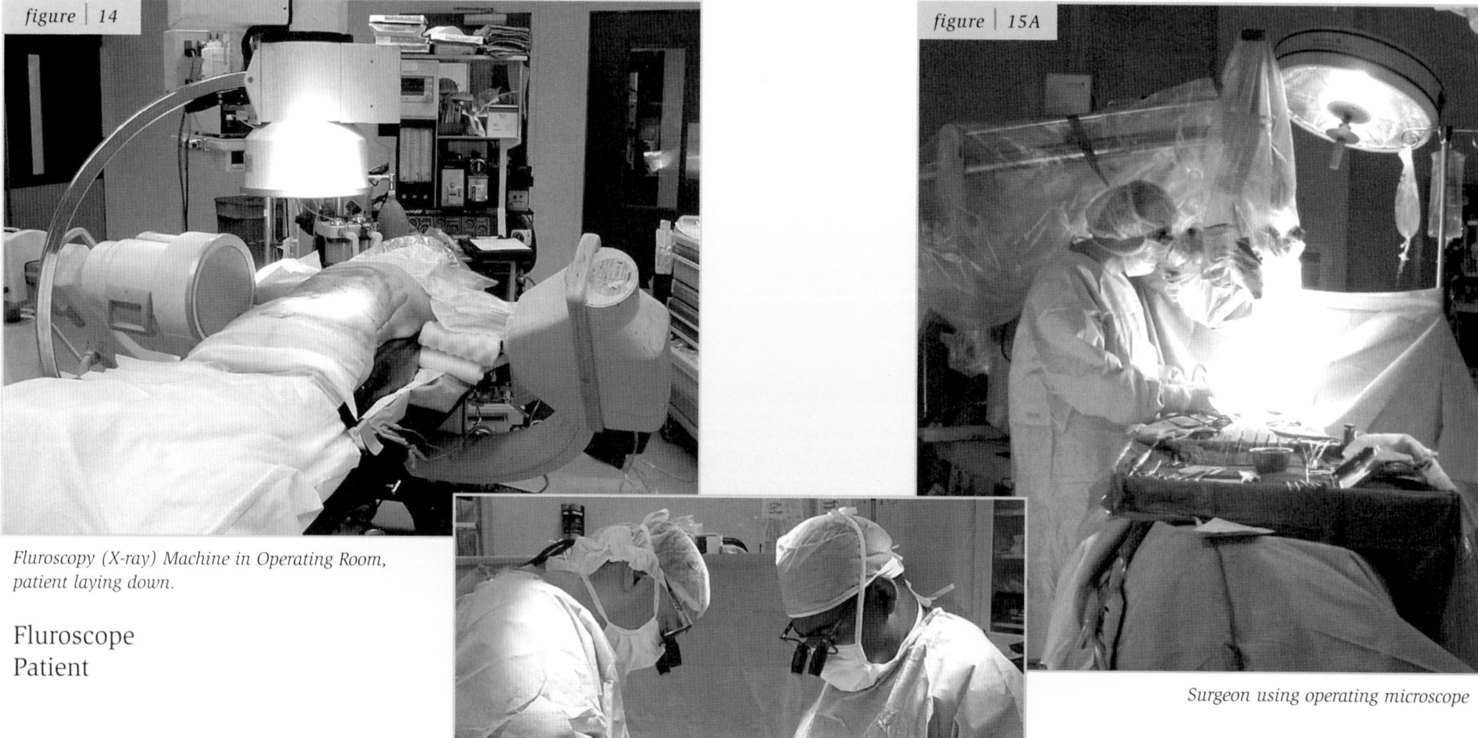
figure | 14

Fluroscopy (X-ray) Machine in Operating Room, patient laying down.

Fluroscope
Patient

figure | 15A

Surgeon using operating microscope

figure | 15B

Surgeons using Surgical Magnification Loops

recognize his or her limitations and be ever alert to new symptoms. It's also important for the golfer to recognize and correct risks that may aggravate and reduce chances of a good surgical outcome, as well as not promote further thoracic disc herniations. Here are some of the avenues that the golfer can follow to help reduce such risks:

- Stop using tobacco products. Such products will only affect the golfer's overall good health, as well as increase the chance of promoting an unhealthy spine.
- Maintain good posture while walking or sitting. This includes at work and at home. There should be armrests on chairs at work and at home. This will help to prevent slouching in the chair.
- Avoid heavy bending, lifting and pulling activities.
- If lifting cannot be avoided, never bend; always lift from the legs.
- Maintain a good exercise program. This includes stretching and warming up before play, and cooling down after play.
- Maintain a weight that's appropriate to one's height.
- Wear low heels and comfortable shoes, and often re-evaluate the golf shoes, once every year. Golf shoes with rubber spikes will provide adequate traction without placing unwanted torsion on the thoracic spine.
- Maintain a healthy diet, including 6 to 8 glasses of water a day.

THE FOURTH THORACIC (T4) SYNDROME

The thoracic T4 syndrome usually refers to pain in the interscapular area (between the shoulders). The T4 refers to the fourth thoracic vertebra and, in this particular situation, the fourth thoracic spinous process. Even though the name T4 refers to the vertebra, it does not necessarily mean that T4 is the only upper thoracic level that can be involved in this particular disorder. In fact, one or more levels between T1 and T7 may be involved in this particular pain-producing syndrome. Most patients will not recall a specific event or activity which brought about their severe discomfort. However, golfers who experience pain between the shoulders often recall a certain moment on the course that elicited discomfort. This syndrome is usually brought about by a postural strain. Shoulder muscle functions, which elevate and depress the shoulders and arms, are usually involved in producing the so-called T4 syndrome. This is because such movements will cause the tendons to strain and, over a period of time, if out of shape, will become inflamed. Many patients will present with pain in the upper part of the chest region and a vague discomfort into the upper extremities. Some individuals will even complain of headaches, which radiate to the back of their heads. Other individuals may have symptoms of numbness and tingling sensations into the arms and hands and, on occasion, weakness. Symptoms may be found in either one arm or both arms. The symptoms are intermittent. Some patients will describe a heaviness and numbness in the arms, hands and upper part of the thoracic spine. They find that the symptoms, in particular pain, are aggravated with movement of the arms and shoulders. Many patients report that raising the arms above the head will bring about discomfort. Some will find that trying to raise a newspaper in front while reading will cause pain. Others will also complain of symptoms when driving in a car.

During the physical examination, local tenderness may be elicited by the doctor's palpating over the spinous processes in the back of the neck from the first thoracic disc to the seventh thoracic disc; that's the area just behind the neck and between the shoulders. Treatment consists of stopping activities that aggravate the symptoms. Use of a nonsteroidal anti-inflammatory medication is usually the first line of therapy to help reduce inflammation. The use of an over-the-counter medication may be beneficial to some patients, while other patients will need an anti-inflammatory medication that's gentler on the stomach. Medications obtained without a prescription at the pharmacy may have more of a chance of causing stomach upsets and problems than those prescribed by a physician. Medications given by the physician are often stronger. Ice packs may be of benefit, particularly with evidence of muscle spasm. Ice packs should only be applied for approximately 20 minutes and never placed directly onto the skin because of the possibility of burning the skin. Some individuals will actually state that ice will aggravate their discomfort and will prefer heat. In most situations the ice pack should be given as the initial local treatment. In the event that the pain does not improve, further evaluation including a visit to a physician will be needed. For patients who have not responded to the use of medications and local therapies, more testing will be needed that will usually include X-rays, MRI, and bone scans. A CAT scan with special views may also be considered. Other forms of therapy will include connective tissue massage and, in certain situations, a local trigger-point injection with steroids.

Exercises to strengthen muscles are very important to help prevent the recurrence of this syndrome. Exercises will include both strengthening and flexibility stretching exercises. Breathing exercises will also be important to prevent recurrence of this syndrome. It is very important that the patient with the T4 syndrome evaluate his or her environment. This particular situation came about because of a postural strain; therefore, the environment should be evaluated to help prevent bad posture. Any activities that will take undue strain off the shoulders should be evaluated. Such simple things as making sure that the chairs at home and work have arms will help to avoid slumping of the shoulders. Use of armrests while driving in a car is beneficial. The good news about this syndrome is that most patients do get better. Exercises and good posture will keep this syndrome away.

The thoracic spine is not immune to tumors or infections. Both spinal disorders commonly cause pain. The discomfort worsens with time and prompts an individual to consult a doctor or healthcare provider. Tests are ordered and a diagnosis is formulated. Any thoracic pain or discomfort that is relentless and fails to improve in a reasonable time needs medical evaluation.

THE LUMBAR SPINE (LOW BACK)

CHAPTER 8

T. Glenn Pait, M.D., F.A.C.S.

I hung around Fred Couples a lot when he was getting his back worked on by Tom Boers, who has become sort of the guru of Tour players with back problems. At an off-season tournament Tom was working on Fred's back, and Fred felt guilty because I was sitting around watching him get his back worked on. Fred said to me, "Tell Tom about your foot."

I said, "My foot hurts a little but it's not a big deal."

And Tom said, "Well, when does it hurt?"

I said, "Only when I walk the golf course. The more I walk, the more the top of my foot hurts."

Tom said, "Does your hip hurt?"

I said, "No, not really. I never really thought about it. Every once in a while when I'm on the side of a hill it feels like it might give out."

And he said, "Well, then your lower back is stiff," and I disagreed with him, and he said again that my lower back must be stiff and that was causing my hip to hurt.

I said, "Sure, whatever," and didn't really pay any attention to it.

Almost exactly a year later, starting off the next year, my lower back went out just like Freddie's, so I started to see Tom and he loosened it up. But he kept worrying about it and the fact that my right hip wouldn't loosen up, and he kept thinking that there must be something wrong with my hip.

Two years later he sent me to get an MRI, and I found that I have arthritis in my hip. It's taken four years of work and stretching to get completely over an injury to my back that if I'd done something at the first signs-might not have caused the back problems I've had since then.

The thing I've learned about back ailments over the last 10 years is that they can show up in other parts of the body. It can show up in my hand, or in my foot, and my advice is that any signs of strange pain should be looked at immediately because it might be coming from the back. Nearly everything comes from the nerve center in your spine, so pay close attention to pains in your body and get them diagnosed as soon as possible.

Davis Love III

The lumbar spine is the low back part of the spine (Fig. 1A and B). When we hear the term low back pain, it's often this part of the spine that is causing the discomfort. The individual vertebrae of the lumbar spine are much larger than those of the cervical and thoracic spine. There are 5 large vertebrae in the lumbar spine. Their shapes resemble kidneys (Fig. 2). They are labeled L1, L2, L3, L4, and L5, the 'L' standing for lumbar (Fig. 3). Some people have an extra lumbar vertebra, which is referred to as L6. An extra vertebra does not offer any advantages or increase disability. The disc interspaces between the vertebrae are labeled just as they are in the cervical and the thoracic spine. Between the L1 and L2 vertebrae is the L1–L2 disc. Between the L2 and L3 vertebral bodies is the L2–L3 disc, and so forth. The lumbar spine is what makes up the small of the low back. This section of the spine is very important for bending. If you take a moment and bend forward and backward, you will find that it's the lower part of your back that's involved in the movement. It's the lumbar spine that's involved in flexion and extension movements of the low back area (Fig. 4).

THE SACRUM (UPPER BUTT BONE)

The sacrum is the triangular bone just below the lumbar spine (Fig. 5). It consists of five elementary, or rudimentary vertebrae. The major difference in this part of the spine is that the vertebrae are fused together; there are no intervertebral discs between the vertebrae. The upper border of the sacrum is called S1, the 'S' meaning sacrum, followed by S2, S3, S4, and S5. As the numbers get larger, the size of the bones gets smaller. The sacrum is unique because it is fused together and articulates with the hipbones. Between the sacrum and the hipbones is a large joint called the sacroiliac (SI) joint (Fig. 5). The front part, or the anterior and upper margin of the first sacral vertebra, S1, bulges forward and is the back part of the pelvis. This part of the sacrum is called the **sacral promontory**. The main purpose of the sacrum is to form a weight-supporting structure, as well as forming part of the pelvis (Fig. 6).

THE COCCYX (TAILBONE)

The coccyx is the end of the spine. It is pronounced *kok'siks*. The coccyx is truly the tailbone that joins together at its base with the lower end of the sacrum (Fig. 7).

LOW BACK (LUMBAR SPINE) DISORDERS

Pain in the lower part of the back or the lumbar spine is very common. If you have never been troubled with pain in this part of the spine you are very lucky. If you have these problems, you are not alone. Eight out of every ten adults will have low back problems sometime during their lifetimes. Once you have had pain in your low back, there is a good chance that you will have another episode. Fortunately, between these episodes of low back pain, people will usually return to their normal activities and will return to playing golf with few or no symptoms. However, playing golf may be one of the reasons for having another episode of back discomfort. Playing golf is a recognized cause of low back pain. Having low back discomfort is a common complaint among professional golfers. Ten to 33% of touring golf professionals play golf with some kind of back problem at any one time. This is an area where physicians and trainers work closely with professional golfers to ensure that their low backs

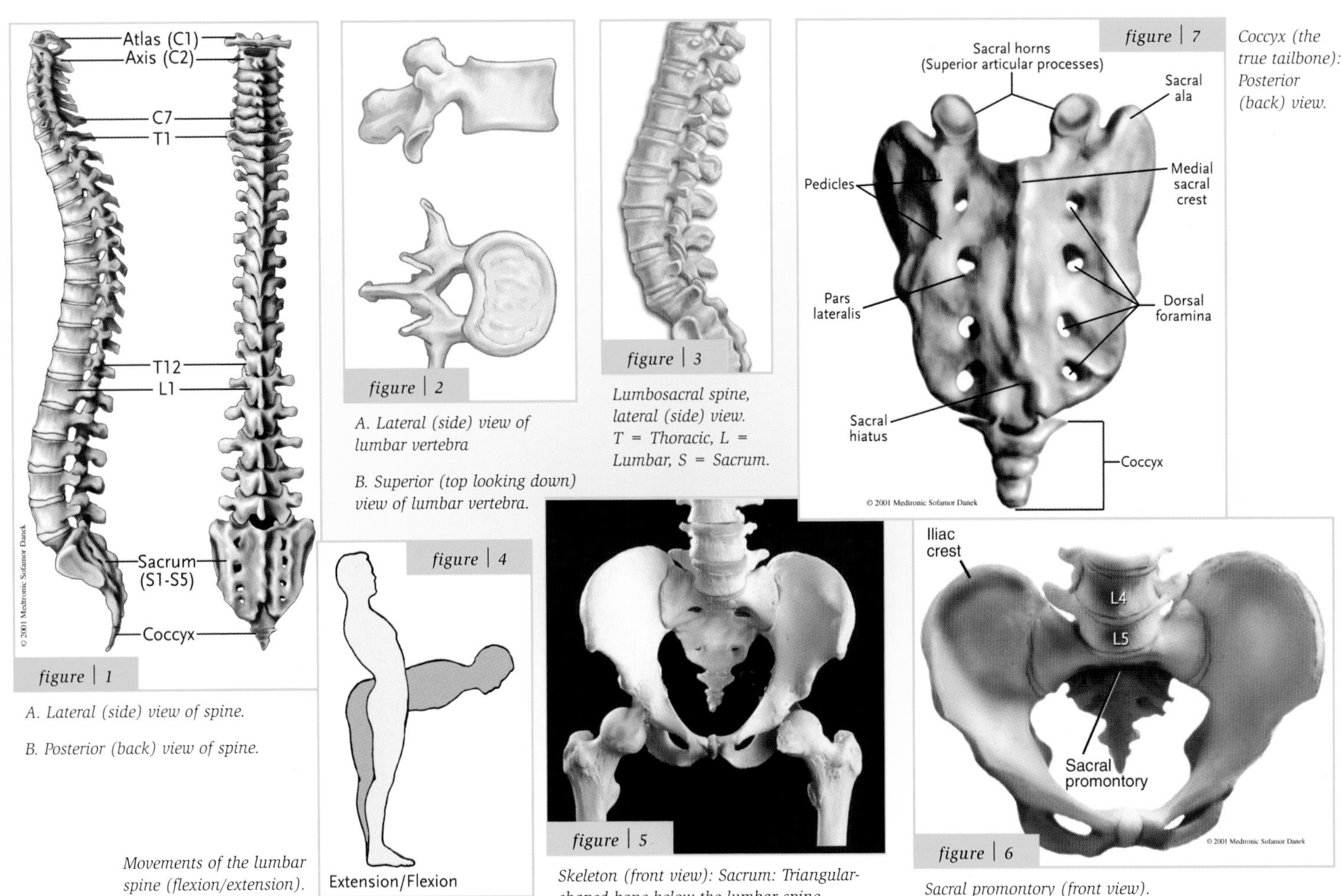

figure | 1

A. Lateral (side) view of spine.

B. Posterior (back) view of spine.

figure | 2

A. Lateral (side) view of lumbar vertebra

B. Superior (top looking down) view of lumbar vertebra.

figure | 3

Lumbosacral spine, lateral (side) view. T = Thoracic, L = Lumbar, S = Sacrum.

figure | 7

Coccyx (the true tailbone): Posterior (back) view.

figure | 4

Movements of the lumbar spine (flexion/extension).

figure | 5

Skeleton (front view): Sacrum: Triangular-shaped bone below the lumbar spine.

figure | 6

Sacral promontory (front view).

are in shape. There are many factors that contribute to the problems in the lumbar spine. First, there is the issue of aging. Not only do we change on the outside as we mature, but our spines also undergo an aging process. All of the elements that make up our spines change with time. Lumbar intervertebral discs undergo numerous changes. The vertebrae show signs of wear and tear. All of the lumbar muscles, ligaments, and tendons mature and age as well. Unfortunately, most golfers do not practice good spine hygiene until they have a problem. Playing golf when you are not conditioned is a good way to shorten your golf career. It is important to understand and appreciate some of the disorders that can arise in the lumbar spine.

With all of today's modern technology, many times the exact cause of low back problems may go undiagnosed. Even the best MRIs and CAT (CT) scans may not shed light on why you are having back pain. Low back troubles can be disabling and interfere with all aspects of living, including golf. Fortunately, very few people turn out to have problems that result in a serious medical condition; most individuals will not need any surgical intervention. There are two types of golfers with low back pain. The first is the golfer who has never experienced low back pain. This is usually a younger golfer who has sustained a muscle sprain/strain or strained ligaments. This type of pain is located in the back and does not tend to radiate into the lower extremities or legs. The first thing that a golfer with this problem needs to do is stop playing. If one continues to play, it may not be too long before he or she is miserable. There is no reason to make it worse. Regardless of the type of treatment, about 80–90% of this type of pain will resolve in about 6 to 12 weeks.

Here are some tips on how to take care of this kind of back pain. First, put your clubs back into the bag and ask someone else to pick up your golf ball. Back at the clubhouse, apply ice to a strained muscle or ligament. An ice compress will soothe a sore muscle or ligament and will help to reduce muscle spasms. Be sure not to apply the ice directly to the skin because of possible skin damage. Put ice into a plastic bag and then wrap the bag with a towel or a cloth. Over-the-counter pain medications such as anti-inflammatory medications are quite helpful. It is a good idea to carry either aspirin, acetaminophen or a non-steroidal anti-inflammatory medication such as ibuprofen in your golf bag; just don't leave it in your bag for years. Read the drug insert and follow the directions in taking the medications before using it. If the pain is quite severe, do not drive home. Ask someone for a ride. A driver with severe muscle spasms may divert attention away from driving and may end up injuring him- or herself as well as others on the road. After the acute episode of pain subsides and the spasms have been reduced, you may apply moist heat. A good way to do so is standing in the shower. Allow the heated water to hit the injured area. Limit the application of moist heat to about 20 minutes. Heating pads and heat lamps are another source of comfort that will help loosen tight muscles. Never use a heating pad on high or fall asleep under a heating lamp. Both can cause burns to the skin. Keep the heating pad on a low setting and the heat lamp at a distance so you do not inadvertently hit it. If you are able to tolerate the over-the-counter medications, continue them for 5 to 7 days, even if you are feeling better. Go the full course of the anti-inflammatory medication in order to achieve the maximum benefits. After the pain has subsided, it doesn't mean that you can go back to the practice range. It means that it is time to practice stretching exercises. One of the reasons that the muscles were injured was because of over-stretching or over-use. Stretching exercises help you to keep on playing your game. If you return too early, you may be leaving shortly thereafter and your absence from the game will be extended.

After you have experienced this type of problem, re-evaluate your situation at work and at home. Note how you sit in a chair and how you travel back and forth to work. For a short period of time, back-support corsets or braces may be helpful in providing comfort and support to your low back. They should be used for short periods of time and only until the pain in the back has subsided. Use of a corset or brace for an extended period of time may actually weaken the back muscles and will increase the rehabilitative time needed before returning to golf. During this period of time, avoid heavy lifting, bending, pulling activities and sex. All of these are muscle/ligament-demanding activities. It is recommended that you not lift anything weighing more than 3 to 7 lbs. Bed rest is recommended for 2 to 3 days only. If you stay in bed too long, the muscles will begin to weaken and may again extend the rehabilitation time. When evaluating your environment: another item that should be investigated is your bed. If you sleep on a waterbed, this is not the time for its use. You need to have a bed that has a firm mattress that will help support the spine and muscles in your back.

If the pain is persistent, worsens or starts to radiate into your legs and over-the-counter medications do not help, then it is time to contact a doctor. The pain may mean that there are other more serious problems. The doctor will obtain a medical history and perform a physical examination and may recommend other studies. You may or may not need to see a physician who specializes in the treatment of spinal disorders.

There are basically two types of specialists who take care of spinal problems: one is a non-surgical specialist and the other is a surgeon. Non-surgical spine specialists include: neurologists, physical therapists, chiropractic physicians, massage therapists, physiatrists, radiologists, anesthesiology pain specialists, and acupuncture physicians. Neurosurgeons and orthopedic surgeons make up the surgical spine specialists.

Here are some other causes of low back pain. Physicians refer to this list as a **differential diagnosis**. This is a long list of possible causes of low back pain. It is important to realize that often a definitive diagnosis of exactly what caused the back pain may not be possible; and a definitive diagnosis may not even matter at all if the back pain goes away. The reason you may want to know the cause of your back pain is to help prevent a recurrence of the discomfort. It is important to recognize that if your pain is not better in a few weeks, it may not get better without some medical help. The problem may be more than a sprain or a strain. With this in mind, here is the list. It's not designed for you to diagnose your own problem, but it is to help bring some insight into what may be causing your problem and allow you to help your doctor.

ACUTE ANNULUS FISSURE (TEAR)

The annulus is the outer layer of the disc (Fig. 8). A tear in the annulus is a very common cause of acute or sudden onset of low back pain. The fissure or tear occurs at a weakened site of the outer covering of the disc (Fig. 9). As we mature the disc changes and the outer layers of the disc become more fragile and easier to tear. This type of injury usually occurs with flexion and with or without torsion or rotation. Many patients will report that the pain began soon after bending or swinging. For the golfer it may occur with the swing or when picking up the ball. Bending, or flexion, is enough to cause a tear in the

figure | 8

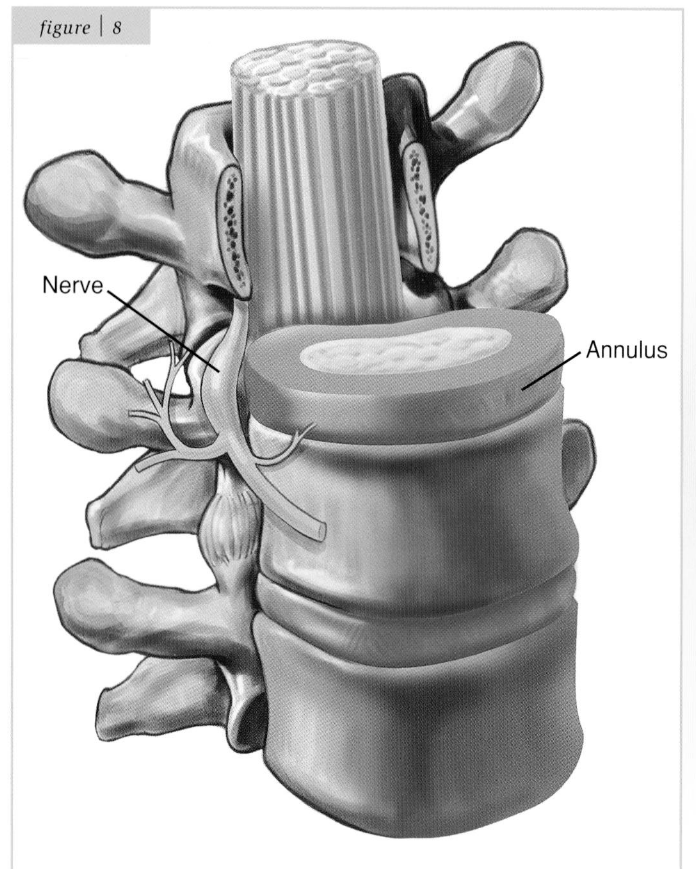

Annulus (outer layer of the disc).

figure | 9

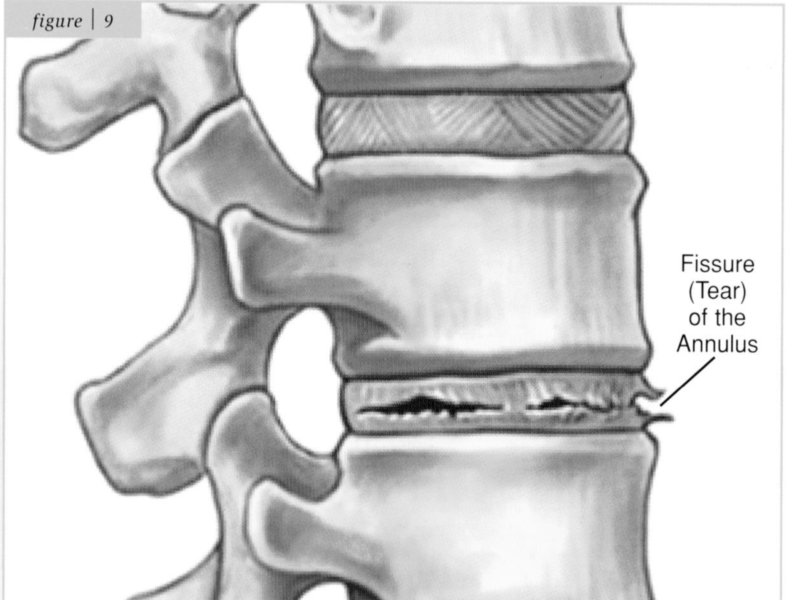

Fissure (tear) of the annulus.

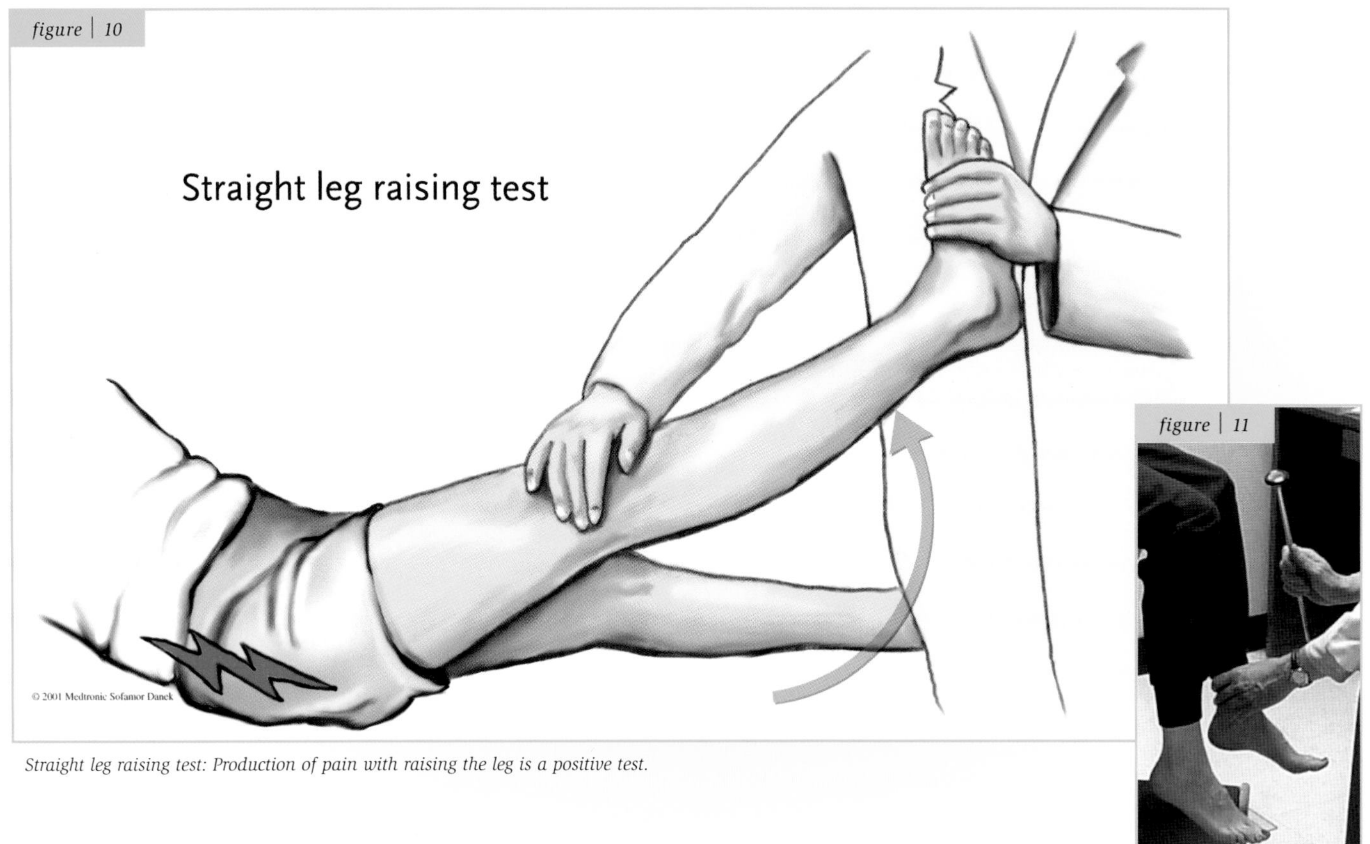

Straight leg raising test: Production of pain with raising the leg is a positive test.

figure | 11

Knee reflex testing with a special reflex hammer.

annulus in certain situations. Some players report that they heard a pop in their back resulting in severe pain. At this point it is most likely that the game will have to be discontinued. You may be tempted to try to tee the ball up. This is not wise. The pain will usually stop the golf game. Sometimes the pain will radiate into the buttocks or gluteal areas. You will not be able to continue your golf game because activities such as bending, twisting, rotating, or even sitting in a cart will do nothing but aggravate the pain. Standing may be the preferred way to move around. It is also not unusual to experience tingling or numbness in the legs. The most common problem that occurs is severe muscle spasms. Golfers may find that with these spasms they may list, or lean to one side or the other. Range of motion, how you rotate or move, will also be very limited. The pain will prompt a call to a doctor, who will need to evaluate the golfer in pain.

After the medical history is taken and during the physical examination, the doctor will perform a straight leg test (Fig. 10). The doctor will raise one leg up straight while the patient is either sitting or lying down, to see if any pain is elicited from the back or leg. The test stretches the nerves in your legs. If the nerves are under pressure, the pain will be much worse. The doctor will test the sensations in the legs with a sterilized disposable pin, particularly if the patient is experiencing any numbness. Reflexes are tested with a special hammer (Fig. 11). The doctor will ask the patient to pull the leg up, kick the leg out, and to pull the leg back and push down as one would on the gas pedal. Usually, the strength is normal. The treatment for an annular tear is not specific and is similar to a sprain or strain treatment. Bed rest is usually recommended for no longer than 2 to 3 days. A non-steroidal anti-inflammatory medication or acetaminophen may be helpful. There are many types of these medications now available over-the-counter, or the doctor may prescribe a stronger anti-inflammatory medication. These medications not only work as an analgesic (reduce pain) but also as an anti-inflammation medication. Acetaminophen will not help the inflammatory aspect of a discomfort, but will help with the analgesic aspects. At times the pain may be so severe that a stronger type of pain medication, an opioid, may be necessary to control the pain. Oral corticosteroids may be recommended in an amount that decreases over a period of days. With severe discomfort that is not affected by these medications, an injection of pain medications into the injured, inflamed spinal area may be helpful.

Physical therapy is an important part of any back therapy. Early physical therapy will often help to bring about a quicker resolution to the discomfort. Physical therapy promotes conditioning, increases muscle strength and flexibility, and leads into other exercise and body mechanics programs that will help prevent a recurrence of the annular tear. Between 4 t012 weeks, the pain should get better and the annular tear should heal itself. The bottom line about acute annular tears is that they are common and most patients do get better.

For those individuals whose function-limiting low back pain does not improve with conservative therapies such as rest, medications, physical therapies, nerve injections, exercises, manipulation therapies, activity changes, braces, and other alternative treatments, intradiscal therapy may be considered. Intradiscal electrothermal therapy (IDET) or intradiscal electrothermal annuloplasty (IDEA) is a minimally invasive procedure that may be helpful for patients who have fissures or tears in the annulus (outer layers of the disc) or bulging of the nucleus pulposus (gel center of the disc). IDET may be considered for patients who have had discogenic low back pain for more than 6 months and failed other less invasive therapies. Individuals who have disc herniations with referred pain into their legs may not be good candidates for this procedure. Individuals with bony spinal canal stenosis or collapsed disc (loss of greater than 50% of the normal disc height) are usually not considered for this procedure. Also individuals older than 55 years or with medical burdens tend to have lower success rates. Golfers who smoke cigarettes do less well because the tobacco use hinders healing.

Pre-IDET studies include an MRI or CT discogram or plain discography to determine the affected disc producing the pain. The procedure involves the placement of a navigable, flexible electrothermal catheter into the diseased disc under X-ray (fluoroscopy) guidance. The heating coils of the catheter delivers an electric current to the disc. The electric current heats the disc to very high temperatures (90 degrees C.) for 15 to 20 minutes. Various theoretical therapeutic mechanisms have been proposed to explain the effectiveness of the procedure, including the modification of the collagen fibers, stiffening of the disc, alteration of the annular fissures, and ablation of the pain receptors of the disc. Usually after a period of observation the patient is allowed to go home. Pain relief varies from patient to patient. Some individuals report relief of back pain within a few days following the procedure; others may take 6 to 8 weeks to notice reduction in their pain. However, some patients do not experience any pain relief. Recovery from IDET may take weeks. An exercise and physical therapy program is usually recommended. The postprocedural rehabilitation program will include progressive flexibility and strengthening exercises. Resuming normal activities should only be started with the approval of a physician and physical therapist. Golf activities can usually be gradually started in about 5 to 6 months after the IDET procedure. The long-term outcomes for patients receiving IDET for their back pain has not been determined. More data is needed to determine the true effectiveness of IDET. Therefore, prior to having this procedure, patients are encouraged to discuss this therapy with their doctor or healthcare providers.

LUMBAR DISC HERNIATION

A lumbar herniated intervertebral disc occurs when the nucleus pulposus (gel) inside the disc is squeezed and moves outward (Fig. 12). The medical name for a herniated lumbar disc is a **herniated nucleus pulposus**. This kind of herniation has many other names, such as a pinched nerve, a disc herniation, a slipped disc, or a clipped disc. A herniated nucleus pulposus presents with a wide array of symptoms, all depending on the location and the size of the herniation and whether or not it occurs suddenly or over a period of time. The intervertebral disc is like a jelly donut with an outside layer (annulus) and an inside (nucleus pulposus) that makes up the gel of the disc (Fig. 8).

Many factors can cause a disc herniation. One is the aging process. There are natural biochemical changes that are occurring in the disc. Just like a donut that is left out of the box, it loses its height; the pasta becomes fragile and cracks, and the jelly shrinks down as the water content decreases. All of these factors affect the strength and resiliency of the donut and the disc. There is nothing you can do about this phase of aging discs besides knowing that they are not as strong as they used to be and that they will rely on their neighboring muscles and joints to help carry the forces placed on the spine. On the other hand, there are particular lifestyle choices that have a bad influence on the discs and spine. One factor is being out of shape and then trying to play golf as if one

figure | 12

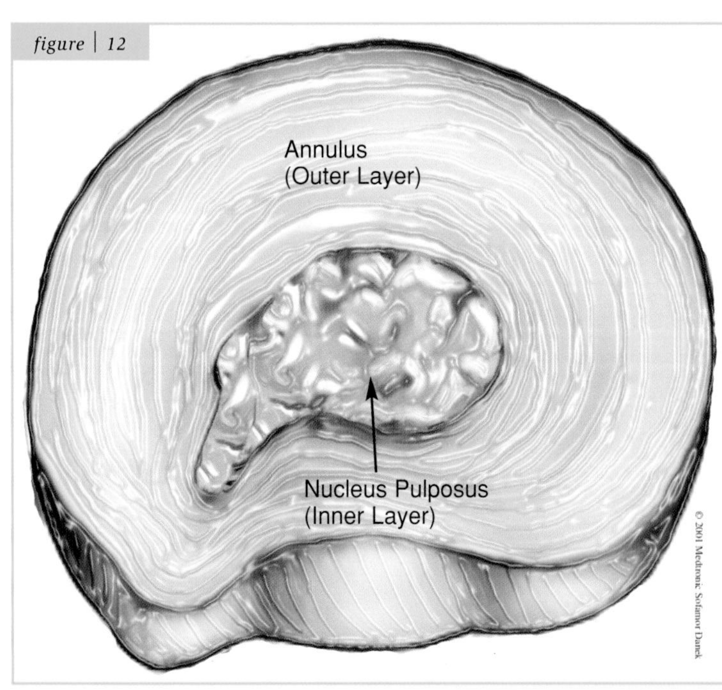

Disc degeneration (internal disruption).

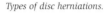

Types of disc herniations. figure | 13

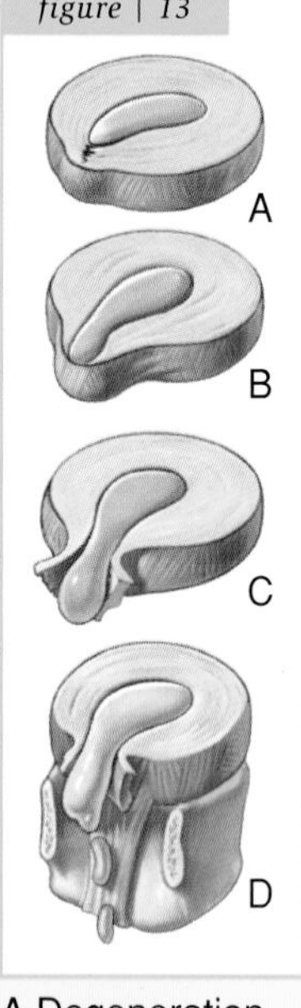

A Degeneration (Internal Disruption)
B Prolapse or Bulging Disc
C Extrusion
D Sequestration Nucleus Pulposus

figure | 14

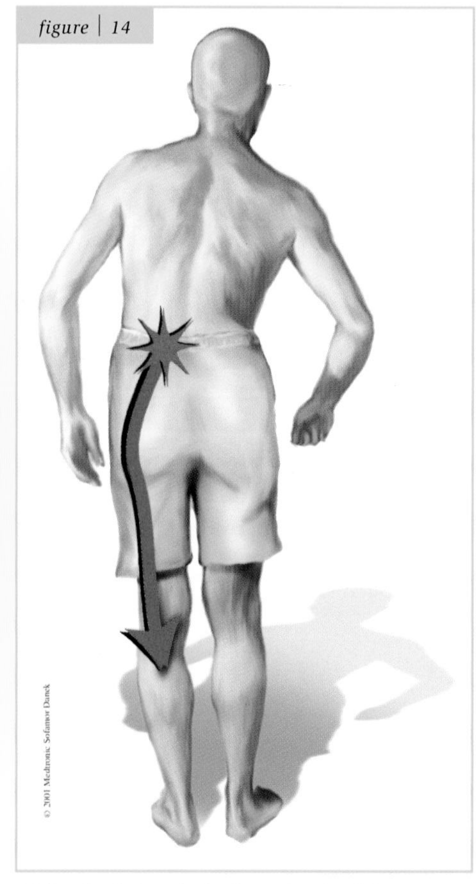

Referred pain into the leg from a herniated disc.

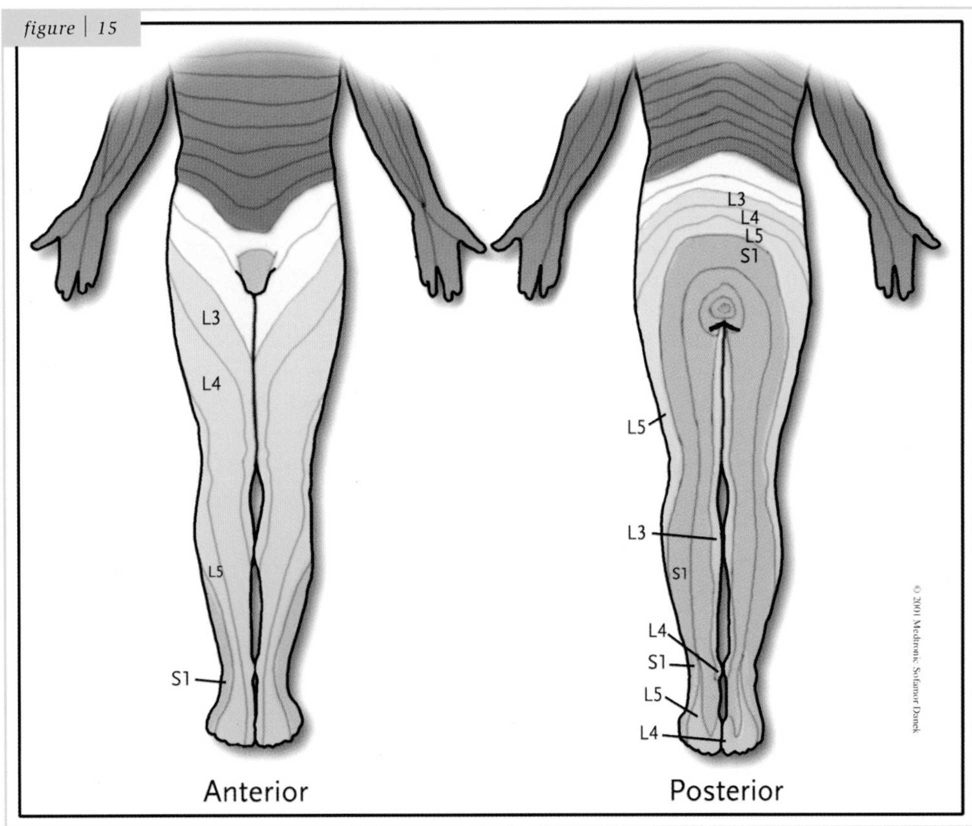

Dermatomal distribution into the legs from nerves.

were 10 to 25 years younger. Poor conditioning has an adverse effect on the body mechanics and places more stress on the lumbar discs. Another major negative influence on the discs is the use of tobacco products, in particular cigarettes. Tobacco will actually speed up the aging process. Finally, another influence on the aging discs is not hydrating, that is not getting enough to drink. We need 6 to 8 glasses of water a day, and we need to eat enough of the right foods (fruits and vegetables). Even though the back is aging, there are aspects of our lives that we can control. Try to cut down on the bad influences on the spine; doing so will increase the length of time that you can play golf.

A disc herniation is the result of maturing or aging. The inside (nucleus pulposus) may suddenly pop out or take weeks to months to migrate through the outer annulus. There are different stages to a disc herniation (Fig. 13). A disc herniation is due to degeneration and internal disc disruption. With age the disc loses water content; the nucleus pulposus dries out. There are also biochemical changes and protein loss that lead to disc disruption and degeneration. The first type of internal disc disruption or degeneration is the herniated disc. The inside nucleus ruptures through the innermost annular fibers, but does not migrate to the annular surface. The second stage of disc herniation is referred to as a **bulging or prolapse** of the disc. If you squeeze a jelly donut just a little bit, the jelly comes just to the surface; this is called a **disc bulge or protrusion**. The disc has not totally herniated, but it begins to encroach on the nerves in the spinal canal. The next stage of a disc herniation is the **disc extrusion**. The gel pushes out of the outer layer of the annulus, but overall is still contained within the disc. Sometimes this may cause severe discomfort if it is pushing on a nerve.

The last stage of a disc herniation is referred to as a **sequestered disc**. The gel inside the annulus ruptures to the outside of the disc. When the nucleus pulposus breaks through and is located entirely outside of the outer ring of the disc, it is sometimes jokingly called a **canal mouse** because a portion of the disc is hiding inside the canal and causing mischief. The disc herniation is usually caused by flexion activities, but can occur with lifting, twisting, bending, or swinging a golf club. Incorrectly lifting an item, no matter how heavy, may overload a disc and cause a herniation. There are times a patient may be unable to say specifically what brought about the herniation. Others will hear a pop in their backs; the annulus may have been torn. The pain is immediate and localized to the low back. Shortly thereafter, leg pain follows. The pain may be in the middle of the back or on one side or the other. It may be referred or radiate into the buttocks or the leg (Fig. 14). The distribution of the pain will depend on the given nerve that is being pinched by the disc herniation. The pattern and referred symptoms and findings on the physical examination can often identify the offended nerve. Dermatomes are the areas of the skin supplied by a particular nerve (Fig. 15). These symptoms usually occur within a short period of time, usually a few days after the onset of the severe back pain. If there is leg pain a nerve is being squeezed or pinched, thus the name **pinched nerve**. Squeezing the nerve will cause the nerve to become irritated and swell, adding to the pain. Pain down the leg usually occurs when the disc herniates out of the side of the annulus. A disc that herniates in the middle of the disc usually causes only back pain. When the disc is very large it may cause a **cauda equina syndrome**. This is an extremely serious type of disc herniation and causes severe pain in the back and sometimes into the back of the thighs and the legs. There may be numbness and tingling sensations that travel down the legs and into the soles of the feet. Weakness may occur and the patient may not be able to move the legs or feet at all; this is known as **paralysis**. An individual with this problem may have trouble initiating urination or may only be able to urinate when the bladder is very full (overflow incontinence). If an individual develops any of these symptoms, he or she must go to the nearest emergency room. This is a medical emergency.

The pain from a disc herniation is caused, in part, from chemical reactions as well as mechanical pressure or pinching the nerve. There are several disc proteins that become very irritating to nerves when they travel outside the disc.

Patients with a disc herniation will have increased pain with almost any activity. Even sitting or standing can be quite painful. Some will report that walking actually lessens the pain, while others state that lying flat and not moving is the best position to lessen the discomfort. There are different symptoms for different people, but one thing is certain, a disc herniation is a most unpleasant experience.

Muscle spasm may be present with a disc herniation. The muscles on one side may appear to be standing up and are quite firm. When muscles are in spasm, they are painful. An individual may also have a list to one side or the other. Usually they tend to move in the direction away from the offending disc. There is one thing for certain, they won't be moving a lot. Their range of motion will be remarkably restricted and a doctor may be able to find differences in the motor strength of their legs. This depends on the level and site of the herniation and what nerve is being pinched. There may be decreased sensation to pinprick along the leg that is experiencing the pain. When the physician uses a reflex hammer to test the reflexes, the reflexes may also be depressed or not very active. Another commonly performed test in the doctor's office is the straight leg-raising test (Fig. 10). If an individual slowly extends the leg out either sitting or lying down and experiences pain in that leg, this is called a **positive straight leg-raising test**. This is **true sciatica**. During the straight leg-raising test the sciatic nerve is stretched, and, if it is also pinched, will cause pain when the leg is elevated 35 to 40 degrees. The doctor will test both legs. The treatment for a disc herniation depends on each patient's situation. In most cases, bed rest is recommended for only 2 to 3 days. Muscle spasms are best treated with ice that has been wrapped in a towel or cloth, for 20 to 30 minutes. Repeat application three times per day. Heavy lifting, bending, pulling or sex is to be avoided, as is golf. If a patient must indulge in golf, computer golf games or TV golf may help with golf withdrawal symptoms.

Use of medications depends on an individual's medical history. If there are no contraindications, the first drugs to be used are the non-steroidal anti-inflammatory medications (NSAIDs). The patient may also need an opioid (a narcotic pain medication) for the pain. If the traditional course of non-steroidal anti-inflammatory medication does not produce enough relief, the physician may try oral steroids that are usually given in a dose pack to be taken over several days. One common dosage of steroids will include tablets that are given 4 tablets per day for 4 days, 3 tablets per day for 3 days, 2 tablets per day for 2 days, and 1 tablet a day for one day. An epidural injection, insertion of a spinal needle near the site of the disc herniation to place medications, is controversial, but may be helpful for some patients. Prior to the use of an epidural steroid, the patient will need to undergo diagnostic imaging tests such as an MRI or CAT scan. Physical therapy may be a very useful form of treatment in the initial stages of pain. The use of ultrasound and massage, as well as the ice packs, will help to reduce the muscle spasms and help alleviate the pain. After the pain has subsided, physical therapy will be valuable for muscle strengthening and dynamic lumbar muscle-stabilization programs. The patient will need to learn exercises that are directed at developing the muscles in the lumbar spine and abdomen. In most cases, disc herniation patients will get better in 4 to 12 weeks. During this time the patient will gradually become more active. The important point is that the patient should not become too active too quickly. There should be no golf yet. He or she must be patient and allow the body to heal. If any patient returns too quickly to normal activities, this may aggravate the situation and put him or her right back into the sick bed. Once cleared by a doctor or health care provider, the patient will need to start all over again with golf. This means taking lessons and having the swing evaluated. Twisting and swinging are causes of disc herniation. Recovering patients should learn the correct bending techniques, particularly for picking up a golf ball. In fact, avoidance of bending is often recommended. Ball pick-up devices are very helpful (Fig. 16). Before returning to golf, disc suffers need to evaluate their golf bag situation. Check its weight. Clean it out. Many golfers have a tendency to fill their bags with too many golf balls. One would be surprised how much weight all those golf balls will add to the bag. Golfers should pay close attention to how they place their golf bags into a car. Lifting a golf bag and placing it into the trunk of a sedan requires a great deal of twisting and bending of the lumbar spine (Fig. 17). It is safer for the spine to put the bag into the back seat of the vehicle. In this manner the bag can be slid into and out of the car (Fig. 18). Sport utility vehicles allow the back gate to open, which provides easier golf bag placement and removal (Fig. 19).

If a patient is not improved in 6 to 8 weeks, then other testing may be needed. The test most often used is Magnetic Resonance Imaging (MRI). Before suggesting an MRI, the doctor will ask the patient if he or she has performed any metal work. If an individual has small metal filings in the eyes or any kind of implants (orthopedic rods, screws or electrical devices such as a pacemaker), he or she may not be able to enter the MRI. An individual troubled with claustrophobia may need a mild anti-anxiety medication or sedative to undergo the test. The MRI is a very helpful imaging test for lumbar intervertebral disc problems.

A golfer with a disc herniation must keep the faith. Only about 5% of all back problems require back surgery. The important point to remember is that a golfer who has a disc herniation history now has a history of a bad back, which means that he or she must continue to observe good spine care. Recognizing a back problem, doing something about it, and then making sure that it doesn't happen again will be the best way to be able to continue playing golf.

Increased Risk Factors for Intervertebral Disc Herniation:

1. Smoking
2. Obesity
3. Unconditioned muscles (abdominal and lumbar)
4. Poor nutrition and under-hydration
5. Poor posture
6. Incorrect listing (spine twisting and rotation)

SURGERY

Most individuals who have low back pain and leg discomfort will not need any surgical intervention. In fact it is a very small percentage of individuals with such problems who require a trip to the operating room.

Patients who do not improve with non-surgical or conservative therapy after about 6 to 12 weeks will need more

Golf ball retrieval suction device. Good to avoid bending, particularly with a bad back.

figure | 16

figure | 17

Lifting a golf bag from the trunk requires bending and stresses the lumbar spine.

figure | 18

Sliding the golf bag along the back seat puts less stress on the spine.

figure | 19

Placing the golf bag into a sports utility vehicle is less lumbar spine strain.

aggressive therapy or surgery. These individuals have pain that is not managed well enough to go about their everyday activities. They find that even the simple joys in life become a great challenge due to the pain produced by any kind of activity, regardless of how subtle or small the activity may be. Getting up and going to work may be a task. Severe discomfort in the back and legs interferes with activities at home, work and the golf course. A spouse or significant other may find that his or her role has become that of caregiver rather than companion or lover. Pleasant activities with family, loved ones, or friends are now out of the question. Constant back and leg pain will not allow much enjoyment. If leg or foot weakness has not improved or has worsened despite medical therapy, surgical avenues will need to be considered.

However, before a surgeon considers any surgery, the surgical benefits and risks will need to be discussed. The patient's complete health history (*i.e.*: any pre-existing diabetes, heart disease, bowel problems, or other medical problems) will need to be investigated by a medical doctor in order to reduce the surgical risks. Once the patient has been given medical clearance, surgical options can be strongly entertained. The patient's physical examination is correlated with a radiological imaging study, *i.e.* MRI, CAT scan, myelogram, discogram. The abnormality on the radiologic studies should correlate with the patient's history and physical findings in order to insure a more successful surgical result. All of the pre-operative tests and studies will be used to assist the surgeon in the operating room and will be of help to the anesthesiologist (the physician who administers the anesthetic medication). Patients must tell their doctors about any of their drug or food allergies. They must also inform their doctors about any of their current and past medications, including any over-the-counter, alternative, or herbal medications. Medicines obtained from alternative health stores contain ingredients that may interact in an adverse fashion with medicines that a physician has prescribed. If a golfer is undergoing any other types of therapy, acupuncture or massage therapy, it's important that his or her surgeon knows about them. The more a physician and surgeon know about a patient, the better the chances of a successful outcome. If a patient smokes, it's best to discontinue use of all tobacco products several weeks before the date of spine surgery. Cigarettes and other tobacco products (smokeless tobacco) contain thousands of toxins that will effect the blood's ability to carry oxygen and may interfere with the healing process after surgery. The use of tobacco also increases the risk of surgical and anesthesia complications. Smokers also have a more difficult time with their respiratory system (lungs) than non-smokers do after surgery. The bottom line is that smokers do not do as well during and after surgery as non-tobacco users.

There are two ways that a surgeon will usually view a lumbar disc herniation surgical patient's back. The person with a first time disc herniation is referred to as a **virgin back**. The second is the patient who has recurrent back herniations. This occurs when residual nucleus pulposus ruptures at the same location as a previous herniation. There is a risk of recurrent herniation after undergoing any lumbar disc surgery. Sometimes a patient with a history of a disc herniation and surgical treatment may have another herniation either the same site or above or below the previous disc herniation site.

The patient who is considered to have a "virgin back" may be a candidate for other surgeries. One type of surgery is called **minimally invasive lumbar disc**

surgery. This surgery uses a very small incision through which a small probe is inserted through the skin of the back and directed down into the herniated disc space (Fig. 20). This is performed with the help of X-ray guidance or a navigating guidance system. The herniated disc material is removed with a suction device or small micro-surgical instruments, and occasionally a laser. Under the very best of conditions, not all of the disk can be removed. It would be like trying to remove all of the jelly from inside the donut through a very small incision; some of the jelly may be left behind. The surgeon may be assisted with a video camera that is placed on the endoscope to better see the disc space. This procedure is called **lumbar endoscopic discectomy**. The minimally invasive disc operations are intended to cause less embarrassment to the back muscles. However, there are certain situations when the minimally invasive procedure must be turned into an open operation. This can occur with occasional bleeding, leaking of spinal fluid, and possible nerve injury. Not everyone is a candidate for minimally invasive surgery, so a patient needs to discuss this with his or her surgeon. Patients who have low back pain *not* caused by a herniated disc will not benefit from removal of a disc. Patients who have severe spinal cord stenosis (severe narrowing of the spinal canal) are not usually considered surgical candidates for minimally invasive procedures. Some patients may have this procedure performed under local anesthetic or intravenous sedation. Prior to considering the lumbar endoscopic discectomy, a patient should make sure that he or she is a candidate for this kind of therapy. One should inquire about other available surgical avenues and the surgeon's success rate with these various surgeries. If any patient has any doubts the surgery, it may be wise to seek another opinion. A surgeon will not be upset or offended when a patient asks for a second opinion. Most surgeons will welcome the option and never give it a second thought. After minimally invasive disk surgery, the patient will be observed in a special holding area, or post-operative room and, when stable, will be allowed to go home.

The other procedure that is commonly used for a disc herniation is called an **open lumbar discectomy**. For this operation, the patient is given a general anesthetic. An incision is made in the middle of the back or to the side of the location of the herniated disc. The incision is carried down through the skin and into the deeper tissues. The muscles are carefully retracted to the sides, exposing the underlying elements of the spine under which the herniated disc may be found. The surgeon will usually use some type of magnification, either magnifying loupes or a microscope, to perform the surgery. Occasionally, the disc can be removed without having to take away any of the underlying bone or lamina. Once the correct site of disc herniation has been located, the surgeon will carefully remove as much of the herniated disc as possible (Figs. 21A and B). Even in the best of situations, all of the inside disc material cannot be removed, even with an open operation. There is always the chance of a recurrent disc herniation. After surgery, the patient will be placed in a post-operative room and observed closely for 6 to 8 hours or up to 24 hours. The patient may or may not go home after this procedure. No matter whether it is a minimally invasive operation or an open operation, patients will not be able to drive themselves home. There is a list of dos and don'ts after surgery, and precautions should be followed as per the surgeon's instructions. After surgery, the surgeon will advise the patient to avoid heavy lifting activities (mainly bending), driving, sex, and golf. The patient will be given a prescribed pain medication and perhaps a muscle

figure | 20

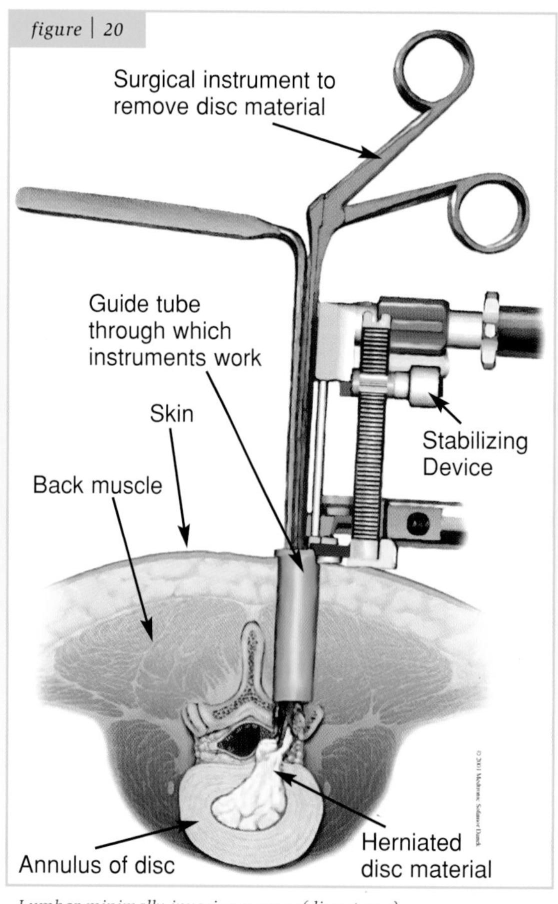

Lumbar minimally invasive surgery (discectomy).

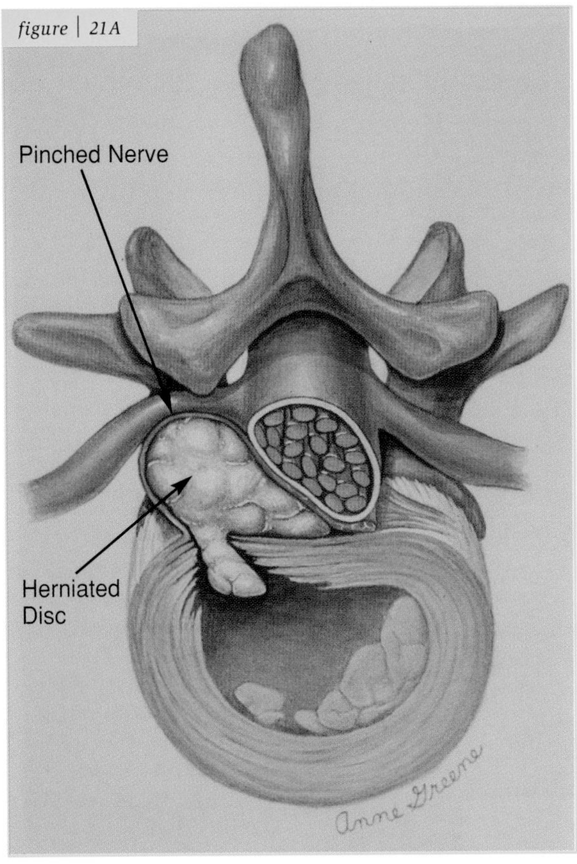

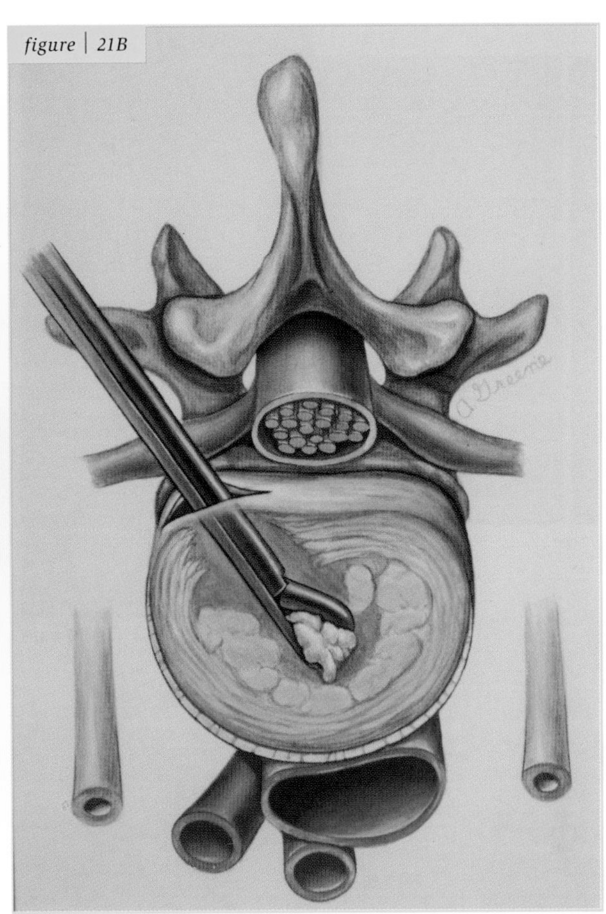

A. Herniated disc material pinching a nerve.

B. Removal of herniated disc material with a surgical instrument.

relaxing medication and sometimes even a gentle laxative. Pain medication may slow down bowel movements and cause constipation. One of the best ways to keep the bowel movements regular and prevent constipation is to eat plenty of fresh fruit and vegetables and drink plenty of fluids. In many cases, the patient will not have any stitches that will need to be removed. The patient needs to discuss this with his or her physician before discharge home. Many sutures will dissolve. The patient may have small bandages (steri-strips) over the incision; these will peel off with time. The surgeon will determine when the patient will be able to take a shower or bath. It is better to take a shower, rather than a bath, because of all the bending and manipulation that it takes to get into the tub. Some surgeons may instruct their patients not to get their incision wet for anywhere from 4 to 7 days. Lifting is another item that a patient and his or her surgeon will need to discuss. Often the patient is instructed not to lift anything heavier than a milk carton. If patients have small children or animals, they should not be lifting them even if they weigh less than a milk carton. The problem is that they will be moving around and it will be necessary to keep them at bay. A follow-up clinic visit will depend on a surgeon's preferences. Some like to see the patient in about 10 days, while others will wait until 6 weeks have passed. Driving and returning to more normal activities can resume in about 3 to 6 weeks. Gentle walking activities will be encouraged, but this does not mean that the individual should strike out on a hike in the woods traveling unfamiliar territory. A good place to do gentle walking is at an indoor track or outdoor track, either in the early morning or early evening hours. Anyone should always take a bottle of water during the walk. It's easy to quickly become dehydrated.

Returning to golf after undergoing any type of lumbar discectomy or disc procedure depends on the surgeon's advice and experience. In most cases, a lumbar discectomy involves removing as much of the nucleus pulposus inside the disc as is safely possible. There is usually very little bone removed in a discectomy and the nearby joint is not removed. A patient's surgeon is the only one who truly knows what has been done to the golfer's back and must be consulted before returning to golf. If the patient is making a good recovery and experiencing minimal pain after surgery, then in about 4 weeks strength training for lumbar and abdominal muscles may be started. Strengthening the abdominal muscles is referred to as **dynamic abdominal bracing**. These are exercises that are needed to play golf. Once these exercises are started and tolerated without any great discomfort, they should be continued throughout the patient's golf lifetime. If a golfer should have any pain after surgery, he or she will need to go a bit more slowly on the strengthening and re-conditioning exercises.

After physical therapy sessions that have lasted 2 to 4 weeks, the patient may be able to look at his/her golf clubs with great enthusiasm once again. The first thing that a returning golfer should do is clean the golf bag out. Remove any unnecessary items that are helping to weigh down the bag, such as used balls, broken tees and the lost sweater. A good way to pass time for post-surgery golfers waiting to get back to playing is to visit their club's golf shop or golfing store. Shopping and looking at new golf clubs and other items is a relaxing and enjoyable pastime. If everything is going well after surgery, the golfer experiences no pain, and the exercises have brought about increased lumbar and muscle strength, then it is time for the golfer to take a lesson. The individual should tell their golf pro exactly what they have been through so he or she can evaluate the mechanics of the patient's golf swing. After completing the pre-golf requirements, the patient should be able to return to swinging with short irons in about 6 weeks. The returning golfer should always remember that he is an ex-patient and should always exercise good judgment and caution when playing.

GOLF AFTER DISC SURGERY

How soon and in what capacity one can return to the golf course after undergoing a lumbar discectomy depends on a number of factors, the most critical of which is the patient. If the patient smokes, is overweight, or has not participated in a pre-operative exercise program, the return to the course will take longer, as these factors show the healing process. If the healing process occurs normally, and the patient does not experience pain or any other problems, flexibility and strength training may begin within four weeks. It is important that this training be supervised by a therapist who understands a golf swing and what it demands from the body.

After two weeks of these exercises, the patient may begin swinging with short irons. Weighted clubs may also be added to this program if the short iron swinging is well tolerated. During this time, upper body cross training with light weights may be recommended, as this is a good time to begin strengthening the rotator cuff and the scapular muscles of the shoulders.

Eight weeks after surgery, the patient should still be working on easy swings with short irons and weighted clubs. It is very important that these exercises are performed gently, and not with the power of one's regular swing. All of these gradual steps need to be followed, even if the training is going very well. If steps are skipped and a patient moves to an exercise for which he or she is not ready, problems are sure to result.

If the exercises and the swinging activity are well tolerated without pain, mid-range irons may be added to the routine. The long irons and woods can be added at 12 weeks post-surgery. When golf clubs are used in a post-operative exercise program, it is important that they be used in a controlled environment. A patient should never go to the practice range during this time, as the temptation will be great to let loose with a full swing, and to exercise too much. Building endurance is extremely important; playing golf while fatigued and while still healing will increase the probability of re-injury.

After twelve weeks of practice in a controlled environment, the patient may return to the practice range, but only with the short irons and only to hit a small bucket of balls. Hitting more than a small bucket of balls is bad for the patient and will not help his or her game. Additionally, if the bucket is emptied too quickly, faster than in 20 to 30 minutes, problems may result. In the first few return visits to the range, the patient should pace him- or herself, enjoying the feel of golf again.

After all the balls are gone, the patient should not continue on to the putting green because putting requires a great deal of bending, for which the spine is not ready. Only after a few trips to the driving range with the short irons should a few minutes of putting be attempted, and only then with either a long putter or a standard putter with a device on the end for ball retrieval (Figs. 16 and 22). It is best to avoid bending to pick up the ball. Squatting to retrieve the ball is acceptable in this situation (Fig. 23).

If the first outing at the practice range goes well, the exact same regime should be repeated 3 or 4 times. At that point, another bucket of balls can be added to the practice. As each driving range has a different number of balls in a bucket; the time limit for this next level

Ball retrieval claw device.

Good method to pick up a golf ball, particularly for a bad back patient.

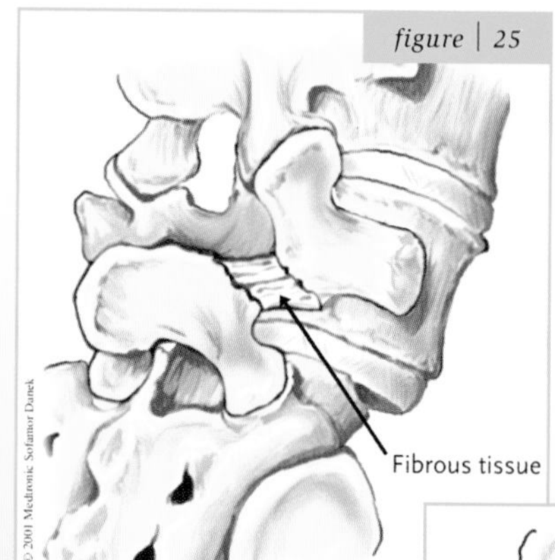

Fibrous tissue in the pars defect preventing healing.

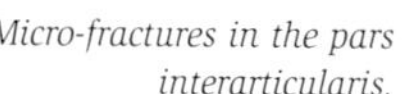

Micro-fractures in the pars interarticularis.

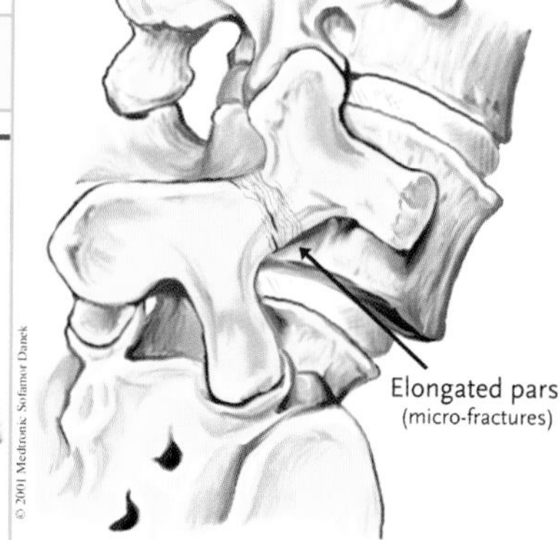

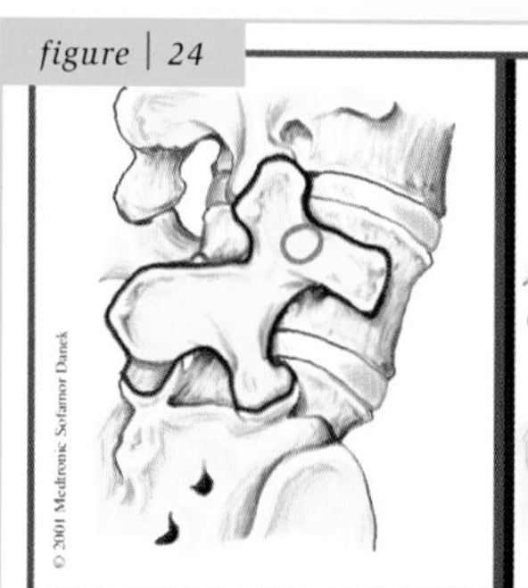

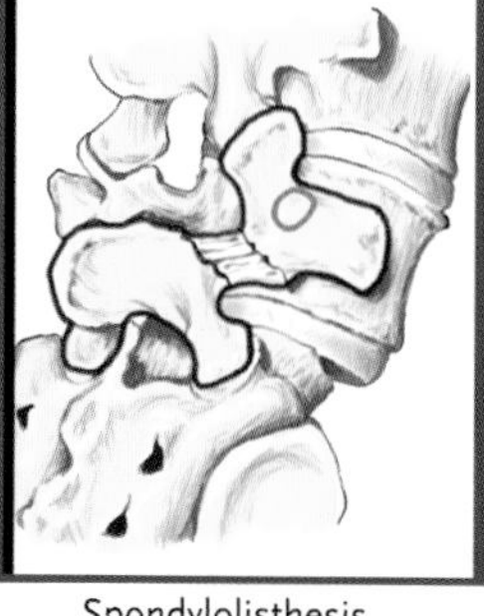

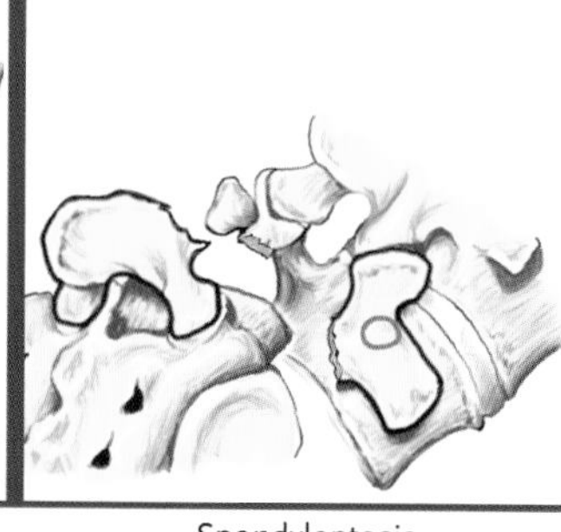

Normal pars interarticularis and types of defects.

of practice should be limited to 30 to 35 minutes, even if there are balls left over at the end of this time period.

These practice sessions should continue for two weeks, staggered by 2 to 3 days between sessions. Finally, after 12 weeks of practice without any problems, 9 holes of golf may be played, but the patient should be prepared for the fact that this short game after spine surgery may be more demanding and the fatigue factor greater than anticipated.

After the return to the course, it is very important that games be limited to 9 holes ONLY for three to four months, and that these games take place no more often than one or two days per week. Even this may seem excessive as the patient deals with healing. Diehard golfers who think they are able to play 18 holes during these months should NOT do so, as this will slow the return to full health.

After three to four months of these shortened games, barring any pain or problems, the patient may finally attempt 18 holes of golf, though only after a consultation with the surgeon, physician, and therapist. Some doctors will suggest that walking the course for the first 18-hole game is acceptable; however, riding in a cart is probably a safer way to return to a full game. If a golfer is determined to walk the course, it should be a familiar course, and a course that is relatively flat, allowing easier walking and easier demands on the spine. Golf bags should be placed on the cart, and not be carried or pulled.

Some suggestions that might make the game easier on the back: Use the red tees or the tees closest to the hole to minimize the temptation to "kill" the ball. Try to stay in the fairway even if it means shorter, safer shots, as angled lies and sand traps cause unsure footing that may cause an injury. Thick rough will cause varied swing resistance that can be quite harmful to a post-operative patient.

The most important thing is to use common sense when easing back into the game. Don't attempt any shot that holds even the slightest risk of injury. Never attempt a shot off a tree root or take an unnatural swing. Continuing to play is your only goal.

SPONDYLOLYSIS AND SPONDYLOLISTHESIS

Spondylolysis and spondylolisthesis are two complicated medical terms that can evoke fear from just looking at the words. Any medical term that looks frightening just to read must indeed be bad. That is not the case. The two terms are closely related, but are not the same spine problem.

Let's look at **spondylolysis** first. Spondylo- refers to the vertebrae or the bony spine, and -lysis means that there is a defect or a break in a bone in the lumbar spine. The defect is usually found in the last vertebra in the lumbar spine at L-5 (lumbar #5). Occasionally, it may be associated with other sites in the spine. The defect in the bone is located in a bone called the pars interarticularis. This is a small, connecting bone that carries a lot of weight by uniting the upper and lower facets in the lumbar spine. The pars interarticularis looks like the neck of a Scottie dog (Fig. 24). The "neck" bone of the dog connects the upper bones (the dog's head).to the lower bones (dog's body). It is a defect in the dog's neck that leads to problems. A defect in this particular site is found in about 5 to 6% of the population. It is more often found in males as compared to females, and when it is present it is usually located on both sides of the bone. There are genetic and traumatic types of spondylolysis. It may show up in childhood between the ages of 5 and 7 years. These are often silent fractures, and many times the child will never know he or she has a defect in the spine. Many patients will not complain of pain or have any unusual signs, *i.e.* limping, loss of movement or other indications that there is a problem. If a child in this age group complains of pain, there may be an abnormality in a bone (**pars**) that is causing the pain. There appears to be a familial tendency for the development of this bony defect. About 30% of children who present with spondylolysis will have a family history of a similar problem.

The origin of this particular defect is thought to begin early in the growth of the spine with a bony defect or weakness of the "pars" bone. With the loss of strength and development of this bone, a fracture may develop and potentially lead to a gap between the two ends of the bone that remain separated by fibrous tissue. The pars may try to heal but not in the proper way, creating a less than satisfactory healing that causes an elongation of the bone that is unable to withstand repetitive pressures. On the other hand, the bone may not heal at all, resulting in a permanent defect between the ends of the two bones (Fig. 25). Twenty-five percent of adolescents who have persistent back pain will demonstrate radiographic (X-ray, CAT scan, MRI) evidence of spondylolysis. The other cause of spondylolysis is due to repetitive trauma or micro-trauma to the low back area. This is commonly found in the athlete. Some physicians believe there is a difference between spondylolysis that is found in the child and that found in the adult athlete. The incidence is higher in the athlete.

The pars defect, or spondylolysis, is most often seen in individuals who are involved in diving, gymnastics, wrestling, weight lifting, football, field and track events, and in athletes in general. All of these sports require repetitive movements that are associated with hyperextension of the lumbar spine; enough to cause micro-trauma and micro-fractures. Over time, this activity will cause stress on the spine and lead to a fatigue fracture of the pars. When the pars interarticularis does not heal correctly, a non-union occurs and the bone is left unstable. In other situations, the pars will unite, but will not form a strong union (Fig. 26). If this happens during childhood, the child will need to be closely followed by the pediatrician or family doctor into maturity to ensure that there are no other complications.

When there is slippage of one bone on another one, a **subluxation**, this is referred to as **spondylolisthesis** (Fig. 24). Spondylo- means bone or vertebra and -listhesis means slippage. Spine specialists sometimes use the "bony hook" concept to describe spondylolisthesis. The hook is made up of the vertebra, the pars interarticularis, and the lower (inferior) facet joints of the spine. The hook is holding the upper vertebra onto the lower spinal elements. When the hook bends or breaks, the upper vertebra can slip forward on the lower vertebra (Figs. 27A and B).

Disc degeneration and aging changes are sometimes associated with spondylolisthesis. The loss of disc height and joint (facet) degeneration may cause an increase in the forces on the vertebrae; particularly the lowest levels of the lumbar and sacral spine (L5 and S1). Such pressures may increase the shear stresses on the vertebra, *i.e.* L5, and cause the upper vertebra to slip forward on the lower vertebra (Fig. 28).

In a child or young individual, the spondylolysis defect usually occurs between the ages of 9 and 14 years and becomes less of a problem thereafter. If a slippage occurs, it does so at the site of the pars defect due to the stress and strain on the low back at L–5. Most people with spondylolysis (bony defect of the pars) have no noticeable symptoms of the problem. About 80% of the individuals will never know that they have a chronic bony defect in their backs. However, they are at a higher risk than the normal population of developing low back pain.

For those individuals in the athletic arena, *i.e.* golfers, the defect is associated with hyperextension that occurs when playing their sport. When athletes playing golf or any other sport involving extension of the back, the defect may cause pain. In fact, any type of hyperextension or bending of the back may cause severe pain. When the lower vertebrae, L-5, creeps forward, slipping off the platform of the sacrum (S-1), the movement will carry with it all of the spinal elements, producing increased distortion and displacement of the nerves associated with this segment of the spine. The slippage of spondylolisthesis is defined by using the **Meyerding grading scale** (Fig. 29A). **Grade 1** means that there is less than 25% slippage of one bone on the other (Fig. 29B). **Grade 2** means there is 25–49% slippage, **Grade 3** means 50–74% slippage and **Grade 4** indicates 75–99% slippage (Fig. 29C, D, E). Grade 5 occurs when the entire vertebra slips completely off the lower vertebra. This type of slippage is called **spondyloptosis** (Fig. 29F). The slipping happens when the disc, ligament, and the pars are not strong enough to prevent bony movements. The forward movement of one bone on the other will narrow the spinal canal. The nerves associated at this level will have less room to function. The nerves are literally pinched, thus causing pain. When the one bone moves on another and produces pain, it is considered unstable and unable to meet the demands put on it by everyday movements, particularly golf.

SYMPTOMS

The symptoms associated with this problem will be different in young people as compared to older individuals. In children and young adults, the pain may come from the bony defect itself. The pain may be present in the low back area and into the buttocks, and can be made worse by activities involving rotation of the spine; including the golf swing. In the older individual, the pain is usually due to the loss of room in the spinal canal due to stenosis. With both the younger and older individual, there may be pain that radiates into the legs and even into the feet. Numbness, and eventually weakness, may become a problem as well as bowel, bladder and sexual problems. There is no doubt that this situation will interfere with activities of daily living and golf. Life is a struggle, but you do not have to be in misery.

When a patient goes for a medical consultation, it is helpful to think of what the doctor will need to know. Date of onset? What were you doing? Where is the pain? Have you ever had pain like this before? Does the pain move into your buttocks or legs? What makes it better? What makes it worse? Having the answers to these questions will help the doctor better evaluate your situation. The physician will do a physical examination. X-rays will show the slippage of one bone on the other. Special angles may be necessary to see the pars interarticularis defect and can be obtained by a side view of the spine. The physician may order other tests such as a CAT scan to show bony defects, MRI to show the soft tissue structures, or a myelogram followed by a CAT scan.

In most cases, no surgery will be needed. The first things that a physician will do will be to restrict a patient's activities, and that means no golf for the time being. Most people respond well to the conservative, non-surgical therapy that restricts activities and uses medication, an exercise program, and the occasional use of a brace. The physician may recommend that the patient see a physical therapist who will demonstrate exercises to help stabilize the abdominal and lower back muscles. It is important for a patient to inform the therapist that he or she is intending to return to golf so the exercises can be structured accordingly. Anti-inflammatory medications can be helpful. In certain situations, an epidural nerve block can be used to control pain.

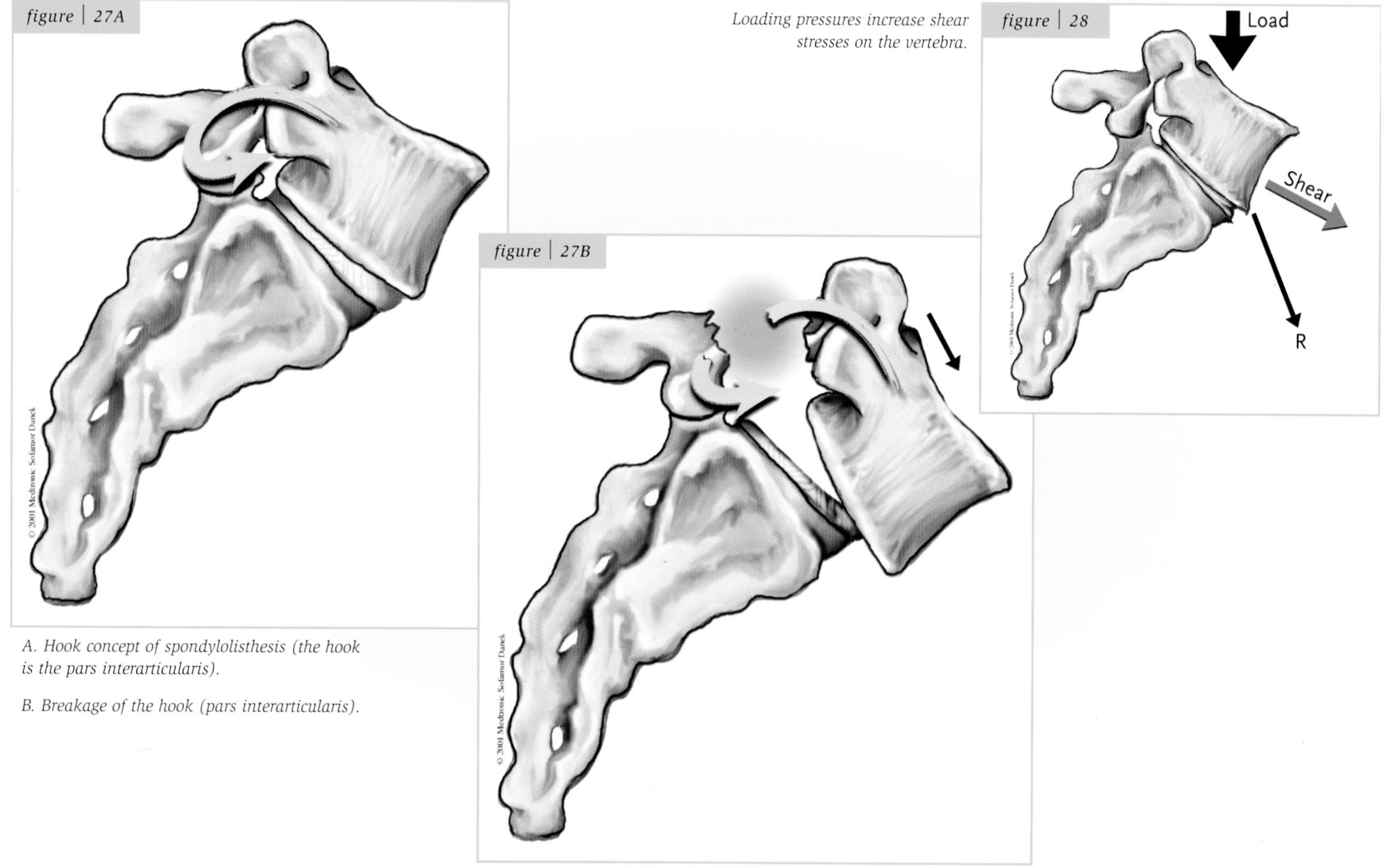

A. Hook concept of spondylolisthesis (the hook is the pars interarticularis).

B. Breakage of the hook (pars interarticularis).

Loading pressures increase shear stresses on the vertebra.

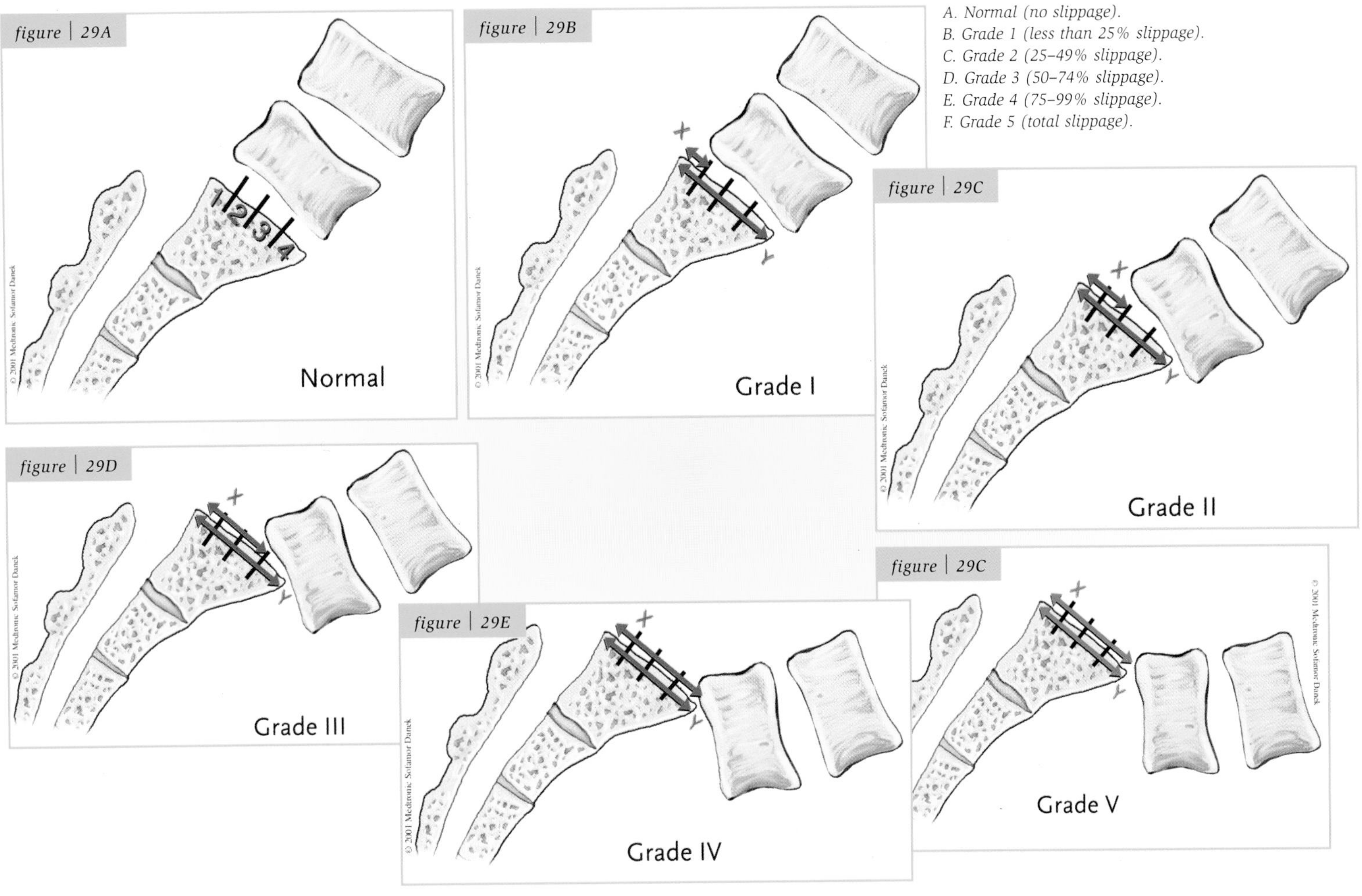

A. Normal (no slippage).
B. Grade 1 (less than 25% slippage).
C. Grade 2 (25–49% slippage).
D. Grade 3 (50–74% slippage).
E. Grade 4 (75–99% slippage).
F. Grade 5 (total slippage).

Once there is no back pain, the patient may consider returning to golf. This should be discussed with the physician and therapist. There should be no heavy lifting, bending, or pulling. Think before doing these activities. It is important to continue the exercises that one learned from the therapist. They will allow a patient to continue with everyday activities as well as with golf.

SURGERY

Only in rare cases will surgical stabilization be necessary, if the pain persists after adequate conservative treatment. When surgically treating spondylolysis and spondylolisthesis, the objective of the surgery is essentially the same. There are abnormal mechanical problems due to the pressure on the spine and symptoms brought about by the pinching of the nerves. There are several different techniques used to treat these problems. There is no single surgery that is best for everyone.

The goal of the surgery is to remove any bone or abnormal scar tissue that may be compressing a nerve, and to stabilize the spine. The mainstay of stabilization is using spine fusion. A better way to think of a spine fusion is to think about a bone graft operation. The surgeon is the farmer who harvests bone seed from the body (usually the hip, rib, or bone bank) and places it at the designated site to bring about stabilization. If bone is placed next to bone, they often grow together. If there is an abnormality between L-5 and S-1, the goal will be to place bone between the two vertebral bodies. The operation can be performed from the front (anterior) or from the back (posterior).

If the patient is medically stable and a candidate for surgery, the surgeon will review the different approaches that will bring about a long-lasting bone graft (bone fusion). In the posterior procedure, the patient is anesthetized and gently placed face down onto padded rolls. Navigational X-ray machines, fluoroscopy, may be used. An incision is made in the low back area and the muscles are moved to the side, exposing the bone. This is called an **open operation**.

After the appropriate levels of abnormality have been identified with X-rays, the surgeon may perform a lumbar laminectomy, removing the bone (the lamina or rooftop and the overgrown facet joints) that is pinching the underlying nerves. In the past, when this part of the procedure was completed, a bone graft or spine fusion was performed. This did not involve placement of any internal fixation devices. The surgeon would roughen-up the bone and then place the bone graft on the roughed-up bone in the hope that this would encourage solid bony fusion. After surgery, the patient was placed into an external body cast or body brace used to prevent movement in order to allow the bone graft to take hold. This is the same as when an arm is broken and a cast is placed on the arm to prevent movement that would disrupt healing. In young children this may be all that is needed to bring about a long-lasting bone fusion. With the advancements in metallurgy and better understanding of the biomechanical workings of the spine, however, different metal devices are now available to act as an internal cast.

Over the past two decades, there have been many ingenious internal fixation devices designed, tested and implanted into patients. These devices consist of bone screws, plates, hooks or rods (Figs. 30A and B). Initially they were made with stainless steel and did a good job, but caused troubles with the taking of post-operative X-rays. Because of the distortion and artifact production on the post-operative X-rays, new metals were needed. Titanium alloys are used today in the construction of bone screws, plates, and rods, and are compatible with

X-rays, CAT scans and MRIs. If a patient had one of these operations more than 10 years ago, he or she probably has stainless steel implants, so the doctor should be alerted.

The screws that are used in the bone implants are called pedicle screws because it is through the pedicle (walls of the vertebrae) that the screws are placed. With the guidance of X-rays, the bone screws are inserted into the middle of the pedicles on both the left and the right sides of the vertebrae. For example, if a patient needed screws placed into the L-5 vertebral body, the screws would be placed into both the right and left pedicles of L-5 and then into the S-1 (sacrum). Taking an X-ray would check the position of the screws. Once the screws are in place, they are attached to titanium bone-rods or plates that are secured to all of the screws (Fig. 31). Bone screws, rods, or plates create a stiff box that holds the vertebrae in alignment, allowing the bone to heal (Fig. 32). This is considered a type of internal brace. The bone screws may be left in place indefinitely, or removed with another operation if there have been problems or complications, *i.e.* screw movement, breakage or the screw's irritating a nerve. It is important to remember that "the operation" is the bone graft or fusion procedure, and the pedicle screws and rods are inserted to help the bone graft grow. The graft is placed between two vertebral bodies after the disc is removed. If the slippage is at the L-5/S-1 level, the L-5/S-1 disc is removed and a bone graft takes its place.

Other surgeons may choose to use an intervertebral bone graft or fusion cage that is either a hollow cylinder or square cage that is made of titanium or carbon. The cages allow the bone graft to be placed inside. The bone cage will sit between two vertebrae and replace the disc, holding the vertebrae in the correct position to allow the bone fusion to grow into solid bone. Using the L-5/S-1 example, the bone graft will grow from the L-5 vertebral body to the S-1 (sacrum). The bone cage helps to spread the two vertebral bodies apart, allowing for more room for the exiting nerves and helping to decrease the instability between the two vertebrae. The intervertebral bone cages are then further secured with bone plates, screws, or rods (Fig. 33). Placing bone grafts through a posterior (back) approach is called a **posterior interbody fusion**.

After surgery a patient may spend some days in the hospital, and may be fitted for a brace. The brace is a heavy, restricting device that is similar to wearing a barrel (Fig. 34). With the development of new fixation devices, braces are used less often and for shorter periods of time.

It will take two to four months for the bone graft to mature and for the patient to be able to increase activities. Total bone healing may not happen for one to three years. The bone healing process varies depending on the individual, his or her age, nutritional status, and smoking habits. Smokers do not do as well as the non-smoker does with the bone healing. Before leaving the hospital, the patient will have to get out of bed and walk around. The doctor will encourage walking. Returning to normal activities will be a gradual process. Heavy lifting, bending, pulling, sex, driving, and golf will be restricted. Usually after this type surgery, thoughts center on walking and bowel function. After extensive spine surgery and pain medications, the bowels may be sluggish. Once the use of pain medication has decreased and the patient is walking and eating fruits and vegetables, the bowels will begin to function properly. After posterior back surgery the patient will usually be sent to an outpatient physical therapy clinic for 6 to 12 weeks. The therapist will assign strengthening exercises and teach the patient how to do them properly.

Returning to golf after surgery will take time. The fusion will start in two to four months, so the patient needs to keep

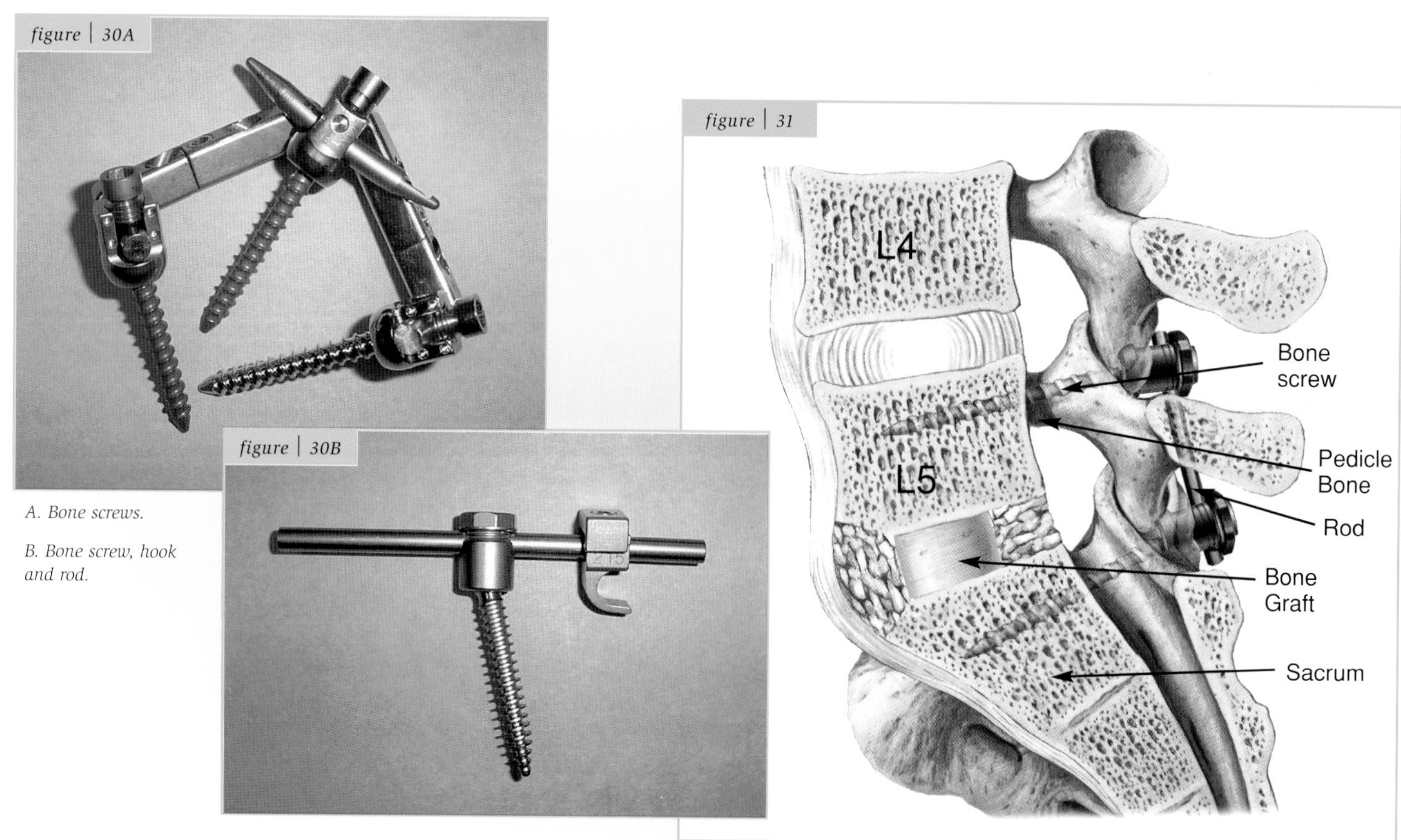

A. Bone screws.

B. Bone screw, hook and rod.

Bone screws placed into the pedicles and attached to rods.

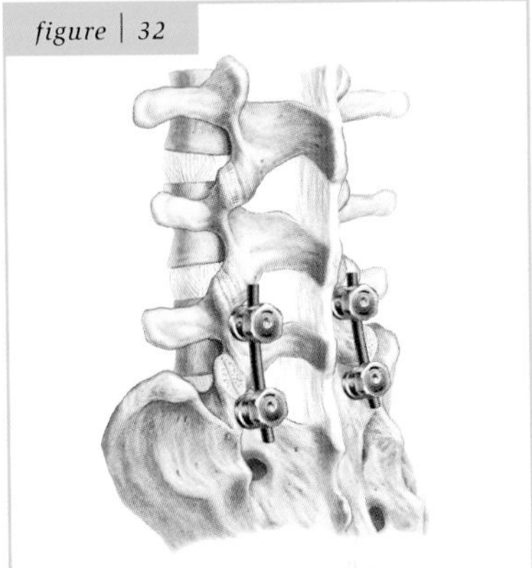

figure | 32

Posterior (back) view of bone screws attached to rods in the lumbar spine.

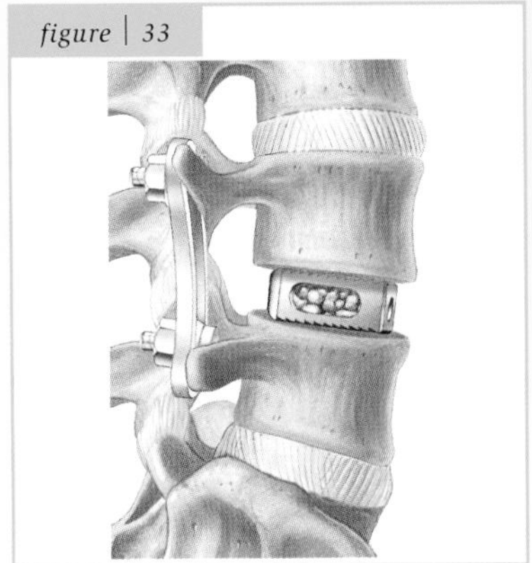

figure | 33

Side view of interbody fusion with carbon bone cage. Bone plates are placed in back of the spine.

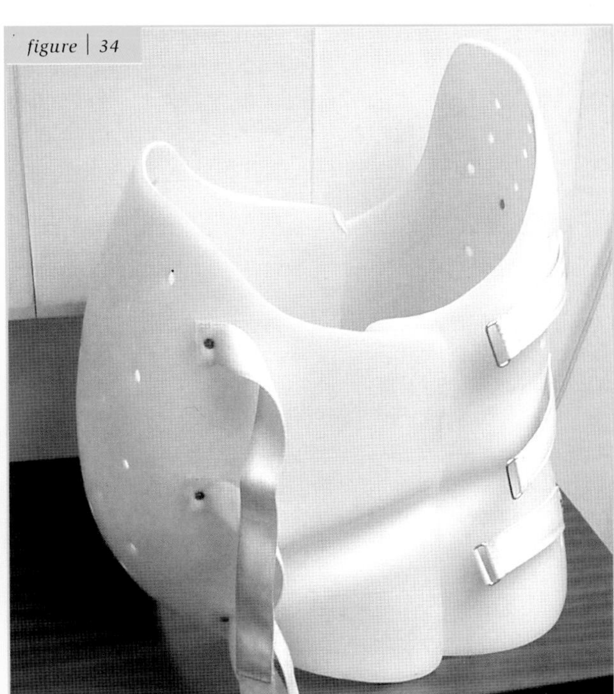

figure | 34

Plastic lumbar brace.

movements to a minimum and follow the physician's and therapist's instructions. For the first 12 weeks there will be no golf at all. Some individuals will be tempted to go out and practice their putting. This is a bad idea. The back muscles are not able to let a person stand up and bend over a putter. There should be *no* putting.

After 12 to 16 weeks, light stretching exercises are started along with abdominal and low back muscle therapy. As progress is made the patient can anticipate being able to play golf in about 24 weeks. The patient should have his or her swing re-evaluated before resuming golfing. After 24 weeks the short irons can be used at a driving range for no more than 20 to 30 minutes. If practice is overdone, a setback can occur. Some surgeons will not even allow a patient to think about golf for at least six months, while other doctors encourage a wait of as long as 9 months.

At 28 weeks, the patient may look at the mid-range irons; at 32 weeks the long irons, woods, and the putter may be considered more seriously. The putter is a very difficult club for the lumbar spine, the reason being that with the classic putter one must bend over to do the putting and to pick up the ball. Eliminate any bending by using an extended putter or by placing a ball grabber on the end of the putter. After a spine fusion operation, the practices must be done in a controlled environment. Most injuries to the back occur at the practice range due to overdoing it. The patient should practice only 20 to 30 minutes starting out, and gradually move to longer practices. After 30 weeks, when the doctor feels that the patient is doing well and tolerating practices, normal play can be resumed. However, this does not mean 18 holes; only very easy 9 holes on a relatively flat course with few sand traps and few up-and-down lies should be attempted. It is important to remember that fatigue often brings about re-injury of the low back, undoing the surgery and the rehabilitation. Playing 9 holes should be done using great control; do not try to kill the ball. Relax and enjoy the golf and the course.

Here are some things to avoid:

- Angled lies (the downhill and uphill)
- Deep bunkers
- Sand traps
- Thick ruff
- Hazards (especially water hazards)

All of the above cause a varied swing resistance that can be difficult for a recovering patient.

Sometimes when a spine surgeon is considering surgery for spondylolisthesis, he or she may suggest that the operation be done from the front, through the abdomen (an **anterior lumbar interbody fusion**). This usually involves the placement of a titanium or carbon cage, or a bone graft. The operation can be done in an open fashion (an incision is made) or it can be done with a closed operation, or a laproscopic approach. In the **open operation**, the surgeon sees the targeted disc. In the **laproscopic operation** the surgeon inserts a laproscope through a small incision and uses special TV cameras that are inserted into the abdomen that allow the surgeon to better visualize the operative site. The surgery happens through the laproscope, making this a less invasive surgery. Unfortunately, this approach may be difficult if not impossible to do in many cases. The surgeon may start the operation using the laproscope and then have to turn the operation into an open operation in order to complete the operation. With either of the above operations, the disc is removed and one or two bone cages are inserted into the disc space. A bone graft may be taken from the pelvis through a small incision and then placed into the hollow intervertebral bone cages that are placed between the two vertebrae.

Intraoperative fluoroscopy X-ray machines are used to insure the appropriate placement of the bone cages. After the front (anterior) part of the procedure has been completed, a second operation may be performed from the back (posterior). Bone screws, rods, and/or plates are inserted in the same way as in the posterior lumbar interbody fusion operation. There are other techniques now being developed that allow the posterior bone screws to be placed less invasively by using special guidance and imaging machines. The goal for both operations is to provide an environment where the bone graft will take, become solid, and last a lifetime.

Returning to golf after undergoing an anterior lumbar interbody fusion will usually follow the same guidelines as the posterior lumbar interbody fusion. However, if a less invasive procedure is used, the period of time for the recovery may be somewhat shorter because there was less muscle disruption, which allows for quicker strengthening of the muscles along with better flexibility. Regardless of the operation, anterior or posterior, open or minimally invasive, it is important for a golfer to be cautious and to heal before returning to play.

SPINAL STENOSIS

Spinal stenosis is the result of narrowing of the spinal canal. It usually occurs in individuals around the age of 60, but may occur in younger people who were born with small spinal canals. A good way to picture spinal stenosis is to use a foot and shoe analysis. The shoe is the spine, the sock is the lining over the spinal cord and nerves (dura), and the foot is the spinal cord and nerves. In spinal stenosis an individual is trying to put a large foot into a smaller size shoe. Things can get tight and cause problems. In most cases there is room between the spinal cord, nerves and the bony edges of the spinal canal. As we mature and age, this space decreases. There are many conditions that will bring about a reduction in the size of the spinal canal in the lumbar spine (low back). Overgrowth in the joints in the spine can reduce the needed space in the spine. Ligaments can harden or calcify and cause a reduction of space. Anything that narrows and causes a reduction of the spinal canal diameter can cause irritation of the nerves. If the spinal cord is located in this area, it too may be subject to pressure. In most cases of spinal stenosis there is a great deal of wear and tear in the lumbar spine from daily activities. These changes are referred to as degeneration.

A common cause of aging in the lumbar spine is the thickening of ligaments that hold the vertebrae together. Another common cause of the canal diameter's being too small is the notorious **bone spur**. Bone spurs, osteophytes, form around the joints when the joints are placed under a great deal of stress. Bulging of aging discs will also contribute to the continued narrowing of the spinal canal. The process of normal aging makes the spinal canal much smaller. In some situations, there is not enough room for the spinal cord and nerves; in the lower back exiting nerves may be irritated. The joints in the lower back tend to get larger, or hypertrophy with age (Figs. 35A and B). This is the body's attempt to decrease the stress per unit across the aging joint. When the joint overgrows, it does so at the foramen, the site where the nerve exits to travel down the legs (Fig. 36). This bony overgrowth can cause pressure and literally pinch the nerves. This all leads to pain. Another consequence of the narrowing of canal diameter is decreased blood flow to the spinal cord and the nerves. Activities such as standing, walking, or moving increase blood flow to the spine and nerves. With decreased space in the spinal canal, the blood flow may become congested, leading to further irritation of nearby nerves.

SYMPTOMS

In the beginning, most symptoms are a mild pain in the low back area. On occa-

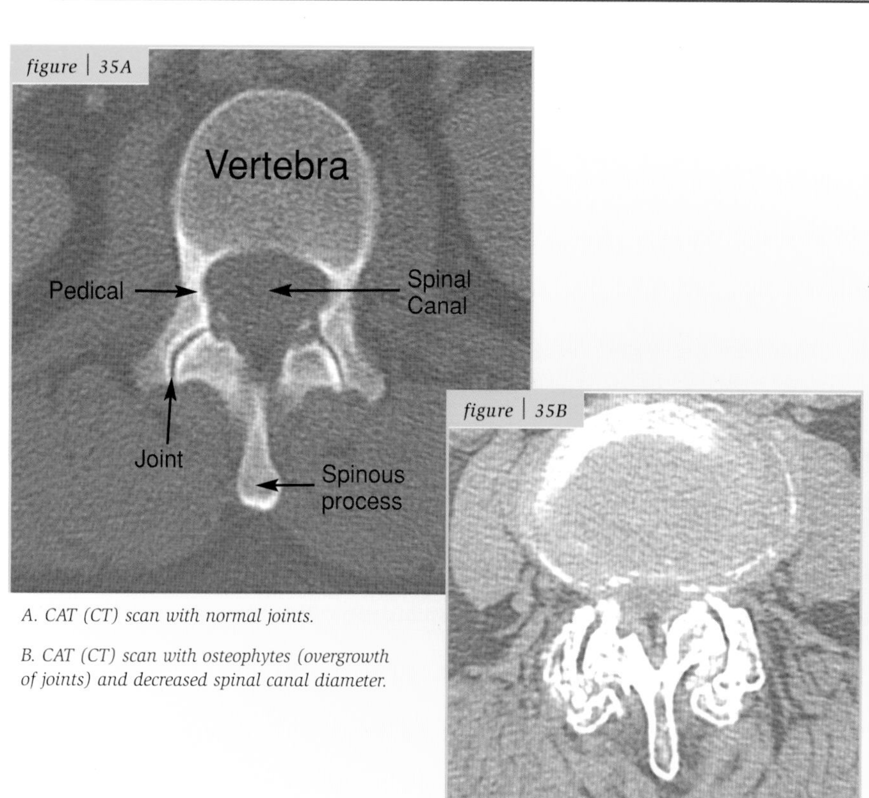

A. CAT (CT) scan with normal joints.

B. CAT (CT) scan with osteophytes (overgrowth of joints) and decreased spinal canal diameter.

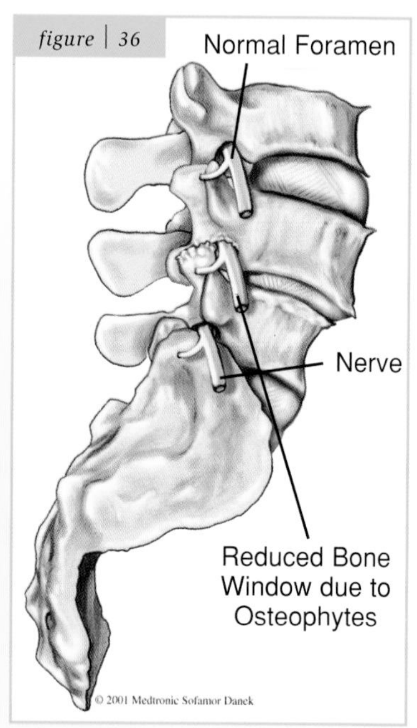

Osteophytes (bone spurs) reducing the bone window (foramen) through which nerves course.

sions the pain can become more severe and will be called moderate. The pain can be constant or it can be intermittent. It may begin in one leg and then progress into both legs. Often, it is worse with walking and better with rest. Physicians and surgeons refer to this type of symptom as **neurogenic claudication**. In some situations, there can be leg pain and no lower back pain at all. Usually there is little or no pain while sitting or lying down. Those troubled with lumbar stenosis are usually not awakened during the night from discomfort. Often, the legs will be described as being heavy, dead, or asleep. Another common finding is numbness or tingling sensations (**paresthesias**). A golfer will notice these problems while out walking the course. The patient may experience what is known as the "shopping cart syndrome" or walking along while leaning over an object (a cart) to help ease the discomfort. The patients are often flexed or "leaning over the shopping cart" and walking. Many individuals will be able to tolerate using a stationary bicycle because they are leaning forward, just as they would do with a shopping cart.

DIAGNOSIS

When an individual is no longer able to get up and walk without severe pain, then it is time to see a doctor. The first thing a physician will do is to obtain a complete history and then perform a physical examination. Before a patient sees a physician or healthcare provider, he or she may want to jot down a few notes:

- Describe the pain (dull, achy, sharp, burning).
- Does anything make it better or worse?
- Does the pain radiate into one leg or both legs?
- Does the pain radiate into other parts of the body?
- Note the intensity of the pain (try to give your pain a number between 0 and 10; 0 = No Pain, 10 = Worst Pain Ever).
- Have there been any changes in bladder, bowel or sexual function?
- Does golfing cause a problem and make the back pain worse?
- Does the awaken the patient from sleep?

The doctor will want to know if the patient was on the golf course and did something that caused the pain to start. After the history has been completed, the physician will perform a physical exam.

PHYSICAL EXAMINATION

The physical examination is an important part of trying to evaluate the possible causes of any pain and discomfort. The physician will try to determine whether there are any other causes for the pain other than those originating from the low back area. The patient will be asked to move the neck, rotate the back, and bend forward and backward to determine the range of movement of the spine. If certain movements cause pain, the patient needs to tell the physician. This will indicate a loss of movement or flexibility of spine. The doctor will look at muscles to see if muscle mass is normal and will ask the patient if he or she has experienced any twitching. The patient will be asked to move the legs, kick the legs, pull them back, and lift them up in order to test for muscle strength. The next part of the examination will be to test the sensory capabilities in the extremities by using a disposable pin. The patient will then be asked to get up and walk around, stand on the heels or toes, or walk in a tandem fashion. A reflex hammer will be used to elicit reflexes from the knee and Achilles tendon. The doctor will also palpate around the spine to evaluate for tenderness. A rectal examination may be performed. After the examination the physician may order certain radiologic diagnostic tests.

DIAGNOSTIC TESTS

Radiologic tests will depend upon what the physician suspects is causing the pain. X-rays of the lumbar spine may be obtained. These X-rays will be helpful in determining aging bone changes in the lower spine. Usually there is decreased height in the space between the intervertebral discs as well as evidence of joint overgrowth (hypertrophy). X-rays may reveal any type of bony compression fracture or any unusual movements in the bones and joints in the back. Bending forward and/or backward for X-rays are referred to as dynamic X-rays.

Some physicians may order an MRI (Magnetic Resonance Imaging) or a CAT scan (Computer Assisted Tomography). The CAT scan is an excellent test to evaluate bony changes in the spine. The CAT scanner is similar to an X-ray because they both use radioactive materials to evaluate and record pictures of the bones of the spine. During the CAT scan the patient will have to lie quietly on the table. If patients think they will be unable to do so, they should tell the physician, the radiologist, or the X-ray technician. Any movement will cause distortions in the images, thus making it difficult to evaluate. The procedure will take several minutes to complete, depending on what the physician or provider has requested.

The CAT (CT) scan produces picture-slices of the spine. The procedure is similar to taking a loaf of bread and then slicing it. Each slice will be evaluated and examined separately by the radiologist. The CAT (CT) scan will reconstruct pictures and display the spine in different views to evaluate for spinal canal narrowing (Figs. 35A and B). The CAT scan is excellent for viewing bone, but not as good at viewing soft tissue, so a myelogram may be performed to see the tissue. The radiologist or doctor will place a needle in a certain area in the lumbar spine and then inject contrast dye. The patient who is allergic to iodine or seafood must tell the doctor. This dye will allow better appreciation of the soft tissue elements than the CAT scan alone. The myelogram is done first and then followed by the CAT scan. The whole procedure is referred to as a post-myelographic CAT scan (Figs. 37A and B).

Magnetic Resonance Imaging, commonly called MRI, is a test similar to the CAT scan. The patient will have to lie on a table. If the patient is having pain and cannot lie still, the study will be of little value. The MRI does not use radiation; rather the images are created by using magnetic and radio waves. The MRI will create pictures in slices that will resemble a CAT (CT) scan. The MRI shows soft tissue better and the CAT (CT) scan shows the bone better (Figs. 38A and B). The MRI will often show soft tissue abnormalities in the nerves or ligaments and will help to rule out any kind of tumor of the spine. The MRI is an excellent test to show the loss of water in a maturing disc and any evidence of a protruding or a herniated disc into the spinal canal. Stenosis can also be seen with narrowing of the spinal canal and the contents within the canal, *i.e.* spinal cord or nerves (Fig. 39A and B). If the patient is claustrophobic, the MRI will cause a great deal of anxiety because the MRI is a long narrow tunnel. There are MRI machines that are more comfortable for people with claustrophobia. These MRIs are called open MRIs. The MRI takes several minutes to perform. Physicians use the MRI and the CAT scan to compliment each other. In many situations, a high quality MRI will eliminate any need for a myelogram.

TREATMENT

Treatment for lumbar stenosis varies with each patient. The radiologic studies, X-rays, MRI, and CAT (CT) scans will demonstrate the degree of the stenosis and whether surgery is needed. Spinal stenosis is a slow progressive problem that didn't occur overnight. Other factors are considered in the treatment of spinal stenosis, such as other medical conditions. Many patients will not need any surgery; they learn to adapt to their problem. Conservative or non-surgical care is the first form of treatment for this form of back problem. A mild pain medication may be prescribed to ease pain. Some of these medications include non-steroidal anti-inflammatory medications. In some situations an epidural corticosteroid injection may give excellent relief. These injections help to decrease the inflammation around the nerves. The epidural injection involves the placement of a long spinal needle into the low back area of greatest concern. To use the shoe and foot analogy, the physician will insert the needle through the shoe but will not go through the sock. This space between the shoe and sock is called the epidural space. It is in this space that the medication will be injected. The medication will travel around the nerves and promote a reduction in the inflamed tissues. Epidural steroids may not work for everyone. For some there may be no relief of pain; for others it is very helpful. The individual will be able to have only three or four of these injections per year. The epidural injections may be the best avenue of care for patients who have other existing serious medical problems. A few select patients who are not surgical candidates and for whom the epidural injections have failed may be candidates for percutanous spinal cold stimulator placement. This means that a special electrical stimulator is inserted through the skin using a special tube. This type of therapy is tried only after the aforementioned therapies have been tried and have failed. For some patients, a rigid lumbar orthosis, or brace, may be recommended. The patient should never sleep in this brace. Many physicians do not feel comfortable using this brace over a long period of time because it may have adverse effects on the muscles, leading to the loss of muscle mass and muscle atrophy. Muscle loss will adversely affect the long-term outcome of therapy and the ability of the golfer to play.

SURGERY

In a small number of patients who do not get better with the conservative therapy, surgery may be considered. Surgery becomes an option if the patient is medically cleared for surgery and the benefits of the surgery outweigh the risks. Surgery is also recommended when the patient's lifestyle has been greatly compromised, he or she is no longer able to walk without pain, and the enjoyment of life and golf is greatly reduced. Other indications for surgery are weakness and/or the loss of strength in the legs, loss or changes in the function of the urinary bladder, the bowels, or in sexual ability. Any trouble controlling the bladder, bowels, or a history of incontinence may mean there is the need for surgical intervention. It is important for the patient to remember that back surgery is a major operation and has all of the complications and risks of any surgical therapies. Ultimately, the decision to have spine surgery rests with the patient, with the help of his physician and input from family. If the patient has experienced any of the above problems, then surgery may be considered.

In most situations, the patient will go to the hospital the day of the planned surgery. Before surgery, nurses and anesthesiologists will evaluate the patient in a holding area. Once in the operating room the patient is administered medications. After the anesthetic has been given, the patient is gently placed onto the operating table on special cushions that are positioned under the chest and abdomen in order to help prevent compression. The operation is called a **lumbar laminectomy**. This means that the lamina will be removed from the bony elements in the lumbar spine (Fig. 40). After appropriate washing and draping of the area, an incision is made in the low back. The muscles are carefully moved to the sides,

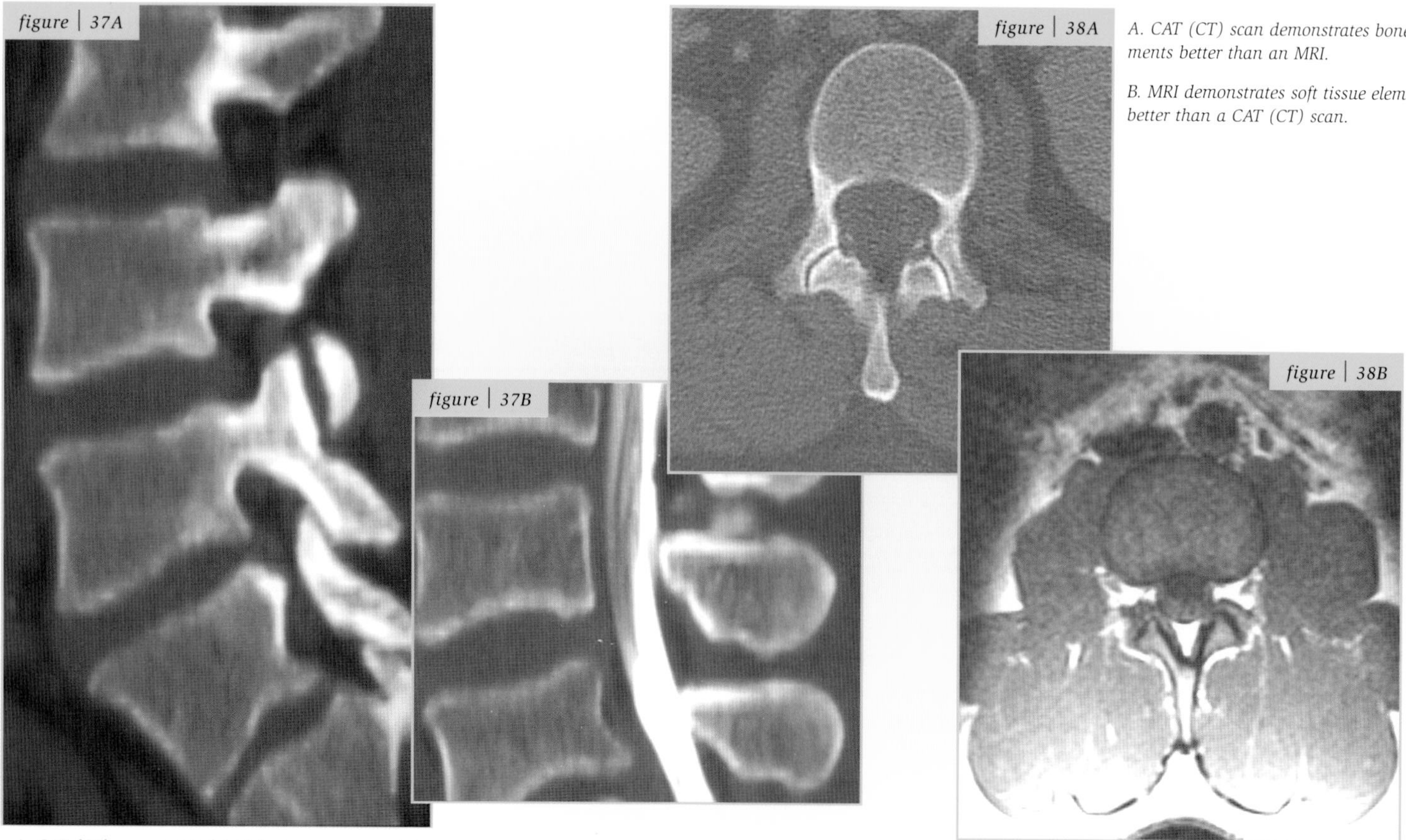

A. CAT (CT) scan: Lateral (side) view–no contrast dye.

B. CAT (CT) scan after myelogram.

A. CAT (CT) scan demonstrates bone elements better than an MRI.

B. MRI demonstrates soft tissue elements better than a CAT (CT) scan.

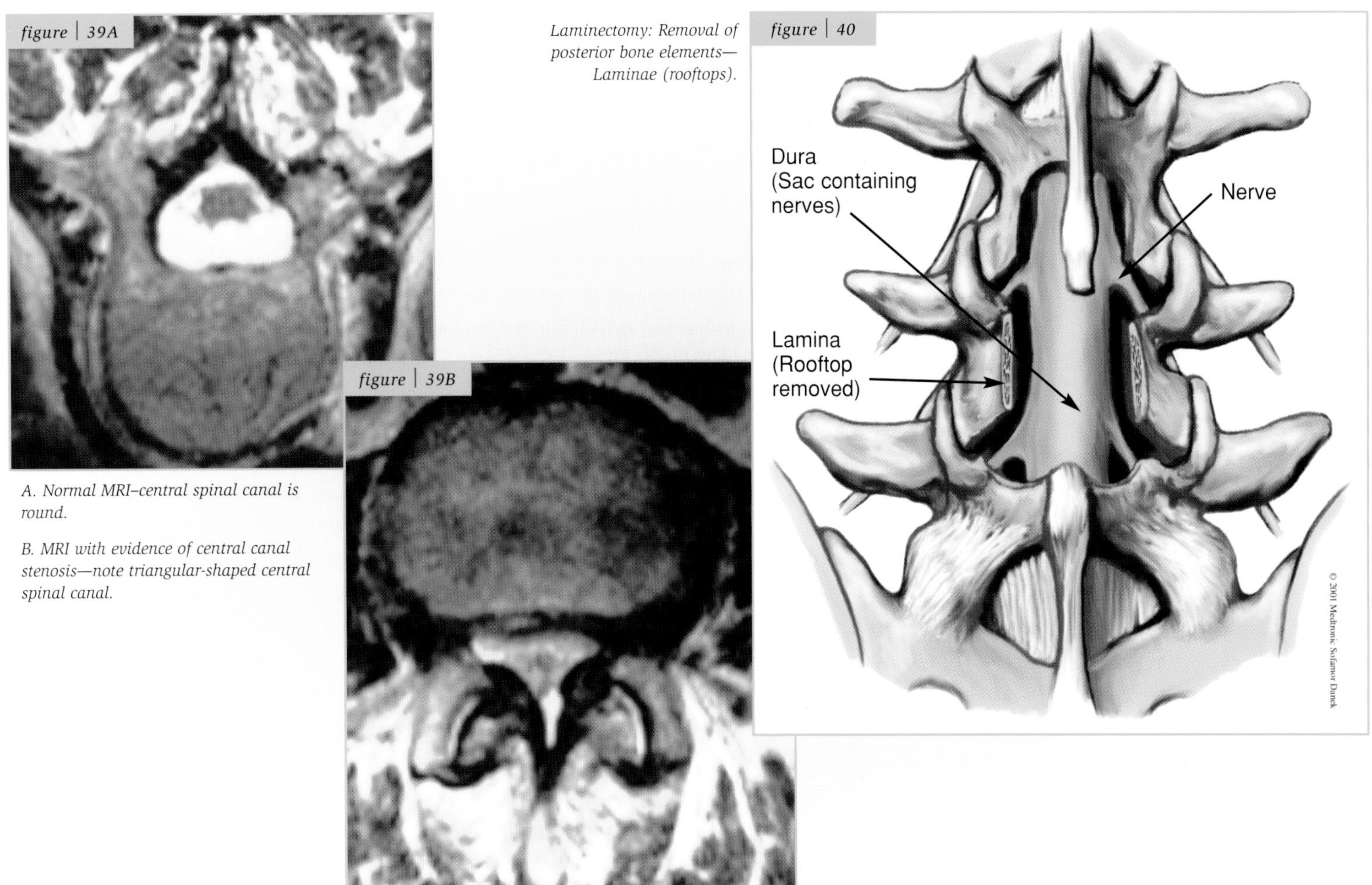

A. Normal MRI–central spinal canal is round.

B. MRI with evidence of central canal stenosis—note triangular-shaped central spinal canal.

Laminectomy: Removal of posterior bone elements—Laminae (rooftops).

exposing the underlying laminae (bony rooftops). Once the targeted laminae are identified, they are removed using a combination of different bone-removing instruments. Usually in a laminectomy only the laminae are removed, but at times small portions of nearby joints will also be removed in order to expose and resect underlying bone spurs. Removing the lamina will enlarge the spinal canal and give the nerves and spinal cord room. Using the foot and shoe analogy, the surgeon cannot give the patient a new shoe (spine). What the surgeon will do is remove the top of the shoe, exposing the underlying sock that contains the foot. In most situations there will not be a need to open up the sock (dura) itself. The surgeon will remove only the necessary amount of bone. If too much of the top of the shoe is removed, there will not be enough support left to walk around in the shoe. If this happens, the patient will need more involved spine surgery that will involve the placement of bone screws and bone rods along with a bone grafting procedure. At the conclusion of the operation, a special dressing will be placed at the incision site. The patient will be turned back to the face-up position and placed onto a surgical bed. Many times the patient will be awakened in the operating room and then taken to the recovery room and observed until the anesthesiologist and surgeon feel that the patient is stable enough to go to a hospital room. The length of the hospital stay will depend on the type of surgery and how the patient responded to the surgery. It is important that the patient not compare himself to others who have undergone a similar operation. Every person heals at a different rate. The surgeon will allow the patient get out of bed in a day or so. The patient may or may not need physical therapy. It is not unusual to experience muscle pain after this procedure; spine muscles were moved to the side in order to expose the laminae. Some people may need a brace or corset after surgery, depending on the surgeon's experience or preference. To aid the patient's efforts to get around, the surgeon may also recommend physical therapy shortly after surgery. This type of spine surgery is a major operation and it will take time to get better. Patients should carefully follow the instructions that were given by the physical therapist, physician, and surgeon.

An exercise program will be started and will be beneficial for recovery from lumbar laminectomy surgery. Physical therapy and exercise programs will be needed prior to returning to golf and will focus on increasing strength, flexibility, posture and coordination. The results from lumbar spinal stenosis surgery can be very rewarding. Guidelines for returning to playing golf after this type of surgery are the same as those for returning to play after surgery for spondylolisthesis. For some patients, the time to return to play will actually be shorter.

SACROILIAC JOINT SYNDROME AND COCCYDYNIA

CHAPTER 9

T. Glenn Pait, M.D., F.A.C.S.

Based on the number of people who have shared their back-pain experiences with me, I must be one of the few golfers who hasn't suffered from debilitating pain in that part of my anatomy, although the ailments I have been afflicted with will some day make good content for another book.

Golf is one of the toughest sports on the spine, and the fear of developing back pain is a motivating factor for me to spend a lot of time in the gym. The golf swing is an unnatural movement, and by all accounts the human body is not well suited for the game. While I freely admit that I don't know all the inner workings of the spine, I do believe the best course of action in preventing injury to the back is to stabilize the lumbar spine with a solid muscular structure.

The lumbar spine seems to be the area of the back that most golfers have trouble with, and this may be because the muscles surrounding the lumbar, known as the thoracolumbar fascia, are perhaps the most difficult muscles in the body to develop. This muscle has been shown to be virtually unreachable by traditional equipment, even the back-extension machines found in most gyms. What's more, even bodybuilders and strongmen who have been tested are often found to have a weak muscular structure of the lower back. Therefore, because of this muscle's inherent weakness, support muscles such as the abs, glutes, and hamstrings, all of which are relatively easy to exercise, must be maintained in top physical condition. Other than finding the limited and expensive pieces of equipment designed to specifically work the thoracolumbar fascia, there is no substitute for keeping these other areas in top shape.

One other thought is that if you can shed those few extra pounds you might be carrying, your back will thank you.

Greg Norman

SACROILIAC JOINT (SI) SYNDROME

The sacroiliac joint (SI joint) is one of two large joints in the pelvis. It is the joint that connects the sacrum (end of the spine) to the large pelvic bone known as the ilium (Figs. 1A and B). The SI joints literally connect the spine to the pelvis. This is a very special type of joint in that it is involved in weight-bearing activities. It is a shock absorber for the spine. It is a unique joint in that it is made up of two different kinds of cartilage, which rub against each other. The surfaces of the SI joint come together like pieces of a puzzle (Fig. 2). This is important because the SI joint helps in walking and golfing. It does so by a self-locking mechanism; this is where the puzzle pieces come together and allow us to move. The joint on one side locks as weight is transferred from one leg to another. The other side allows stretching, so as we move with one leg, the SI joint puzzle pieces come together and lock. On the other side the SI joint allows stretching. It is this locking and stretching mechanism that aids in walking.

The sacroiliac joint is often an overlooked source of low back pain. Dysfunction or inflammation in the joint can cause localized pain that may mimic other common causes of low back pain. It can either exist as a pain generator all by itself, or may actually be associated with other spine problems. The demands of axial load-sharing placed upon the SI joint are also common demands on other parts of the spine; therefore, it's not uncommon for more than one site to be affected by changes of aging.

The most common cause of SI joint dysfunction is from an injury such as a fall or slip while pushing or swinging any item. Any traumatic event that stretches or tears ligaments around the pelvis can lead to SI joint problems (Fig. 3). Repetitive motion such as a golf swing can lead to wear and tear of the SI joint. Over time, the joint will become inflamed. This sets up the perfect environment for arthritis. In some people, the SI joint problems arise from a birth defect. The bones that comprise the sacrum never grow or fuse together correctly or totally, thus a so-called false joint develops. As the individual grows, becomes more active, and engages in sporting activities, he or she has a greater chance of having SI joint problems than others may.

Women have more SI joint problems than men; the reason is pregnancy. Hormones of pregnancy cause connective tissues in the body to relax. This tissue relaxation is needed to allow the pelvis to stretch during childbirth. This pelvic stretching causes the SI joint to become overly mobile. If the joint remains more active or mobile than normal, changes develop which can lead to dysfunction.

Another cause of SI joint dysfunction or pain is infection. Infections spread to the SI joint through the blood system. Predisposing conditions for infection in the SI joint include trauma, pregnancy, and infection elsewhere in the body, a weakened immune system, and any other condition that weakens the body and exposes it to infections. Blood circulation in the SI joint is somewhat sluggish; therefore, this is an excellent place for infection. Infection in this area is often referred to as **osteomyelitis** (bone infection). With this condition, any type of weight-bearing or hip movement will cause severe pain.

Other medical conditions that can cause SI joint pain include gout or pseudogout (false gout), tumors, and different types of arthritis.

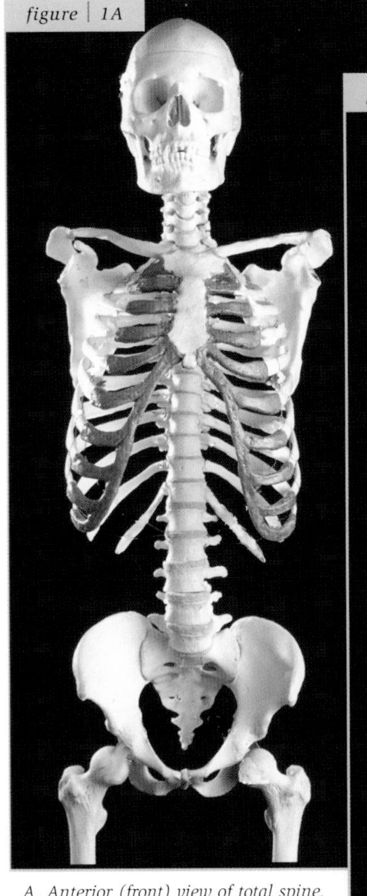

figure | 1A

figure | 1B

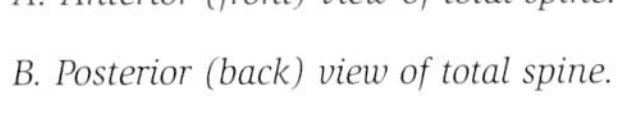

A. Anterior (front) view of total spine.

B. Posterior (back) view of total spine.

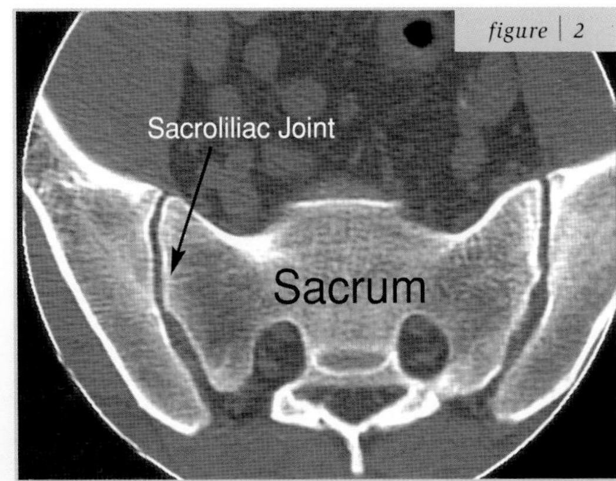

figure | 2

CAT (CT) scan of the sacroiliac joints; joints come together like puzzle pieces.

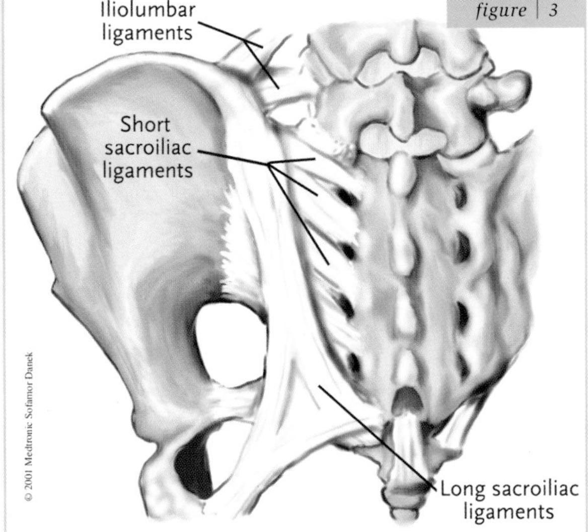

figure | 3

Posterior (back) view of ligaments of sacroiliac joints.

Sacroiliac joint dysfunction can cause many symptoms. The pain is usually only on one side (unilateral), and is worsened by bending, prolonged sitting, or traveling. Often the pain is alleviated by standing and walking. The pain can be sharp, dull, or constantly aching. It may also be referred or travel to the buttocks, groin, or back of the thigh. Sometimes the pain is noted even below the knee. Some SI joint sufferers report numbness, tingling and a burning sensation into the buttocks and the leg.

All these symptoms are very similar to symptoms caused by the facet joint, arthritis, stenosis (lumbar spine narrowing), disc herniations, and tumors (masses), to just name a few. Therefore, a doctor is needed to help determine if the problem is truly arising from the SI joint. In order to further evaluate the SI joint, the doctor will obtain a complete history and physical examination. A common physical finding on the examination is tenderness over the SI joint. The doctor may also perform several other different types of maneuvers to provoke pain by mechanically stressing the SI joint. The physician will test the movement of the hip and legs in order to determine the pain generator. A positive test is a test that will produce pain. Such a test is only significant when correlated with the history and other physical findings during the examination.

Special blood tests are ordered by a doctor to evaluate for an infection in the joint. Such tests usually include a complete blood count and an erythrocyte sedimentation rate. X-rays may be obtained to evaluate the bony elements surrounding the SI joint. However, the notation of joint changes on a plane x-ray is useless unless correlated with the patient's history and physical examination. This is because some 25% of all individuals over the age of 50 will have abnormal-appearing SI joints. The SI joint is involved in a great deal of wear and tear of living; therefore, over time, it demonstrates changes of maturing or aging.

Radionuclide scans may better reveal evidence of an inflammation or an infection than plane x-rays. Radionuclide testing will also help to reveal whether or not a tumor is present. Such abnormalities usually appear on the bone scan as hot spots. Computed axial tomography (CAT scan) will clearly demonstrate any bulge or soft tissue abnormalities of the sacroiliac joint. Magnetic resonance imaging (MRI) may be performed to demonstrate the presence of any abnormal soft tissue. In certain situations, the physician may need to better appreciate this very complex large joint. The doctor may do so by using a fluoroscopic injection into the SI joint. The doctor will inject the painful SI joint with a local numbing anesthetic medication. The SI joint is fairly deep under the buttocks, and it is covered by some rather large muscles. Therefore, it's very difficult to inject actually into the SI joint without some type of radiological guidance. A fluoroscope is a special type of x-ray machine that will allow the doctor to place the needle into the correct site. Sometimes this can be done using a CAT (CT) scan to help guide the positioning of the needle. Once the needle is in the correct position, an anesthetic is injected into the joint. If the pain goes away, this may indicate that the SI joint is indeed involved in the production of pain and may actually itself be the so-called "pain generator." The doctor may also choose to place a cortisone (steroid) injection into the SI joint. The cortisone is a very powerful type of anti-inflammatory medication that will help to reduce inflammation caused by arthritis. For some patients, the SI joint injection will provide long-lasting relief and they may not need further treatment. For others, the benefits may be short-lived.

The treatment for sacroiliac joint syndrome is to restore the joint to a more normal state, which will hopefully bring resolution of the discomfort. The treatment for a new onset of SI joint discomfort is rest. The patient will be advised to avoid all arduous activities or movements that bring about discomfort. This means—no golf. For the acute discomfort at the SI joint, ice may be beneficial. It's important when placing ice that it only be placed for approximately 20 minutes, and it should never be placed directly onto the skin. Placing ice directly onto the skin will damage the skin; therefore, the ice must be placed into a protective sleeve. The ice will help to control pain caused by inflammation. The ice works by causing vasoconstriction, which means it narrows the blood vessels and therefore reduces the blood flow to the painful site. Some physicians and physical therapists will use ice massage to help decrease the discomfort. Ice massage is done by rubbing an ice cube over the tender site. This is entirely different from putting ice over the tender site and leaving it. During the ice massage, the ice cube is actually in constant movement; therefore, there is less chance of damaging the underlying skin. An easy way to perform an ice massage is to take a paper cup and fill it with water; the cup should be placed into a freezer. Once the water has frozen, the edge of the cup can be peeled away revealing the underlying ice. Don't take the entire cup away; the bottom of the cup will be used as a handle or handgrip to better apply the ice. The ice massage should only continue for approximately 3 to 5 minutes or until the skin begins to feel numb and the pain subsides.

For some individuals, the ice will actually cause more pain; these individuals may wish to try to using heat. Heat causes vasodilation, just the opposite of the cold. Vasodilation means that the blood vessels are enlarged. Increasing the diameter of the blood vessels allows more blood to flow to the painful SI joint. Increased blood supply to the given area will increase the oxygen, which helps in the healing process. Heat is usually applied in the form of a hot pack or a heating pad. It's very important not to fall asleep using a hot pack or heating pad for fear that, if the heating packs are left unattended, they may cause injury or burns to the skin. Another excellent way to provide heat to a painful site is in a warm shower or bath. And some individuals find that using topical creams that increase the blood supply to the skin can also be very beneficial as well. If the discomfort is not alleviated with the above-mentioned therapies, the physician may order physical therapy, which may involve the use of ultrasound. An ultrasound machine produces a high frequency sound wave that changes to heat as it passes deeper into the body tissues. Ultrasound allows a physical therapist to reach deep-seated tissues that are more than two inches below the surface of the skin. Another form of therapy that may be helpful for SI joint dysfunction is **massage therapy**. Massage therapy will allow muscles to relax and also increase the circulation of blood to a painful site.

Physical therapy is needed to plan a series of mobilizations and manipulations and pelvic muscle strengthening exercises, which will help to stabilize and strengthen the unstable sacroiliac joint. An exercise program is very important for any patient with an SI joint dysfunction or syndrome. The exercise program is designed to promote trunk and hip flexibility and hamstring strengthening. Joint mobilization or manipulation will also be of added value to SI joint syndrome sufferers. Physical therapy is the keystone for long-term stabilization of a dysfunctional SI joint. Throughout the course of treatment for the SI joint, medications may be very helpful. The most commonly used medication is a non-steroidal anti-inflammatory drug. These medications often benefit and will complement other treatments. The non-steroidal anti-inflammatory medications may be used for as long as two weeks, or longer if recommended by a physician.

It's very important that a patient with an SI joint syndrome be taught exercises that he or she will be able to continue on an independent basis. Exercises will help to improve muscle strength and endurance. Usually, in approximately six weeks, an individual with an SI joint syndrome will improve. In certain individuals, various types of orthotic devices (braces) have been prescribed. For a very small group of patients in whom no form of medical therapy has brought about any type of abatement of their discomfort, surgery has been considered. Surgery in this particular situation usually involves placement of a bone graft (fusion) and internal fixation devices (bone screws). However, patients undergoing surgery for sacroiliac joint problems are very few, and before a patient undergoes such surgical intervention, a second or third opinion by other doctors is strongly recommended.

COCCYDYNIA (PAIN IN THE TAILBONE)

The coccyx is the end of the spine. It is formed by the fusion of the last 3 to 5 rudimentary vertebrae. The first coccygeal vertebra has a base for articulation with the sacrum. The other bones in the coccyx are only remnants; the last coccyx vertebra is only a mere button of bone (Fig. 4).

Coccydynia is truly a tailbone pain (Fig. 5). The discomfort is located between the buttocks. There are two types of coccydynia. One is called **true coccydynia**, and the other is **pseudococcydynia**, or false coccydynia. The most common cause of true coccydynia is trauma. The trauma is usually a fall. Patients either slip or fall backward and land on their buttocks, causing a fracture of the coccyx bones. Another cause of coccydynia is childbirth. In fact, postpartum (after birth) coccydynia is a well-known problem. Other causes of coccydynia include infections, pilonidal cysts, tumors, and anal intercourse. Prolonged pressure due to poor posture while sitting has also caused pain in the coccyx. In many cases no cause can be found.

Pseudococcydynia is a false tailbone pain. This means that the pain is felt in the coccyx area, but is actually located elsewhere and is referred to the coccyx. Irritation or inflammation of pelvic structures may cause false coccydynia. Such irritation may arise from infections, disc herniations, inflammation of the bladder, prostate, urethra or cervix, and tumors of the rectum, bladder or prostate.

The most common symptom of coccydynia is pain. The pain is worsened by sitting or changing positions. Usually, lying down relieves the discomfort. Pain that awakens an individual from sleep may suggest a more serious problem, such as a tumor. In fact, any pain of the spine that awakens an individual from a night's sleep must be evaluated. Tumors of the spine will often disturb an individual's rest at night.

The first step to a diagnosis of coccydynia is a complete and thorough history and physical examination. A history of falling onto one's tailbone certainly is very strongly suggestive of a fracture of the coccyx. The physical examination will include not only the regular testing of muscle strength and the sensory examination using pins, but also a complete rectal examination. Rectal examination is needed to palpate the prostate and rectum. A digital examination will help to rule out a tumor or growth in the rectum. A female patient will need to undergo a pelvic examination to look for a mass or tumor in the vagina or uterus. For true coccydynia, the rectal examination may elicit pain from the movement of the coccyx.

X-rays of the sacrum and coccyx may reveal a fracture, dislocation, or bony

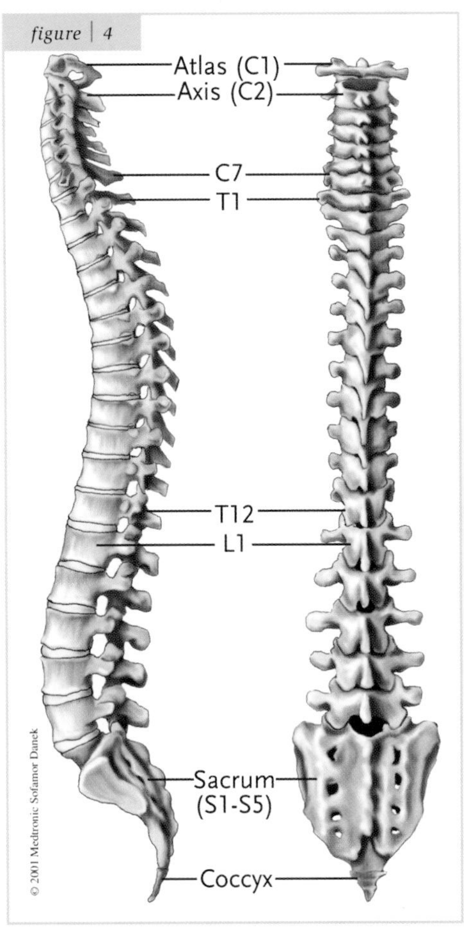

A. Lateral (side) view of spine.

B. Posterior (back) view of spine.

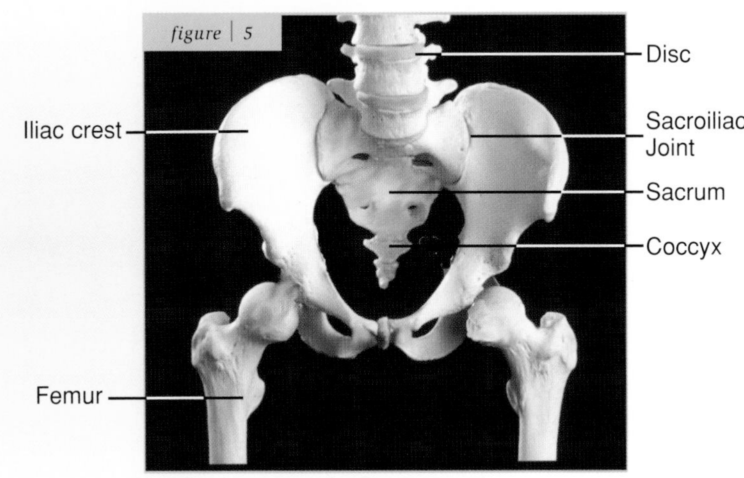

Anterior (front) view of coccyx (true tailbone).

abnormalities in the coccyx and nearby sacral area. In some situations, a radionuclide bone scan can be helpful, and a recent fracture or area of inflammation may reveal itself as a so-called hot spot on the scan. Computed axial tomography (CAT scan) with special reconstruction views may also demonstrate bony abnormalities of the coccyx area. Magnetic resonance imaging (MRI) is less often used; however, if there is suspected pseudococcydynia, the MRI will be helpful to evaluate for any tumors or other soft tissue abnormalities.

One of the first lines of treatment for coccydynia is use of a medication to reduce the inflammation and discomfort. One of the most commonly used medications is the anti-inflammatory. There are now numerous medications that are available in drugstores and pharmacies. It's best to check with your doctor or pharmacist before using such medications because of potential harmful side effects, particularly stomach bleeding. A physician may prescribe a newer type of anti-inflammatory medication. Some of the newer anti-inflammatory medications may be gentler on the stomach. Anti-inflammatory medication is usually given for 7 to 14 days or, in certain situations, longer if the physician feels that it would be helpful. Patients with coccydynia are also instructed about seating modifications. Often this involves the use of an inflatable doughnut or a well-padded seat when sitting. Some patients with persistent, recalcitrant coccydynia are treated with a local steroid or cortisone injection. In certain patients, injection of steroids may provide long-lasting relief and benefits. For a small group of patients who have intractable, incapacitating coccydynia that does not respond to conservative measures, surgical therapy may be considered. Surgery in this particular situation is a **coccygectomy**. The outcome with surgery varies from patient to patient. Surgical intervention should never be considered as the initial form of therapy for coccydynia, and it is wise to obtain a second surgical opinion before undergoing such a procedure. Patients who suffer from recalcitrant post-traumatic coccydynia appear to do better than those with other causes of coccydynia. Women suffering postpartum coccydynia had acceptable outcomes and, in certain studies, 75% of these patients improved. The patients who experience idiopathic (not knowing what causes it) coccydynia did less well with surgical intervention.

Usually, coccydynia responds to conservative therapy, and when the pain in the tailbone resolves an individual will be able to return to golf. In fact, some individuals are able to continue to play golf when they have coccydynia; they just cannot sit in a golf cart. For these golfers walking is just what the doctor ordered.

SPINAL DEFORMITIES AND THEIR EFFECT UPON GOLF

CHAPTER 10

Richard E. McCarthy, M.D.

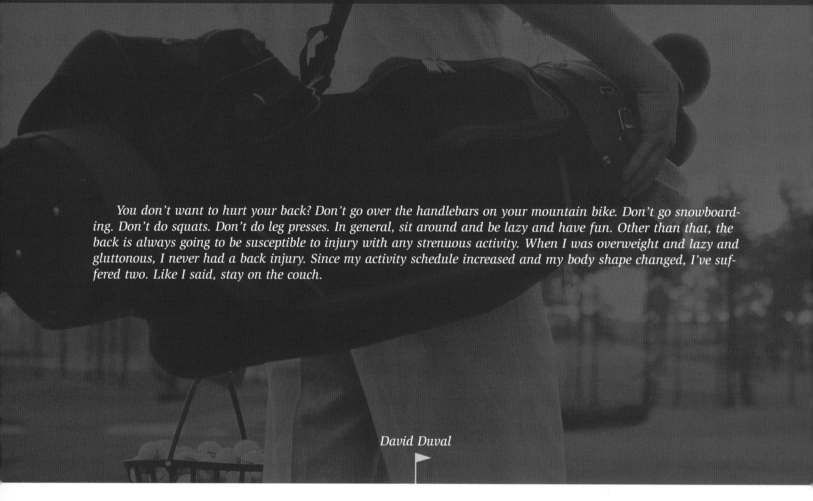

You don't want to hurt your back? Don't go over the handlebars on your mountain bike. Don't go snowboarding. Don't do squats. Don't do leg presses. In general, sit around and be lazy and have fun. Other than that, the back is always going to be susceptible to injury with any strenuous activity. When I was overweight and lazy and gluttonous, I never had a back injury. Since my activity schedule increased and my body shape changed, I've suffered two. Like I said, stay on the couch.

David Duval

Golf is a game requiring the coordination of precise movements of the musculoskeletal system (bones and muscles) in order to bring a powerful force to project a ball down the fairway. The full potential of the musculoskeletal system is brought to bear in this endeavor. Spinal deformities greatly impact upon the balance, motion, and alignment of the musculoskeletal system in the wonderful game of golf.

The purpose of the spine is to align the individual in space, to act as a protective column for transmission of information to and from the brain through the spinal cord and throughout the body and extremities, and to act as a framework upon which to attach the numerous muscles required to coordinate and power the individual (Fig. 1). The vertebral column consists of the soft tissue structures, such as discs and ligaments, that hold the vertebral bones together in proper alignment (Fig. 2A and B). Each individual vertebral bone is joined to the adjacent one by two movable joints in the back (facet joints) and the relatively immobile segment in the front known as the disc (Fig. 3). The disc consists of an annulus, a tough fibrous circular structure that surrounds a soft gelatinous center, and the nucleus pulposus, which acts as a shock absorber between the bones (Fig. 4). This shock absorber system resists excessive force placed upon the vertebral column (Fig. 5). Discs, of course, can wear out in time and produce degeneration of both the anterior vertebral column and the posterior facet joints.

The proper alignment of the vertebral column in space includes a normal forward curvature of the upper cervical area of the vertebral column known as cervical lordosis. Below this in the thoracic spine, there is a gentle sloping in the posterior direction referred to as kyphosis. These normal curves are balanced by a reversal of this curve in the lower lumbar spine, referred to as lumbar lordosis or swayback (Fig. 6). The balance produced by these normal curves holds the head properly aligned over the torso and the pelvis. The vertebral column joins the pelvis at the sacroiliac joint, the junction between the sacrum, the lowest portion of the vertebral column, and the iliac wing that is the broad portion of the pelvis just below the waist (Fig. 7). Any change in this spinal alignment that produces an alteration in this balance and alignment is referred to as a **spinal deformity**. Too much forward curvature in the alignment of the vertebral column is referred to as **kyphosis** (Fig. 7). Too much side deviation and curvature is known as **scoliosis** (Fig. 8). The excessive swayback that can occur in the low portion of the spine characteristically is referred to as excessive **lordosis.** An example of thoracic kyphosis can be seen in elderly individuals who have experienced compression, wedge-shaped fractures of the vertebral bodies in their elderly years secondary to weakened osteoporotic bone coupled with minor trauma (Fig. 9).

Scoliosis produces a spinal deformity characterized by a frontal plain curve to the side that occurs in approximately two percent of the population. Many individuals have "a touch of scoliosis" that does not amount to a significant curvature, and for many the curvature is so small that it is not even recognized by the individual. The most common type of scoliosis is referred to as **idiopathic** scoliosis and is inherited genetically. There is no correlation between the severity of the scoliosis curvature in the parents and their child. A mother or father with a minor degree of curvature can have a child with a significant curvature and vice versa.

Scoliosis can occur anywhere in the vertebral column, but is most commonly

Numerous muscles attach to the spine to bring about movement.

figure | 1

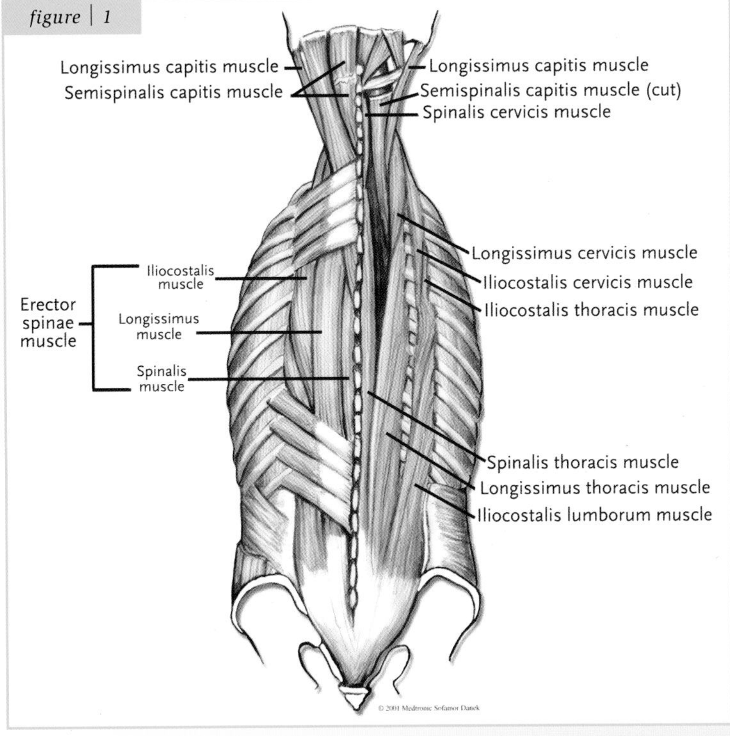

figure | 2A

figure | 2B

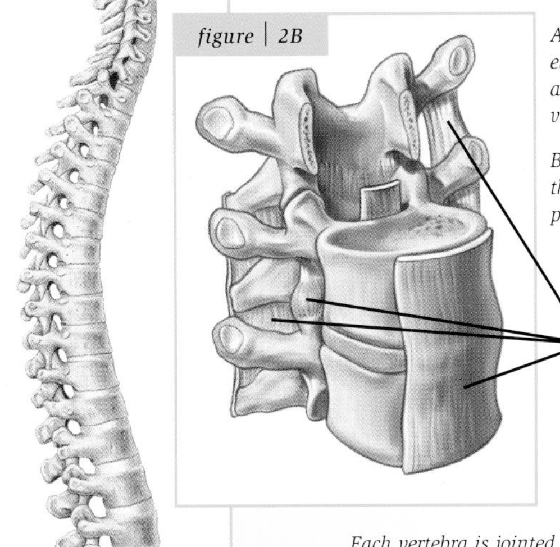

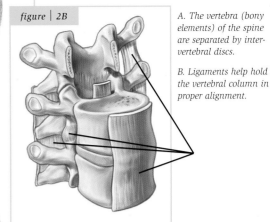

A. The vertebra (bony elements) of the spine are separated by intervertebral discs.

B. Ligaments help hold the vertebral column in proper alignment.

Each vertebra is jointed to the adjacent one by facet joints and the intervertebral disc.

figure | 3

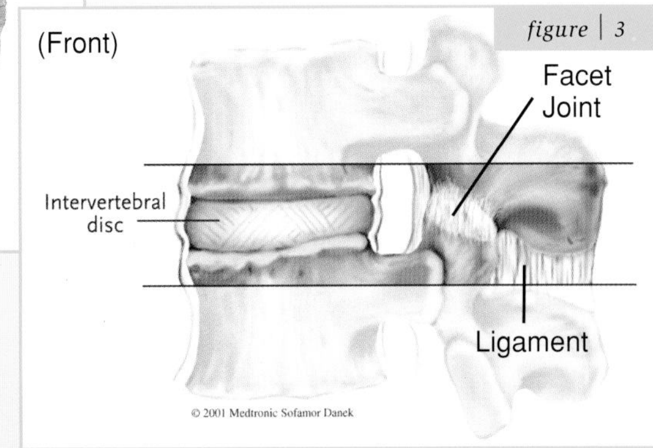

figure | 4

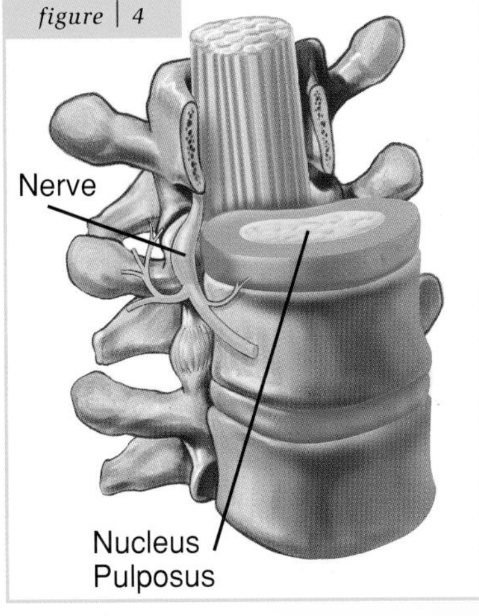

The annulus surrounds the nucleus pulposus.

figure | 5

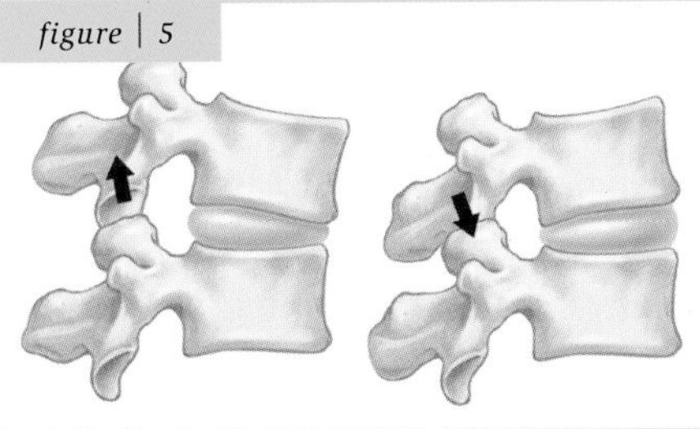

The intervertebral disc acts like a shock absorber to resist loading forces.

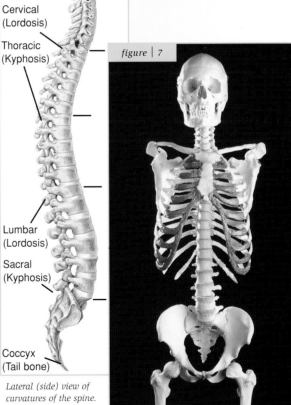

figure | 6

Cervical (Lordosis)

Thoracic (Kyphosis)

Lumbar (Lordosis)

Sacral (Kyphosis)

Coccyx (Tail bone)

Lateral (side) view of curvatures of the spine.

figure | 7

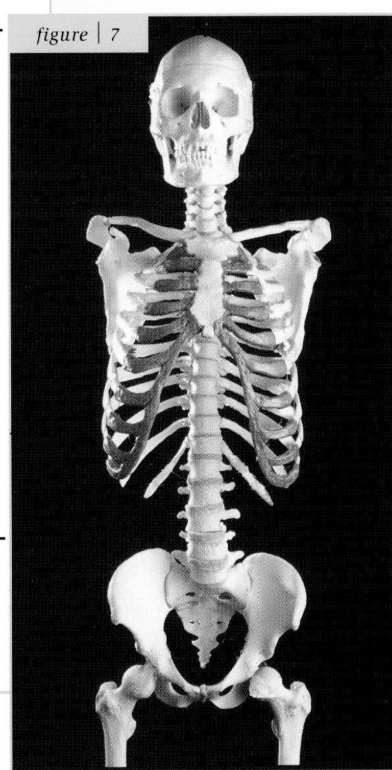

The vertebral column joins the pelvis at the sacroiliac joint.

figure | 8

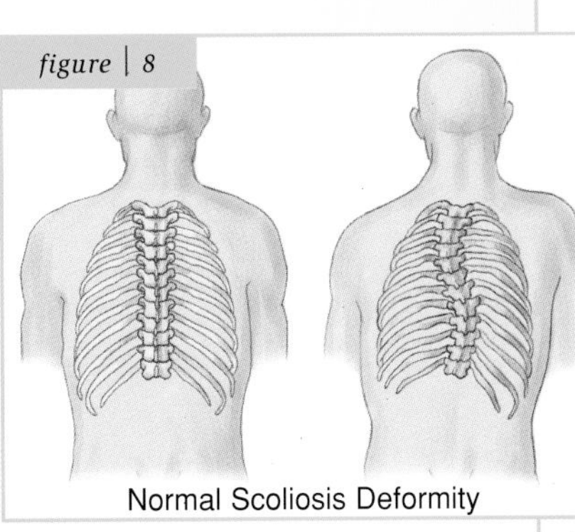

A change in normal spinal alignment is a spinal deformity.

figure | 9

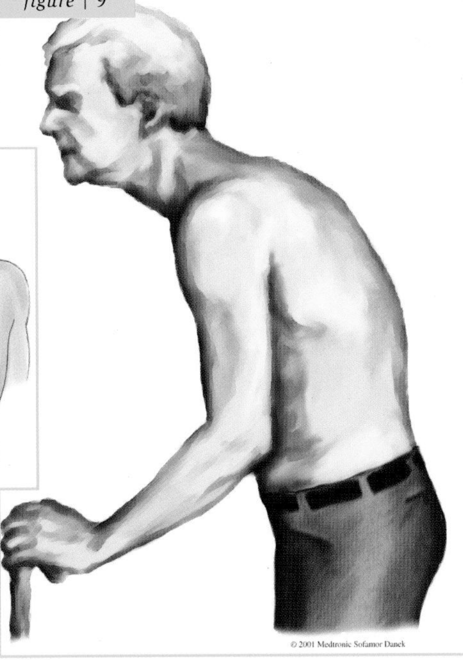

Thoracic kyphosis with too much forward curvature of the spine.

seen in the thoracic (middle spine) and thoracolumbar (junction between the middle and lower spine) spine, or occasionally in the lumbar spine. In the adult onset type scoliosis due to degenerative changes (aging), the curve occurs more commonly in the lumbar spine (Fig. 10). Degenerative scoliosis can be quite painful, can limit motion, and can produce both primary and secondary stiffness in other areas of the spine. The latter stiffness is associated with muscle spasm and splinting from pain, which can decrease motion in adjacent spine levels. Adults with idiopathic type scoliosis commonly experience pain in the thoracic and thoracolumbar areas of the spine in the midline or slightly off to the side, generally below the apex (top) of the curve; occasionally this requires surgical intervention (Fig. 11A and B). The more severe forms of scoliosis can be associated with a limitation in pulmonary function, *i.e.* lung function due to rib compression on lung space (Fig. 13). This can limit one's overall ability to function athletically. The combination of **thoracic lordosis**, *i.e.* the reverse of kyphosis, and scoliosis can produce a further impact upon limitation of space in the chest cavity allowed for breathing. Scoliosis is associated with a rotational component at the apex of the curve that produces a rib hump which pushes the ribs backward on the side of the convexity of the curve (Fig. 12A, B, and C). This deforms the rib cage and squeezes the underlying lungs. The facet joints, which normally occur between each vertebral level for movement, are thrown out of alignment due to scoliosis and in this misaligned position can become stiff and painful due to degenerative arthritis (Fig. 15). This long-term effect of scoliosis can limit one's ability to rotate the torso during the mid and late phases of the golf swing. This is not normally seen in younger individuals with this disorder because the stiffness takes years to develop, and naturally the larger the curve the greater the area of stiffness.

Frequently adults with scoliosis are plagued by spinal pain around the area just inside (medial to) the shoulder blades in the area of the rhomboid muscles. The movement of the scapula riding over the irregularly shaped underlying ribs can produce a bursitis in the bursa membrane underlying the scapula. Patients with this disorder will note an aching, sometimes burning, sensation beneath the medial border of the scapula on either side of the spine, but most frequently on the side of the rib hump. This may limit one's ability to fully extend the arms during the early and late swing or to rotate the shoulder girdles during the middle phases of the swing. Certainly the stiffness imposed by degenerative facet joints in the spine can limit rotation of the torso, also.

One of the secondary effects of lumbar scoliosis is to shorten the torso by decreasing the distance between the thoracic spine and the pelvis, bringing the ribs closer to the pelvis (Fig. 17). Characteristically adults with scoliosis will notice an out-of-balance posture seen most dramatically in swimsuits or tight clothing, where the center of gravity of the upper torso is off to one side away from the center of gravity of the pelvis (Fig. 18). In its more painful form, the scoliosis can produce such shortening of the torso that the ribs are pushed against the inner wall of the pelvis.

It should be noted that malalignment of the lumbar spine can be seen on a temporary basis in painful conditions such as a ruptured (herniated) disc or a lumbar muscle strain. These are not to be confused with structural scoliosis, since once the underlying cause of the painful condition is resolved the alignment of the spinal column returns to normal.

If the scoliotic spinal curve occurs in the lower lumbar segments, it can affect the junction between the sacrum and the pelvis (Fig. 13). A misalignment of the sacroiliac joints between the sacrum and the pelvis can occur producing pelvic obliquity. Sacroiliitis, or inflammation of these joints can occur and be associated with pain and stiffness.

The second most commonly known condition of spinal deformity about the

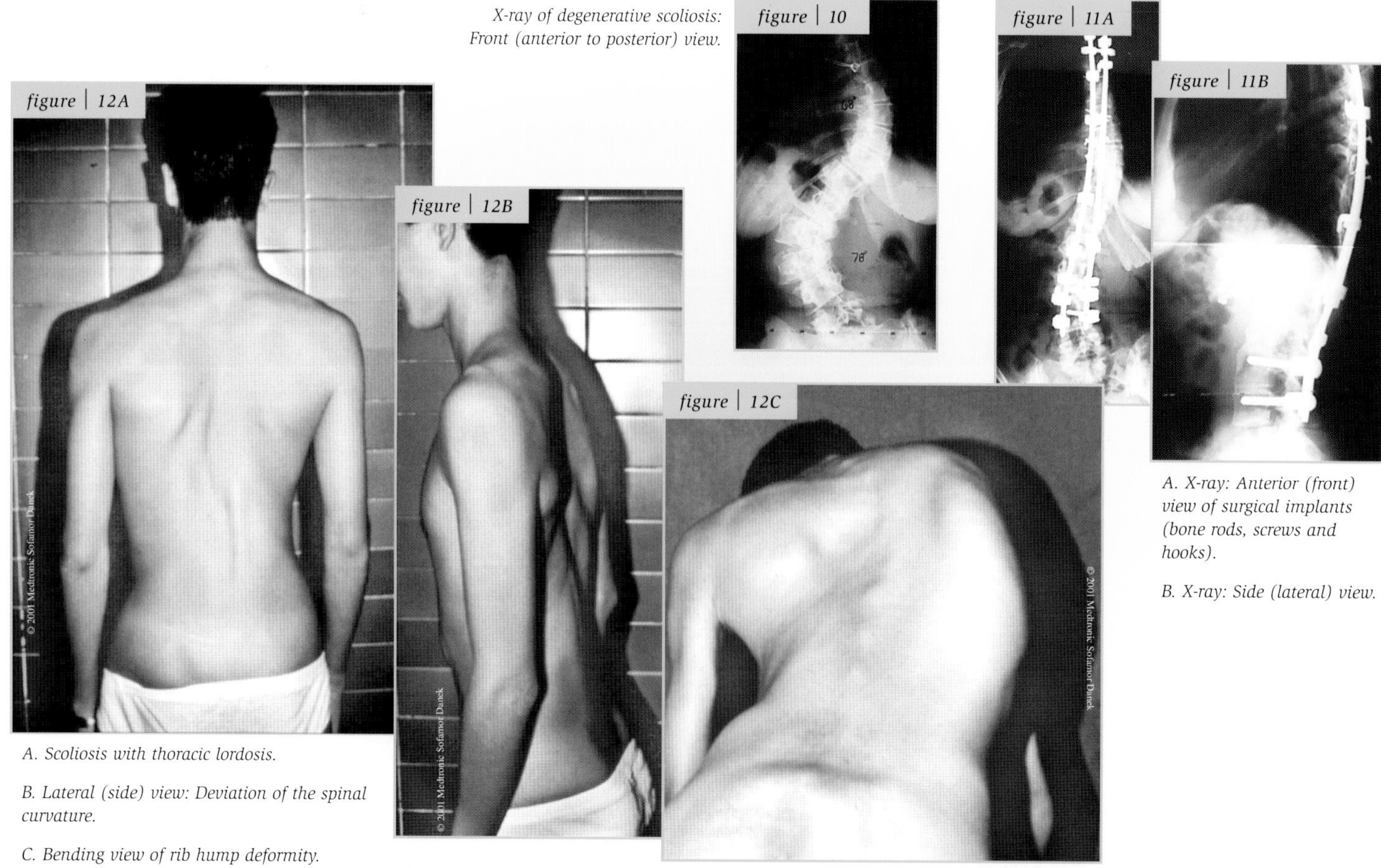

X-ray of degenerative scoliosis: Front (anterior to posterior) view.

A. X-ray: Anterior (front) view of surgical implants (bone rods, screws and hooks).

B. X-ray: Side (lateral) view.

A. Scoliosis with thoracic lordosis.

B. Lateral (side) view: Deviation of the spinal curvature.

C. Bending view of rib hump deformity.

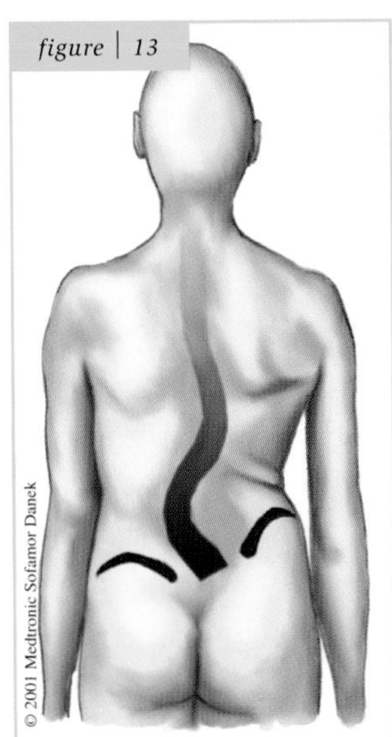

Posterior (back) view of scoliotic spinal curvature.

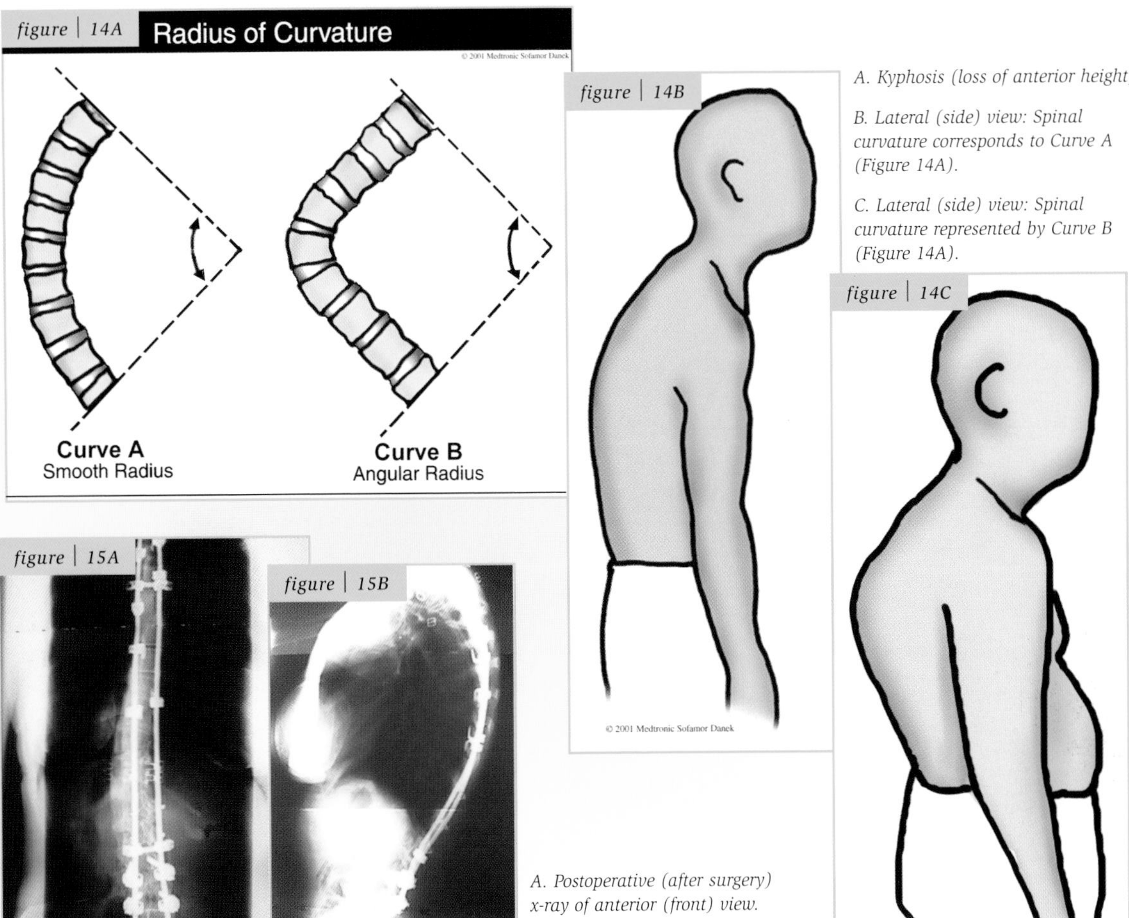

A. Kyphosis (loss of anterior height)

B. Lateral (side) view: Spinal curvature corresponds to Curve A (Figure 14A).

C. Lateral (side) view: Spinal curvature represented by Curve B (Figure 14A).

A. Postoperative (after surgery) x-ray of anterior (front) view.

B. Postoperative lateral (side) view.

spine is **kyphosis**, which has many causes. Kyphosis occurs because of a loss in height in the anterior, front, portion of the vertebral column (Fig. 14). The loss in height can occur in the vertebral body itself or the disc space. These conditions can occur with fractures, tumors, infections, or even just changes in the bone strength, such as is seen with osteoporosis. There are even primary arthritic joint conditions that can produce an excessive degree of kyphosis, such as **ankylosing spondylitis**. This is a generalized form of inflammatory arthritis affecting primarily the spine and often the hips. This is associated with a rounded, sometimes extreme forward-bent kyphosis, sometimes leaving the individual with his head and face looking downwards. Only corrective osteotomies (surgical cutting of the bones) of the vertebral column can bring the individual into a more functional position. This tends to affect men more commonly in their middle years. Hip arthritis can be greatly helped by joint replacements, which will also improve spinal alignment by eliminating the forward bend position at the hip joint. Abnormal spinal curves of scoliosis can cause spinal dysfunction. This dysfunction often produces pain and limits activities of daily living and golf.

TREATMENT

After careful evaluation with both physical and radiographic studies (plain X-rays and CAT scans), a treatment plan can be formulated. This can then allow for enhanced function and improve the rehabilitation process in which trunk strength, muscle coordination, and balance are stressed. Truncal strengthening exercises involve muscles of the thighs, hips, and trunk, which play a key role in balance and strength for the lumbar spine and trunk during the golf swing. The trunk strength provides a synchrony of motion between the upper and lower extremities in that there is a controlled unwinding of the upper body relative to the trunk and legs during the golf swing. Maximizing the mobility of the vertebral column with structural deformities is key to accomplishing this. This is done through stretching those mobile segments not involved in the deformity and maximally strengthening the musculature of the trunk and shoulders. Achievement of this may in fact help in the overall balance and health of the individual.

Surgery plays a role in the treatment of spinal deformities when there is a need to stabilize a curve to prevent deterioration, to treat arthritic pain through bone grafts (fusion) to stop motion in the affected segment, or to realign the spinal alignment through correction of the deformity. Surgery can be accomplished with immediate stabilization using spinal implants, rods, hooks, screws, and wires, which in many cases prevent the need for braces or casts after surgery (Fig. 15A and B). With modern techniques, patients are mobilized within a few days of surgery and return quickly to a functional status.

Walking for exercise is begun immediately, advancing to one mile a day within three weeks. The patient can progress to gentle upper extremity strengthening within six weeks, and begin swinging a golf club gently within two months. Chipping can commence at three months and slowly advance through the irons, holding off the woods until after four to six months after surgery. Maximizing physical conditioning prior to surgical intervention will undoubtedly lead to a quicker recovery and earlier return to golf. Returning to golf will ultimately depend on the patient and his or her medical status. A patient should only start to play after approval by a physician or other healthcare provider. Utilizing a cart and playing for exercise rather than score will promote a safe and gradual return to the game we love to play.

MALADIES OF THE UPPER AND LOWER EXTREMITY IN GOLF

CHAPTER 11

By Jack L. VanderSchilden, M.D.

One thing I found out about seven years ago was I had a misaligned back because I had flat feet, and one was flatter than the other. Once that was diagnosed, I started wearing innersoles in my walking shoes, in running shoes, and in my golf shoes. Now that I have appropriate footwear, it has improved my whole body alignment and my back as well.

Retief Goosen

Although the low back shows a predilection to injury in the golfer, many participants are affected by injuries to either the upper or lower extremities. In this chapter we will deal with three areas in the upper extremity—the shoulder, the elbow, and the wrist. In the lower extremity we will deal predominantly with the hip and knee. Even though injuries to the back are probably the most debilitating to the golfer, injuries to these other joints can severely affect your game.

INJURIES TO THE SHOULDER REGION

The shoulder joint is a ball-and-socket joint. The ball is at the top of the humerus or upper arm bone. The socket comes off the wing bone or the scapula and is called the glenoid (Fig. 1). In contrast to the hip, the shoulder has a very large ball and a small socket. This allows for a great deal of motion in multiple planes, which permits you to swing a golf club fluidly. To supplement the stability about the shoulder, there is a large amount of soft tissue both in the front and the back of the shoulder. It is injuries to this soft tissue that can totally compromise your golf game.

The most common injury one sees about the shoulder in golf is an injury to the rotator cuff. The rotator cuff is a group of three muscles in the back of the shoulder that allow you to bring your arm away from your body, as in the back swing (Fig. 2). When the rotator cuff of your dominant arm is inflamed or injured, this can severely hamper your back swing, totally modifying the fluidity of your golf swing in general. Your follow-through can be greatly affected because of inflammation in the non-dominant shoulder.

The rotator cuff degenerates as a natural part of the aging process (Fig. 3). Degeneration begins at approximately age forty. Therefore, injury or inflammation to the rotator cuff is not an unusual injury in the golfer from middle age and on. In the initial stage of this injury, one notices achiness about the shoulder, usually in the back, after playing golf. This may resolve after taking some over-the-counter (non-steroidal) anti-inflammatory medication such as aspirin or acetaminophen (Tylenol®). Rest alone will usually provide some significant relief in the early stage of the injury.

The problem arises when the pain becomes more prevalent and begins to affect a participant's golf game. The shoulder will ache throughout the round and for an extended time after completion of the round. At this point the golfer may also be developing shoulder pain at night, which either awakens the individual or makes it very difficult for him or her to fall asleep. This second stage of the problem, with continued pain, is a precursor to a possible tear in the rotator cuff. At this point, see your doctor or healthcare professional, for medical intervention is necessary.

The second stage may persist for an extended period of time, but will eventually lead to a tear in the rotator cuff. Although a high percentage of rotator cuff tears can be dealt with non-surgically, the injury may result in an inability to play golf for an extended period of time.

In treating problems with the rotator cuff, the most common drugs used are anti-inflammatories, either prescription or non-prescription. Another aspect of the treatment, which is extremely important, is a structured physical therapy program. When the rotator cuff becomes inflamed, the soft tissues actually swell (Fig. 4). There is very little clearance in the shoulder joint in a normal individual. When inflammation arises, the clearances

This is the normal anatomy of the shoulder region. Please note the acromion is the roof of the shoulder that covers the ball of the upper arm. The rotator cuff resides between the acromion and the ball. (Reproduced with permission from Sports Injuries: Their Prevention and Treatment, 3rd Edition, by Lars Peterson and Per Renström, published by Martin Dunitz Publishers, London, UK.)

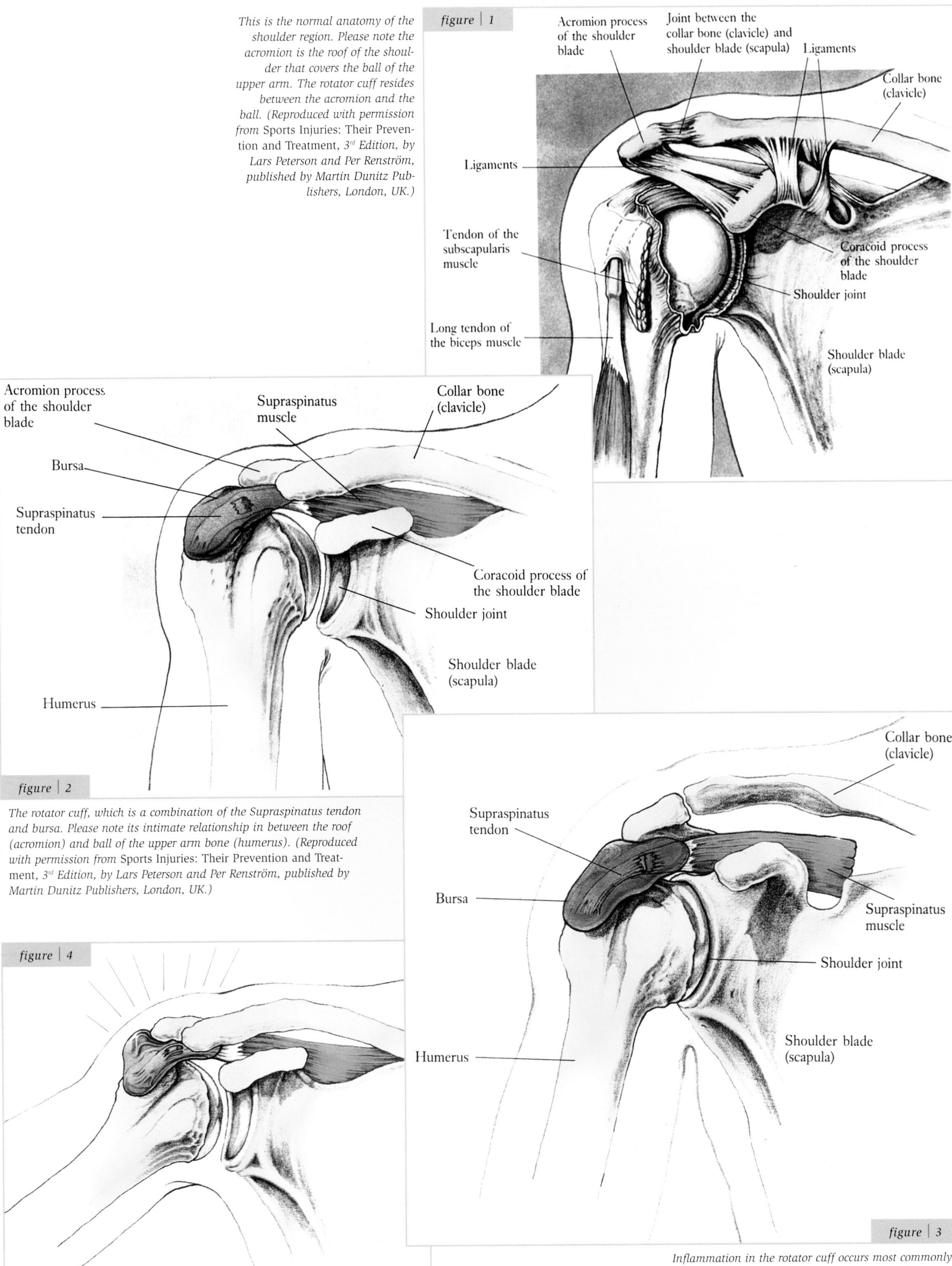

The rotator cuff, which is a combination of the Supraspinatus tendon and bursa. Please note its intimate relationship in between the roof (acromion) and ball of the upper arm bone (humerus). (Reproduced with permission from Sports Injuries: Their Prevention and Treatment, 3rd Edition, by Lars Peterson and Per Renström, published by Martin Dunitz Publishers, London, UK.)

Inflammation in the rotator cuff occurs most commonly between the acromion and the ball of the humerus. (Reproduced with permission from Sports Injuries: Their Prevention and Treatment, 3rd Edition, by Lars Peterson and Per Renström, published by Martin Dunitz Publishers, London, UK.)

Bringing the arm away from the body (abduction) narrows the space between the roof and the ball, effectively pinching the rotator cuff even more. This is called impingement and may eventually lead to a tear of the cuff. (Reproduced with permission from Sports Injuries: Their Prevention and Treatment, 3rd Edition, by Lars Peterson and Per Renström, published by Martin Dunitz Publishers, London, UK.)

become even smaller, therefore pinching the rotator cuff with motion, which results in an injury to the structure. This is referred to as "impingement." A rehabilitation program will not only help strengthen the cuff, but will help reduce the swelling and therefore return the function to a more acceptable level. The judicious use of steroid injections can be of great benefit as well.

Another problem that one sees about the shoulder in the golfer is an unstable shoulder joint, although this is much less common. Instability means that the ball can either slide too far forward or backward out of socket (Fig. 5). It is far more common for the ball to slide too far forward and rather unusual for it to slide too far backward. This entity would be most symptomatic in the non-dominant shoulder on the follow-through of the golf swing. During the follow-through, your non-dominant shoulder would have the feeling that the ball is slipping too far forward. The good news is that most instability problems can be rectified with an aggressive physical therapy regimen and perhaps some modification of your swing.

Another problem that one can see in the shoulder in the golfer, depending on his or her age, is degenerative arthritis (osteoarthritis) in two separate areas. One joint that degenerates with time is the A-C joint where the collarbone meets the shoulder bone (Fig. 1). This area does show degeneration over time, even in the normal individual, and can cause a significant amount of pain. Also, bone spurs may form on the undersurface of the joint, pushing down into the rotator cuff and resulting in tendonitis or a tear of the cuff (Fig. 3). Another area where this can occur is on the undersurface of the acromion, or roof, of the shoulder. Spurs can develop on the undersurface, pushing down into the rotator cuff with resultant injury (Fig. 3). When these entities occur, they sometimes will require surgical intervention to deal with the spurring and injury to the rotator cuff. Prior to surgical intervention, however, a thorough rehabilitation program should be considered along with anti-inflammatory medication and a possible steroid injection into the shoulder.

ELBOW INJURIES

Although elbow injuries in golf are relatively uncommon, they can be quite debilitating when they do occur. Injuries can occur to the inside (medial), outside (lateral), or back (posterior) portion of the elbow (Fig. 6).

An injury to the inside portion of the elbow is sometimes referred to as "golfer's elbow" or medial epicondylitis. The epicondyle is the small bump on the inside of your elbow where your forearm muscles (flexors) attach (Fig. 7). This attachment point can be irritated, usually in the dominant arm, at the point of impact with the club on the ball. A large nerve runs just behind this area. This happens to be the ulnar nerve or the "funny bone" nerve. This nerve can also get irritated, resulting in numbness and tingling down the arm into the ring and little fingers. It can give you very significant pain on the inside of the elbow as well.

Injury to the outside of the elbow is called lateral epicondylitis, or "tennis elbow." Although commonly referred to as "tennis elbow," this entity can occasionally be seen in the golfer. The bump on the outside of the elbow is the attachment point for the extensor muscles, the considered muscles on top of the forearm which allow you to cock your wrist in an upward direction (Fig. 7). This entity usually occurs in the non-dominant arm and is symptomatic with follow-through. The most common symptom here is constant pain on the outside of the elbow, which may even occur at rest in severe cases.

Pain in the back of the elbow is usually derived from one of two sources. The triceps muscle, which is the huge muscle in the back of the arm, ties into the back of the elbow joint. This allows you to straighten the elbow with significant

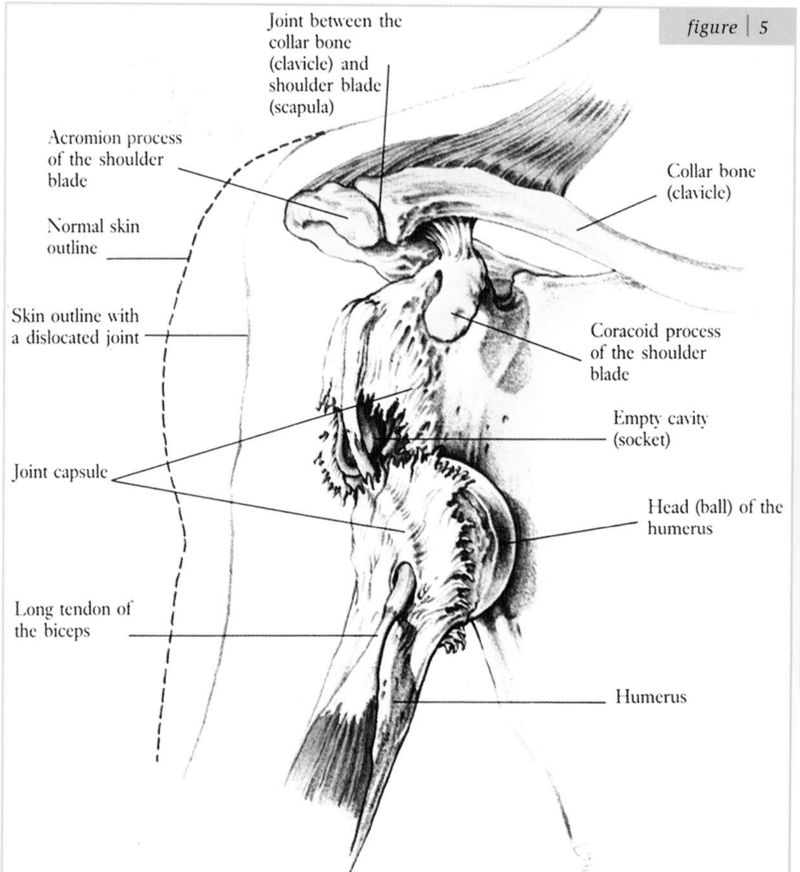

This depicts an anterior (frontal) dislocation of the shoulder. Please note the severe disruption of the soft tissues about the shoulder. A subluxation is a mild form of this injury where the ball tries to come out the front but does not quite leave the joint completely. (Reproduced with permission from Sports Injuries: Their Prevention and Treatment, *3rd Edition, by Lars Peterson and Per Renström, published by Martin Dunitz Publishers, London, UK.)*

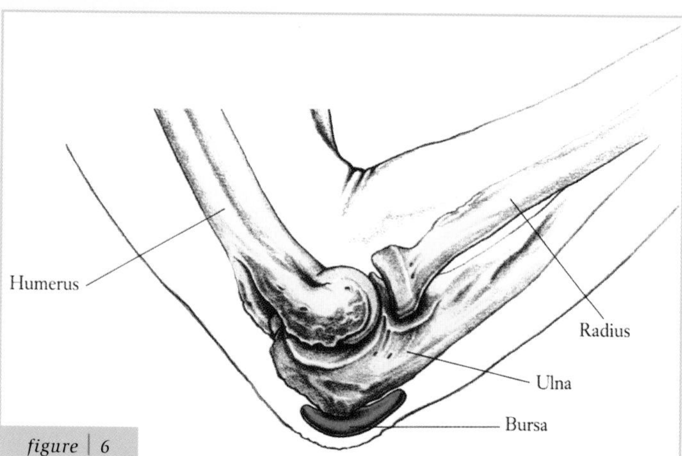

This is the normal bony anatomy of the elbow. Please note the humerus (upper arm bone) and the radius and ulna in the forearm. The radius allows rotation of the forearm and the ulna acts as a hinge along with the humerus. (Reproduced with permission from Sports Injuries: Their Prevention and Treatment, *3rd Edition, by Lars Peterson and Per Renström, published by Martin Dunitz Publishers, London, UK.)*

Lateral epicondylitis is inflammation of the muscle attachment on the outside of the elbow (lateral or external epicondyle). Medial epicondylitis occurs with inflammation on the attachment point of the forearm muscles to the inside of the elbow (medial or internal epicondyle). (Reproduced with permission from Sports Injuries: Their Prevention and Treatment, *3rd Edition, by Lars Peterson and Per Renström, published by Martin Dunitz Publishers, London, UK.)*

figure | 7

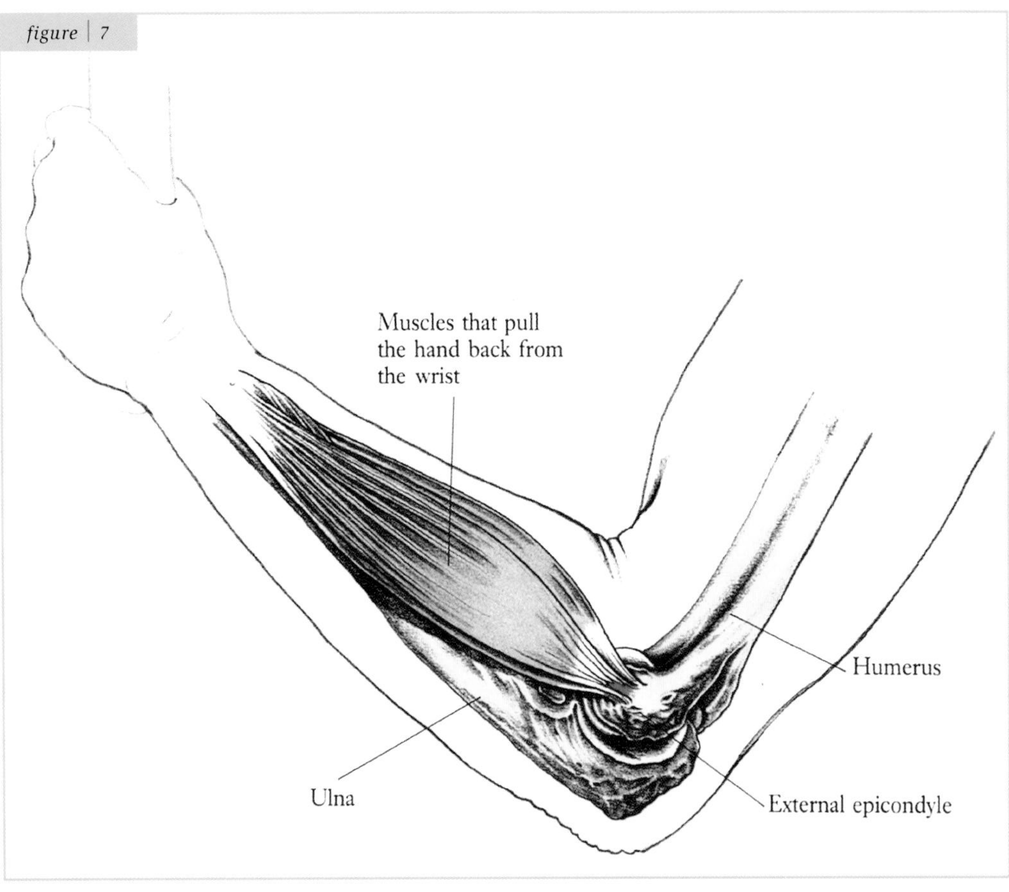

power. In the region where it attaches at the back of the elbow, one can develop inflammation; this is, however, a relatively rare problem in the golfer. A more common problem in the back (posterior) region of the elbow is a loose body or a small piece of the joint that has broken off and is floating about the elbow. These loose bodies have a tendency to lodge in the back portion of the elbow, causing significant pain and catching or popping when straightening the arm. If you are experiencing symptoms of catching or popping about the elbow, I would strongly recommend that you visit your doctor or healthcare professional for an X-ray. A high percentage of these loose bodies will show up on a plain X-ray or MRI examination.

Treating elbow problems can be quite difficult. Both medial and lateral epicondylitis must be treated with rest (splinting), anti-inflammatory medications, and a physical therapy or strengthening program. This may require several weeks of rest and a prolonged strengthening program, even after one has returned to playing golf. In some cases, the use of a tennis elbow splint may be of benefit. A steroid injection may also be considered, with surgery as a last resort.

A right-handed golfer, in the worst case scenario, may well suffer from "tennis elbow" in the leading left elbow and "golfer's elbow" in the following right elbow.

WRIST INJURIES

Wrist injuries are, unfortunately, too common and very debilitating in the golfer. These injuries can result from overuse or injury. The most common etiology of injury to the wrist is secondary to the club face's hitting an immovable object such as a stone or a stump. Also, hitting out of extremely heavy rough or wet sand can overload the wrist, resulting in an injury.

There are numerous tendons that pass through the wrist that allow your fingers to function. These tendons are both on the top (dorsum) or bottom (palmer) portion of the wrist. A golfer can inflame these areas quite readily with overuse, poor technique, or injury.

Overuse will cause significant pain and swelling about the wrist, making it virtually impossible to play golf. One needs to seek advice from his or her doctor in dealing with this problem. It will usually require rest (splinting), anti-inflammatory medication, and perhaps physical therapy. Rest is by far the most important therapeutic regimen a golfer can entertain for this entity. Therefore, when a golfer experiences wrist pain, he or she should not continue to play until the cause of the pain has been determined, treated, and the pain has totally resolved.

A golfer can also develop carpal tunnel syndrome, which is a compression on one of the major nerves that provide function to the hand—the median nerve. Acute or chronic inflammation in the wrist can reduce the space in the tunnel where this nerve passes. The nerve is then subjected to excessive pressure, causing symptoms of a dull ache with pain and numbness radiating in the thumb, index finger, and middle finger. The symptoms will generally get worse at night and are often described as the hand's having "gone to sleep." Sensation in the hand is diminished and muscular atrophy (loss of muscle mass) can occur if this condition is persistent. People with this condition find it extremely difficult to grip a golf club. Initial treatment for this entity is rest (splinting) and anti-inflammatory medication. Refractory cases sometimes will require surgical decompression with usually a very good result. The surgery requires cutting the ligament that is squeezing the median nerve. There are general techniques to cut the ligament. It's always best to discuss this with your surgeon. You may return to play when your surgeon allows—usually 6 to 8 weeks.

A ligamentous injury to the wrist can occur when, as previously mentioned, the face of the club hits a rigid object. This can send a tremendous shock up the shaft of the club, and the wrist takes the brunt of it. This can result in a ligamentous injury between two of the multiple bones about the wrist. Also there is a small piece of cartilage in the wrist called the triangular fibrocartilage complex (TFCC). This can be injured with the aforementioned mechanism of injury. Treatment may entail prolonged rest (splinting), anti-inflammatory medications, and therapy. Surgery, either open or arthroscopic, may be required in refractory cases.

If the pain in your wrist is persistent and compromising, you should absolutely seek the help of a doctor. Wrist injuries are difficult to diagnose and sometimes complex to treat. They must be treated appropriately or they will totally compromise a golfer's ability to play. Prolonged rest and immobilization is sometimes required. High dose anti-inflammatory medications and steroid injections may be recommended. Surgery is usually a last resort.

One other condition I would like to mention is pain at the base of your thumb, either while playing golf or at rest. As we age, it is very common to develop arthritis in the joints at the base of the thumb, usually in the dominant hand at first and then going to the non-dominant hand. This is far more common in women than men and is a degenerative or arthritic process and not due to injury. If pain is perceived at the base of your thumb, the diagnosis can be easily made with an X-ray and physical exam. Judicious use of anti-inflammatory medication and sometimes splinting will provide relief and allow you to return to the golf course in a hopefully expeditious fashion.

INJURIES TO THE HIP

Although injuries about the hip are relatively uncommon in the golfer, they certainly can be debilitating.

The hip is a ball and socket joint. It differs from the shoulder in that the ball is small and is engulfed by the socket (Fig. 8). This provides excellent stability, but less motion than in the shoulder.

A very common problem is inflammation or bursitis of the greater trochanter. The greater trochanter is a bump on the outside portion of the femur or thighbone adjacent to the hip. This is the point of attachment of the large muscle groups of the buttock muscles that control your pelvis and allow you to shift your weight while swinging a golf club. Therefore, these muscles are of utmost importance in the golfer (Fig. 9).

At the attachment point one can develop tendonitis or an inflammation. This can result in bursitis, which is an inflammation of the fluid-filled sac (bursa) that surrounds the attachment point. This malady can cause very significant pain on the outside or lateral aspect of the hip. The tenderness can occur with pressure over a small area around this structure. The pain can be precipitated by pressing the leg outward against resistance or shifting the weight side to side, as with a golf swing. The treatment for this entity may include anti-inflammatory medication as well as steroid injection. A judicious use of a steroid injection in this instance is definitely warranted, in that it can markedly diminish the discomfort and allow the individual to rehabilitate more aggressively. A physical therapy regimen is sometimes recommended not only to strengthen, but also to stretch the adjacent tissues.

When dealing with hip problems, one also has to consider degenerative arthritis (osteoarthritis) of the hip in the middle-aged and older golfer (Fig. 10). As we age, degeneration of the joints in the lower extremity, especially the knee and hip, is not uncommon. This usually can

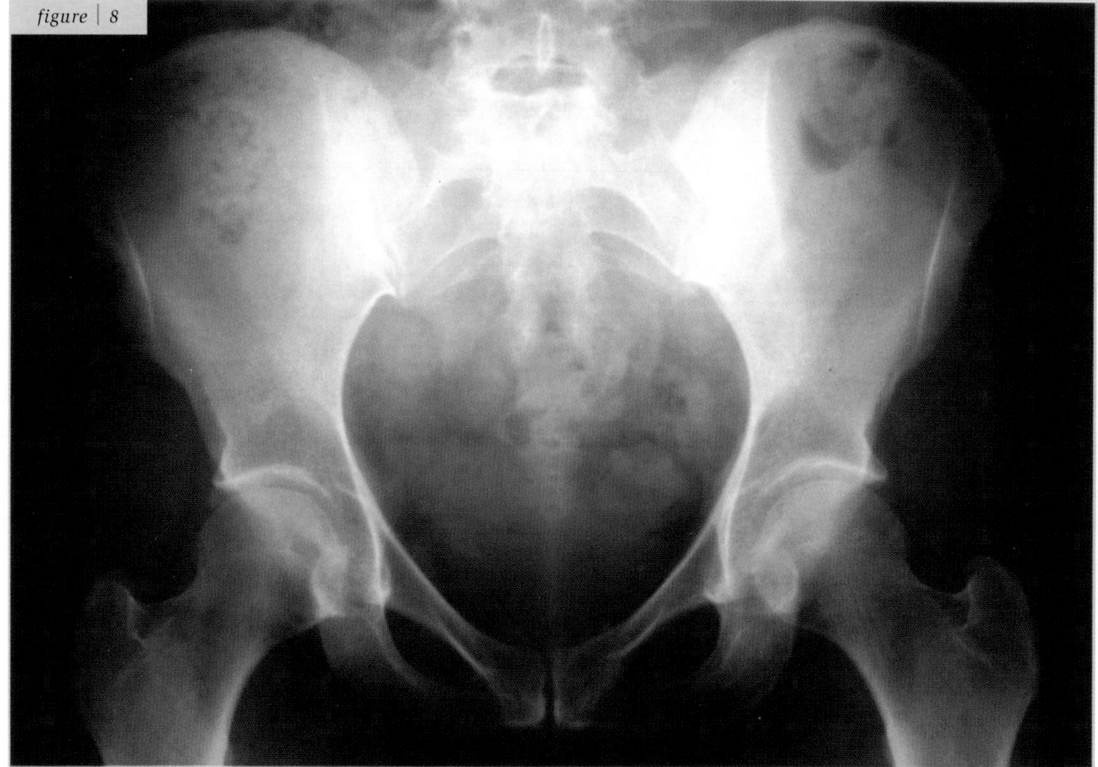

figure | 8

This is a frontal X-ray of the pelvis to include both hip joints. Please note the ball-and-socket nature of the hip joint with the smooth contour of both the ball and the socket. Also there is a dark space in between each which is where the smooth cartilage surface of the ball resides.

figure | 9

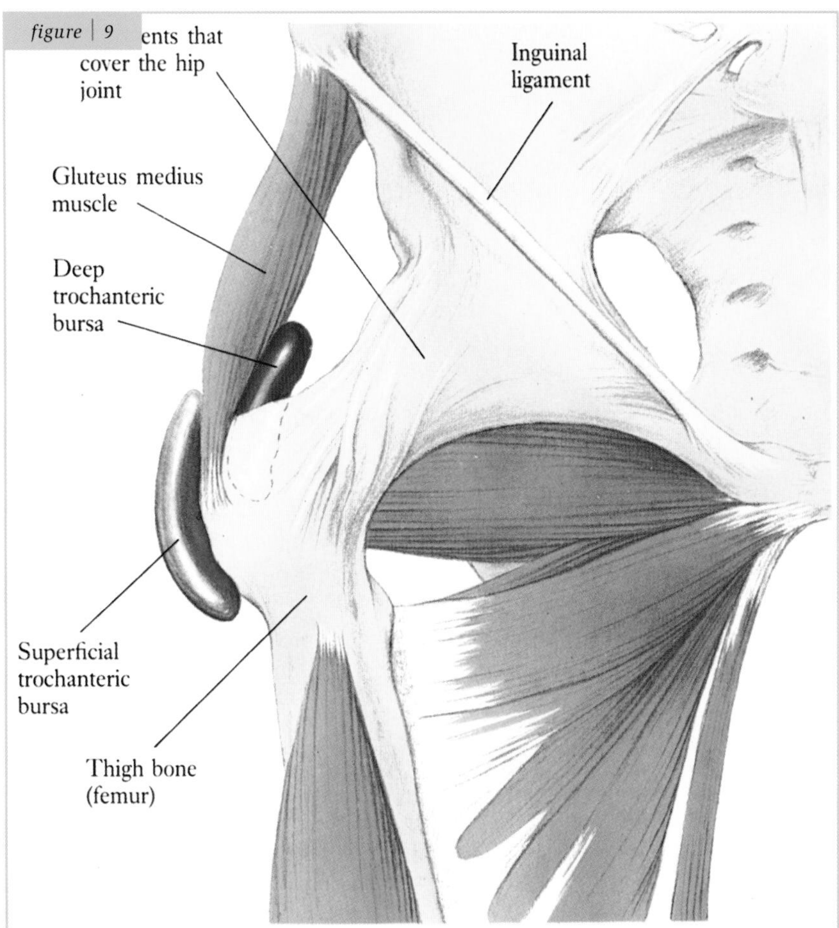

Trochanteric bursitis is inflammation at the attachment point on the outside of the thigh bone of the muscles coming out of the buttock. Please note that this is not adjacent to the hip joint, but is to the outside of the thigh where the pain can be quite significant. (Reproduced with permission from Sports Injuries: Their Prevention and Treatment, *3rd Edition, by Lars Peterson and Per Renström, published by Martin Dunitz Publishers, London, UK.)*

figure | 10

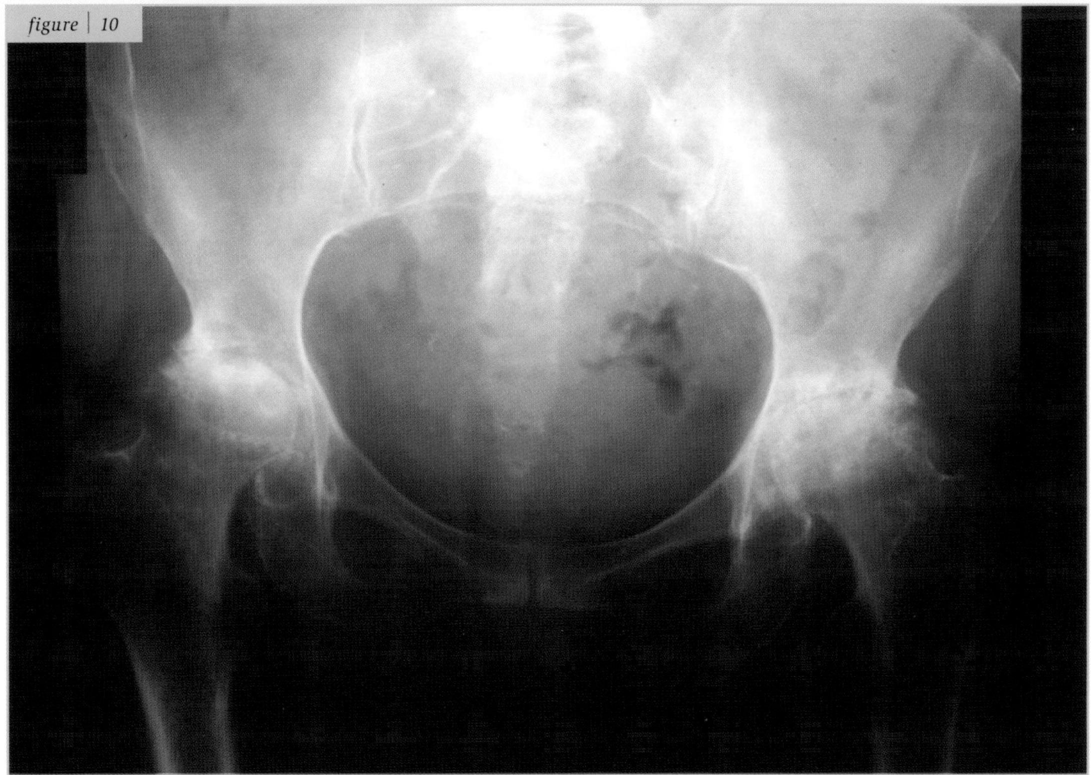

This X-ray depicts severe arthritis of both hip joints with the loss of contour of both the ball and the socket. Spurring is noted throughout both hips and there is no dark space in between the ball and the socket noting a total loss of the cartilage cover of the ball.

begin during the fifth and sixth decade, or sooner if a previous injury is noted. The classic symptom for arthritic pain in the hip is groin pain on the affected side. The pain may be nothing more than an ache, or it may become intractable. It can be a constant ache directly in the groin region, exacerbated with twisting of the hip inwards and outwards.

Arthritis about the hip will severely affect anyone's golf game. The diagnosis can often be made with a good physical exam and X-rays. Treatment is usually anti-inflammatory medications combined with weight loss, if needed. Also, if you are used to walking the course, the use of a cart may be indicated. You also might have to diminish frequency of play (1 to 2 times per week on non-consecutive days) in order to allow the affected joint to rest.

If the degenerative arthritis becomes extreme, total joint replacement is sometimes recommended. This will allow you to return to the golf course only after an extensive rehabilitation program, but it will allow you to do so with markedly reduced pain in the affected hip. A hip replacement entails replacing the ball with a space-age metal and the socket with a metal and polyethylene construct called the "cup" (Fig. 11). Depending on the type of hip replacement performed, one should be able to return to the game within 3 to 6 months.

INJURIES TO THE KNEE

The knee is the second most commonly injured joint in athletics, after the ankle. Yet most debilitating injuries to athletes do occur to the knee. Golfers are not immune to injuries about the knee. Actually, golf is a fairly tough sport on the knee, due to a great deal of rotation that occurs through the knee when swinging a golf club. Although we don't have the complex and devastating ligamentous injuries to the knee in golf as we do in other sports, there are still several areas that can be affected by the rotation of the golf swing.

The knee has two cartilage pads (menisci), one on the inside and one on the outside, that provide shock absorbency between the thighbone (femur) and shinbone (tibia). There are also four major ligaments to provide stability. One on the inside and one on the outside provide stability side-to-side. Two ligaments in the center of the knee provide front-to-back and rotational stability. The kneecap (patella) is in front of the knee, imbedded in tendons that run from the thigh muscles to the shinbone (Fig. 12).

The most common problem with the knee in golfers pertains to problems of the patella or kneecap. Pain in the region of the kneecap or widespread pain in the joint and behind the kneecap can occur during exertion or load. Walking up or down hills can exacerbate this pain. Also the rotation associated with the golf swing can cause significant discomfort. The etiology of this discomfort can be multifactorial. It can be due to weakness in the thigh musculature, constricting structures to the outside of the kneecap, malalignment of the lower leg during development, and flat feet—yes, flat feet. Excessive pronation, or flat feet, can increase the inward rotation of the lower leg, which alters the alignment of the leg and the direction of the pull of the thigh muscles.

It is beyond the scope of this chapter to help one self-diagnose what entity is causing his or her kneecap problems, but most problems can be dealt with in the following fashion. A thigh muscle-strengthening program is usually recommended by the healthcare professional. Also bracing may help one significantly. Anti-inflammatory medication is commonly prescribed. And for the flat foot, orthotics (arch supports) are definitely indicated. The orthotics can be off-the-shelf or custom-made to one's foot. These can be inserted in your golf shoe, as well as your regular shoes, to help correct the malalignment in your lower extremity. I don't know how many patients have told me, "I can't believe that these arch supports are really making my knee and hip pain go away."

We have two cartilage pads within the knee, on the inside (medial) and the outside (lateral) (Fig. 12, 13). Although

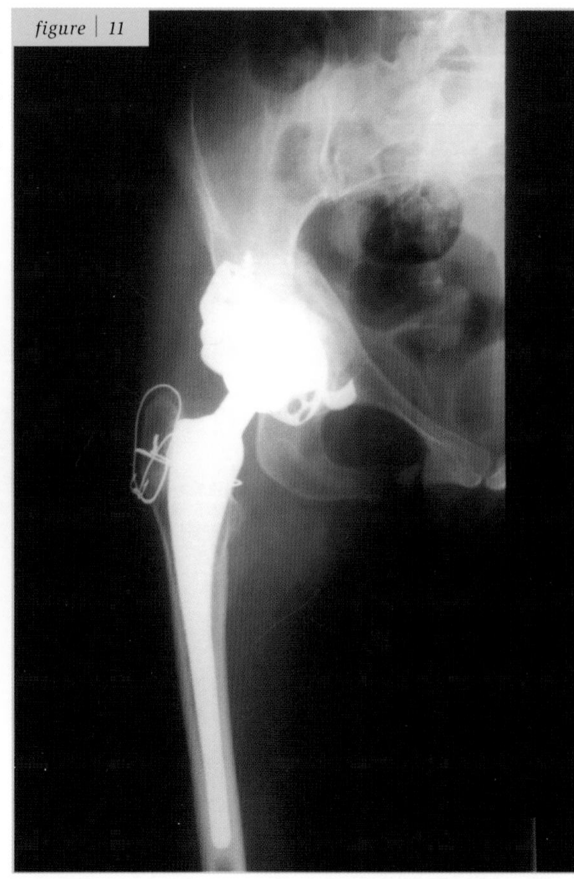

figure | 11

This is a total hip prosthesis inserted for severe arthritis of the hip. The ball is attached to a stem and cemented into the thighbone. This is made from a metal alloy. The socket portion is plastic with a metal backing that is inserted into the pelvic bone.

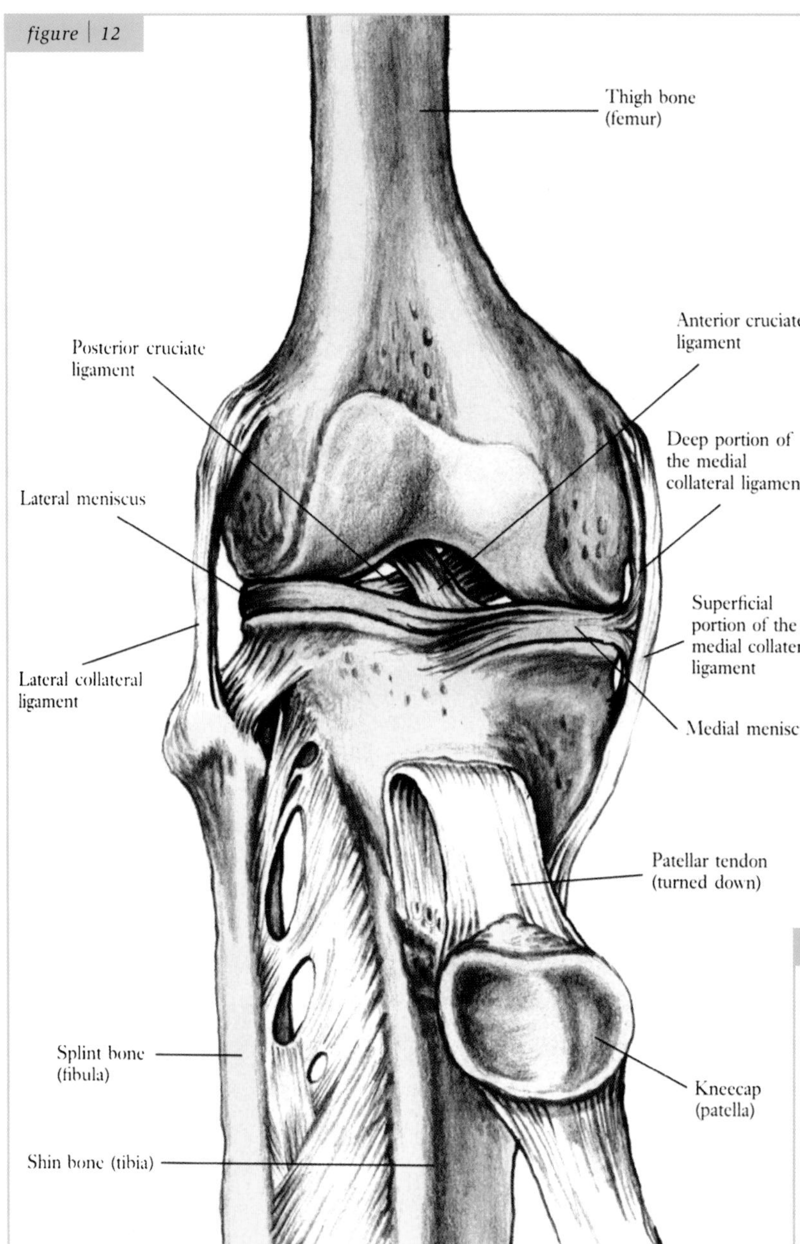

Frontal view of the normal anatomy of the knee. Please note the outside of the knee correlates with the fibula or splint bone. (Reproduced with permission from Sports Injuries: Their Prevention and Treatment, *3rd Edition, by Lars Peterson and Per Renström, published by Martin Dunitz Publishers, London, UK.)*

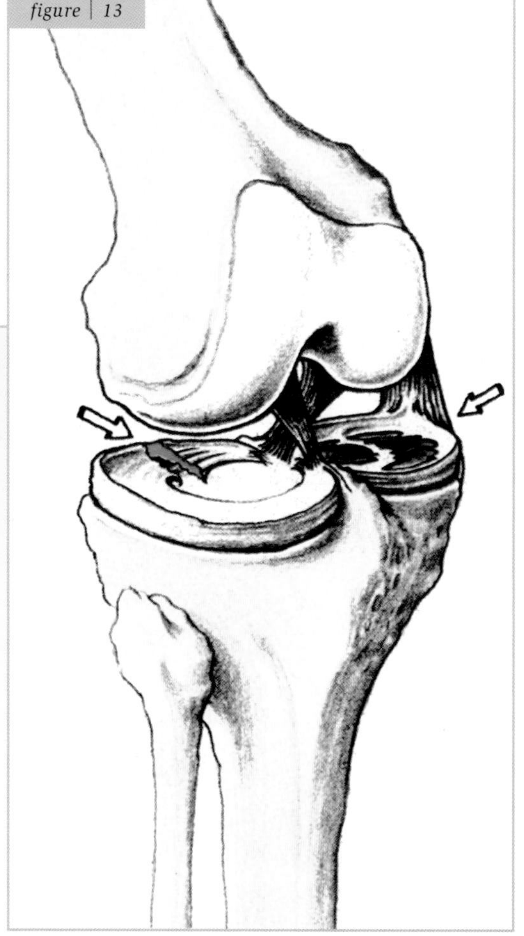

This depicts a tear in both the inside and outside cartilage pads (menisci). The inside pad (medial meniscus) is most commonly injured in all athletic endeavors, including golf. (Reproduced with permission from Sports Injuries: Their Prevention and Treatment, *3rd Edition, by Lars Peterson and Per Renström, published by Martin Dunitz Publishers, London, UK.)*

the catastrophic injuries to these structures do not occur in golf as with other sports such as football or basketball, injuries can occur from repetitive small injuries. We call these degenerative-type tears, and they occur most commonly on the inside of the knee. The classic symptom for this entity is pain to the back and the inside of the knee that is exacerbated by twisting. This may also cause very significant discomfort at night while just lying in bed.

A torn cartilage is often diagnosed by a physician via clinical examination and/or MRI (Magnetic Resonance Imaging). The symptoms will sometimes improve with rest, yet they may return without notice at any time. An arthroscopic examination of your knee may be recommended to remove the torn portion of the cartilage and leave the remainder of the structure behind to perform its job as a shock absorber for the knee. An arthroscopy is when a small tube is inserted in the knee to visualize the pathology (Fig. 14, 15, 16). The injured structure can be dealt with via special instrumentation (Fig. 17). The beauty in this procedure is that it will allow you to return to golf in 4–6 weeks, after a post-operative rehabilitation program.

As in the hip, degenerative changes of the knee are very common, especially with a previous injury (Fig. 18, 19). Men will usually develop arthritis on the inside of their knees first. Women generally develop arthritis on the outside of their knees. The reason for this is that men become "bowlegged" and women become more "knock-kneed" with age, generally speaking. When the knees begin to angle either in or out, it puts excessive pressure on that portion of the joint, with resultant degeneration.

Depending on the degree of arthritis, the treatment regimen is multifaceted. First and foremost is weight reduction, if necessary. Carrying excessive weight puts tremendous stress across both the knee and the hip. Anti-inflammatory medications are an advised treatment. Glucosamine and chondroitin sulfate have become popular over the last couple of years for arthritis. Both medications can be bought over-the-counter at any pharmacy. If you take these medications, always tell your doctor. There are presently ongoing studies looking at the efficacy of glucosamine in the arthritic patient. Preliminary data does show that it is of some benefit. One must take 1500mg of glucosamine a day (500mg 3 times per day) at a minimum to be effective. Doses of no more than 3000mg are recommended. Steroid injections can be used judiciously. They certainly should not be abused. Hyaluronic acid injections, or commonly called visco-supplementation, can be used in the knee. Hyaluronic acid is Mother Nature's natural lubricant in the knee. This can be injected into the knee to help the symptoms of degenerative arthritis. This seems to help in approximately 80% of individuals. It has provided some dramatic relief in some people, but has been disappointing in others, and there is no predictor as to whether it will work with one patient or another.

As previously noted, one must look at the foot when trying to assist the knee. A very flat foot or a very rigid, high arch may cause abnormal stresses in the lower leg, making one's knee pain significantly worse. Both of the entities can be dealt with via orthotics (arch supports). Also knee bracing may be of some benefit in the arthritic individual. Even though most knee braces provide minimal support, they can improve symptoms during activities such as golf.

As a last resort, total knee replacement may be considered. This requires replacing the end of the femur or thigh bone with a large piece of metal. The top of the tibia or shin bone is replaced with polyethylene and the undersurface of the kneecap or patella is replaced with polyethylene as well (Fig. 20). Knee replace-

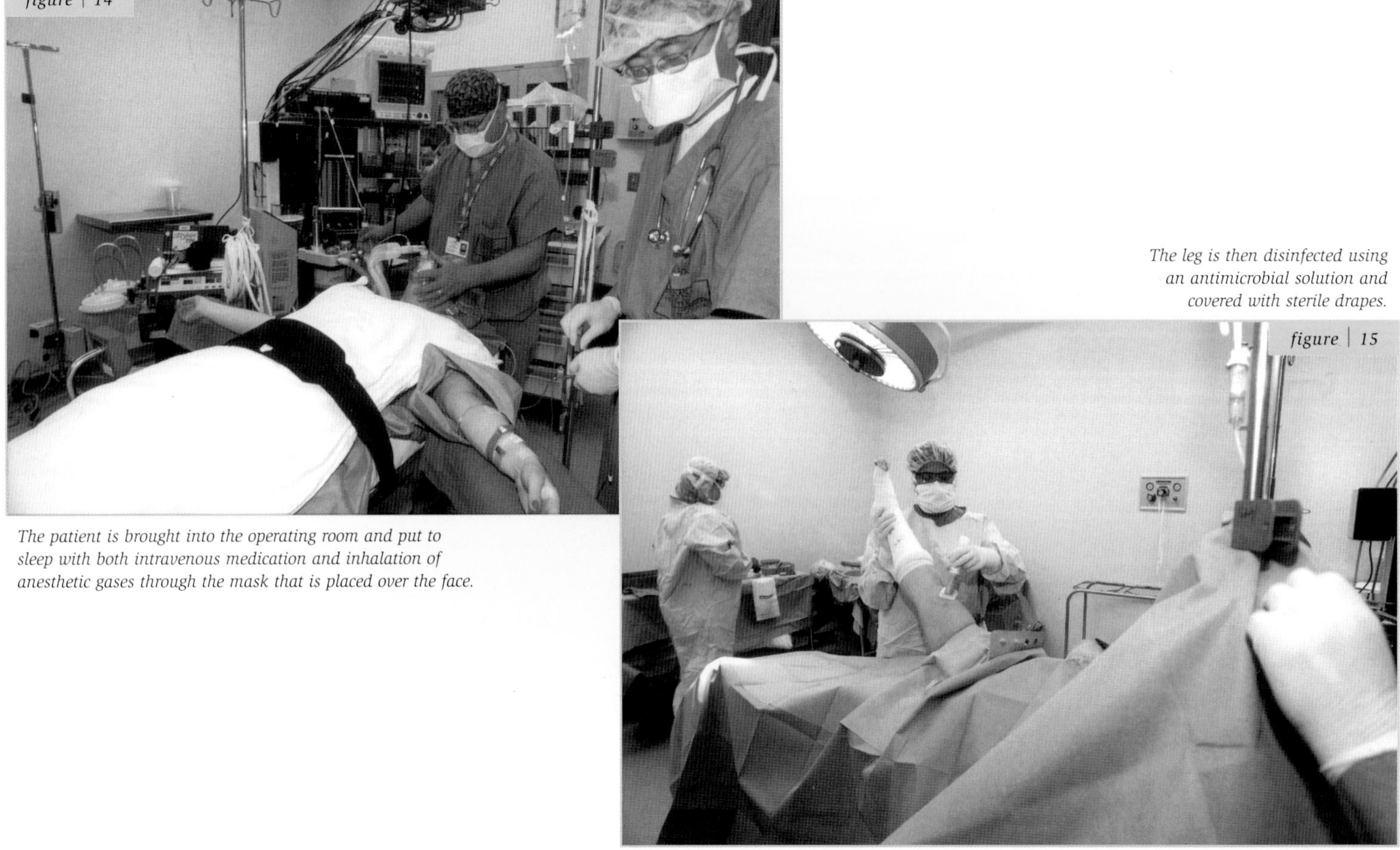

figure | 14

The patient is brought into the operating room and put to sleep with both intravenous medication and inhalation of anesthetic gases through the mask that is placed over the face.

figure | 15

The leg is then disinfected using an antimicrobial solution and covered with sterile drapes.

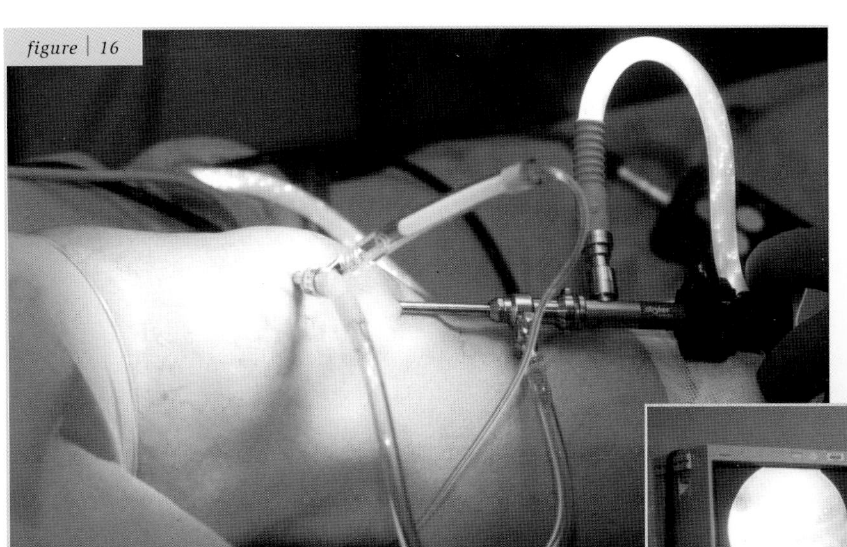

figure | 16

The arthroscope is then inserted in the knee after making a small incision. Please note a supplemental drain coming out from just above the knee. This enables the solution that is pumped through the arthroscope to escape, allowing for a continuous flow of fluid within the joint. The arthroscope is then attached to a camera and visualization of the structures inside the knee is readily apparent on a monitor.

figure | 17

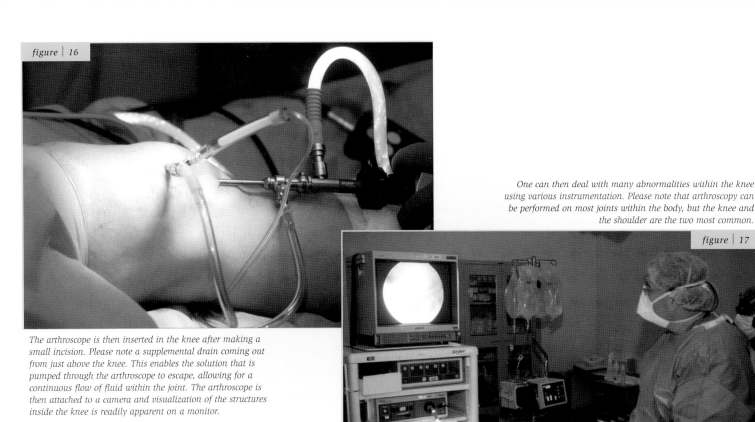

One can then deal with many abnormalities within the knee using various instrumentation. Please note that arthroscopy can be performed on most joints within the body, but the knee and the shoulder are the two most common.

ments have a very good track record for relieving a significant amount of pain about the knee—just ask Joe Namath, who has two knee replacements and plays golf almost every day. Although this is a very big operation, as is a hip replacement, one can usually return to golf in three to four months after a thorough rehabilitation program. I also recommend that one use a cart when playing, in lieu of walking the course after a hip or knee replacement. One must also note that a change in your swing will occur after joint replacement. Even though the prostheses are very good for relieving pain and improving function, they're not quite as good as what Mother Nature gave you. Therefore, the fluidity of your swing may be somewhat modified.

MISCELLANEOUS RAMBLING

There are several small topics that do not fit into any specific area of this chapter.

Some braces may be of benefit for specific conditions. Perhaps the classic is a tennis elbow splint which may help significantly for tennis elbow on the outside of the elbow or golfer's elbow on the inside of the elbow. One must be warned not to apply this device too tightly about the forearm. One can compress a rather significant nerve if the brace is applied inappropriately, causing pain and numbness.

Another entity that can help reduce symptoms is a neoprene knee sleeve. Neoprene is a heavy-duty rubber, basically the same material that a wet suit is fabricated from. A knee sleeve made from this material doesn't provide much structural stability to the knee. Yet it does provide warmth and also can actually fool the knee into thinking that it is more stable than it really is. This is due to a feedback mechanism to the brain that will indirectly enhance the stability about the knee. The one downside to neoprene is that it is extremely warm in the summer. Some manufacturers have developed these sleeves out of Lycra, which is much better tolerated than the neoprene here in the South.

Another item that has gained popularity recently is magnet therapy. No one is quite certain how magnets decrease pain and increase function, but for some people they have offered significant improvement. There is an ongoing study at Vanderbilt University comparing magnet therapy with the traditional modalities. Hopefully in the near future we will have a scientific basis for the perceived improvement.

My personal philosophy in using homeopathic remedies is that if it makes you feel better then don't hesitate to use them. As long as they are safe and don't have any potential to hurt you in any way, I see no reason why the individual shouldn't use one of the many homeopathic therapies now offered.

I would now like to discuss some nuances of golf equipment. Most new golf club grips are absolutely outstanding. Yet with continued use over an extended period of time, they can wear just like anything else. When your grips do wear it requires you to grab the club harder, increasing the forces in your forearms. This may give you a predilection for developing either tennis or golfer's elbow. We recommended to runners that they replace their running shoes intermittently so as to prevent lower leg problems. I would implore you to replace your golf grips if severely worn, to help prevent upper extremity problems. Also, thicker grips may be used for the arthritic hand.

Some of the newer golf club bags on the market have a double strap, very similar to a knapsack. If you carry your clubs when you play, it is preferable to use the double strap so that it distributes the weight of the bag over both shoulders as well as centering the weight to place less stress on your neck and upper thoracic spine. I would like also to warn you about placing a heavy golf bag deep into your auto trunk. Lifting a heavy golf bag from the trunk puts an incredible amount of stress both on the shoulders and lower back. Many authorities recommend placing the clubs in the back seat of your four-door automobile to allow you to slide the bag in and out with significantly less stress on your spine.

A deep bunker or very long rough can pose a tremendous hazard for the golfer. The deep sand bunker can certainly cause difficulties in the arthritic knee and hip. It also can pose significant problems for the player who has undergone a total hip or total knee replacement. The shifting in the sand poses inordinate stresses about the joints and can certainly cause a great deal of pain.

Thick rough is especially tough on the wrist and elbow of the golfer. When faced with either of these two entities, I would highly recommend taking a Mulligan and moving the ball out of the heavy rough or deep sand. It may not be the purist's form of golf, but it certainly is a safer form.

SPECIAL DIAGNOSTIC STUDIES

In recent times the addition of the MRI has been a tremendous help in assisting physicians diagnose sports-related injuries. The MRI is exceptionally sensitive at picking up soft tissue injuries such as an injured rotator cuff in the shoulder, or a torn ligament and/or cartilage pad in the knee. I would like to show you three examples of MRI's, each of a different anatomical area.

The shoulder (Fig. 21) is readily visualized with the MRI. As you can see, the upper portion of the humerus, or arm bone (h), sits underneath the roof of the shoulder or acromion (a). The rotator cuff is demonstrated by "r c." The collarbone, or clavicle, is designated by "c." The socket of the shoulder, or glenoid, is seen labeled as "g."

The knee (Fig. 22) is a joint where the MRI is extremely valuable. The femur or thighbone is labeled "f." The tibia or shinbone is labeled "t." The meniscus or cartilage pad is well visualized and labeled "m." One of the major ligaments in the knee, the anterior cruciate ligament or ACL, is labeled "1."

The hip (Fig. 23) is another area where the MRI can be extremely helpful. The main structures that are visualized are the acetabulum or socket of the hip. This is demonstrated in "a." The ball of the hip or upper part of the femur is labeled "h." The remainder of the thighbone or femur is designated as "f."

As previously mentioned, the MRI is extremely sensitive and helpful for diagnostic purposes. Due to the cost, it is usually reserved for patients who pose a diagnostic dilemma, but it is another tool that your physician has in his armamentarium to assist you in the care of your sports-related injury.

THERAPEUTIC EXERCISES

In this last section I would like to demonstrate some exercises, both therapeutic and prophylactic, for the shoulder.

As part of a therapeutic regimen, restoring range of motion and strength is absolutely imperative.

While the inflammation is resolving, one can begin with range of motion exercises. The most traditional are Codman's exercises: making small circles in both a clockwise and counterclockwise fashion (Fig. 24). I prefer performing these exercises three times per day, ten times in each direction both clockwise and counterclockwise.

Putting your hand behind your back with your thumb up (Fig. 25) will help stretch the front portion of the shoulder. It is imperative to reach up as high as possible with the palm out.

A cross-chest maneuver is very effective in stretching the back portion of the shoulder (Fig. 26).

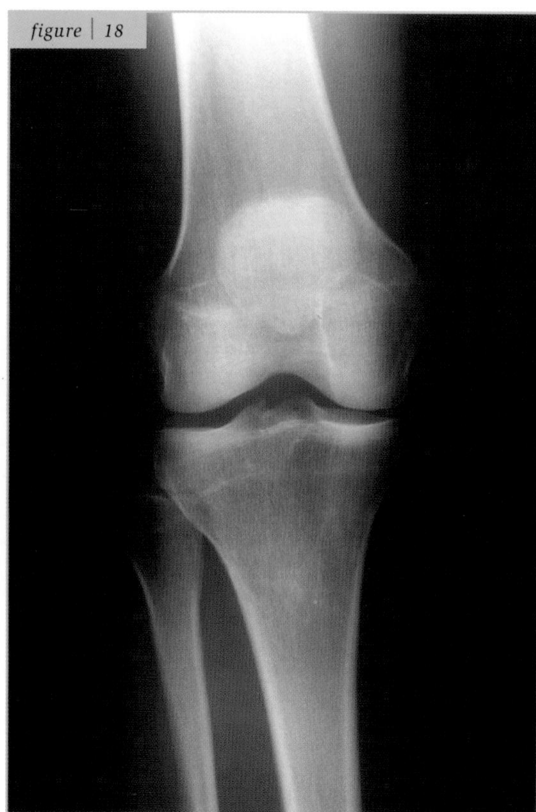

This is a frontal X-ray of the knee with the thigh bone in the upper portion of the picture and the shin bone, the large bone in the lower leg. Please note the smooth contours of the ends of both joints with the nice space in between both bones. Also note the round structure near the center of the knee. This is the kneecap, seen from the front.

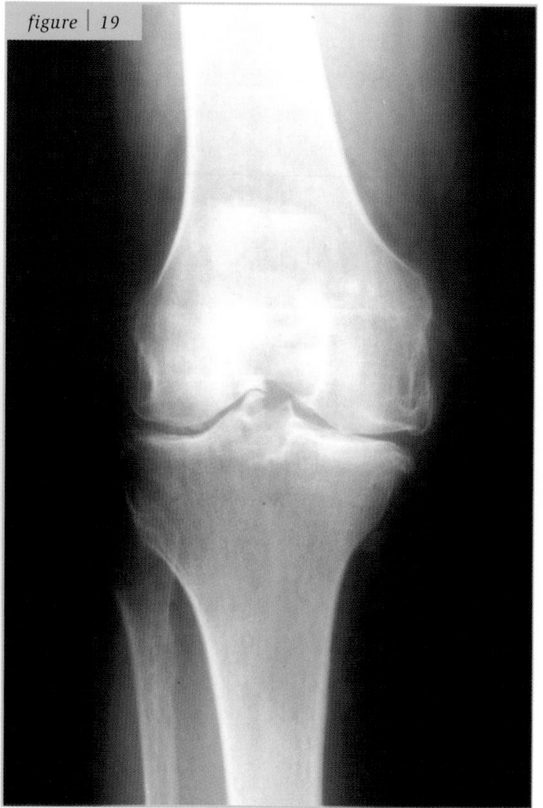

This X-ray demonstrates very severe arthritis affecting both the thigh bone and shin bone. Note the loss of contour of both bones and spurring of both bones as well.

figure | 20

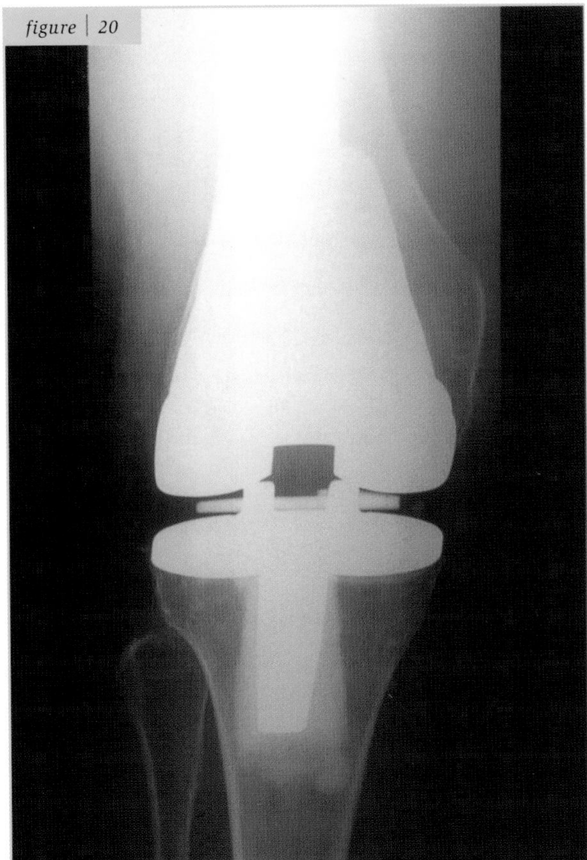

This X-ray reveals a total knee replacement in the previous patient. A large piece of metal allow is cemented at the end of the thighbone. A plastic and metal structure is cemented on the top of the shinbone and a plastic component is placed on the under surface of the kneecap (not shown).

figure | 21

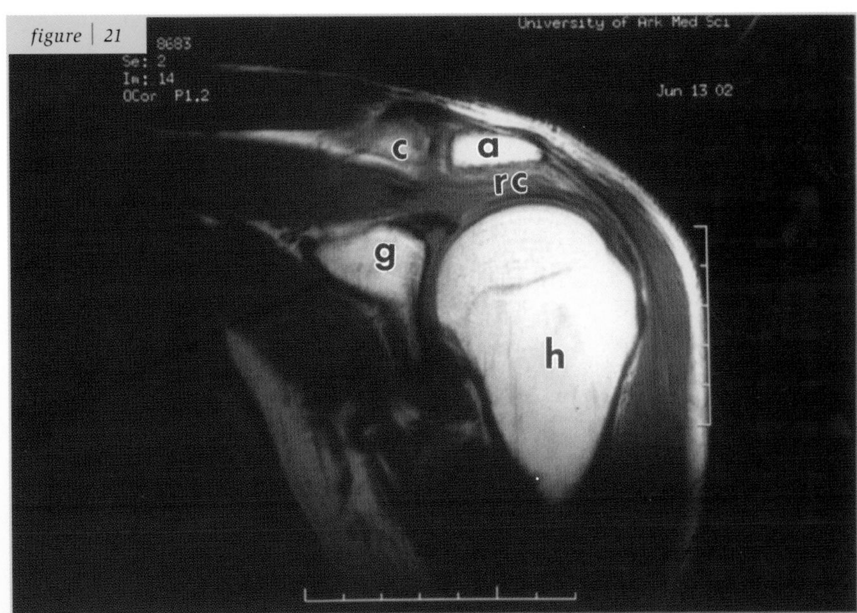

figure | 22

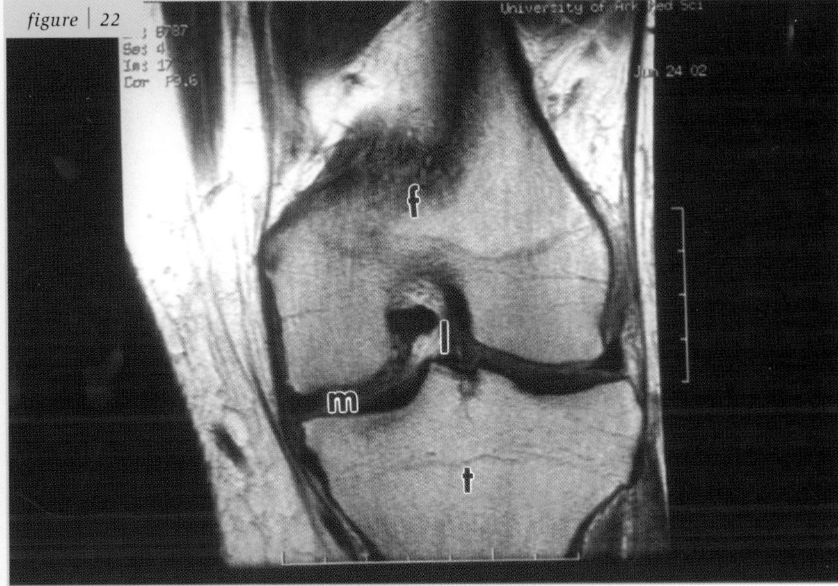

figure | 23

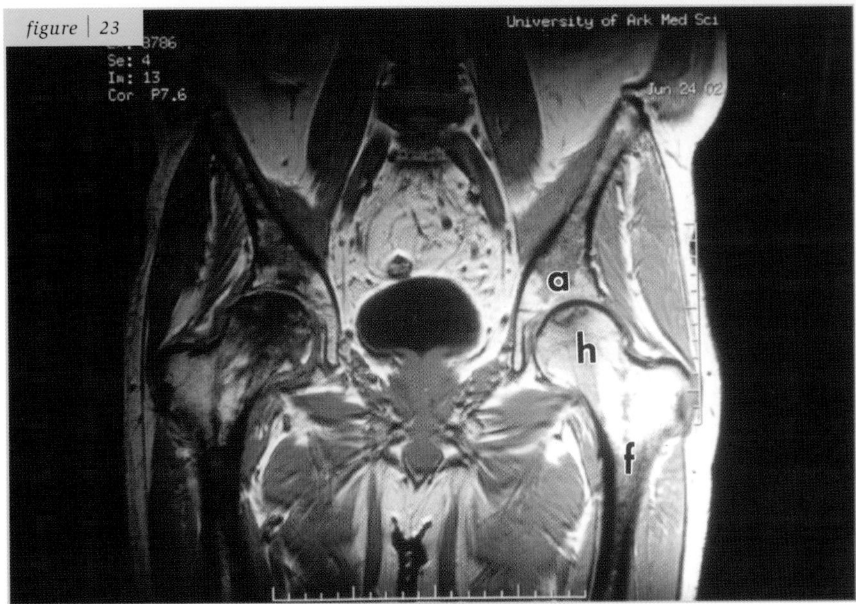

figure | 26

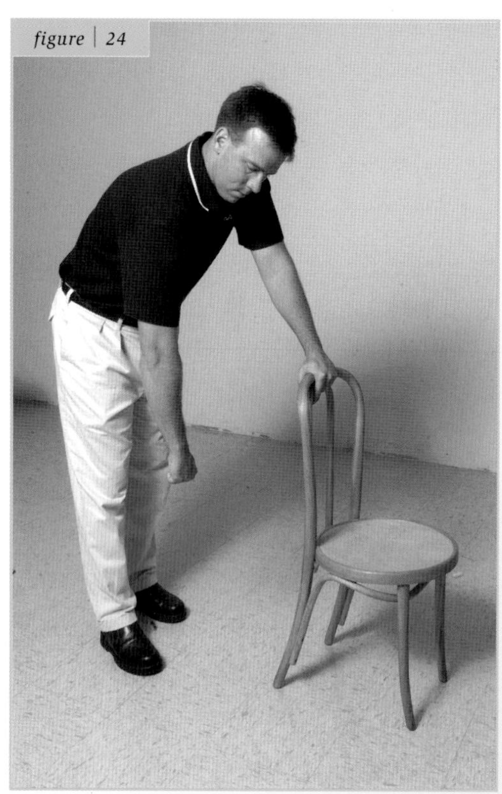

figure | 24

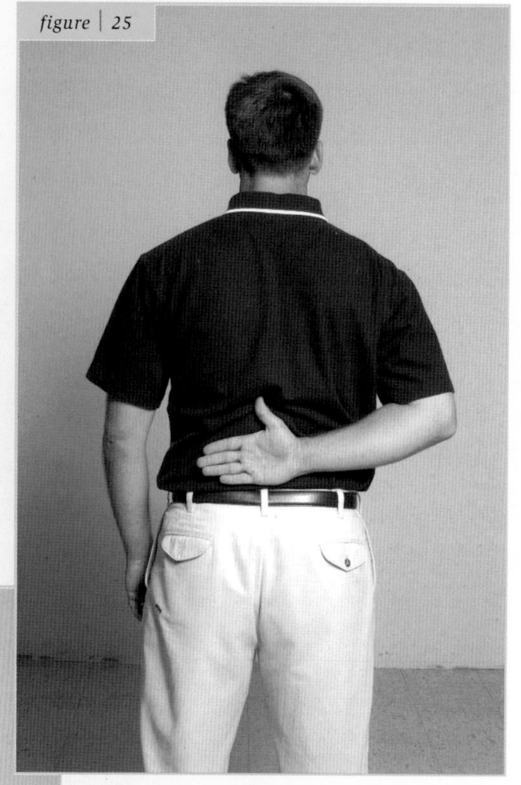

figure | 25

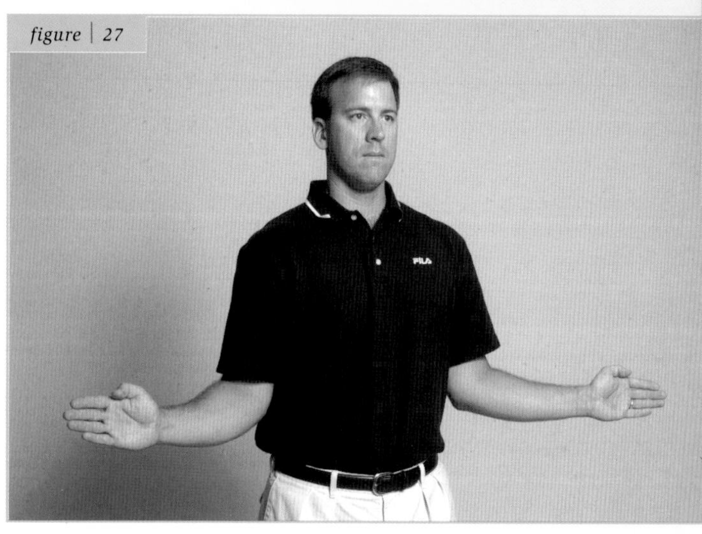

figure | 27

figure | 28

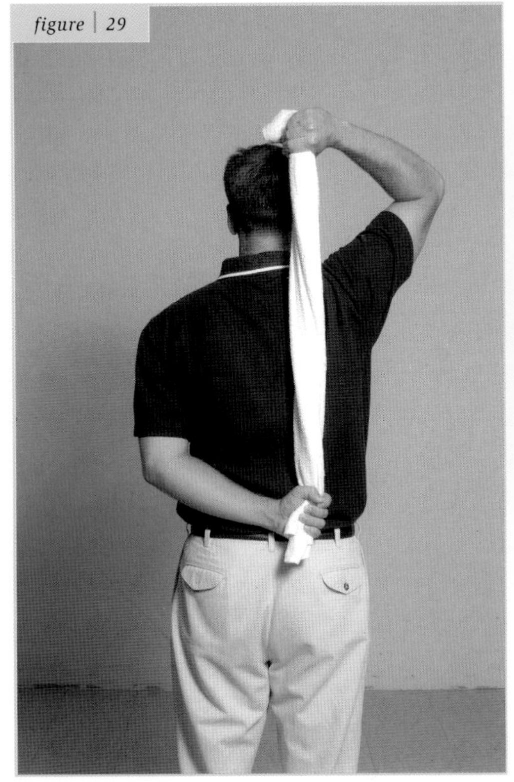
figure | 29

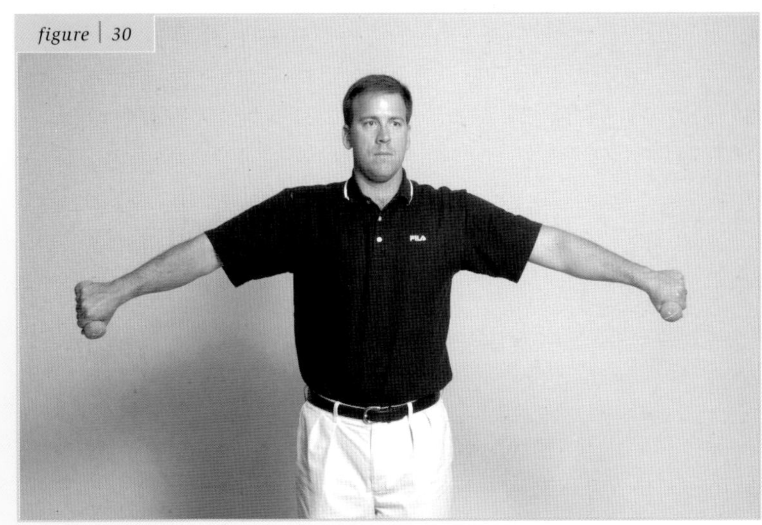
figure | 30

figure | 31

Another exercise entails placing your arms to your side with your elbows close to your body. Slowly move your hands away from the body while keeping your elbows in and your arms bent to 900 (Fig. 27).

The next range of motion exercise entails assisting your injured arm overhead with the uninjured arm (Fig. 28).

Another very effective range of motion exercise entails stretching with the assistance of a towel. The towel is placed behind the back. The good arm is at shoulder level and the towel is raised as high as possible to assist motion in the affected lower arm (Fig. 29).

As previously noted, all these exercises should be performed three times per day for ten repetitions when used therapeutically. When used as a prophylactic measure, one time per day, three to four times per week is permissible.

Strengthening exercises go hand in hand with the range of motion exercises. For these particular exercises, a 2 to 5 lb. dumbbell weight, elastic tubing, or cans of food are adequate.

The first strengthening exercise (Fig. 30) is performed with your palm facing your body. Please do not elevate the weight above shoulder level. Actually it is best to elevate the arms to just below shoulder level with the elbows straight and the thumbs turned toward the floor. The arms should also be approximately 300 forward flexed. The exercise, again, should be performed three times per day for ten repetitions.

The last exercise entails lying with the injured shoulder toward the ceiling (Fig. 31). The elbow must be held close against the body. The weight should be slowly raised toward the ceiling and then lowered to its initial position. All exercises should be performed slowly and deliberately.

These tips will improve the quality of your golf game and keep you injury-free. If any pain is persistent in the region of a joint for greater than seven to ten days, contact your healthcare professional. Most mild inflammation should usually resolve during this period of time. After sustaining an acute injury, apply ice for at least the first 48 hours, 20 minutes on and 20 minutes off, 2 to 3 times per day. Heat should not be used in the acute situation. It's greatest benefit is with a chronic malady, such as a stiff shoulder or knee. Remember, ice should never be placed directly on the skin.

HAND AND WRIST INJURIES IN GOLFERS

CHAPTER 12

Randip R. Bindra, M.D. F.R.C.S.

One back story I can share occurred when I flew to Australia last year for the Accenture Match Play championship. From Louisiana, it was a three-hour flight to Los Angeles, then a two-hour delay there. Another 14 hours to Auckland, New Zealand, then four more hours to Melbourne. It was a total of 26 or 27 hours to get there, and when we arrived I felt stiff and had a sharp pain in my lower left back. I couldn't straighten up completely. I went to the therapists and they worked on me for three or four days. Every time I tried to swing the club, I'd catch a flinch in the back.

The therapists went so deep that I was bruised. They worked hard to get that pain out of my back, but it just wasn't coming out that week. I probably shouldn't have played, but I'd traveled all the way over to Australia, so I tried anyway. My first match went four extra holes. I got beat on the 22nd hole.

I haven't had any real bad problems with my back lately because I've worked hard on trying to keep my hamstrings looser and trying to keep my pelvis level. I would recommend that golfers keep their hamstrings loose because that will greatly reduce the tension on the back. My hamstrings have a tendency to get really tight, and my back stays stiffer because of that. You need to make sure that you keep your muscles stretched so you can turn easier during the swing and the whole motion of the golf swing will work better.

I also utilize the fitness trailer a lot and the guys in there help me get stretched. I also take anti-inflammatories all the time.

Hal Sutton

Although seemingly a benign sport played at one's own relaxing pace, golf is associated with more hand and wrist injuries than is commonly recognized. Almost one in three golfers will experience pain in their hands or wrists during their careers. Fortunately most of these problems are not of a serious nature and can be easily remedied. This chapter highlights the common problems and suggests preventive measures that allow continued enjoyment of the sport.

Injuries that occur to the hand or wrist can be divided into two broad categories: Chronic or longstanding problems caused either by overuse or incorrect technique, and acute or sudden injuries that could happen while swinging a club.

ANATOMICAL STRUCTURE OF THE FOREARM AND WRIST

It is important to understand the structure of the hand and wrist and the overlying muscles to better understand the injuries that can affect them. The muscles that bend the fingers into a fist and bend the wrist forward towards the palm are called the flexor muscles, and constitute the bulk of muscles under the lighter skin on the front of the forearm. These muscles originate from the bony prominence on the inner side of the elbow referred to as the medial epicondyle (Fig. 1). This is the so-called "funny bone," named after the tingling sensation in the hand if the sensitive ulnar nerve running behind it is struck. Near the wrist, the muscles narrow down into tendons and then run along each finger to attach to bone.

The muscles that straighten the fingers and thumb and bend the wrist backwards away from the palm are called the **extensor** muscles and are situated in the forearm deep to the darker skin on the back of the forearm. These muscles are attached to the bony prominence on the outer side of the elbow referred to as the **lateral epicondyle** (Fig. 2). The tendons of the extensor muscles are closely held down to bone at the level of the wrist with a strap of firm tissue or **retinaculum** that covers a two-inch area at the back of the wrist and stops them from bowstringing. The tendons under the retinaculum are lined with smooth **synovial** tissue that lubricates them and allows frictionless gliding under the retinaculum.

The pliability of the wrist is due to eight small bones arranged in two rows of four bones each. The first row joins with the radius and ulna, the two bones of the forearm. The second row of four bones form a joint with the bones of the hand (Fig. 3). The special arrangement of these small bones allows for the good range of wrist motion so essential when swinging a club.

The two bones of the forearm, the radius and ulna, are arranged side-by-side with the ulna bone located on the side of the little finger. When turning the forearm over, the radius rotates around the ulna and is held in place with strong ligaments, of which the most important component is a tough triangular piece of cartilage, the **triangular fibrocartilage** that connects these two bones at the level of the wrist.

CHRONIC INJURIES

Golf is a sport enjoyed by people of all ages, with differing body types and levels of fitness. Overuse or incorrect technique over a long period of time can result in chronic problems with pain around the elbow or wrist and will affect not only your game, but also make daily tasks difficult.

The only injury named after the sport is "golfer's elbow," or **medial epi-**

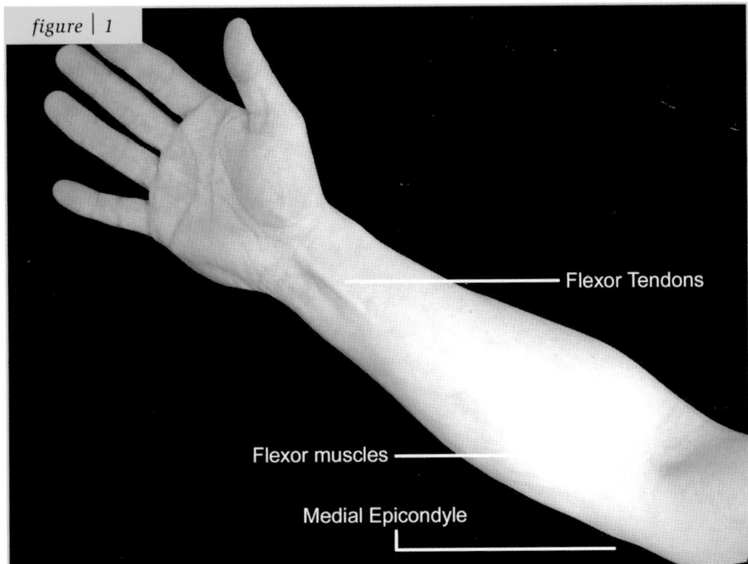

The front of the forearm, demonstrating the flexor muscles.

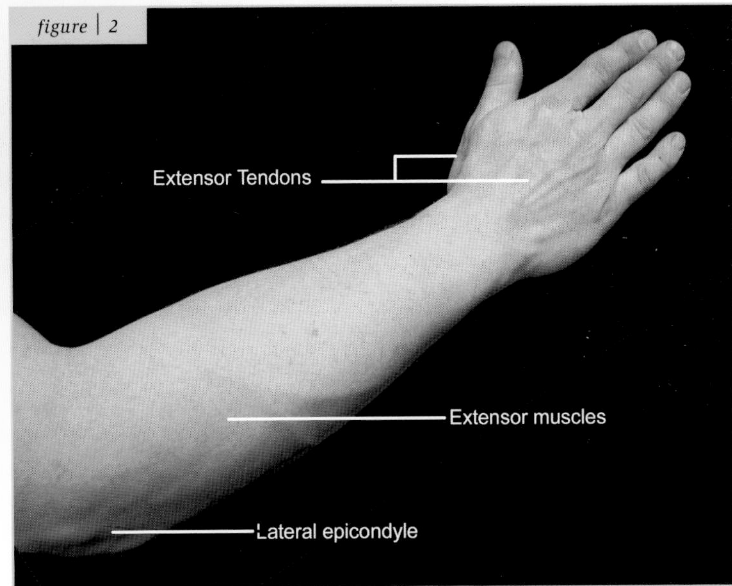

The back of the forearm, showing the extensor muscles.

condylitis, an inflammation of the flexor tendons at their point of origin from the medial epicondyle. Such an inflammation can also affect the extensor muscles at the lateral epicondyle, referred to as **lateral epicondylitis,** or more commonly, "tennis elbow." Tennis elbow is the most common cause of pain around the elbow in golfers and manifests as soreness in the outer aspect of the elbow that is aggravated by twisting movements of the wrist. A commercially available strap worn on the upper forearm, along with a period of rest and medication, is usually effective in early stages. If the pain persists, seek an expert opinion.

Too tight a grip or improper positioning of the hands can affect the natural movement of the wrist during the golf swing and result in repetitive undue stretching of the tendons around the wrist. Repetitive overstretching of the tendons causes inflammation of the synovial sheath that lines the tendons at the wrist retinaculum. The result is a soft, painful swelling around the tendons referred to as **tenosynovitis**. Movements of the wrist that stretch the affected tendons are exquisitely painful, while other movements may not be affected. The tendons at the base of the thumb are commonly affected; not only do they affect your golf swing, they will also make all tasks requiring gripping, pinching or twisting quite uncomfortable.

In its early stage, tenosynovitis will settle with rest and an appropriate splint that effectively immobilizes the wrist and thumb, along with a course of anti-inflammatory medication that you have used before and can tolerate. If these measures fail to resolve the problem within three or four weeks, it is wise to seek the opinion of a specialist to confirm the diagnosis and consider other treatment options, such a steroid injection into the inflamed tendon sheath, physical therapy and, if all else fails, surgical release of the tendons.

Chronic problems recur if the underlying cause is not treated. Before you return to your game, it is very important that you seek the help of a golf instructor who will help you make the appropriate modifications to your equipment and technique to minimize chance of a recurrence. It is also important to perform a warm-up of stretching exercises of your wrist muscles, both before and after a game. This is especially true for the "weekend" players who move from their desks to a strenuous round of golf on the weekend and injure the muscles that are not properly conditioned.

ACUTE INJURIES

Golfers can, like anyone else, hurt their hands or wrists if they trip or fall onto their hands. Almost exclusive to golf is an uncommon injury in the wrist, a fracture of the hook of the hamate bone. The hamate is one of the small bones of the wrist located in the palm in line with the little and ring fingers (Fig. 4). The fracture occurs with a missed hit, when the club mistakenly strikes the ground or hits a stone or other object concealed in the rough. The force intended for the ball is instead transmitted via the club handle to the palm, where it can break the hook of the hamate. The symptoms are sudden pain in the wrist worsened by making a fist. Movements of the little finger are more noticeably painful. Because the hamate hook cannot be clearly seen on ordinary x-rays, the injury is often missed on the first visit to the emergency room and is often picked up weeks later after the pain fails to settle and a CT scan is obtained (Fig. 5). These injuries cannot be prevented, but it is important that a severe blow to the hand which causes pain in the wrist should be evaluated by a specialist and appropriate imaging studies be obtained.

A tear in the triangular cartilage between the radius and ulna at the wrist can occur after a fall or twisting injury or may be the result of repetitive forceful impact between the wrist bones and the tip of the ulna. Pain is noticed more on the inside (little-finger side) of the wrist and is most noticeable when gripping and swinging the club. Tears of this nature usually do not respond as well as tendonitis to rest in a splint and physical therapy. If the diagnosis is suspected, specialized studies such as MRI scans are required. The tear can also be directly visualized by arthroscopy (keyhole surgery) of the wrist, at which time it is possible to deal with small tears.

OTHER PRE-EXISTING CONDITIONS

The pursuit of golf can bring to the surface other pre-existing problems in the wrist that become painful from the stresses and strains placed on the wrist during a round of golf.

Such a condition is **carpal tunnel syndrome**, which affects people of all ages and is due to pressure on the median nerve that runs down the front of the wrist (Fig. 4). This presents with a feeling of "pins and needles," or aching in the hand after prolonged gripping of the golf club. A persistent numbness in the fingers or weakness of the hand indicates long-standing and a more serious nerve compression. In early stages, this condition can be helped with rest in a splint and anti-inflammatory medications. If carpal tunnel syndrome is suspected, early assessment by a specialist is recommended to avoid irreversible loss of nerve function in the hand. Surgery for this condition is effective in resolving the symptoms and is often eventually required.

Arthritic conditions in the hand can also be aggravated by a strenuous round of golf. The basal joint of the thumb is one of the commonest joints in the body to be affected by osteoarthritis (Fig. 3). This pain usually is localized to the arthritic bone and the joint is often tender to local pressure. Often, other joints such as the joints at the tips of the fingers are simultaneously involved. Both arthritis and tendonitis can present with pain and swelling around the wrist, but arthritis is apparent on X-rays. Arthritis is not curable, but fortunately can be remedied with simple measures such as use of a strap or brace along with anti-inflammatory medications. Most people find that they can continue to enjoy their game within the limitations imposed by arthritis. Surgery is helpful if the joint remains persistently painful between games; it needs to be scheduled carefully, however, as it can involve a prolonged convalescence period.

PREVENTION

To summarize, not all injuries are preventable, but stretching exercises can be helpful in prevention of some common problems and must become a part of your routine before and after a game. It is important to seek the help of an instructor if you develop a problem, and to consult a specialist if you have pain that persists after you have tried rest and splints for a few weeks. These simple measures will ensure a trouble-free and enjoyable, long golfing career.

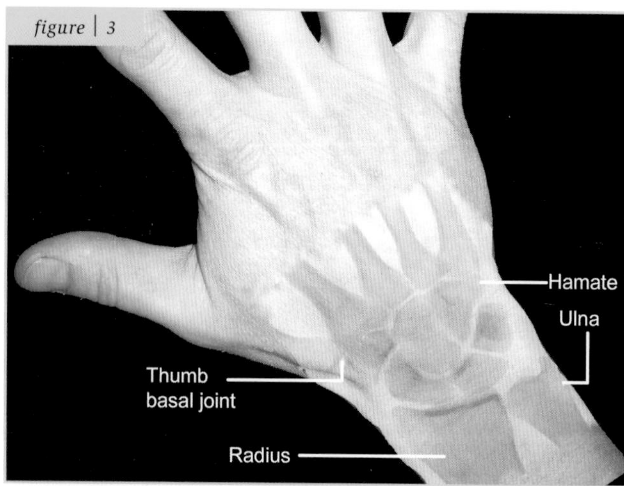

The skeletal structure of the forearm and wrist.

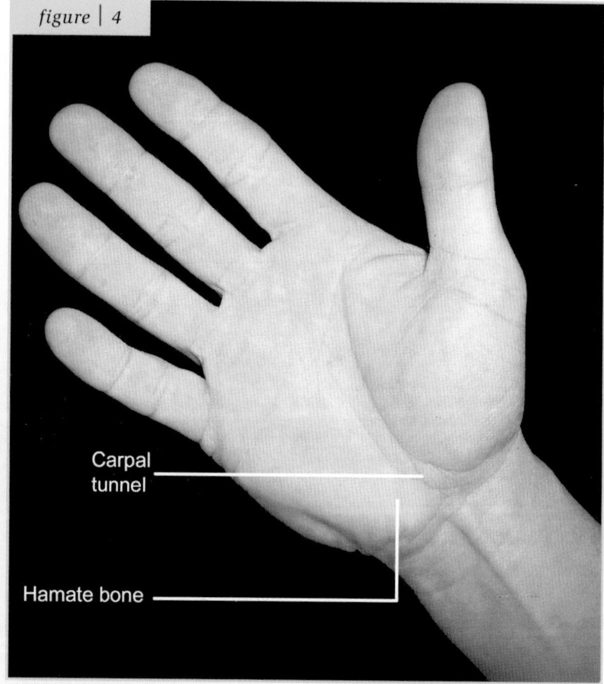

Close-up view of the front of the wrist and hand.

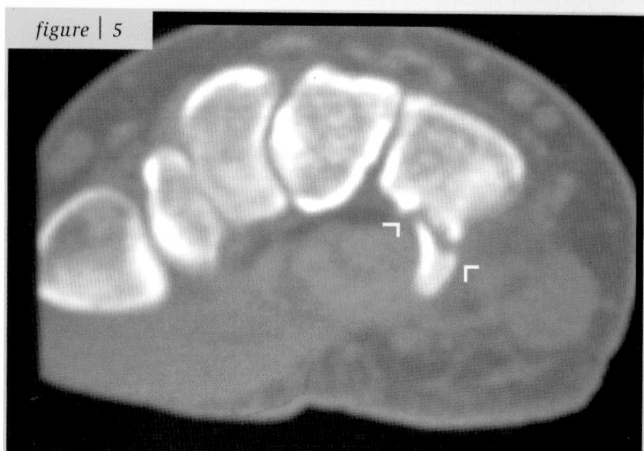

CT scan of the wrist, demonstrating a hamate hook fracture (white arrows).

YOUR FEET AND GOLF

CHAPTER 13

Ruth L. Thomas, M.D.

As was the custom at the time in Germany, when I was 18 years old I was drafted into the National Service. For the first three months I shared a room with seven other young men, rose at 5 A.M., and endured the very strict, very demanding training. One day in the middle of January, with snow and ice on the ground, I was required to go on a march carrying a 30-pound backpack and a rifle. After marching for hours, our leader yelled "airplane attack," which meant that immediately everyone was required to drop flat on their bellies so as to avoid being a target. After repeating this exercise 20 or 30 times in a row, my back started to hurt and I fell on my side and rolled to my belly. Unfortunately, this was the incorrect procedure, and my leader decided to make me do it until I got it right. Even though I managed to march back to the barracks, this was the beginning of my back problems. The next morning I was paralyzed and had to be taken by stretcher to the hospital, where I spent four weeks, the first two with my legs in traction. Already a golf professional, I thought my career was over at 18. Since then, I have had back pain every day of my life.

Bernhard Langer

The feet of a golfer, as for most of us, are one of the most neglected aspects of the body. In fact, if you're like most people, you never pay much attention to your feet until they give you problems. Good foot action is a sign of a good golfer. Unhealthy feet, even a painful callus or corn, will affect any golfer's game. A foot problem will impede both the timing and the balance of the golf swing, and will greatly compromise the golfer's performance. Golfers must be able to stand and firmly plant their feet on the grass or sand, balance themselves, and engage in a golf swing. This all requires healthy, non-painful feet. For the golfer who walks 18 holes, this will provide the opportunity to walk at least 4 to 5 miles. Any type of foot problem will no longer allow walking; therefore, the golfer will miss a great opportunity to enjoy other health benefits, such as a cardiovascular workout. With painful feet, this becomes impossible. Therefore, it is helpful to understand some of the basic foot anatomy and to recognize common foot problems which could compromise any golfer's game. It's important not to ignore the foundation upon which the game of golf stands, our feet.

ANATOMY

The foot is a very complex structure. Each foot is made up of 26 bones. In fact, the bones of the feet make up almost one-quarter of the total number of bones in our entire bodies. There are some 33 joints in the feet; these joints allow the foot to be flexible. There are 20 muscles located throughout the foot; these muscles allow foot movements. Numerous tendons connect the muscles to the bones. When muscles contract they pull the tendons, which pull the bones, which allows the feet to move. There are more than 100 different ligaments in the feet. The ligaments hold the bones together. In fact, some ligaments in the foot may well be the strongest in the entire body. Most people's feet are very ticklish; there is a good reason for this. There are numerous nerve endings in the foot; it's very important for the foot to be sensitive. The nerve endings allow the feet to be sensitive to what we walk on.

The foot is divided into three subdivisions: the **forefoot**, the **mid-foot**, and the **hind-foot**. The **forefoot** is made up of five metatarsal bones and the phalanges (the bones in the toes). Each toe has three phalanges, except for the big toe, which has two phalanges. The three phalanges, or bones of the toes, are designated as **proximal**, **middle**, and **distal**. Proximal means that it's closer to the heart. The big toe, or the hallux, has two bones, the proximal and the distal. The digits of the toes and their metatarsal bones are numbered 1 to 5: the big toe is the first toe and the little toe is the fifth toe. The big toe, or the first metatarsal bone, is an extremely important bone. It is the big toe that bears most of the weight and plays a very important role in propulsion. This is why it's the shortest and the thickest (Fig. 1).

The **mid-foot** is comprised of five of the seven tarsal bones of the foot. The tarsal bones all work together as a group. It is the tarsal bones that conform to the surface on which an individual walks. The talus bones connect to the metatarsals. Ligaments rigidly connect the tarsal bones and the metatarsals to each other. The metatarsals are connected to the phalanges. The phalanges are the bones of the toes. The joints between the metatarsals and the first phalanx of each toe are called the **metatarsal pha-**

langeal joints. It is these joints that form the ball of the foot. The ball of the foot is very important for walking. For those with an interest in more detailed anatomy, the five tarsal bones of the mid-foot are the **navicular**, **cuboid**, and **cuneiform** bones (Fig. 2).

The **hind-foot** contains the remaining two tarsal bones: the **talus** and the **calcaneus**. The calcaneus is the largest of the seven tarsal bones and is called the heel bone. The talus is another large bone that rests on top of the calcaneus; it forms the pivot of the ankle. The calcaneus, or heel bone, is a very complex bone. On its upper surface are smooth facet joints, which connect with corresponding joints on the talus to form what is called the **subtalar joint**. The rear part of the calcaneus consists of a large rounded projection of bone that forms the back of the heel. It is this calcaneal tuberosity, or bone projection, which is the attachment site of the Achilles tendon. The underside of the calcaneus is the surface that comes into contact with the ground during weight bearing, or walking. A fat pad cushions the calcaneus, or heel bone. The talus sits on top of the calcaneus, and connects with the ends of the tibia and the fibula (two bones of the lower leg) to form the complex ankle joint (Fig. 3).

The muscles of the foot, just like the bones of the foot, are very complex. Muscles in the feet are classified as either **intrinsic** or **extrinsic**. The intrinsic muscles of the foot are the muscles inside the foot; they are responsible for the movement of the toes. The extrinsic muscles are located on the outside of the foot. Their tendons cross the ankle to insert onto bones of the feet. Both the intrinsic and extrinsic muscles of the feet help to support the arches of the feet.

Each foot has two arches. The **transverse arch** is also known as the **metatarsal arch**. The second arch is called the **longitudinal arch**. There are two parts to the longitudinal arch; one is the inside (medial border) of the foot, and the other is on the outside (lateral border) of the foot. The longitudinal arch is at a right angle to the transverse arch. The longitudinal arch flattens when standing and shortens when not bearing weight, such as sitting or lying down. The longitudinal arch is located at the instep of the foot. Some people are said to be "flat-footed;" this means that their arches are always relaxed and low, whether they're standing up, lying down, playing golf, or seated. Having relaxed arches, or flat-footedness, rarely causes problems. It is those individuals who have a so-called "high-arched" foot, which is rigid, who may experience pain.

The foot is a weight-bearing structure that allows walking. The foot must be a very adaptive structure in order to adapt to standing, running, putting, or swinging a golf club. The multiple bones and other soft tissue structures of the foot give it pliability, which allows it to move. Every golfer has his or her own swing. The same is true about walking; everyone has a different style of walking, but the basic movements are the same. It is the big toe that pushes an individual forward and helps to maintain balance. The metatarsal bones allow the foot to adapt to walking surfaces, and in a normal walk, the body weight is centered over the feet.

ANKLE ANATOMY AND HINDFOOT

The ankle is a complex structure comprised of three bones: the **talus**, the **tibia** and the **fibula** (leg bones). Each one of these bones is joined together by ligaments. The joint below the ankle joint (between the talus and calcaneus) is the subtalar joint. The ankle joint enables the foot to bend up and down. The subtalar joint allows the foot to move from side to side (Fig. 4).

TENDONS

The most famous of all the tendons is the **Achilles tendon**. It is one of the largest tendons in the body. It is important for

figure | 1

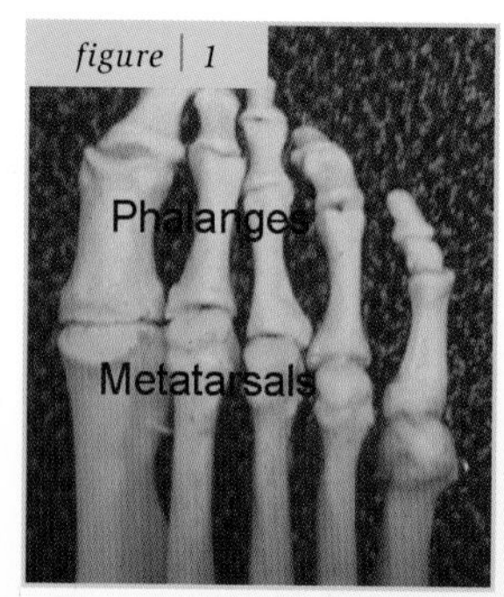

figure | 2

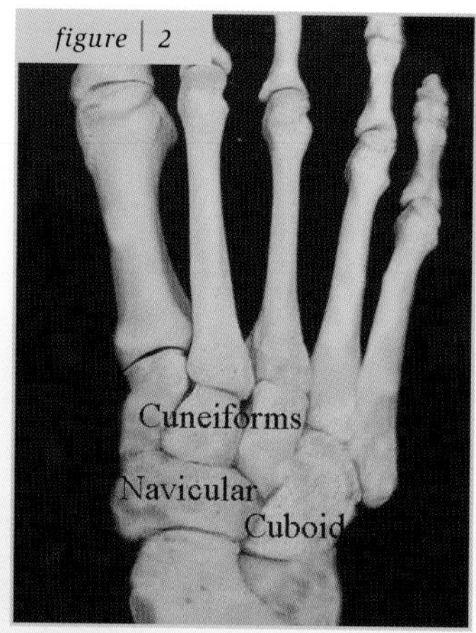

figure | 3

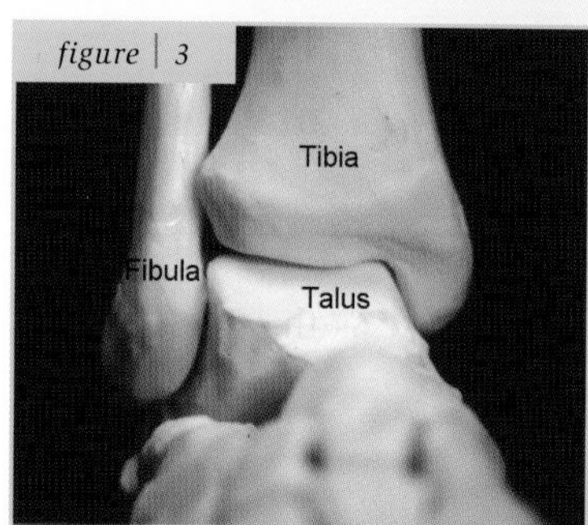

figure | 4

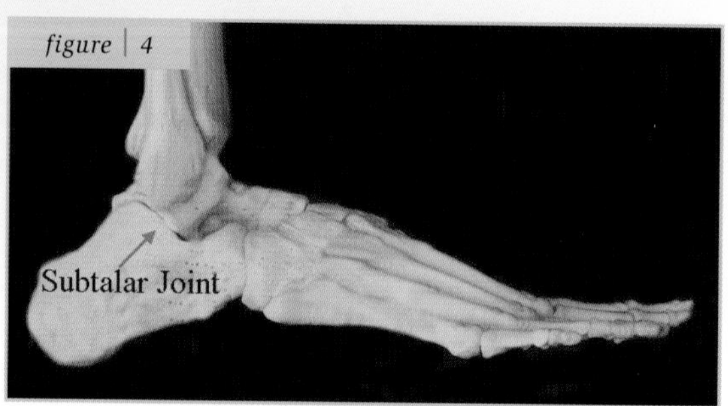

figure | 5

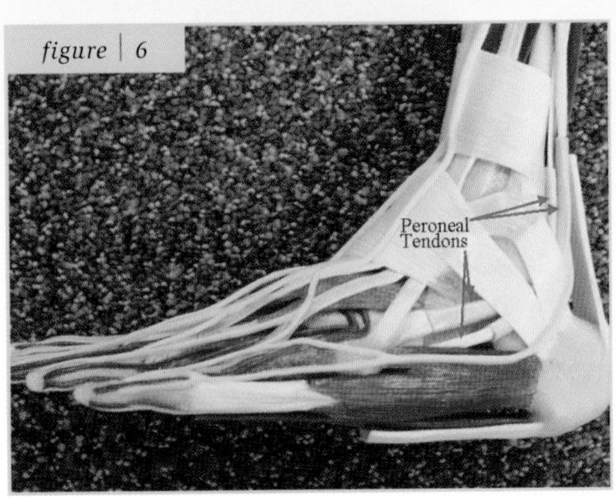

figure | 6

walking, jumping, running, and the golf swing. It attaches the large calf muscles to the calcaneus, or heel bone (Fig. 5). The Achilles tendon allows us to rise up on our toes. Another important tendon of the ankle/foot complex is the **posterior** (back) **tibial tendon**; it attaches a smaller muscle of the calf to the underside of the foot. It is this tendon that provides the dynamic arch of the foot and allows the foot to move downward and inward. The **anterior** (front) **tibial tendon** attaches to bones on the front surface of the foot and allows us to raise the foot. There are two peroneal tendons located on the lateral side of the ankle. These tendons turn a sharp angle just below the fibula bone before inserting into the lateral and underside of the foot (Fig.6). These two tendons seem unusually susceptible to tendonitis in golfers. This is probably related to the rotational component of the hindfoot during the swing. Altogether, there are some 13 tendons that cross the ankle. They are responsible for the remarkable array of movements of the ankle, foot, and toes.

PROBLEMS

For most golfers, the problems associated with their feet and ankles are usually transient in nature and will respond to self-treatment and rest. For those recalcitrant problems that are not responsive, a physician consultation may be needed. No golfer should continue to play golf with painful feet. When giving your history to a treating physician, supplying answers to the following questions may be very helpful.

1. Is this complaint related to a recent injury, or is it more chronic in nature?
2. When does the pain occur; is it during or after your golf game?
3. What have you done about it; how have you treated it? Medications? Braces? Exercises?
4. Has there been a recent change in your golf game; have you purchased new shoes or changed your swing? Are you playing on a different terrain?
5. Are you using orthotic devices in your shoes? How do they help? Are they rigid or flexible?

An examination for foot problems will also include a physical examination of the entire lower extremity, or leg, and the lumbar spine and back. The patient will be asked to walk, stand, and sit for different components of the examination. Not only will the foot and ankle be examined thoroughly, but also leg muscles will be tested, and the Achilles tendon will be examined for tightness. Leg length inequality will also be noted. The physician may also order x-rays to evaluate the bones of the ankle and foot. If after a thorough physical examination and review of x-rays additional information is needed to make the correct diagnosis, then a bone scan, CT scan, or MRI may be added to the evaluation.

COMMON ANKLE INJURIES: LATERAL (SIDE) INJURIES

Pain located around the lateral aspect, or outside of the ankle, can be secondary to many causes. Frequently, pain in this area is due to an ankle sprain. An ankle sprain occurs when ligaments in the ankle joint are stretched beyond their limits and are torn. The most common cause of an ankle sprain is applying weight to a foot when it is turned inward (inverted) or turned outward (everted). This may happen when standing on an uneven surface. The typical sprain involves injury to the lateral, or outside, ligament complex. A **high sprain** refers to an injury to the ligaments connecting the tibia and fibula bones. This type of sprain occurs more frequently with an external (outside) rotation injury to the ankle. It is called high because it is located above the typical ankle sprain. A high type of ankle injury can be very slow to heal. Tenderness on the inner side of the ankle after a sprain usually indicates a more severe injury. Ankle sprains are classified by the degree of severity. Ankle sprains are divided into three types: **Grade 1**—stretch and/or minor tear of the ligaments without laxity (loosening); **Grade 2**—a tear of the ligament plus more movement or laxity; and **Grade 3**—a complete tear of the ligaments, which causes a great deal of movement.

TREATMENT OF ANKLE SPRAINS

When an ankle sprain occurs, it means that golfing activities should shop. Continuing to play golf with an ankle sprain is only inviting further injury, which will prolong any type of rehabilitation. The first step of treatment for an ankle sprain is to follow the **R.I.C.E.** treatment plan: **Rest**, **Ice**, **Compression**, and **Elevation** are the best immediate and most effective treatments for ankle sprains or strains. Ankle sprains will cause a great deal of swelling, or edema, around the ankle; therefore, it's important to minimize swelling. Applying ice to the injured ankle is very helpful, but it's important to never apply ice directly to the skin; doing so may damage the skin itself. The ice should be wrapped in a protective device such as a plastic bag or towel. The ice should be applied for about 20 minutes. After the ankle has been cooled down, the ankle should be immobilized in an ACE bandage and then elevated. Over-the- counter non-steroidal anti-inflammatory medications (NSAIDs) can be very helpful to alleviate the pain and inflammation of an ankle sprain. Aspirin can help to reduce pain and inflammation. Non-steroidal anti-inflammatory medications and aspirin should only be used if an individual does not have any sensitivities or contraindications to their use. It's very important to read the inserts that accompany these medications. If there are any questions about their use, or their use with other medications including herbal supplements, a pharmacist or physician should be consulted. Acetaminophen is also helpful to reduce pain; however, it will not help with inflammation. An ankle sprain will become evident with the appearance of bruising, or collection of blood, at the injury site. Full weight bearing should be avoided until the bruising and the swelling begin to dissipate and it no longer hurts to walk on the foot. At this particular time, a rehabilitation program can be started; this program will include gentle stretching exercises of the Achilles tendon complex, strengthening of the outside ankle muscles, and balancing skills to improve proprioception (the body's awareness of its parts in space). One simple exercise is to draw the letters of the alphabet with your toes. Any exercise program should be continued for several months to reduce the risk of re-injury and to avoid chronic pain problems. Any ankle sprain that does not respond to self-treatment in one to two weeks may indicate a more serious problem and will need a thorough evaluation and diagnosis by a physician.

PERONEAL TENDONITIS

Another cause of lateral ankle pain is peroneal tendonitis. The peroneal tendons run just behind the outside ankle-bone (fibula) and obliquely across the outside back one-third of the foot. Acute injury to the peroneal tendons is uncommon, but degenerative changes in the tendons occur frequently with age. Golfers seem unusually susceptible to peroneal tendonitis, probably related to the rotation of the hindfoot during swing. Symptoms of peroneal tendinitis are primarily located just behind the ankle bone and along the course of the tendons on the outside portion of the foot. Initially rest, NSAIDs, and activity modification are sufficient to allow improvement. However, either of the peroneal tendons can develop degenerative tears leading to chronic pain along the course of the tendon. Mild symptoms are treated with NSAIDs and a program of rehabilitation. Warm-up exercises and stretching are emphasized. A laced ankle brace with medial and lateral supports reduces available motion and reduces stress on the tendon. High-top basketball shoes can be helpful because they also restrict ankle inversion. More significant pain requires near-complete rest of the peroneal tendons using a boot walker (removal cast) for several weeks. If initial conservative measures fail, operative repair of the tendon tears is recommended.

ACHILLES TENDON PROBLEMS

The Achilles tendon is the largest in the body. It is the tendon that is most exposed. **Achilles tendonitis** (inflammation) is a very common problem among athletes. Achilles tendonitis is a chronic problem; it occurs primarily from overuse. As the tendonitis worsens over time, pain becomes fairly regular and is aggravated with almost any activity, particularly golfing. The worst thing that a golfer can do when he or she is experiencing pain in the Achilles tendon is to ignore early discomfort and continue to play anyway. If the Achilles tendon becomes sore and achy, it is an indication to discontinue all golfing activities and pay attention. Another cause of Achilles tendonitis is **tight, weak calf muscles**. Overuse of these muscles can lead to fatigue. The more fatigued the calf muscles are, the shorter and tighter they will become. This tightness will stretch the Achilles tendon and can lead to inflammation, or tendonitis. At the first sign of Achilles tendon pain or discomfort, all golfing activities should be stopped; this includes practicing and putting. Strengthening the calf muscles will help to reduce stress on the Achilles tendon. Toe raises, balancing on your toes, and wall-stretching exercises can be very helpful in this situation.

Insertional Achilles Tendonitis occurs where the Achilles tendon inserts into the heel bone (calcaneus). This type of tendonitis may be associated with a bony prominence of the heel bone. The heel counter of the shoe often aggravates it. In certain situations, the tendon at its junction with the bone may become calcified. X-rays of the ankle and foot may demonstrate a bone spur extending into the tendon from the insertion (Fig. 7). The first treatment for this type of tendonitis is **non-operational treatment**; this includes use of NSAIDs, ice massage, contrast baths, and immobilization of the ankle and the foot with use of a boot-walker or a cast during the acute period of inflammation (Fig. 8). Physical therapy can be helpful in this particular situation. Occasionally, orthotic devices or a simple heel lift can be effective. If non-operative measures fail, **operative treatment** may be indicated. Surgery involves the removal of the prominent bone, debridement (cleaning) of the Achilles insertion and the surrounding inflamed bursa (joint sac), and removal of any spur (Fig. 9).

Another type of tendonitis is called **non-insertional tendonitis**. The problem occurs about one to two inches (2–5 cm) above the site of insertion of the tendon and is not associated with shoe wear pressure (Fig. 10 and 11). The pain is often worse in the morning and after exercise. Over time, the pain can become constant with any activity such as walking, running, or golfing. Non-insertional tendonitis can occur in three stages. In the **first stage**, the irritation of the tendon is limited to the tissue surrounding the tendon, and is called **peritendonitis**. Many of these cases will resolve with rest and conservative treatment. Most do not require surgical therapy. Conservative treatment includes use of the non-steroidal anti-inflammatory medications

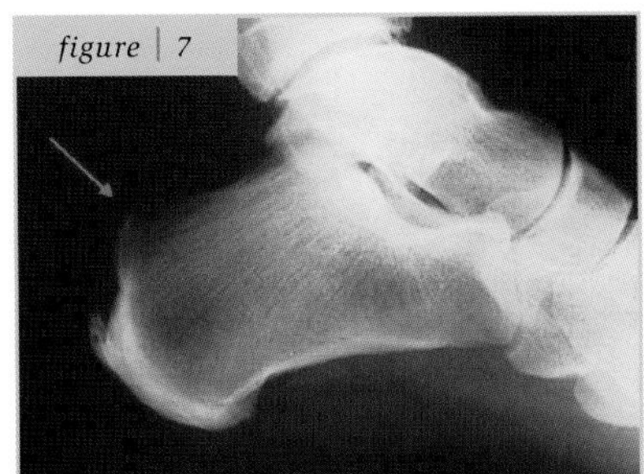
figure | 7

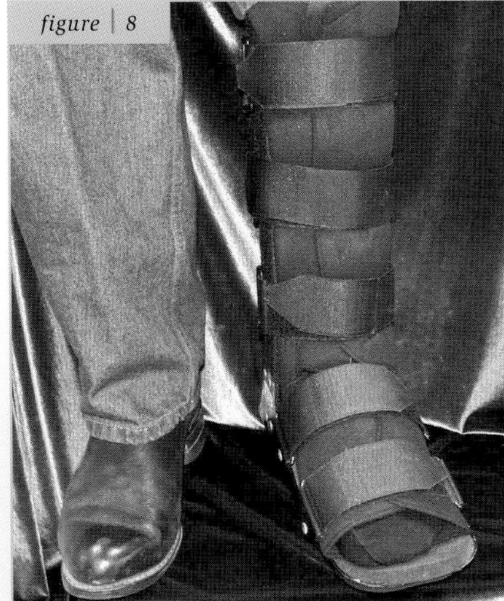
figure | 8

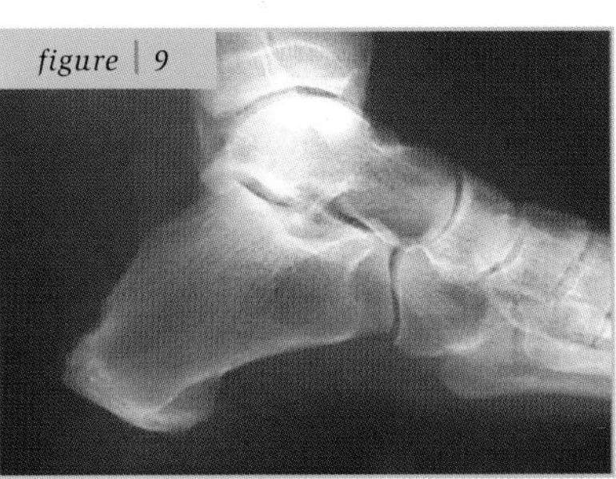
figure | 9

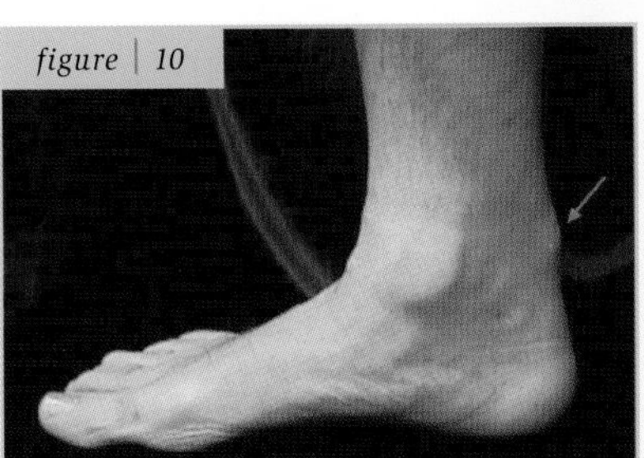
figure | 10

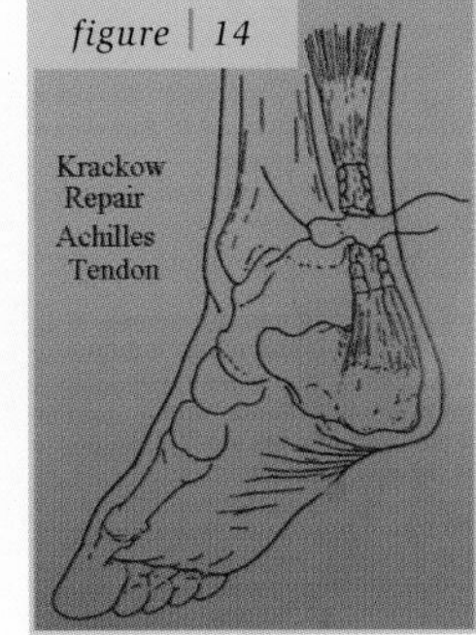

figure | 14

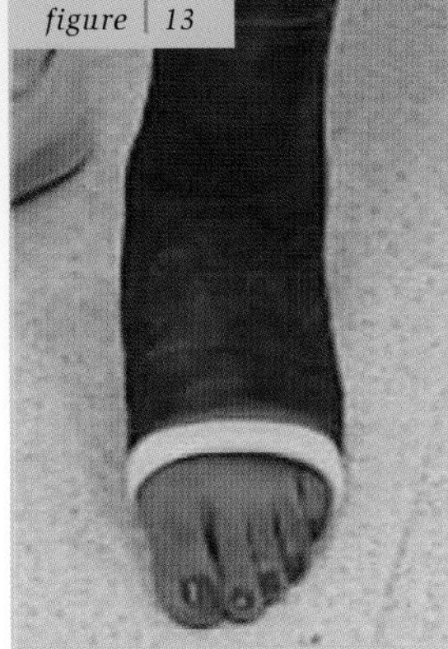
figure | 13

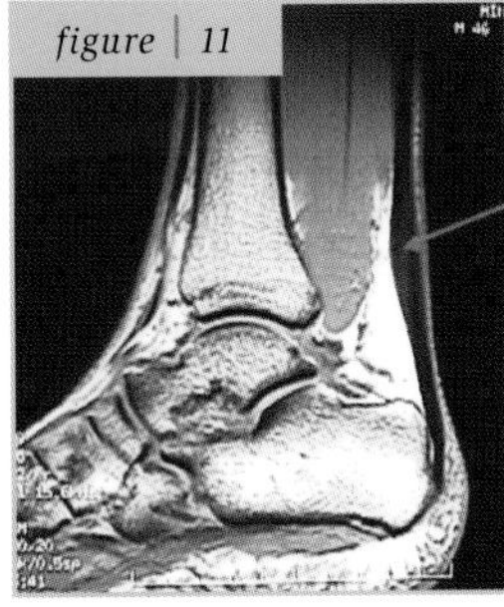
figure | 11

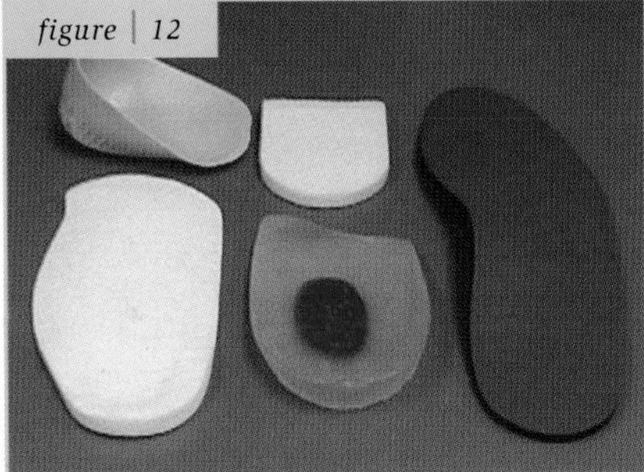
figure | 12

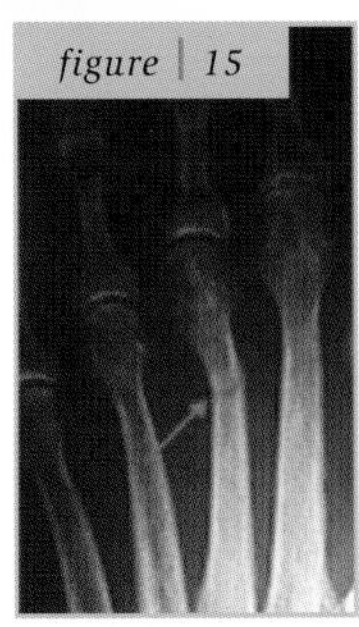
figure | 15

(NSAIDs), ice massage, electrostimulation, and contrast baths. A physician or therapist often provides electrostimulation. When the pain becomes severe, temporary use of a heel lift can be helpful (Fig. 12). The **second stage** of insertional tendonitis involves both **peritendonitis** (inflammation of soft tissues around the tendon), and **tendonosis** (inflammation of the tendon itself). In this stage, a portion of the Achilles tendon itself is diseased and has developed an area of nodularity (dysfunction). This stage of tendonitis is at risk for rupture. If an individual is symptomatic, with worsening pain and limitation of activities, surgical therapy may be indicated. The **third stage** of insertional tendonitis is one of **pure tendonosis**. These patients experience rupture of the tendon without warning symptoms. Most patients are middle-aged, and are amateur athletes. When the tendon is examined, it is found to have evidence of chronic degeneration. Achilles tendon rupture usually occurs when the force on the tendon is greater than the tensile strength that the tendon can bear. The most common patient for an Achilles tendon rupture is usually a middle-aged amateur athlete, or golfer with silent tendon degeneration, or aging changes. Most ruptures of this tendon occur from a combination of forceful stretches of the tendon with contraction of the calf muscles. Many patients report a sudden, often audible "pop" that usually occurs during a rapid push-off maneuver, and a sudden loss of calf strength. It can also occur with sudden dorsiflexion, or pushing down of the foot, such as stepping in a hole. There is usually little warning, and often the pain can be quite severe. Individuals who have experienced a rupture of the Achilles tendon will not be able to lift up on their toes; although they may be able to point the toes when not weight-bearing. Partial tears of the Achilles tendon may be treated without surgery; this usually involves immobilization or casting of the foot and ankle for up to 12 weeks (Fig. 13). After a few weeks of rest, golfing could be continued, but only while protected in the cast or a brace. Protection must be continued until the Achilles tear is healed. A heel lift or bracing device may also be required for up to six months to one year following removal of the cast. Rehabilitation is very important after this type of injury to regain flexibility, endurance, and muscle strength. A completely ruptured Achilles tendon will often require surgical repair. Surgical intervention requires re-attaching the ruptured tendon (Fig. 14). Golfing must be discontinued at least 3 months, and not resumed until a strong rehabilitation program has allowed full recovery of calf strength and ankle range of motion. A returning golfer should use a cart initially until all tenderness has resolved.

STRESS FRACTURES

A stress fracture is a **non-displaced fracture** through a bone, caused by repeated episodes of recurrent stress. Non-displaced fractures are bones that are broken, yet they remain in their normal position. In displaced fractures, the bones are not only broken, but are no longer in their normal positions and, in fact, are out of alignment. Stress fractures seldom displace by more than a few millimeters (Fig.15). The stress fracture is an **overuse fracture**. Ninety-five percent of all stress fractures occurring in athletes occur in the lower extremities. Stress fractures are most commonly associated with high-impact sports such as running, track, gymnastics, and basketball. However, any sport in which there is repetitive stress of the foot striking the ground can lead to a stress fracture. Rapidly increasing the intensity of a workout can lead to a stress fracture. Women are more likely to experience a stress fracture than men; this is due to less bone mass in women than in men. Women with a history of osteoporosis are at greater risk for stress fractures than others. Stress fractures are associated with a sudden onset of pain and a pinpoint site of severe tenderness. Most stress fractures are difficult to diagnose by X-rays with the first onset of symptoms. Over time, as a fracture begins to heal with the formation of new bone, the X-ray findings may become more obvious and the diagnosis can be made easily (Fig. 16). If the x-rays remain negative and there is strong clinical evidence for a stress fracture, a bone scan may be needed. A bone scan will almost always diagnose a stress fracture within one week of the onset of pain (Fig.17). A negative bone scan does not necessarily rule out the possibility of a stress fracture. The most important treatment for a stress fracture is reduction of activity (no golf), rest, and protection from movement. This can usually be accomplished with a wooden shoe, a boot walker, or an orthotic device within the shoe (Fig.18). Individuals will need to refrain from engaging in any arduous activities during the six to eight weeks that it usually takes for most stress fractures to heal. If any activity, including golfing, is resumed too quickly, the stress facture can worsen and become a more difficult problem to treat. Re-fracture or re-injury can lead to chronic problems in which the fracture may not heal properly. The fracture is considered healed when the fracture site becomes non-tender. The discomfort is well managed by using acetaminophen. There is some evidence that use of non-steroidal anti-inflammatory medications may slow fracture healing and accordingly should be avoided temporarily. A stress fracture usually requires surgery, only if it fails to heel over many months. Returning to golf should be under the advice of a physician or physical therapist. Here are a few tips to help prevent stress fractures:

- Slowly increase activity, particularly sports. For the returning golfer, this means initially using a golf cart instead of walking. The first time out on the course should include only nine holes.
- Maintain a healthy diet and adequate hydration. Incorporate calcium-rich foods into meals.
- Use proper equipment; do not use worn out or old golfing shoes.
- When returning to golf, if pain develops, stop immediately. If the pain continues or worsens after a few days of rest, a physician consultation is needed.

PLANTAR HEEL PAIN

A common foot problem for the athlete and non-athlete alike is **plantar heel pain**. Heel pain can affect golfers of all ages. It develops as a response to repetitive stress on the heel. It is an **overuse syndrome** with chronic inflammation. With each step, the fat pad beneath the heel bone (calcaneus) is asked to absorb forces equal to 110% of the body's weight. After age 40, the fat pad tissue will gradually deteriorate. Shock absorbency is reduced. Plantar heel pain that develops because of reduction of this shock absorbency usually radiates throughout the entire heel and is more uncomfortable with activities on harder surfaces. A cushioned heel cup or a shock absorbent athletic shoe is the most effective treatment (Fig. 12).

Heel pain syndrome is plantar heel pain more localized to the origin of the plantar fascia (a very thick fibrous structure that helps support the arch) from the plantar front portion of the heel bone (Fig. 19). With overuse, tiny tears develop in the plantar fascia. The body responds with an inflammatory reaction in an attempt to heal these tears, and a chronic inflammatory situation develops. There may be local swelling and tenderness, which can extend into the arch area of the foot along the plantar fascia. The pain is most acute with the first steps in the morning and with the first steps after sitting for a prolonged period of time.

figure | 16

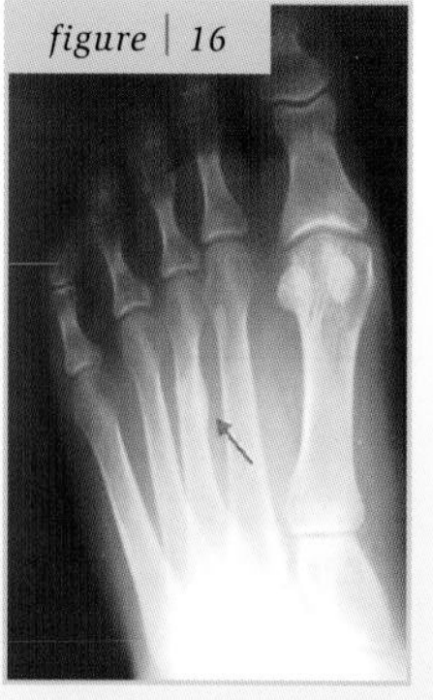

figure | 18

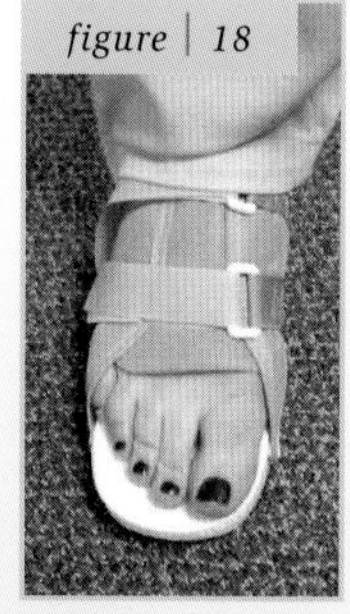

figure | 17

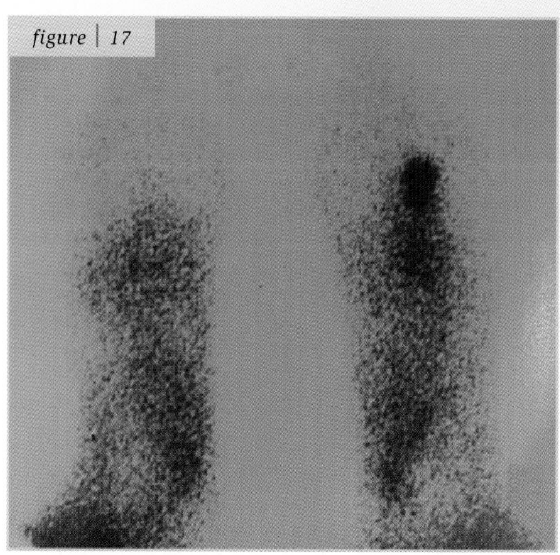

figure | 19

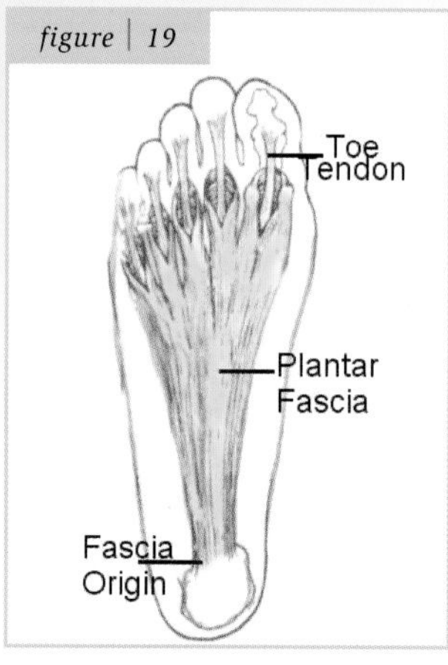

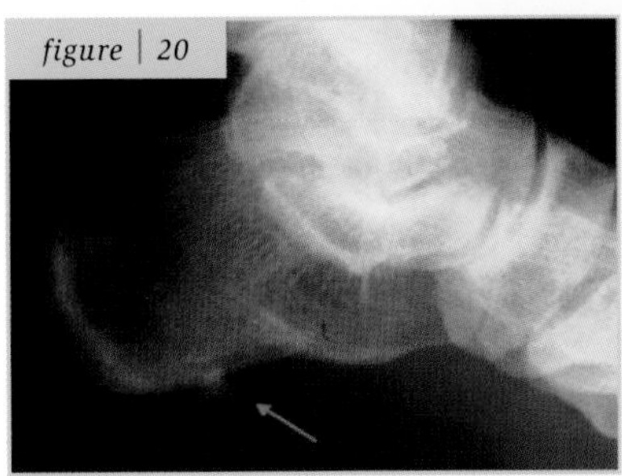
figure | 20

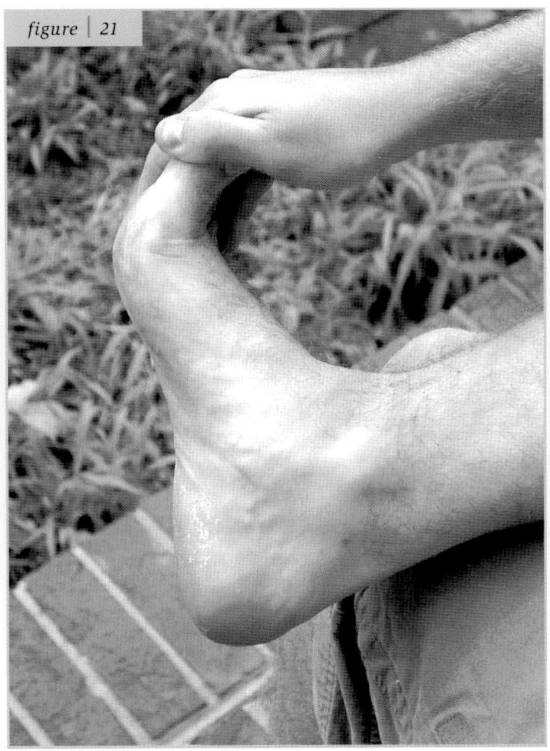
figure | 21

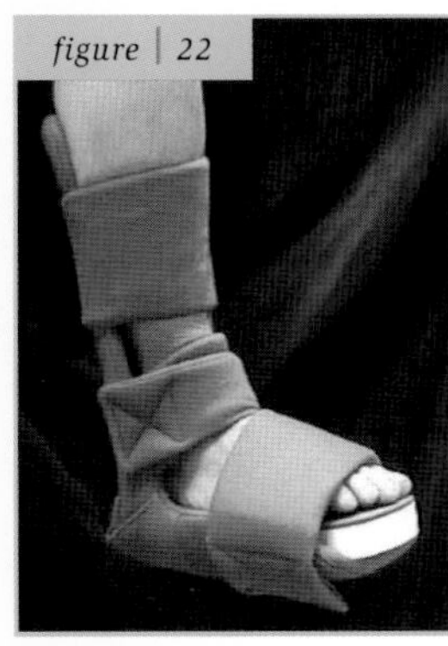
figure | 22

The pain is intensified by long periods of walking and standing. Heel pain syndrome may occur more frequently in individuals who are overweight. Frequently, plantar heel pain is blamed on the presence of a heel spur seen extending from the plantar front edge of the heel bone on a lateral X-ray (Fig. 20). There is no positive correlation between the presence of a heel spur on x-ray and symptoms. Treatment begins with a cushioned heel or well-molded arch support (Fig. 12). NSAIDs, over a few weeks, can often help to break the cycle of chronic inflammation and reduce the pain. The most important aspect of treatment is slow, gentle stretching of the heel cord and the plantar fascia (Fig. 21). Slow stretching increases the blood flow to the diseased area, improving cellular nutrition. Tissue elasticity is increased and the tendency for recurrent tears is markedly reduced. Stretching should be divided into multiple short sessions of about five minutes each, disbursed throughout the day. Total time stretching for a 24-hour period should equal or exceed 30 minutes. If these preliminary steps do not prove successful in management of heel pain syndrome, then additional measures, including steroid injections, a night splint to hold the foot in a neutral position for a slow nighttime stretch, or a walking cast may be helpful (Fig.22). Ninety-five percent of individuals with heel pain syndrome will respond to conservative, non-operative therapies. Very few cases ever require surgical intervention. The surgical treatment for a recalcitrant case or condition is release of the plantar fascia. Every attempt should be made to avoid this procedure, particularly in athletes and golfers, as release of the plantar fascia may have a detrimental effect on overall function. Release of the plantar fascia can reduce the arch height. It is also known that release of the plantar fascia will lead to increased mid-foot stresses, which can bring about a new, "different" foot complaint.

Another cause of plantar heel pain is entrapment of a branch of the lateral plantar nerve, or nerve to the abductor digiti minimi muscle (little toe). Pain with **nerve entrapment** usually occurs where the nerve curves sharply around the plantar aspect of the foot. Pressure can result from the sharp edge of the fascia covering the abductor muscle to the great toe. Localized tenderness is in the same area of the heel as heel pain syndrome or plantar fasciitis. Early morning pain complaints are less and pain usually increases at the end of the day or after prolonged activities. Weakness in the ability to pull the little toe outward and away from the foot may be noted. Pressure over the area where the nerve is entrapped can lead to a tingling sensation traveling up on the inside of the ankle. Treatment is the same as heel pain syndrome, or plantar fasciitis. If surgery is needed, the fascia covering the great toe abductor muscle must be released.

NERVE ENTRAPMENT

Nerves can be compressed or pinched by bony structures or by increased pressure within a compartment of muscles in the leg or within the foot. This problem often manifests during a sporting event. When pain occurs in the second or third web space of the forefoot, it may indicate irritation or compression of a nerve in that web space. With time, irritation of the nerve can cause the development of a **neuroma**. A neuroma is a thickening of the nerve and, in this particular situation, is called a **Morton's neuroma**. It develops when a nerve between the two metatarsal heads is compressed, or pinched, and bruised. This is often caused by wearing shoes with pointed toes, or by repeated trauma or blows to the foot. Frequently, the pain is described as a "burning" or an "aching" sensation. The pain may radiate out of the tip of one of the three middle toes. There may also be a numbness of one of the middle toes. Quickly removing the shoe and massaging the foot will usually bring relief. The first step for any treatment of a neuroma is to wear a wider shoe. A metatarsal pad placed just behind the metatarsal heads, or ball of the foot, can sometimes be helpful. An arch support can also reduce pressure to the metatarsal bones. In certain cases, a cortisone injection can be quite helpful, both from a diagnostic perspective as well as therapeutic. However, multiple injections can lead to re-absorption of the plantar fat pad, making the bony prominences even more prominent. If pain persists, then surgical therapy may be recommended. The enlarged or damaged part of the nerve is removed; this will bring about permanent numbness in this area. Golfing should be discontinued after surgery until the incision is completely healed (2 to 3 weeks). When first returning to golf after surgery a cart should be used until all tenderness resolves.

There are other nerves in the foot that can also be compressed by bony structures and ligaments. A physician or other healthcare provider should evaluate any persistent pain, numbness, or tingling sensations in the foot. An orthopedic surgical consultation may be needed.

The **tarsal tunnel** is a space on the inner side of the hind-foot, just below the bony prominence of the end of the tibia. The nerves, blood vessels, and tendons that supply the bottom of the foot travel through this area and are contained beneath a fibrous roof (tunnel) (Fig. 23). Large nerves going to the bottom of the foot can become compressed in this space. This most commonly follows an injury to this area, but can occur spontaneously. Burning and numbness in the bottom of the foot are the most common symptoms. Occasionally, the pain is focused in the heel. Initial treatment includes wider shoes, arch supports, heel cord stretching, and activity modification (less golf). If the fifth toe cannot be spread away from the fourth toe, or if numbness of the plantar surface of the foot or toes develops, then a consultation with a physician is recommended. It may be necessary to open the fibrous "roof" to take away pressure from the nerves. Tarsal tunnel release surgery should only be tried when all other non-operative measures have failed.

BUNIONS

The term bunion is derived from the Greek word for "turnip" and commonly is used to refer to enlargement around the great toe joint. This enlargement can occur when the normal first metatarsal head becomes uncovered as the great toe deviates laterally toward the lesser toes (hallux valgus) or with spur formation associated with great toe joint arthritis (hallux rigidus).

Hallux valgus is the more common "bunion" deformity. It occurs more frequently in women and is felt to be associated with years of improper shoewear. However, there is also a genetic contribution to this deformity and individuals can develop hallux valgus without wearing tight shoes. As the great toe deviates laterally toward the lesser toes, the metatarsal head becomes uncovered (Fig. A). This metatarsal prominence can become red, swollen, and painful with shoewear pressure. Over time the matatarsals may spread apart and additional bone may develop over the medial metatarsal head prominence. This can lead to increasing pain (Fig. B). Wider shoes are the first step in treatment. Women may benefit from combination-last sole shoes with a wider forefoot and narrower heel. A shoemaker can often stretch leather shoes to accommodate the deformity. Surgery should only be considered when shoewear changes fail to relieve chronic pain, or when the bunion is associated with a crossover 2nd toe deformity (Fig. C). A bunion with associ-

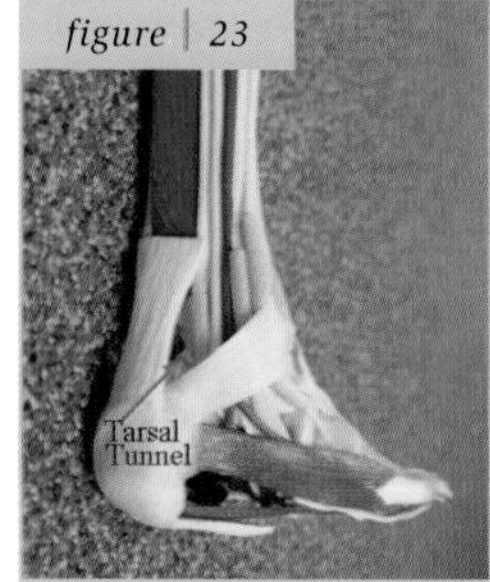

figure | 23

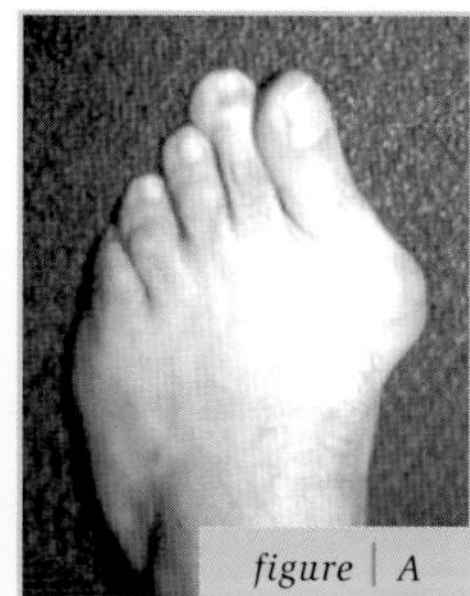
figure | A

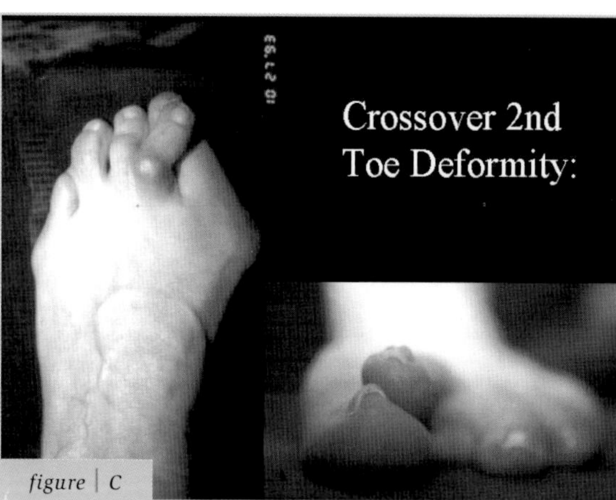

figure | C

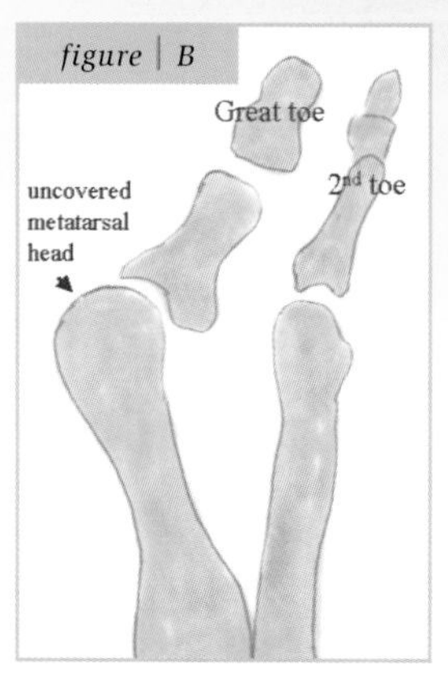

figure | B

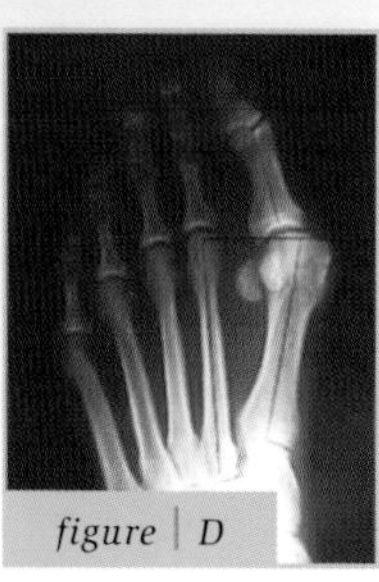
figure | D

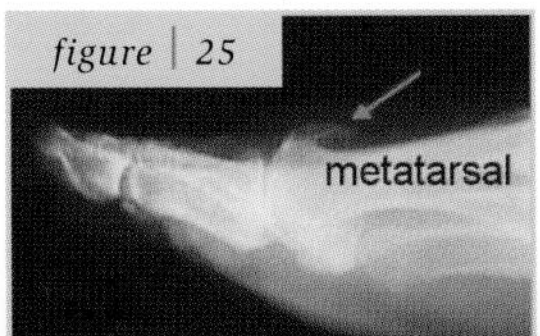

figure | 25

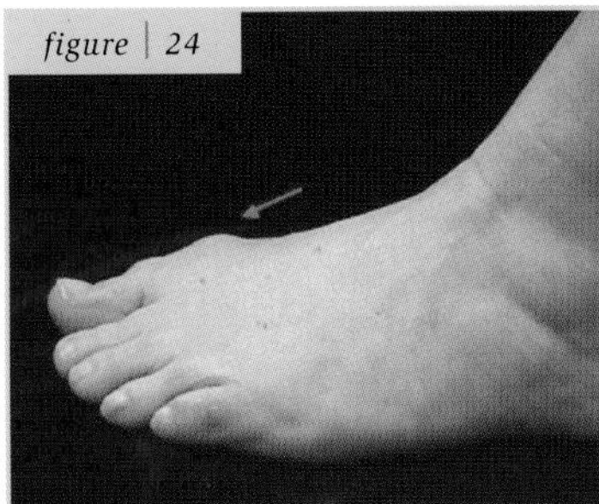
figure | 24

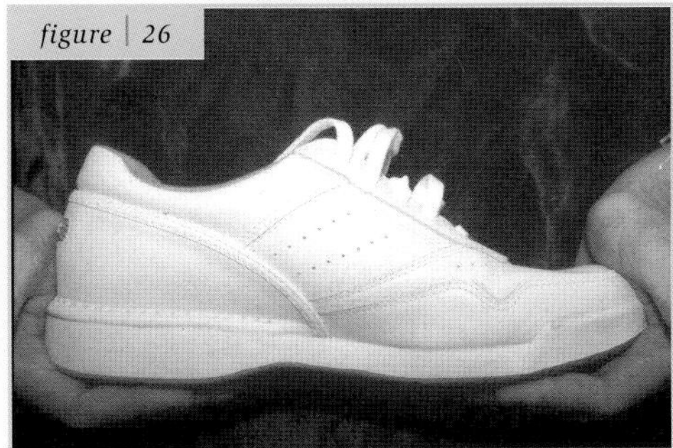
figure | 26

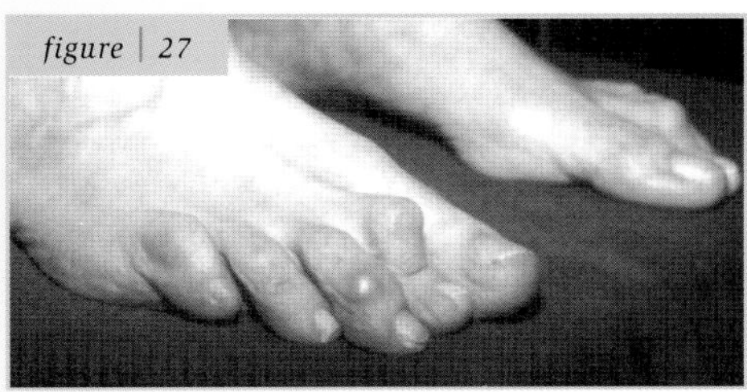
figure | 27

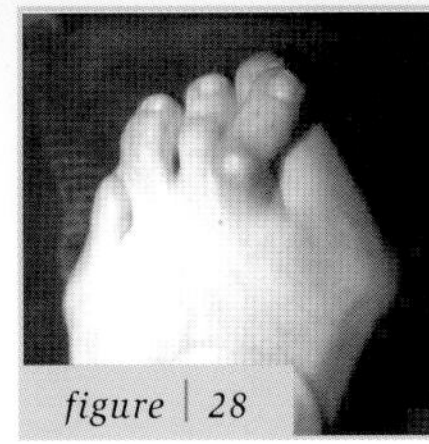
figure | 28

ated crossover 2nd toe deformity should be corrected early before the combination deformity becomes fixed and increasingly difficult to correct. There have been many surgical procedures described for the correction of hallux valgus. Standing X-rays are used to measure the spread of the metatarsals and the degree of lateral deviation of the great toe (Fig. 23D). These two measurements are the basis for the surgical procedure chosen. With simple procedures weight bearing can begin immediately after surgery. More complex procedures often require 4 to 6 weeks of no weight on the operated foot. Weekly foot dressings by the operating surgeon may be required to maintain the correction gained at surgery. There is often a mild to moderate loss of great toe joint motion after hallux valgus surgery and, although usually not a problem for golfers, this could be detrimental for runners or dancers.

Hallux Rigidus: Hallus rigidus is a medical term for **arthritis of the great toe joint**. It is common, especially in older athletes. Arthritis in this toe joint is characterized by loss of movement, pain, redness and swelling at the base of the big toe (Fig. 24). Severity of the problem can range from small osteophytes, or bone spurs, around the joint visible on x-ray, and reduced range of motion of the joint, to severe joint destruction with very limited motion of the joint (Fig. 25). The first step in management of hallux rigidus should be modification of the shoe wear. A stiff-soled shoe will reduce the motion occurring in this joint with daily activities, and will simultaneously help reduce the pain. A rocker-bottom can be added to the sole to increase the ease of walking without great toe motion (Fig. 26). All shoes should be stretched to reduce pressure over the bump on the top and inside portion of the great toe. If shoe wear modification fails to reduce symptoms, then surgical removal of the osteophytes may be recommended. Sometimes joint fusion should be considered. Most orthopedic foot and ankle surgeons do not recommend Silastic™ implants. Use of a non-steroidal anti-inflammatory medication may help to relieve the inflammation of the joint. Cortisone may also be injected directly into the joint to help with inflammation and pain.

CLAW TOES, HAMMERTOES, AND MALLET TOES

Claw toes, hammertoes, and mallet toes involve varying degrees of contracture at one of the joints of the lesser toes. Early on, the deformity may be flexible, but with time the deformity becomes fixed. Typically callus forms over the prominent toe joint and the deformity becomes painful (Fig. 27). Treatment includes relieving pressure over the painful area. Roomy shoewear is needed. Padding and shaving of the callus provide temporary relief. Deformities of the lesser toes do not require surgical intervention unless pain cannot be controlled with conservative measures. If surgery is required it involves removal of the prominent bone and realignment of the soft tissues (tendon and capsule) to straighten the toe. One exception to the "no surgery required" recommendation is the case of the crossover 2nd toe. This deformity is often a combination of claw toe and hammertoe deformities, with the 2nd toe crossing up and over the great toe (Figure 28). Although shoe wear choice can contribute to pain with a crossover toe, the deformity is thought to be rooted in a genetic predisposition. If the deformity is allowed to progress the 2nd toe will eventually dislocate at the metatarsophalangeal joint and correction becomes much more difficult. This deformity often occurs in combination with a bunion deformity. To surgically correct the 2nd toe the bunion will have to be addressed too, so that the 2nd toe has room to lie flat between the great toe and 3rd toe. This is one of the few instances when a non-painful bunion deformity should be corrected.

SKIN AND NAIL DISORDERS

Foot blisters are well known to anyone who regularly participates in sports. It's considered by most to be the "price you pay, when you play." Friction blisters occur when shearing forces are rapidly applied to the skin. Fluid or blood accumulates beneath the epidermal (outer) layer of the skin, and above the dermal (second) layer of the skin (Fig. 29). This occurs more frequently with ill-fitting shoes. Careful fitting of the golf shoe is very important. Care must taken to relieve any pressure over bony prominences and to prevent sliding and pistoning of the foot within the shoe. Always wear socks, as they act as an interface to dissipate shear stresses between the shoe and the skin. Don't wear extra-large socks, as they bunch up and cause pressure within the shoe. Look for a well-fitted, absorbent sock. Foot powders can be useful for drying the surfaces between the toes. Wear socks made from synthetic blends. If a blister forms, it's important to keep the blister from enlarging and to avoid infection. The signs of infection include: very red, warm skin around the blister; possible red streaks leading away from the blister; and any drainage, particularly pus, from the blister. A small blister usually does not cause any major discomfort. Larger blisters are those that tend to be painful. It is usually more comfortable to drain such blisters. The skin covering should be left intact to provide protection, speed healing, and help prevent infection. If the blister is to be drained, the blister first needs to be cleaned with rubbing alcohol or antibiotic soap and water. Usually, a straight pin is the most available instrument to drain a blister. The straight pin should be cleaned with an alcohol solution and then placed over a flame until the tip of the pin glows red. Don't immediately use the hot pin on the skin; it should be allowed to cool before puncturing the edge of the blister. The fluid from the blister is released by applying gentle pressure. Make sure that you wash your hands before puncturing the blister and applying pressure. Pressure should be applied with a clean dressing or bandage. After the blister has been drained, an antibiotic ointment such as Bacitracin® with Polymyxin B (double antibiotic ointment) or Bacitracin® alone is usually helpful. The blister should be covered with a clean bandage and changed daily. Moleskin (a soft material, often with an adhesive backing, used especially on the feet to protect against chafing) can be used for padding until the blister heals.

"Athlete's foot" (tinea pedis) is a very common fungal infection of the feet in golfers. It is more common with men than with women. It usually involves the spaces between the toes. Several types of fungi that thrive in warm, humid environments cause the condition. The initial clinical picture is a superficial whitish scaling of the skin that is not painful (Fig. 30). The infection leads to cracked, sore and itchy areas of the skin. The moist environment within the golf shoe encourages fungal spread to the damp spaces between the toes and symptomatic infection follows. Treatment involves topical anti-fungals. The most effective agents contain miconazole, tolnaftate, haloprogin, or clotrimazole. Many of these can be purchased as over-the-counter medications. Aeration of the foot is very important to control this infection. A synthetic blend sock that allows perspiration to evaporate will help to prevent the build-up of moisture in the golf shoe. A cotton sock allows increased absorbency; however, the moisture may be trapped in the shoe. Between golfing events, shoes should be allowed to dry completely in a well-ventilated area. Alternating shoes can be beneficial. For the golfer who plays daily or several

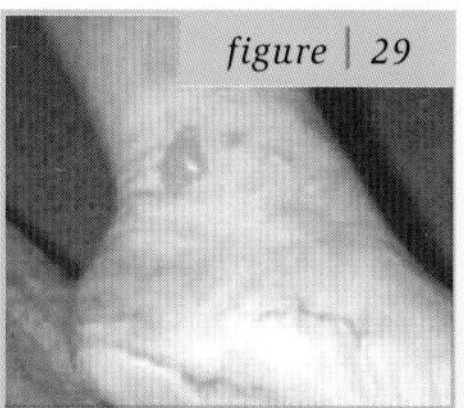
figure | 29

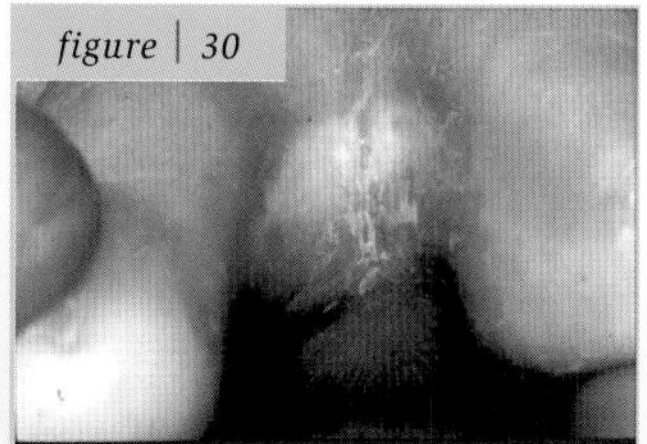
figure | 30

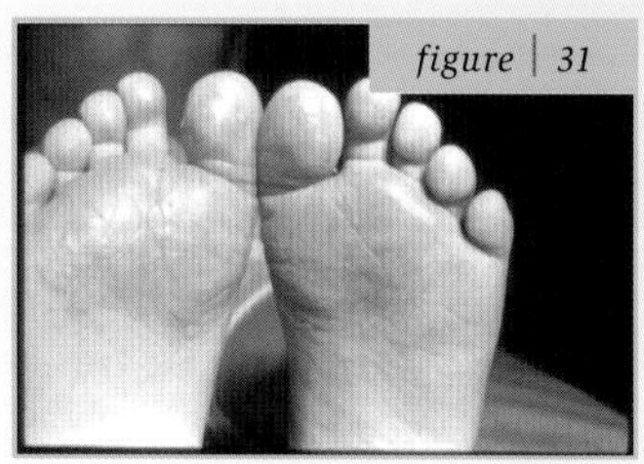
figure | 31

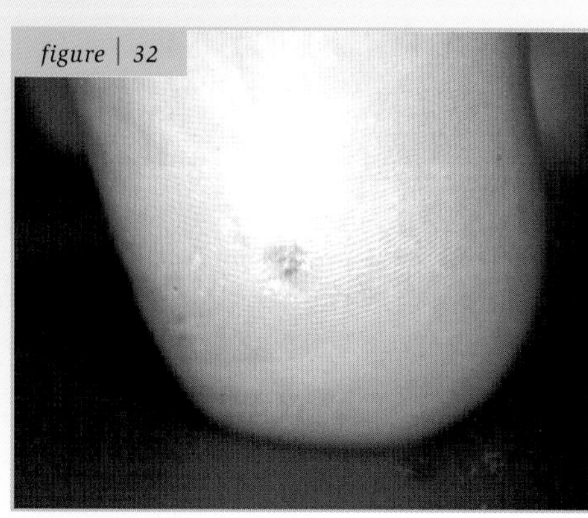
figure | 32

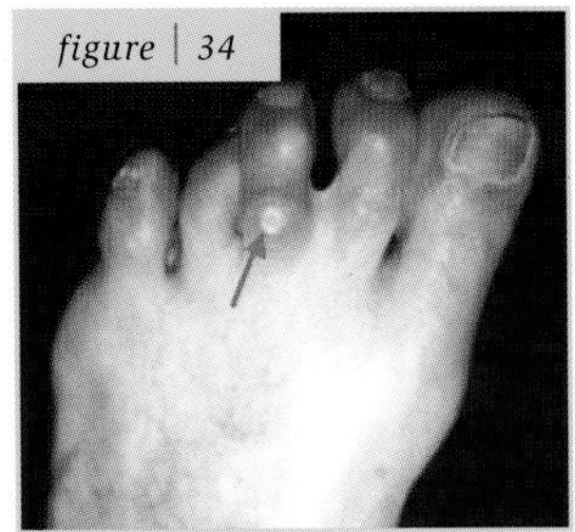
figure | 34

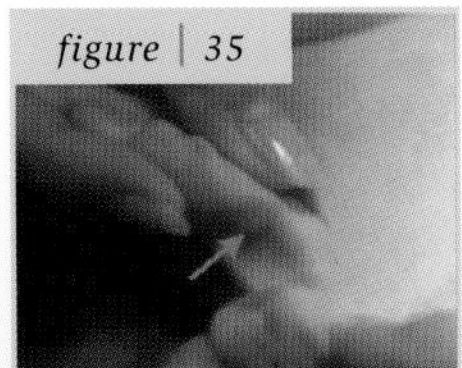
figure | 35

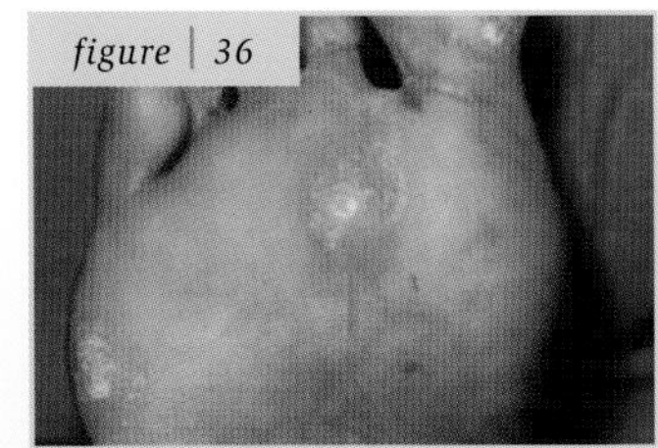
figure | 36

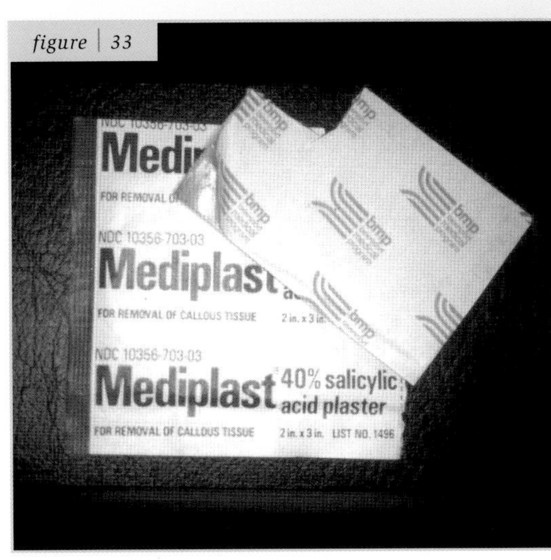

figure | 33

figure | 37

times a week, having more than one pair of golf shoes can be very helpful in preventing fungal problems. Occasionally, an individual will develop an allergic reaction to the construction material of the golf shoe. This can be confused with athlete's foot (Fig. 31). This occurs most frequently with rubber components. Moisture within the shoe exacerbates the problem. Changing shoewear or using drying agents is recommended.

Plantar warts are identified by tiny hemorrhages within the core of the wart after trimming the callus (Fig. 32). Warts can be confused with calluses secondary to increased areas of weight-bearing pressure. Calluses represent a thickening of the skin layers in response to chronic pressure or to an irritating substance that has become trapped in the skin. Warts also involve thickening of the skin layers, but this thickening is caused by the presence of a virus within the skin cells. Warts are characteristically painful with side-to-side squeezing, while calluses are more painful with direct pressure. Salicylic acid (aspirin) solutions applied directly to the wart can assist in reducing the associated callus size and, accordingly, decrease pain. The life expectancy for a plantar wart is two years. If possible, conservative measures, including salicylic acid and padding, should be used to "wait out" the wart (Fig. 33). If this is unsuccessful, multiple treatment options by a physician are available, including electrocautery, liquid nitrogen, and laser. Surgical excision should be seen as a last solution as it can lead to a painful scar. Absorbent socks that allow evaporation and drying solutions can help in prevention by reducing the moist environment loved by wart viruses.

A few unlucky individuals will experience **excessive sweating** (hyperhidrosis) of the soles of the feet; this can lead to skin maceration, blistering, and athlete's foot. A physician can assist in managing this problem by using a topical solution of 20% aluminum chloride (hexahydrate) and anhydrous ethyl alcohol (Drysol®) applied at bedtime and removed each morning for a 10-day course. Maintenance therapy is continued once each week. If this is not helpful, a dermatologist should be consulted.

There are two types of **corns**. A **hard corn** occurs over a bony prominence secondary to pressure between the underlying bone and the shoe (Fig. 34). Ill-fitting shoes are the most common culprits. Temporary padding with corn pads can be helpful. Replacement shoes must be deep enough and wide enough to eliminate pressure on the toes. With aging, the clawing of the little toes increases. Close attention to shoe wear becomes increasingly important. A **soft corn** occurs between the toes where moisture softens the callus. There may be an area of central ulceration (Fig. 35). Padding to separate the toes with lamb's wool, foam, or moleskin can help control pain. Shoes with a large toe box can reduce pressure between the toes. Permanent control of the corns requires surgical correction removing prominent bone.

An **intractable plantar keratosis** is a **callus** beneath one or more of the metatarsal heads (Fig.36). The callus can be discrete or diffuse. **Discrete calluses** are usually secondary to prominence of the plantar portion of the metatarsal head itself, while **diffuse calluses** usually result from misalignment of the forefoot bones. Treatment involves callus care using a pumice stone or callus file, after bathing when the callus is soft, followed by alteration of the shoe to reduce pressure to the callused area. Occasional use of a salicylates solution can provide more aggressive debridement of the callus. Metatarsal pads placed strategically within the shoe will spread the metatarsal heads and unweight the heads by allowing weight bearing through the metatarsal pad (Fig. 37).

Onychomycosis refers to **fungal toenails** (Fig. 38). In the earliest stages, there is only slight discoloration of the nail. It usually begins in the tip of the nail. The nail gradually thickens and becomes distorted with ridges. Debris begins to form beneath the nail. The nail can become a problem rubbing within the golf shoe. Oral anti-fungal agents are available; the drug must be taken for many months to allow complete re-growth of the nail. Once the drug is stopped, rapid return of the fungus is often seen. The anti-fungal medication can be harmful to the liver, and regular blood studies must be obtained to observe for possible problems during treatment. An alternative method of treatment involves removing the involved portion of the nail and treating the nail bed with twice daily debridements with a toothbrush and then painting the nail bed with a topical anti-fungal agent. This method of treatment has no systemic side effects, but is time-consuming and requires meticulous nail care. Fungal infections can also be managed by routine nail buffing and trimming to prevent rubbing in the shoe and ignoring the underlying fungus. Fungal toenails do not pose a serious health threat.

Onychocryptosis refers to **ingrown toenails** (Fig. 39). Many factors can contribute to the development of ingrown toenails. There can be a genetic predisposition with increased curvature of the nail. Excessive moisture, poor nail care, and trauma can all contribute to this problem. A small spike of nail protrudes into the nail fold and starts the inflammatory process. To treat, the spike must be trimmed leaving a smooth margin. The foot is then soaked twice a day for 20 minutes in lukewarm soapy water. After soaking, the nail fold should be gently pushed away from the nail edge using a cotton swab or cuticle pusher. Antibiotic ointment can be applied in the groove. Oral antibiotics are seldom required. Future nail care should emphasize the need to allow the edges of the nail to grow out to the end of the toe so that a spike will not be left behind to irritate the skin fold. The nail should be cut straight across and not in a concave fashion (Fig. 40). After each bath, care should be taken to push the nail fold away from the nail edge. Frequent recurrences should prompt physician attention. A portion of the nail matrix can be ablated to prevent growth of the offending side of the nail.

Subungual hematoma refers to blood accumulation beneath the toenail (Fig. 41). The toenail may appear black. Most frequently, this occurs in the great toe when it hits against the end of the shoe. Ill-fitting shoes should be replaced with large toe-box shoes. If the hematoma, or blood collection, beneath the nail is painful, relief can be obtained by a small drill hole using a trephine or large bore needle through the nail plate, which will allow release of the accumulated blood.

PROPER FOOT CARE

Proper care of your feet, on a daily basis, can help prevent foot problems and maintain a healthy golf game. People with diabetes or poor circulation in their feet must take extra precautions. They must inspect their feet more often and should be tuned in to complications associated with their diseases. An infection in a diabetic patient or an individual who has poor circulation in the lower extremities can cost them much more than their golf game—it could cost them their feet. Good foot care is mandatory for any golfer with a history of diabetes or poor circulation. Individuals with diabetes or poor circulation should inspect and examine their feet in a thorough fashion at least once a day. They should check for any cuts, cracks or redness. Individuals with such problems may have a decreased appreciation of sensation in their feet and, therefore, may not be aware that anything has happened to

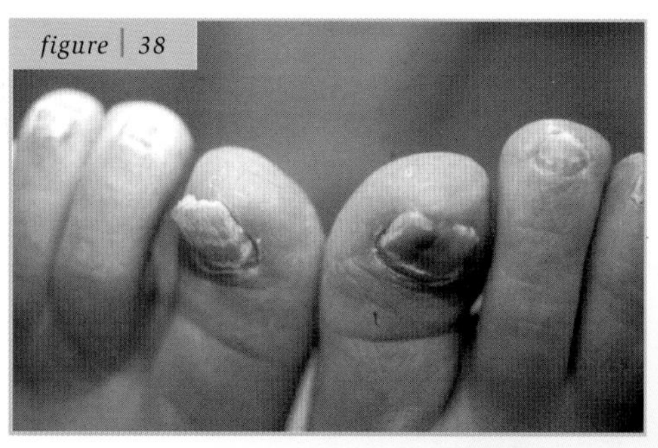
figure | 38

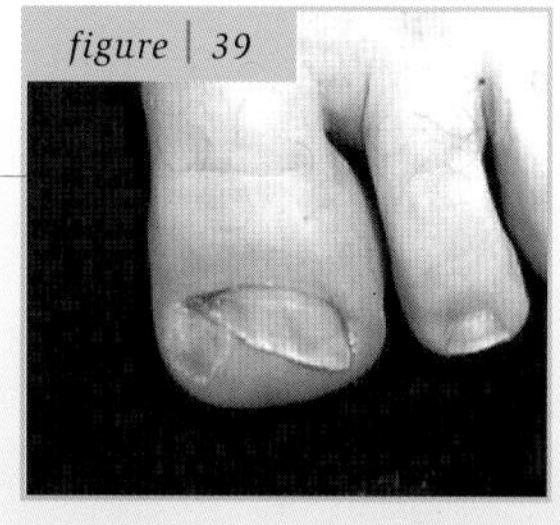
figure | 39

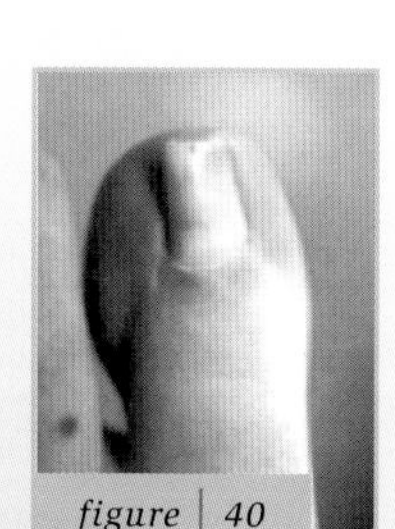
figure | 40

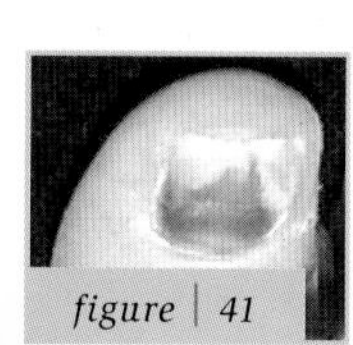
figure | 41

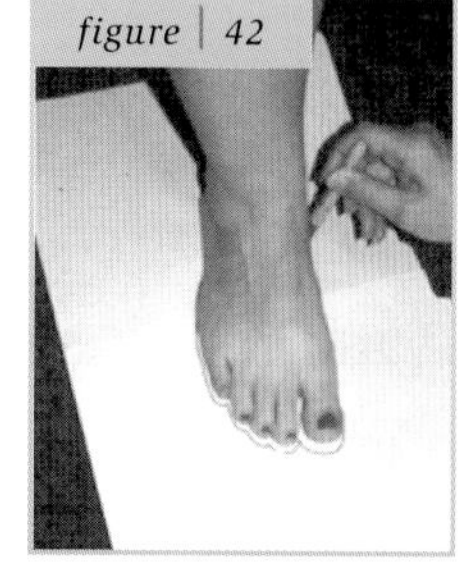
figure | 42

figure | 43

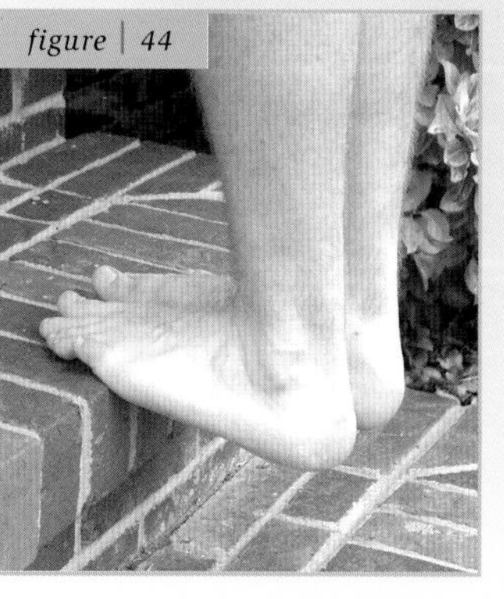
figure | 44

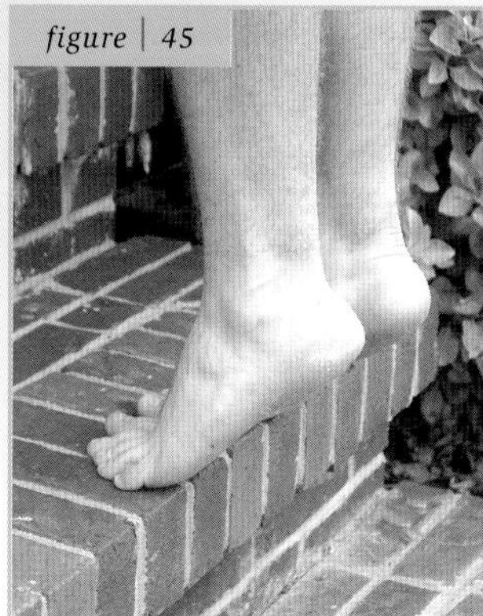
figure | 45

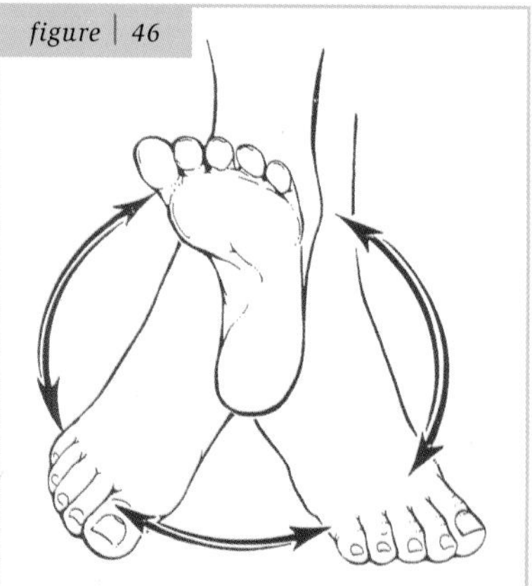
figure | 46

their feet. Therefore, checking the feet is very important. They should also never wear tight-fitting socks, stockings or shoes. It's also a good idea for these individuals, as well as others, before putting on a pair of shoes, always to check to make sure there's not anything foreign, such as a stone, a piece of plastic, or an insect or spider in the shoe. Individuals with diabetes and poor circulation should always check their feet at the end of a round of golf. In fact, golfers should always check their feet at the end of nine holes. If there's evidence of any redness, skin changes, blisters, tingling, or worsening numbness in the feet, it's probably best not to continue to play. Individuals with these problems can enjoy golf with good foot health, but it does take extra precautions. They're worth it in order to continue to be able to play golf.

It's important that all golfers become more aware of the importance of their feet. Here are a few hints for good foot care:

- Inspect your feet thoroughly every day, at least once a day. Check for any unusual redness, cracks, cuts, or discoloration.
- Feet should be washed on a daily basis. All soap should be thoroughly rinsed off and the feet dried. It's important to make sure that the foot is dry between the toes. Toes are often forgotten in the drying process.
- Trim all toenails straight across, and do not cut them too short. Don't pick or pull the toenails off. Don't cut out or dig at the corners.
- Wear clean socks or stockings. Never wear socks that are too tight, too small, moist or soiled.
- If a golfer has a tendency for sweaty feet, it's a good idea to carry, in the golf bag, a change of socks. Don't feel embarrassed to change a wet pair of socks; nobody likes to play golf with wet socks. Changing the socks may prevent unwanted infections. Sweaty feet may also respond to over-the-counter foot powder. An anti-fungal foot powder may be very helpful to prevent athlete's foot and fungal infections.

Buying the right golf shoe is very important. Wearing an ill-fitting or wrong sized shoe can cause or aggravate any foot problems. Wearing the right shoe can help prevent and sometimes correct many foot problems. Wearing the right shoe is vital for foot health and a golfer's game. In fact, ill-fitting shoes can often be reflected in the scorecard at the end of the day. The final score is often not the desired one. Here are a few tips on buying the right shoe:

- Never buy a shoe that's uncomfortable. If the shoes don't feel right, don't buy them. Aging causes changes in the foot, therefore, always measure both feet every time you buy shoes. Never assume that the size of shoe that you bought last time will be appropriate and correct this time. Measure both feet; foot sizes are not always equal. And always buy shoes for the bigger foot. A minimum of 1/4 inch (.64 cm.) to 3/8 inch (.97 cm.) in front of the greater toe should be left when measuring the length of the shoe.
- Go shopping late in the afternoon; feet swell to their largest size after a day's activity. Therefore, when looking for new golf shoes, buy them at the end of the day, or better yet, at the end of 18 holes. Never buy shoes the morning you intend to play. Wear your usual "golf" socks to insure adequate room within the shoe.
- The toe box should always be large enough to allow you to wiggle all your toes easily. A golfer's forefoot should never be wider than the golfing shoe.
- The heel should fit snugly, and the instep should never have a large space.
- It's important to buy golf shoes every year. Through the season, the shoes often lose much of their shock absorbency.

With aging, the feet tend to change. The fat pad lessens and shock absorbency decreases. The feet tend to spread in the forefoot; thus the forefoot should never be wider than the shoe itself. An easy, simple way to determine whether the forefoot has enough room is to take the forefoot test. Stand with your foot on a white piece of paper, *i.e.* Xerox® or printing paper. Ask someone to trace carefully around your foot while you are putting all of your weight on this foot. Remove your foot, and make sure your foot shape has been well traced and the tracing is easily seen. Then place your shoe directly over the tracing. If your forefoot is wider than the shoe, the shoe is too small (Fig. 42). Wearing the right size shoe will make a world of difference when playing golf.

Good foot care is important for one's health, as well as one's golf game. A painful foot will impede and will most assuredly hinder any golfer's game. Foot pain will take the pleasure out of playing golf. Any foot pain which is not resolved with self-treatment, continues to be present for more than two or three consecutive rounds, and is worsening, needs further evaluation. A physician or healthcare provider will be able to care for many foot ailments; however, with more complex problems of the feet, a visit to an orthopedic surgeon or a podiatric sports physician may be indicated. Good foot care and properly taking care of any foot problems will allow an individual to play healthier golf, and healthier golf means better golf.

PRE- AND POST-GAME EXERCISES

Relaxed, limber calves and feet can improve your golf game and prevent injury. A set of warm-up exercises may be beneficial in achieving this relaxed state. Slow, gentle stretches are better than quick, jerky movements. Begin with a slow Achilles stretch by leaning against a wall with the leading knee bent and the back leg straight, heel down against the ground (Fig. 45). You should feel the stretch in your calf. Hold for at least 10 seconds, then repeat with the opposite leg. Follow this with a slow stretch of the plantar fascia by standing on the edge of a step, using your forefoot only, then allowing your heels to drop as far as can be comfortably achieved. Hold this position for about 10 seconds (Fig. 46). Follow this by rising up onto your toes and holding for several seconds (Fig. 47). This strengthens the Achilles tendon and the other muscles around the ankle that stabilize the hindfoot. Repeat this toe-rise exercise 25 to 50 times in a slow, controlled manner. Increased strengthening can be achieved by doing this same exercise one leg at a time. If you have problems with ankle instability, these toe rises, combined with balancing exercises involving standing on one foot and responding to changing stimuli (such as a bouncing ball), can be very helpful.

Stretch of the plantar fascia can also be achieved while sitting by grabbing the toes and bending them into extension until the tightness of the fascia can be seen and felt in the plantar aspect of the foot (Fig. 21). Again, a slow steady stretch to a count of 10 is better than quick, short stretches. The final exercise includes clockwise and counterclockwise movements of both ankles to increase mobility and flexibility (Fig. 48).

These simple exercises before and after golfing allow pre-game warm up and post-game cool down, and when performed regularly will likely decrease the incidence of injury to the feet.

ARTHRITIS

CHAPTER 14

T. Glenn Pait, M.D., F.A.C.S.

I am no stranger to back problems. Actually, mine go back to the middle 1960s and originated with an aching hip that acted up so much in 1966 that it forced me to withdraw after two rounds of 71 at New Orleans. The hip bothered me off and on over the next few years and caught me severely at the PGA Championship at the NCR course in Dayton in 1969. I aggravated it badly when I pressed a long-iron second shot on a par-five hole early in the round, ended up with an 82, and had to drop out. My doctors eventually determined that it was a lower-back problem. I increased my exercise routine at that time and have followed a fairly rigorous routine ever since. I have had other ailments, but the exercise really seems to have helped the back trouble immensely.

Arnold Palmer

Arthritis is a medical problem that is very familiar to many golfers. It is an inflammation of the lining of joints (*arthr* means joint, *itis* refers to inflammation). The term arthritis includes a group of inflammatory and degenerative conditions that cause stiffness, swelling and pain in joints. Arthritis affects approximately 80% of individuals over the age of 55. It attacks millions of people every day and prevents many golfers from enjoying the game. Some individuals will suffer only intermittently, while others will be less fortunate. Every move will become a painful occurrence. Arthritis interferes with the day-to-day movements of everyday living. It is estimated that some 1.5 million people in the United States will suffer a partial disability from arthritis and another 1.5 million will become totally disabled. There are 70 million missed workdays each year because of this disease, and 500 million days annually of restricted activities due to arthritis. This includes golf.

Muscles and skeletons make possible the movements of life. We take for granted all of those graceful and smooth sliding motions of our bones and joints until that movement is painful and hampered. Body movements and arm swings are possible because of joints. Joints are formed where two or more bones meet (Fig. 1). Most joints move freely and are called synovial joints. These joints are found in our limbs. The bones are held together by ligaments that form a fibrous capsule. Another kind of joint is a semi-movable joint that is found in the spine and pelvis. Here the joint surfaces are fused into a toughened pad of cartilage that has less movement and flexibility, but provides greater stability (Fig. 2). In order for the joints to move freely they must be lubricated. Without lubricant, friction builds up and impedes joint movements. The joints need a lubricating substance in order for bones to glide and move freely without friction. The joint membrane secretes the needed lubricating material. This fluid is stored in packets called **bursae**. In youth, joints have an ample supply of this lubricating, cushioning fluid to cover all bony surfaces. With age, the bursae produce less lubricating fluid, which leads to joint stiffness. The bones that are connected at a joint site are covered with a flexible cartilage. In a normal, healthy joint the slipperiness of the cartilage and the cushioning synovial fluid allows the bones to move easily and with virtually no friction. The joints need just the right amount of lubricating fluid to cover the cartilage. Too much lubricating fluid is just as bad as too little. With age, joints change. Changes occur due to hereditary factors, injury, trauma, infection, and autoimmune diseases. Even an adverse reaction to a drug can sometimes bring about changes in joints. There are now more than 100 different types of arthritis.

OSTEOARTHRITIS

Osteoarthritis is the most common form of arthritis. It is a chronic disease that causes breakdown of the cushioning cartilage in joints and the formation of new bone at the margins of the joints. This new bone growth is sometimes in the form of bone spurs (Fig. 3). Osteoarthritis is very frequently called **degenerative joint disease** (DJD). It is sometimes referred to as **hypertrophic osteoarthritis**, an overgrowth of bone associated with aging. About half of the population over the age of 65 will have this type of arthritis. By the age of 70, almost all individuals will have some type of osteoarthritis. For some golfers, arthritic

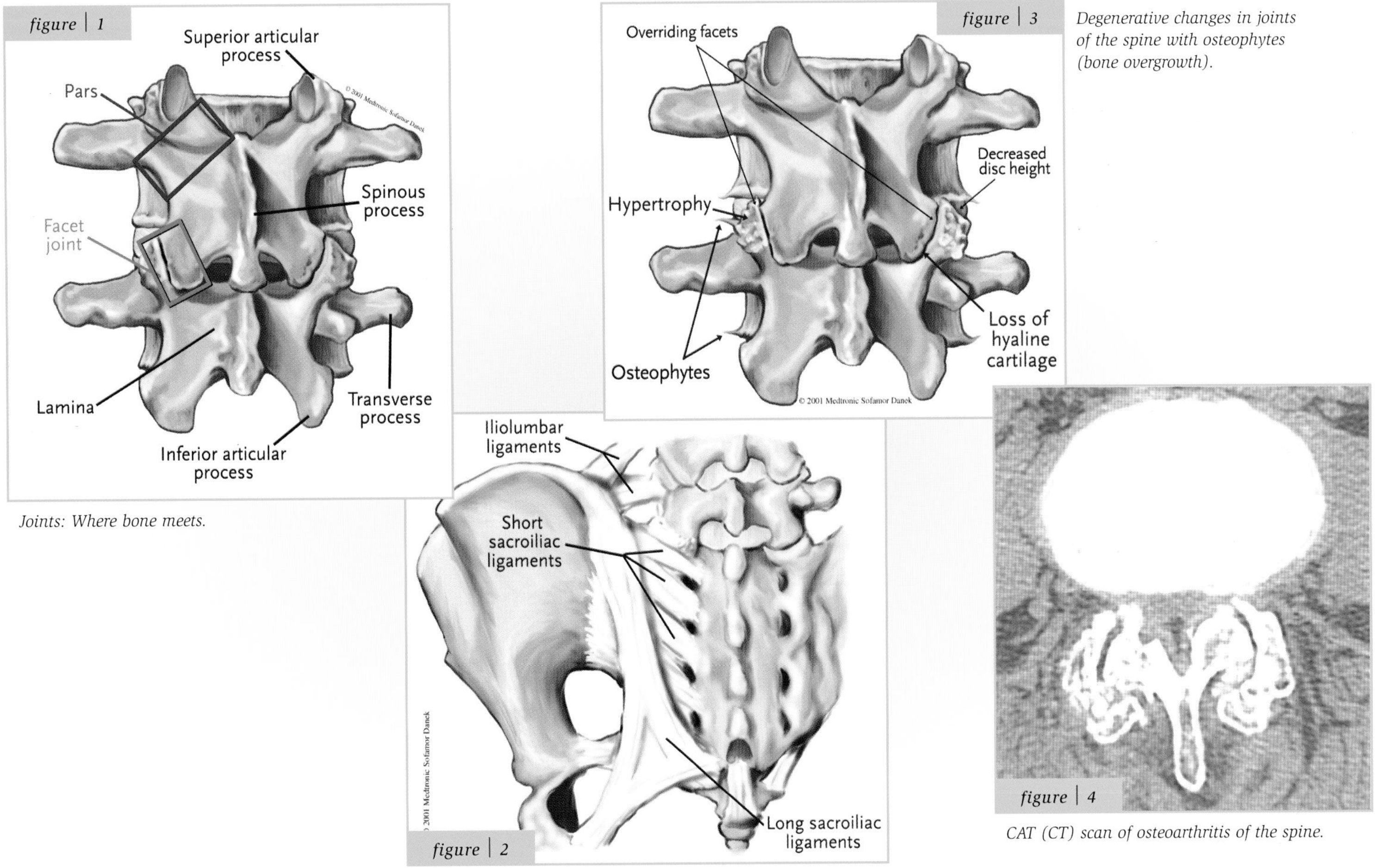

Joints: Where bone meets.

Ligaments of sacrum.

Degenerative changes in joints of the spine with osteophytes (bone overgrowth).

CAT (CT) scan of osteoarthritis of the spine.

symptoms may begin in the 30s or 40s. However, for most individuals the onset of symptoms usually begins around middle age. Before the age of 55, osteoarthritis occurs equally in both sexes. After age 55, it appears that women are more affected than men. With osteoarthritis, the cartilage and affected joint become roughened and worn down. Over time, the cartilage completely wears down and bone begins to rub on bone during movement. Bone rubbing on bone causes pain. Bone spurs tend to form around joint deterioration in an attempt to limit or prevent painful movements.

The joints most affected by osteoarthritis include the spine, fingers, hands, hips, knees, and toes (Fig. 4). In certain situations, osteoarthritis is the result of an injury. Obesity with extra weight on joints makes the joints work harder and wear down sooner. Occupational duties or misuse during sporting activities can promote osteoarthritis. Finally, misalignment of the joints, such as being bow-legged or knock-kneed, causes osteoarthritis. The symptoms are gradual and subtle. There is often a dull, deep aching sensation in the hands or feet; this discomfort is worse after exercising or golfing. Once the activity is stopped, the pain will usually disappear. Patients may notice swelling of the joints that is accompanied by limited movement. Often, there will be morning stiffness after a night's rest that is accompanied by achiness and discomfort in the joints. After an individual gets out of bed and starts moving, the stiffness may decrease, only to return in the evening. With movement, there may be a grating of the joint. Many people with arthritis say that they can predict changes in the weather by the pain in their joints. Such pain is sometimes referred to as **barometric pain**.

TREATMENT

The goal of any treatment is to alleviate the pain, maintain or improve the affected joint's mobility, increase the strength of the joint, and minimize long-lasting disability of the joints caused by the disease. Treatment begins with patient education. It's important that a patient understands the "do's" and "don'ts" of his or her daily activities. Weight loss is an appropriate goal for patients with osteoarthritis. Less weight placed on arthritic joints reduces the stress loads on the joints. The specific treatment depends on which joint is affected. In most situations, the first line of treatment is medications such as non-steroidal, anti-inflammatory drugs (NSAIDs). These drugs can be used only if the individual is not sensitive or allergic to the medications. Some types of NSAIDs can be bought over-the-counter. NSAIDs work by blocking the production of pain-producing substances called prostaglandins. It may take days to weeks before a user is able to tell if the medication will be of any benefit. Sometimes an individual may feel better after only one or two tablets. When using over-the-counter anti-inflammatory medications, it is important that an individual discuss their use with a physician, healthcare provider or pharmacist. Many of the non-steroidal anti-inflammatory medications are difficult for people to use because they can cause stomach disorders. These medications block prostaglandins not only at sites of inflammation, but also in the stomach where they protect the stomach from irritation. Stomach irritation can cause pain and bleeding, which can be life threatening. Renal or kidney problems are also of concern for many users. There is a new class of drugs called **cyclo-oxygenase (COX-2) inhibitors** that have the needed anti-inflammatory effects but are gentler to the stomach. These drugs are selective inhibitors that block prostaglandins at only the sites of inflammation. They do not inhibit the prostaglandins that protect the stomach. The new COX-2 inhibitors can only be obtained with a physician's prescription.

Another medication that can be helpful for controlling pain and inflammation is aspirin (ASA). Aspirin is a NSAID that belongs to the family of drugs called salicylates. To control the pain and inflammation ASA must be used on a regular schedule and usually at higher doses than the other NSAIDs. Many people can not tolerate the long-term use of ASA due to stomach problems. It is recommended that patients take ASA and NSAIDs with food to help prevent stomach disorders. For those individuals who can not use ASA or NSAIDs because of stomach problems, derivatives of ASA, non-acetylated salicylates, may be helpful and cause fewer stomach upsets. These medications include salsalate and magnesium trisalicylate; both require a doctor's prescription.

For severe pain, analgesics are often recommended. These medications help decrease the joint pain; however, they do not reduce the inflammation. Acetaminophen (brand Tylenol® and others) is a commonly used medication for aches and pains. It is very effective for many users, but must be taken cautiously because it can cause serious liver problems. In fact, acetaminophen overdoses are a frequent emergency-room admission. Other frequently prescribed analgesics are propoxyphene (Darvon® and other brand names) and tramadol (brand Ultram®). Long-term use of analgesics is not recommended due to possible drug dependency. Another undesirable side effect is constipation; therefore, a stool softener and fresh fruits and vegetables may be very helpful when using analgesics.

Topical capsaicin is a medication that may be very helpful for some sufferers of osteoarthritis. Capsaicin may reduce pain-generating substances at the nerves, thus reducing pain. Local burning may occur with initial use, but generally ceases with continued use.

Sometimes steroids such as glucocorticoids can be beneficial when injected directly into the joint to help reduce inflammation and swelling. Patients should rest the injected joint for about 2 to 3 days before playing a gentle round of golf. For some individuals such injections can deliver enough relief so they can return to a gentle game of golf. Injections of steroids can only be given a few times a year because of possible harmful side effects that can accelerate the cartilage deterioration of the joint. For this reason the same joint is usually not injected more frequently than every 3 months. However, not all arthritic golfers are candidates for steroid injections. For select individuals, an artificial joint fluid can now be injected into the knee and may relieve the pain for up to several months.

There are also other drugs that are used to combat osteoarthritis, many of which can be obtained over the counter at the drug store. These drugs include glucosamine and chondroitin sulfate. There is some evidence that they may be helpful in controlling pain; however, they do not appear to grow new cartilage.

Medications cannot do the job by themselves; they need to be accompanied by lifestyle changes that include exercises. Exercises are important to maintain joint and overall body mobility. Any treatment for osteoarthritis should involve physical and occupational therapies to provide exercise treatment for the joints that are affected. Physical therapy increases the strength of muscle groups surrounding the involved joints. Increased strength of the muscles will help to maintain joint stability, reduce or prevent injury, and allow better golf. Water aerobic activities and other exercises in the water are effective for increasing mobility. Swimming is an ideal exercise for maintaining joint flexibility and increasing endurance. Since the water supports the body, muscles can be exercised without stressing and straining

figure | 5

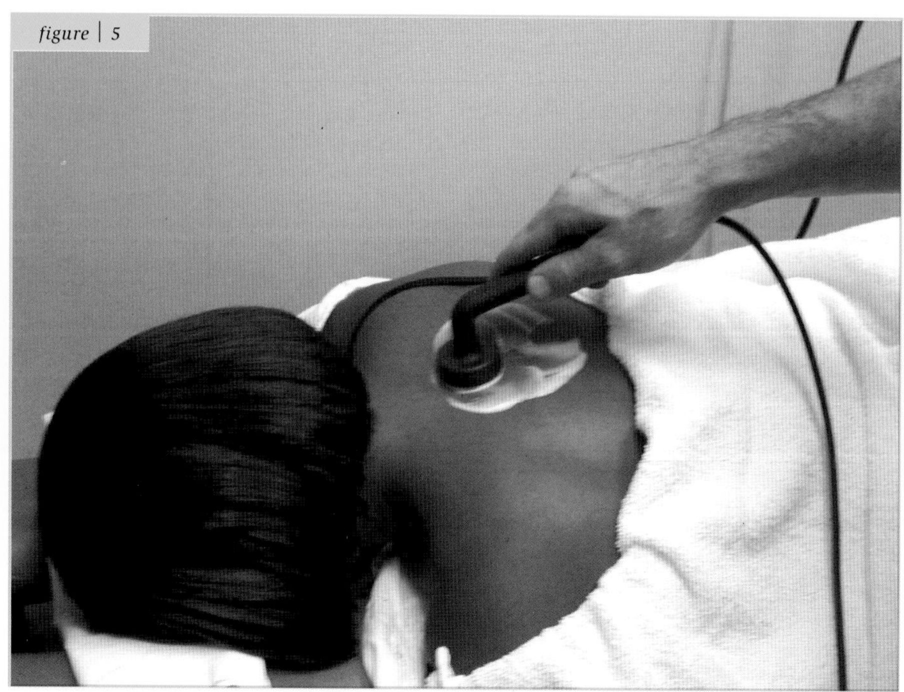

Ultrasound treatment.

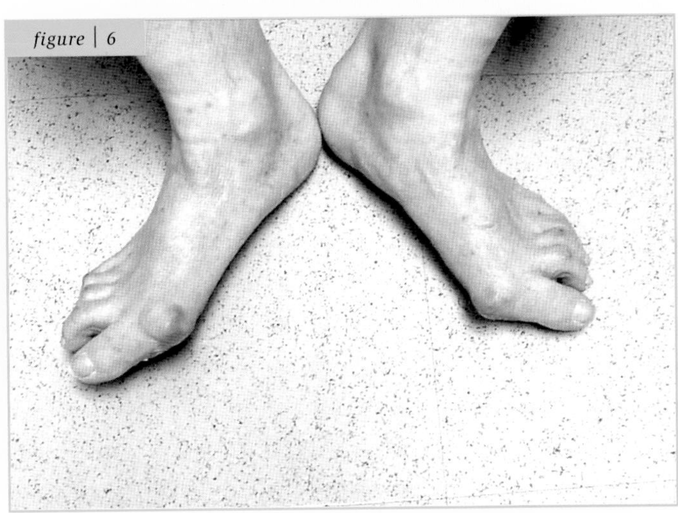

Rheumatoid arthritis of the feet with swollen, inflamed joints.

joints. Sometimes, merely getting into the water and walking in the shallow end of a pool can be helpful. Water exercises are best learned from a therapist. Some athletic clubs or YMCAs will offer water activities and exercises. It is important to be involved in an exercise program because the exercises help to improve muscle strength and maintain motion in stiff joints. The exercises learned during physical therapy must be continued at home. Usually, the benefits of therapy will be seen in about three to six weeks. Heat, ultrasound, and massage techniques may help to reduce and control pain (Fig. 5). Good nutrition and careful weight control are also important when treating osteoarthritis. Weight loss for overweight individuals will decrease the mechanical stress on the joints, which will be of benefit to the spine and legs.

SURGERY

Surgical treatment for osteoarthritis is indicated when medical treatment and physical therapy fail to bring about improvement in the quality of life. Surgical procedures include joint debridement, arthrodesis (fusion), osteotomy (bone removal), and arthroplasty (joint replacement). Surgery is intended to replace or repair damaged joints in severe situations for which medical treatment options have failed. Surgical options may include arthroplasty. Arthroplasty will be either total or partial replacement of a joint with an artificial joint. Arthroscopic surgery involves trimming the torn or damaged cartilage and then washing out the joint. Surgery is indicated only when the disease has become severe and debilitating. If the problem is in the spine and bone spurs are the problem, surgery may be needed to decompress or remove the pressure on nerves and the spinal cord. This may include the placement of bone screws, rods, or plates with bone grafting (fusion).

RHEUMATOID ARTHRITIS

Rheumatoid arthritis (RA) is a chronic inflammatory disease that attacks the lining or synovial membrane of the joints and the surrounding tissues. It can also affect other organs in the body. It is a systemic disorder, meaning that it affects the whole body. The exact cause of RA is not known; however, the body's immune system plays a role in the inflammation. The inflammation causes joint deterioration. The immune system is the body's defense against invading foreign agents such as bacteria and viruses. In RA, the immune system is defective. For some reason, the immune system attacks organs and joints. Immune system cells travel through the bloodstream to the joints and organs. Once in the joints, an inflammatory process develops. The inflammatory cells produce enzymes, antibodies and other molecules (cytokines) that attack the joint and invaded organs. Just as in many other diseases, it may be genetically related. However, the genes associated with RA are not passed directly from parents to children. The inherited genes make an individual more susceptible to the disease. Fortunately, most people with the inherited gene will not be plagued with rheumatoid arthritis. Several factors such as infection, hormonal changes, trauma, and environmental elements may play a role in the development of RA. The disease can occur at any age. Most often the onset is between the ages of 25 and 55 years. Women are affected about three times more often than men are. Today, about 1 to 2% of the total population will be affected by rheumatoid arthritis.

Rheumatoid arthritis has many faces, and the effects on each individual will vary considerably. RA can become a debilitating disease that affects the quality of life. RA most often affects the joints in the wrists, fingers, knees, feet and ankles (Fig. 6). However, it can also attack special joints in the neck. The joints in the neck that are often affected are the upper cervical spine levels (C1–C2) where the head and the neck unite. Ligaments in the neck may develop laxity that can cause abnormal spinal movements. Such increased neck movements produce instability, which causes pain. Rheumatoid arthritis will impact both sides of the body equally. When the disease becomes more severe, it will attack larger joints. The inflammation will cause the joint to secrete more fluid, which over a period of time will become red, warm, tender, swollen, and painful to move (Fig. 7). The natural history of the disease is varied. It may even change over time in the same individual. RA can go into spontaneous remission over weeks to months in about 10 to 20% of patients. More than 50% of the individuals will experience a recurrence of the disease. In some patients the disease is mild with periods of worsening called flares. Between the flare-ups the patient usually returns to normal health. Other patients will experience continued worsening of their joints and a normal state between the attacks does not occur. During active flares of RA, patients are easily fatigued, lose their appetites, and may run a low-grade fever. About one in 10 individuals with RA has a single episode of pain during an active period of the disease that is followed by a long remission period. The cartilage in the joint will become rough and pitted. One to two years after the onset of the disease bone, ligaments, and tendons are attacked and destroyed. Such destruction leads to joint deformity and disability. The deformities normally associated with RA are best seen in the fingers, wrists, elbows and knees, and can be permanent (Fig. 8). These deformities are due to cartilage destruction, bone erosions, and tendon inflammation and rupture. When the tendons in the neck are involved with RA, they become unstable and may require surgical intervention.

Approximately 20% of patients with rheumatoid arthritis will develop **rheumatoid nodules** (Fig. 9). These are painless, hard, oval or round tissue masses that appear under the skin and are found at pressure points such as the fingers, elbows, feet, and over the spine.

One of the systemic complications of RA includes **anemia**. Anemia is a low blood count, which results when the bone marrow fails to produce enough red blood cells. Taking iron supplements will not help with RA because iron utilization in the body becomes impaired. Other blood abnormalities include platelet or blood clotting cell disorders. The platelets can be either too high or too low. A serious complication of RA is **vasculitis**, an inflammation of blood vessels. Any vasculitis should never be ignored because it can be life threatening. Vasculitis of the brain can cause a stroke. It can also produce a nerve problem (neuropathy) that causes numbness and tingling in the extremities. The heart can be affected, leading to heart failure or heart attacks. In addition to the inflammation of the blood vessels of the heart, the outer lining of the heart can be attacked. Inflammation of the lining of the heart is called **pericarditis**. When the muscle of the heart is involved, this is called **myocarditis**. Both of these conditions are serious and can lead to congestive heart failure. If the blood vessels of the stomach are involved with RA, it can cause stomach ulcers that can hemorrhage. When skin is attacked, ulcers and infections form. Another organ that may be involved with rheumatoid arthritis is the lung; this occurs in about 20% of patients with RA. Inflammation of the lining of the lung can bring about **pleuritis**, which causes an accumulation of fluid on the lung. Finally, RA can cause dryness of the eyes and mouth due to inflammatory processes of the tear glands and salivary glands. This is referred to as Sjogren's or Sicca syndrome. Patients with rheumatoid

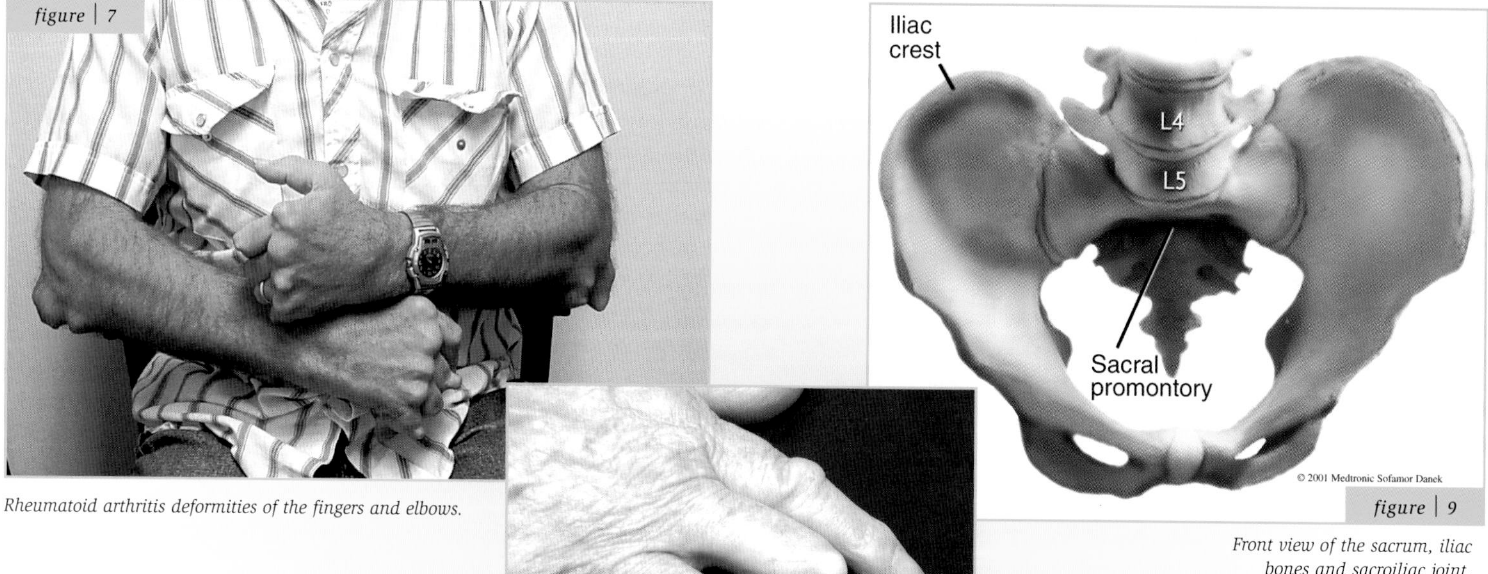

Rheumatoid arthritis deformities of the fingers and elbows.

Rheumatoid nodules of the fingers.

Front view of the sacrum, iliac bones and sacroiliac joint.

arthritis must be screened by an ophthalmologist to ensure that the disease is not invading the eyes.

There are many symptoms produced by rheumatoid arthritis. Fatigue is a common problem. A patient will often feel a general discomfort, sick all over, accompanied by lethargy. Joint pain, stiffness, and swelling are indications of an underlying inflammatory process. Pain is always an indication of underlying problems. Pain in the wrists, knees, elbows, fingers, toes, ankles or neck should alert an individual to the possibility of RA. RA can cause morning stiffness that lasts several hours, a loss of appetite, and a low-grade fever.

TESTS

One of the first tests ordered to evaluate for arthritis is a blood test called a **rheumatoid factor**. This test is frequently negative in the first year of symptoms. Eventually the tests become positive in approximately 75 to 80% of people who have symptoms consistent with rheumatoid arthritis. Another blood test is the **erythrocyte sedimentation rate (ESR)**. This is a non-specific test that indicates a possible underlying inflammation. A **CBC** (complete blood count) may reveal anemia (low hematocrit) and abnormal platelets. Another blood test is the **C-reactive protein (CRP)**. This can be positive in individuals who have no detectable rheumatoid disease. These tests are often helpful in making a diagnosis; however, there is no single test that can establish or exclude rheumatoid arthritis. If there is an inflamed, swollen joint, a doctor may have an analysis done on the fluid surrounding the joint by using a needle to draw off the fluid. The synovial fluid analysis is very helpful in the diagnosis of RA and other types of inflammatory arthritis. Finally, a synovial tissue biopsy may be needed when the diagnosis of RA is elusive.

TREATMENT

Rheumatoid arthritis has no cure. The treatment is life long and includes the use of medications, physical therapy, and possible surgical intervention. The goal of any treatment is to bring about a better quality of life by reducing pain and increasing mobility. RA is a disease that will not go away by itself. It cannot be ignored. Aggressive early treatment of RA can help to delay the onset of serious joint destruction. The initial therapy involves rest, anti-inflammatory medications, and exercises. Anti-inflammatory agents have traditionally been the first lines of therapy for RA to decrease pain and inflammation promptly. Because of significant patient variability in the efficacy, multiple agents may be prescribed before the most effective anti-inflammatory medication is discovered for an individual. RA causes inflammation; therefore, an anti-inflammatory medication will be very helpful. Aspirin is also a helpful drug in treating RA; it helps with both pain and inflammation. Non-steroidal anti-inflammatory drugs (NSAIDs) such as ibuprofen, fenoporfen, indomethacin, Naprosyn® and others have been used. In fact, many of these drugs are now household words. There are other non-steroidal medications called COX-2 inhibitors, but they are prescription medications. They are widely used medications and are often helpful in relieving pain and decreasing the inflammation associated with RA. The most common side effects of these medications are gastrointestinal bleeding and kidney problems. Because of gastric side effects of other NSAIDs in certain individuals, the COX-2 inhibitors are often the anti-inflammatory drugs of choice. These new medications are gentler on the stomach and are less likely to cause stomach bleeding. If an individual is allergic to aspirin, he or she may not be able to use other anti-inflammatory medications because they too can cause adverse allergic reactions. Such a patient may benefit from acetaminophen. However, acetaminophen is not without its complications. It can cause liver problems. Any user of medication must be aware of the drug's possible side effects. For many patients with RA the NSAIDs alone will not be adequate long-lasting treatment. Other medications will be needed to combat the inflammatory disease.

Other drugs involved in the treatment of rheumatic arthritis include **disease-modifying anti-rheumatic drugs** (**DMARDs**) or second-line drugs. These drugs are aimed at altering the course of the disease, thus preventing joint damage. These drugs often need to be given for weeks to months before improvements can be appreciated. DMARDs are administered aggressively in an effort to halt early, irreversible damage to joints. Usually a single DMARD is started. If it is ineffective, serial DMARDs are given until the destructive disease process is controlled. Other physicians start the therapy by giving low dosages of multiple DMARDs. After control of the disease is achieved, therapy is slowly decreased or withdrawn, and the patient is maintained on the least toxic DMARD that subdues the inflammation and pain.

Gold compounds were one of the early types of DMARDs. Gold was first used to treat infections, particularly tuberculosis, in the early 1900s. At that time tuberculosis was thought to be a cause of rheumatoid arthritis. Therefore RA patients were treated with gold therapy. High doses of gold benefited the patient, but caused unacceptable side effects. Lower doses proved to be better with good control of the inflammatory process and fewer side effects. However, gold therapy still produced toxicity in about 30% of the patients using it. Gold therapy is given as injectable gold salts (Myochrysine®, Solganol®) or taken by mouth in gold pills, auranofin (Ridaura®). The gold pills have a lower incidence of serious toxic side effects. Gold therapy is not as prescribed today as it once was because of newer available drugs.

Antimalarial drugs have been used to treat rheumatoid arthritis for numerous years. They were developed initially to treat malaria. When they were found to relieve inflammation, joint swelling, and pain, they became useful medications to benefit patients with RA. The most commonly prescribed antimalarial drug is hydroxychloroquine (Plaquenil®). Patients should have a baseline eye examination before starting antimalarial medications and will need regular eye examinations to check for possible retinal damage, which could cause decreased color and peripheral vision. Eye examinations should be performed every 3 to 6 months. When loss of vision is evident, continued loss of vision can progress despite discontinuing the drug. Therefore routine eye evaluations are very important. However, such eye problems are rare.

A very commonly used medication is methotrexate. It was introduced as a cancer chemotherapy treatment in the 1940s. The use of methotrexate increased because its onset of action is faster than other DMARDs. In fact, improvement can be seen in just a few weeks. It can be given in pill form, liquids, or as injections. Individuals using methotrexate need to be followed closely by their doctor. Methotrexate can cause liver damage and abnormalities of bone marrow functions. Patients should not use alcohol because the combination with methotrexate can increase the risk of liver problems. An unusual side effect of methotrexate is inflammation of the lungs (pneumonitis). This is a more common problem in smokers. Any patient who develops a dry or hacking cough and fever must call his or her doctor at once. This side effect is generally reversible, but can be life threatening. Methotrexate can cause birth defects. Men and women should stop the use of methotrexate 90 days before planning pregnancy.

D-penicillamine (Depen®, Cuprimine®) is an oral medication that is less often given to patients because of its many potential side effects. Toxicity usually is related to dosage and generally appears in the first year of treatment. Kidney toxicity and hematologic (blood) disorders may develop; therefore frequent blood tests will be needed while the patient is treated with penicillamine.

The oral therapies include medications such as D-penicillamine, and antineoplastic or anti-cancer drugs such as Methotretrax (Rheumatrex®). It may take weeks or months for the benefits from these medications to become apparent. It is important when taking these medications that the patient is followed for toxic side effects. Close monitoring by a medical team is very important.

Sulfasalazine is an antibiotic and anti-inflammatory drug combination. It was development specifically in the 1930s to treat RA. Side effects include rashes, gastrointestinal intolerance (stomach upset), blood disorders, and liver problems (hepatitis). Spermatogenesis may be affected. Most side effects are reversed with discontinuation of the drug. Patients with an allergic reaction to medications containing sulfa cannot take sulfasalazine.

Minocycline (Minocin®, Dynacin®) is an antibiotic medication that has anti-inflammatory properties. It is usually more effective in the early stages of RA. Minocycline may interfere with certain birth control medications. Patients who are allergic to tetracycline cannot take minocycline.

A relatively new medication used to treat RA is leflunomide (Arava®). Like other DMARDs it can cause side effects that include skin rashes, stomach upsets, hair loss, and liver problems. Women and men who wish to become pregnant must discontinue taking leflunomide because it may cause birth defects. Both men and women must use reliable birth control methods while taking leflunomide.

Azathioprine (Imuran®) is an immunosuppressive medication. RA involves the immune system by attacking organs; therefore, drugs that suppress the immune system may be tried for patients with poor response to other therapies. It was the first such drug approved for the use in RA patients. It often takes weeks to months to be effective. Toxicities depend on the dosage. Side effects include blood and liver disorders; thus safety screening of blood tests (CBC, liver function) will be needed every 3 to 4 months. A serious possible side effect is the risk of cancer in patients with prolonged use of azathioprine.

Cyclophosphamide (Cytoxan®) is a very potent and toxic immunosuppressive drug used to treat rheumatoid arthritis. It is generally reserved for patients with severe complications of RA. It can increase the risks of certain cancers in patients. Patients will need very close monitoring when using this medication.

The treatment of rheumatoid arthritis is a large field of medical research. New medications are currently being introduced. Promising new drugs are called biologic response modifiers (BRMs). Etanercept (Enbrel®) and infliximab (Remicade®) are BRMs. These drugs act by inhibiting an anti-inflammatory causing protein called tumor necrosis factor (TNF). Etanercept is also used in children and teenagers (age 4 to 17 years) with juvenile arthritis. Both of these drugs are intended for use in patients with moderately to severe RA. Individuals taking these medications must be followed closely for side effects.

New BRMs are being developed to treat RA. One such modifier is anakinra. It blocks the activity of another inflammatory RA chemical called interleukin-1. RA research is continuing to reveal other components of the inflammatory response and more drugs are under investigation that will benefit RA patients.

For numerous years, rheumatoid arthritis patients have been treated with glucocorticoids (cortisone, prednisone). In fact, steroid treatments for RA patients have been used since the 1940s. Corticosteroids were so dramatically effective in the treatment of RA that the Nobel Prize was awarded for the work with these agents. For many patients, steroids have provided an improved quality of life. These drugs are related to cortisol, a hormone needed to live and function. Cortisol controls body functions such as blood pressure and pulse. However, high doses of glucocorticoids may cause serious side effects that include easy bruising, osteoporosis (brittle bone disease), cataracts, weight gain, increased susceptibility to infection, diabetes, high blood pressure, cataracts, glaucoma, facial changes, and even psychosis. Many of the unwanted side effects of steroid use are directly related to the dosage and the length of use of the drug. Corticosteroids can be helpful, but can cause other medical problems. Research for the medical treatment of rheumatoid arthritis is an ever-expanding field with new medications just over the horizon. These medications will, hopefully, allow better pain management, improved quality of life, and fewer side effects. Any long-term use of a medication, even an over-the-counter medication, requires close monitoring.

SURGERY

Surgery is indicated for severely affected joints. The most successful joint surgery is on the knees and the hips. Surgical treatment may include removing the lining of the joint (synovectomy). Other surgery may involve total joint replacement with a prosthesis or artificial joint. Surgery can help to relieve joint pain, correct deformities, and improve joint function. Total joint replacement can be very successful, and may mean the difference between being active or totally dependent on others. If surgical avenues can offer help, procrastination can complicate the situation and lead to less successful outcomes.

PHYSICAL THERAPY

In addition to medications, lifestyle changes will be needed for those with rheumatoid arthritis. It is important that a physician or physical therapist structure the patient's exercise program for those who have joint dysfunction. Initially, heat and cold treatments can be helpful. When joints are inflamed, the joint cartilage is prone to injury and irreversible injury. Therefore it is very important that joint protection is understood and practiced by the patient. Golf is out of the question during this vulnerable period. Splints or orthotic devices may be needed to protect, support, and align the joints. Water aerobics can help to increase joint mobility and aid in joint strengthening. Physical and occupational therapists will both be needed to help treat those with RA.

Aggressive medical and surgical treatment can improve the quality of life for those who have rheumatoid arthritis. The course of the disease will vary between individuals. People who develop RA at a young age seem to have a more difficult time and demonstrate a more rapid course of the disease. People who have a positive rheumatoid factor and/or subcutaneous nodules also may have a more severe course of the disease. The goal of treatment is to halt the occurrence of RA. It is most likely to occur in the first year. As time passes and the disease does not ease up, it is unlikely to do so. About 20% of individuals who develop arthritis will go into remission. It is important that this disease is treated and not ignored.

ANKYLOSING SPONDYLITIS (AS)

Ankylosing spondylitis (AS) is a special type of arthritis that causes inflammation of the spine. Ankylosing means to become stiff or rigid. Spondyl- means the spine, and -itis means inflammation. The inflammation of the spine is referred to as spondyloarthropathy. This condition is chronic and usually progressive. This arthritis attacks the spine and the sacroiliac joints. The sacroiliac joints are large joints located in the low back area where the iliac bones of the upper buttocks and the sacrum (tailbone) come together (Fig. 9). Any type of inflammation will cause pain and stiffness. In this situation the pain and stiffness will be located in and around the spine as well as the sacroiliac joints. As the disease progresses chronic inflammation (spondylitis) will cause changes to occur in the ligaments and the bones of the spine and joints. The inflammatory process will cause new bone formation to occur at the attachments of tendons and ligaments to the bone. The medical term for this is **enthesopathy**; this means that the ligaments and the tendons that attach to the bone will fuse or cement together. Once the backbones, ligaments, and tendons are fused they become rock hard, resulting in total loss of mobility in the spine. Ankylosing spondylitis can cause inflammatory points away from the spine. It can affect the eyes, heart, lungs, and kidneys. AS is also called ankylosing spondylitis or rheumatoid spondylitis, plain spondylitis or Marie-Strumpell disease (named after the physicians who first described the disease).

Scientists and physicians do not know what causes this disease; however, genetic factors appear to play some role. There is usually a familial clustering with this disease, meaning that if an individual has this disease, then other members of the family have a higher incidence of the disease. There is a 10% risk of developing ankylosing spondylitis for an HLA-B27, tissue antigen, positive child. This is a common genetic marker among individuals with ankylosing spondylitis. This marker is found in a higher than expected frequency of individuals who have this kind of spondylitis. AS typically attacks adolescents and young adults. Symptoms usually begin in the early 20s and rarely after the age of 40. Men are at greater risk than women are. The onset of symptoms is often insidious with morning stiffness. The pain is intermittent hip or lower back discomfort. Individuals may be awakened at night with discomfort; will note stiffness and will need to walk off the discomfort. Activity tends to alleviate the pain caused by stiffness. Symptoms may be aggravated with rest, and bending over may ease the pain. The disease varies from individual to individual. Even though the symptoms may begin in the low back area, they may also involve the entire spine, shoulders, hips, and feet. When the spine is involved, there will be decreased movement in the affected areas. If the inflammation travels to the ribs, chest pains may occur. Other internal organs may be involved in the inflammatory process of AS. A urinalysis (urine test) will be performed to look for abnormalities in the kidneys. Advanced AS can led to deposits of a protein-type material called amyloid from the kidneys. Over time, the amyloid build-up can lead to kidney failure. Some patients may have a low-grade fever, while others may experience weight loss, fatigue, anemia, and eye inflammation (iritis). In severe cases, the heart and heart valves may be attacked. Other diseases of internal organs may mimic AS, so laboratory testing may be needed to further determine what disease is causing the problem.

Laboratory evaluation will be needed for making the diagnosis of ankylosing spondylitis. The HLA-B27 tissue antigen will show up positive in 90% of patients who have AS, as compared to 5 to 8% positive testing in the general population. Another test that is obtained is called an erythrocyte sedimentation rate (ESR); this test is non-specific, but is elevated or high in approximately 80% of individuals who have AS. A rheumatoid factor test will be positive for patients with RA and absent for those with AS.

Radiological studies will consist of plain X-rays, bone scans, and computer-aided tomographies (CAT scans). These tests will demonstrate the characteristic changes or fusion in the bones. X-rays will be obtained of the sites where pain is noted. X-rays of the spine will show a so-called "bamboo" spine. The vertebral bodies of the spine will appear "squared" and the anulus fibrosis (outer layer of the disc) will be ossified or calcified (Fig. 10A and B). Other tests may include an EKG to evaluate the heart. A chest X-ray may also be helpful. An ophthamological consultation examination will be needed for those individuals who have eye involvement from AS.

The goal of treatment of ankylosing spondylitis is to reduce the discomfort and pain, and to bring about an improved quality of life for the sufferer. Many patients will assume a hunched-over posture because an upright posture will cause pain. Posture training and range of motion exercises are essential. Abdominal and back exercises will help to maintain a more correct posture, so a physical therapist will be needed to help with increasing spine and joint flexibility. Other exercises will include breathing exercises to enhance lung capacity. Water aerobics and swimming will often provide some pain relief and muscle strengthening. A firm bed and sleeping without a pillow is sometimes recommended. Even with the best of treatment, some patients will continue to develop a stiff spine. If the process continues, it is important that the spine fuses in the upright position, not in the bent-over position. An upright position will allow a better quality of life. It is beneficial for individuals who smoke to stop smoking. Smoking affects the bones and joints of the spine, and causes breathing problems. With this particular disease, it is important to maintain good lung capacity, which would be compromised by smoking.

TREATMENT

There is no single drug that will cure ankylosing spondylitis, but there are many medications that can improve the quality of life. The non-steroidal anti-inflammatory medications (NSAIDs) are medications that help with the pain and inflammation. For some people, aspirin is a powerful pain and anti-inflammatory medication, but can be tough on the stomach. NSAIDs have been of great value to individuals with all kinds of arthritis; AS is no exception. Taking NSAIDs depends on the individual. Some patients respond well to a non-steroidal anti-inflammatory medication called indomethacin (Indocin®). A major side effect of non-steroidal anti-inflammatory medications is related to stomach problems such as upset, nausea, diarrhea, abdominal pain, and bleeding ulcers. Therefore, such medication should be taken with food in order to minimize the side effects. Patients taking NSAIDs must be followed for other potential complications like kidney problems. There are other medications that can be prescribed for patients with more severe AS. One medication is Remicade® (infliximab). This medication is an antibody that will block tumor necrosis factor-alpha (**TNF-Alfa**), a substance made by cells that promote inflammation. The TNF protein promotes inflammation that is associated with fever, pain, tenderness and swelling. By blocking the action of this tumor necrosis factor, Remicade® helps to reduce the signs and symptoms of inflammation. Another medication that is helpful in attacking the TNF protein is Enbrel®. This medication helps to remove the TNF protein from the blood and joints. If the TNF factor is removed there will be less inflammation and less swelling and pain. Another medication that has been promising in treating AS and other types of arthritis is Arava®. This medication helps with the reduction of inflammation. It does so by suppressing the immune cells that are responsible for producing inflammation. For certain individuals, methotrexate has proven to be helpful as it has with other types of arthritis. There are other drugs that are waiting in the wings; however, they are experimental and are not yet available outside of research trials. For select patients who are not doing well with established lines of therapy, they may want to ask their doctor about any ongoing clinical trials for which they may be a candidate for treatment.

Physical therapy is important in the care of any individual with AS. Exercise will help to maintain an upright posture and maintain joint flexibility. A preferred exercise is swimming. Swimming reduces the weight and strain on the spine and will help to reduce the pull of gravity. Patients with AS should try to swim as often as possible. Throughout the day, they should try to perform some type of stretching exercises; this will help to alleviate stiffness. Patients may find that mid-day and evening will be the most appropriate times to perform these exercises. Patients with AS should try to keep their spines as straight as possible, particularly when they are walking or sitting. The physiotherapist will be helpful in establishing exercise routines, as well as advising about correct posture. At work, the AS patient should sit in an appropriate chair: one with a solid seat and an upright firm back. Armchairs will help prevent a rounded, stooped posture. Patients should avoid soft cushioned chairs and sofas; they encourage bad posture, which leads to more back discomfort. When patients are sitting in a chair, they should pull their shoulders back to help maintain an upright posture. Some people use a brace or corset to keep the back rigid; this can be harmful over a long period of time because it can lead to muscle disuse. At night, patients should have a good firm mattress with a pillow under both the neck and legs for good spine alignment. The use of heat or cold is up to the individual. Many find that a hot or warm shower in the morning will help to reduce stiffness and pain. Showers can be very helpful before performing stretching exercises. Taking a bath may be somewhat more difficult. Sitting in a bathtub will encourage bad posture. Other individuals with AS may find that cold is better at reducing the pain than heat. If an ice pack is used, the pack should be wrapped in a protective towel or bag. Patients should not use it for more than 20 minutes, and never place an unwrapped ice pack onto the skin, as it could cause burns. Driving with AS can be somewhat of a task due to the immobile spine, particularly if it involves the neck. Extra care will need to be exercised while driving. If patients have to drive for long distances, they may need to stop every two hours to stretch and place a cushion under their backs to maintain a comfortable position.

It is important, with any type of arthritis, that patients remain physically active. Swimming is an excellent way to exercise in a relatively gravity-free environment. It is best to avoid contact sports such as football or wrestling. High-impact sports such as tennis, basketball, volleyball, and all net ball sports and step aerobics should be avoided. AS should not limit a prepared individual from playing golf; however, the golf activity should be modified. A patient with AS should discuss his or her condition with a golf professional. An AS golfer should avoid heavy lifting, bending, and pulling activities. The golf bag should not be overly burdened with unnecessary items. Old golf balls should be removed from the bag. When in doubt about engaging in an athletic activity, first discuss it with a physician. AS is a lifelong problem and requires continued care and commitment to engaging in the

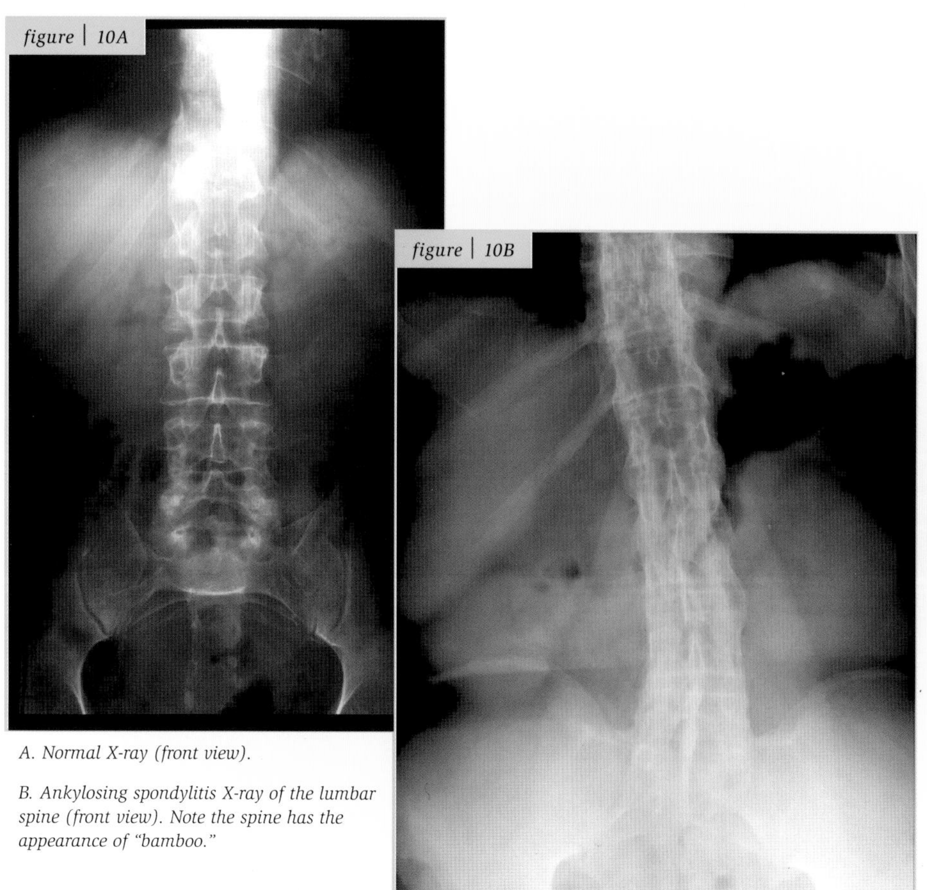

figure | 10A

figure | 10B

A. Normal X-ray (front view).

B. Ankylosing spondylitis X-ray of the lumbar spine (front view). Note the spine has the appearance of "bamboo."

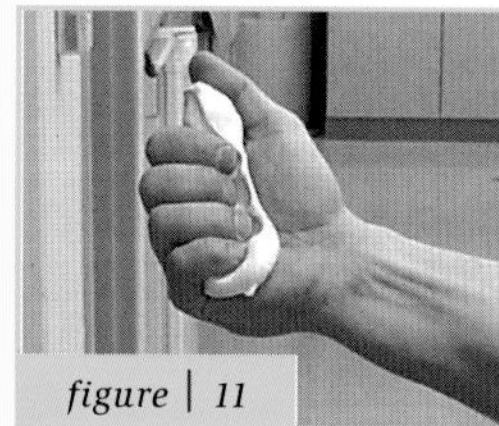

figure | 11

Hand putty.

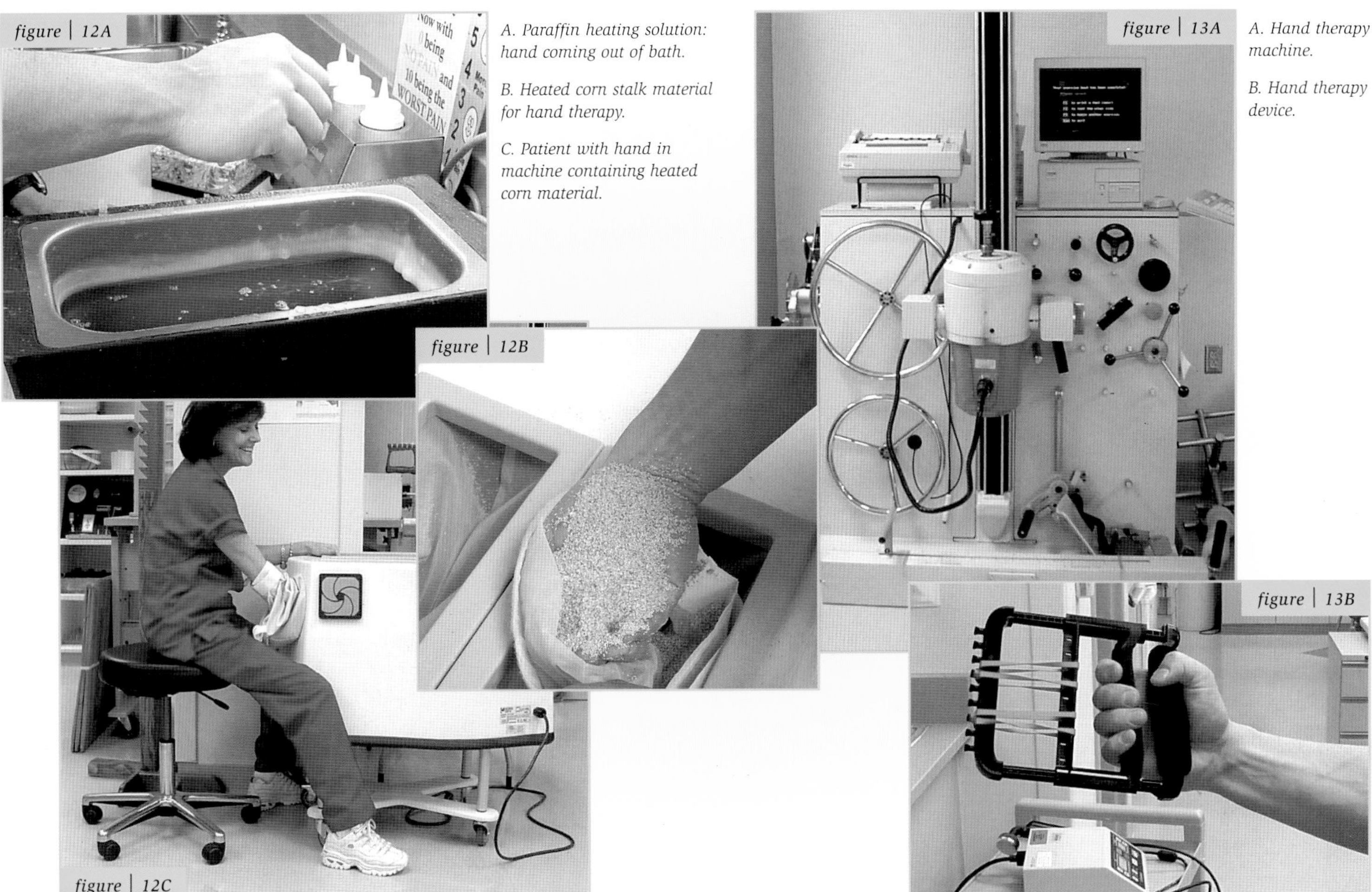

figure | 12A

figure | 12B

figure | 12C

A. Paraffin heating solution: hand coming out of bath.

B. Heated corn stalk material for hand therapy.

C. Patient with hand in machine containing heated corn material.

figure | 13A

figure | 13B

A. Hand therapy machine.

B. Hand therapy device.

necessary activities that will promote a healthier life.

Golf is a most enjoyable sport. For the arthritic patient who has many physical demands, it can have health-enhancing effects. Playing golf can provide a means to increase the strength of the extremities and spine, and increase the mobility of the arms, spine, hips, and legs. Golf benefits the range of motion in the joints and provides improvement in coordination and balance.

If a golfer has any type of arthritis, adaptation is the key for continued play. It is important to plan ahead before teeing off. It's a good idea for arthritic golfers to talk to a doctor, physical therapist, occupational therapist, and golf professional about what they will need, especially special aids, to play golf. The arthritic patient will need an extra degree of help to continue playing golf in a pain-free environment. If a golf professional has any hesitation about instructing an arthritic patient, the patient should find a professional who works with arthritic patients. The Arthritis Foundation recommends the following equipment modifications for patients with arthritis.

1. Use clubs with lightweight graphite shafts because they absorb the shock better.
2. Use a lower-compression ball. The golfer will need to discuss ball types with a professional and experiment. When a harder ball is struck, it has a tendency to jar the joints and cause pain. It's like hitting a rock with a club.
3. A parameter-weighted head on the club will provide better shock absorption.
4. A proper grip is very important. Arthritis often affects the hands, so grip adjustments will improve the handling of the club. The arthritis in the hands will limit the patient's ability to maintain a strong grip throughout the golf swing. The inability to maintain an effective grip will bring about a twisting of the club at impact. A mid-sized or larger grip may feel more comfortable for the golfer. Another easy way to adjust the grip size is to use athletic tape to build up the grip to a comfortable size. There are also air-cushioned grips that incorporate air chambers into the grip allowing for a more comfortable feel. Positioning the thumb around, instead of on top of the shaft may allow more wrist movements and lessen discomfort of sore joints.
5. Wearing wrist braces and gloves on both hands to stabilize the wrist joints can ease arthritis in the hands. Speaking to an occupational therapist is helpful.
6. Wear comfortable walking shoes or spike-less golf shoes.
7. Hand putty can be carried and used between play to massage and loosen up hands (Fig.11).
8. A paraffin heating solution or heated corn shuck material can be very helpful to ease painful joints. (Fig.12A, B, and C). Hand therapies and strengthening devices will increase endurance (Fig.13A and B).
9. Hand exercises will benefit the golfer's grip (Fig.14).

Once all of the equipment modifications have been completed, it is on to the golf course. It is important to take only the clubs that are most frequently used. Before arthritic golfers tee up, it's important to loosen up. An easy exercise is simply walking around for about 15 minutes. Warm-up exercises are key to the completion of an enjoyable round of golf: easy practice swings, gentle trunk twisting, hamstring stretches are all good warm-up exercises. Walking from the first tee to the green and back is a good warm-up exercise. Arthritic sufferers should arrive at the course early. They will benefit by going to the driving range and taking 10 to 20 easy swings. The Classic swing with an upright follow-through is less stressful and more comfortable than the Modern swing with a reverse-C follow through (Fig. 15 A and B). The first club out of the bag should not be the driver. Arthritic golfers should start out by hitting higher-lofted clubs like a pitching wedge and slowly work up to the woods. It is important, whenever they hit the ball, even on the practice range, to avoid striking the ground; this will only jar tender joints and cause pain. Arthritic golfers should consider using tees whenever they hit the ball. This will help to avoid hitting the ground and jarring joints. The goal is to enjoy golf and have a pain-free round. The arthritic patient who fatigues easily should consider riding in a motorized cart rather than walking and should never carry the bag. It is a good idea to have an attendant take the golf bag out of the car and place it into the golf cart. If the patient is able to walk, a pull-cart should be used. The patient with arthritis is very tuned into his or her joints and body. It is important that arthritic golfers continue to listen to their bodies as they play golf. They should not be embarrassed by not completing the full 18 holes of golf. Playing a flatter, less hilly course will be easier on the patient's joints. For some, the 9-hole course will be just what the doctor ordered. Some golf courses offer 9-hole leagues. Playing from the 150-yard markers may help to prevent early fatigue. It is not unusual for the arthritic golfer to experience stiffness in the joints after a round of golf. A nice warm bath or a soak in a hot tub will provide relaxation for the muscles and ease the aching joints.

There are many types of arthritis. Each one affects individuals differently. The course of the disease for each individual will also be different. The outcome for each case of arthritis can not be totally predicted. It is important to recognize and not ignore the early symptoms and signs of arthritis. Any aches or pains in any joint, including the spine, that do not go away within a reasonable time should be further evaluated. Early diagnosis, testing, and treatment are the best ways to promote continued health while living with arthritis. If arthritis patients are to continue playing golf, they must remain motivated and committed to treatment and work closely with their doctor, therapist, and golf professional. Treatment of arthritis is multidisciplinary; a team is needed to allow the patient to maintain a functional and active lifestyle that includes golf.

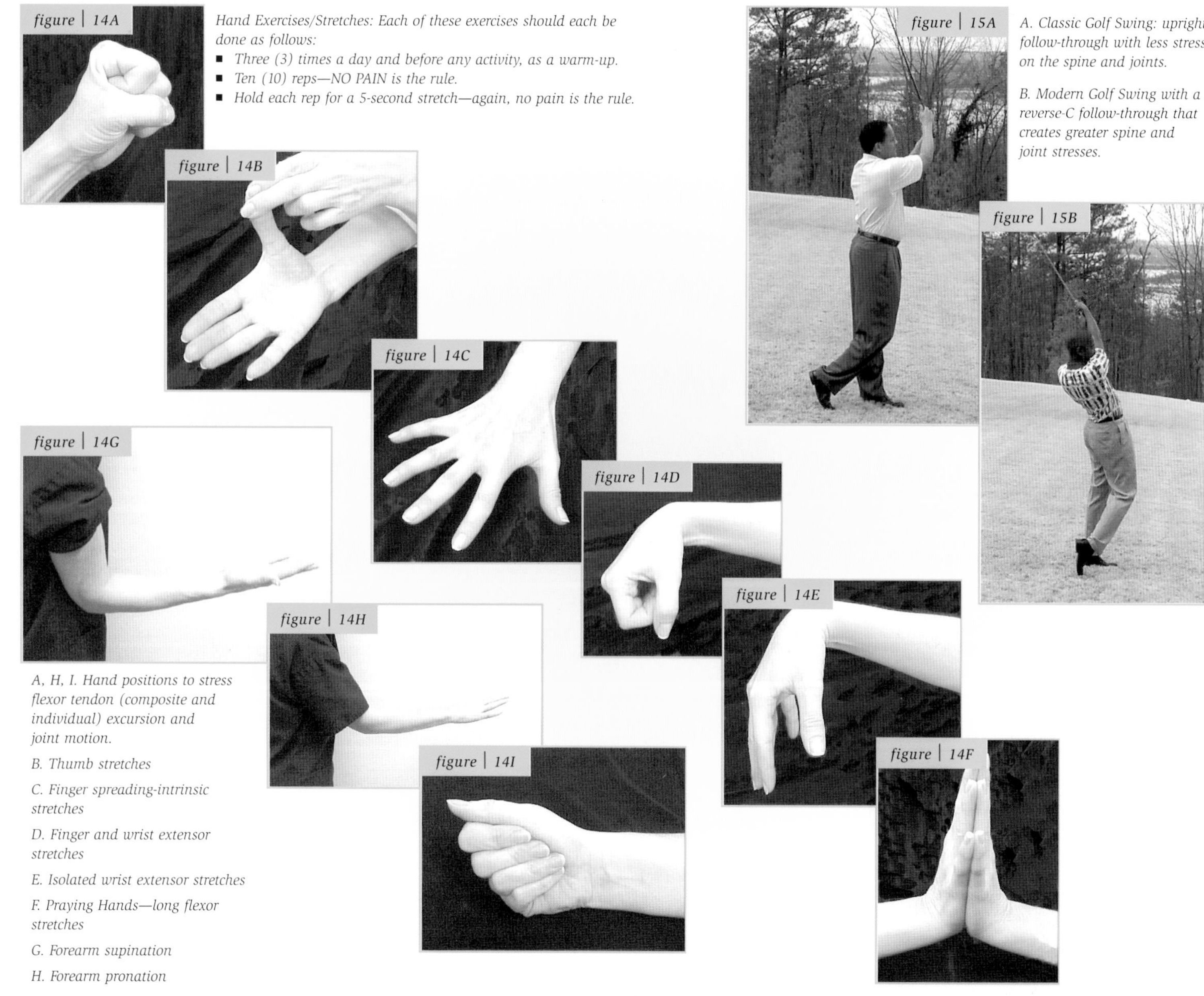

figure | 14A

Hand Exercises/Stretches: Each of these exercises should each be done as follows:

- *Three (3) times a day and before any activity, as a warm-up.*
- *Ten (10) reps—NO PAIN is the rule.*
- *Hold each rep for a 5-second stretch—again, no pain is the rule.*

figure | 14B

figure | 14C

figure | 14D

figure | 14E

figure | 14F

figure | 14G

figure | 14H

figure | 14I

A, H, I. Hand positions to stress flexor tendon (composite and individual) excursion and joint motion.

B. Thumb stretches

C. Finger spreading-intrinsic stretches

D. Finger and wrist extensor stretches

E. Isolated wrist extensor stretches

F. Praying Hands—long flexor stretches

G. Forearm supination

H. Forearm pronation

figure | 15A

figure | 15B

A. Classic Golf Swing: upright follow-through with less stress on the spine and joints.

B. Modern Golf Swing with a reverse-C follow-through that creates greater spine and joint stresses.

OSTEOPOROSIS

CHAPTER 15

T. Glenn Pait, M.D., F.A.C.S.

I've tried everything in the world on my back but voodoo, and I've even considered that. And that's the honest truth. After three surgeries on my back, I think it's critical to keep the hamstrings and buttocks loose. I definitely stretch them every day before I leave the room, and that seems to help as much as anything.

Fuzzy Zoeller

Osteoporosis is an age related disorder that causes a decrease in the bone mass of the skeleton. It is a bone-thinning disease. The loss of bone mass is called osteopenia and can lead to biomechanical problems. Bones with osteopenia will have an increased susceptibility to fractures. These can occur in vertebrae (back bones), hips, wrists and arms. Sometimes fractures can occur with minimal trauma.

Osteoporosis is a result of a defective remodeling system of the bones. Bone is a living tissue. Just like any other cell in the body, bone cells die and are replaced by younger, healthier cells. When we lose bone mass, it is because the dead cells are not replaced by new cells. If bone loss continues and the cells are not replaced, over time fractures will likely occur. The normal process for bone remodeling, when bone cells dies and are replaced, takes about 3 to 4 months. If there is evidence of osteoporosis, this process can take from 2 to 4 years.

Osteoporosis is a serious health risk. As the population ages, osteoporosis becomes a serious health threat. More than 323 million individuals aged 65 years or older are at risk world-wide. Some 20 million Americans have osteoporosis, with more than one million broken bones that are caused by osteoporosis. Some 500,000, or about 45% of all of the osteoporotic fractures, will occur in the spine and, in particular, in the vertebrae. Another 225,000, or 20% of osteoporotic injuries, will occur in the hips. The distal forearm will account for 14%, or about 172,000 broken bones. Another 24% of fractures will appear at other bony sites. Spine fractures are 10 times more common in women than men. 18% of women over 50 will develop osteoporosis and the resulting fractures, and 27% of women over the age of 65 need to be concerned about osteoporotic problems. When all of the math is said and done, one out of every three women over the age of 65 years can expect to have a fracture of a bone in her spine. The bony changes brought about by fractures will be permanent and will change the shape of the vertebral bodies (back bones), affecting the strength of the bone. The inability to support the demands placed upon the spine, due to osteoporosis, is a limiting factor to playing golf.

Rapid formation of bone mass occurs in the fetus and in the infant. During childhood, until around the age of 11 in females and 12 in males, bone formation slows down. Then in adolescence there is a growth spurt during which there is tremendous bone formation. The majority of the formation of bone-mass levels is achieved by the ages of 18 to 20, with only a small amount of bone mass added from then until the age of 28. Once the peak bone mass has been attained, it is maintained by a process called remodeling. This is a process that occurs throughout our lifetimes. Remodeling is the tearing down of small parts of the bones and then re-forming them. The breaking down of bones is called **resorption** and is performed by large bone cells called **osteoclasts**. Osteoclasts are found in the central part of the bone and are continually removing small portions of bone at the edge of the bone surface. Not far away are other bone-forming cells called **osteoblasts**. There is a tug-of-war between the breakdown by the osteoclasts and the re-building by the osteoblasts. Beginning around the age of 35, more calcium is taken away from our bone bank than is deposited. At first, bone loses calcium very slowly. The osteoblasts (builders) become less efficient at building bone than the osteoclasts are at removing bone. As we age, this becomes more of a problem. Bone banks are robbed of their calcium more quickly than it can be re-deposited. Osteoporosis is a silent thief. There are no obvious signs of the bone bank's being robbed. When the bank has suffered too many withdrawals, it becomes weak, and the risks associated with breaking bones increase, causing pain, disability and deformity. Broken bones typically occur in the spine, the hip and the wrist.

CLASSIFICATION OF OSTEOPOROSIS

Osteoporosis may be classified either as primary or secondary osteoporosis. The primary osteoporosis has two types.

Type I occurs in post-menopausal women, and is six times more common in women than men. This type of osteoporosis usually occurs about 15 to 20 years after menopause and commonly occurs between the ages of 51–75 years of age. Estrogen deficiency is a primary factor in women who have this type of bony problem. In Type I, there is a loss of the spongy tissue (cancellous bone) located inside the vertebral bodies. The outside of the bone, which is harder, is called cortical bone; in Type I osteoporosis there is some sparing of the outer bone. Don't be misled by the fact that this type of osteoporosis occurs six times more in women than men; it does occur in men. In men, it is linked to a testosterone deficiency, indicating that hormonal factors, as well as aging, are associated to osteoporosis. Vertebral spine fractures are the most common fractures in Type I osteoporosis (Figs. 1A and B).

Type II osteoporosis affects not only the inside cancellous (spongy tissue), but also the harder outer bone. This is more age-related than Type I osteoporosis and is found in both men and women over the age of 70. This bony disorder is associated with a deficiency in dietary calcium and a decline in vitamin D. There is also decreased activity in the parathyroid glands. There are four parathyroid glands that are imbedded in the back of the thyroid glands in our necks that produce parathyroid hormone that helps to regulate calcium levels in the blood. A drop in the calcium level in the blood stimulates an increase in the secretion of parathyroid hormone that acts on various organs to raise calcium levels. This condition will typically develop after the age of 50. Over-production of parathyroid hormone is called hyperparathyroidism, which can be likened to a bone-stealing hormone. In order to get more calcium, the hormone removes it from the bone. This causes an increase in the levels of calcium in the blood, which results in weakened bone, which increases the likelihood of fractures. Hip fractures are the most common result of Type II osteoporosis. Genetic factors play a role here. There are other problems that cause Type II osteoporosis; hyperparathyroidism is one, and hyperthyroidism is another that causes many functions of the body to speed up. Diabetes may also cause osteoporosis. Diabetes is a disorder in which the pancreas does not produce enough insulin. Finally, long-term use of steroids, in particular oral corticosteroids, may also lead to osteoporosis. If a golfer has any of these hormonal problems, it is best to check with a doctor before playing golf.

There are other diseases that can lead to loss of bone mass. One of the most common is **multiple myeloma**. This is an unusual and life-threatening cancer of the bone. This condition affects plasma cells, or white blood cells, that are involved in the production of antibodies that fight infections. The plasma cells undergo changes and become cancerous. When this happens, they begin to multiply in an uncontrolled fashion (Fig. 2). People who have this disease are very susceptible to infections. The abnormal plasma cells destroy bone tissue and release calcium into the blood stream.

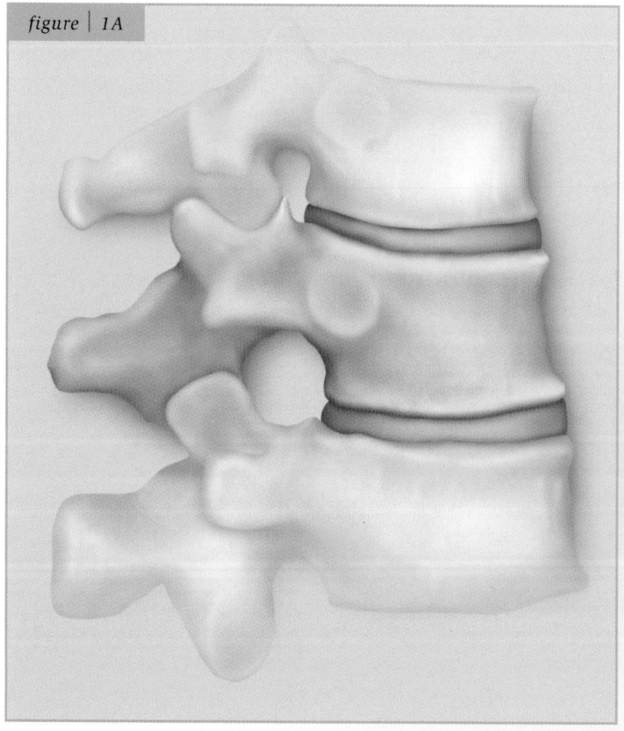

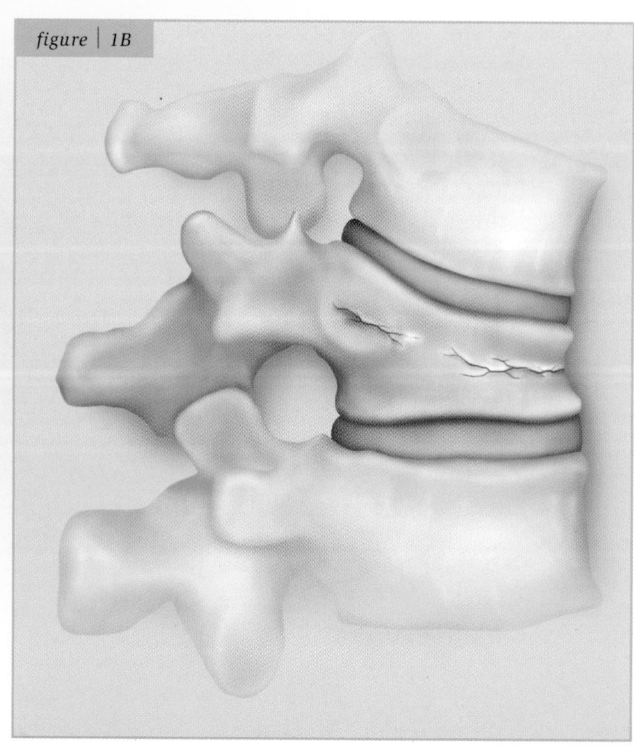

A. Normal vertebra.

B. Compression fracture of vertebra.

figure | 3A

A. Normal CAT (CT) scan: solid bone.

B. CAT (CT) scan with multiple myeloma: moth-eaten bone.

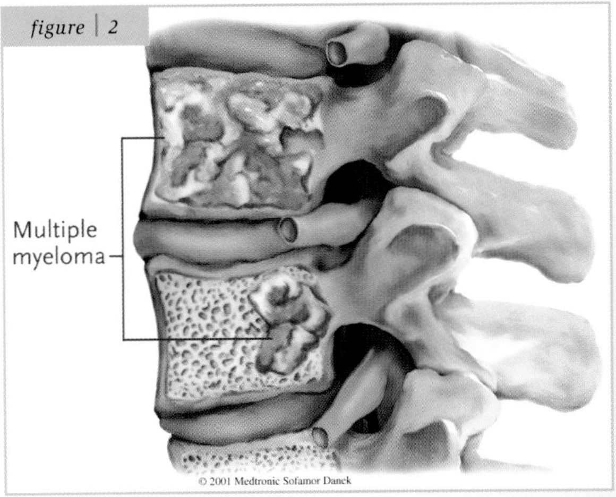

Multiple myeloma.

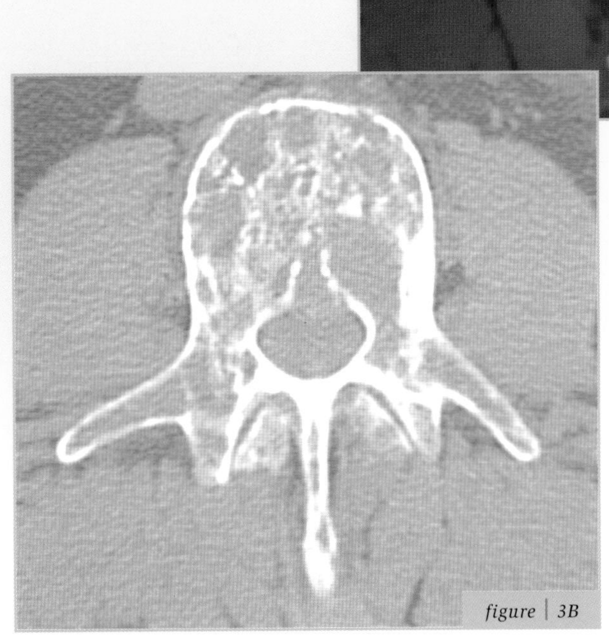

With the loss of calcium, bone fractures are frequent. Leukemia is another kind of bone marrow cancer where abnormal blood cells multiply at an uncontrollable rate. In every type of leukemia, there are cancerous blood cells that accumulate in the bone marrow. The loss of bone marrow to the abnormal white blood cells will bring about secondary osteoporosis (Figs. 3A and B).

The bone-thinning disease of osteoporosis will affect many individuals who want to play golf; understanding some of the risk factors of the disease may help to predict the chance of getting osteoporosis. There are three basic ways to develop loss of bone mass: heredity, other medical problems, and lifestyle related risk factors. Here are some of the risk factors of osteoporosis:

1. Gender: Women have a much greater chance of losing bone mass than men
2. Race: Individuals of Asian or Caucasian descent are more likely to experience bone loss.
3. Aging.
4. Genetics- Family history of osteoporosis and fractures increase risk.
5. Post-menopause: Men and women are both subject to this change, with women being at increased risk due to the reduction of estrogen.
6. Body Frame: Very thin individuals who are underweight for their height have a greater risk of developing a skeletal problem.
7. Medication: Certain medications over a long period of time will contribute to the loss of bone mass. Drugs that are commonly known to aid the development of osteoporosis include: anti-seizure medications; steroids; anti-coagulants (blood thinners); immunosuppressants; and thyroid hormone suppressive therapy.
8. Medical disorders: Diabetes; hormonal disorders; thyroid and parathyroid diseases; kidney disease; and others.
9. Down's Syndrome.

The above lists medical risk factors for osteoporosis for which patients will probably have no control. There are certain lifestyle risk factors that individuals do have a degree of control over to help reduce the chances of osteoporosis. At the top of the list is the use of tobacco, including smoking or chewing tobacco. Tobacco use should be discouraged in all cases. The use of more than seven ounces of alcohol per week will slightly increase the risk of hip fractures. Sedentary lifestyle with little exercise contributes. Individuals with low calcium intake who consume more than 2 to 3 cups of caffeine coffee per day will increase their chances of osteoporotic problems. Not enough calcium in a diet is bad for bones; golfers should consume at least 300mg per day of calcium (about 11 ounces) or one glass of milk. Poor vitamin D or no vitamin D intake will lead to problems with bones. This can be remedied by eating fortified cereals or milk, or egg yolks. Finally, high phosphorus intake is another risk for developing osteoporosis. High levels of phosphate will decrease the level of calcium in the body systems, thus promoting the parathyroid glands to increase parathyroid hormone production, which steals calcium from bones. A good source of phosphorous is in cola soft drinks; drinking too much cola can cause unwanted problems. Individuals who eat a lot of meat demonstrate a greater loss of bone mass than do vegetarians who avoid meat. The reason for this is that meat is one of the main sources of dietary phosphate.

MATURING AND OSTEOPOROSIS

There are many factors that determine the fate of bones: genetics, nutrition, sex, physical activity, race, and metabolic diseases. Bone mass peaks during the third decade of life. After the fourth decade of life, we begin to lose bone mass, a continuous process throughout our lives. Loss of bone happens at a rate of 0.3 to 0.5% per year and is greater for women than men. After menopause, there is an increase in bone loss of about 2–3% a year for the next 10 years. For men, the accelerated bone loss occurs later in life, usually in the 60s, at a time when golf is of more importance in their lives. Osteoporosis is a disorder in which there is too much bone loss and not enough bone being made. A good way to think about osteoporosis and our bones is to use an asphalt-paved street as an example. Over a period of time, there is wear and tear on asphalt streets. Potholes develop. In a community that is healthy and financially sound, potholes are filled in a timely fashion. Traveling down a road that has been well maintained insures that moving vehicles will not be damaged. If potholes are not filled, the chance that we will hit one and damage our car increases. With osteoporosis, potholes develop and are not filled, increasing the risk of trouble. We are losing bone and not being able to repair it. The strength of bones, particularly bones in the spine, depends on the amount of bone mineral density (bone mass). A reduction of the bone mineral density will subject the spine to increasing harm. It has been shown that a reduction of one-third of normal bone mineral density reduces the strength of vertebral bones to one-ninth of normal. A further reduction of bone mineral density to one-half of normal will bring about a reduction in the strength to one-fourth of normal. The forces that are placed on the bones may become too much, and fractures will occur.

SYMPTOMS

In some medical circles, osteoporosis is not considered to be a problem until the disease becomes symptomatic. When too much bone loss occurs and the bone fails to adjust to the changes, a fracture occurs. Predisposition to osteoporosis may not necessarily cause back pain until we are well into our 70s or 80s. The most common occurrence that produces pain is a vertebral body compression fracture (Fig. 1B). Many times the pain will be quite severe and last for weeks to months. Such bony fractures can happen with minor activities, such as bending over or hitting a golf ball. A compression fracture causes a loss in height of the vertebral body that can lead to a kyphosis (humped back) (Fig. 4). This disorder is often referred to as a "dowager's hump," an exaggeration in the angle in the spine. After the pain has resolved, several months later one may notice this hump in the back. The pain may not be at the site of the hump, but rather lower down in the back. Changes in the angulation of the spine will cause bony compensation elsewhere in the spine. The fracture that occurs in the upper back will cause compensation in the lower back, with an increase in the lumbar curvature. The spinal biomechanics are now altered, causing pain most often in the lower back due to the fact that the facet joints are being stretched to allow for the increased curvature. In most cases, the pain in the low back will go away but may take up to nine months. During this period of time, golfing activities will either need to be curtailed or discontinued.

Osteoporosis is often referred to as a silent disease, because bone loss occurs without our ever knowing that it is happening. Often there are no symptoms or problems. Most people do not know that they have osteoporosis until their bones become so weak that any activity, even a minor fall, sudden movement, or strain causes a fracture. A fractured or collapsed vertebra may not be noticed until there is severe back pain. Osteoporotic patients may have a severely stooped posture.

Osteoporosis is called **brittle bone disease**; the term osteoporosis literally means porous bone. Osteoporosis, brittle bone, is a disease that is characterized by low bone mass and changes in the bone tissue structure (Fig. 5A and B). Both men and women suffer from osteoporosis. Osteoporosis may contribute to an

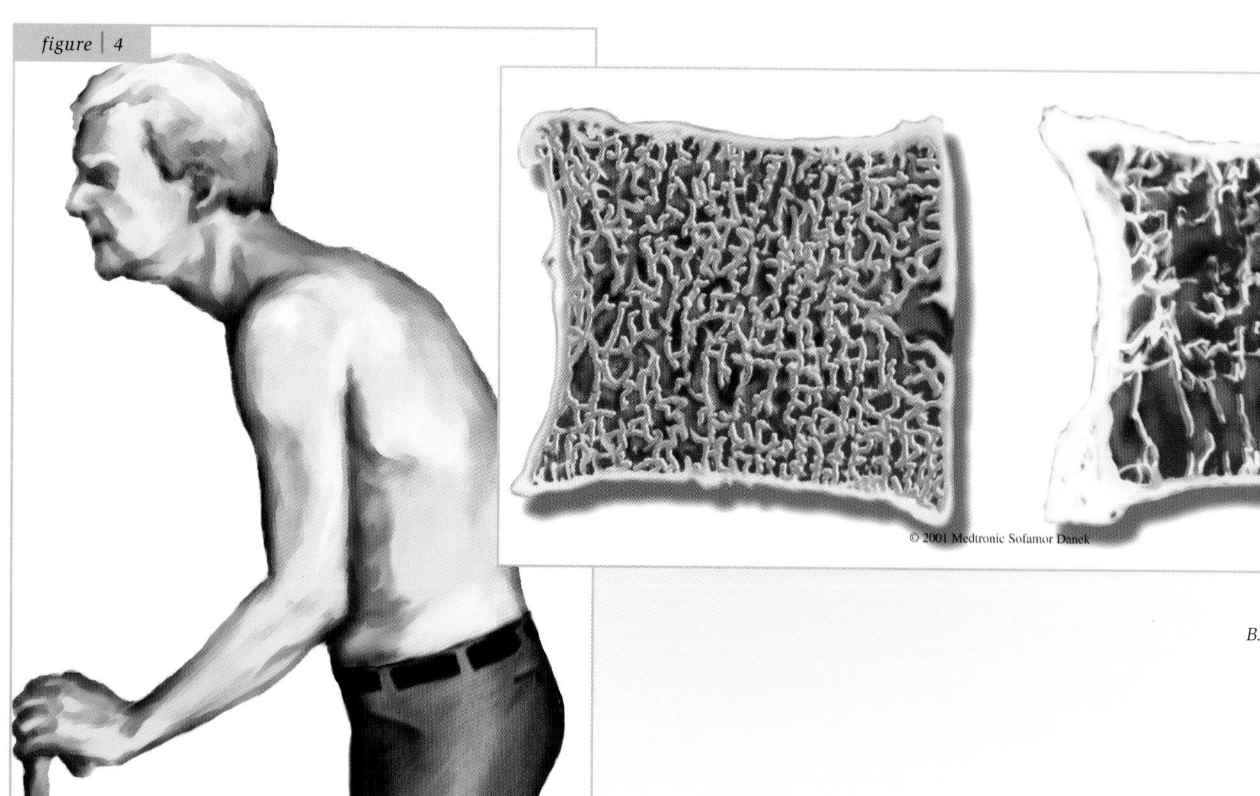

figure | 4

Kyphosis (humped back) due to compression fracture.

figure | 5AB

A. Normal bone.

B. Osteoporosis (Brittle Bone)

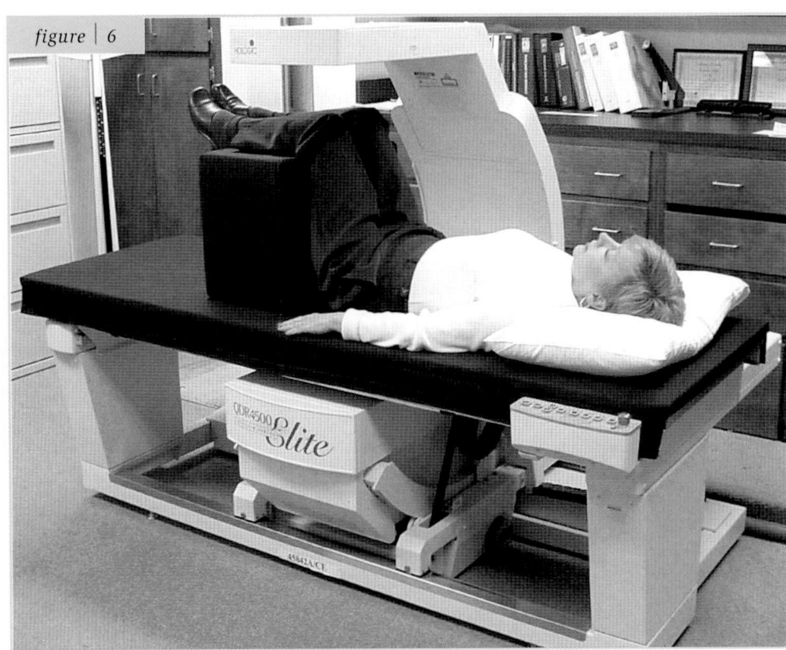

Patient undergoing testing for bone mineral densitometry.

estimated 1.3 million bone fractures every year in people over 45. Some 10 million people already have osteoporosis and another 18 million have low bone mass. This places these people at an increased risk of complications for broken bones and fractures. ***One out of every two women and one in eight men over the age of 50 will have an osteoporotic-related fracture in their lifetime.*** As our population matures, this number will only get larger. Osteoporosis is different from many other diseases in that there is no one single cause. The overall health of our bones is a function of many things. It may depend on how well the bones were formed as a youth or the level of exercise that our bones enjoyed over our developing years. After our bones have reached the maximum bone density, it is important that we learn ways to prevent bone loss.

DIAGNOSIS

If an individual is at risk of osteoporosis and develops severe back pain, it is time to see a doctor. For post-menopausal women it is a good idea to discuss osteoporosis with their doctor, even without any signs of osteoporosis. All women should be aware of the many preventive steps that may help decrease the risk of developing osteoporosis and subsequent bone fractures. This is very important for the woman golfer. To help with a diagnosis of osteoporosis, a complete physical examination will be done that will include height, weight, and spine. A doctor will check the entire length of the spine to check for any hidden fractures. A loss of height occurs with aging. To check how tall you were *before* losing any height, you will be measured from middle fingertip to middle fingertip. The difference between the distance from finger to finger and your current height is the amount of height lost over the years. The diagnosis of osteoporosis is primarily based on a special X-ray called densitometry (Fig. 6). This will give an accurate measurement of bone mineral densitometry (BMD). The World Health Organization (WHO) has established criteria for making the diagnosis of osteoporosis, as well as determining levels that may help to predict the chances for osteoporosis. These criteria are based on comparing a patient's bone mineral density (BMD) with that of a 25-year-old woman. BMD levels that fall below the average for the 25-year-old woman (stated statistically as 2.5 standard deviation below the average) are diagnosed as osteoporotic. The measurement of BMD has proven to be very helpful in the diagnosis of osteoporosis and osteopenia. Plain X-rays may be useful if there is a suspicion concerning a bone. Individuals with proven osteoporosis, by either a fracture history or a bone mineral density of greater than 2.5 standard deviations below the average, need some form of specific drug therapy for the disease. All patients with osteoporosis and osteopenia need to be evaluated for dietary habits, medical therapies, and lifestyle changes before they return to playing golf.

MEDICAL TREATMENTS FOR OSTEOPOROSIS

There is no single cure for osteoporosis; however, over the last several decades new avenues of therapies and medications have been discovered.

Exercise: Exercise plays a major part in maintaining good bone health. Bone is a living tissue and it needs exercise to maintain a healthy state. Bones respond to stresses that are placed on them. When muscles pull on bone, it stresses the bone. When the normal stresses that are placed on bones by normal activities are removed, the bone will lose bone density. Therefore, exercise has a positive effect on bone density. Weight-bearing exercises such as walking, running, jogging and dancing are exercises that are recommended for good health. These activities benefit bones. A regular program of brisk walking may assist bone maintenance. Weightlifting may also help, even though it is not a high impact exercise. Before beginning any exercise program, it is important to check with a doctor. Exercises help to maintain bone mass. Exercises must be continued in order to prevent bone loss. Golfers need to periodically revisit exercise activities with a physician or trainer. Exercising 3 to 5 days a week for at least 30 minutes will help to reduce bone loss.

Calcium: Skeletons are calcium bone banks. Bones contain 99.5% of the total calcium in the body. The calcium in bones is available to the bodies should it be needed it for other purposes. Calcium is needed for many functions in the body, including the heart, muscles, and nerves. Calcium allows these structures to function properly. It is also needed to for blood to clot. Not enough calcium will contribute to the development of osteoporosis Young girls and women consume less than half of the amount of calcium that is recommended to grow and maintain healthy bones. Depending on an individual's age, many physicians recommend a daily intake of between 1000 and 1500 mg. Women over the age of 19 need about 1,000 mg. of calcium every day. Postmenopausal women should have a daily allowance of calcium of between 1,200 to 1,500 mg. Many golfers will need to supplement their diets because most are deficit in calcium. Today the average daily diet contains about 600 to 700 mg. of calcium. The first thing that needs to be done when calcium is lost is to replace it. The daily recommended calcium intake will vary according to age, sex and menopausal status. The best way to increase calcium intake is to change diets or use supplemental calcium pills. Any daily calcium supplemental pill should also contain vitamin D. Vitamin D will help with the absorption of calcium in the stomach. Calcium citrate is somewhat better absorbed than calcium carbonate, which has to be taken with food. It's best to check with a physician, nutritionist, or healthcare provider before adding supplements to one's diet.

Vitamin D: Vitamin D deficiency may also contribute to osteoporosis and subsequent fractures. Sources of Vitamin D include such foods as egg yolks; fortified milk; fortified cereals; and fish such as halibut, mackerel, sardines, shrimp, and salmon. Cod liver oil is also a source for vitamin D. Vitamin D and calcium go hand in hand. Vitamin D is needed to absorb calcium from foods. If we do not have enough vitamin D then it is difficult for our bodies to absorb the calcium from the foods that we eat. If we don't get enough calcium from our dietary habits, then our body will go to our bone bank to remove calcium. Vitamin D comes from two sources: our skin when it is exposed to direct sunlight, and from diets. It is now recommended that a daily intake between 400–800 i.u (International units) per day is needed. Another good way to get vitamin D is through fortified foods. Check the labels; many dairy foods are now fortified with vitamin D and vitamin C.

Medications: There are four medications that are currently used for osteoporosis and are grouped into two categories. The first category is comprised of agents that limit the rate of bone loss and are referred to as **anti-resorption drugs**. The second group promotes bone formation and are called **bone-forming drugs**. Today, only the anti-resorbers are approved in the treatment of osteoporosis.

Calcitonin: Calcitonin is a hormone that is naturally produced in the thyroid glands. It is a strong inhibitor of bone cells called osteoclasts. The osteoclasts are the bone cells that are involved in breaking down the bone; any medication that will stop or slow down the activity of osteoclasts is beneficial for individuals with osteoporosis. Synthetic calcitonin is helpful in patients with a high rate of bone loss. The greatest disadvantage of the use of calcitonin is that it has to be given as an injection. Synthetic calcitonin is a hormone, and hormones are made up of proteins. When a protein is placed into the stomach and intestines, it is digested; therefore, it will not have an opportunity to work. There is, however, a new type of calcitonin that can be sprayed into the nose and quickly absorbed into the blood stream. Most individuals tolerate the nasal spray better than the injections.

Biophosphonates: Biophosphonates are a group of drugs that are **anti-resorptive**. They inhibit the breakdown of bone and slow down bone removal. These drugs may increase the amount of bone density and reduce the risk of fractures, particularly in the spine and the hip. They slow down the osteoclastic activity that is responsible for the resorption of bone. These drugs may bind to the inner linings of the bones, thereby preventing the osteoclasts from removing bone. They act as gate keepers. The disphosphonate drug most commonly used for preventing and treating osteoporosis in post-menopausal women is Alendronate, most commonly known as **Fosamax®**. This drug may cause stomach problems (gastrointestinal problems), so it is best to take it with a full glass of water and plan on sitting up for at least half an hour after taking the medication to prevent possible stomach problems.

Hormone Replacement Therapy (HRT): Hormone replacement is approved for the prevention, treatment, and the management of osteoporosis. Estrogen replacement hormone therapy (ERT) is most often used. ERT involves the use of estrogen replacement following menopause in women, as a means to conserve bone mass. Hormone replacement therapy (HRT) can help to reduce bone loss, increase bone density in the spine and hip, and help prevent hip and spine fractures. Estrogen replacement is given orally or with a patch that is placed on the skin. Protection against hip fractures requires about 5 years of estrogen therapy. Once the estrogen is stopped, bone loss will return along with the risk of fracture. Once started, hormone replacement therapy should continue under a doctor's direction, in order to maximize benefits. For women who still have an intact uterus, estrogen therapy is given with progesterone hormones. When estrogen is taken alone, it may increase the occurrence of endometrial cancer (cancer of the lining of the uterus). For women without a uterus, estrogen replacement therapy is continuous, but without progesterone hormones. The best time to begin estrogen-hormone replacement therapy is when bone turnover or loss becomes more frequent; this typically occurs during early menopause. Many doctors feel that the bone-preserving benefits of estrogen and HRT can still be achieved even when it has been started several years after menopause. It is very important that, in people over 45 years of age, medications for either the prevention or the treatment of osteoporosis be given under a doctor's supervision. Hormone replacement therapy (HRT) is certainly not for everyone. There are significant risks associated with this type of therapy such as cancer, hypertension, blood clots and strokes. Any individual considering HRT must discuss the benefits and risks with his or her doctor before undergoing therapy.

MEDICATIONS FOR OSTEOPOROSIS

Alendronate Sodium (Fosamax®): Alendronate is a biophosphonate. Alendronate is perhaps better known by its brand name, Fosamax®. This medication is used for the prevention and treatment of osteoporosis. It has been shown to reduce bone loss and increase bone density in both the spine and the hip, thus reducing the chance of fracture. This medication must be taken on an empty stomach. It is strongly recommended that before patients take this medication, they should drink a full glass of water and wait 1/2 hour before eating or drinking anything else, and remain upright for at least 1/2 to 1 hour after taking the medication. This medicine may cause heartburn or irritate the esophagus. Another benefit of Alendronate is that it is helpful in the treatment of osteoporosis brought about by the long-term use of steroids. This pertains to both men and women.

Risedronate Sodium (Actonel®): Risedronate is in the same class as Alendronate. It is a biophosphonate. This medication is better known in some circles by its brand name, Actonel®. This medication is taken on a daily basis to slow down bone loss and increase bone density, thus reducing the rate of bone fractures. Because it is a biophosphonate, it must be taken on an empty stomach with a large glass of water. After taking the medicine, individuals should stay upright and not eat or drink for 1/2 to 1 hour. Side effects of this medication are usually related to stomach problems that include an upset stomach, constipation, diarrhea, bloating, gas, and occasionally headaches. If an individual has any unusual symptoms after taking the medication, it is best to call a health care provider. Risedronate has also been approved to treat steroid induced osteoporosis just like Alendronate.

Raloxifen (Evista®): There is a new type of medication used to help prevent bone loss. This new drug is Raloxifen. It is in the class of drugs called Selective Estrogen Receptor Modulators (SERM). These new selective modulators have been found to be helpful in managing the amount of bone loss from the spine, hip and the elsewhere by increasing bone mass. The medication does not do this overnight, but rather takes several years. After 3 years of using this medication the risk of spine fractures appears to be reduced by about 50%. Raloxifen's brand name is Evista®. There are some added beneficial effects of this medication in that it brings about changes in blood lipids that may help to protect against heart disease. Unlike estrogen replacement therapy, elective receptor modulators do not appear to stimulate uterine or breast tissue, so the risk of cancer from these medications is less. These medications are relatively new, however; it may take several more years to determine whether they do or do not affect the uterine and breast tissues, possibly resulting in cancer. Raloxifen is usually given in a pill form and is taken once a day with or without meals. Side effects from this medication are hot flashes and blood clots.

Calcitonin (Miacalcin®): Calcitonin is a naturally found hormone that is involved in the regulation of calcium and bone metabolism. It has been found to be quite helpful in women who are at least 5 years beyond menopause. Calcitonin is also sold under the name brand of Miacalcin®. This hormone has been shown to slow down the loss of bone and increases spine bone density. In some situations it may even help to relieve the pain that is associated with bone fractures. Calcitonin has been helpful with spinal fracture sites but may not be helpful at other sites in the body. Calcitonin may be given as an injection of 50 to 100 I.U. daily, or by a nasal spray of 200 I.U. daily. The nose is an excellent absorptive surface, so Calcitonin is easily delivered through a spray; it may, however, cause a runny nose. Calcitonin that is given as an injection may cause an allergic reaction at the injection site. Other side effects include flushing of the face and hands, frequency of urination, and nausea. Taking medications to treat and prevent osteoporosis is a serious matter. To reduce unwanted and unpleasant side effects, a patient must always follow the doctor's directions. It is never too late, regardless of age, to begin thinking about good bone mass. Healthy bones mean a healthier life style that will translate into better golf.

COMPRESSION FRACTURES DUE TO OSTEOPOROSIS

Osteoporosis is known as brittle bone disease. It is given this distinction because the bones are brittle. If the osteoporotic bone is left untreated, over time, the bone will give way and lead to a fracture. This happens when the spine can no longer support the weight that is placed upon it. Spinal vertebrae become so weakened that they can no longer support the body's weight. If you think of the vertebrae as soda cans that are stacked on top of each other, the added weight on top may compress one of the cans. The compression is a fracture. The most common cause of vertebral compression fractures is osteoporosis. Other fractures may be due to trauma or spinal tumors.

Every year about 1.5 million people suffer from vertebral compression fractures due to osteoporosis. In most cases, osteoporosis is a primary disorder of the bone, but such fractures may also be due to the long-term use of certain medications, such as steroids and blood-thinning Heparin therapy. Any broken bone will cause pain. A compression fracture in any of the bones in the spine may cause severe pain that could become disabling and lead to a stooped posture. With any fracture, it is important to determine exactly what has caused the bony defect. In most cases of a fracture, the patient will find that lying flat in bed will bring about some degree of alleviation of the pain. Sitting up or trying to stand will be almost impossible. Anyone with severe pain must consult a doctor or healthcare provider. Often, just touching the site of the fracture will help to locate it. The provider will order an X-ray to determine the type of fracture (Fig. 7). An MRI (magnetic resonance image) is helpful in appreciating fractures caused by osteoporosis and will often provide insight into other underlying problems, in particular, any tumor (Fig. 8). Metastatic tumors, tumors that have traveled from other organs, or tumors that have arisen from the spinal bone can be ruled out by an MRI. Bone scans may also be obtained to evaluate for fractures at other sites.

Physicians previously had little to offer patients with spinal fractures. If the fracture was caused by osteoporosis, the patient was usually placed in bed, given pain medications, and fitted with a brace. This is typically the first line of treatment for a fracture that has been caused by osteoporosis, or brittle bone disease. Prolonged bed rest may lead to a more difficult, lengthy rehabilitation. Medications, in particular pain medications, come with complications. Thinking and judgment may become cloudy, and constipation becomes a problem. The brace itself is usually a thoracic-lumbar-sacral orthotic (TLSO) device that is made of a hard outer shell with straps to secure it together (Figs. 9A and B). Braces are not comfortable. It's like wearing a barrel. Patients need to wear the brace whenever they are up and out of bed, even if it is to get up and go to the bathroom in the middle of the night. Sleeping in a brace is a bad idea and will cause a breakdown of skin. Patients are instructed to use the brace only when up and out of bed. When they are sitting in a chair that is more than 45% upright, they need to wear the brace. If patients have any arthritic problems in the hands, they will likely have a great deal of difficulty putting on the brace by themselves. For many people, a brace is a two-man job, and is often the first line of treatment for individuals who have sustained fractures due to osteoporosis. Today there are other thoughts about the conservative line of therapy of bed rest, medications and prolonged use of a brace. Some

figure | 7

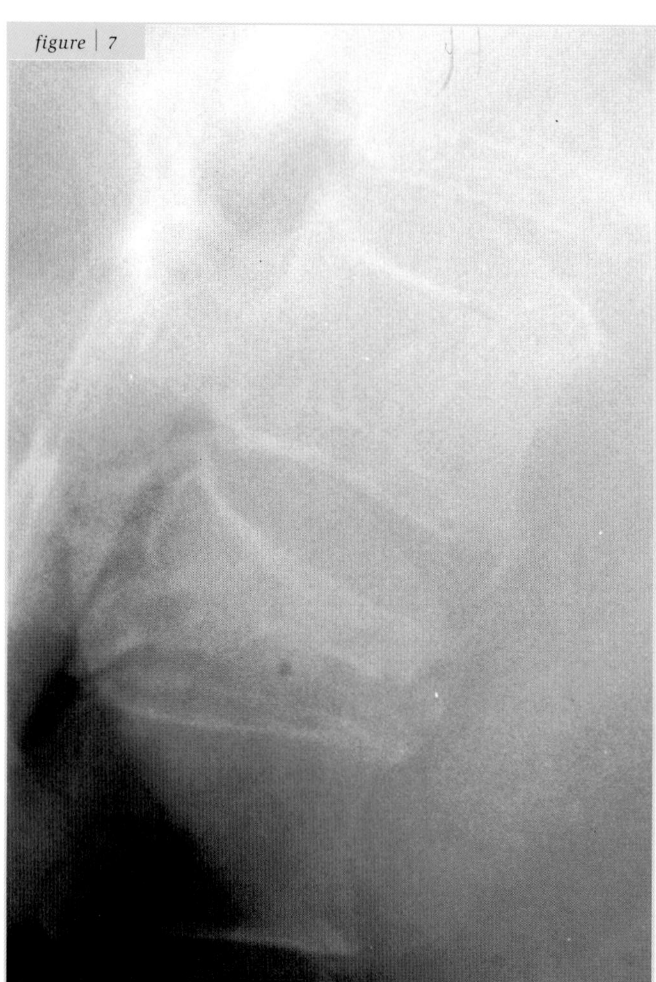

X-ray: Lateral (side) view of compression fracture of vertebra.

figure | 8

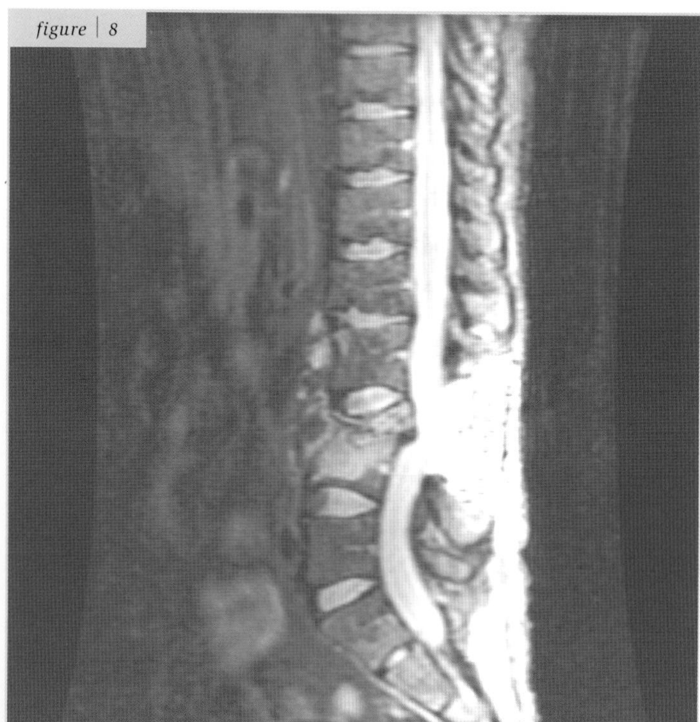

MRI: Sagittal (side) view with fractures of lumbar vertebra 3 and 4 (L3 and L4) due to multiple myeloma.

figure | 9A

figure | 9B

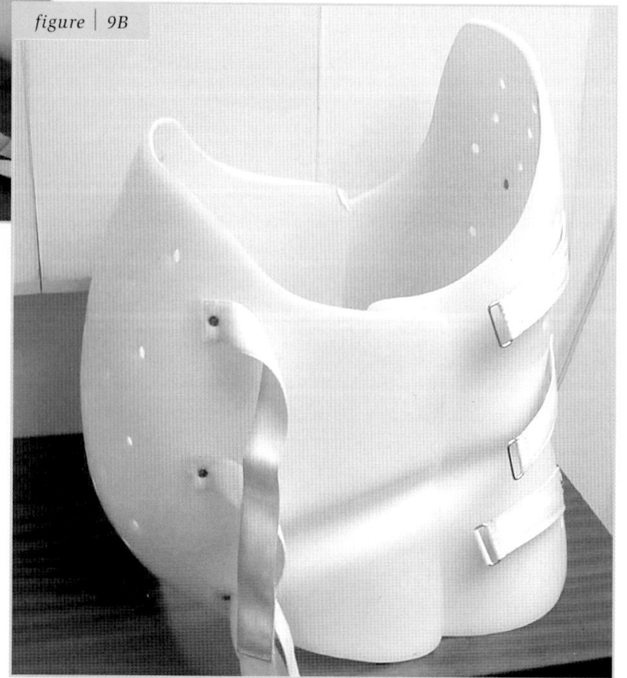

Thoracic-Lumbar-Sacral orthosis (TLSO)
A. Front view
B. Side view

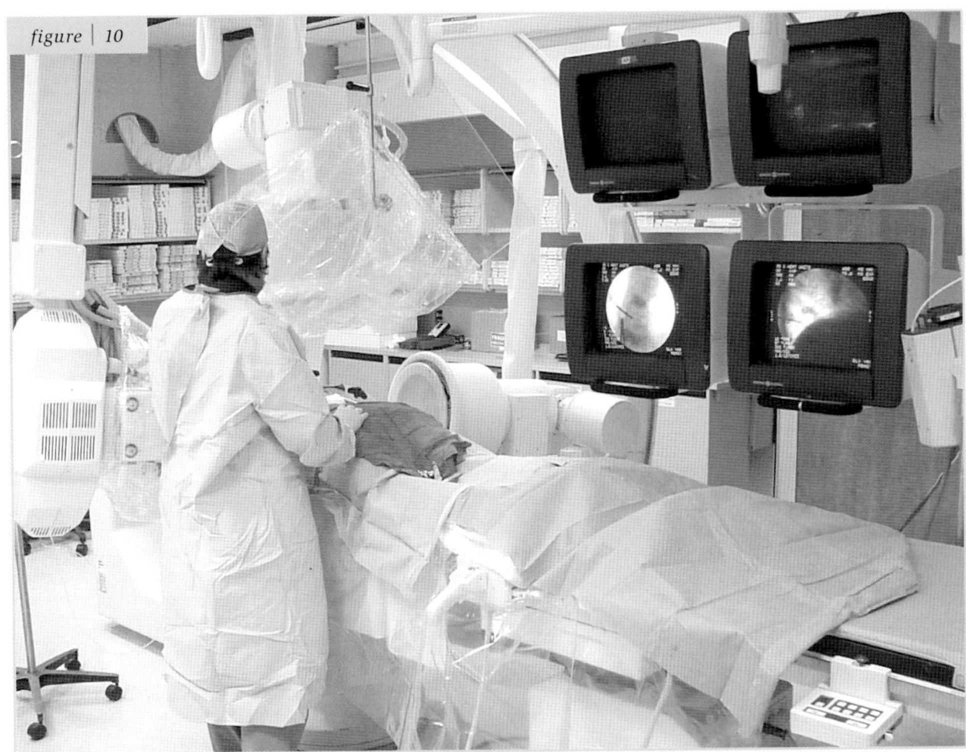

figure | *10*

Vertebroplasty in X-ray suite.

patients may be candidates for a **vertebroplasty**. This procedure involves the injection of surgical cement into the compressed or fractured vertebra. The procedure was first developed in France in 1986, finding its way to the United States in the 1990s. Over the last decade, the technique has been refined. Vertebroplasty is gaining popularity among many spine specialists, including neurosurgeons, orthopedic surgeons, spine radiologists, and pain specialists. The procedure is considered a minimally invasive procedure, which means that it does not involve making a big incision into the patient's back to expose the broken bones. However, it is important to understand that the procedure is not totally free of complications.

Vertebroplasty is intended to help reduce pain and restore function in selected individuals with spinal fractures caused by osteoporosis. It is very important, before a patient undergoes a vertebroplasty, that an MRI and a CAT (CT) scan be obtained. The MRI will demonstrate the soft tissue and the inside of the bone in order to evaluate for a possible tumor. The CT scan will demonstrate the bony architecture. Both of these studies will be used to help the doctor evaluate the patient's candidacy for the vertebroplasty procedure.

A vertebroplasty can be performed in an X-ray suite or in an operating room, depending on the preference of the physician (Fig. 10). Vertebroplasty is a technique where a bone cement is injected into the broken or fractured vertebral body. The procedure is not used to treat any other malady of the spine, such as a ruptured disk or other degenerative spine disease. It is indicated in the treatment of symptomatic painful osteoporotic compression fracture and certain spine tumors.

Vertebroplasty is not for everyone who has a compression spine fracture. Many individuals with compression fractures will have other medical problems. This procedure is performed with the patient in the prone position (face down). Some individuals may not be able to tolerate lying in this position. Individuals with pulmonary or lung problems may not be able to adjust to being on their stomach for a long period of time. The doctor will usually check the patient at his office to determine if he or she is a candidate for this procedure. In an office trial, the patient is placed in the prone position to determine whether he or she will be able to tolerate the procedure. A complete laboratory profile will also be obtained before the patient can undergo the procedure, even though this is a minimally invasive procedure. The physician needs to know the patient's blood count, platelet count, a partial thromboplastin time, a prothrombin time, and a bleeding time. These tests help to assure that the patient does not have any bleeding problems during the surgery.

The procedure is performed in either a radiological suite or an operating room. Special X-ray machines (fluoroscopy) will guide the physician to the fracture site. Needles are placed into a vein and the pain medication is given. During the procedure, the patient's heart rate, blood pressure, and oxygen levels are continuously monitored. Sometimes oxygen is given through a small nasal cannula or prong. After the X-rays have identified the targeted fracture site, the area will be cleaned and covered with a sterile drape. There are two ways that the procedure can be done: one is to give the patient a mild sedative that will leave the patient awake, or the patient will be given general anesthesia to put him or her totally asleep. If the patient is awake during the procedure, the skin will be numbed. Once the targeted area has been localized, a small incision is made just off the midline. A bone needle is then passed through the muscles and tissues of the back.

The fluoroscopy machine allows the physician to guide a spinal needle into the collapsed vertebral body. Once the needle has been put into place, a small amount of X-ray dye is injected into the vertebral body to insure that the needle is in the correct position. Next a small amount of polymethylmethacrylate (PMMA) is often mixed with an antibiotic to reduce the chances of infection. Barium or Tantalum is mixed into the PMMA to allow the bone cement to be seen on the X-ray. The bone cement, the antibiotic, and the Barium or Tantalum are all mixed together. Once mixed, they are placed into a special syringe or delivery system device that is then connected to the needle located in the vertebral body. The bone cement is slowly injected through the needle into the vertebral body (Fig. 11). The bone cement sets up very quickly and provides immediate stability and strength to the vertebral body and can bring about immediate relief of the bony pain (Fig. 12). In most cases the procedure is done on an outpatient basis, taking between one and two hours to complete, allowing the patient to go home the same day. The patient is kept in a recumbent or resting position for about two hours after the completion of the procedure. If the pain relief is acceptable and there is no evidence of muscle spasms, the patient will be allowed to sit up. It is important that, when the patient is finally allowed to stand up, he or she does so with assistance. As with any surgery, this procedure does come with some risks. The risks are minor and should be discussed with the doctor prior to the procedure.

After vertebroplasty was developed, further refinements of the procedure occurred and new techniques were developed based on the initial vertebroplasty. One new technique is called **Kyphoplasty**. It too can be used to treat patients who are immobilized by pain from a vertebral compression fracture. It is also labeled as a minimally invasive procedure. Kyphoplasty is performed in either a radiology suite or an operating room under a general anesthetic or under sedation with local pain-relieving medications. The fluoroscopy X-ray machines are also in the operating room to guide the surgeon. Kyphoplasty, like vertebroplasty, uses a spinal canula or needle to inject bone cement. There is a difference, however. Kyphoplasty uses a bone balloon to restore the height of a broken bone and to help to reduce the bone abnormality or deformity (Fig. 13). Vertebroplasty is intended to stabilize the fracture, but will not restore height or reduce the deformity. Kyphoplasty, just like vertebroplasty, involves the placement of special needles into the compression fracture. Kyphoplasty involves the insertion of one or two needles. Two small incisions are made at the sight of the fracture bone. Special bone catheters are then placed into the fracture. Through these special bone probes a small drill is inserted; the drill prepares the fractured bone site. Once the drilling is completed, the drill is removed and the bone balloon is inserted (Fig. 14). The balloons are then inflated with a saline solution until they expand to the desired height (Figs. 15A and B). The balloons create a space (Fig. 16). The balloons are then removed and the bone cement (PMMA) is placed into the vertebral body (Fig. 17). This procedure may allow restoration of height of the broken bone; vertebroplasty, on the other hand, cannot restore the bone's height. The postoperative care for Kyphoplasty is the same as vertebroplasty.

Hospitalization is usually not required after undergoing a vertebroplasty or Kyphoplasty, unless the patient is medically burdened (has many medical problems), is extremely frail, or needs additional monitoring after the procedure. When the patient leaves the hospital there may be a dull aching sensation at the needle insertion site. This will usually abate after about 24 to 48 hours. Sometimes putting an ice pack on the site can be helpful. This usually means

figure | 11

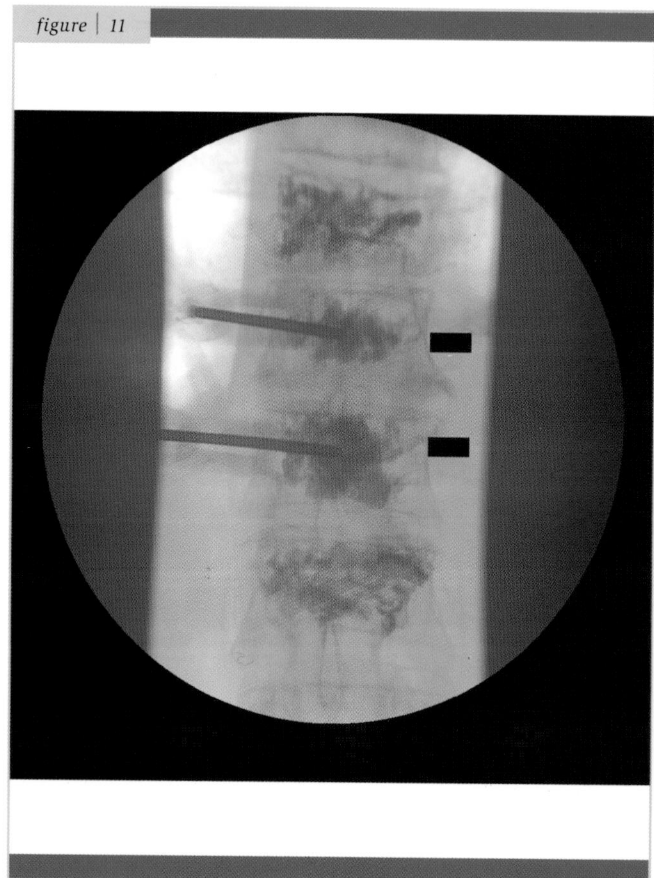

Fluoroscopy (X-rays) viewing needles injecting bone cement (PMMA) into vertebra.

figure | 12

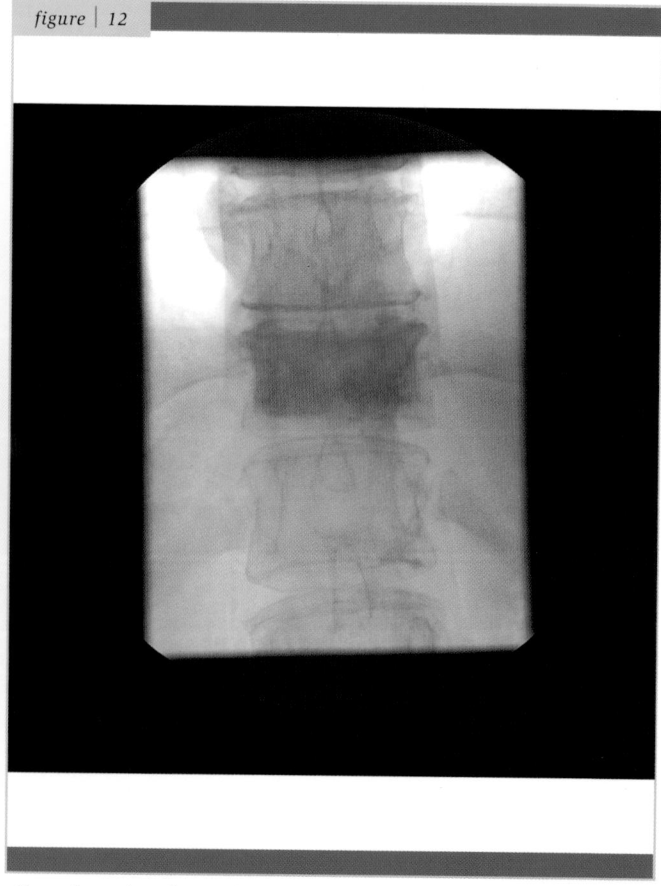

X-ray: Front view after vertebroplasty.

figure | 13

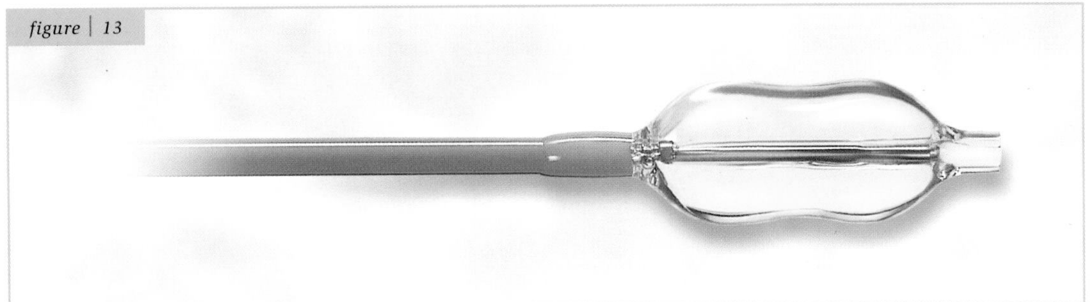

Bone balloon for Kyphoplasty.

figure | 14

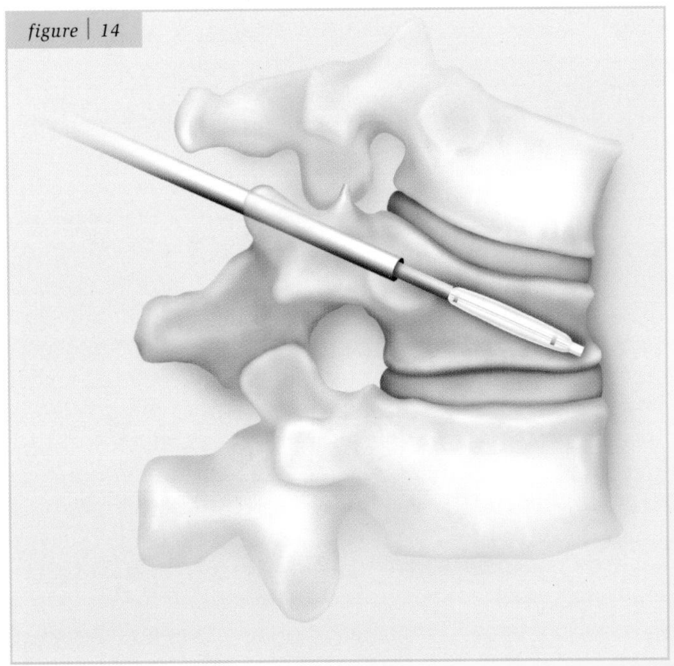

Insertion of bone balloon into the vertebral fracture.

figure | 15A

figure | 15B

figure | 17

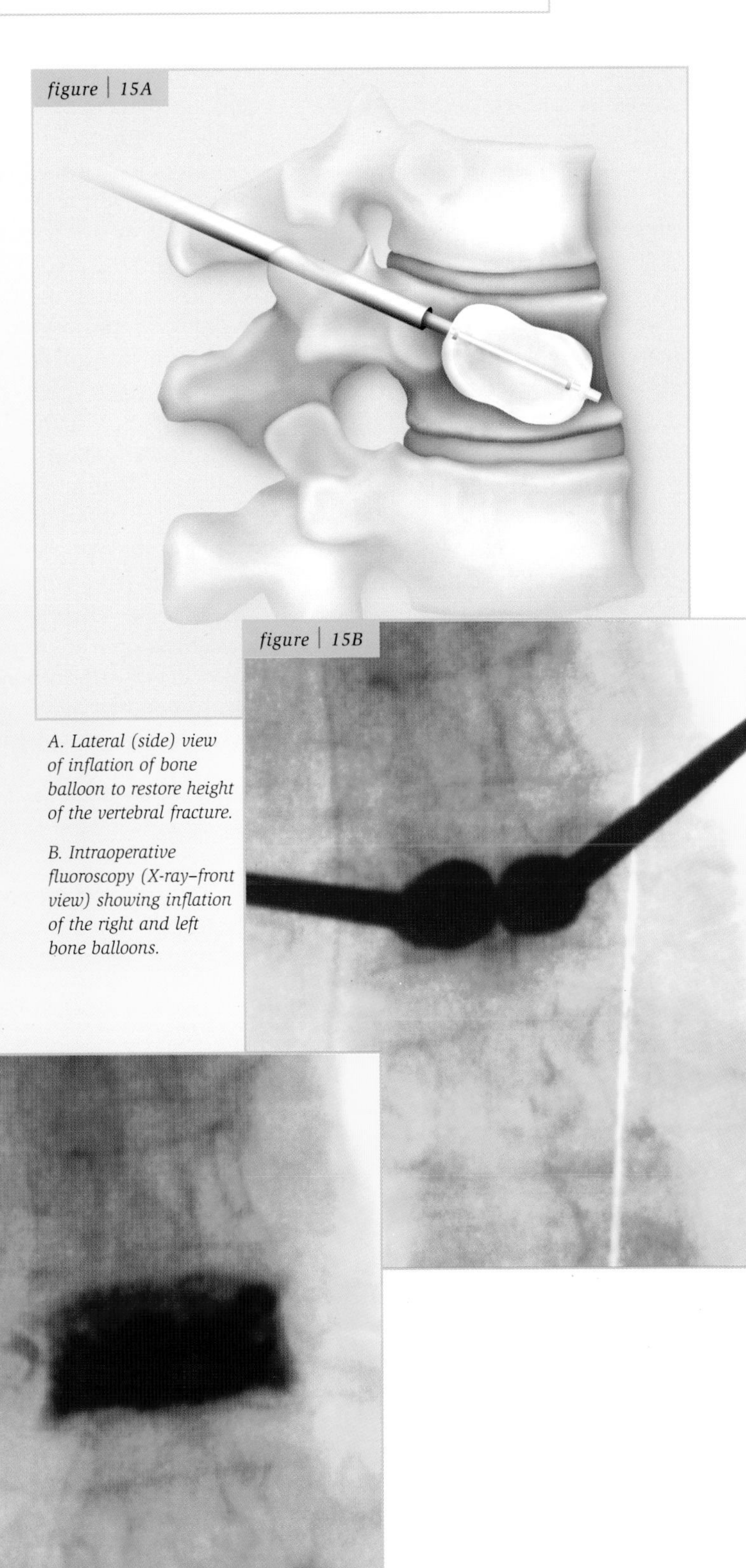

A. Lateral (side) view of inflation of bone balloon to restore height of the vertebral fracture.

B. Intraoperative fluoroscopy (X-ray–front view) showing inflation of the right and left bone balloons.

Intraoperative fluoroscopy (X-ray) showing bone cement in corrected vertebral fracture.

figure | 16

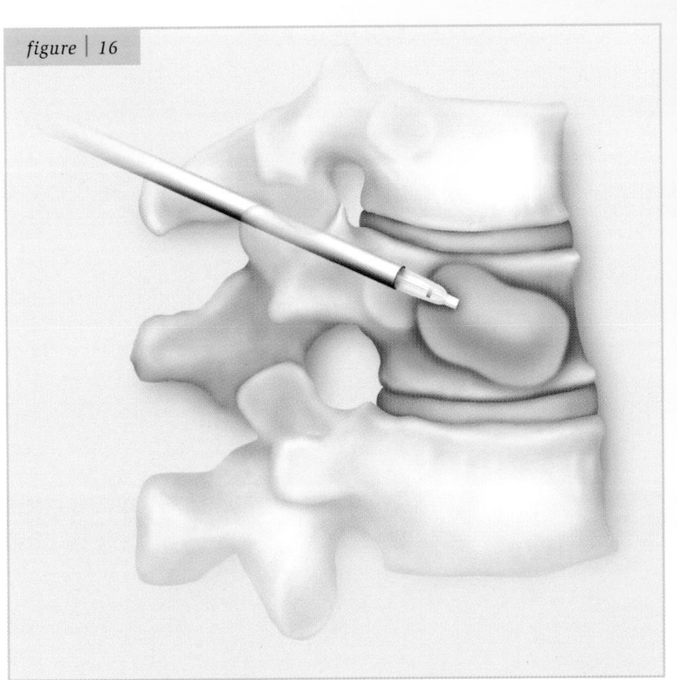

Bone balloon deflated and removed after restoring height of the fractured vertebra; a space has been created for placement of the bone cement.

that the muscles are experiencing some type of spasm. Acetaminophen or non-steroidal anti-inflammatory medications may be helpful in this situation. If a patient is at home and experiences recurrent back pain, chest pain, fever, or chills, a physician should be called immediately. If after undergoing the procedure, the patient notices that his or her legs feel funny, numb, or heavy, or if the patient experiences loose bowels, or loses bladder control, this is a medical emergency. Some of the dye could have leaked out of the vertebra and could be pushing on the spinal cord or important nerves in the back. It needs to be evaluated immediately. Usually the patients that are selected and screened as candidates for vertebroplasty or Kyphoplasty do well and regain satisfactory levels of activity and daily living.

Both vertebroplasty and Kyphoplasty use bone cement that is injected into the fractured or compressed bone. In some situations multiple levels of compression fractures are injected with bone cement. Both procedures are intended to bring about immediate relief of pain. Kyphoplasty has the potential of restoring height to the bone. After the patient has undergone a vertebroplasty or Kyphoplasty, he or she is encouraged to remain active by walking. Many times a patient who has undergone this procedure will benefit by a consultation with a physical therapist to help restore bone strength and activity levels. Vertebroplasty and Kyphoplasty are both options for patients with certain osteoporotic fractures. Both procedures are alike in many ways. Many physicians, surgeons and radiologists are performing the techniques and find that the procedures are safe and provide welcomed relief for patients who are suffering from osteoporotic compression fractures. Many physicians now believe that vertebroplasty or Kyphoplasty, performed on select patients, is the first line of therapy for osteoporotic problems over the more traditional bed rest. Bracing and pain medications would be the second choice of therapy. Vertebroplasty and Kyphoplasty are procedures for the injection of a bone cement-like material into a collapsed vertebral body. Many patients will become symptom-free immediately or within just a few days. Over the next several weeks, more than two-thirds of the patients will show a marked improvement in their daily activities and will find that they require less pain medication.

The above-mentioned procedures do not stop the underlying disease process itself. The cause of the fracture is still present. An osteoporotic vertebral body compression fracture may not be an isolated event. There may be other potential fracture sites; therefore, the cause of the osteoporosis must be treated with continuous medical evaluation along with long-term medical treatment to prevent future fractures.

SURGERY FOR OSTEOPOROTIC FRACTURES

In most cases, surgeons will do anything to avoid operating on the spines of individuals with osteoporosis. This is because the fractured bone can be removed, but it is often difficult to reconstruct the spine. There are two ways to approach a fractured vertebral body with an open operation: by going in from the side, or through the back. In certain situations, an endoscope may provide a minimally invasive avenue for treatment of such fractures. The endoscope is a special tube through which the surgeon is able to see the fracture and remove it. But, there is still the problem of reconstruction. The problem lies not so much in the operation, but in the bone near the fracture. Osteoporosis is often not an isolated problem. There may be brittle bone throughout the spine, but only one site is fractured. Fractures can be removed, but again, putting the patient back together is another story. After the fractured bone has been removed, there are special cages made of either titanium or carbon that can be inserted into the site of fractured bone removal (Fig. 18). These bone cage implants are further stabilized by using screws above and below the fracture site, and are attached to a plate or a rod (Figs. 19A and B). Bone screws that are inserted into brittle bone have an increased chance of pulling out. They

figure | 18

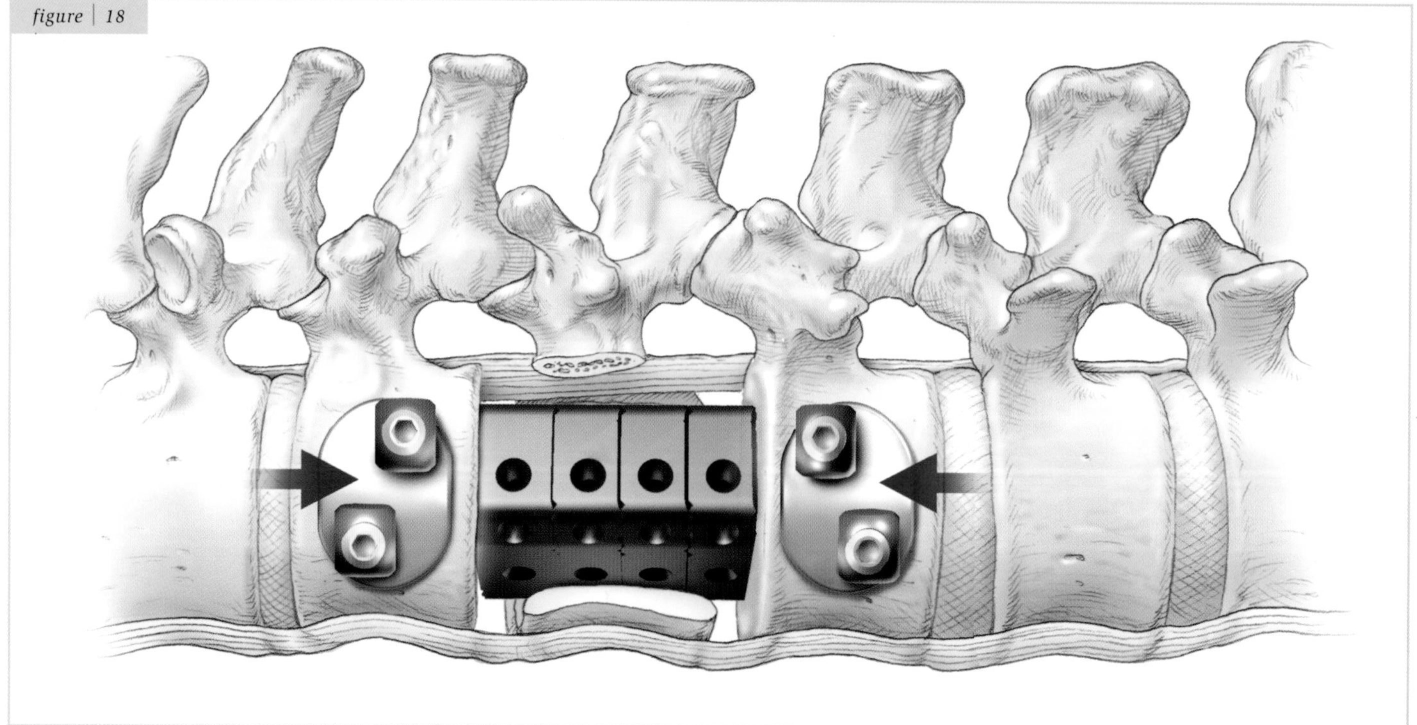

Carbon bone cage inserted between normal vertebrae after fractured vertebra surgically removed.

figure | 19A

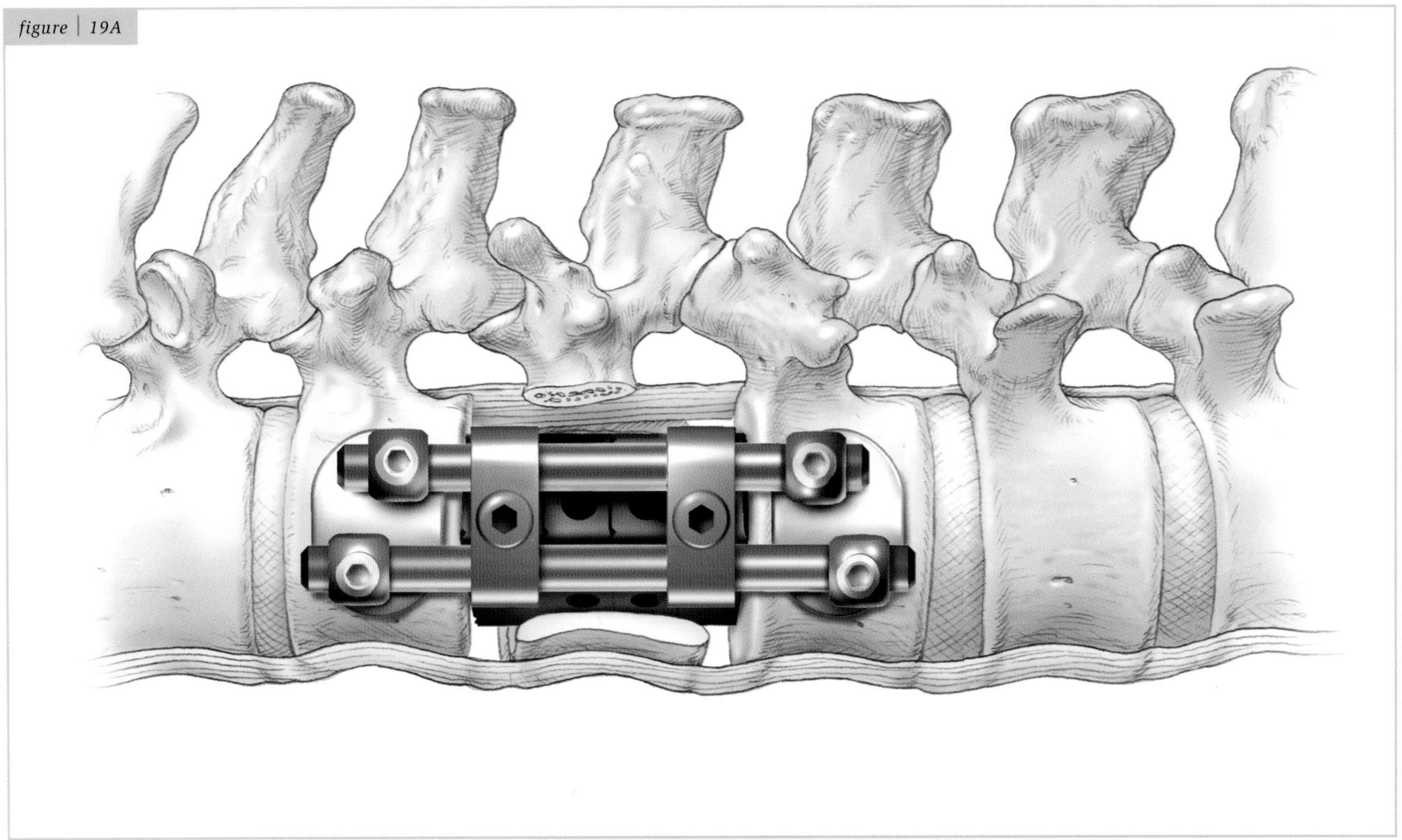

A. Titanium bone rods placed after bone cage insertion.

B. X-ray (front view) of bone rods and screws: carbon cage is not visible, but bone graft (rib) is easily seen.

figure | 19B

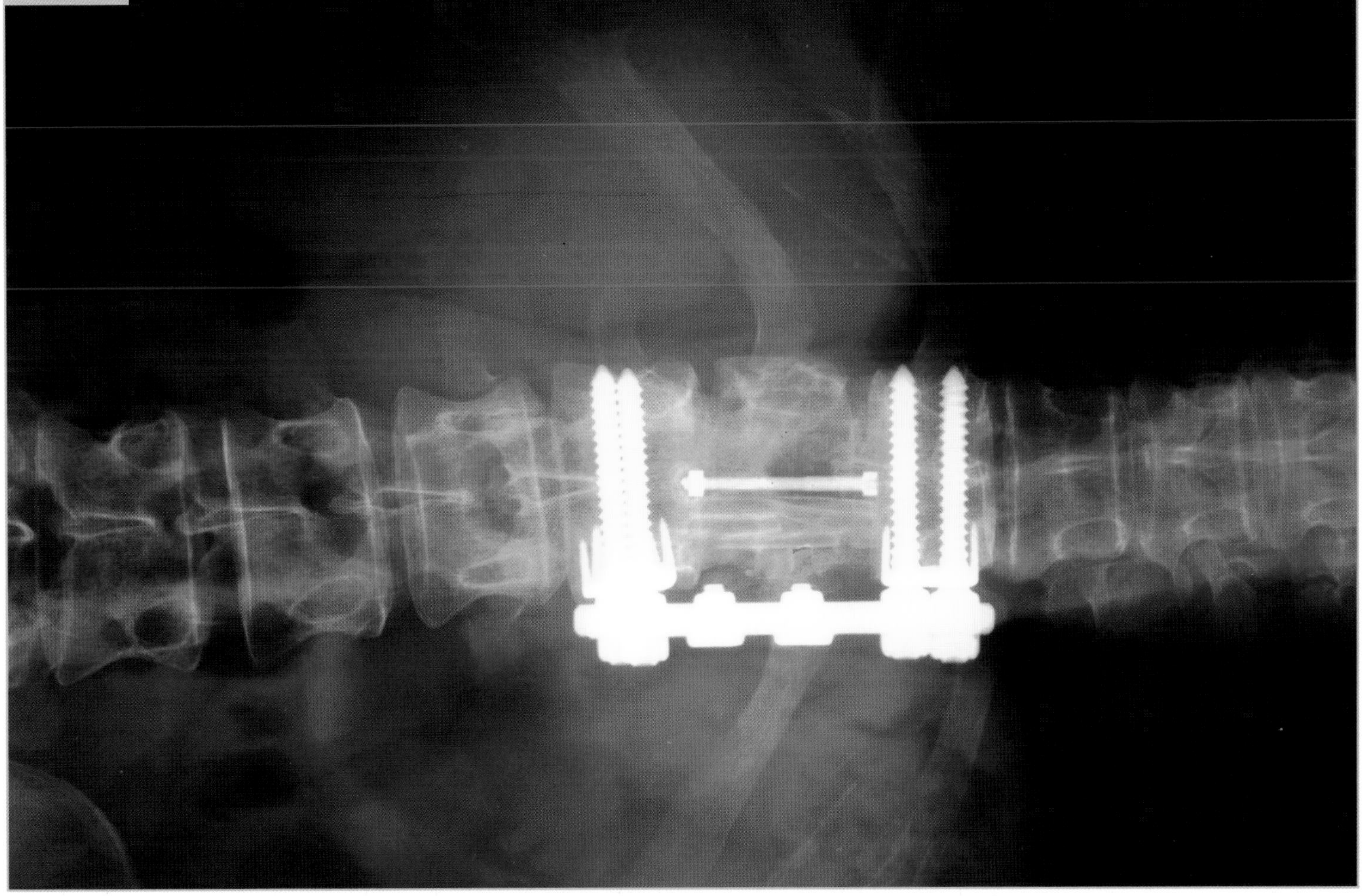

also may not be able to hold the bone in a secure fashion. In most cases, the surgeon will want to augment the brittle non-collapsed bone sites by using bone cement, just as in a vertebroplasty. Surgical procedures for osteoporotic fractures are usually reserved for the more severe fracture cases in which the fractured bone is pushing against the spinal cord or nerves, causing severe pain and neurological problems such as weakness in the extremities or loss of bowel and urinary bladder function. Such surgical treatments will require a longer rehabilitation time. After surgery, the patient may or may not need to wear a brace. Depending on the degree of weakness, the patient may require hospitalization in a rehabilitation facility. If osteoporosis is diagnosed, it is important not to ignore it. Treatment is essential in preventing potential catastrophic fractures that may require aggressive surgery.

GOLF AND OSTEOPOROSIS

Osteoporosis is a major public health problem for millions of Americans. Osteoporosis is a silent bone thief. Many men and women have osteoporosis and do not know it. It is a bone-thinning disease that can cause debilitating fractures of the spine, hip and wrist; all of which are important for the golfer. It is important to practice good spine hygiene to help prevent osteoporosis. Such prevention begins in childhood and continues throughout our lives. If you are at risk for osteoporosis and its consequences, such as fractures, you need to talk to your doctor about brittle bone disease. Bone mineral density (MBD) tests are safe and painless, and will help to measure the strength of bone, an important part of good golf health. With the information that is provided by the BMD testing a physician will be able to better predict the likelihood of fractures and determine the appropriate care. The BMD test is the best way of predicting the chances of breaking a bone from osteoporosis. Therefore, if you are at risk for osteoporosis, talk to your doctor about undergoing a bone density test. If you have osteoporosis, you will want to talk about treatments that could include medications and special exercises.

Golf is a unique sport. Many golfers hope to be able to play throughout their lives. But will golf be safe for those with osteoporosis of the spine? It is a difficult question for a sufferer. Should he or she stop playing golf? There is no easy answer. It is recommended that a sports medical history be obtained from individuals, especially post-menopausal women, who wish to start playing golf or who are currently playing golf. The demands on the spine from playing golf certainly are great. The trunk twisting and the lateral bending are known to increase the load on the spine. Therefore, it is safe to say that if a golfer has osteoporosis, his or her golf game should be modified. It is important that such patients tell their physician or health care provider that they would like to continue playing golf. They may have to play nine holes instead of the usual 18 holes. The osteoporotic golfer will need to take lessons from a golf professional, making sure that the pro knows that the golfer has osteoporosis. The game should become a gentle game. Some individuals may need to wear a back support or brace. The brace will not only add support to the spine, but it will serve as a reminder of what activities or movements should be avoided. The bottom line: if a golfer has osteoporosis, he or she is at an added risk for a bone fracture from playing golf. One may not need to give up the game, but will need to take special precautions while playing golf. Finally, patients with osteoporosis should continue to play only with a physician's approval. Weight-bearing exercises such as jogging, walking and weightlifting can all stimulate bone growth and make bones healthier. Regular exercises are important in helping to maintain balance, which will not only keep an individual from falling and breaking a bone, but will also help his or her golf game.

TUMORS OF THE SPINE (NEOPLASMS)

CHAPTER 16

T. Glenn Pait, M.D., F.A.C.S.

I was enjoying a round of golf one morning at Lakeside Country Club in Los Angeles, when I was suddenly attacked by my lower back. I could not continue playing and I was very depressed. I phoned my orthopedist and he had an opening that day.

After administering treatment, my doctor said, "Don, there's someone here I think you should meet." He took me into another room, where who should be sitting there but Lana Turner. Wow! Lana Turner, my pin-up girl since World War II! After a nice visit with Miss Turner, during which I flirted shamelessly, I thought to myself on the way home: "See, every cloud has a silver lining." So the next time you are attacked by your back, don't be depressed. Who knows, you might meet your Lana Turner.

Don Knotts

Whenever pain along the spine cannot be associated with any type of musculoskeletal injury such as lifting, pulling, or other traumatic occurrence, a tumor of the spine is always a possibility. No one wants to talk about tumors; in fact many people are not even aware of exactly what a tumor is, except that just the word itself often brings about fear.

A tumor is an uncontrolled growth of cells, which will cause an excess of tissue. It is this extra tissue that makes up a tumor. The exact cause of such abnormal tissue growth is often unknown. There are benign tumors and malignant tumors.

As in any field of medicine and science, there are theories about tumors. Some tumors may be hereditary, which means that they are passed from one generation to another generation. Other tumors are the possible reaction to traumatic events in life, which result in abnormal tumor growth. Yet another theory relates such growth to possible exposure to radiation. No one knows exactly what causes a tumor in every situation, except that it is a fact of life for many patients.

Tumor cells develop because of damage to deoxyribonucleic acid, DNA. DNA is found in every cell and directs all of the activities of cells in the body. In most situations, when DNA becomes damaged the body is able to repair it. In tumor cells and cancer cells, however, the damaged DNA is not repaired or fixed. This is why people can inherit damaged DNA, which means they can inherit the cancer or tumor-producing cells. And in certain situations, radiation or exposure to carcinogenic substances, like cigarettes, damages an individual's DNA.

For the golfer, a tumor is crabgrass growing in a beautiful fairway or green. Crabgrass starts off as a very small, single plant doing no harm, and isn't noticed by most people walking on it. With time, it grows, multiplies and, before long, there's a whole patch of crabgrass. Now it's noticeable! The crabgrass continues to grow and soon will encroach upon the good grass. It will steal its water and food supplies, and eventually the good grass dies and the bad grass is left behind. In the body, cells grow, divide, and die in a very orderly fashion. During the developmental years normal cells divide more rapidly; they do so because we're growing. In the adult years cells in most of the body divide only to replace the dying cells or to repair sites of injuries. However, cancer cells, just like crab grass, also grow, multiply, and divide, but instead of dying they outlive the normal cells, and by outliving the normal cells, they continue to grow and produce more new abnormal cells. Then, just like the grass, they occupy the site where normal, well-behaved cells used to function. This growth of cells is a tumor.

Spine tumors are classified as either primary or secondary. Primary spine tumors are those in which the abnormal growing cells have originated in the bony spine. Secondary spine tumors originated at another site in the body and traveled to the spine to grow. A good way to envision what's happening in this situation is to use the crabgrass analogy. The crabgrass is growing on the 16th fairway. It blooms, a strong wind comes along, and the crabgrass seed is carried over to the 8th green. The seeds take hold and find a wonderful place filled with water and vitamins to grow. The seeds did not originate in the 8th green; they came from the 16th fairway, but now they've found a home. The crabgrass has traveled from its original growing site; it is secondary crabgrass, just like a secondary spine tumor.

PRIMARY BONE TUMORS

Primary bone tumors are a rare occurrence. Primary tumors are further classified as either benign or malignant. Benign means good, or non-cancerous; however, benign tumors can also cause problems. They can grow, destroy good bone, and cause pain. They do not have a tendency to travel elsewhere. On the other hand, malignant tumors are bad tumors. These tumors have a tendency to grow and to spread. Malignant bone tumor cells may begin to grow in the bone and metastasize (spread) to other parts of the body. It is a rare occasion for a so-called benign tumor to become cancerous and spread to other parts of the body. If the tumor is benign, not growing, and is not located in an eloquent part of the spine such as next to the spinal cord, no further treatment may be required. It is advisable periodically to assess or check on the tumor with special radiological studies, such as computed axial tomography (CAT or CT scan) or magnetic resonance imaging (MRI). If the benign tumor is producing pain or enlarging with pressure on the spinal cord or nerves, surgical removal may become necessary. Benign tumors include the following: hemangioma, giant-cell tumor, aneurysmal bone cyst, osteoblastoma, and osteoid osteoma. Even benign tumors have the potential to degenerate and travel elsewhere, which is often referred to as monastic degeneration. Fortunately, most of the benign tumors can be treated or followed successfully. Primary bone tumors of the spine are rare and account for approximately 0.04 percent of all tumors.

BENIGN PRIMARY BONE TUMORS

Hemangiomas of the spine are common benign primary bone tumors. In fact, about 10% of the population will have these tumors in their spines and never know. These tumors are benign blood vessels or vascular lesions (Fig. 1). Rarely do they come to clinical notice. Oftentimes they are found incidentally. Sometimes when a patient is involved in an automobile accident, X-rays of the spine and other bones are obtained and the hemangioma is found (Fig. 2 A, B, and C). Only in rare cases will any further treatment be needed. There is no reason that finding this abnormality on an incidental X-ray should change one's golf habits. However, it would be advisable to follow up with a physician. If there are any concerns, a specialist such as a neurosurgeon, orthopedic surgeon, or oncologist can be consulted. For most individuals in whom the hemangioma is significant clinically, back pain will be the presenting complaint. If the hemangioma is large and causing problems, medical or surgical treatment may be needed. Hemangiomas are a type of blood vessel abnormality that may be addressed with vertebroplasty. This is a procedure in which a needle is guided to the site of the vascular lesion and bone cement is injected. This may bring about alleviation of the discomfort caused by the hemangioma and prevent more complex surgical intervention. Surgery will depend upon the site of the hemangioma and its location. If it's located in a vertebra, which is where most are located, surgery may be directed from an anterior approach; however, going posteriorly, or through the back, is also an option. This depends on a surgeon's experience and preference.

Giant-cell tumors are very slow growing tumors and are often found in the anterior part of the spine (Fig. 3). Even though they're under the label of benign tumors, they may demonstrate a locally aggressive behavior. Such tumors occur in any age population, but are most common in ages 20 to 40 years. These tumors are best evaluated with computed axial tomography (CAT scan) and magnetic resonance imaging (MRI) (Figs. 4A and B). The MRI will demonstrate the

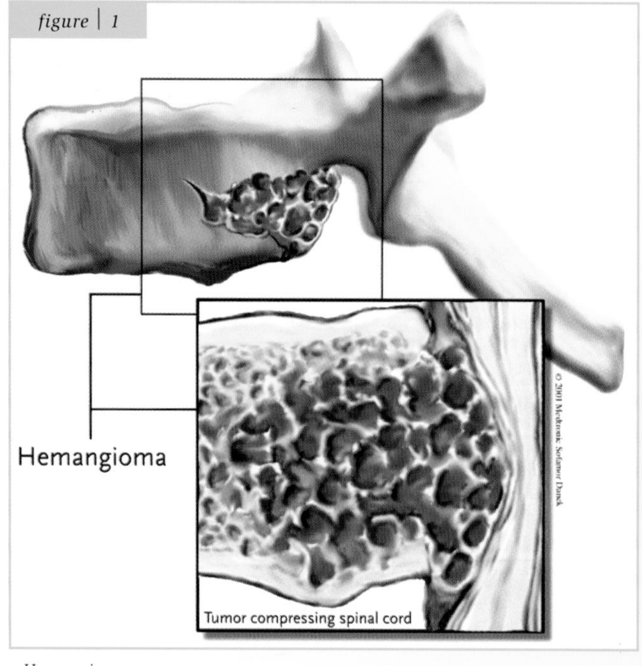

Hemangioma

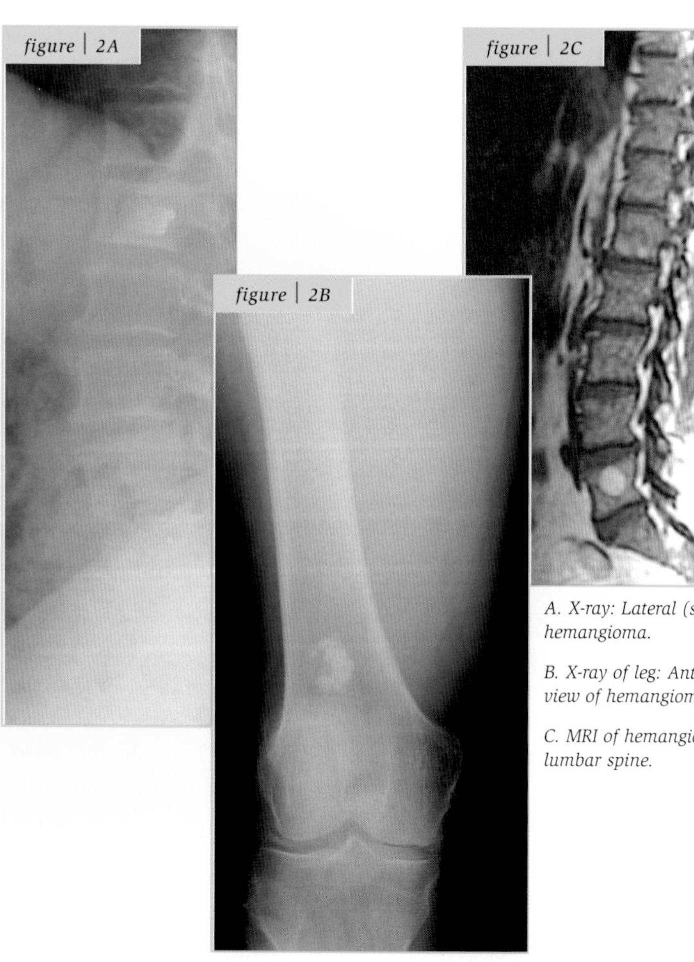

A. X-ray: Lateral (side) view of hemangioma.

B. X-ray of leg: Anterior (front) view of hemangioma.

C. MRI of hemangioma of the lumbar spine.

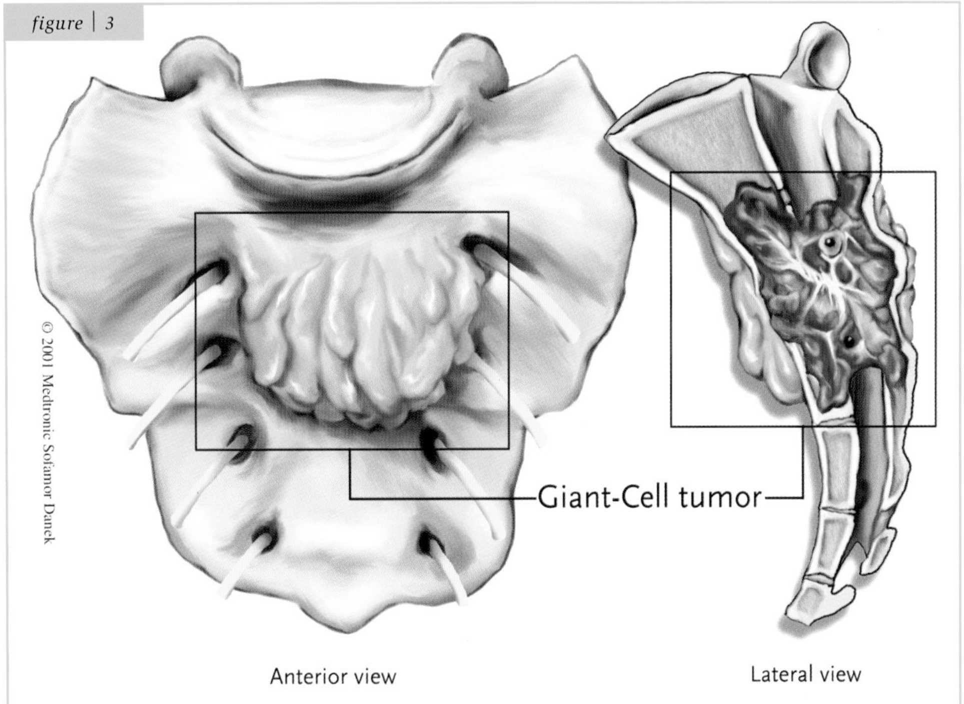

Giant bone cell tumor.

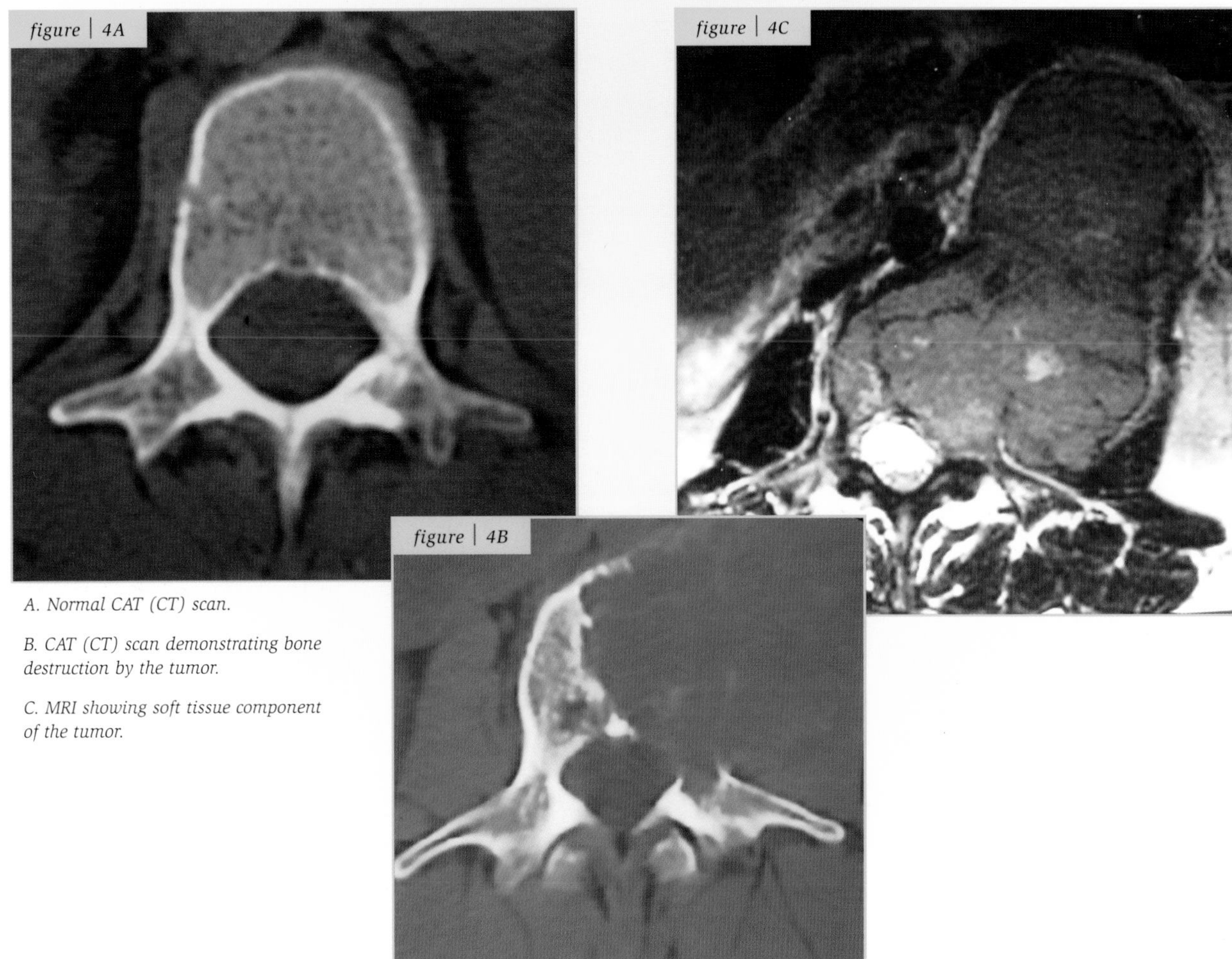

A. Normal CAT (CT) scan.

B. CAT (CT) scan demonstrating bone destruction by the tumor.

C. MRI showing soft tissue component of the tumor.

degree of soft tissue involvement of the giant-cell tumor (Fig. 5). This tumor should not be ignored. The treatment is generally surgical and is directed towards total, complete resection. Sometimes surgeons refer to this as an en block procedure, which means total removal. Since these tumors are usually found in the vertebra, an anterior approach is usually needed. After removal of the tumor, spine reconstruction will be needed. This type of surgery will usually involve a surgical team. In certain situations, the surgical team will involve a spine surgeon (neurosurgeon and/or orthopedic surgeon) and a vascular or general surgeon. After the tumor has been resected, reconstruction of the spine may be required. Reconstruction can be accomplished by using a large piece of bone harvested from the patient's hip, or placement of a reconstruction cage made of either titanium or carbon. After the spine has been remodeled using bone or cages, an internal fixation device is usually placed. There are many types of internal fixation devices now available, including plates or rods. Today these devices are made from titanium. Titanium is an inert, durable metal that allows better post-operative radiological evaluation. This type of metal implant causes less artifact production than the older stainless steel devices. Fewer artifacts or less interference means a better quality CAT scan or MRI. Any added therapy, i.e., radiation, will depend on each individual situation. A team of physicians, including an oncologist as well as spine surgeons, will help in such a decision.

Aneurysmal bone cysts are often found in the posterior elements, back sections, of the spine (Fig. 6). These tumors usually affect older adolescents, but can occur in any age group. It's referred to as an aneurysmal bone cyst because an aneurysm is a kind of blood blister. The blister is located inside the bone. As the bone cysts enlarges it expands the bone. Treatment is usually surgery for total excision of the lesion.

Osteoid osteomas are benign tumors (Fig. 7). Patients often present in their second or third decade of life. Surgery is the treatment of choice. When the tumor is removed oftentimes the pain is alleviated. Recurrence of this tumor is unusual.

Osteoblastoma is just a larger osteoid osteoma. By definition, an osteoid osteoma is less than 2 cm (0.79 inch) in diameter; the osteoblastoma is bigger. They too have a tendency to invade the posterior elements of the spine (Fig. 8). Surgical resection is recommended. They do have a tendency to recur more often than their smaller counterparts.

MALIGNANT PRIMARY BONE TUMORS

Malignant primary bone tumors are those tumors that arise from bone itself and have a tendency to spread elsewhere. One of the most common primary bone tumors is **multiple myeloma.** Certain physicians may not include multiple myeloma as primary bone tumors; however, for the context of this discussion, it will be included in malignant primary bone tumors. It arises from inside the bone, in the bone marrow (Fig. 9). Multiple myeloma is a very aggressive tumor. It causes osteoporosis, brittle-bone disease, because it eats away the bone to the extent that the bone is no longer able to withstand stress or loads placed on it. The result is a fracture. Multiple myeloma is the most common type of bone cancer. Patients are usually more mature, between the ages of 50 and 80 years. Historically, the prognosis for this type of bone cancer was poor; however, today, with better methods of diagnosis and chemotherapy, the prognosis has improved. Surgical decompression and reconstruction of the spine is performed only in unusual cases. Surgical considerations would occur only if there is evidence of gross instability or tumor compressing the spinal cord, leading to neurological compromise (inability to

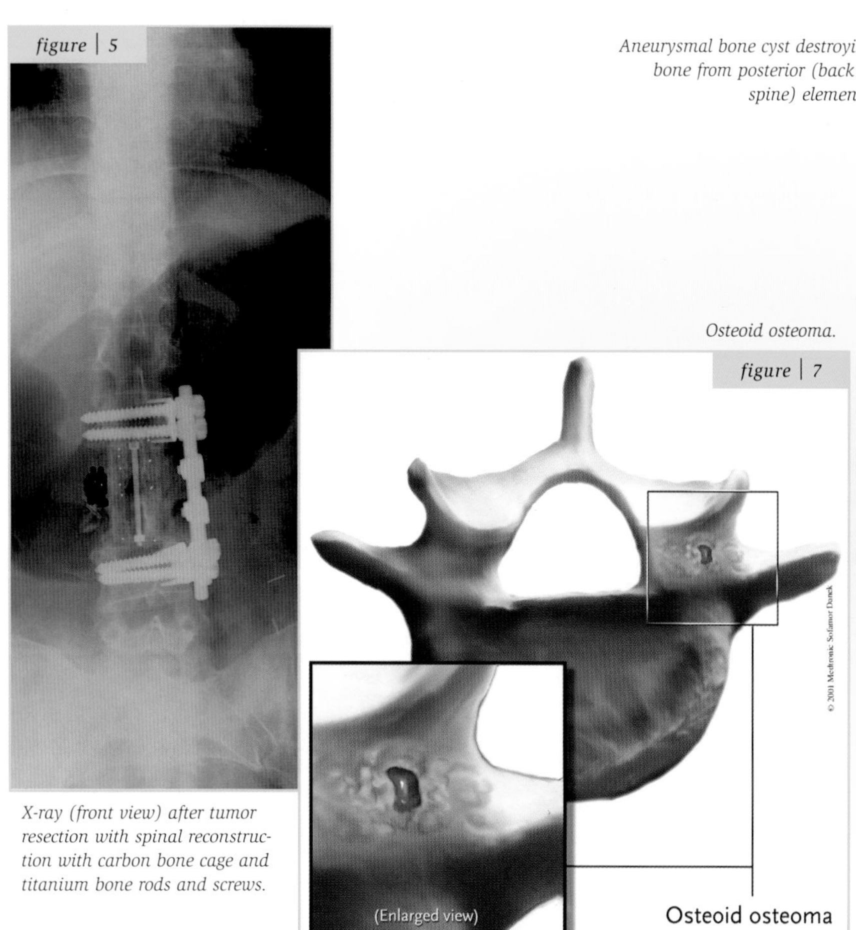

X-ray (front view) after tumor resection with spinal reconstruction with carbon bone cage and titanium bone rods and screws.

Osteoid osteoma.

Aneurysmal bone cyst destroying bone from posterior (back of spine) elements.

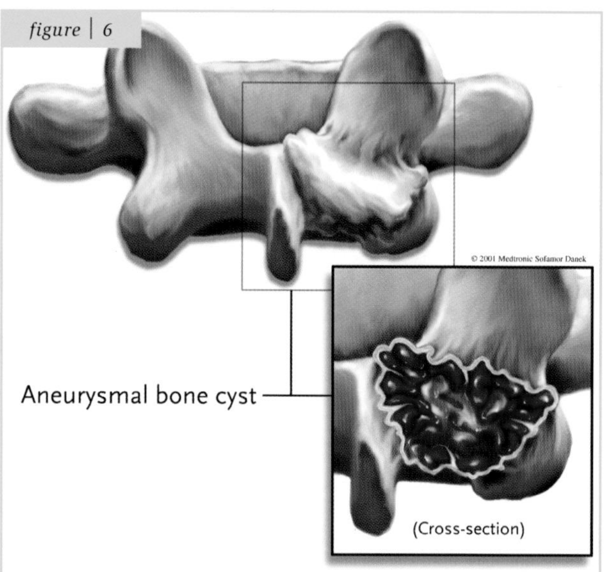

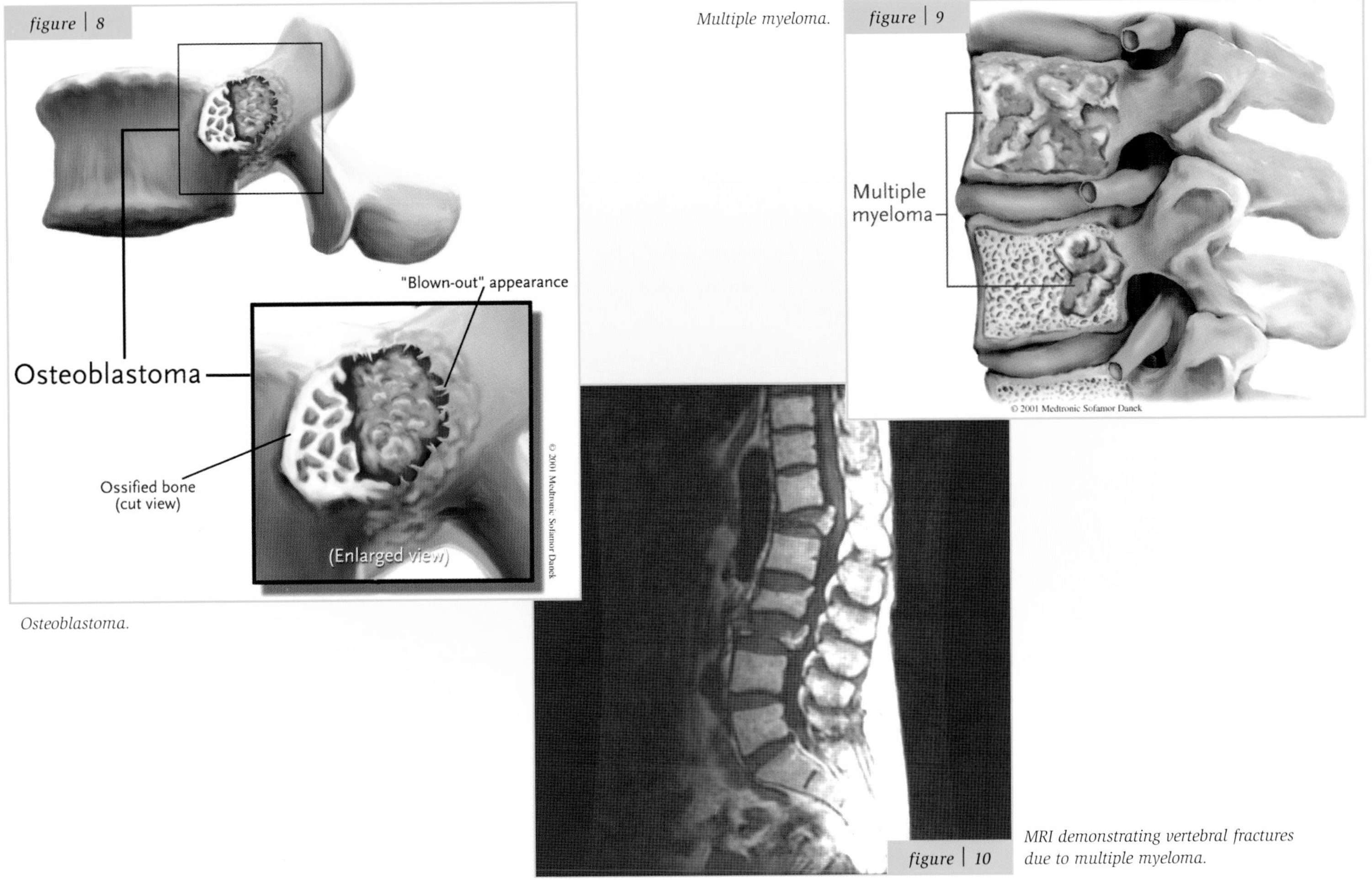

Osteoblastoma.

Multiple myeloma.

MRI demonstrating vertebral fractures due to multiple myeloma.

move arms or legs and/or loss of urinary, bladder or bowel function) (Fig. 10).

A **plasmacytoma** is a solitary region of myeloma and carries somewhat of a better prognosis than the multiple myeloma categories (Fig. 11). Surgery to reconstruct the patient who has multiple myeloma, or a large plastmacytoma, will involve much planning. It is best to consult a spine surgeon with experience in such reconstruction. The surgeon will be faced with brittle bone that may not be able to be stabilized with metal fixation devices. It's like putting a screw into a hollow wall; there's just not much for the screw to purchase and to hang onto. An experienced spine surgeon is needed in this situation.

Lymphomas are a group of diseases that arise from the lymphatic system. The lymphatic system includes the spleen, tonsils, thymus, and bone marrow. The lymphatic system is involved in defending the body against disease and infections. Lymph is a colorless fluid that travels throughout the body in very thin vessels. Lymphocytes, white blood cells, are suspended in the fluid. These cells attack diseases and infections. Small, bean-sized organs called lymph nodes connect the network of lymphatic vessels. These small nodes are concentrated in the armpits, groin, chest, and abdomen. Lymph nodes filter the lymph fluid and initiate the body's immune response. For unknown reasons, lymphocytes can begin to multiple in an uncontrolled fashion and become malignant. The abnormal cells can travel to any organ and grow into a lymphoma. A lymphoma is a group of varied tumor types. Some are slow growing and others are rapidly expanding tumors. Lymphomas are classified as either Hodgkin's Disease (named after the physician who first reported the disease in 1832) or non-Hodgkin's lymphomas. Hodgkin's disease usually occurs in individuals between the ages of 15 and 30, or after 50. Non-Hodgkin's lymphomas rarely attack people younger than 45 years old. Early signs of lymphomas include painless swollen lymph nodes in the neck, groin, and armpits. Some patients note a sensation of fullness in the abdomen and neck. Blood tests and urine studies are helpful in the diagnosis of lymphomas. Radiological tests such as magnetic resonance imaging (MRI) will help to locate and guide biopsies of the suspected tumor sites. Therapy depends on a multitude of factors: the presence or absence of symptoms, the patient's age, and other medical burdens. Different anticancer drugs and radiation therapies are used to treat lymphomas. When lymphomas involve the spine, the patient often experiences pain that prompts further testing, including CAT (CT) scans and MRIs (Figs. 12A, B and C). In certain cases, spinal surgery may be needed due to instability caused by bone destruction from the expanding lymphoma.

Ewing's sarcoma is a highly malignant tumor (Fig. 13). Sarcomas arise in bone, muscle and cartilage. Fortunately, they are relatively rare tumors. Ewing's sarcoma is often found in children between the ages of 5 and 9, and young individuals between 20 and 30 years old. It has a predilection for the sacrum. The five-year survival rate or prognosis for patients with Ewing's sarcoma is generally poor. Multi-agent chemotherapeutic drugs and radiation therapy will be needed and, in certain situations, surgical decompression and subsequent stabilization with bone screws and rods may be needed to improve the patient's quality of life. However, the success rate is lees than 20% of the patients even with the multiple therapies.

A **chordoma** is a rare type of spine tumor. It is very slow growing and, by the time of diagnosis, it has usually been present for a long time. It is a very invasive tumor that destroys surrounding healthy bone. In certain situations, it will spread or

Plasmacytoma in vertebra.

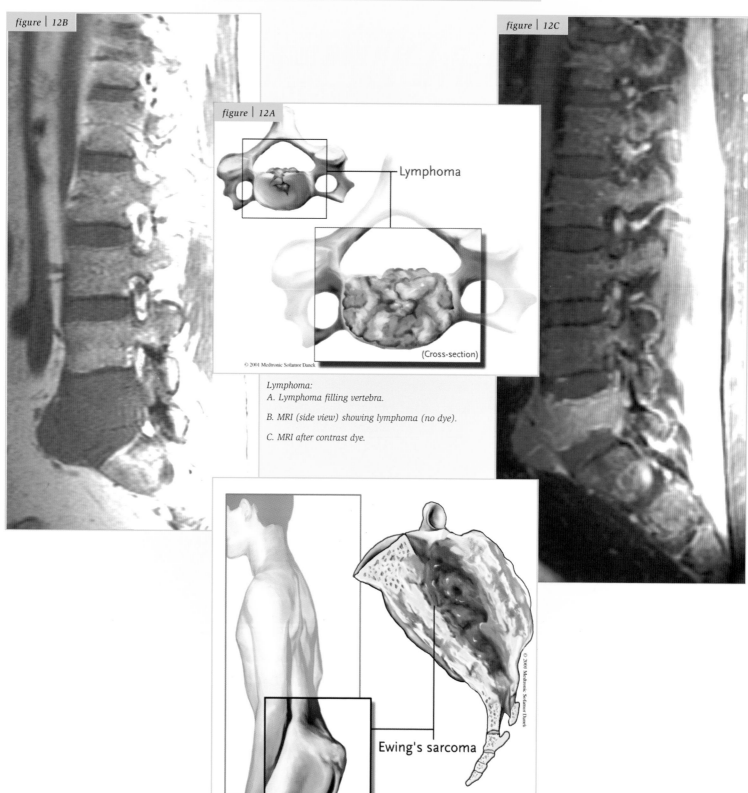

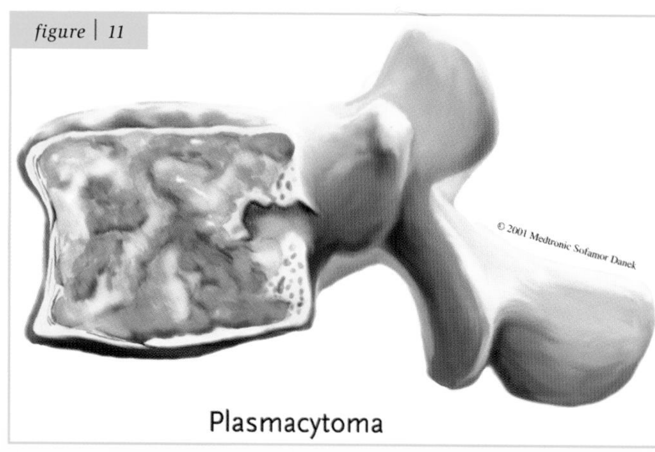

figure | 12B

figure | 12C

figure | 12A

Lymphoma

(Cross-section)

© 2001 Medtronic Sofamor Danek

Lymphoma:
A. Lymphoma filling vertebra.
B. MRI (side view) showing lymphoma (no dye).
C. MRI after contrast dye.

Ewing's sarcoma

© 2001 Medtronic Sofamor Danek

figure | 13

Ewing's Sarcoma.

A. Chordoma of sacrum.

B. MRI with chordoma in the sacrum.

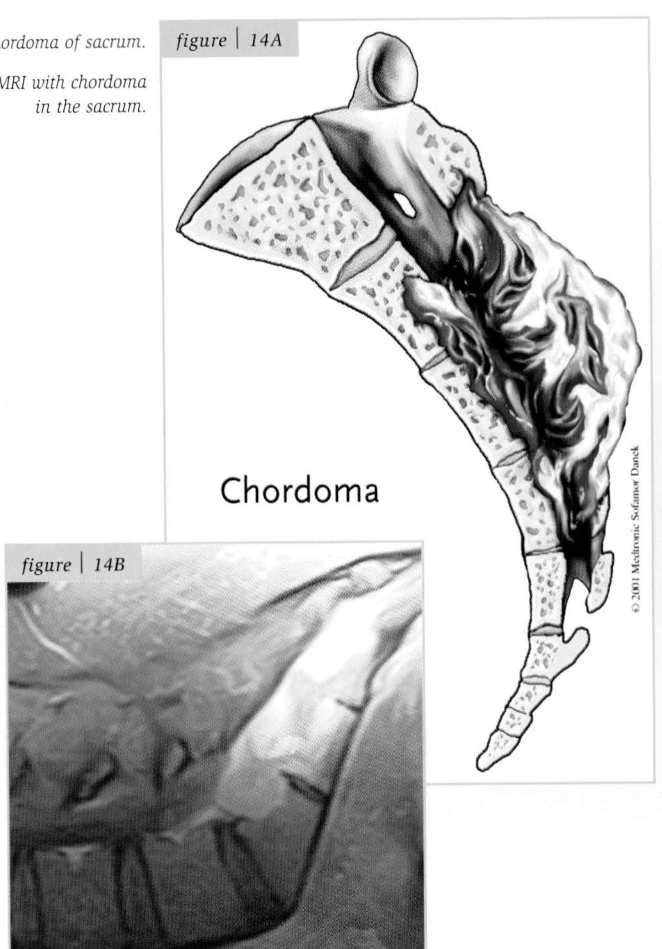

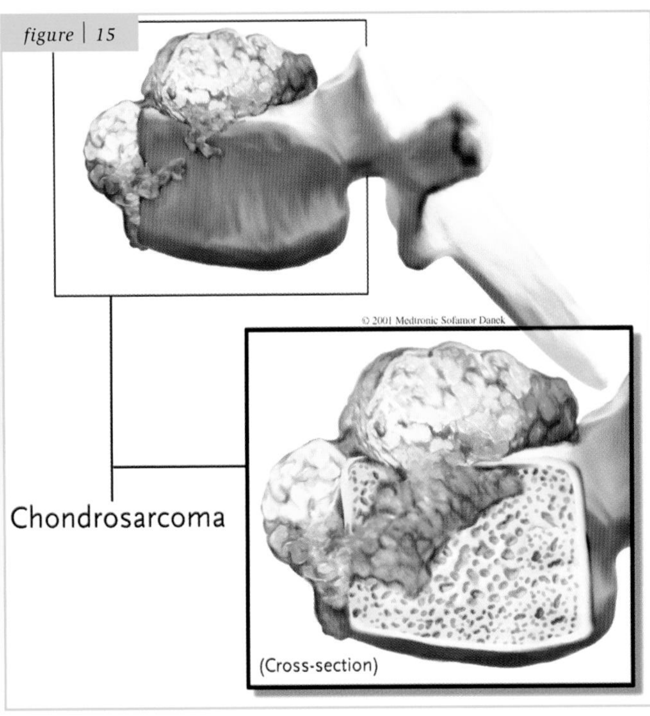

Chondrosarcoma of spinal vertebra.

metastasize. A chordoma is usually diagnosed in patients between the ages of 50 and 70 years of age. It can be found anywhere along the spine, particularly the base of the skull, the upper spine, and the sacrum (Figs. 14A and B). Total surgical excision is the treatment of choice. It is important that a patient with a chordoma be treated by a multi-disciplinary team, including an oncologist and surgeon with experience with such lesions.

Chondrosarcomas fall into the slow-growing malignant tumor category. They originate in cartilage (Fig. 15). They are often diagnosed in patients over the age of 40 years. Surgery is the avenue to follow with this type of spine tumor. These tumors tend to be recalcitrant and resistant to radiotherapy and chemotherapy. Spine reconstruction and internal fixation may well be needed during surgical excision of a chondrosarcoma.

METASTATIC BONE TUMORS

Metastatic bone tumors are the most common tumors of the spine. These are the crabgrass of tumors. There are approximately one million new cases of cancer every year, and about 50% of patients with cancer will develop metastatic tumors to their spines. The spine is the third most common site for cancer to spread. The most common sources of metastatic spine tumors include cancers from the lung, breast, prostate, thyroid, and kidney (Figs. 16 and 17). Cells from these cancers travel to the spine and invade the vertebrae. The spine is filled with blood, which brings nutrients; thus the spine is an excellent site for tumors to grow.

There are two routes by which cancerous tumor cells can spread to the spine. The first is through the blood system. In the second, those cancer cells may actually metastasize directly into the spine itself. These tumors can cause many problems: they can destroy normal bone and cause spinal instability. The tumor can grow at a very rapid pace and put pressure on the spinal cord and nerves. Any patient with a history of cancer who develops back pain has metastatic spine lesions or tumors, until proven otherwise. Radiological evaluation will include X-rays, but X-rays may not show the entire picture. X-rays usually demonstrate bone destruction when approximately 30 to 50% of the bone has been destroyed by the tumor; therefore, an individual with a history of cancer will need more than just X-rays.

Magnetic resonance imaging (MRI) is an excellent imaging tool to evaluate for the presence of metastatic bone tumors (Fig. 18). The MRI will demonstrate the soft tissue elements of the tumor, and will be able to approximate the size of the tumor. The MRI, just like the X-rays, may not reveal the whole picture. Computer axial tomography (CAT or CT scan) will be needed to evaluate the bony architecture and changes in the bone caused by the tumor (Figs. 19A and B). More powerful MRIs will better visualize the bony elements and may reduce the need for the CAT scan. Individuals who cannot undergo an MRI because of a history of metal body implants and/or pacemakers, may need to have a myelogram followed by a CAT scan. A myelogram is an insertion of a needle into the spinal canal for injection of a contrast dye. The CAT scan will be able to pick up the contrast dye and determine whether or not the dye is being displaced by a tumor. Nuclear bone scans (radio-nuclide imaging) are sensitive tests that allow visualization of the entire skeletal system, but they are not specific for neoplastic or cancer disease (Fig. 20). Bone scans are very useful to stage or evaluate other sites of the skeleton for metastatic disease. Today, more medical centers are using positron emission tomography, PET scans, to detect early tumor sites.

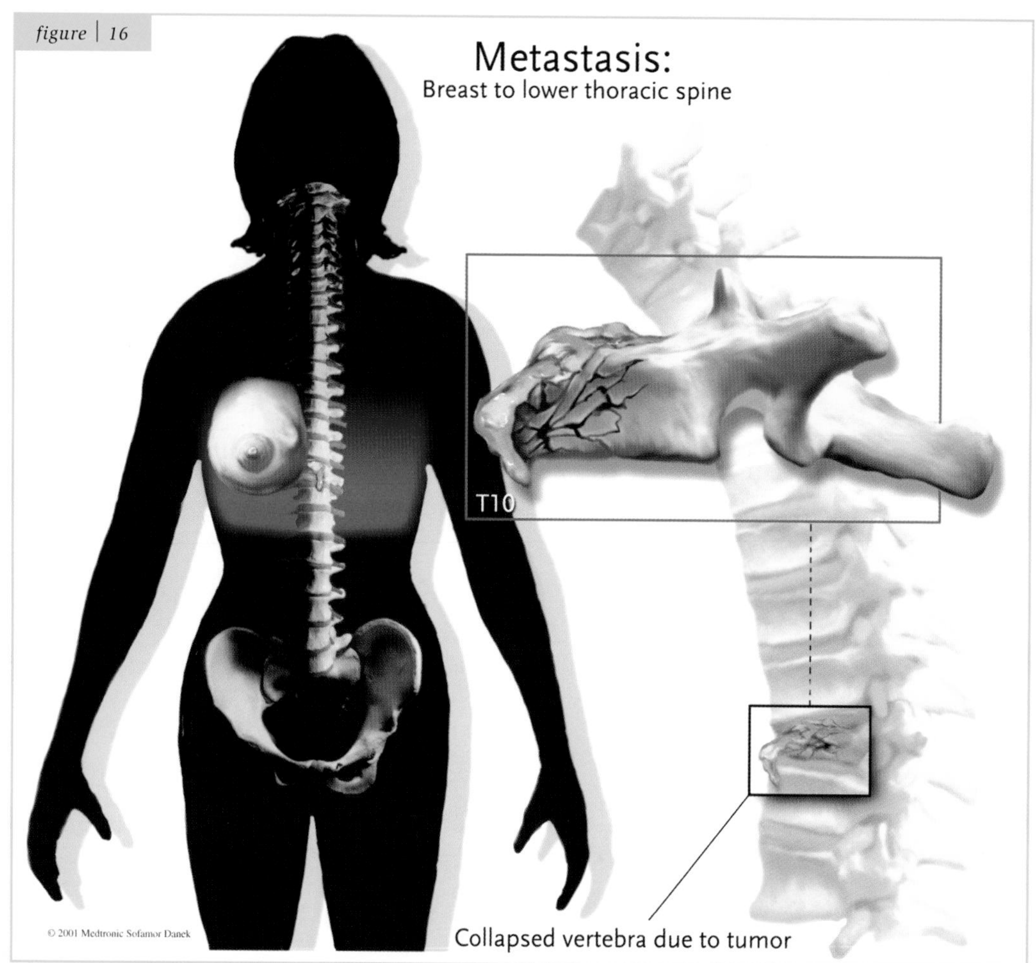

Metastatic bone tumors.

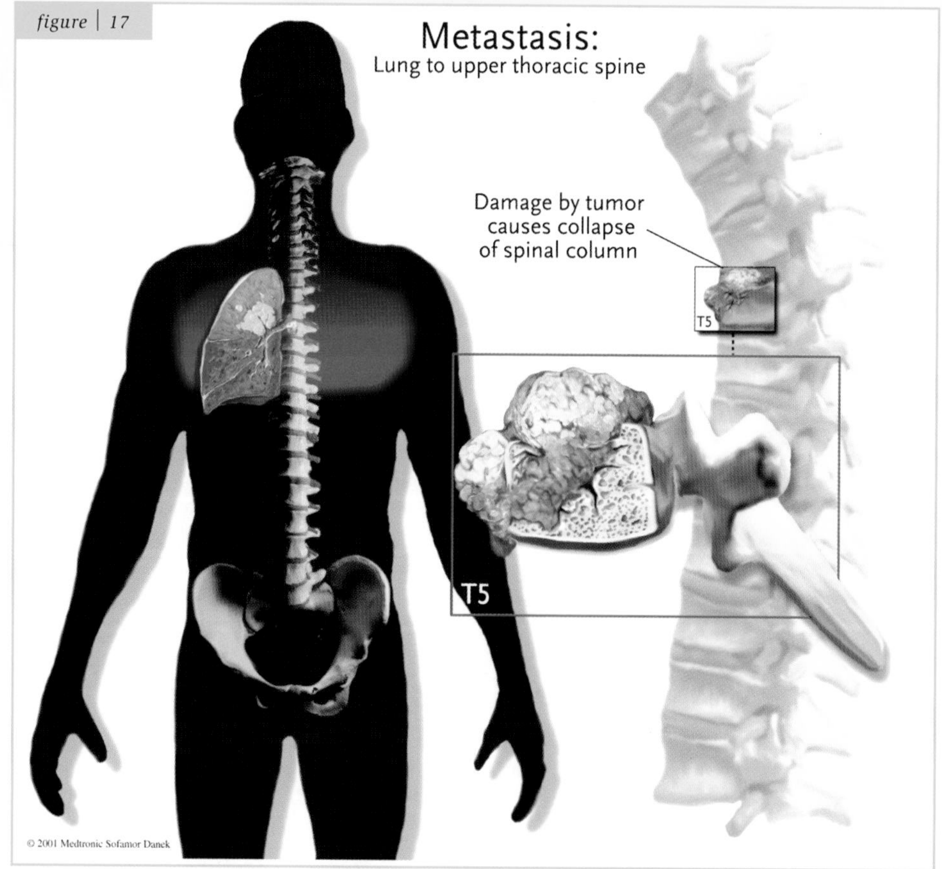

Metastatic bone tumors.

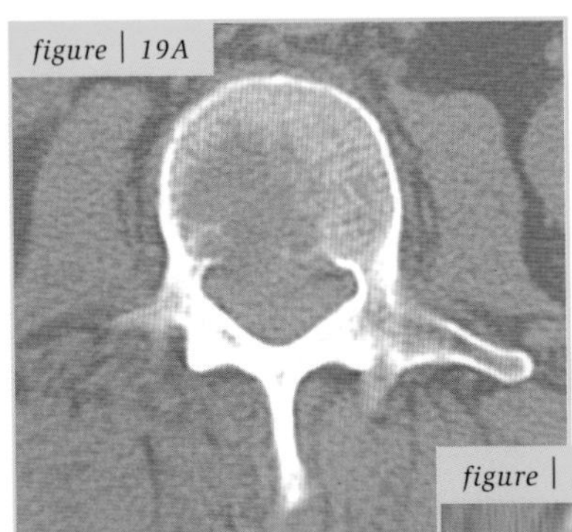

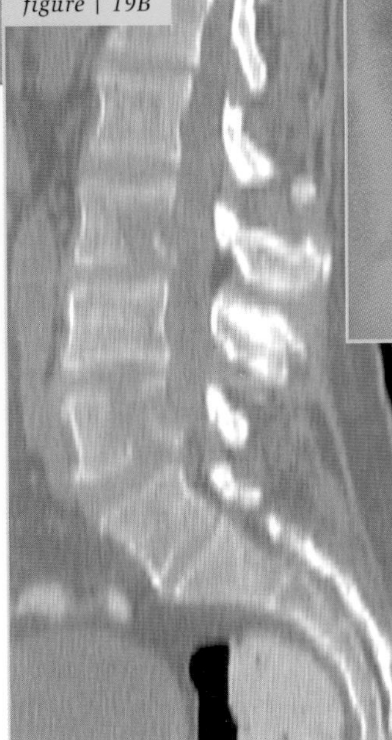

A. CAT (CT) scan demonstrating bone destruction.

B. CAT (CT) scan (side view) showing bone destruction.

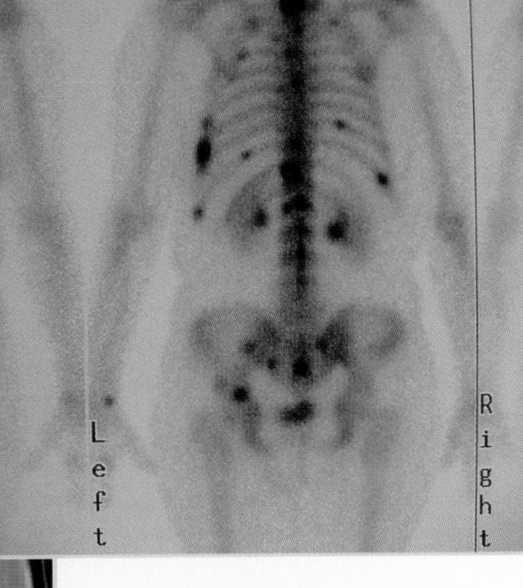

Nuclear bone scan with multiple metastatic lesions.

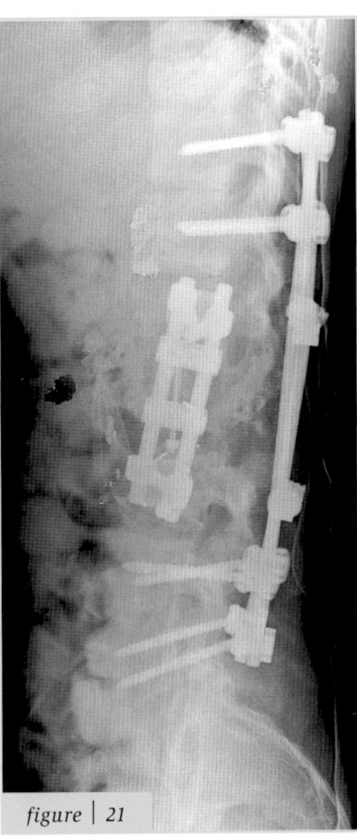

X-ray: Lateral (side) view showing bone rods and screws in front and back of spine.

Treatment for metastatic cancerous tumors will need a multidisciplinary team that includes the patient's family doctor and medical specialists (medical oncologists, radiation oncologists), surgical specialists (spine surgeons-neurological or orthopedic), nurses (oncology and spine), psychiatrists, psychologists, and social workers. Often the patient's religious leader is a member of the team. The primary member of this team is the patient and his/her family. The treatment team will direct their care not only to the primary patient, which is the patient with the cancer, but also to the other patient, the family members that are also affected by their loved one's illness.

Unfortunately, disease never attacks a single individual; it also attacks all the loved ones, family members, and others who care for the patient. The decision to operate on metastatic tumors of the spine depends upon the patient, the type of cancer (whether or not it is sensitive to other treatments such as radiation and/or chemotherapy), the cancer size and location, and spine stability or instability. Surgical decision-making is based on a multitude of factors, but first and foremost is the care of the patient. Will the patient be able to undergo a spinal procedure? In certain situations, if there is only one tumor site, surgical intervention may be very worthwhile and perhaps should be strongly considered. If there are multiple sites, the oncology team will be greatly involved in decisions regarding therapy. Vertebroplasty or Kyphoplasty (injection of bone cement into the site of the metastatic tumor) has been recommended with certain tumors. Not all patients with metastatic spine tumors are candidates for such bone cement injections. Surgical therapy depends upon the location of the tumor. It is often stated, "Go where the money is." If the tumor is located in front of the spine, going anteriorly is certainly an option. Surgery will require removal of the tumor, reconstruction of the spine with either a metal (titanium) or carbon cage, and internal fixators with bone screws, rods, or plates. On the other hand, if the tumor is primarily located in the posterior elements, back of the spine, a posterior approach is needed. Reconstruction with rods, screws, or plates may be needed. Sometimes surgery in front and back is required (Fig. 21).

Some physicians and surgeons will recommend a biopsy of the tumor. This is a percutaneous biopsy and can be performed using computer tomography (CAT or CT scan) or fluoroscopy. The procedure can be performed in a radiological suite or an operating room. Obtaining a sample of the tissue prior to surgical intervention may be helpful, but this is a topic that should be discussed with the oncologist and the surgeon. If there is any question about the type of tumor cells present at a given location in the spine, a percutaneous biopsy is a consideration. In certain cases, it will be impossible to obtain a piece of the tumor tissue in a percutaneous, closed procedure; therefore, an open procedure will be needed. In this situation, the patient is taken to the operating room and is either given a general anesthetic or sedated. In certain situations, local numbing medication may be used. It all depends on the tumor location and whether or not it is easily accessible.

SYMPTOMS

Most patients with spine tumors will present to their physician or health care provider with a complaint of pain. The pain is often not associated with a history of trauma, and the patient may be unable to give an exact time at which the pain started. At first, it may have been thought that the pain was nothing more than a pulled muscle. However, over a period of time, using nothing more than over-the-counter medication (aspirin and/or nonsteroidal anti-inflammatory medications), the pain continues to get worse. The pain may cause relentless discomfort and is not associated with any particular position. The pain is present despite the activity of the patient and, in certain situations; the back pain will awaken a patient from a night's rest. If the tumor is causing pressure on a nerve, the pain may travel into an arm or a leg. The patient may also experience numbness and heaviness, or a tingling sensation in an extremity or extremities. If the spinal cord has pressure on it, this may cause weakness. If the tumor is located in the cervical spine, neck, it may cause weakness in the arms and the legs. If it is located in the thoracic spine, mid-back, it may cause problems with leg pain and weakness. Tumors in the lumbar spine, low back, or sacrum, may also cause leg pain and/or weakness. When symptoms such as loss of urinary bladder or bowel control are involved, further evaluation is absolutely indicated; these signs should never be ignored.

One of the greatest allies of cancer is denial. If any pain in the spine is causing a compromise of one's daily activities and not allowing one to enjoy life, including playing golf, medical evaluation is needed and could be life-saving. The evaluation of any patient suspected of having a spine tumor will include X-rays, computed axial tomography (CAT or CT scan), bone scans, and magnetic resonance imaging (MRI). A physician will order special laboratory tests, such as a complete blood count.

Treatment for spine tumors has improved. Better imaging with MRI and CAT scans has allowed earlier recognition of spine tumors, which means earlier treatment. Advancements in medicine, medical oncology, radiation oncology, and surgery have come about over the last fifty years. Individuals with symptomatic and invasive spine tumors are living longer and have a better quality of life, which includes playing golf.

Individuals who have benign primary bone tumors for which no therapy has been recommended and who are being followed periodically by their physicians, will be able to continue playing golf so long as they remain asymptomatic (no pain or other problems). However, it's always best to check with a physician before picking up the clubs. Individuals, who have bone tumors that require other avenues of therapy such as radiation, chemotherapy, or surgical intervention, will need to be followed closely by their treating physicians and health team. They should consider returning to golf only after treatment for the tumors has been completed, and only with the consent of the treating medical and physical therapy team. New frontiers in the medical, oncological, radiological, and surgical treatments of spine lesions allow new hope for all spine tumor patients, as well as for golfers with a spine tumors.

INFECTIONS OF THE SPINE

CHAPTER 17

T. Glenn Pait, M.D., F.A.C.S.

It was back in September of 1994 when I injured my back from a car ride. We were playing in the PING Cellular One championship in Portland. I was staying with a friend for the week and had about a half-hour commute to the golf course. I was traveling along the freeway on the way to the course two hours before my tee time of 12:20. There happened to be a terrible wreck that caused me to sit in traffic for over a half-hour. I just stressed out tremendously, thinking that I was going to miss my tee time. By the time I arrived at the course, my back was extremely tight from worrying and sitting in one position for so long. Now it was 11:50, which left me only 30 minutes to stretch, change from the sweats I was wearing, and practice. My caddie grabbed my clubs and I went running to the locker room to change. Along the way I dropped my shirt, and when I quickly reached over to pick it up, I herniated a disc and that was the beginning of my back problems. Nevertheless I tried to hit balls on the driving range, but after three shots the pain was so bad I left crying. The next morning, I could not get out of bed and my left foot was going numb. I eventually had to have surgery one month later and was out of competition for five months in all. Backs are so tricky. You're never sure as a golfer whether your back is hurting because you are swinging badly, or you are swinging badly because your back is hurting.

Kristi Albers, LPGA Tour

Infections of the spine can lead to major problems if they are not promptly recognized. Fortunately, infections of the spine are a relatively rare occurrence. However, a spine infection must be included in the differential diagnoses or different causes for any patient with neck or back pain.

There are certain individuals who are more susceptible to spine infections than others. Included in this group are intravenous drug abusers, individuals whose immune system is compromised (HIV/AIDS patients), and elderly patients. There are patients who are compromised because they are medically burdened. In this particular situation the immune system is more challenged. Their ability to ward off infections is markedly reduced. Patients with rheumatoid arthritis who have been given long-term steroids and diabetes mellitus patients fall into this category. Organ transplant patients who are also given immune compromising medication to prevent rejection are also quite susceptible to infections of the spine. Other patients who may be suspect for infections when presenting with neck or back pain include those who are malnourished, have cancer, are obese, and are smokers. Finally, the odds increase for any individual who has undergone any recent invasive medical procedure, such as a urinary tract diagnostic procedure using surgical instrumentation.

In the early stages of a spine infection, the diagnosis can be difficult and require special tests. Blood tests may be very helpful. A complete blood count (CBC) may demonstrate an elevated white count (WBC). White cells are blood cells that help fight infections. Blood cultures are helpful to detect the presence of bacteria in a patient's blood A blood culture is obtained by taking a small amount of blood from the patient, sending it to a laboratory, and placing it into special culture tubes. If the blood culture is positive, the infecting organism can often be identified and its sensitivity to different antibiotics can be determined, allowing for the best treatment. Some organisms or bacteria are more sensitive to antibiotics than others. Other blood tests include inflammatory (infection) markers. Two of the best markers for infection are the erythrocyte sedimentation rate (ESR) and the C-reactive protein (CRP). These markers are elevated in approximately 80–90% of patients who have infections. These markers can also be helpful later on. They can serve as a baseline, so that any subsequent tests will indicate whether or not the patient is responding to a particular type of therapy or antibiotics. If the markers fall during the patient's treatment, the treatment is likely to be successful in eradicating the given infection.

Radiological studies are very helpful in evaluating a patient with a spinal infection. Often the individual presenting with spine pain, neck, or back pain will undergo an X-ray. Plain X-rays will usually be normal in the first 2–4 weeks after the onset of the infection. For an X-ray to demonstrate the presence of an infection, 50–60% of the bone involved in the infection will need to be destroyed. Today, the most sensitive and specific type of radiological imaging study to evaluate for a spinal infection is magnetic resonance imaging (MRI). Different MRI settings allow infections to be better visualized and diagnosed (Figs. 1A and B). The MRI may be enhanced with an I.V. contrast dye called **Gadolinium**. If a patient is sensitive or allergic to iodine or shellfish, it is important that he or she tell the doctor and the radiologist, because Gadolinium contains iodine. The Gadolinium is helpful in evaluating for an infection because the infection causes an increase of blood flow to the infected site, either to the vertebral body or to the disc space. This will be picked up by the Gadolinium, just like a sponge's soaking up water. No test is 100% accurate; however, in most cases, the MRI does an excellent job of routing out the site of an infection of the spine.

Other radiological tests that are not as specific as the MRI includes bone scans. Bone scans can be useful in demonstrating the overall skeleton as well as the spine. The bone scan is helpful when a patient cannot undergo an MRI scan. A bone scan is a reliable test in determining a possible infection; however, it cannot distinguish an infection from a tumor or trauma. The bone scan will show an area of increased activity that is referred to as being hot. An MRI is better able to define an area of the spine as either normal, degenerative, affected by a tumor, or involved with an infection. Computerized axial tomography (CAT scan) is often performed to better appreciate the bony elements of the spine of an individual with a suspected infection (Figs. 2A and B). In some situations, a biopsy and aspiration will be needed. This means that a sample of the site of suspected infection needs to be harvested. This can be done in a radiology suite by using a spinal needle that is guided to the targeted infection site by either a CAT scan or a special X-ray called fluoroscopy (Fig. 3). Prior to needle placement, the patient's skin site is numbed with medication. This is a closed biopsy or radiological biopsy; a surgical scalpel is not used. There are special situations when an open or surgical biopsy will be needed. When the possible infection is located in a very difficult or dangerous site to biopsy, direct visualization may provide a safer route to provide a specimen.

Many patients will ask, "How in the world did I get an infection of my spine?" Most infections travel to the spine through the blood system. For this reason, there is an increased risk for infection, particularly for compromised individuals who have undergone a urinary tract procedure such as a cystoscopy. There is a rich network of arteries and veins around the spine. These blood vessels provide a hematogenous route for infection.

Patients who have infections of the spine will complain of severe back pain. The pain may or may not radiate into the legs. There is often a delay in the diagnosis of an infection of the spine because the early signs are quite subtle. As the infection spreads and more of the spine is involved, the pain worsens. The pain is unrelenting and can be localized. When the physician examines the spine, a point of localized tenderness upon palpation may give a hint as to the location of the infection. Patients will also demonstrate a limitation in the range of motion in the spine. The patient may not want to move at all due to the severe pain. There may or may not be an associated fever. In fact, temperature elevation is rarely present. The key to a diagnosis is a high suspicion for individuals who are susceptible to an infection.

Infections of the spine can be inside the bone, the disc, or the spine canal. Infection in the bones of the spine is called vertebral osteomyelitis. An infection of the bones of the spine, the vertebral bodies, can cause instability. If the bones continue to be destroyed by the invading infection, the bones will collapse. A good way to think about an infection of the bone is to imagine termites invading a wall. If the termites continue to eat away at the wall, the floor above will eventually collapse. Bone collapse may cause pressure on the spinal cord. This collapsed bone can result in significant deformity of the spine, which may produce significant pain (Fig. 4).

Vertebral osteomyelitis is caused by microorganisms. Bacterial infections are

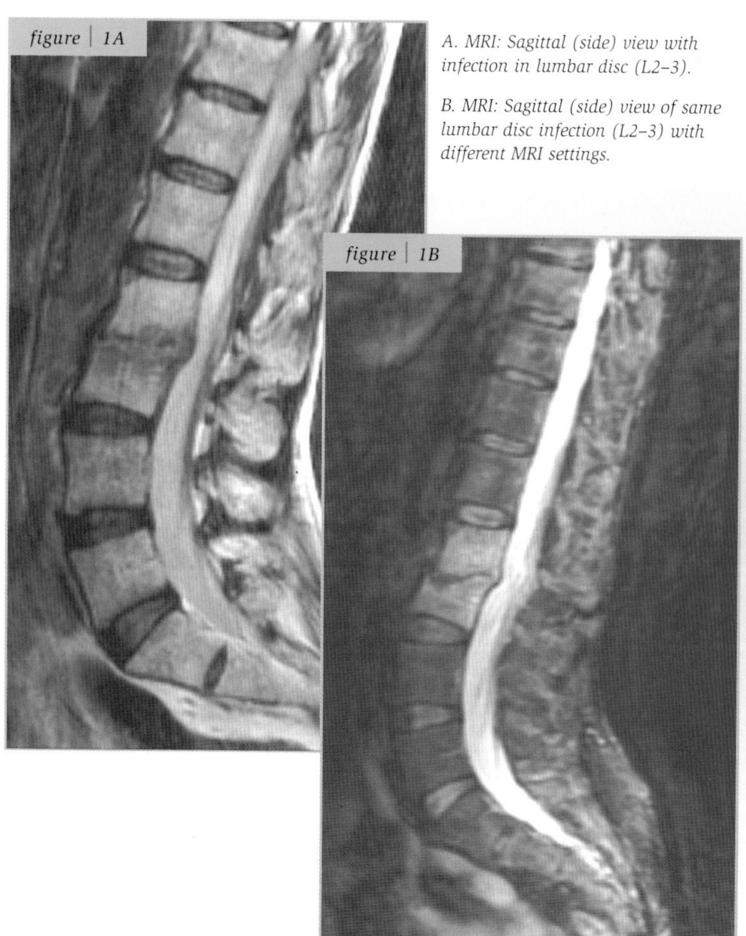

A. MRI: Sagittal (side) view with infection in lumbar disc (L2–3).

B. MRI: Sagittal (side) view of same lumbar disc infection (L2–3) with different MRI settings.

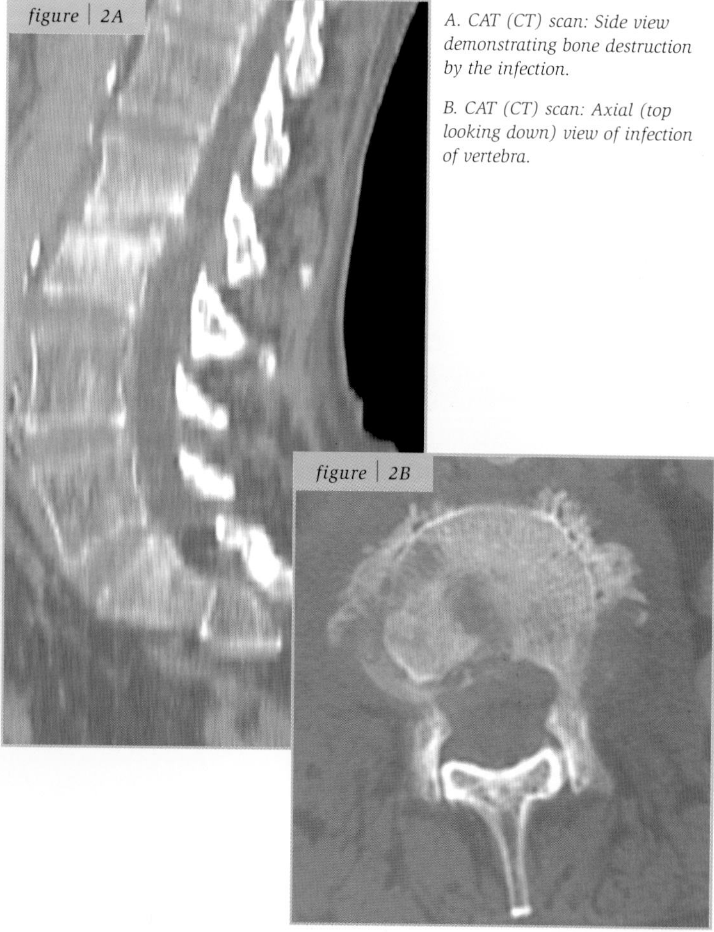

A. CAT (CT) scan: Side view demonstrating bone destruction by the infection.

B. CAT (CT) scan: Axial (top looking down) view of infection of vertebra.

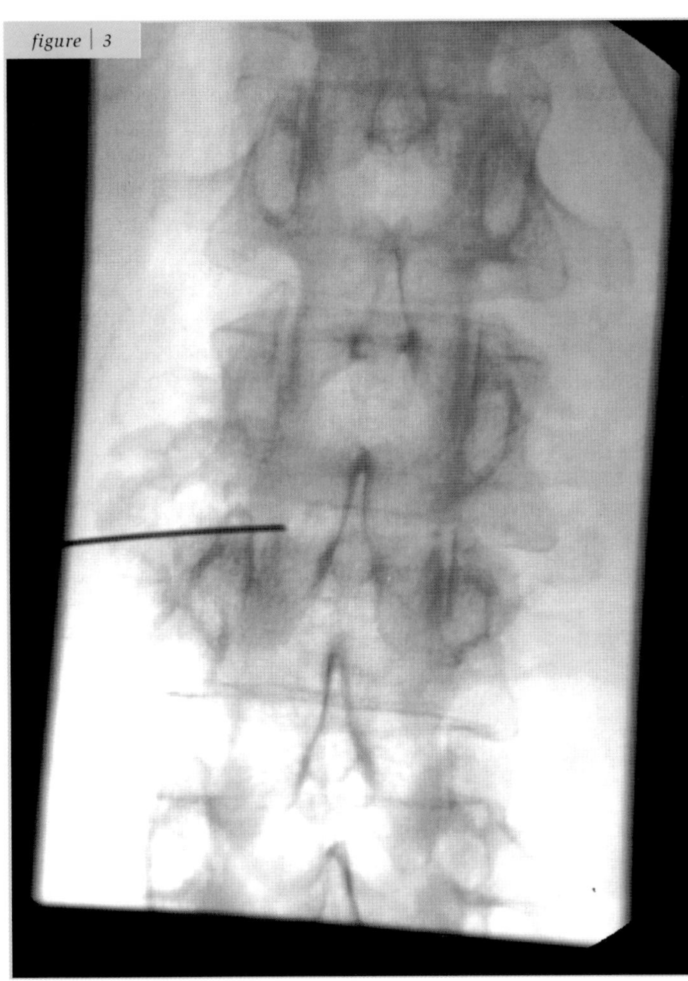

figure | 3 X-ray (fluoroscopy) guided needle biopsy and aspiration of spine infection.

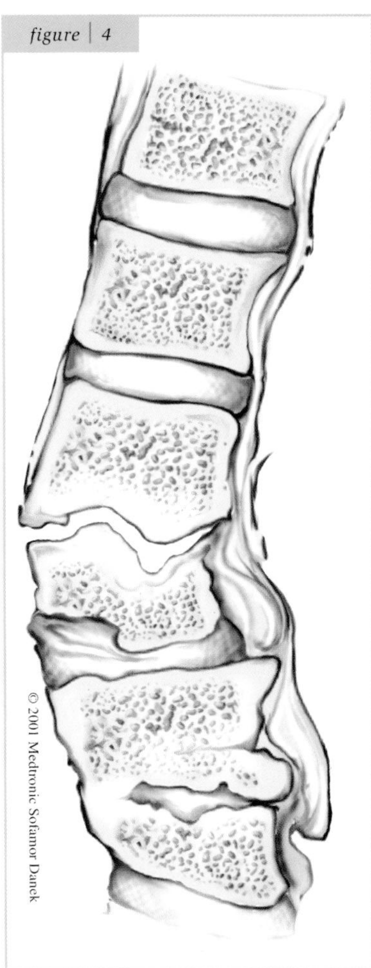

figure | 4 Infection of the disc and bone destruction due to osteomyelitis.

by far the most common cause of this type of infection. However, there are some types of fungal infections and tuberculosis (Pott's disease) which invade the spine. Individuals at high risk for this type of spine infection include diabetics, intravenous drug users, those with chronic renal or kidney problems, alcoholics (malnourished), and individuals with skin infections, bacterial endocarditis (infections within the heart), lung infections (pneumonia, chronic bronchitis), any local infection, dental work, and any previous spine surgery. At times, vertebral osteomyelitis can arise independently of any of the above-mentioned causes, particularly in medically burdened elderly individuals. The treatment for osteomyelitis when there is no evidence of nerve or spinal cord pressure is long-term antibiotic therapy and immobilization by a brace. In certain situations where the spine is considered unstable, surgery may be needed. If the spine is not stabilized, the patient is at risk for injury to the spinal cord. Another indication for surgery would be pus at the infection site that puts pressure on the spinal cord. Surgery would be directed towards the site of most of the infection. The surgery can be performed from in front, with the removal of the infected bone to be followed by reconstruction with a bone cage or bone graft and possible internal fixation with rods and/or screws. Some surgeons prefer not to place instrumentation near or in front of the spine where the abscess or infection is located. Instead they will place screws at a site removed from the infection. If the infection is in front of the spine, the infection or abscess will be evacuated and the bone screws will be placed in the bone on the backside (pedicles). In summary, this means that the bone grafting is done through the anterior column (in front) and is followed by posterior instrumentation and bone screws in the back (posterior). After surgery a brace may be needed. When surgery is not recommended and the patient is placed into a brace, the brace will provide needed stability for the spine while the infection is being treated with antibiotics. It is usually worn for 6–12 weeks until bone heals. This is the same situation even after surgery. If a rigid brace is used, it should only be worn when the patient is up and out of the bed. It is important not to wear the brace while in bed or to sleep in it, because skin abrasions, breakdown, and even skin infections can occur. A new infection is certainly not needed. A patient should always discuss the wearing of their brace with the doctor. Extended use of the brace may require periodic adjustments and refitting.

Another site of spine infection is the disc. If the disc is involved with infection it is referred to as **discitis**. Discitis is a relatively rare problem or sequelae of spine surgery, particularly disc removal. In many cases, there will be no specific cause for the infection. The bacterial that is most likely to infect the spine is **Staphylococcus Aureus**. Individuals with an infection of the disc space will complain of severe back pain and will not move. The pain is relentless. It is worse when standing upright or walking and can be relieved somewhat by lying in bed, but remains a problem nevertheless. Pain management is very important with a spine infection. Patients can also experience fever and chills. Many individuals can point to the infected site because of the pain. Even the lightest touch will cause severe pain. Magnetic resonance imaging (MRI) is an excellent test to evaluate for discitis. If there is any doubt about the presence of an infection, a biopsy will be needed. The needle aspiration will be placed into a culture dish and grown to determine the needed antibiotic treatment. Sometimes an organism does not grow, so the physician will prescribe a broad-spectrum antibiotic to treat the disease. This means that this antibiotic will kill many types of bacterial organisms. In most cases a disc infection is treated with immobilization with a brace, pain medications and the appropriate antibiotic. The good news is that the prognosis for most disc-space infections is good and will improve with time. If the infection does not improve with antibiotic therapy, surgical debridement of the infected disc may be necessary. Surgery can be performed by going in the back, through the side, or through the front, depending on the location. The choice of the procedure and the route the surgeon approaches the infected disc depends on the location of the disc, *i.e.* neck, thoracic spine, or lumbar sacral spine. The need for stabilization with the placement of bone grafts and possible bone screws, rods or plates depends on the site of the infection as well as the degree of bony destruction and the resulting spinal deformity.

The third site of spine infection is inside the spinal canal. Such a collection is referred to as an **epidural abscess**. This means that the infectious material (pus or granulation tissue) is located inside the spine but outside the covering of the nerves and spinal cord (dura). An infection-producing microbe causes epidural abscesses. Bacterial infections are by far the most common; however, infections caused by fungus and tuberculosis may be seen.

Epidural abscesses are often associated with osteomyelitis. Infection begins in the bone, destroys the bone and forms pus. The pus breaks through the bone cortex that may extend to the spinal cord or nerves. In these cases weakness, loss of sensation, or loss of bowel and urinary bladder function may be seen. The onset of these symptoms will need immediate medical and possible surgical intervention. The best radiological study to evaluate for an epidural abscess is the same as with osteomyelitis or disc-space infection, the MRI. The MRI will demonstrate the size of the abscess and the degree of pressure on the spinal cord. It is very important with an epidural abscess that the offending organism be identified and antibiotic therapies begun promptly. If there is evidence of weakness or bowel and bladder changes, surgical intervention may be needed to relieve or take pressure off of the spinal cord. The MRI will help guide the surgeon to the site of the infection.

If spine infections are recognized early and treated promptly and appropriately, the prognosis is generally excellent. It is important for the patient to have patience. It will take time to get better. It is also valuable to find out the reason for the infection to help insure that such problems do not easily recur. Anyone with a spine infection will not be playing golf any time soon. The infection will need to be eradicated and the bone will need to heal before the golfer can return to the greens and fairways. X-rays and CAT scans help to demonstrate bone healing and remolding. In time the patient will become more active, feel better, and want to get back into the routine of daily activities. This is a good sign. The patient should not return to golf unless released by his or her physician. Physical therapy for strengthening exercises will be needed. After the patient has been given the go-ahead to play golf, it is best to start back slowly. First, talk to a professional, obtain guidance and take some lessons. Golfers returning to play after spine infections should follow the guidelines for returning to golf after spine surgery.

TRAUMATIC FRACTURES OF THE SPINE

CHAPTER 18

T. Glenn Pait, M.D., F.A.C.S.

In 1983, I developed problems with a herniated disc in my lower back. After winning the McDonald's Kids Classic, I flew to Tulsa the next week for the U.S. Open. During the first round of the tournament, my back went out. My left foot was numb and I was lying on the ground between shots. After the doctor told me not to play anymore, I was out for eight weeks. A highly recommended chiropractor in Los Angeles was my savior from fusion surgery and what could have been the end of my career. After seven weeks of living in a hotel room in Los Angeles and undergoing daily flexion traction, I was back in the game. That, coupled with a regimented exercise program to strengthen the abdominal muscles, has stopped the degeneration of the disc through the years.

Beth Daniel, LPGA Tour

Ours is an extremely mobile society. Travel has become an integral part of most of our lives. We travel to work, travel back home, and travel to the golf course. Some of us travel from state to state, and still others travel from country to country. Today, we even have space travelers. In fact, golf was the first sport to be played on another celestial body—the moon. During the Apollo 14 Moon Mission of 1971, Astronaut Alan B. Shepard, Jr. dropped two golf balls onto the surface of the moon. Using a six-iron in one hand and a swing encumbered by a bulky space suit, he hit the balls for about 200 to 400 yards.

All of this travel stems from our need to get somewhere, the sooner the better. Our desire to save time translates into speed, which creates a market for ever-faster vehicles, whether bikes, cycles, cars, or planes. One of the consequences of our haste, however, is accidents, and accidents are a common cause of fractures of the spine. Even when we're not traveling from one location to another, we're working hurriedly, often under great pressure. Any event that creates disproportionate stresses on the spine can stress the bone past its breaking point, which translates into a fracture.

Fractures are either minor or major. Minor fractures are injuries to parts of the spine that do not cause bones to move in a manner that could cause harm to nerves or the spinal cord. Minor fractures usually do not require surgical treatment. Major fractures are more severe, and need more evaluation and treatment. Major fractures involve segments of the spinal bones that will allow the injured bones to migrate and possibly damage important nearby structures, such as the spinal cord. Any fracture to the spine will curtail all golfing activities. In most situations, the patient will immediately know that something's just not right. That stressful, traumatic event is often remembered and not soon forgotten. A fracture can occur anywhere along the spine: the neck (cervical), the upper back (thoracic), the lower back (lumbar), the sacrum and coccyx (tailbone) (Fig. 1).

The symptoms of a fracture of the spine depend upon where it occurs. If it is a minor fracture, the symptom is often only pain. The pain is usually a sharp burning sensation, and almost any type of movement will aggravate the discomfort. In most situations, after the precipitating event, the pain will become quite severe and will prompt the patient to seek medical attention. After a traumatic event, the patient should be kept flat and should not be moved. Medical help and an ambulance should be called. If the pain involves the neck, the head must not be moved. If the accident occurs at home, two towels rolled side-by-side can be placed along the patient's neck and a piece of tape placed from one towel across the patient's forehead to the next towel in order to keep the neck in proper alignment. The patient should be instructed not to move. If the pain is in the spinal column below the neck, again, the patient should be kept flat and not allowed to stand or move.

There are many types of fractures of the spine. Fractures can occur in the anterior (front) or posterior (back) part of the spine (Fig. 2A and B). Some are called stable fractures and others are referred to as unstable. A stable fracture means that a bone has been broken, but the injured bony segment has not been displaced out of alignment and does not have a deformity that would compromise its ability to withstand stresses and loading forces. A stable fracture will cause pain, but should heal without surgery

(Fig. 3). An unstable fracture is a more serious matter. The injured bone has been disrupted or the anchoring ligaments around the spine have been damaged to the extent that the fractured bone has a great chance of moving and potentially causing neurological injury (damage to the spinal cord and nerves) (Fig. 4). An unstable fracture cannot tolerate any further stress or other types of spinal loads without further collapsing. A good way to think about fractures of the vertebral bodies is to envision that the vertebral bodies are soda cans. The soda cans are stacked on top of each other with a jelly doughnut (the intervertebral disc) separating the cans. When normal pressure is placed on the can, the can tolerates the load and will not change its shape. As more pressure is added to the soda can, the can itself will begin to deform. As the load on the can increases, the can's deformity increases. Initially, there is only a slight change in the configuration of the can; therefore, the can will still be able to support the column of cans. It is still stable. As the stress forces are increased, the deformity increases and the chances that the can will be able to continue to withstand the added loads are greatly reduced. The forces acting on the can eventually will crush it. The can will lose its height and its sides will rupture. The can has fractured. The can is no longer able to support the weight of the other cans above and below it. It is unstable.

This same mechanical problem may happen in a fractured spine. A vertebral body subjected to stresses and forces that it is unable to tolerate will fracture (Fig. 5A, B, and C). It has been pushed beyond its "breaking" point. If the broken can is placed onto its side, it is no longer under severe stress. The same situation occurs in a fractured spine. Therefore, an injured individual should not sit upright or stand because any added stress to the fracture may cause more deformity and increase the risk of more injury. That's why it's important to lie down. Lying down will help prevent any further deformity of the injured bone. It's extremely important for an individual with a suspected spinal fracture to lie flat. An often-used classification system to determine the stability of an injured vertebra is based on a three-column theory of the spine developed by a spine surgeon named Denis. The Denis technique divides the spine into three distinct columns: anterior (front), middle, and posterior (back). The anterior column includes the anterior ligament and the anterior two-thirds of the vertebral body and the disc. The middle column comprises the back third of the vertebral body, the disc, and the posterior ligament. The posterior (back) column is made of the pedicles (walls of the vertebra), facet joints, and spinal ligaments (Fig. 6). The middle column is the key to the determination of stability and safety of a fracture. If the middle column is not involved in the fracture, the fracture may be stable. If the anterior and middle columns or the posterior and middle columns are injured, the spine is unlikely to be stable. In such a situation the spinal cord and nerves are at risks of injury. In addition, the fractured bony elements may progress, fracture more, and cause a spinal deformity. Many times such deformities are pain-producing sites.

The spine is a bony column that protects the spinal cord and nerves. If the spine becomes damaged and unstable, the spinal cord and nerves are at risk for injury. Once a patient has been transported to an emergency department, numerous physicians, nurses and other healthcare providers will become part of the patient's care. It is helpful for a patient or witness to the trauma to try to remember as much as he or she can about the event. The physician will ask many questions that will help to determine what type of injury the patient may have sustained. Some of the common questions that will be asked are:

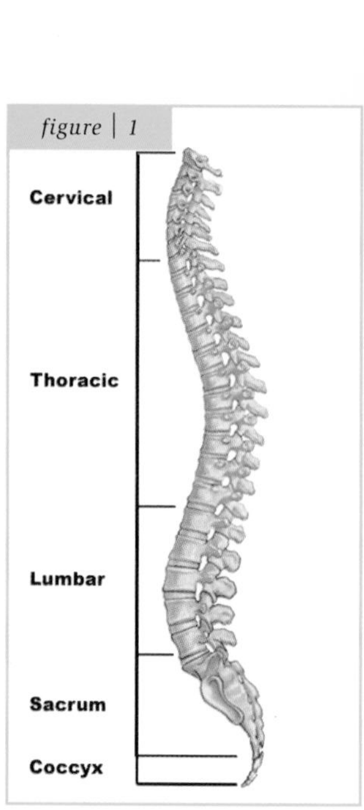

Fractures can occur anywhere along the spinal column.

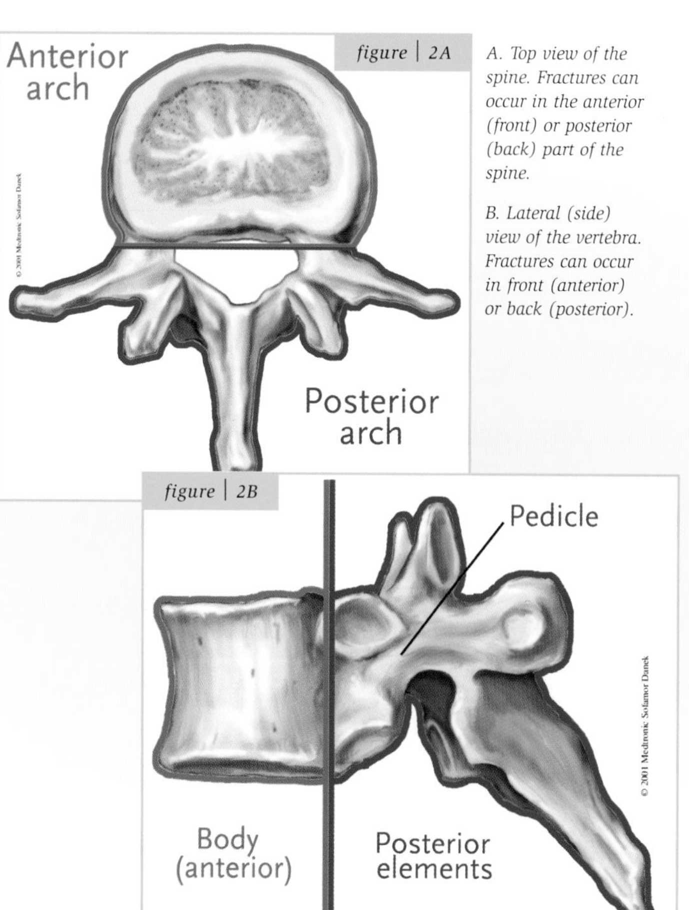

A. Top view of the spine. Fractures can occur in the anterior (front) or posterior (back) part of the spine.

B. Lateral (side) view of the vertebra. Fractures can occur in front (anterior) or back (posterior).

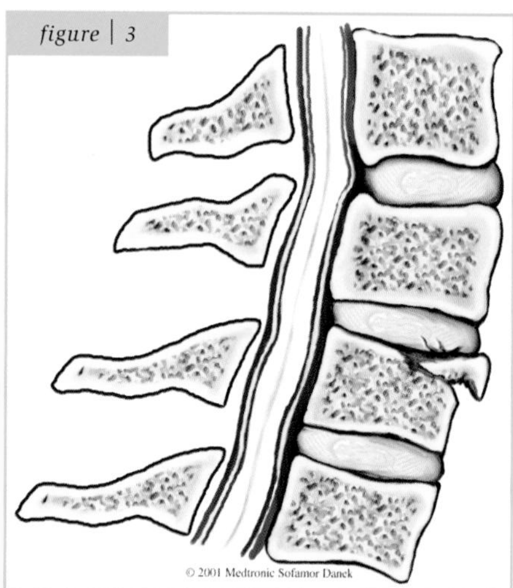

Stable fracture: Anterior (front) part of vertebra is fractured, but still able to support the weight of the vertebra above and below.

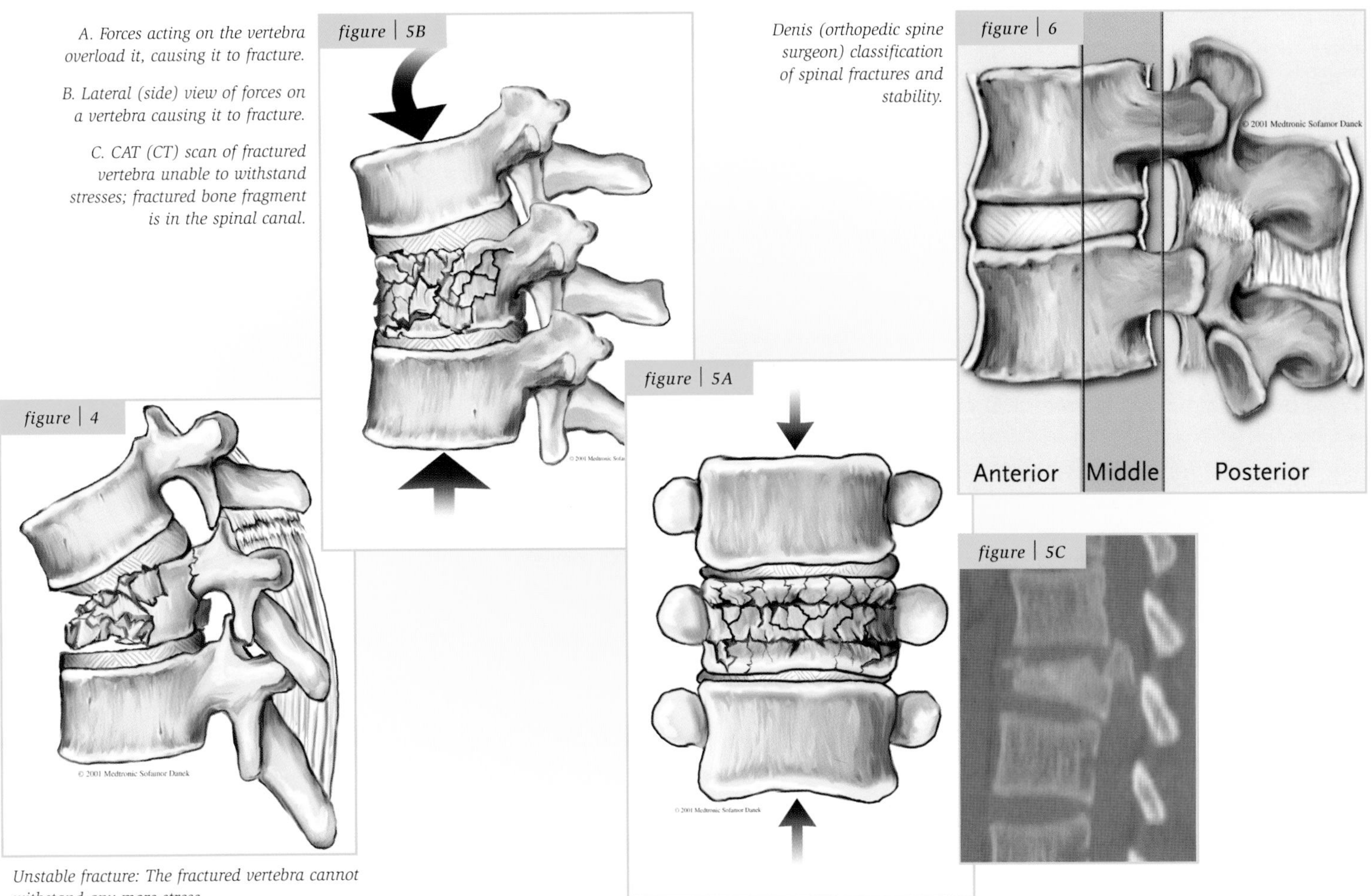

A. Forces acting on the vertebra overload it, causing it to fracture.

B. Lateral (side) view of forces on a vertebra causing it to fracture.

C. CAT (CT) scan of fractured vertebra unable to withstand stresses; fractured bone fragment is in the spinal canal.

Denis (orthopedic spine surgeon) classification of spinal fractures and stability.

Unstable fracture: The fractured vertebra cannot withstand any more stress.

1. What is your name?
2. How old are you?
3. Where do you live?
4. Do you know where you are?
5. Do you know what happened?
6. Did you lose consciousness?
7. Where is the pain?
8. Do you have pain in the neck or back?
9. Do you have any numbness, tingling, burning, sharp sensations or pain in your arms or legs?
10. Did you lose control of your bowels or bladder?
11. Can you more your arms and legs?

If a patient fell and hit his or her head, resulting in loss of consciousness, it is important that this information be related to the healthcare providers. Other common questions asked of a patient with a suspected spinal fracture are: "Where do you feel the pain?" and "How bad is the pain?" A zero to ten (0–10) scale is used by many physicians and healthcare providers (Fig. 7). The zero means that the patient has no pain at all. A ten on the pain scale is the most severe pain. If the pain radiates from the neck into the arms or from the back into the legs, it is important that the physician knows this information. The physician will also want to know if there is any numbness or tingling sensations associated with the pain. The physician will ask the patient about breathing or coughing: do they make the pain worse? A very important question is whether or not the patient has had any problems with his or her urinary bladder or bowels since the accident, meaning incontinence or retention. Loss of control of urine or inability to urinate may indicate a spinal cord injury.

The treating doctors will perform a physical examination. They will look at the patient's head and eyes, and they'll gently palpate the neck. The ambulance team will probably put a cervical collar on the patient's neck. The patient, family or friends should never remove it; only a doctor should do this. The doctor will also gently palpate along the patient's entire spinal column. He'll also perform other examinations including testing reflexes, sensation with pinpricks, and a rectal examination. The more information a healthcare team can harvest, the better chances they have of finding the problem. Any point-tenderness found on the examination will allow the doctor to pinpoint the site of a possible fracture. X-rays will be obtained of the cervical, thoracic and lumbar spine.

X-rays are taken from many different views. If there is evidence of an unstable fracture of the cervical spine (neck), special medical tongs may be attached to the patient's head to keep the fractured bones from moving and causing more injury. Depending on the findings of these X-rays, a doctor may suggest other testing. It's common to further evaluate a suspected spine fracture with computerized axial tomography (CAT or CT scan). A CAT (CT) scan will allow a radiologist and physician to examine the bony architecture of the spine in more detail. Special slices taken of the spine will allow better evaluation of each single segment. The CAT scan can also be programmed to obtain other views of the spine, i.e., reconstruction views. These views will demonstrate the bones of the spine from a side view. This representation of the spine is referred to as a sagittal reconstruction view (Fig. 8). The type of fracture and the degree of bony compromise are important pieces of information needed by the treating doctors in order to determine whether or not the bony fracture is stable and what subsequent treatment will be needed. The CAT (CT) scan often provides a better overall image than X-rays of the bony elements of the spine.

In certain situations, other testing will be needed. Magnetic resonance imaging (MRI) may be recommended. The MRI will be able to reveal and demonstrate soft tissue structures better than the CAT (CT scan). The MRI will allow the radiologist and treating physicians to evaluate the spinal cord and the spine better than the CAT scan. The MRI will demonstrate if the spinal cord has been bruised or injured (Fig. 9). In addition, the MRI will reveal ligamentous injury. The ligaments are the ropes that bind the vertebral bodies together. Some fractures may have an associated ligamentous injury. The presence of a ligamentous injury may alter the course of therapy. If a ligament has been damaged to the extent that it has been torn, it may not be able to hold the bony structures in alignment and may allow the bones to move too much. Such abnormal movement may cause damage to nerves or the spinal cord and surgery may be needed. In an acute traumatic spine situation X-rays, CAT (CT) scans and MRIs usually provide added information to direct therapies. However, there are some situations in which a fracture is not acute; it may have happened weeks or months ago. The patient usually recalls the event, but the pain was not of a nature that prompted immediate evaluation. It's just a constant nagging pain that now brings the patient to the doctors. The CAT scan or MRI may give some indication that the fracture is not new. An old fracture may need no further therapy. In some situations, another test may be called upon to answer the question when there is doubt; such a test is a nuclear bone scan. This test may help determine the age of the fracture. All the information put together will help the doctor determine what course of therapy will be needed for each individual patient.

If a fracture is determined to be a minor fracture and is not unstable, which means that it's not prone to move in any abnormal fashion, the patient will be treated conservatively with medical management. If the injury is in the cervical spine, the patient may be placed into a collar. There are many types of collars or braces, ranging from soft to more rigid (Fig. 10A and B). A soft collar offers a slight amount of support. Its main job is to remind the patient that he or she has a problem and should not do certain activities. Other collars are also available; they are firmer collars ranging from Styrofoam to hard plastic. The patient will wear the collar depending upon what type of fracture and how long it will take the fracture to heal. The patient must always wear the collar as instructed by his doctor. Removal of the collar or brace should only be done with the instruction of a physician.

If a fracture of the cervical spine is unstable but does not require surgical therapy, a halo device may be needed. Such a device is affixed to the patient's skull with screws; these screws are then attached to a carbon halo or circular device, which is then affixed to a vest (Fig.11). It is almost like putting a patient into a birdcage. The patient will remain in the halo 24 hours a day and follow-up X-rays of the cervical spine will be obtained to determine the healing stages of the fracture. Healing may take three to four months. Individuals who smoke may have a longer period of time in the halo because cigarette smoking will impede bone healing. Some patients who need a halo device may opt for surgical therapy because they just will not be able to tolerate being placed into such a device. Fractures lower down in the spine, the thoracic (mid-spine), or the lumbar spine, may need a firmer orthotic device made of plastic and called a thoracic-lumbar-sacral orthotic device (TLSO) (Fig. 12A and B). The common feature of these orthotic devices—cervical, thoracic or lumbar—is that they're never comfortable. Nobody likes being placed into such a device, but if the device allows a fracture to heal, and to heal with good alignment, then it's worth putting up with the inconvenience. Meticulous care of the skin under the collar or any orthotic device is extremely

figure | 7

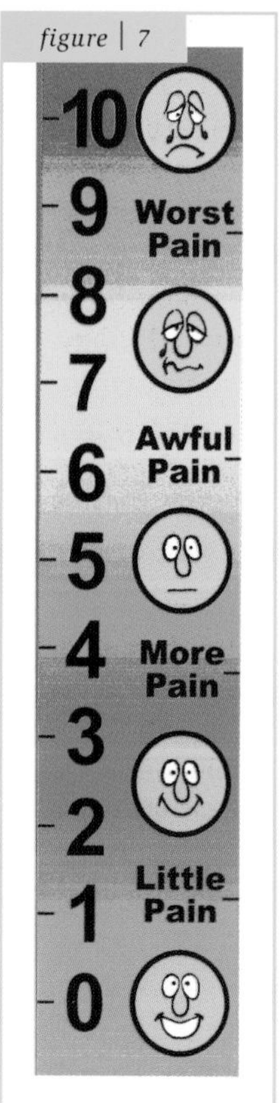

Pain scale often used by physicians and healthcare providers.

figure | 8

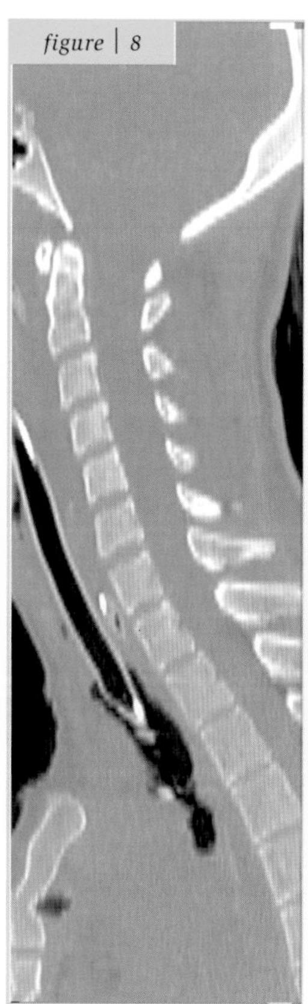

CAT (CT) scan: Sagittal (side view) reconstruction of the cervical spine (neck).

figure | 9

MRI: Lateral (side) view demonstrating a fracture of the cervical spine (neck) with spinal cord edema.

figure | 10A

figure | 10B

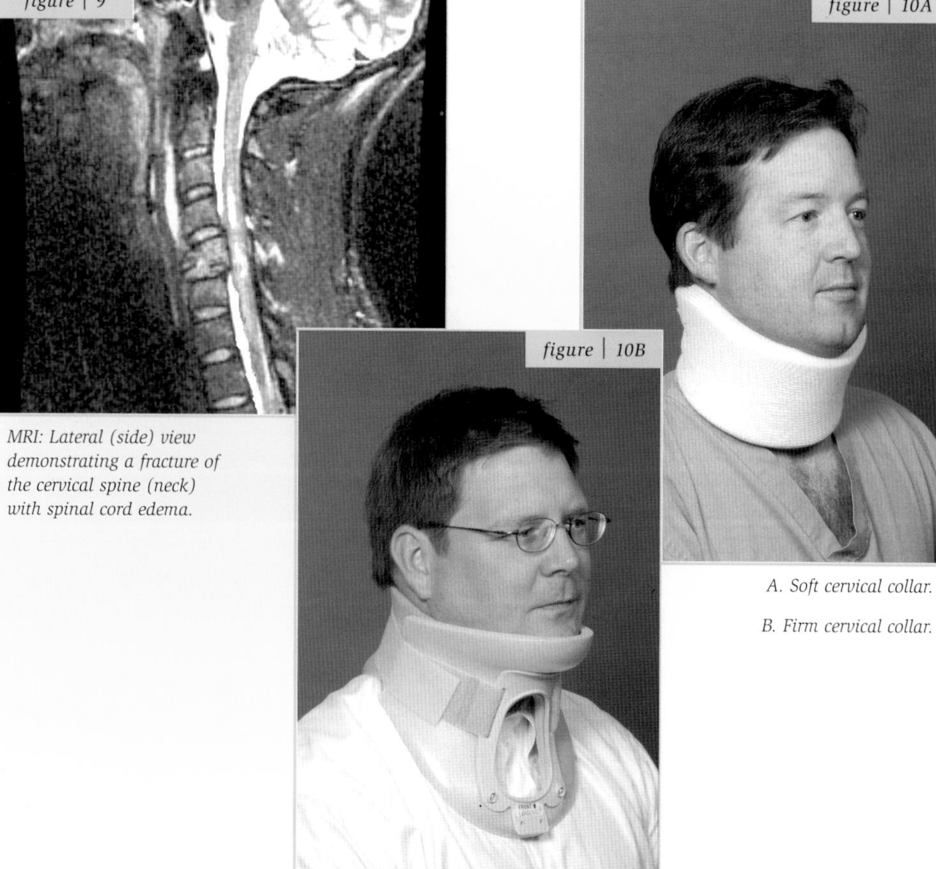

A. Soft cervical collar.

B. Firm cervical collar.

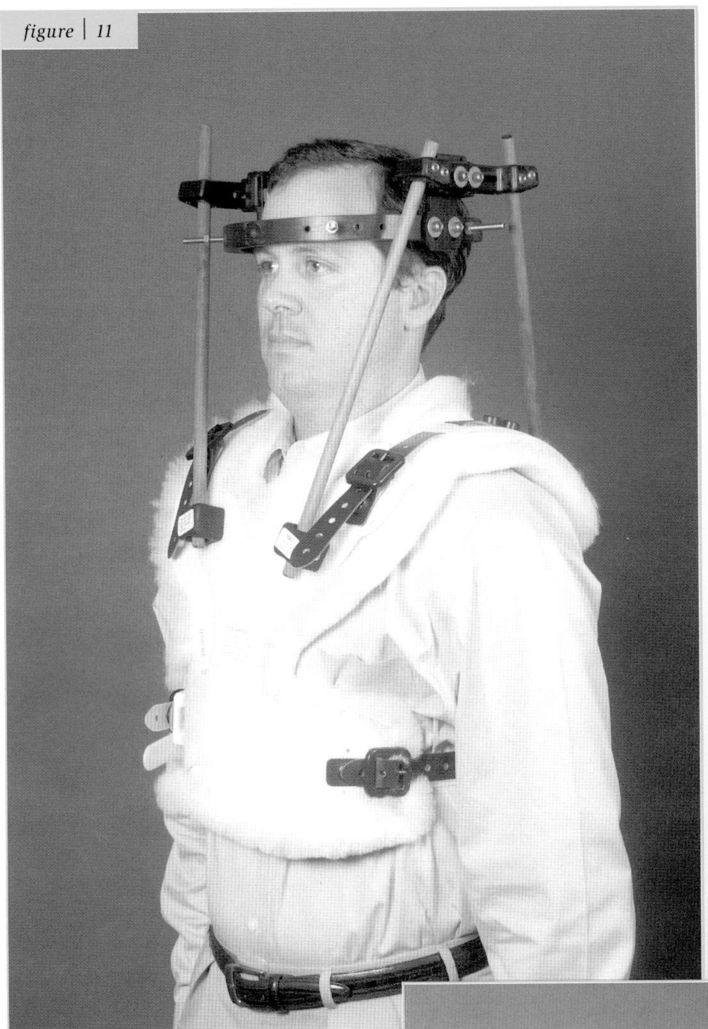

figure | 11

Halo device with fur-lined vest. MRI compatible, able for patient to be placed into an MRI.

figure | 12A

figure | 12B

A. Thoracic-Lumbar-Sacral Orthosis (brace), front view.

B. Thoracic-Lumbar-Sacral Orthosis (brace), side view.

important in order to prevent breakdown of the skin and infection.

If a fracture is determined to be unstable due to the degree of bone that is fractured or allowed abnormal movements, which could further compromise the spinal cord or other nerves, surgical intervention will be recommended. Advancements in surgical techniques and the development of newer implants have allowed better reconstruction of the spine after traumatic events. Today, there are numerous types of metal spine plates, bone screws, rods, hooks and bone cages (Fig. 13A, B, C, D, and E). In addition, advancements in carbon engineering have brought about the use of carbon bone cages for some types of spinal reconstruction (Fig. 14A and B). All metal implants are usually made of a material called titanium. Titanium is a metal that will allow better imaging and radiological tests after surgery. Carbon implants provide a good view of bone healing.

The fracture site, the type of fracture, and its location will determine the avenue through which the surgery will be performed. If a fracture is in the front of the neck, the surgery most likely will be performed from in front of the neck; however, there are also techniques to stabilize the spine from the back. The same situation exists for the rest of the spine; if there's a fracture in the front, oftentimes the surgeon will address the fracture from the front or side of the spine (Fig. 15). If the fracture is in the back, the surgery will be addressed from the back with placement of rods, screws or hooks (Fig. 16A and B). Sometimes due to severe unstable spinal fractures placement of internal devices will be needed both in front and back of the spine (Fig. 17). These devices are referred to as "hardware." Regardless of the type of fracture, a bone grafting procedure will be needed. The surgeon is like a farmer; he or she is planting bone seeds into a patient so the bone seeds will mature and grow into a solid, healed bony structure. The patient is the soil; therefore, it is the patient who will actually do the fusion. If the patient smokes, bone healing will be delayed; thus, it is important for any patient undergoing reconstructive spine surgery with bone grafting procedures to seriously think about stopping this habit. The bone used in bone fusion surgery is harvested from the patient, usually from either the ribs or hips (the iliac crest). In certain fractures, the bone graft used is actually the broken bone, the fractured bone itself. This broken bone can be placed into a bone cage, either metal or carbon. The cage will be placed into the site from which the fractured or broken bone was removed. This is the spine reconstruction part of the surgery. The next phase of spine surgery involves internal fixation. The internal fixators are either rods or plates that are attached to the uninjured, neighboring, bone in the spine using bone screws (Fig. 18A, B, C, and D). It is these devices that will provide a safe environment for the spinal cord and nerves and the best spinal alignment for the bone graft to grow into a solid, long-lasting, healed bone. From a clinical perspective, usually a bone graft procedure will become clinically stable in about three to four months. In many situations, after undergoing spinal reconstruction, the patient will be placed into an external orthotic device, i.e., collar or brace. At the end of three to four months, if radiological studies demonstrate that the implants remain in good alignment and the bone graft appears to be healing, the patient may be allowed to slowly wean himself or herself from the orthotic device (Fig. 19). It will usually take bone a year and sometimes three years to become totally healed. This doesn't mean that the patient will have to wait one to three years before he or she can return to most of the activities of daily living. Therefore, following a physician's instructions is extremely important.

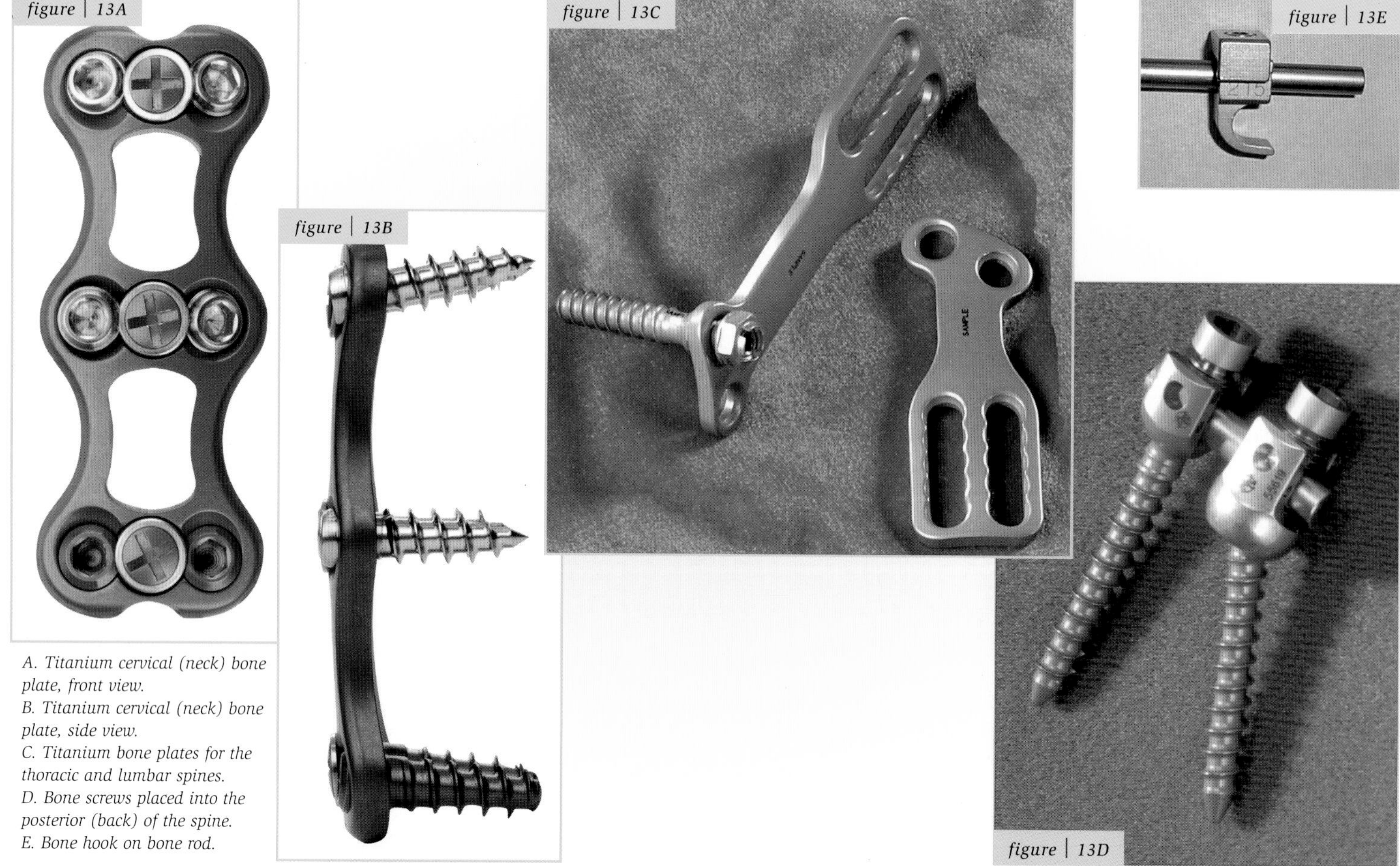

A. Titanium cervical (neck) bone plate, front view.
B. Titanium cervical (neck) bone plate, side view.
C. Titanium bone plates for the thoracic and lumbar spines.
D. Bone screws placed into the posterior (back) of the spine.
E. Bone hook on bone rod.

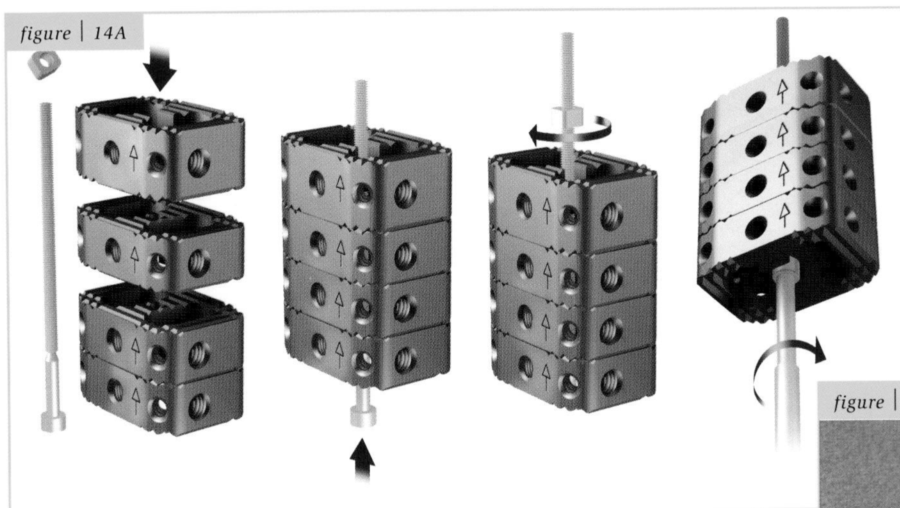

figure | 14A

figure | 14B

A. Stackable carbon bone cages. Cages are available in different sizes. They are stacked to the needed height and locked together with a titanium rod.

B. Carbon and titanium bone cages for reconstruction of the spine.

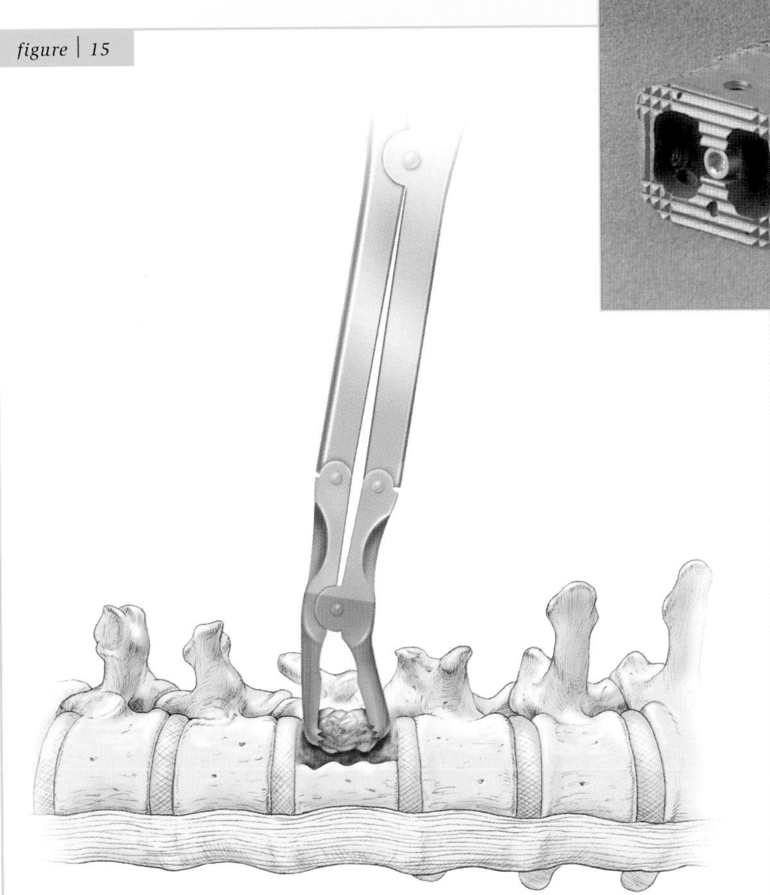

figure | 15

Removing bone fracture with a surgical instrument.

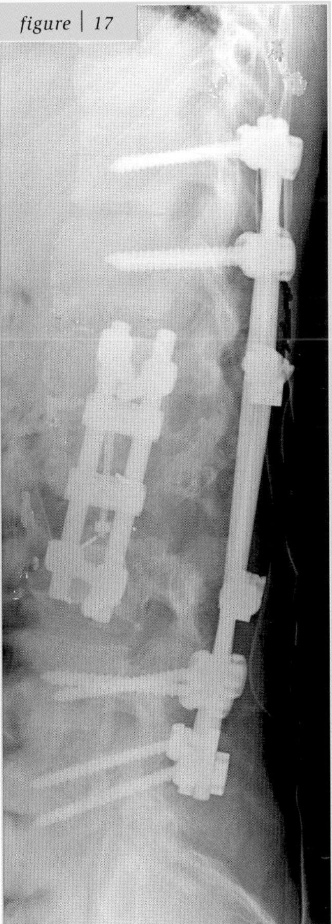

figure | 17

Lateral (side) view of surgical implants in front and back of the spine

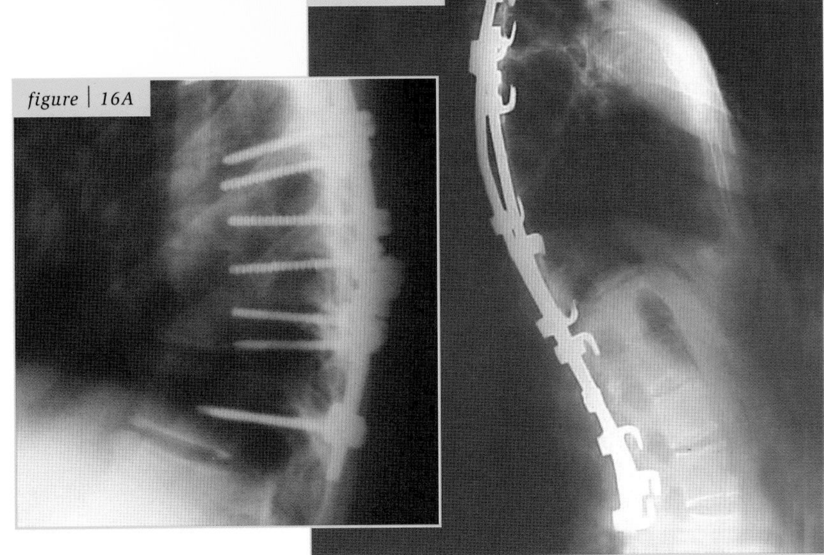

figure | 16A

figure | 16B

A. X-ray: Lateral (side) view of bone screws and rods in the back of the spine.

B. X-ray: Lateral (side) view of bone rods and hooks in the back of the spine.

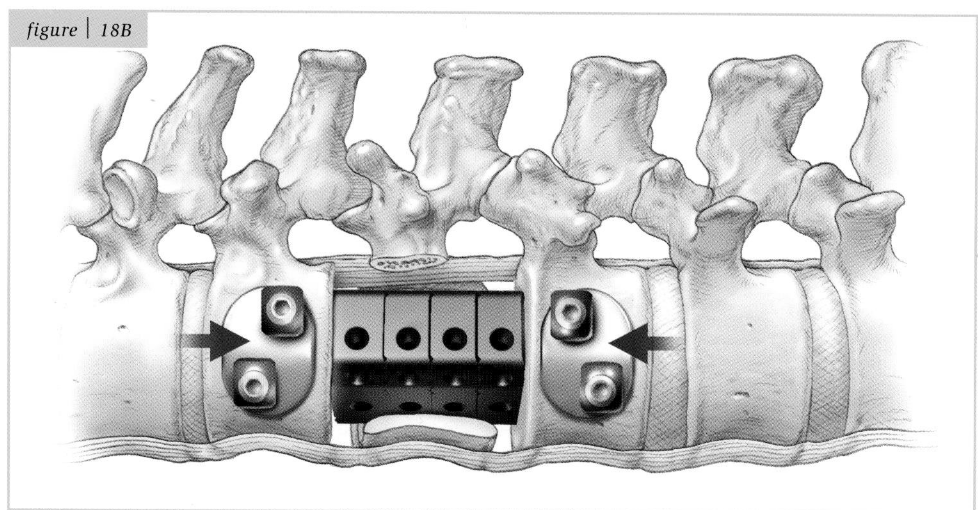

figure | 18B

A. Surgical instrument placing bone screw into vertebra.

B. Carbon cage placed into site of removal of fractured vertebra.

C. Attachment of bone rods to bone screws in vertebra.

D. Completed operation with insertion of carbon cages, bone screws and bone rods.

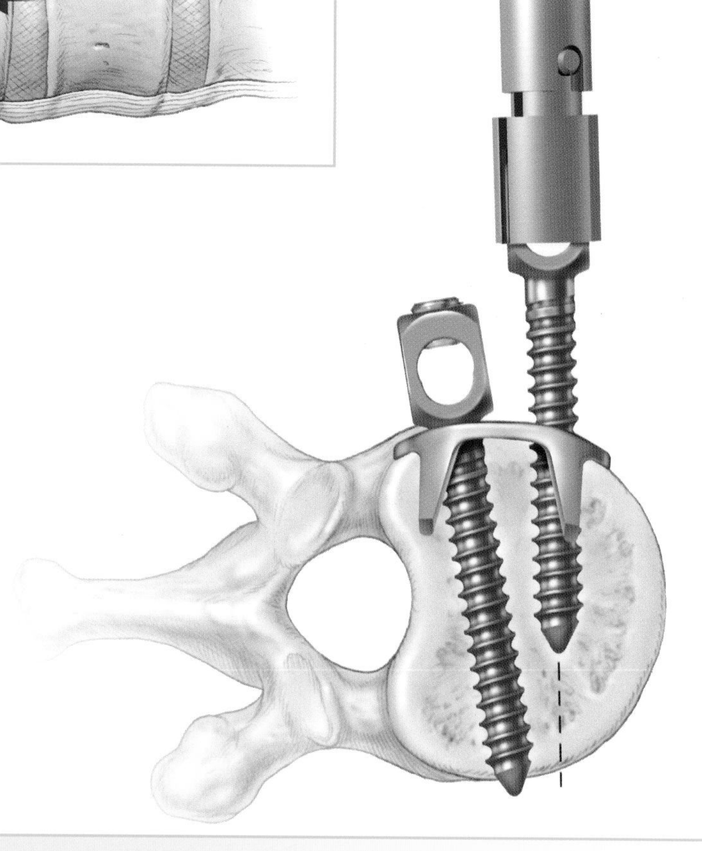

figure | 18A

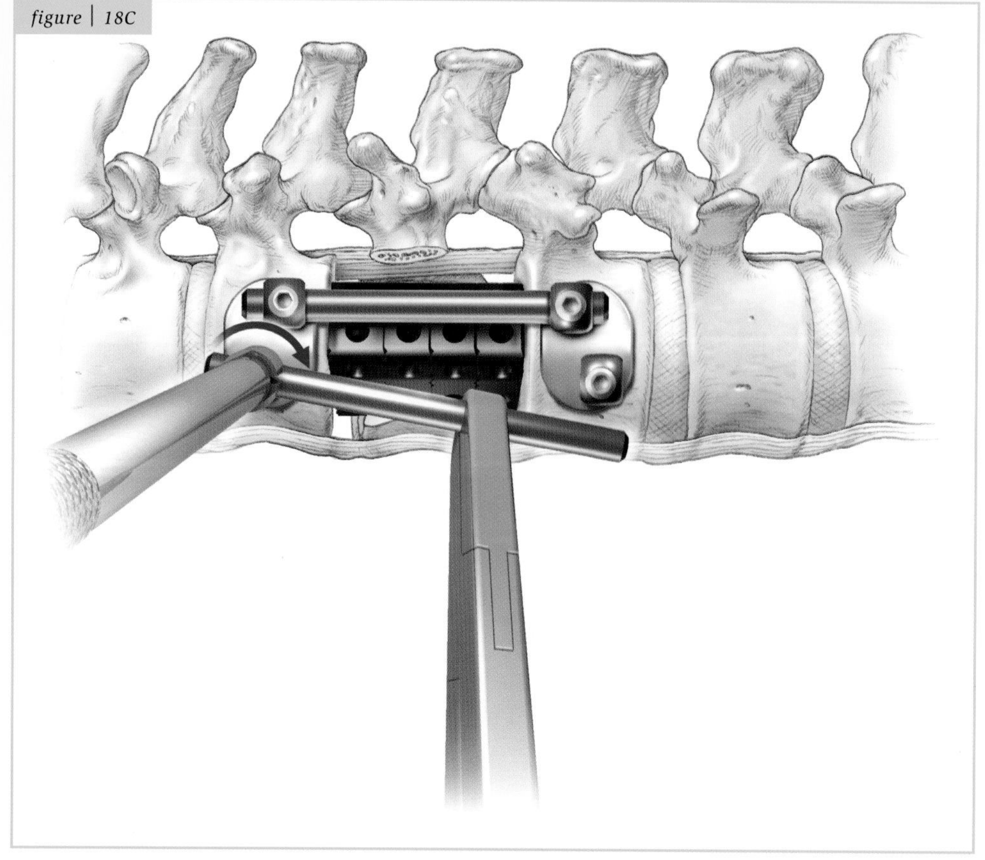

figure | 18C

figure | 18D

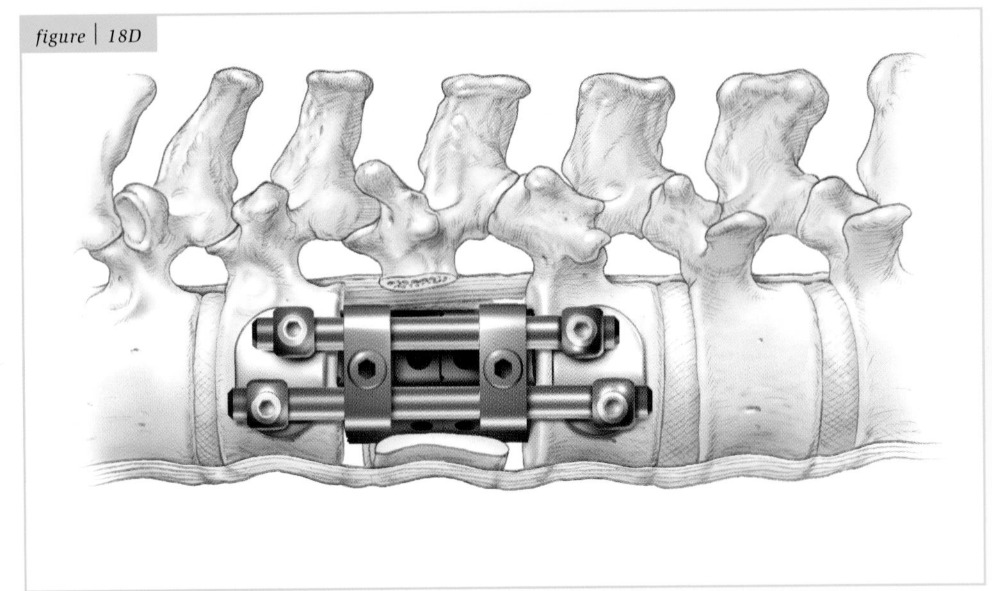

figure | 19

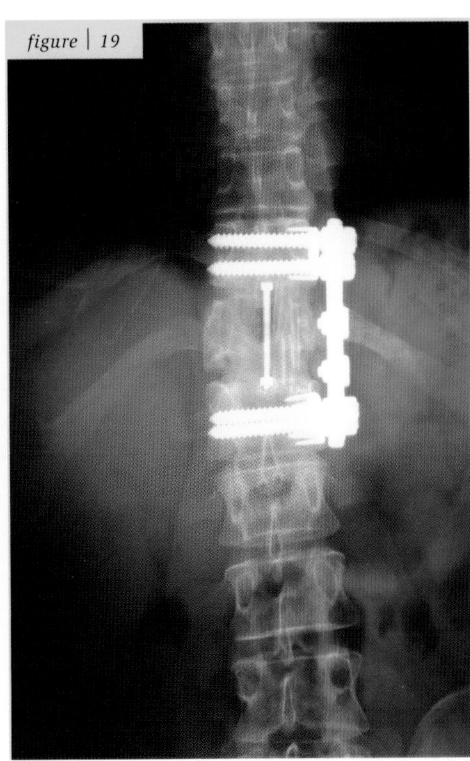

X-ray (front view) of carbon bone cage (Radiolucent) and titanium rods and screws.

If a patient does not need surgery and is treated with external orthotic devices, he or she will then be followed very closely by the treating doctor with physical examinations and radiological studies. If, after a period of time, the X-rays demonstrate that healing is taking place, the patient will then be weaned from the collar or brace; this means that each day he or she will wear such an external device less often. It is at this time that the patient may be referred to a physical therapist. The physical therapist will help to strengthen the musculature that was trapped within the confines of the brace or collar. Muscle within such bracing devices may become lazy; it certainly has not been exercising and most assuredly is not ready to jump into all the routines of daily living, including playing golf. This is where the physical therapist can help. The golfer needs to tell the therapist about his or her future intentions of returning to the game. A therapist with a special interest in the mechanics of golf will be very helpful. One should never return to playing golf without the okay of a doctor and physical therapist. If the patient has undergone surgery, it will take a longer period of time to return to golf. Again, a physical therapist with a special interest in golf will be needed. Playing golf with an implant is not impossible; it will take more work on the part of the golfer to build up important muscles needed to play a safe, painless round of golf. Depending upon what type of surgery was performed, either in front or back, the therapist will direct attention to those muscles first, and other muscles needed to play golf.

Returning to golf after sustaining a traumatic fracture requires commitment and dedication. Strengthening and flexibility exercises become extremely important if a golfer is to continue to play golf years beyond the traumatic event. Readjusting the golf thermostat will become a vital part of playing golf after sustaining a traumatic event, even more so if surgery was needed. Everything has changed. The golfer should start all over again, from top to bottom. The first thing needed to return to golf, after the patient has been released by his doctor and physical therapist, is to find a golf professional with experience teaching individuals with spinal problems. In fact, it may be helpful for the professional or the trainer to call, with the patient's permission, the physical therapist and the doctor to discuss exactly what has been done, what progress the patient has made, and what muscles and other structures were involved or compromised from the traumatic fracture. Such communication will be very helpful for the golfer, the released patient. The individual will need to evaluate his or her entire golf life. This includes shoes, clothing, clubs and golf bag. Here are some guidelines that may be helpful getting ready to play golf:

1. Check the golf bag. The golfer should only place needed items into the bag. The golf bag should not be a portable life support bag.
2. Don't overload the golf bag with too many balls. Unnecessary golf balls will only add weight to the bag. Old golf balls should be removed or stored elsewhere.
3. Choose a golf ball wisely. Golf balls are either hard or soft. The old compression rating for a golf ball was usually expressed as 90 (soft) or 100 (hard), with no unit of measurement after the number. A postoperative golfer should choose a softer ball, not a hard ball. Hitting a very hard ball will be like hitting a rock. A softer ball, when returning to golf, will often be better tolerated. As muscles become stronger and the golfer's confidence improves, ball selection may change.
4. The returning golfer should have the swing weight of his or her clubs re-evaluated. A golf professional will be needed.
5. If a golfer travels to the golf course in a car with a trunk and usually put his or her clubs into the

trunk, he or she shouldn't do this anymore. Put the clubs in the back seat; it's easier to slide the clubs in and out of the trunk than placing them into or taking the clubs out of the trunk (Fig 20A and B). In fact, in the beginning, it is best that the golfer not put the clubs into the car at all. He or she should ask a family member or a neighbor to help. And when the golfer arrives at the course, an attendant should be asked to take the clubs out of the vehicle. There's no reason to get into the heavy bending and struggles of a filled golf bag.

6. Riding in a cart depends on the golfer. For some patients the vibration of the cart may not be comfortable. Walking may be better. Walking and riding may be the answer. There is no law that states that both golfers must ride at the same time. The returning postoperative golfer should not carry a golf bag. Pushing a cart may be better tolerated than pulling. Electric or battery-powered walking carts may be the answer for some players. The golfer will still be able to walk, but without the strain of pulling or pushing a cart. If the golfer experiences discomfort or pain, he or she should not continue to play.
7. Aim for only nine holes. Playing from the 150-yard marker may help to prevent early fatigue.
8. It's very important, before the golfer approaches the first tee, that he or she performs warm-up exercises. In fact, it's helpful to walk from the clubhouse to the first tee and back again about three times. This will help to get things going, so to speak.
9. Make sure to follow all the other health rules of playing golf. All golfers should be well hydrated before, during, and after play. They must carry bottles of water in the cart during the round.
10. If during play, the golfer becomes fatigued, he or she need not feel ashamed to call it a day. The golfer is on the course to enjoy being out on the course again, have fun, and not to cause injury that will fill the up coming night with pain and misery.
11. After completing a round of golf, cool-down and stretching exercises should be performed.

Even though a golfer may have experienced a spinal fracture, perhaps requiring surgery with surgical implants, in many cases he or she will be able to return to golf after the fracture has healed (Fig. 21). For the golfer who sustained a spinal cord injury from the spinal fracture golf is still possible. The golfer with a history of a spine fracture should know the limitations of the spine. A golfer wishing to play golf forever must listen to his or her body. If golf causes pain for the player, a physician should be consulted. A golfer returning to play after a spinal fracture must be patient. It will take time to build up endurance and return to full play.

Many disabled individuals play and enjoy golf. The United States Golf Association, in the *Rules of Golf,* includes a section on golfers with disabilities. This applies to players who use wheelchairs, crutches, canes, and other devices for movement. Special golf aids and carts are available for spinal cord injured golfers as well as players who are visually impaired, amputees, joint replacement patients, and others with neurological diseases of the brain and spinal cord. Patients who have had certain strokes may also return to the links with special help and instruction. Many times the love of golf and the desire to play are strong motivating forces that assist the patient throughout rehabilitation and beyond.

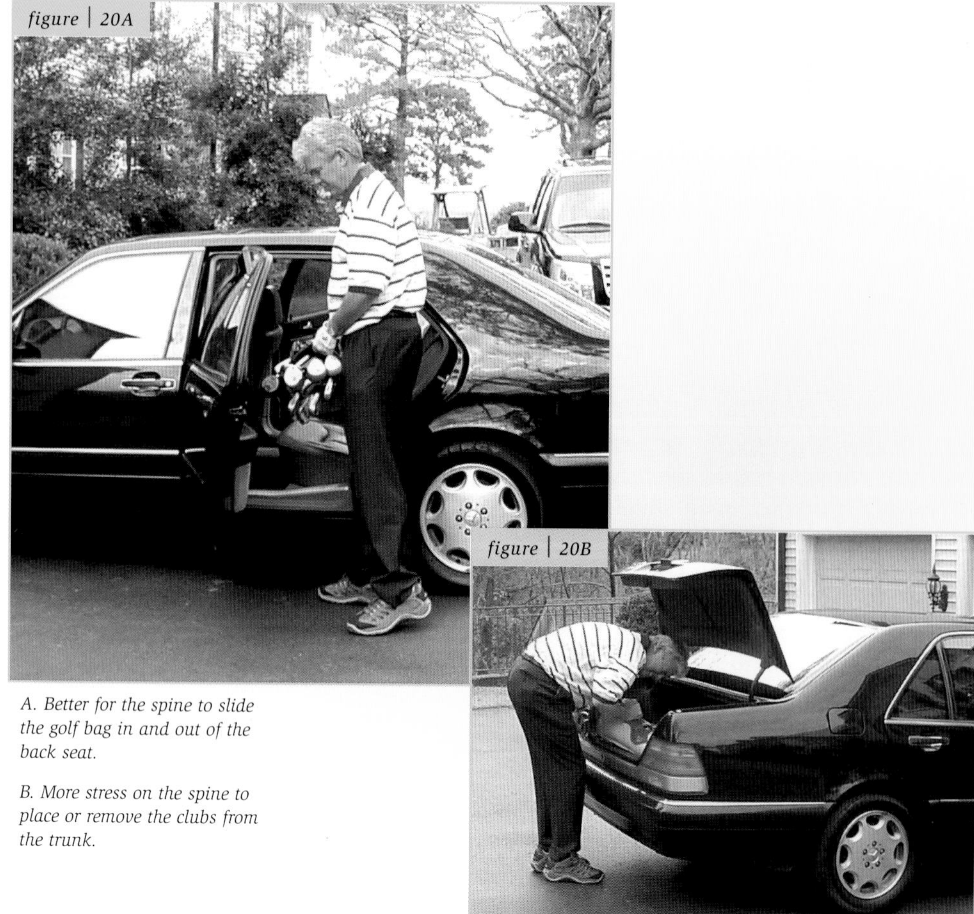

figure | 20A

figure | 20B

A. Better for the spine to slide the golf bag in and out of the back seat.

B. More stress on the spine to place or remove the clubs from the trunk.

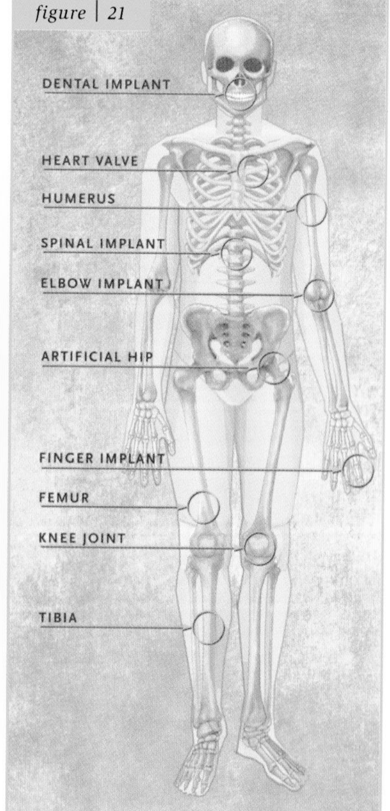

figure | 21

Body sites for different surgical implants. In most cases, the golfer will be able to return to play.

DIZZINESS, VERTIGO, AND YOUR GOLF GAME

CHAPTER 19

John L. Dornhoffer, M.D.

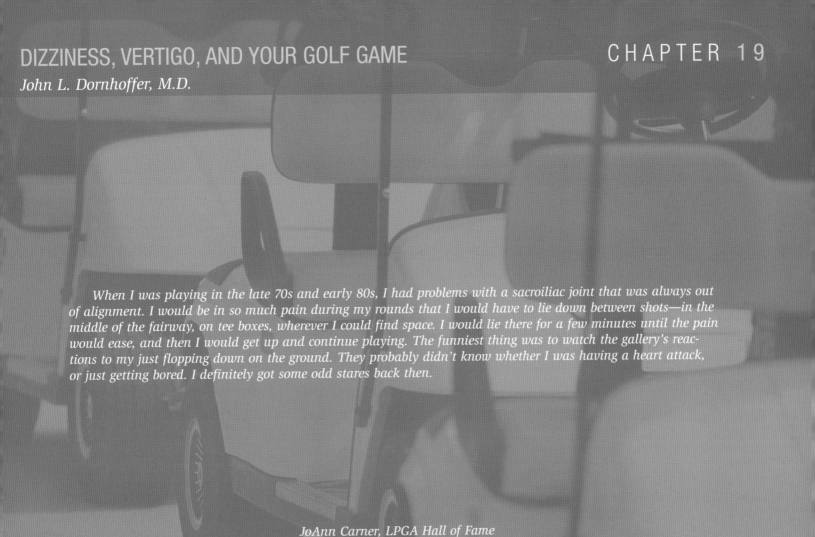

When I was playing in the late 70s and early 80s, I had problems with a sacroiliac joint that was always out of alignment. I would be in so much pain during my rounds that I would have to lie down between shots—in the middle of the fairway, on tee boxes, wherever I could find space. I would lie there for a few minutes until the pain would ease, and then I would get up and continue playing. The funniest thing was to watch the gallery's reactions to my just flopping down on the ground. They probably didn't know whether I was having a heart attack, or just getting bored. I definitely got some odd stares back then.

JoAnn Carner, LPGA Hall of Fame

OUR PERCEPTION OF BALANCE: DIZZINESS VERSUS VERTIGO

One of the many changes that occur with increasing age is an increased incidence of dizziness and vertigo. These two conditions are not the same. Whereas dizziness is a sensation of being off-balance, vertigo is a sensation of spinning with dizziness and is commonly associated with nausea, vomiting, and blurred vision. All of us have experienced dizziness at some point in our life, and many of us have experienced the sensation of vertigo or motion associated with our dizziness. The first condition can be more of a nuisance, but vertigo can be a truly debilitating condition, having a huge impact on quality of life—and the game of golf.

Our perception of balance represents a complex interaction between the balance system in the inner ear, the input from the eye, and input from proprioception, or our ability to feel what position our joints are in space. The brain acts as a computer to integrate all this information from these three systems and give us what we call balance. The balance system in the inner ear is able to recognize two types of motion: angular motion, which is sensed by the semi-circular canals in the inner ear, and linear motion, which is sensed by the otolithic organs. The otolithic organs are the part of the inner ear that contain little flecks of calcium, called otoliths. The otoliths allow us to sense gravitational pull and determine which direction is "up." Thus, in a zero-gravity environment, such as on the space shuttle, astronauts have a problem with balance because the otoliths are "unweighted" (floating). This conflicts with the information from the other two input systems (the eye and proprioception) and, as a result, many astronauts experience vertigo and motion sickness.

POSITIONAL DIZZINESS: CAUSES AND CURES

Many things can cause positional dizziness. A blood pressure that is too low, which can be a side effect of some high blood pressure medicine, can cause something called orthostatic hypotension, which is due to not enough blood getting up to the brain when positional changes of the head are made. This typically occurs when changing from a down to an upright position and is very brief. Dizziness due to orthostatic hypotension most commonly occurs in golfers when standing up after bending over to tee a ball or after retrieving a putt. This condition is usually only a minor nuisance and can be prevented by adequate hydration, especially on hot days. Water is the best thing for hydration; some beverages, such as alcohol and coffee, have chemicals that actually cause dehydration and should be avoided. It is important to recognize, however, that orthostatic hypotension can in some cases be severe enough to cause blackouts and falls. If a person experiences severe tunnel-vision or eminent blacking-out with standing, he or she should see a doctor to check the blood pressure while sitting and standing to assess this problem. Frequently, minor adjustments in lifestyle and medicines can take care of the problem.

A condition called vertebral-basilar artery insufficiency can likewise cause some positional dizziness that is related to decreased blood flow. This is frequently associated with a general increase in arteriosclerosis. With this condition, two blood vessels, the vertebral arteries, which supply oxygen to the part of the brain that provides balance, are affected.

These vessels, which travel through the spine, are pinched off when an individual looks up, causing dizziness and blacking out. This usually does not cause too much trouble with the golf game, but can cause problems with activities involving extreme upward gaze, such as changing a light bulb. This can be diagnosed by a doctor with something called a carotid Doppler and is usually treated with mild lifestyle changes. If severe, surgery can be performed to release the vessels from their bony canals.

A problem with the central nervous system, such as stroke and Parkinson's disease, can likewise cause some dizziness. The treatment of these conditions is individualized and is usually based on physical therapy.

BENIGN PAROXYSMAL POSITIONAL VERTIGO

Another condition that can affect a person's golf game causes positional vertigo, as opposed to the positional dizziness caused by the conditions described above. This is known as benign paroxysmal positional vertigo (BPPV) and is very common. If 100 people over age 65 are seen in a clinic specializing in balance disorders, over one-third will have this condition. In BPPV, the otoliths become detached from the otolithic organ and become lodged in a portion of the inner ear called the posterior semi-circular canal, which senses angular motion. When the otoliths become lodged in this portion of the inner ear, the individual notices brief but profound spells of vertigo when provocative head positions are made. The movement most likely to bring about the vertigo is rolling onto the affected ear while lying prone. Typically, after a delay of a few seconds, the individual will experience a crescendo of vertigo lasting approximately fifteen seconds, which then goes away.

Other head positions can also bring on the vertigo. For example, the next most provocative head position would be looking up or looking down; finally, looking over the shoulder will typically cause some disequilibrium and imbalance. All of these provocative head movements are common physical movements during a game of golf. In fact, golfers with BPPV typically describe attacks of vertigo when they step up to the ball and look down. After the sensation of vertigo subsides, the golfer is able to strike the ball. However, when he or she looks up to follow the ball, the vertigo recurs for a brief period of time, making it very difficult to track the shot. This is especially troubling during putting, when it is necessary to look up at the hole and down at the ball several times to ensure a straight shot.

Many factors are felt to contribute to BPPV, including increasing age, other types of ear problems, and trauma. This disease is seen more frequently in the aged, but it is certainly also common in younger individuals. Fortunately, BPPV is very easy to treat.

The treatment for BPPV is called canalith repositioning. As the name implies, the goal of the treatment is to move the otoliths back inside the otolithic organ, where they belong. The treatment, which can be done in just a few minutes, is associated with over a 95% success rate with one repositioning session. It is quite straightforward, can be done in any medical clinic, and has been in use in this country for over two decades.

The first step is to confirm the diagnosis and determine which ear has the loose otolith(s). This is done by an examination called the Dix-Hallpike. In order to do this test a person begins by sitting in the upright position on a bed or examination table. The individual then turns his or her head to one side and lies back until the head is able to hang over the edge of the bed or exam table while turned at a 45-degree angle, as seen in the illustration (Fig. 1). If BPPV is present in that ear, the room will start to spin after several seconds. The spinning will increase until it finally goes away in

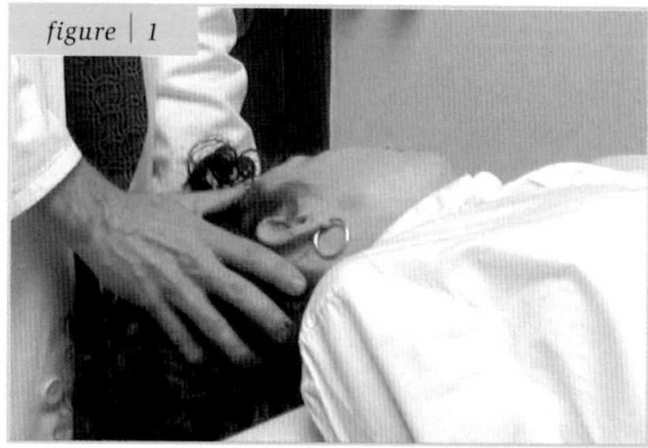

figure | 1

Canalith–left ear.

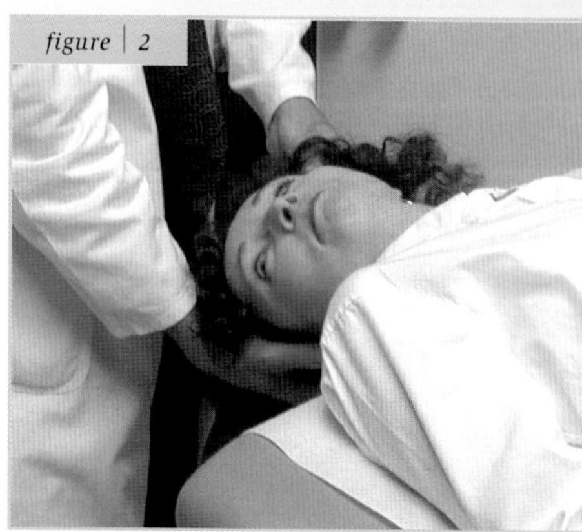

figure | 2

Canalith #2.

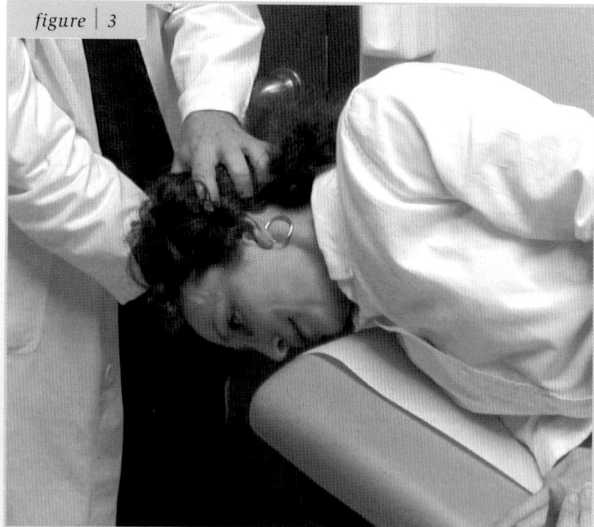

figure | 3

Repositioning canalith.

about 10 to 15 seconds. Each ear is checked, and the ear that causes the vertigo to occur (*i.e.,* left ear down or right ear down) will be the ear with the loose otolith. In addition to the vertigo that occurs while performing the Dix-Hallpike maneuver, there is a physical finding, called rotary downbeat nystagmus, that is associated with the vertigo. This is a jerky movement of the eye that is characteristic of this condition.

Once the diagnosis is made, a canalith repositioning can be performed. The patient lies in the same position as with the Dix-Hallpike. Once the vertigo subsides, and after approximately 30 seconds, the head is turned to the opposite side at 45 degrees while the individual remains in the supine position (Fig. 2). After waiting one minute, the head is rotated further in the same direction so that the individual's nose is now pointing toward the floor at 45 degrees (Fig. 3). After a minute or so, the person then rotates on his back and proceeds to sit up. This may cause a little bit of disequilibrium or imbalance for several hours, but by the next morning the person is usually feeling fine and the dizziness is completely gone.

Although canalith repositioning is quite simple, it is also quite effective in treating BPPV. Physicians reported a greater than 90% success rate in one trial using this technique. Although there is a 30% chance that BPPV can return over the next 5 years, it can be treated just as easily and effectively as the first time.

After treatment of BPPV with canalith repositioning, it is usually possible to return to the game of golf immediately. Even though most people are completely symptom-free the next day, it is sometimes helpful to stagger a bit after a bad shot. The explanation that you have "rocks loose" in your head usually results in a Mulligan instead of an argument.

REHABILITATION OF THE SPINE

CHAPTER 20

Thomas A. Boers, PT, MT

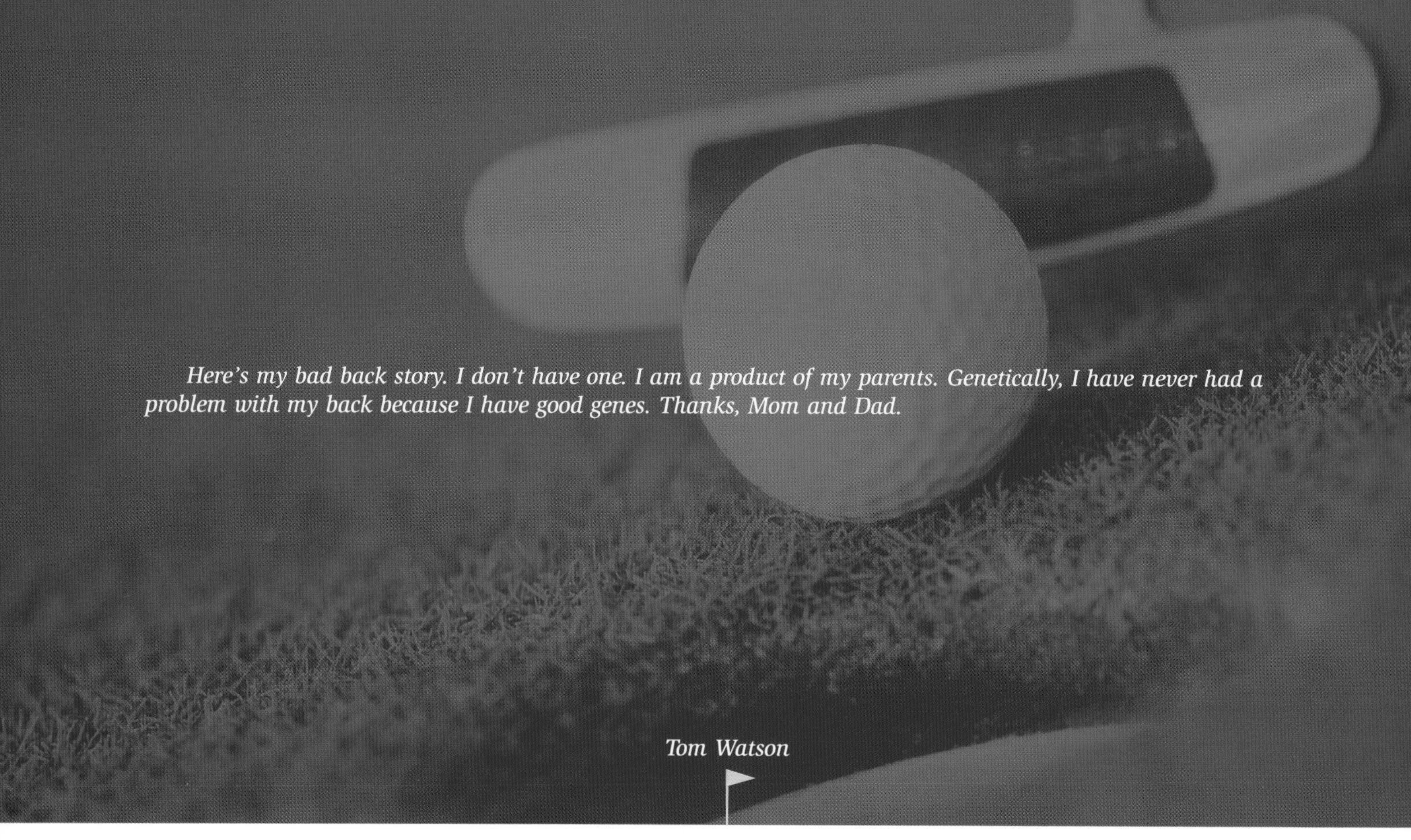

Here's my bad back story. I don't have one. I am a product of my parents. Genetically, I have never had a problem with my back because I have good genes. Thanks, Mom and Dad.

Tom Watson

Golf has the image of being bad for the spine. The contrary is true. A bad back is not good for golf.

Rehabilitation requires five steps:

1. Range of motion within the facet joints of the spine
2. Flexibility
3. Strength
4. Cardiovascular stamina
5. Coordination

Rehabilitation involves three types of spine problems:

1. Non-surgical back
2. Post-operative spine
3. General conditioning

RANGE OF MOTION

Rehabilitation of the spine requires several elements. The spine has to be able to perform multiple movements in order to be productive. It takes determination, commitment, and effort to recondition a painful, degenerative or postoperative spine.

The range of motion of the spine is probably the most overlooked aspect in the rehabilitation of the spine. It is also the most frequent cause of lower back pain. Flexibility, strengthening and cardiovascular rehabilitation exercises are not nearly as effective without the full range of motion in the facet joints (Fig. 1). The range of motion of the spine is a much more complicated physical examination than that of the knee or shoulder; therefore, it is often deferred.

The mechanics of the lumbar spine work like a kinematic chain reaction. Bending forward (flexion) or backward (extension) occurs in all spinal segments, including the sacroiliac joints and hips (Fig. 2). The major reason for loss of motion in the spine is overload in one or more of the facet joints. There is a subconscious protection mechanism (reflex) that protects the joint capsule from tearing. The muscles surrounding the joint disallow the motion in one or more directions. This reflex mechanism cannot be resolved by stretching exercises alone; often a physical therapist (manual therapist) has to unlock the involved facet joint in order to restore the normal range of motion. The spine is very clever in compensating for lost segmental motion; it simply bypasses the area of protected motion (Fig. 3). It takes extra muscle energy to do this, causing muscle spasms. The associated inflammation produces pain. It is very difficult to try to move an area of the spine that is protected by its own muscles. It is much easier to bypass it!

FLEXIBILITY

Flexibility has to do with muscle lengthening or stretch capacity. There are only a few muscles during the golf swing that are really challenged. Stretching exercises are used to get the muscles ready and warmed up before playing in order to prevent injury. Special attention must be paid to those muscles that have to be stretched during the golf swing; like the Left Shoulder Rotator Cuff muscles (right-handed player) in the back swing and Left Hip muscles at time of impact and follow through.

STRENGTHENING

The muscle strength of shoulders, back, and hips will play a very important part in injury prevention as well as maximizing a player's golf abilities. The key muscles involved are the stabilizers. Each joint is supplied with two types of muscles: the prime movers (muscles that actually make the joint move) and the stabilizers. The stabilizing muscles provide the necessary stability or compression to the joint that

Lateral (side) and posterior (back) views of the spine.

Movements of the spine.

Motion segment of the spine: The intervertebral disc and facet joints connecting any two adjacent vertebrae (functional unit of the spine).

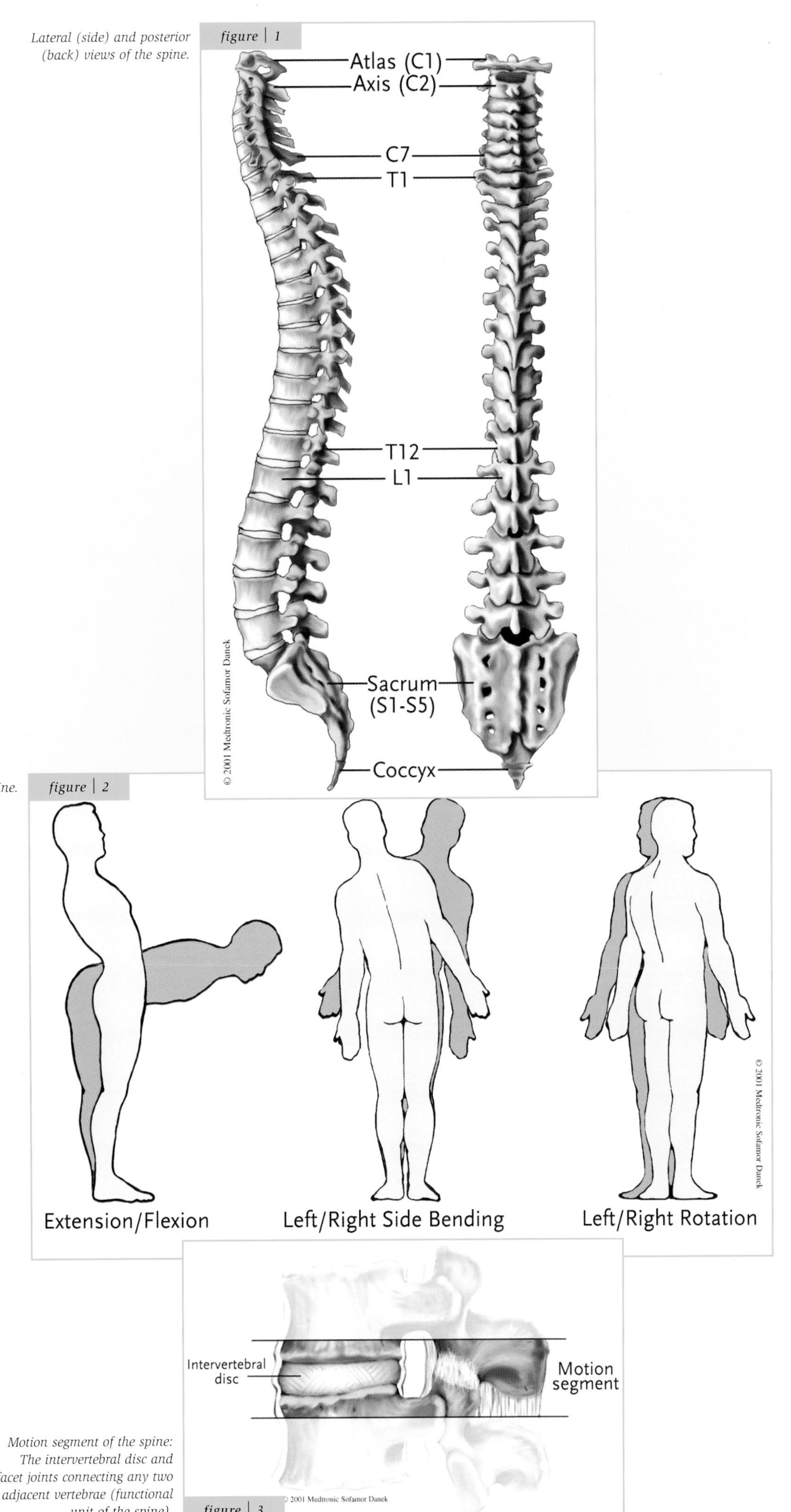

will enable the prime movers to act. There is no movement possible without the stabilizers' working.

CARDIOVASCULAR RECONDITIONING

Stamina allows us to play for as long as we need without losing form. Repeating the golf swing, especially in demanding terrain and possibly for more than one day, demands cardiovascular fitness. Aerobic exercises require a certain amount of repetitions over an extended period of time.

COORDINATION

It has been proven that the amount of energy spent swinging a golf club by a professional golfer is significantly less than a high handicapper. The reason is economy; the professional does not waste movement. Sound fundamentals and practice are key ingredients to reducing unnecessary energy. This does not mean that everybody has to swing the same way.

RANGE OF MOTION EXERCISES

Full range of motion is end-range in the joint without muscle guarding. The repetitions are relatively low, 5 to 10 repetitions per exercise. Especially in the early phase of rehabilitation, the joint capsule should not be overloaded; however, the exercise can be repeated several times throughout the day.

Extension:
- Prone on elbows (Fig. R1–1)
- Full prone press up (Fig. R1–2)
- Supine extension over Swiss ball (Fig. R2–14)
- Sitting lordosis (Fig. R1–3)
- Sitting kyphosis (Fig. R1–4)
- Standing extension (Fig. R2–12)

Flexion:
- All fours flexion (Figs. R1–5, R1–6)
- Sitting bent over (Fig. R2–11)

Rotation:
- Side-lying rotation (Fig. R2–1)
- Lateral Bending: (Fig. R2–9)

FLEXIBILITY EXERCISES

Flexibility exercises are important in the warm-up phase prior to playing golf. Exceptions are for those muscle groups (rare in the spine) that are truly contracted, thus making it impossible to swing the golf club along the correct plane. Important for the spine and hips are the Left Lateral Hip musculature as well as the Left Lateral Abdominal wall muscles (abdominal obliques and quadratus lumborum).

The exercises are held to a total of about 30 seconds in one or more repetitions with each of the muscle groups stretched. After 30 seconds, the muscle has reached its lengthening capability.

Flexion:
- Single knee to chest (Fig. R1–7)
- Double knee to chest (Fig. R1–8)
- Hamstring stretch (Fig. R2–8)

Rotation:
- Pelvic rotation supine (Fig. R1–9)
- Sitting rotation legs crossed (Fig. R1–11)

Lateral Bending:
- Standing lateral glide (Fig. R2–9)
- I–T band stretch (Fig. R2–10)
- Hip extension (Fig. R2–2)
- Hip abduction (Fig. R1–15)

STRENGTHENING EXERCISES

Strengthening exercises for the spine are divided into two groups. The first group is the stabilizers. The second group is the prime movers.

The **prime movers**, those muscles that actually make the motion, can only do so if the spinal joints are appropriately stabilized. The weakness occurs much more frequently in the stabilizers than in the prime movers. The **stabilizers** are all muscles that provide a rotational component.

The more repetitions per time with the strengthening exercises, the better. The goal is to fatigue the muscle groups that are exercised.

Stabilizing Exercises:

Spine:
- Abdominal obliques supine (Figs. R1–12, R2–3, R2–4)
- Prone Superman (Figs. R1–13, R1–14)

Hip:
- External/internal rotators (Fig. R2–13)

Prime Movers Exercises:

Spine:
- Abdominal crunches, upper and lower (Fig. R2–7)
- Back extensions prone (Fig. R2–4)
- Reversed sit-ups (Fig. R2–6)

Hip:
- Flexors, extensors and abductors (Figs. R3–1, R3–4, R3–5, R3–3, R3–2)

BACK TO GOLF AFTER SPINE SURGERY

Lumbar Laminectomy, Laminotomy:

The post-operative exercises following spine surgery are largely determined by the surgeon's preference and the post-operative symptoms. It is not uncommon to have residual sciatica or other nerve involvement, which will influence the post-operative rehabilitation course.

Post-operative exercises should contain the following:

- Range of motion for flexion and extension (see previous segment)
- Strengthening of the stabilizers and prime movers (see previous segment)
- Cardiovascular rehabilitation (walking)
- All exercises are initially done without gravity-loading.

Two to three weeks after surgery, rotational exercises for range of motion and flexibility are begun. The amount of spine degeneration will determine how many gravity-loading exercises can be done safely. There is significant stress on the spine in rotational with flexion gravity-loaded exercises. The spine's tolerance of loading forces depends on the energy absorption qualities of the intervertebral disc and facet joints, regardless of the muscle strength. Gravity-loading exercises may need to be avoided in the severe degenerative spine.

The first step in returning to golf is swinging the golf club at home. Take a 9- or 8-iron and produce a slow motion mini-golf swing, gradually progressing to a full swing before the speed factor is added to it. Swing-weighted clubs are not recommended in this phase. Stretch the back frequently in extension to unload the posterior structures.

It is safe to return to playing golf, if proper rehabilitation has been completed. The time frame will be around 6 t012 weeks, depending on the extensiveness of the surgery (one level disc surgery vs. multiple disc operations) and the preoperative conditioning status.

Rehabilitation after Lumbar Fusion

The rehabilitation and the return to golf after lumbar fusion (bone graft) surgery is far more complicated. Most bone fusion surgeries involve the placement of internal fixation devices such as bone screws, plates or rods. Bone fusion with fixation devices will cause the loss of motion segments in the spine. The goal of such surgery is to eliminate a given mobile segment of the spine that produces pain. This loss of motion may reduce pain; but it has to be taken into consideration, not only for postoperative exercises, but also for the golf swing. Most fusions will take approximately three to four months to begin to consolidate and at least 8 months to begin to solidify. Total bony fusion may not be achieved until one to four years after surgery. Smokers will take longer to heal. However, usually after three to four months the bony fusion is strong enough to allow the golfer to begin thinking about returning to playing. The return to golf exercises can be started after three to four months when the bone fusion shows signs of consolidation. The exercise program in the first three months is dependent on the surgical approach: whether

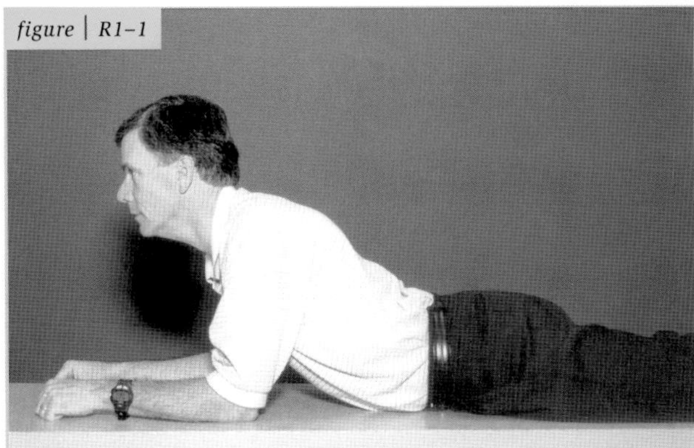

Prone on Elbows
Starting position:
Prone.
Raise up on elbows.
Relax lower back and hold for 5 counts, then return to prone position.

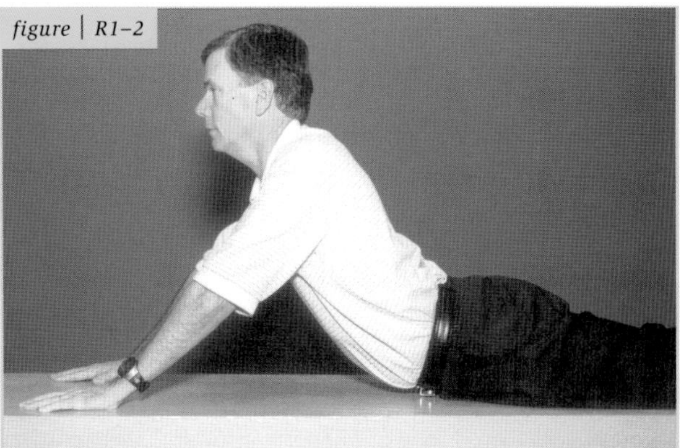

Full Press Up:
Starting position:
Prone.
Raise up on hands with elbows fully extended.
Relax lower back and hold for 5 counts, then return to prone position.

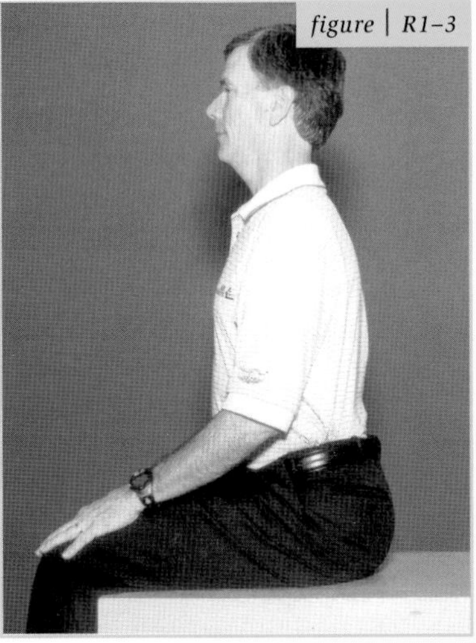

Sitting Lumbar Extension:
Starting position:
Sit straight.
Roll pelvis forward, arching the lower back, hold for 3 counts, then relax.

Most golfers will recognize our "model" in these photos as 1987 Masters Champion Larry Mize.

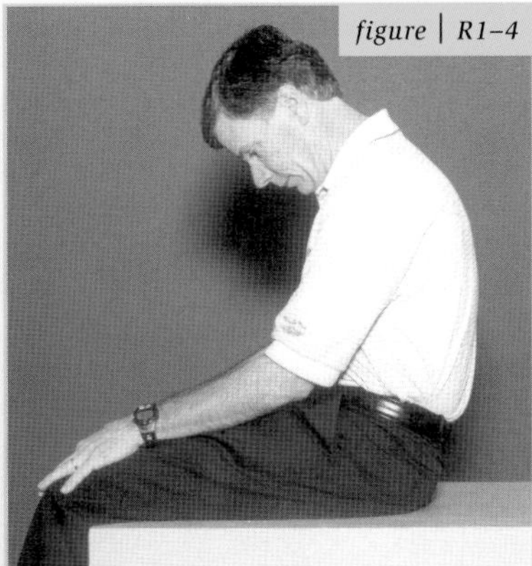

Sitting Lumbar Flexion:
Starting position:
Sit straight.
Roll pelvis backward, fully flexing the lower back, hold for 3 counts, then return to starting position.

Cat Stretch:
Starting position (5):
All fours.
Round the back and slowly sit on heels, hold for 5 counts, and return to starting position.

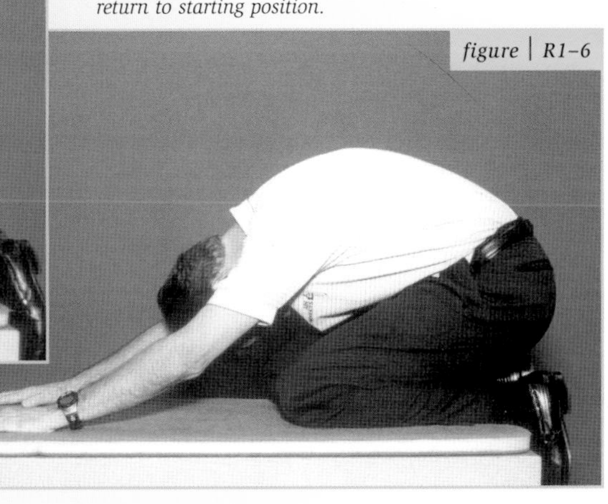

Upper Hamstring Stretch:
Starting position:
Supine, maximum flexion of the hip, hold hands behind the knee.
Extend knee until feel pull in the upper hamstring.

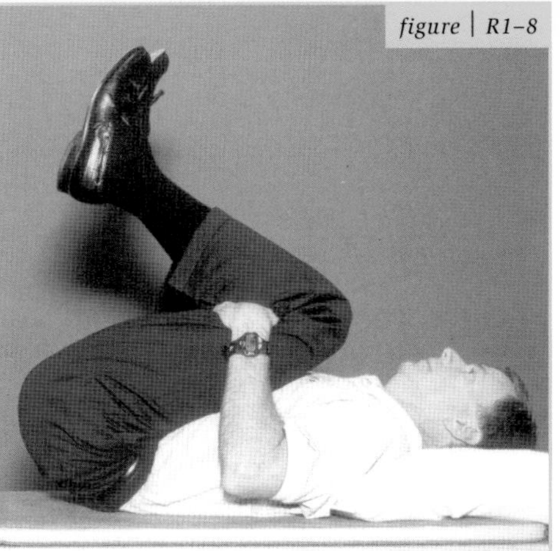

Double Knees to Chest:
Starting position:
Supine with knees in bent position.
Pull both knees toward chest, hold for 5 counts, then return to starting position.

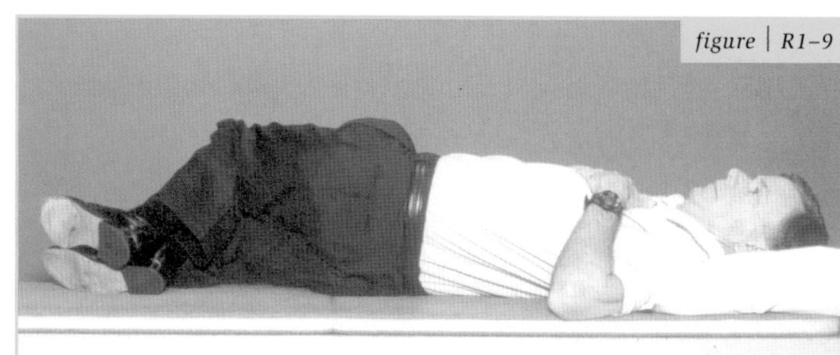

figure | R1-9

Pelvic Rotation:
Starting position:
Supine with both knees bent. Rotate both knees to one side, hold for 3 counts, then repeat on the other side.

figure | R1-10

figure | R1-11

Sitting Lumbar Rotation:
Starting position:
Sit with one leg bent and crossed over the other leg. Rotate back in the opposite position, hold for 5 counts, then repeat on the other side.

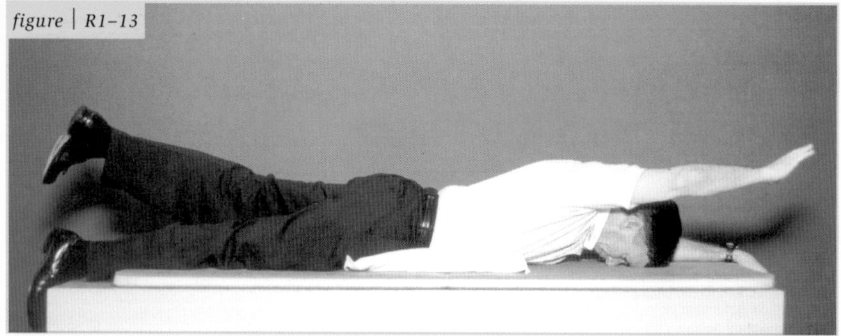

figure | R1-12

Abdominal Obliques Strengthening:
Starting position:
Both hands behind head, both knees bent. Bring R-knee and L-elbow together, switch and bring L-knee and R-elbow together.

figure | R1-13

Prone Pointer:
Starting position:
Prone with pillow under stomach. Raise R-arm and L-leg together, hold for 2 counts, then switch.

figure | R1-14

Prone Pointer on All Fours:
Starting position:
On all fours. Raise L-arm and R-leg together, hold for 2 counts, then switch.

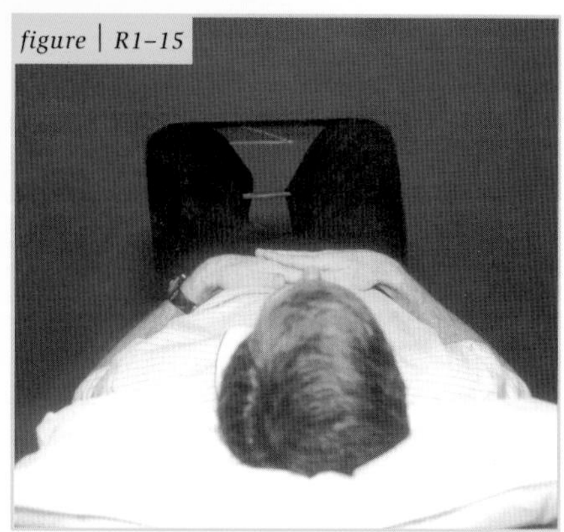

figure | R1-15

Hip External Rotation Strengthening:
Starting position:
Supine with knees bent, theraband around knees. Pull both knees apart, hold for 5 counts, then relax and repeat.

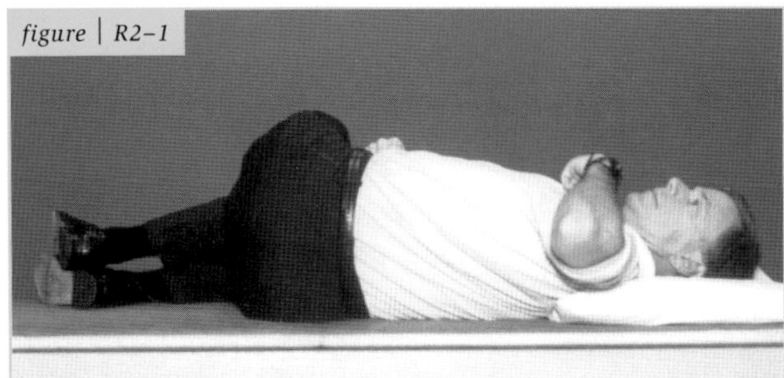
figure | R2-1

Upper Lumbar Rotation:
Starting position:
Side-lying with knees bent in 90° position.
Arch lower back and rotate shoulders backwards, hold for 3 counts, then return to starting position.

figure | R2-2

Hip Flexor Stretch:
Starting position:
Supine, hold hands behind R-knee; L-leg straight or hanging of the table.
Pull R-knee to chest until feel pull in L-front hip.

figure | R2-3

Abdominal Oblique Strengthening (Dead Bug modified):
Starting position:
Supine, L-arm above head and both knees flexed.
Press lower back into the table, bring L-arm to vertical position, bring R-knee up to a vertical position, hold for 2 counts, then switch.

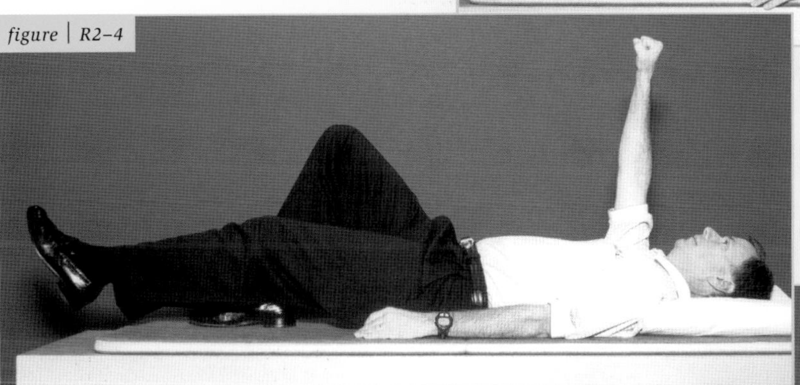
figure | R2-4

Abdominal Oblique Strengthening (Dead Bug modified):
Starting position:
As in #3, keep legs straight, lift leg slightly off the ground.

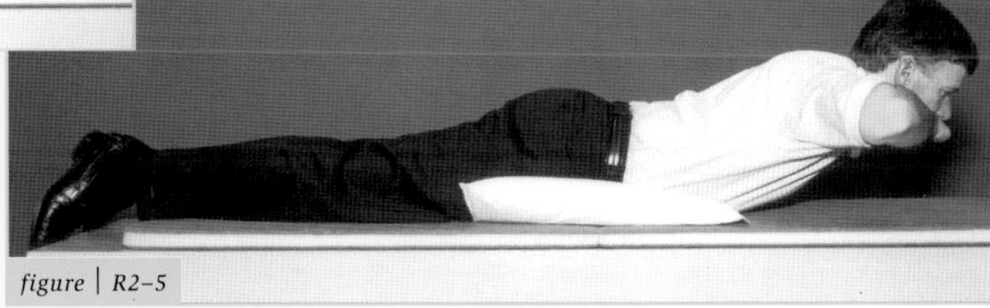
figure | R2-5

Prone Extension:
Starting position:
Prone with pillow under stomach.
Raise both arms and upper back from table, hold for 2 counts, then repeat.

figure | R2-6

Reversed Abdominal Curl:
Starting position:
Supine with knees bent.
Flatten lower back against table, raise both legs off the table, hold for 2 counts, then relax and repeat.

figure | R2-7

Abdominal Crunch:
Starting position:
Supine with both knees bent.
Raise head and shoulders, point fingers to knees, hold for 2 counts, then relax and repeat.

figure | R2-8

Lower Hamstring Stretch:
Starting position:
Supine, hold both hands behind one knee.
Straighten knee until feel pull in hamstring, hold for 5 counts, then relax and repeat.

figure | R2-9

Lateral Side Bend Stretch:
Starting position:
Stand.
Slide hand down on leg as far as possible, hold for 3 counts.

figure | R2-10

figure | R2-11

Sitting Flexion:
Starting position:
Sit on stool or Swiss ball.
Slouch lower back and flex forward as far as possible; hold for 3 counts, then roll slowly up to starting position.

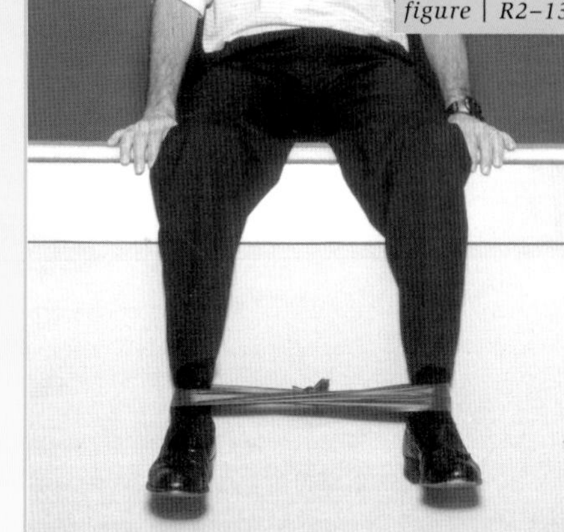

figure | R2-13

Hip Internal Rotation Strengthening:
Starting position:
Sitting with theraband around both ankles.
Spread both ankles apart while knees stay stationary; hold for 3 counts, then relax and repeat.

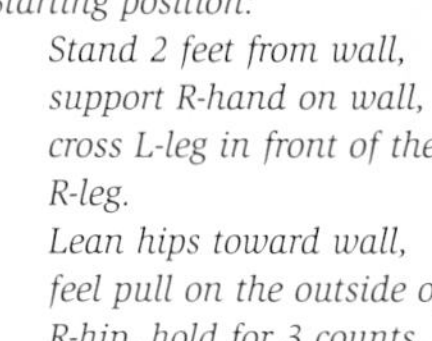

I–T Band Stretch:
Starting position:
Stand 2 feet from wall, support R-hand on wall, cross L-leg in front of the R-leg.
Lean hips toward wall, feel pull on the outside of R-hip, hold for 3 counts, then relax and repeat.

figure | R2-14

Passive Lumbar Extension:
Starting position:
Lie supine on Swiss ball.
Roll body over the ball in extension, hold for 5 counts, return to starting position, then repeat.

Standing Extension:
Starting position:
Stand with hands on hips.
Push hips forward to extend the lower back, hold for 3 counts, then return to starting position.

figure | R2-12

figure | R3-1

Hip Flexor Strengthening:
Starting position:
Stand facing wall, theraband around L-foot.
Raise L-foot toward wall, hold for 2 counts, return to starting position, then repeat.

figure | R3-2

Standing Hip Abductor Strengthening:
Starting position:
Stand with theraband around ankles.
Side-step with knees straight.

figure | R3-3

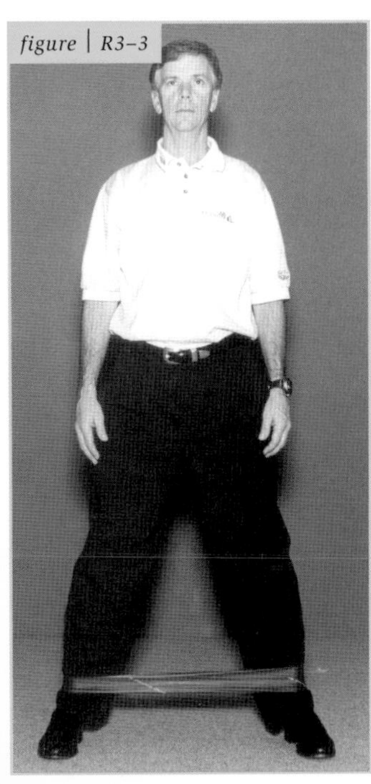

Wall Slides:
Starting position:
With back against wall or Swiss ball.
Squat down until knees bent to 45°, hold for 3 counts, raise forefoot up while straightening back up.

figure | R3-4

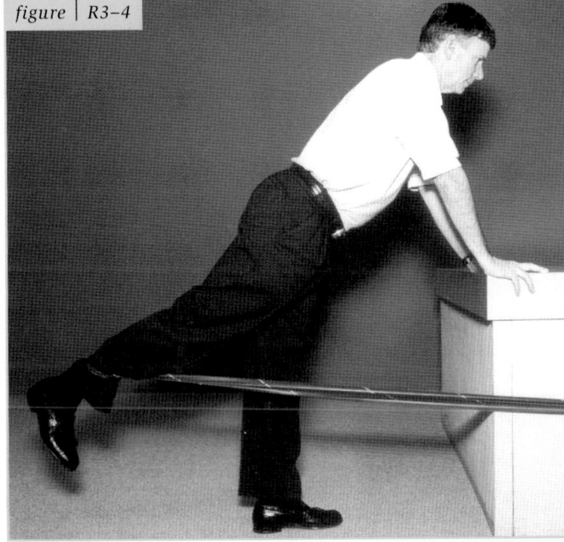

Hip Extensor Strengthening:
Starting position:
Stand and support with hands forward.
Put theraband around foot, extend leg and hold for 2 counts, relax and then repeat.

figure | R3-5

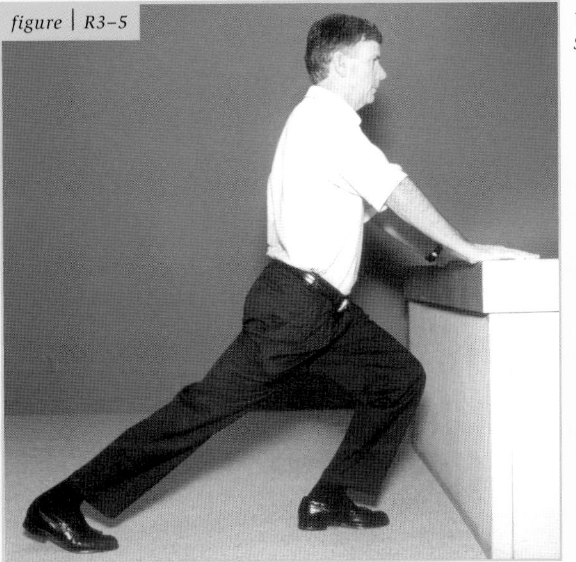

figure | R3-7

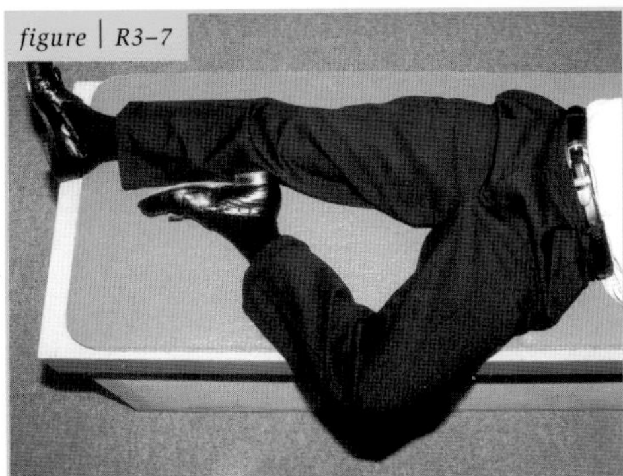

Standing Quadriceps Stretch:
Starting position:
Stand.
Bend one knee while holding hip straight with use of one hand, hold for 5 counts, relax and then repeat.

figure | R3-6

Passive External Rotation:
Starting position:
Supine with one leg flexed.
Bring flexed leg toward the table, hold for 5 counts, return to starting position, then repeat.

figure | R3-8

the surgeon operated through an anterior (front), posterior (back) or a combined (front and back) approach. Another important consideration is whether the spinal disorder required the placement of instrumentation. Most surgeons have their own protocols for the first 6 to 12 weeks. It's important that the patient discuss with the surgeon his or her desire to return to playing golf.

The anterior interbody fusion, in general, allows for early flexion-type range of motion exercises to restore the flexion movement above and below the fusion segments (Figs. 4A and B). Extension and rotation exercises are delayed till after bone fusion consolidation. Posterior fusion surgery with instrumentation allows, in most cases, for gentle extension exercises after 4 to 6 weeks.

Return-to-golf exercises are based on the same principles as the post-laminectomy exercises:

- Restore range of motion above and below the fusion.
- Maximize the rotational flexibility above the fusion and the hips.
- Strengthen and condition the trunk and leg musculature.
- The exercise program needs to take the multiple level fusions in consideration.

Back Range of Motion:

Extension: (after 3 months)

- Prone props with elbows extended forward to diminish the stress on the fusion
- Sitting extensions
- Standing extensions (maintain center of gravity as much forward as possible)

Flexion:

- All fours flexion
- Supine, double/single knee to chest
- Sitting, bend over

Rotation:

- Side-lying rotation with lower back extended (rotation of upper lumbar spine).

Lateral Side Bending:

- I–T stretch

Hip Range of Motion:

Extension:

- Supine, hip flexor stretch
- Standing, hip flexor stretch

Flexion:

- Supine, single to chest

Rotation:

- Number 4 stretch
- Supine, internal rotation stretch

Back Strengthening:

Stabilizers (Abdominal oblique muscles):

- Supine, rotational crunches.

Back rotators (Multifidus muscle):

- Prone, superman
  Many variations are possible including different tools like an exercise ball, hand weights, rubber tubing, etc.

Hip Strengthening:

Abductors, rotator muscle groups:

- Supine, resistive abduction exercises with theraband.
- Side-laying, abduction/adduction.
- Supine, external rotation hips (knees bend) with theraband resistance.
- Sitting, internal rotators resistance with theraband.
- Standing, side stepping with theraband.

Flexibility Hip:

- Upper/lower hamstring stretch
- Quadriceps stretch

Conditioning:

- Walking program 45 minutes
- Stair stepper
- Elliptical trainer

GOLF SWING CONSIDERATIONS

How can we swing with minimal stress in the lower back? It is very difficult to make changes without the feedback of someone who knows. It is often very helpful to have a visual tool. The "One piece take-away" is where hips and shoulders turn simultaneously. The hips will run out of turn before the shoulders will. It is important to utilize this hip turn first because it will avoid lower back twisting. This move also encourages one to keep the arms in front of the body. The lifting of the arms to get the club in 3/4 position also does not cause rotation of the lower back. The rotation actually

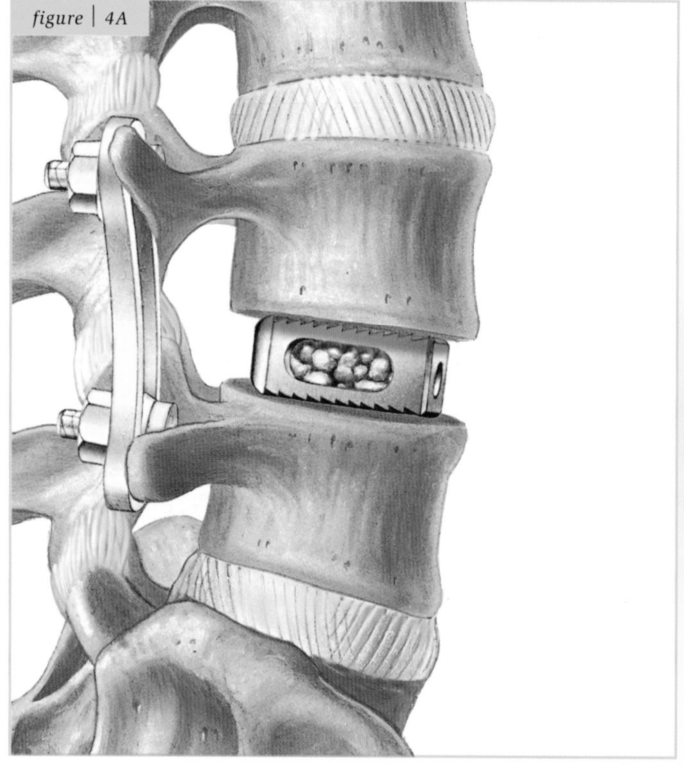
figure | 4A

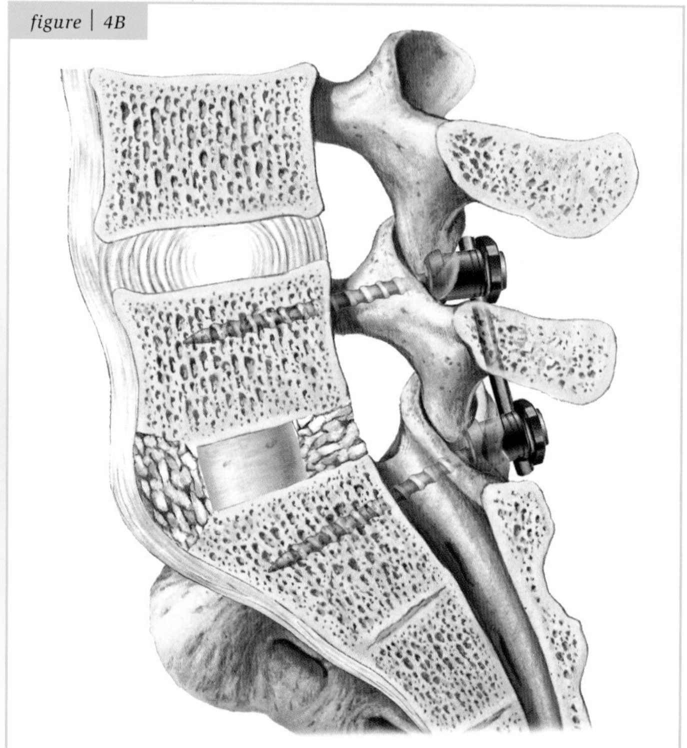
figure | 4B

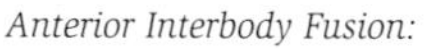
Anterior Interbody Fusion:
A. Carbon bone cage filled with bone grafts, with bone screws and bone plate in back.
B. Bone grafts with bone screws and rods in back.

A. Inverted (reverse) "C" golf swing: Avoid with bad back.

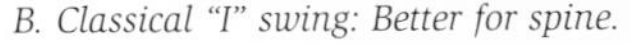

B. Classical "I" swing: Better for spine.

happens in the hip joints. A full turn needs to be avoided. On the downswing, a rotation with the shoulders is initiated without releasing the club (coming over the top). The critical moment is at impact; the so-called hitting against the left side needs to happen without significant side-bending (Figs. 5A and B).

RETURN TO GOLF AFTER TOTAL HIP SURGERY

Total hip surgery has made life with golf possible for many osteoarthrosis patients. There are several different surgical techniques for hip reconstruction. The different approaches and whether the hip is cemented or not do not make any difference in the long-term functional outcome. In the first 6 to 8 weeks after surgery, the total hip needs some protected weight-bearing, especially in the noncemented hip, to ensure that early loosening is prevented. Hip dislocations are also rare after this time frame.

In the first weeks, as preparation for the return to golf, the exercise program needs to focus on avoiding the hip flexion contracture and return of hip abductor strength. The hip flexion contracture is common prior to surgery as a result of the osteoarthrosis process in the hip. It prevents the patient from standing upright and causes a limping gait. We encourage the patient, after total hip replacement, to lay flat for approximately 45 minutes or to tolerance and slowly straighten the hip out. Patients should avoid long sitting episodes that encourages the flexion contracture.

There are several surgical approaches that violate the muscles on the outside of the hip (hip abductors). The hip abductors play a vital role in stabilizing the pelvis during the gait. A limping gait is a result of weak, insufficient hip abductors. Strengthening exercises are begun as soon as possible. In some total hip replacements, this is delayed due to the surgical approach (*e.g.* total hip with trochanteric osteotomy).

Therapy to strengthen the hip muscles can be intensified after 6 to 8 weeks. The focus is placed on the hip flexors, abductors and extensors, of which the abductors are most often the weakest.

Hip abductor strengthening:
- Standing hip abduction with ankle weights
- Standing hip abduction in **closed chain** (raise "good" leg from the floor, hike the hip)
- Side stepping with theraband

Hip flexor strengthening:
- Standing forward hip flexion against resistance (theraband)
- Walking against resistance of theraband

Hip extension strengthening:
- Standing hip extension with resistance of theraband
- Mini squats

CONCLUSION

Returning to playing golf for the postoperative patient is a great challenge. Preparation for the return begins in the preoperative period. The golfer needs to discuss with the surgeon his or her desire to continue to play after surgery. Possible **prehabilitation** or conditioning exercises that will better prepare the patient for the procedure and after surgery may be helpful for certain individuals. After surgery, any golfer will need to recognize and accept that he or she has undergone a body biomechanical change that will affect his golf game. **Rehabilitation** is the key to again swinging a club or stroking a putter. The golfer must be patient, follow the instructions of his or her doctors and therapists, and remain committed to returning to playing golf.

FOOD AND WATER FOR THE GOLFER

CHAPTER 21

Carolyn E. Kennedy, M.S., R.D.

I have had back troubles since 1973, very early in my professional career. I ruptured a disk and it became a chronic problem that eventually ended my career at age 38. However, some of my best playing years came as I was fighting through the pain. I had surgery in 1985, after my competitive days were over, that helped greatly. As serious as my back problems were throughout my career—and certainly at the end of my career—the injury may have been a blessing in disguise because I would not have been home as much to watch my son go through high school and grow up, nor would I have gotten the opportunity to start my television career.

Judy Rankin, LPGA Hall of Fame, Television Commentator

Golfers come in all sizes, shapes and ages: young, mature, heavy, lean, well-conditioned, fit, and less fit. Some have better health than others, some are medically burdened, and some have even undergone surgery. But all golfers, regardless of their medical status, have one common interest—golf. For all of these different types of golfers, good nutrition, drinking water, and regular exercise are critical factors influencing their golf performance.

More and more golfers are becoming health conscious. They exercise on a regular basis and are eating healthier. Historically, golf was not considered a strenuous sport; in fact, it was considered a game of leisure. Golfers never gave much thought to good nutrition and hydration maintenance. The "before the tee" meal usually consisted of doughnuts, biscuits, eggs, pancakes and coffee. At the clubhouse an assortment of crackers, candy bars, chips and soft drinks were available to help sustain the golfer through 18 holes or more. It is now well recognized that a good diet is an essential part of any sport. Golf is a sport; it is a sport that requires endurance. It is a sport that takes players over different, challenging terrains. The golfer is challenged by short and long holes, grass, sand, hills, water, and wooded environments. It is a type of long hike; therefore, just as for any long hike, the golfer must be prepared. This includes eating and drinking wisely. Mature golfers know what they enjoy eating. They have developed eating habits, habits for work and play. Eating is one of the great pleasures of life. In youth, we never give a great deal of time to analyzing what food goes into our bodies. However, sometime in middle-life, in the 40s, people begin to think about what they eat. Many begin to search for the perfect, miracle, health diet: the diet that will promote longevity, increase endurance and slow down the process of aging. Bookstores are lined with dieting manuals. Unfortunately, no such "perfect" exists for everyone. A diet is like a golf swing—we all have one. A diet is a habit around which daily food choices are made. Diets are a highly individual activity. Diet influences long-term health and impacts the aging process. With maturity, cells in our bodies lose degrees of functioning. Organs, muscles and nerves gradually deteriorate. In middle-life, most people require fewer calories than when they were younger. That's why it's so much easier to gain weight as we get older.

When planning a day of golf, the last thing you probably want to worry about is eating right. While golf may not be considered an ultra-endurance event, you are still burning calories, especially if you are walking on a hilly course. In fact, a 175 lb. man who golfs (without a cart) for about 59 minutes burns approximately 300 calories. Any sport, regardless of the intensity, requires that you fuel yourself adequately in order to maximize your performance. In addition, providing your body with an optimal diet can improve endurance and overall health. Whether you are a serious golfer or just love to play the game, you owe it to yourself to know the basics of good nutrition in order to maintain optimal health and top performance.

The basics of good nutrition start with the six basic types of nutrients: carbohydrates, protein, fats, minerals, vitamins, and water. Of these six only carbohydrates, fats and protein provide us with energy.

Carbohydrates are a source of energy from sugars and starches. Carbohydrate-rich foods are the best source of fuel for athletes, and they are the primary source of energy when you are exercising at high intensities. Each gram of carbohydrate provides about 4 calories, and a serving of carbohydrate provides about 80 calories. Examples of serving sizes are one slice of bread, 1/2 cup cooked pasta or rice, 3/4 cup dry cereal, 1 piece of fruit. It is recommended that athletes get 55 to 60% of their calories from carbohydrates. Carbohydrate-rich foods include grain and cereal products, fruits, vegetables, and legumes. Not only do these foods provide energy, they are also naturally low in fat and an excellent source of fiber. Some carbohydrates like cookies, cakes, pastries, and donuts contain a goodly amount of fat and are not the best choice for a healthy diet. Once in a while these foods are okay, but it is best to eat them only occasionally.

Protein is also an energy source, but its main function is to build and repair body tissues. Protein as an energy source is used when not enough carbohydrate energy is available. This is an inefficient process and is not the ideal fuel for an athlete. Protein is similar to carbohydrates in that it provides 4 calories per gram: a serving of protein can provide 55, 75, or 125 calories depending on how much fat the protein contains. For example: a high fat meat like a hot dog would provide about 75 calories with most of the calories coming from fat. A 3 oz. serving of chicken would provide about 55 calories per ounce, or 165 calories. When choosing protein-rich foods, it is best to choose meats low in fat like chicken or fish more often than high-fat ground beef or luncheon meats like bologna or salami. Protein is also found in foods like tofu and beans. Choosing a meatless meal once or twice a week is a good way to cut down on your fat intake and still get the protein that your body needs. It is recommended that 15% of your calories come from protein.

Fats are a source of stored energy and are utilized by the body mainly during low-intensity activities like walking or slow jogging. Fats from animals, like butter or lard, are usually saturated fats and contribute to heart disease and some cancers. Vegetable fats like canola oil, olive oil, or corn oil are generally unsaturated and are less harmful. Animal fats and high-fat foods should be consumed sparingly, although we do need some fat in our diets. You should aim for only about 25% of your daily calories from fat. A gram of fat provides 9 calories, which is much more than the 4 calories provided by carbohydrates and protein. A serving of fat would be 1 teaspoon of oil or 1 teaspoon of butter; each serving of fat provides 45 calories. Be careful of foods that appear to be low in fat, but actually are not. Muffins, biscuits, and many other baked goods are typically high in fat and should be eaten only occasionally.

Vitamins and minerals are also nutrients, but they do not provide the body with energy. Vitamins and minerals are contained in the foods we eat. The next time you are in the grocery store, pay attention to all the different colors of the produce. What you are actually looking at are the vitamins in the fruits and vegetables. The vitamins include vitamin A, D, E, K, C and B complex. The vitamins are responsible for regulating chemical reactions in your body. Exercising does not increase your need for vitamins; they do not provide energy. Minerals are substances obtained from foods that regulate body processes and combine in many ways to form structures in the body, like bones. Some common minerals include calcium, sodium, iron, chloride, potassium, iodine, fluoride, magnesium, phosphorous, chromium and zinc. Like vitamins, minerals do not provide energy. The American Dietetic Association recommends that you obtain your vitamins and minerals from the food you eat; if you do this, you don't need a supplement to prevent deficiencies. Generally people who are concerned enough about their diet to take a supplement don't need one. However, if you want to take a supplement for "insurance," it is not likely to harm you. Be careful of supplements that have megadoses of vitamins and minerals. Anything greater than 10 times the daily value listed on the label is considered a megadose. Your body cannot absorb these megadoses, and in some cases the levels may be toxic. It is best to stick with a standard single one-a-day multivitamin.

Water is a nutrient that does not provide energy, but is essential for your body to function properly. Water makes up about 60–70% of your body weight; it normalizes body temperature, carries nutrients to and waste away from your cells, and is necessary for body cell functions. If you are planning a long day of golf, it is important to make sure you are well hydrated. Don't wait until you feel thirsty to hydrate; by the time your thirst mechanism is triggered, you are already dehydrated. In addition, as people age their thirst sensation becomes less sensitive. Take advantage of the water that most courses have available, especially during the summer months. Beverages that contain caffeine or alcohol have a dehydrating effect, causing you to urinate frequently and lose valuable fluid. An occasional beer or soft drink is fine, but make sure that you are quenching your thirst with water. Drink at least 2 cups (16 oz.) of water the night before your golf game, and on warm days ingest at least 1 to 2 cups (8–16 oz.) about 30 to 60 minutes before tee time. Once you start playing, you should try to drink about 1/2 cup (4 oz.) of water every 15 to 20 minutes, especially in extreme temperatures. If it's possible to drink the water chilled, this is recommended because chilled drinks will be better absorbed. One way to provide the chilled water source during a round of golf is to place a water bottle into the freezer the day before you play. The next day, take the frozen water bottle out, place it into a plastic bag and take it with you to the course. Throughout the round, the ice will melt, providing the chilled, cooled water. There are also plastic athletic bottles with central cores, which can also be frozen. The frozen core is placed into the bottle and then water is poured into the bottle. The frozen core provides chilled water during the game. Sports drinks are unnecessary unless you are exercising at high intensities for an hour or more. Water is inexpensive, readily available, and will do a better job of hydrating you during low-intensity activity. An easy way for a golfer to determine that he or she is doing a good job of rehydrating is to weigh before playing. At the end of the round the golfer needs to re-weigh. If the pre-weight and the after-weight are the same, the golfer has done a good job replacing the lost body fluids. It is very important for golfers who plan to play daily or on a vacation do this weighing exercise. If golfers lose more than 3 pounds in just a few days of golfing, they are losing too many fluids. They are becoming dehydrated. Drinking more water is needed.

Water means hydration. Golfers often forget how important maintaining adequate hydration is for their golf health. Golfers lose fluids when playing: they sweat. If the humidity is higher than normal for a given day, the body's cooling ability is reduced. Therefore, the golfer sweats more and will to need to drink more fluids (the right kind of fluids, which means water). If fluid replacement is neglected, heat-related injuries, including heat stroke, may occur. Before beginning any round of golf, the player must be well-hydrated. That does not mean tanking up on coffee or caffeine-laden drinks. These drinks are diuretics, which means they make you urinate. Therefore, drinking diuretics before playing golf means that, on the first tee, the golfer begins with a negative hydration factor. There are some golfers who must have their morning coffee; in fact, they cannot begin a day, more less a round of golf, without coffee. So, have your coffee, but try to drink only 1 or 2 cups of caffeinated coffee. In fact, it may be better to drink half decaf and half caffeinated on your golf days. Avoid caffeinated beverages after the round has been completed.

Alcoholic beverages are never good for golfers while they're playing. Alcohol, just like coffee, is a diuretic and it causes fluid loss. This applies to all types of alcoholic beverages including wine, beer, and others. Also, avoid alcoholic drinks for at least two hours after playing. Coming off the course, the golfer needn't lose more water. Water is the fluid replacement needed by the playing golfer.

All golfers, when playing a new course, will study the topographical map; they will take into account the length of a hole, its par and hazards. It's also an important idea to find out where the "watering holes" on the course are located. Watering holes do not mean hazards, but places where drinking water can be obtained. Better yet, golfers should carry their own water supply. Bottled water is now easily available and comes in all sizes. Now, there are some golfers to whom plain water just isn't very appealing. Therefore, the next best thing is to take along one of the many sports drinks; these drinks often contain glucose and sugar polymers. The added sugar and carbohydrates are intended to help maintain a high energy level. If a golfer plays multiple days in a row or in a very humid hot climate, such drinks may be very helpful. The flavor of the sports drink is essentially the golfer's choice. It's very important that any golfer with a history of medical problems and those who have undergone any type of surgery pay very special attention to their hydration and water needs.

When deciding what foods to eat, try to keep these three basic guidelines in mind:

1. **Variety:** Don't restrict yourself to the same foods every day. If you do this, you miss out on important vitamins and minerals. Each food offers its own special mix of nutrients. For example, an orange contains vitamin C and carbohydrates but has no protein or calcium, and chicken offers iron and protein but no vitamin C. Your health and performance will be best if you concentrate on variety.
2. **Moderation:** Everyone likes a candy bar or soda once in a while and these foods, in moderation, can fit into a healthy diet. Just make sure that these nutrient-empty foods are balanced out with nutrient rich foods at your next meal. For example, compensate for a high-fat hot dog and a cola at lunch by choosing a lean piece of chicken and vegetables at dinner. There is no bad food, but don't let junk food make up the bulk of your diet.
3. Wholesomeness. It is best to choose natural or lightly processed foods as much as possible. For example, whole wheat bread instead of white, baked potatoes rather than potato chips, grapes instead of grape juice. Natural foods will most likely have more nutritional value and fewer additives.

Fueling yourself adequately for a long day of golf requires that you eat some type of breakfast. Don't wait to eat until you take a break at the ninth hole; by then you may be half-starved and are more likely to choose a high-fat hot dog and a soda. Some fast, easily portable breakfast ideas are bananas, bagels, graham crackers spread with peanut butter, raisins and peanuts, bran muffins, or yogurt. If you are able to bring a snack with you on the course, try a granola bar or Fig Newtons® or fruit rather than a candy bar. Taking the time to make wise nutritious choices will pay off by improving your endurance and performance and, ultimately, your overall health.

ALTERNATIVE MEDICATIONS FOR GOLFERS (SAFETY, EFFICACY, AND HERB-DRUG INTERACTIONS)

CHAPTER 22

Bill J. Gurley, Ph.D.

Just as you can't neglect any part of your golf game-chipping, long irons, driving, sand shots, putting—so you can't ignore any part of your body when you play professional golf. The minute you 'turn your back' on your back, it will flare up like a scorned woman and make you pay the price. While the older guys on the Tour may have their own brand of wisdom, the young bucks today understand that the best favor they can do for their bodies is to spend hours in the gym and fitness trailer.

Peter Jacobsen

Dietary supplements have literally taken the American healthcare system by storm. A variety of these types of products currently fill the shelves of our nation's pharmacies, grocery stores, convenience stores, shopping malls, health food stores, and even Wal-Mart. Who among the reading audience hasn't heard a radio advertisement or seen a television infomercial touting the benefits of one type of dietary supplement or another? The marketers of dietary supplements would have us believe that their products are the proverbial panacea. Oftentimes, however, the marketing hype for these products far outpaces any scientific evidence to support such claims. It is important for consumers to understand that dietary supplements are an extremely lucrative industry in the United States. For example, in 1998, sales of echinacea exceeded $300 million; sales for ginseng amounted to almost $300 million; *Ginkgo biloba* topped $250 million; garlic and St. John's wort passed the $200 million mark; and saw palmetto approached $150 million. In 2001, estimates for herbal (botanical) supplement sales exceeded $8 billion. That same year projected sales for the dietary supplement industry as a whole, which includes not only the botanicals but also vitamins and minerals, were over $20 billion. Several surveys over the last few years have asked individuals why they consumed dietary supplements, and about 1/5th of all respondents stated that they used supplements to treat a health problem; about 1/4th stated that they used dietary supplements to prevent health problems; and half of those surveyed stated they just used supplements to enhance overall health. Furthermore, 65 to 70% of those surveyed believed that botanical medicines are safe. Consumers often say "Well, these products are 'natural,' so they must be inherently safe." Of course, many things that are natural may not be inherently safe. Poison mushrooms and rattlesnakes immediately come to mind. Not to be facetious, but just because something is *natural* doesn't necessarily mean that it's going to be *safe!*

Based on recent data from the Centers for Disease Control, about 40% of the population is estimated to take dietary supplements, and this includes vitamins, minerals and botanicals. Recent articles in the medical literature, one of which stated that about 50% of all emergency department patients ingested botanical supplements, have corroborated these estimates. Moreover, a number of other surveys conducted between 2000 and 2002 indicate that between 30% and 60% of all hospital patients use botanical supplements on a regular basis. This is not surprising, given that retail sales for botanical supplements have doubled every two years since 1991, with the exception of 2001, when sales started to level off, due in part to negative reports in the media. A lot of this negative press was on target because a number of supplement brands that are on the market are just plain bad products. Others, however, appear to show much promise.

The types of products that can be found in the marketplace range anywhere from conventional dosage forms containing crude botanical material, like capsules and tablets, to more elegant drug delivery systems, such as transdermal patches. Newer classifications of supplements known as nutriceuticals and functional foods account for much of the boom in supplement use. Functional foods are basically food items that have botanical supplements added to them. For example, grocery stores may carry potato chips supplemented with ginkgo biloba, or candy bars containing ginseng, or soups containing St. John's wort. There is a wide variety of soft drinks that contain botanical supplements. Whether or not these supplemented soft drinks are any better than their non-herbal counterparts remains to be seen, since many of them contain very little of the herbal ingredients, often only enough to allow a claim to be made, or to put the herb name on the label. Products like "Mango Passion Crisp," a breakfast cereal containing the herb St. John's wort, a flower containing anti-depressive compounds, and kava, a plant with natural sedative properties, can claim to be an herbal "de-stress cereal" designed to support emotional and mental balance. Now let's be practical; that's asking a lot of a breakfast cereal! Virtually no scientific studies support claims made for many functional foods. This further illustrates the point that many manufacturers add botanical supplements to everyday food items merely as a marketing ploy to improve sales.

Occasionally, supplements are formulated as elegant drug delivery systems. One example is "Slender Strip," a transdermal patch designed to deliver an extract of the herb *Fucus vesiculosus* across the skin. According to the advertisement, placing the patch on one's arm for a designated period of time supposedly facilitates weight-loss without the need for exercise, without skipping meals, without taking dangerous diet pills, and without having to eat boring foods or smaller portions. According to the ad, it's just a fast and easy effective weight loss product. Of course, the advertisement fails to mention that no scientific studies have ever been conducted, let alone demonstrated that *Fucus vesiculosus*, when delivered transdermally, has any efficacy with regard to weight loss. But then, why let a small detail like that get in the way of a good marketing ploy?

Let's not forget those products "designed" to boost your sexual potency (botanical aphrodisiacs). One with a particularly catchy name is "Horny Goat Weed." Now, the fact that a company would name its product "Horny Goat Weed," I think, speaks volumes. An interesting tidbit about one of the ingredients in "Horny Goat Weed," a plant known as *Tribulous terestris,* is that goats and sheep grazing on it in Australia and New Zealand sometimes develop a neurological disorder that local farmers refer to as "the staggers." Whether or not development of "the staggers" is part of the desired response to "Horny Goat Weed," I'm not sure, but again, many of these products borrow some science, mix it with anecdote, and run with it. Whether these products are safe and/or efficacious is often anybody's guess. There is a whole cottage industry centered on "natural alternatives" to Viagra® and, as will be discussed later, many incorporate naturally-occurring pharmacological agents that can interact negatively with a wide variety of conventional medications. Advertisements for dietary supplements claiming to increase breast or penis size, cure baldness, promote weight loss, *etc.*, abound. As one might expect, the best-selling and most-heavily promoted supplements are those associated with mood, food, sleep, or sex.

The reason these types of products exist is because of the Dietary Supplement Health and Education Act of 1994, also known as DSHEA. By passing DSHEA the U.S. Congress defined dietary supplements as being distinct from conventional drugs or food additives. According to the act, a dietary supplement is a product other than tobacco added to the total diet that contains at least one of the following: a vitamin, mineral, herb or botanical, amino acid, metabolite extract, or any combination of those above, which is a fairly broad and encompassing definition. One of the most important things that the Dietary Supplement Health and Education Act did was to limit the role of the Food and Drug Administration (FDA) with regard to regulation of these products. DSHEA exempts dietary supplements from the pre-market approval process that conventional medications undergo. The end result is that dietary supplements are not required to undergo any safety and/or efficacy testing prior to entering the marketplace. This is in stark contrast to the conventional pharmaceutical industry, which has to subject new drugs to years of safety and efficacy testing, in both animals and humans, before obtaining FDA approval. This is a very important distinction between dietary supplements and conventional medications because, as we'll see later, many botanical supplements contain a number of pharmacologically active ingredients. One of the other important aspects of DSHEA is that it placed the burden of proof for safety of dietary supplements squarely upon the shoulders of the FDA. In other words, the FDA, and not the supplement manufacturers, must prove that a dietary supplement is unsafe for human consumption before it can be removed from the market. This policy places an undue burden on the FDA because: 1) the agency is understaffed with regard to testing the thousands of supplements on the market; and 2) the burden of proof for safety should be shouldered by the supplement companies, not a regulatory agency.

The Dietary Supplement Health and Education Act also allowed manufacturers to make structure-function claims. Such claims can be made without FDA approval as long as the label does not claim to diagnose, mitigate, treat, cure, or prevent a specific disease. Labels must also identify the product as a "Dietary Supplement." Whatever label claims have been made by the individual manufacturer for efficacy, the following statement must be included: "This claim has not been evaluated by the Food and Drug Administration," and, again, "This product is not intended to diagnose, treat, cure, or prevent any disease."

Demographically, the greatest consumers of dietary supplements are college-educated, middle-aged white females; however, use in children as well as the elderly has increased significantly in the last 3 to 4 years. Most consumers don't consider botanical supplements as drugs, even though many herbs contain pharmacologically active ingredients and are natural sources of several drug entities. Consumers are also less likely to link herbal supplements to some type of adverse health event. A number of recent surveys have shown that people are less likely to link an adverse health event to a botanical supplement, as opposed to a prescription or non-prescription (also known as over-the-counter or OTC medicines) drug product. A very compelling statistic, at least with regard to the medical community, is that less than 30% of patients reveal their use of botanical supplements to healthcare professionals (*i.e.* nurses, physicians, pharmacists, *etc.*) The main reason that an individual decides to supplement his or her diet with these types of products is often based on the recommendation of a friend or a relative, and the second-most popular reason is due to television and magazine ads. The airwaves and print media are literally filled with ads for botanical supplements making, in many instances, extraordinary claims based on little or no scientific proof.

Patients and healthcare professionals frequently view dietary supplements as being innocuous. In fact, there are a large number of botanical dietary supplements, particularly single-ingredient products, that are innocuous; on the other hand, however, there are a number of instances where certain products can be quite dangerous. With regard to efficacy, there are a number of clinical trials that have been conducted or are currently ongoing for a variety of dietary supplements. There are large studies sponsored by the National Institutes of Health investigating the utility of St. John's wort in treating depression. So far, St. John's wort appears to be efficacious at treating mild to moderate depression, although it doesn't appear to be very effective at treating severe depression. Many studies have addressed garlic's efficacy in lowering blood cholesterol. Interestingly, there are just as many trials to show that garlic may be efficacious as there are trials to show that it has no efficacy. And as we'll find out later, these equivocal findings are due to variability among various garlic products. There have been a number of other trials investigating the use of *Ginkgo biloba* in treating mild senile dementia and various circulatory disturbances. A host of studies also seems to indicate that saw palmetto is an effective treatment modality for benign prostatic hyperplasia. To medical professionals and the general consumer, the results of these studies can be very confusing. Some studies indicate that certain supplements are effective, while an equal number may demonstrate no efficacy. Much of the confusion lies with the quality of the study design and the quality of the supplement. Much unlike conventional prescription and OTC medications, the quantity of so-called "active" ingredients in dietary supplements can vary considerably among brands. Consumers are often unaware of this discrepancy and assume that dietary supplements displayed on shelves in pharmacies and grocery stores are held to the same standards of quality and consistency as OTC drug products. They are not. The FDA regulates OTC drug products (Motrin®, Sudafed®, Zantac®, *etc.*), and when purchasing these medications consumers can rest assured that what's on the label is actually in the product. This is not always the case with dietary supplements.

Variability in phytochemical (*i.e.* plant-derived chemicals) content is not uncommon for botanical supplements. Much of this depends on the location in which the plant is grown, the time of harvest, environmental conditions during the growing season, *etc.*, as well as how the plant is processed after harvest and during its formulations as a dietary supplement. Different brands can vary dramatically with regard to "active phytochemical ingredients," and even the same brand can vary dramatically from lot to lot. Such inconsistencies contrast greatly with conventional nonprescription drugs that are regulated by the FDA. For example, federal regulations mandate that Motrin® capsules containing 200 mg of ibuprofen must be consistent with the label claim for content. OTC products must also exhibit lot-to-lot consistency. Because dietary supplements are not regulated as rigorously as conventional medications, oftentimes the labels are not indicative of actual content. This is not only true for St. John's wort, but also for milk thistle, ginseng, *Ginkgo biloba*, ephedra products, glucosamine, *etc.* Literally every brand of dietary supplement on the market is suspect for product inconsistency. Obviously certain brands are better than others, and some supplement companies go to great lengths to assure quality and consistency. Some suggestions on selecting dietary supplements will be provided at the end of this chapter (see ***Useful Tips for Selecting Dietary Supplements***).

When used as single ingredient products, there are a number of potentially safe botanicals. These include echinacea, feverfew, garlic, *Ginkgo biloba, Panax ginseng*, saw palmetto, St. John's wort, and valerian, to name a few. However, there are a number of unsafe botanicals that can still be purchased on the market: these include colt's foot, comfrey, sassafras, chaparral, and germander, all of which can be fairly potent liver toxicants. A discussion of individual supplements and their safety concerns will follow later in this chapter.

Poor safety profiles for some botanicals stem from the misidentification of particular plant species. It's not uncommon for some of the smaller dietary supplement companies to have personnel with little or no experience in botany or pharmacognosy (the science of medicinal plant use). Thus, it is not surprising that separate batches of raw product can be misidentified. Two recent and tragic examples illustrate this point. The first occurred five years ago when a company purchased a batch of *Digitalis lanata* that was mistakenly identified as plantain. *Digitalis lanata* is the natural source of a very potent cardiac drug, digitalis, and as expected a number of individuals who consumed this particular product experienced very severe cardiac toxicity. Another more recent example occurred in Belgium when a manufacturer of botanical weight-loss products inadvertently included *Aristolochia fangchi* with the formulation. For years the scientific and medical community had been aware that aristolochic acid, a chemical found in *A. fangii*, produced kidney failure and tumors of the urinary tract in experimental animals. Not surprisingly, many women who ingested the contaminated product developed various grades of kidney dysfunction, and a number developed cancer of the urinary bladder. So again, misidentification of plant species stemming from a lack of proper regulation can plague certain botanical supplements.

Another more compelling safety issue, particularly with regard to Chinese herbal medicines, is adulteration of supplements with conventional drug products. The list of adulterants found in Chinese herbal medicines is extremely long. For example, some of the drugs found in Chinese herbal medicines that were not indicated on the label include benzodiazepines (Valium®); corticosteroids; digitalis; ephedrine; diuretics (hydrochlorothiazide); non-steroidal anti-inflammatory agents (indomethacin, phenylbutisone, aspirin); barbiturates; anti-seizure medications (Dilantin®); thyroid hormones; and a variety of pesticides that have been banned in the United States. Some of the most prevalent adulterants in Chinese herbal medicines, and even several domestic supplements, are heavy metals. These include, but are not limited to, mercury, lead, cadmium, and arsenic. The practice of drying plant materials over coal-burning fires may contribute to the arsenic contamination problem, since the arsenic content of coal in certain regions of China is more than 1000 times greater than that in the United States. Even domestically produced supplements sometimes list heavy metals as part of their ingredients. For example, a product called Virgin Earth Herbal Rain Forest™ lists more than 70 "organic-derived liquid minerals" on its label including cadmium, cesium, lead, mercury; arsenic, osmium, thallium, thorium, and strontium, just to name a few. One might think that the likelihood of these products' containing enough heavy metals to be problematic is quite small. A 16 year-old female was admitted to a hospital with a diagnosis of liver cancer, but she and her family decided to forego conventional chemotherapy and opted for an alternative regimen they had discovered on the Internet. One component of this alternative cancer chemotherapy regimen was something known as "cancer-kill mineral salt." She began ingesting 5 grams of this substance on a daily basis. Two weeks later she was readmitted to the emergency room with severe nausea, anorexia and syncope (fainting). An electrocardiogram revealed a very unusual heart arrhythmia. One of the physicians recognized this particular arrhythmia as one associated with cesium overdose. Following up on their suspicions, the level of cesium in her blood and urine were determined. The cesium concentrations in her blood were a hundred times greater than normal, and her urine concentrations were a thousand times greater than normal. After stopping the quack medicine, her heart rhythm eventually returned to normal. This episode illustrates another example of the risks some supplements pose whose claims of safety and/or efficacy are unsupported by scientific evidence.

Other factors that consumers need to be aware of are that many products contain multiple botanicals. It's not uncommon to find 10, 12, or even 50 different herbal ingredients in a particular product. In turn, each botanical ingredient may have hundreds of unique phytochemicals. The end result is a product with hundreds of unique chemical entities ,each possessing its own pharmacological activity. In effect some products can best be described as a veritable pharmacological Pandora's box. A classic example of an herb exhibiting multiple phytochemicals is *Panax ginseng,* in which more than 400 different chemicals have been identified. More importantly, most botanical supplements are formulated as concentrated plant extracts. Supplement companies extract the active ingredients from various herbs, concentrate them in a liquid or powder form, and package them as tablets, capsules, or liquids. Thus, these unique phytochemicals with diverse pharmacological activity are concentrated so that their effects are enhanced. For supplements with a proven track record of safety and efficacy, this procedure can be beneficial. For those individuals also taking conventional medications concomitantly with botanical supplements, however, this process may increase the risk of adverse herb-drug interactions. The use of multiple supplements can contribute to herb-drug interactions, or even herb-herb interactions. In other words, the more supplements one takes, the greater the likelihood of interactions with prescription and/or nonprescription medications, or other dietary supplements.

HERB-DRUG INTERACTIONS

One of the most important things to realize when taking self-prescribed dietary supplements is the potential for these products to interfere with conventional medications. It has been estimated that more than 15 million adults take prescription medications concurrently with herbal remedies or high-dose vitamins, which constitutes about 20% of all prescription users. This estimate includes nearly 3 million adults aged 65 years or older. The elderly are also the greatest consumers of conventional medications; therefore, senior citizens (*e.g.* senior golfers) may be at an increased risk for herb-drug interactions when taking botanical supplements in conjunction with conventional medications.

With regard to botanical supplements' potentially affecting the safety and efficacy of conventional medicines, consumers must realize that herbs contain a wide variety of pharmacologically active phytochemicals, many of which, when taken orally, can be readily absorbed from the gastrointestinal tract into the circulating blood stream. For example, a number of unique chemicals found in garlic, ginseng, Ginkgo biloba, kava, St. John's wort, saw palmetto, *etc.* are readily absorbed after oral ingestion of these supplements.

Herb-drug interactions can be classified into two major categories: (1) pharmacodynamic and/or (2) pharmacokinetic. Pharmacodynamic interactions include those in which a botanical supplement has pharmacological properties very similar to a conventional medication such that the effect of the conventional medication may be exacerbated. For example, Ginkgo biloba and dong quai contain naturally occurring chemicals known as coumarins that have anti-coagulant (blood thinning) properties. Conventional anti-coagulant drugs like aspirin, Warfarin, heparin, and others, if taken in conjunction with certain botanical supplements, may result in bleeding episodes or hemorrhages due to an excessive anticoagulation. On the other hand, botanicals like ginseng and danshen can lower blood glucose, and if taken along with conventional medications designed to lower blood glucose, a profound state of hypoglycemia may result as evidenced by fainting or even coma.

Following are some examples of botanicals that may give rise to pharmacodynamic herb-drug interactions.

Ginkgo biloba is touted for its ability to improve memory, treat mild dementia, and improve blood circulation. The efficacy of most ginkgo-containing products, however, is somewhat mixed; much depends upon the individual brand and whether or not it contains enough active ingredients to be effective. A number of interactions with conventional medications have been reported for ginkgo, and most involve anti-coagulants such as Warfarin, aspirin, dipyridamole, clopidigrel, and heparin. Ginkgo interacts with these medications because naturally-occurring molecules known as ginkgolides inhibit a protein in the body known as platelet-activating factor. Inhibition of platelet activating factor causes blood cells not to clot as well. The consequence of taking ginkgo with conventional anti-coagulants is an increased risk of bleeding.

Pharmacodynamic interactions may also involve ***Panax ginseng***, often referred to simply as **ginseng**. The indications for ginseng products are very diverse, ranging from aphrodisiac to energy booster to cancer prevention. The efficacy for most indications is questionable. The few controlled clinical studies conducted with ginseng have been inconclusive; however, a number of herb-drug interactions can occur. The interaction mechanism is somewhat unclear on account of the many different phytochemicals present in ginseng. Ginseng may potentiate the effects of Warfarin and other anti-coagulants, which can lead to bleeding episodes. It may potentiate the blood glucose lowering effects of conventional anti-diabetic medications, resulting in pronounced hypoglycemia. Ginseng is also suspected of interacting with a certain class of antidepressant medications known as monoamine oxidase (MAO) inhibitors. When taken with the MAO inhibitor phenelzine (Nardil®), manic episodes may ensue. Due to the limited research on herb-drug interactions involving ginseng, avoid taking it with conventional medications.

A number of dietary supplements marketed to increase sexual desire, performance, and potency include a product called **yohimbe** bark, which is indicated as an aphrodisiac and to treat impotence. The efficacy of yohimbe is questionable, although some reports suggest it is useful in treating certain types of mild erectile dysfunction. There are, however, a wide variety of interactions that can occur with yohimbe and conventional medications. Pharmacodynamic interactions involving yohimbe are the result of a potent pharmacological agent found in the plant called yohimbine. Yohimbine increases blood pressure, and if taken with prescription anti-hypertensive medications (diuretics, angiotensin converting enzyme (ACE) inhibitors, calcium channel blockers, *etc.*), yohimbe counteracts their effectiveness, resulting in poor blood pressure control. Yohimbe has been implicated in an interaction involving the drug terazocin (Hytrin®), which resulted in an individual's developing a priapism (a prolonged and painful penile erection that is considered a medical emergency) that required surgical intervention. This particular interaction illustrates the unanticipated side effects that can sometimes occur between dietary supplements and conventional medications.

Licorice root is a common ingredient of many multi-component botanical supplements. The powdered root or extract is indicated for the treatment of bronchitis and gastritis, although its efficacy for these ailments is quite poor. A number of interactions can occur with chronic use of licorice root products. The interactions stem from a chemical found in licorice called glycyrrhizic acid. Long-term use of glycyrrhizic acid causes the body to retain sodium and deplete potassium, which can lead to the development of hypertension (elevated blood pressure). As such, it can interact with diuretic anti-hypertensive medications (such as hydrochlorothiazide, Lasix®). Because of the potassium depletion qualities of licorice root, it may also interfere with anti-arrhythmic drugs as well as digoxin. Thus, the consequences of prolonged use of licorice root-containing supplements may be elevated blood pressure, hypokalemia, or incidences of arrhythmias.

One of the more popular dietary supplements is **kava kava**. Kava contains a class of chemicals known as kava lactones that possess sedative properties. Kava appears to be a fairly efficacious natural sedative, assuming the particular brand has sufficient active ingredients. Due to its sedative properties kava kava may exacerbate the effects of conventional sedatives like Valium®, Xanax®, and other benzodiazepines. Caution should be exercised when taking kava with alcohol or certain antidepressant medications (*e.g.* amitriptyline, imipramine, doxepin). The consequence of such interactions is over-sedation. A more recent health concern regarding kava is possible liver toxicity. In Europe, several cases of liver failure have been linked to kava ingestion, prompting its removal from the European market. Some evidence suggests the kava-associated liver damage may stem from interactions with conventional drug products. Again, avoid using kava with prescription and nonprescription medications. Individuals with liver dysfunction should also avoid kava products.

Pharmacokinetic interactions constitute the second major class of herb-drug interactions. Pharmacokinetic interactions occur when phytochemicals in botanical supplements increase or decrease the activity of drug metabolizing enzymes and drug transport proteins in the liver and small intestine. The major classes of drug metabolizing enzymes in humans are known as cytochrome P450 enzymes (CYP). An important group of drug transport proteins known as P-glycoproteins (Pgp) act as drug efflux pumps. Pgp prevents many drugs from being absorbed by pumping them out of the cells lining the small intestine back into the gut lumen. By modulating the activity of CYP and Pgp, dietary supplements may affect how much of a conventional drug product is absorbed into the blood stream from the small intestine, or how quickly a drug is metabolized by the liver and removed from the body. In short, the therapeutic effects of many conventional medications can be enhanced if the metabolic enzyme or transport protein involved in regulating a drug's absorption or elimination is inhibited. Herb-mediated inhibition of CYP and/or Pgp may lead to increased blood concentrations of the drug, resulting in toxicity. On the other hand, herb-mediated induction of CYP or Pgp activity results in less drug absorption and/or increased metabolism. The end result is that adequate blood concentrations of the drug are not maintained and the drug is rendered ineffective. In either case the consequences can be potentially dangerous.

Following are examples of some popular botanical supplements whose interactions with prescription medications can be classified as pharmacokinetic in nature

To date, the most important botanical supplement, with regard to pharmacokinetic herb-drug interactions, is undoubtedly *Hypericum perforatum* or **St. John's wort**. St. John's wort is indicated in the treatment of mild depression. Many clinical studies suggest that St. John's wort is an effective treatment modality for mild depression, making it one of the few botanicals with a proven track record in clinical settings. However, one drawback to St. John's wort is that a chemical present in the plant, hyperforin, induces (boosts) the activity of perhaps the most important cytochrome P-450 enzyme in man, CYP3A4, as well as Pgp. Together CYP3A4 and Pgp are responsible for the metabolism and transport of almost 70% of all conventional medications. St. John's Wort increases the activity of CYP3A4 and Pgp in some individuals by as much as 100%. CYP3A4 and Pgp are present in high concentrations in the small intestine and the liver; therefore, many medications are either metabolized or their transport is inhibited in these organs before reaching the systemic circulation. Drugs taken concomitantly with St. John's wort are metabolized and back-transported to a much greater extent in the small intestine, such that less than half of a normal dose may be absorbed. Some evidence suggests that women may be more susceptible to the inductive effects of St. John's wort than men. This may be very important, particularly with regard to oral contraceptive use, because most oral contraceptives are metabolized by CYP3A4. Thus, women taking oral contraceptives along with St. John's wort run the risk of negating their birth control.

Other examples of St. John's wort's ability to negate the effects of conventional medicines have been observed in organ transplant recipients. The oral absorption of cyclosporine, an immunosuppressive drug used to combat rejection following organ transplantation, is severely curtailed in individuals self-medicating with St. John's wort. As a result, effective blood levels of the drug are reduced and organ rejection can ensue. Many cases of organ rejection have been reported throughout the world in transplant patients who self-medicated with St. John's wort. Other drugs whose efficacy is severely affected by St. John's wort include digoxin in the treatment of congestive heart failure; indinavir in the treatment of HIV infection; Warfarin in the treatment of blood clots; simvastatin in the treatment of hypercholesterolemia; and a host of others. On the other hand, St. John's wort may actually exacerbate the activities of certain antidepressive medications, producing a condition known as serotonin syndrome. This is because St. John's wort's mechanism of action is very similar to that of drugs like Prozac®, Paxil®, and Zoloft®, drugs known as serotonin re-uptake inhibitors. The bottom line is that St. John's wort should not be taken with *any* conventional medication. By itself, St. John's wort may be effective and has a fairly good safety profile, although there have been some reports of photosensitivity and enhanced susceptibility to sunburns.

Another problem with many St. John's wort supplements is that the content of hyperforin (the agent responsible for CYP3A4 and Pgp induction) is often unknown and not indicated on the product label. Most products are standardized to contain a known and uniform amount of another phytochemical called hypericin. Unfortunately, hypericin has no antidepressive activity, nor does it affect the cytochrome P-450 activity. So, standardizing St. John's wort supplements to hypericin tells the consumer nothing about the interaction potential of the product. Some brands standardized to hypericin contain a very small amount of hyperforin, while others contain substantial amounts. Even specific brands can vary considerably in hyperforin content from lot to lot.

Garlic is primarily indicated as a supplement for lowering blood cholesterol. The efficacy of garlic preparations for treating hyperlipidemia is somewhat mixed. There are just as many studies that demonstrate efficacy as there are studies showing no effect. Much of this inconsistency has to do with the particular garlic product under investigation. There are three main categories of garlic products: garlic oil, garlic powder, and aged garlic extract. Garlic oils appear to have very little efficacy in lowering blood cholesterol, and the efficacy of garlic powder is also questionable. Aged garlic extracts, however, do appear to bring about modest reductions in blood lipids. The safety profile for garlic preparations is also very good.

With regard to drug interactions involving garlic, these too appear to be product dependent. What little research is available at present suggests that garlic can modulate various CYP enzymes. For example, certain garlic powder products appear to induce CYP3A4 much like St. John's wort. Some small studies indicate that ingestion of garlic powder for a prolonged period of time can reduce the effective concentrations of certain HIV drugs like saquinavir. Other studies indicate that garlic oil supplementation can inhibit another drug metabolizing CYP2E1, but the clinical significance of this effect remains to be determined.

Echinacea is one of the most popular botanical supplement sold in the United States. Echinacea is indicated for the prevention of various types of infections, colds, *etc.*, and there appears to be some laboratory evidence that it can stimulate the cellular immune system. In the few studies that have been conducted, the effectiveness of echinacea at preventing colds has been, as you might expect, mixed. Some products appear to be better at stimulating the immune system than others, which is probably a reflection of whether or not the particular brand has sufficient quantities of "active" ingredients. As previously stated, different brands and different lots may vary with regard to content. There are possible herb-drug interactions associated with echinacea. Of concern is the use of echinacea in organ transplant recipients and its possible interference with immunosuppressant medications. Stimulation of the cellular immune system may place transplant patients at risk for possible organ rejection. To date, no interactions of this type have been documented in the medical literature; nevertheless, because patients are less likely to report supplement usage to health care providers and individuals are also less likely to link adverse drug reactions to dietary supplements, the possibility exists. Some evidence also suggests that echinacea can inhibit CYP3A4, but the clinical significance of this interaction is not well documented. Still, caution should be used when taking echinacea with prescription medications. Echinacea is also a member of the ragweed family, and therefore some individuals may develop allergic reactions to the supplement. In Australia, several serious allergic reactions that resulted in anaphylactic shock have been linked to echinacea.

Milk thistle is touted for its ability to protect the liver from the effects of certain toxins and for the treatment of cirrhosis. While this appears to be true for certain animal studies, its utility in humans remains in question. Laboratory studies suggest that milk thistle can inhibit CYP3A4 and thus possibly exacerbate the effects of many drugs metabolized by this enzyme. No conclusive studies in humans have confirmed this potential interaction; nevertheless, combinations of prescription drugs and milk thistle supplements should be avoided. Milk thistle appears to be relatively safe, even with long-term use.

HERB-HERB INTERACTIONS

Another category of interactions involves those dietary supplements whose phytochemical content can interact with other components in the same formulation—an herb-herb interaction, if you will.

Perhaps the most notorious example in this category is those supplements formulated with **ephedra** ***(Ma huang)*** and natural sources of caffeine. Ephedra-containing dietary supplements are marketed as diet aids, weight-loss products, energy boosters, and exercise performance enhancers. Over 300 different brands of ephedra supplements are sold in the United States. Some of the more popular brands include Metabolife™, Ripped Fuel™, Xenadrine RFA-1™, Stacker II™, and Yellow Jackets™. Ephedra is a natural plant source of ephedrine alkaloids, which include the drugs ephedrine, pseudoephedrine, norephedrine, methylephedrine, and norpseudoephedrine. The vast majority of ephedra-containing supplements are formulated with multiple botanical ingredients, one of the most prevalent being natural sources of caffeine (*e.g.* guarana, green tea, kola nut, mate). Because ephedrine alkaloids and caffeine are potent central nervous system stimulants and cardiovascular stimulants, there's a potential for interaction with a wide variety of medications. Ephedra-containing supplements raise blood pressure and may antagonize the effects of anti-hypertensive medications. Ephedrine alkaloids can also raise blood glucose and may interfere with oral hypoglycemic agents and insulin. Due to the risk of hypertensive crisis, a life-threatening condition, ephedra supplements are contraindicated with certain antidepressive medications known as monoamine oxidase inhibitors (*e.g.* Nardil®, Parnate®). Because these products contain a large number of phytochemicals on which very little research has been conducted, consumers are best advised not to take them in combination with any conventional medication.

It is the opinion of this author and many other health care professionals that ephedra supplements should be avoided altogether. FDA regulated, nonprescription drug products containing combinations of ephedrine alkaloids and caffeine were removed from the market in 1983 due to the risk of serious adverse health events. In the 1980s combinations of ephedrine alkaloids (*e.g.* norephedrine) and caffeine were linked to a number of heart attacks, strokes and seizures. Since that time it has become well known that ephedrine and caffeine potentiate each other's pharmacological activity. Moreover, other naturally occurring ingredients in ephedra-containing supplements boost this activity even more so. One example is the catechins, a group of phytochemicals found in high concentrations in guarana and green tea that are readily absorbed into the blood stream along with ephedrine and caffeine. Catechins inhibit an enzyme important in the breakdown of certain neurotransmitters (*e.g.* noradrenaline) that are responsible for some of ephedrine's and caffeine's activity. By doing so, catechins increase the magnitude and duration of cardiovascular and central nervous system stimulation. A large number of other phytochemicals are also likely involved in some of the toxicity associated with these products. Sadly, the ephedra manufacturers are not required to do any toxicological studies on their multi-ingredient products prior to releasing them on the market.

As a result of DSHEA, however, these combinations can now be sold in the guise of a dietary supplement. Unfortunately the adverse health risks could not be legislated away by DSHEA. Thousands of serious adverse health events have been reported to the FDA and various Poison Control Centers around the country regarding these supplements. Case reports linking ephedra supplements to heart attack, stroke, seizure, psychosis, and even death have appeared in the scientific and medical literature. While many of these products are advertised as "fat burners" and thermogenic diet aids, their principal mechanism of action is as an appetite suppressant. Very little research has been conducted on the efficacy and/or safety of these supplements. The few studies that have been conducted indicate that a modest weight loss (5 to 10 lbs.) can be achieved over several months. Many of the subjects, however, voluntarily withdrew from the studies due to treatment-related side effects. Such side effects included heart palpitations, nervousness, elevated blood pressure, insomnia, headache, and chest pain. In short, most health care professionals believe that the benefit of a possible modest weight loss does not outweigh the potential health risks associated with these products.

As far as the exercise performance-enhancing ability of these products is concerned, no scientific and/or clinical studies have been conducted to verify such claims. However, extreme caution is urged when combining ephedra-containing supplements with vigorous exercise, or exercise in hot and/or humid environments. Such practices may lead to serious adverse health effects like heart attack, stroke, or hyperthermia. As a result, the NFL and NCAA have banned the use of ephedra-containing supplements. Of course, not everyone who uses ephedra supplements will experience a serious adverse health effect; in fact the majority of users will probably not. Unfortunately, there is no way to discern who will or will not be adversely affected. Therefore, everyone, golfers included, should weigh the benefits versus the risks of ephedra supplements before contemplating their use.

MISCELLANEOUS DIETARY SUPPLEMENTS

Aside from the herb-drug and herb-herb interactions documented above, many other dietary supplements have yet to be studied for their interaction potential. Many of these appear to have a good safety record, and others exhibit some evidence of clinical efficacy. Below are a few more popular dietary supplements that deserve mention.

Glucosamine and **chondroitin** supplements are primarily indicated in the treatment of osteoarthritis and knee joint pain. As the golfing population ages, more players are likely to self-medicate with glucosamine and chondroitin supplements. Glucosamine and chondroitin are slowly but incompletely absorbed from the small intestine into the systemic circulation. Nevertheless, a number of small clinical studies have demonstrated a modest effect of glucosamine/chondroitin on relieving joint pain associated with osteoarthritis. Some data suggests that glucosamine should be used with caution in diabetic patients due to its ability to cause insulin resistance in animals. The only study examining this issue in humans demonstrated no effect of glucosamine on insulin resistance in humans. Again, much of the study results depend upon the particular product under investigation and whether or not sufficient quantities of glucosamine and chondroitin were available. Like all dietary supplements, glucosamine and chondroitin suffer from the problem of whether or not their contents coincide with the label claim.

Creatine is one of the more popular exercise performance enhancing supplements, particularly among high school and collegiate athletes. Creatine is believed to increase strength and endurance, but the scientific data to support these claims is equivocal. Some studies indicate that creatine can increase strength among powerlifters during short bouts of exercise, and may slightly increase the speed and endurance of trained sprinters. Most of these studies have been in trained athletes; thus it is difficult to ascertain whether or not these results can be translated to the non-professional athlete. Creatine is produced naturally in the liver and transported to muscle via the blood. There is no evidence to suggest that creatine supplementation directly stimulates protein synthesis in the muscle. Any perceived increase in muscle mass is the result of water retention within the muscle. Although large doses of creatine are often recommended (approximately 20 grams per day), prolonged use of such doses is unwarranted and not beneficial. After the first two days of "loading" with creatine (*e.g.* 20 grams per day) subsequent doses should be limited to 2 grams per day. Daily supplementation regimens exceeding 2 grams per day provide no physiological advantage and may reduce endogenous creatine production in the liver. Excess creatine is not utilized by the muscle and is ultimately excreted into the urine. As a result, excessive creatine use may result in elevated laboratory tests for kidney function (*i.e.* serum creatinine tests). Patients should advise their physicians of creatine use prior to any laboratory analyses of blood and/or urine. There is some concern among physicians about creatine's ability to increase an athlete's susceptibility to hyperthermia; therefore, caution is warranted in those individuals combining creatine and vigorous exercise in hot and humid environments. To date, no serious interactions between creatine and conventional medications have been reported.

Saw palmetto is indigenous to the United States and is indicated in the treatment of benign prostatic hyperplasia. Several controlled clinical trials attest to the utility of saw palmetto in increasing urinary outflow in men diagnosed with benign prostatic hyperplasia. Saw palmetto is another example of a dietary supplement with a proven track record of clinical usefulness. Of course, not all saw palmetto brands are alike. Owing to product variability the effectiveness of the supplement will vary. As of yet, no potentially harmful herb-drug interactions have been noted for saw palmetto.

The root of **black cohosh** is indicated for the treatment of premenstrual discomfort, as well as menopausal symptoms. As might be expected, the efficacy is mixed and product dependent. Whether or not Black Cohosh can interact with conventional medications remains to be seen.

USEFUL TIPS FOR SELECTING DIETARY SUPPLEMENTS

Only a few of the more popular dietary supplements out of hundreds that are on the marketplace have been addressed in this brief chapter. To assist the consumer in wading through the jungle of information and misinformation about specific dietary supplements, several good references are available in bookstores and via the Internet. Some to consider are: *Tyler's Honest Herbal: A Sensible Guide to the Use of Herbs and Related Remedies* by Steven Foster and Varro Tyler; *Tyler's Herbs of Choice: Therapeutic Use of Phytomedicinals,* by James Roberts and Varro Tyler; *What the Labels Won't Tell You* by Logan Chamberlain; *Herb Contraindications and Drug Interactions* by Francis Brinker.; *Rational Phytotherapy: A Physician's Guide to Herbal Medicine* edited by Volker Schulz, Rudolf Hansel, and Varro E. Tyler; *Herbal Medicine: Expanded Commission E Monographs* edited by Mark Blumenthal, Alicia Goldberg, and Josef Brinckmann.

If there is doubt as to the quality and consistency of a particular brand, one might also consider contacting the company and asking a representative to provide evidence that supports claims for quality and consistency. Those companies that practice good manufacturing procedures and who pride themselves in product quality will gladly provide supporting documentation. Those that cannot, or will not, are best avoided.

In summary, when considering the purchase and use of dietary supplements, consumers are best advised to heed the Latin adage *caveat emptor*—let the buyer beware.

A BACK "EXPERT" OFFERS ADVICE

CHAPTER 23

By Jack Sheehan and Randy Henry

Now that I'm 65, just watching the young players on the PGA Tour swing at the ball hurts my back. Actually, I've been fortunate because I've worked out my whole life, and all things considered, my back has held up pretty well through all my years of playing golf. Now if someone could find a cure for my allergies, I'd give them a vat of Texas Tea. Musta been all those animals my purty cousin kept around the mansion.

Max Baer Jr. (Jethro Bodine from The Beverly Hillbillies)

It's a scene branded in memory. We're on the first tee at Downriver Municipal in Spokane, Washington, on an early spring day in 1975. My pal Randy Henry is addressing his tee shot. His stringy blonde hair hangs in his eyes. A Marlboro dangles from a corner of his mouth, its ash less than an inch away from setting his head on fire. His feet wiggle a few times before he draws the club back. His upper body is motionless. When he starts his downswing, I hold my breath.

Whack! The ball sails off the tee with a slight hook, 200 yards down the middle.

Not bad for a guy in a body cast.

We played about five holes before the laws of physics won out. Randy tried to hit a 2-iron from an elevated tee on a par-three hole; when he pitched forward and nearly toppled over a rocky cliff, looking for all the world like the Tin Man before Dorothy found the oil can, we decided it was time to wave the towel. The 50-pound cast wrapped around his frail 120-pound frame made the challenge of swinging a golf club nearly impossible, but that hadn't stopped him from trying. As we pulled him to his feet, Randy argued that he was pretty sure he could continue, but I reminded him of the old golfers' joke about hitting a shot and dragging George, and he agreed that it was poor etiquette to make his opponent lug him around. I was glad I'd forked over a 10-spot for an electric cart, or I'd never have gotten him back up the hill.

Had any of Randy's doctors been around that day, they would have readmitted him to the hospital and had me arrested for violating every tenet of common sense. But it's hard to say no to a good friend who insists on playing golf, even though his back is broken in nine places.

And after all, I had a cinch bet. He wanted only two strokes a side.

Randy's infirmity was caused by an horrific car accident that took place on June 30, 1974. Following a weekend golf tournament, Randy was riding from Spokane to Hayden Lake, Idaho, in a car driven by his girlfriend Gail. At the Washington/Idaho border, a drunk driver crossed the center median and three lanes of traffic and struck them head-on. Gail was killed instantly; Randy's spine was shattered.

When I saw him the next day in the hospital, the word from the doctors was that he'd never walk again, that he was darn lucky to have survived. His back had been so pulverized they didn't know where to begin treatment. One vertebra stuck out through his stomach, and two protruded through the skin on his back. An intern told Randy, without knowing a thing about his personal life, that the lumps on his back were the size of golf balls. Randy asked him what compression. The intern didn't get the joke.

Two days later, Randy felt a tingling sensation in his toes. That same afternoon, he told me he was going to be just fine, that we'd be playing golf in a few months. He was right.

The following year, sometime after our aborted round at Downriver Muni, Randy underwent a 16-hour surgery at the University of Washington Medical Center. A team of international specialists, headed by a British doctor from Korea named Dr. Gunn, worked on him—from the front *and* the back. They collapsed his lung and diaphragm, removed three of his ribs, and took bone grafts from his hip. They then sewed him up, rolled him over onto his stomach, and went into his back, grafting pieces of rib and hip onto his spine. Next, they implanted steel rods on either side of his spinal column, and inserted pulleys into his shoulders and down into his hips.

My friend was now truly bionic.

"For a few years after the operation, I could never make it through security checks in airports," Randy says. "Once a security guy had me strip down to my boxers, but when he saw all the scars, he couldn't wait for me to get my clothes back on."

Within a year of his accident, Randy became a PGA apprentice and took a club job in Kellogg, Idaho. Later, he took a similar position in Klamath Falls, Oregon. Before long, he had gained a reputation as an excellent instructor. Having played golf in various stages of infirmity—wearing braces and slings and casts—he became particularly adept at working with golfers who suffered from bad backs, neck injuries, and a variety of other ailments. Who better to work with gimpy golfers than a devoted student of the golf swing who had come back from a shattered back injury?

Through the late 1970s, Randy tinkered with different golf clubs, trying to find a set that would fit the swing his body was capable of executing. He also noticed that by having his students try different shafts and swing weights, he could get dramatic results. He studied hundreds of hours of old film on great players, and used computer technology to analyze his students' swings. He became convinced that teaching could not be separated from technology.

"Too many golfers today, whether in excellent shape or suffering from aches and pains, are limited by their equipment," he says. "I saw that through years of teaching. I'd have a student making good swings, with very little reward. Many times, they'd be playing the same clubs and shafts as the touring professionals, and they couldn't move properly. When I would put a club in their hands that allowed them to move, the rewards were dramatic and immediate."

His six years as a PGA club professional were the training ground Randy needed to prepare him for the golf-club manufacturing business. In 1982, he moved back to Hayden Lake, where his family had always kept a summer home. In partnership with Jim Griffitts, he formed Henry-Griffitts Inc., specializing in custom-fit and custom-built golf clubs.

Without doing any advertising, and by just allowing his sophisticated swing analysis and club-fitting techniques to speak for themselves, Randy Henry has built a highly respected company with annual revenues in the seven figures. Through the years, he has worked with a number of PGA Tour and Senior PGA Tour and LPGA players, not only finding them the precise equipment for their swings and body shapes, but also as an instructor who can spot the smallest swing flaws and get them back on track. Among the top players Randy has helped are Peter Jacobsen, Scott McCarron, Homero Blancas, Tom Shaw, John Brodie, Sandra Palmer, Tracy Hansen, and dozens of others.

Randy Henry may be the most knowledgeable person in the world when it comes to fitting clubs and offering swing advice to golfers with bad backs.

"A general statement about the challenge of swinging a golf club with back problems is that the swing should be more *around* the body, rather than vertical," Randy says. "Think of the difference between a forehand in tennis and a lob shot. In the forehand, the knees are slightly bent and the back is straight, so there's no real tension on the back. But in the lob, where the arm comes nearly straight up, the back must be bent. An amateur player who practiced lob shots for an hour would have a sore back. It's similar in golf. Swinging around the body, with an erect spine and most of the turn taking place in the shoulders and hips, creates very little stress on the back. But a swing like that of Fred Couples, which is extremely vertical and with the reverse C, or bent-back position, creates a lot of strain on the back. It is not surprising at

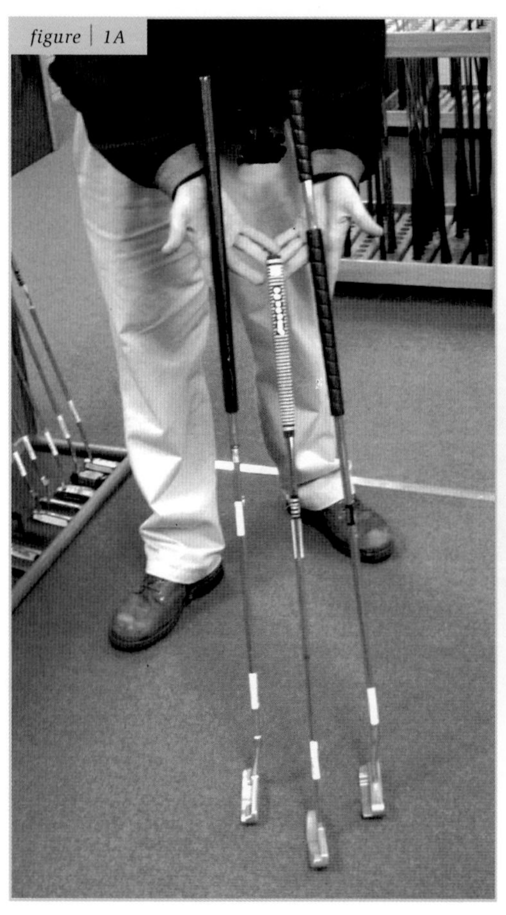

figure | *1A*

figure | *1B*

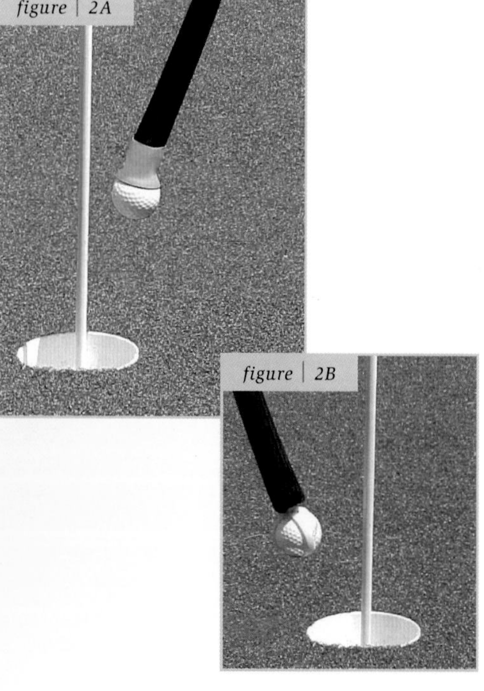

figure | *2A*

figure | *2B*

figure | 3A
figure | 3B
figure | 3C
figure | 4

all that Couples has experienced back problems throughout his career. It almost hurts to watch him swing."

Randy suggests that golfers with infirmities should use lightweight, longer shafts to ease the strain. More clubhead speed—the major determinant in acquiring distance—is generated by longer clubs, and the lightweight shafts, including beryllium, graphite, and titanium, reduce the impact of the clubhead hitting the ground. The newer technology shafts, in essence, are shock absorbers.

"Clubs with a lower deflection-point on the shaft also will help golfers get the ball in the air better," Randy says, "and the biggest challenge for hurting golfers is getting the ball off the ground."

Henry also suggests that the bigger headed metal woods can reduce back strain. Because these clubs have a much bigger sweet spot, golfers will feel less impact even with a slightly off-center hit.

And Randy is a big advocate of long putters, or the latest fad—belly putters—to keep golfers more erect while putting. "Golfers with bad backs often ignore practicing putting," he says, "because the strain of staying bent over for long periods of time is intolerable to them. But with these longer putters, the degree of bend in the waist is greatly reduced, and practicing becomes far more pleasurable" (Figs. 1A and B).

Henry also likes those inexpensive suction-cupped or plastic claw devices that are attached to the grip end of a putter, as a convenient way of retrieving the ball from the cup (Figs. 2A and B). "I don't know how many players through the years have told me they threw their backs out from the simple act of picking a ball out of a cup," he says.

Here are some other quick thoughts from Randy about easing back strain on the golf course:

- Make certain that your shoes fit properly, and don't wear golf shoes for more than one or two years. Also have your feet measured each time you buy a new pair, because feet do change size and shape.
- In transporting your golf clubs, it's much easier to pull them from a back seat than a traditional car trunk. SUVs, which have a back storage space that's much higher, are much more back-friendly than the trunk of a standard vehicle (Figs. 3A, B, and C).
- If you carry your golf bag, use the new model bag with a double shoulder strap that is carried like a backpack (Fig. 4). The single shoulder strap can be hard on the spine and requires unnecessary bending from the side. If you prefer a pull-cart, alternate the arms you pull with.
- Amateur golfers should recognize that a golf bag is not a portable life-support system, but rather a tool kit that should be well organized and efficient. Carry only what's needed and thereby reduce strain, especially if you are going to be packing the bag over your shoulder for 18 holes. Remove old golf balls and carry only those you plan on using. Don't lug rain gear or sweaters or other clothing on perfect days with clear skies. Using a bag with a leg-stand will protect you from additional side-bending and lifting. And leave the big bags for the pros, who are paid to endorse products and logos on them and have caddies to carry for them. Amateur golfers are much better off with what are commonly referred to as "Sunday bags."
- Look into softer grips on your clubs. Anything that softens the impact of hitting the ball can be helpful.
- You've probably heard this many times before, but muscle-stretching exercises , both prior to and immediately following a practice session or round of golf, are a must. When I see a golfer go to the driving range and immediately take out a driver and start blasting balls, I cringe thinking of the damage he or she is doing to the spine and discs. I would even suggest that the 19th hole not be refreshments in the clubhouse, but a brief walk around to the first tee or around the clubhouse to reflect on the day as well as to cool down.

I know my grandfather was a great advocate of stretching both before and after a round of golf, and he always stayed pretty limber. There's nothing more important than keeping the muscles and limbs loose both before and after a round of golf. As a native Scot, he played in a lot of cold weather early in his life, and he understood that loosening up is even more important when the thermometer drops.

Tommy Armour III

How often have your heard golfers comparing notes during a casual round about their various back aches and pains? And whenever we golfers are asked for advice from a fellow golfer, do we simply say, "I don't know. I'm not a doctor"? Probably not. It's more likely that we share with the fellow sufferer our own home grown remedies or cures, despite the fact that we have an entirely different ailment.

Take a few moments to answer these questions posed by the North American Spine Society and you'll learn more about your back in 20 minutes than you ever will swapping anecdotes with your golf partners.

Back Pain Risk Scale

What are YOUR Chances of having back pain?
Take this quiz to find out.

1) How old are you?
Under 30 - *add 0*
30 to 39 - *add 1*
40 to 65 - *add 2*
Over 65 - *add 3* 1)__________

Back pain affects 80% of people over the age of 30 at some point in their lives.

2) Do you smoke?
Yes - *add 1*; No - *add 0* 2)__________

Smoking contributes to the potential for back pain.

3) Are you overweight?
No - *add 0*
If yes and 0-5 lbs overweight - *add 1*
6-10 lbs overweight - *add 2*
11-15 lbs overweight - *add 3*
16-20 lbs overweight - *add 4*
more than 20 lbs - *add 5* 3)__________

Excess weight increases your chance of developing back pain.

4) How often do you exercise?
0 times per week - *add 3*
1 time per week - *add 2*
2 times per week - *add 1*
3 times per week - *add 0*
4-7 times per week - *deduct 1* 4)__________

Regular exercise can help prevent back pain.

5) How often do you lift heavy objects?
0 times per month - *add 0*
1-2 times per month - *add 1*
3-4 times per month - *add 2*
5-6 times per month - *add 3*
7-8 times per month - *add 4*
more than 8 times per month - *add 5* 5)__________

Lifting heavy objects can contribute to strain on the back; be sure you are using proper lifting techniques.

6) Have you already experienced back pain?
Yes - *add 3*
No - *add 0* 6)__________

Once you have back pain, there is a greater chance it will return.

TOTAL________________

SCALE:

0	Congratulations! You are doing what you can to prevent spine pain.
1-4	Low risk – You are doing many things right to prevent spine pain.
5-8	Potential risk – You should change some habits.
9-12	Moderate risk – See a doctor to learn more about prevention.
13-16	Significant risk – You need to change habits now to prevent spine pain.
17-20	Serious risk! Spine pain is likely.

For more information and to find a spine specialist near you, visit the North American Spine Society Web site at www.spine.org, or call toll-free (877) SpineDr.

Back Quiz for Women

How well do you know your back? Take this quiz to find out.

How should you protect your back when lifting a heavy item like a toddler?
a) Keep your back straight.
b) Stand with your feet parallel.
c) Hold your load close to your body.

c) Hold the load close to your body to avoid straining your back when lifting.

Is it normal for a child to get back or neck pain?
a) Yes, they have the same tendencies as adults.
b) Yes, especially when they are very young.
c) No, unless they have an injury or illness.

c) No, unless they have an injury or illness. Spine problems, as well as diseases like meningitis, can cause neck pain.

Can wearing high heels cause spine problems?
a) No, not likely.
b) Yes, definitely.
c) Sometimes.

c) Studies suggest a correlation between heel height and the potential for spine problems. If you have a back problem, avoid heels.

Can having osteoporosis cause spine pain?
a) Yes, it will lead to spine problems.
b) No, but it may lead to problems.
c) Yes, especially in the low back.

b) Osteoporosis does not ***cause*** *spine pain, but it may lead to fractures or other conditions that can cause pain.*

Does bad posture cause back pain?
a) Yes, it causes back pain.
b) No, but it can make back pain worse.

b) Bad posture can aggravate back pain. Standing or sitting up straight uses your stomach muscles and takes pressure off your back.

True or false? If a woman has chronic back pain, she should not get pregnant.

False – Although carrying a child will put additional strain on your back, there are ways to deal with it. Ask your doctor.

The best time to stretch is:
a) In the morning.
b) Throughout the day.
c) After work.

b) Throughout the day. Stretching keeps your muscles flexible and helps avoid injury.

True or false? Strengthening abdominal muscles may prevent back pain and provide some relief if you already have back pain.

True – Abdominal muscles help support the back, so strong "abs" can keep your back fit.

How well did you do? The more you know, the better chance you have of avoiding back pain - which affects 80% of the adult population and is the second most common reason people visit their doctors. If you have back pain or want to know how to avoid it, consult a spine care specialist.

For more information and to find a spine specialist near you, visit the North American Spine Society Web site at www.spine.org, or call toll-free (877) SpineDr.

Know Your Back!

Do you know how to take care of your back? Take this quiz to find out.

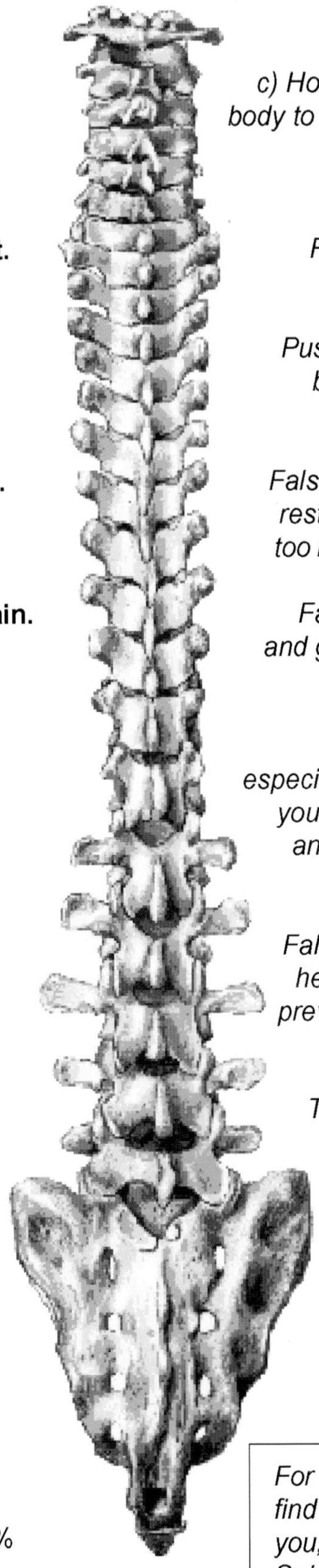

How should you protect your back when lifting?
a) Keep your back straight
b) Stand with your feet parallel
c) Hold your load close to your body

c) Hold your load close to your body to avoid straining your back when lifting (especially heavy objects.)

True or false? Back belts allow you to lift more weight.

False – Back belts ***do not*** *make you stronger!*

Which is better for your back: pulling or pushing?

Pushing is better than pulling because your body weight provides the thrust.

True or false? Prolonged bed rest will cure back pain.

False – While a brief period of rest may help, staying in bed too long will weaken muscles.

True or false? Heat is best for acute (severe) back pain.

False – Anti-inflammatories and gentle stretching are best, followed by an ice pack.

True or False?
Being overweight can contribute to back pain.

True – Excess weight, especially in the stomach, shifts your center of gravity forward and puts additional strain on your back muscles.

True or false? If you have back pain, you should not do weight-bearing exercises.

False – Strength training can help alleviate back pain and prevent further injury, but ask your doctor for guidance.

True or false? Strengthening abdominal muscles may prevent back pain and provide some relief if you already have back pain.

True – Abdominal muscles help support the back, so strong "abs" can take some of the strain off your back muscles.

The best time to stretch is:
a) In the morning
b) Throughout the day
c) After work

b) Throughout the day. Stretching keeps your muscles flexible and helps avoid injury.

How well did you do? The more you know, the better chance you have of avoiding back pain – which affects 80% of the adult population and is the second most common reason people visit their doctors. If you have back pain or want to know how to avoid it, consult a spine care specialist.

For more information and to find a spine specialist near you, visit the North American Spine Society Web site at www.spine.org, or call toll-free (877) SpineDr.

Ten Tips for a Healthy Back

Follow these simple guidelines to keep your back in good shape.

1) **Standing**
Keeping one foot forward of the other, with knees slightly bent, takes the pressure off your low back.

2) **Sitting**
Sitting with your knees slightly higher than your hips provides good low back support.

3) **Reaching**
Stand on a stool to reach things that are above your shoulder level.

4) **Moving Heavy Items**
Pushing is easier on your back than pulling. Use your arms and legs to start the push. If you must lift a heavy item, get someone to help you.

5) **Lifting**
Kneel down on one knee with the other foot flat on the floor, as near as possible to the item you are lifting. Lift with your legs, not your back, keeping the object close to your body at all times.

6) **Carrying**
Two small objects (one in either hand) may be easier to handle than one large one. If you must carry one large object, keep it close to your body.

7) **Sleeping**
Sleeping on your back puts 55 lbs. of pressure on your back. Putting a couple of pillows under your knees cuts the pressure in half. Lying on your side with a pillow between your knees also reduces the pressure.

8) **Weight Control**
Additional weight puts a strain on your back. Keep within 10 lbs. of your ideal weight for a healthier back.

9) **Quit Smoking**
Smokers are more prone to back pain than nonsmokers because nicotine restricts the flow of blood to the discs that cushion your vertebrae.

10) **Minor Back Pain**
Treat minor back pain with anti-inflammatories and gentle stretching, followed by an ice pack.

The more you know, the better chance you have of avoiding back pain – which affects 80% of the adult population and is the second most common reason people visit their doctors. If you have back pain or want to know how to avoid it, consult a spine care specialist.

For more information and to find a spine specialist near you, visit the North American Spine Society Web site at www.spine.org, or call toll-free (877) SpineDr.

Exercises for a Healthy Back

Use these simple exercises to keep your back in good shape.

Regular aerobic and weight-bearing exercise (3-5 times per week) will improve your overall fitness and decrease the likelihood of back injury.

Follow these simple rules:
1) Do each exercise slowly.
2) Do each exercise twice a day.
3) Start with five repetitions of each exercise, and work up to ten repetitions.
4) If an exercise increases your back pain after five repetitions, stop.
5) Always remember to begin and end your exercise session with stretching!

Consult your doctor before starting any exercise program.

Modified Sit-up - Strong abdominal muscles protect your back! Slowly raise your shoulders off the ground while keeping your chin tucked. Touch your fintertips to your knees and hold for the count of five. Do not arch your back.

Straight Leg Raise - This strengthens your legs and abdominal muscles. Lie on your back with one knee bent so the foot is flat on the floor; keep the other leg straight and slowly raise it 8" off the floor. Hold for five seconds, lower and relax; repeat five times then change legs.

Leg Lifts - Lie on your right side (on the floor) with your right leg bent slightly. Stretch your right arm flat in front of you and use it for balance. Align your shoulder and hips. Slowly lift your left leg 8-10 inches then lower slowly. Repeat five times. Turn over and repeat on your left side, raising your right leg.

Neck Press - This is an isometric exercise to strengthen your neck. Press your palm against your forehead, then use your neck muscles to push against your palm. Hold for ten seconds and repeat six times. Then press your palm against your temple and use your neck muscles to push against your palm, holding for ten seconds and repeating six times on each side. Then cup both hands behind your head and use your neck muscles to press back into your hands. Hold for ten seconds, and repeat six times.

Isometric Abs - This easy way to strengthen your stomach muscles can be done standing or sitting. Exhale and pull your abdominal muscles in as tightly as possible. Hold for five seconds then release; repeat ten times.

Aerobic Exercise - Aerobic exercise raises your heart rate with continuous, rhythmic movement and, done regularly, will increase your stamina and strengthen your heart and lungs. It should be done 3-5 times per week for at least 20 minutes. Walking is the best place to start, but bicycling, jogging and swimming are good options, too.

The more you know, the better chance you have of avoiding back pain – which affects 80% of the adult population and is the second most common reason people visit their doctors. If you have back pain or want to know how to avoid it, consult a spine care specialist.

For more information and to find a spine specialist near you, visit the North American Spine Society Web site at www.spine.org, or call toll-free (877) SpineDr.

Seven Back Pain Warning Signs

If you answer "Yes" to any of the following questions, you should consult a spine specialist.

To find one, visit our Spine Care Finder at www.spine.org.

1) **Has your low back pain extended down your leg?**

If the pain persists and is severe, it is a sign that something is compressing a nerve running from your back to your leg.

2) **Does your leg pain increase if you lift your knee to your chest or bend over?**

If so, there is a good chance a disc is irritating a nerve.

3) **Have you had severe back pain following a recent fall?**

A fall may cause damage to your spine. Chances of injury increase if you have osteoporosis.

4) **Have you had significant back pain lasting for more than 3 weeks?**

Often, pain will go away with basic treatment. However, if your pain persists you should consult a spine doctor.

5) **Have you had back pain that becomes worse when you rest, or wakes you up at night?**

If this is accompanied by a fever, it may be a sign that there is an infection or other problem.

6) **Do you have persistent bladder or bowel problems?**

Bladder and bowel problems may be due to many causes, but some spine problems may cause these symptoms.

7) **Do you get numbness or weakness in your legs while walking?**

These problems can be caused by a narrowing of the spinal canal. This is called spinal stenosis.

Some of things you can do to keep your back healthy include: Quit smoking, maintain a normal weight and exercise at least three times a week.

If you have back pain or want to know more about avoiding it, consult a spine care specialist.

For more information and to find a spine specialist near you, visit the North American Spine Society Web site at www.spine.org, or call toll-free (877) SpineDr.

Strength Training for the Elderly

It's never too late to start!

Recent studies have shown that even 90- to 100-year-old nursing home residents can benefit from a regular program of strength building exercises.

What are the benefits?

Better balance. Strength training can help improve balance – a key issue for the elderly who are at risk for falls. Particularly, hip muscle strength reduces the risk of a fall. If you can't rise out of a chair without using your hands, you need to strengthen your hip muscles.

Faster responses. Exercise can increase the ability of muscles to respond quickly and efficiently, which may also play a role in preventing falls.

Reduced risk of osteoporosis. Weight-bearing exercises help build and maintain bone mass, reducing the likelihood of osteoporosis.

Improved quality of life and mental alertness. Studies show that people who exercise regularly enjoy a higher quality of life and increased mental alertness. Even patients who have minor mental impairments after a stroke have shown small improvements in thinking with exercise.

Beginning a strength training program does not have to be complicated! Starting off with a difficult routine is associated with a higher dropout rate. The goal is to increase physical activity.

Walking around the block, or taking longer walks at the local shopping mall, is a good start.

Swimming is also an excellent choice as part of an exercise program.

Exercise with hand-held weights or training machines build strength. Common household items (like small canned goods) can be used instead of hand weights.

Ask your doctor or physical therapist to prescribe an exercise program that matches your abilities.

The more you know, the better chance you have of avoiding back pain – which affects 80% of the adult population and is the second most common reason people visit their doctors. If you have back pain or want to know how to avoid it, consult a spine care specialist.

For more information and to find a spine specialist near you, visit the North American Spine Society Web site at www.spine.org, or call toll-free (877) SpineDr.

Back Pain During Pregnancy

What to expect while you're expecting.

Half of all pregnant women can expect some back pain. Back pain develops for two reasons. One is simply the added weight caused by the pregnancy. Another may be that the extra weight is carried in the front of the body, shifting your center of gravity forward and putting more strain on the low back. The muscles in your back may have to work harder to support your balance.

How can you minimize the discomfort?

1) *Stick with your exercise program.* Find out from your doctor what abdominal and back strengthening exercises are safe for you, and how long you can maintain your regular exercise program. Swimming is an excellent way to keep fit and relieve the stress on your back from the extra weight of pregnancy.

2) *Lifting.* If you have to pick something up, kneel down on one knee with the other foot flat on the floor, as near as possible to the item you are lifting. Lift with your legs, not your back, keeping the object close to your body at all times. Be careful, though – it may be easier to lose your balance while you are pregnant. Whenever possible, get assistance in lifting objects.

3) *Carrying.* Two small objects (one in either hand) may be easier to handle than one large one. If you must carry one large object, keep it close to your body.

4) *Sleeping.* Sleeping on your back puts 55 lbs. of pressure on your back. Placing a pillow under your knees cuts the pressure in half. Lying on your side with a pillow between your knees also reduces the pressure.

How can you deal with the back pain related to pregnancy? Fortunately, most back pain related to pregnancy is self-limited and will resolve. In most cases, medication is not a very good option. Do not use any medication during pregnancy without permission of your physician. Some treatment options include learning exercises to support muscles of the back and pelvis, use supportive garments that may be helpful with certain causes of back pain in pregnancy, and use of spot treatments such as heat and cold. If your pain persists despite these measures, or you develop any radiating pain, numbness, tingling or weakness in your legs, you should consult with a spine physician with expertise in women's health issues and/or pregnancy related disorders. They will be able to assist you in diagnosing and treating your specific problems.

The more you know, the better chance you have of avoiding back pain – which affects 80% of the adult population and is the second most common reason people visit their doctors. If you have back pain or want to know how to avoid it, consult a spine care specialist.

For more information and to find a spine specialist near you, visit the North American Spine Society Web site at www.spine.org, or call toll-free (877) SpineDr.

Are You at Risk for Osteoporosis?

Signs to look for if you don't have any symptoms

Bones are made of living tissue. Old bone tissue is constantly replaced by new bone tissue. At some point after age 30, more bone tissue is broken down than is replaced. Osteoporosis occurs when much more bone is destroyed than is replaced, which makes bones very weak.

In the early stages of osteoporosis, you usually have no symptoms. ***These are signs that you could be at risk:***

Family history – If someone in your family has osteoporosis, you have a 60-80% chance of developing it. Hip fractures in particular are a clear indication of bone weakness. Your chances for a hip fracture double if your mother had a hip fracture.

You are shorter than you used to be – It is common between ages 60 to 80 to lose ½ to one full inch of height from lost disc elasticity. However, a spine fracture could result in additional loss of height. Multiple fractures also can cause the spine to form a curve known as a "dowager's hump."

Back pain – Persistent back pain could be a sign of a spinal fracture. Weak vertebrae can fracture and collapse without warning, even during everyday activities.

Chronic medical problems – If you suffer from rheumatoid arthritis, hyperthyroidism, hyperparathyroidism, diabetes or liver disease, your chances of having osteoporosis increase.

You do not get enough calcium – Calcium is normally excreted from the body every day. When we don't replace it, the body steals calcium from bones. This can contribute to the development of osteoporosis. Milk and dairy products as well as leafy green vegetables provide the calcium bones need.

Smoking – If you smoke, your risk of an osteoporotic fracture is double that of a non-smoker. Cigarette smoking reduces calcium absorption and prevents new bone growth.

Alcohol consumption –Poor nutrition leading to bone loss is common with excessive alcohol use.

Low body weight – Being too thin can be a sign that you have low bone mass, putting you at risk for osteoporosis.

Frequent dieting – Extreme changes in diet and frequent fluctuations in weight can cause loss of muscle and bone density in addition to fat. Lost fat and muscle can come back, but bone could be gone forever.

The more you know, the better chance you have of avoiding back pain – which affects 80% of the adult population and is the second most common reason people visit their doctors. If you have back pain or want to know how to avoid it, consult a spine care specialist.

For more information and to find a spine specialist near you, visit the North American Spine Society Web site at www.spine.org, or call toll-free (877) SpineDr.

Preventing Osteoporosis

Simple steps to protect your bones

The best prevention begins in childhood. However, it is never too late to make small but effective changes that can stave off or even reverse bone loss.

Your risk of developing osteoporosis depends on how much bone mass you build between ages 25 and 35 (peak bone mass) and how quickly you lose it as you grow older. The higher your peak bone mass, the more bone you have "in the bank" and the less likely you are to develop osteoporosis during normal aging.

Getting enough calcium and vitamin D (which is essential for absorbing calcium) and exercising regularly can help ensure that your bones stay strong.

Calcium – The skeleton contains 99% of the body's calcium. Calcium is necessary for proper functioning of the heart, nerves and muscles and is involved in vital functions from blood clotting to muscle contraction. As profoundly important as calcium is to these essential body functions, your skeleton's health is so dependent on this mineral that it uses all but 1% of your body's calcium. A diet low in calcium contributes to your risk for osteoporosis. Milk and dairy products as well as leafy green vegetables provide the calcium bones need.

Vitamin D is necessary for the body to absorb calcium. Not getting enough vitamin D can cause your body to use the calcium stored in your bones. Sources of vitamin D include fortified milk, cod liver oil, egg yolks, liver and fatty fish such as salmon.

Exercise is crucial to good bone health. In particular, weight-bearing exercises (including but not limited to weightlifting, jogging, walking, hiking, stair climbing and push-ups) help increase bone strength. Please check with your doctor before beginning any exercise program.

Lifestyle – ***Stop smoking.*** There are many dire health consequences of using tobacco. Add bone loss to that list. ***Limit alcohol.*** Excessive alcohol consumption is linked to increased bone loss. ***Avoid fad diets.*** Fad diets often restrict food consumption to the point that you may not be consuming what your body needs. Eat a well-balanced diet and consult with your doctor for advice if you need to lose weight.

The more you know, the better chance you have of avoiding back pain – which affects 80% of the adult population and is the second most common reason people visit their doctors. If you have back pain or want to know how to avoid it, consult a spine care specialist.

For more information and to find a spine specialist near you, visit the North American Spine Society Web site at www.spine.org, or call toll-free (877) SpineDr.

A BRIEF OUTLINE OF GOLF HISTORY

CHAPTER 25

Jackson T. Stephens and T. Glenn Pait, M.D., F.A.C.S

I first hurt my back almost twenty years ago in an incident that had nothing to do with golf. But the weakness left behind has caused me to injure it many times since, usually in cold weather, and often in ways that kept me off the golf course or affected my game, because swinging the club aggravated the injury. Three things have helped to virtually eliminate the problem: 1. Regular exercise to strengthen abdominal muscles. You don't have to have washboard abs to be strong enough to ward off back pain. We can all be constantly contracting our abs and building their strength as we go about our daily business. 2. Stretching the big leg muscles—the quads, hamstrings, and calves. When these muscles are tight they put enormous pressure on an already weak back. On a trip to Africa last year, my back was so sore I could hardly walk up a flight of steps to a meeting. I stopped and stretched my quads and hamstrings (always sucking in my gut, but still breathing). My mobility immediately returned, pain free. 3. Strengthening the middle muscles of the back to ensure better posture and alignment, thus reducing pressure on the back. The easiest way to do this is to go to an open doorway, put your arms, elbow to palm, against sides, stick your chest out, don't drop your head forward and lean in. You can increase the effectiveness of this by doing it on your toes. If you do it for one or two minutes a day, you'll be amazed at how much those middle muscles will do to keep you erect and keep the pressure and pain off your back.

President Bill Clinton

An understanding of the history of any field provides a greater appreciation of the subject. To know some of the many avenues undertaken by the early participants of the subject will most assuredly awaken within the disciple of the topic a need to learn more. A picture taken today of any modern golfer may grace the pages or the compact discs of tomorrow as an historical photograph, for we are all making history every day in our own ways. The following outline will, hopefully, open the doors of interest to a few golfers who will want to learn more about the history of the wonderful sport of golf.

MILESTONES OF GOLF

Chinese:

A. The Song Dynasty (960–1279), Shepherds, tending cows, played a game with wood clubs. They hit rocks or a ball of some type into rabbit holes. They would drink wine while they played. When the wine was gone, the game was over. Usually they hit about 18 balls before the liquor was drunk. This may have resulted in the rule of 18 holes for the game.
B. The Ming Dynasty (mid-to-late 1300s), introduced *suigan,* a game of hitting a ball with a stick while walking. Silk traders may have carried this game to Europe (Fig. 1).

Roman Empire (1st Century):

The Roman armies overran Europe and crossed the English Channel to occupy England and Scotland. Soldiers must be entertained, and so they played games. These Romans played a team sport called *paganica.* They used curved clubs to hit a moving wool- or feather- filled leather ball. They engaged in this activity in an open countryside. This may have been the beginning of several club and ball sports in many European countries (Fig. 2).

Holland (13th Century to early 18th Century):

The Dutch played a game called *colf.* The game originated in a small village of Loenen aan de Vecht around 1297. The object of the game was to hit a ball toward a door. Almost any door would do for this game. All one had to do was to hit four targeted doors. However, the fairways to the doors were often more than forty-five hundred yards. *Colf* certainly brought new meaning to "who's knocking at my door!" Due to personal and property damage, these Dutch "colfers" were forbidden to play within the village. They were sent to the countryside. *Colf's* increased popularity prompted the development of better clubs and balls. There are numerous paintings by Dutch artists depicting players hitting balls with clubs. *Colf* was played until the early 19th century (Fig. 3).

Britain:

Cambuca was played in the mid-fourteenth century. This game was conducted by hitting a small wooded ball with a club or a mallet. In 1363, Edward III banned *cambuca* and other time-consuming sports. This game clearly took valuable time away from soldiers who needed to work on military skills. Golf-like sports were restored as legal games after the introduction of gunpowder, which lessened the importance of archery. A stained-glass window, circa 1350, in the Gloucester Cathedral illustrates an early player (Fig. 4).

Italy and France:

In the 14th century, *jeu de mail* was a popular open country game that was played with long-handled mallets and wooden balls. In fact, it resembled croquet. The *jeu de mail* players gathered

figure | 1

A scroll from the Ming Dynasty depicts Chinese playing Suigan; perhaps the first golfers.

Roman armies in the First Century played a game called Paganica.

figure | 2

figure | 3

"Colfers" on the ice near Haarlem; by Adriaen van de Velde (1636–1672)

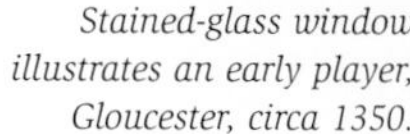

Stained-glass window illustrates an early player, Gloucester, circa 1350.

figure | 4

figure | 6

Match at Blackheath, 1869, by Frederick Gilbert.

figure | 5

Jeu de Mail was a popular open-country game.

along a roadway and tried to hit the ball to a specific target. The winner accomplished the task using the fewest strokes. This game was played in England but was never as popular as in France (Fig. 5).

Holland (1425):
The Dutch made sheepskin-covered balls filled with animal hair, usually cow's hair, to play hand tennis (*kaatsen*). *Colfers* quickly recognized that these tennis balls were well-suited to their game. Soon the production of Dutch sheepskin balls greatly increased.

King James II of Scotland:
In 1457, the King issued a decree, "that fute-ball and golfe be utterly cryed downe, and not be used." His Royal Highness was concerned that his archers were playing too much "golfe" and not practicing enough with their bows.

Holland (1486):
Dutch companies increased their importation of wool from Scotland. Dutch seamen took their colf clubs and balls along with them during their travels. The eastern coasts of Scotland were well-suited for the game of *colf*. These early links were formed when the sea receded leaving wastes of sand. Sea birds found the sandy beaches perfect resting-places. Where there were birds there were droppings, which provided the seeds and fertilizer for the growth of grass. The land was of little value except to the birds and the local rabbits. It was destiny that these tracts of land with natural holes provided by rabbits and grass seeds from birds were to become the links that brought forth modern golf.

King James IV of Scotland (1503):
The King married a daughter of Henry VII and signed a treaty of peace with England. Golfers were allowed to pick up their clubs instead of their weapons.

England (1604):
James VI of Scotland succeeded to the English throne as James I. The new King greatly influenced the spread of golfe throughout his New Kingdom. The King appointed William Mayne as the royal club maker for the rest of his life. Soon the king was purchasing new clubs and golfe balls.

Royal Blackheath (1608):
The first links outside of Scotland to later become a golf club. However, the Honourable Company of Golfers was not officially established until 1766 (Fig.6).

Golf (1650):
The word golf, spelled as we spell it today, became well-known along the eastern coast of Scotland.

America (1650):
Colf was played in the Dutch colony of New York.

Scotland (1682):
The Prince of Wales became involved in a strong discussion with certain English nobleman about the history of golf. The controversy lead to a golf challenge and the winner would determine the correct history of the game.

Holland:
The Dutch, in the 18th century, replaced *colf* with *kolf*.

Edinburgh, Scotland (1744):
The first golfing society to organize a true club, the Honorable Company of Edinburgh Golfers. Club members realized that they would need formal recognition if they were to be a lasting organization. Such recognition came from the Town Council in the form of an official prize, a Silver Club, which would be competed for annually. The competition for the Silver Club was the first such a tournament ever held in golf. This first

competition was held at the famous Links of Leith until 1831. In 1836 the club moved to the Musselburgh links (Fig. 7).

Golf Rules (1744):

The Silver Club tournament prompted the need to establish codes of rules and standards to guide uniform and fair play. Thirteen articles for play were agreed upon which captured the essence and spirit of golf. The Edinburgh Company's tournament was a very important turning point in the maturing of golf as an established sport. It was the first time that the game would be played under approved articles and rules (Fig. 8).

The Society of St. Andrews Golfers (1754):

Some form of the game of golf was played on Scotland's sandy links along the North Sea since the 13th century. There is written evidence of golf at St. Andrews from 1522. However, it was not until 1754 that some twenty-two golfers formed the Society of St. Andrews Golfers for the benefit of their health. They were quick to organize their own Silver-Club tournament. They adopted the thirteen articles of golf from the Edinburgh Company. All members wore bright red coats during play to identify themselves as golfers to passersby. They were the first club to protect their course from pedestrian and animal abuse. They forbade all types of wheeled or animal travel over the links during play. In the beginning, a round of golf at St. Andrews consisted of twenty-two holes (Fig. 9).

St. Andrews Golf (1764):

The twenty-two holes for a round were changed to eighteen holes. This number of holes per round would soon become the accepted standard throughout the golfing world.

The Musselburgh Society of Golfers (1811):

The first women's-only golf tournament.

The Calcutta Club (1829):

Scottish missionaries began their travels to India. They took their beloved golf with them, and soon a club was formed in Calcutta.

The Royal and Ancient Golf Club (1834):

King William IV of England become the patron of the St. Andrews Golf Club and declared that it be known as the Royal and Ancient Golf Club. Such an honor from His Royal Highness placed the club into a very special category.

India to Scotland (1848):

James Paterson, a Scottish missionary, sent his brother, Robert, a statue of the Hindu god Vishnu. The statue was packed with a material called gutta percha. The material was quite moldable and so young Robert, a student and golfer, made himself a new golf ball. The Pattern brothers, three in all, introduced the world to a new, improved golf ball. The ball became affectionately know as the "gutty." This affordable little ball truly resuscitated the sport of golf.

Pau, France (1856):

During the Peninsular War English troops played golf for entertainment and exercise. Years after the war's end, many veterans returned during holidays without their weapons but with their golf clubs to the meadows of Pau. This French town became the first tourist golf course and the retired soldiers the first golf vacationers.

St. Andrew's Ladies Golf Club (1867):

The first organized woman's golfing society. In less than twenty years the club would have some five hundred members (Fig. 10).

Royal Montreal Golf Club (1873):

Four young golfing immigrants from Edinburgh established the first golf club in North America in Montreal. Alexander Dennistoun, his two brothers, Scots and John, and David Sidey committed themselves to the development of golf in their new country. They maintained close ties

figure | 7

Edinburgh Castle (1746–1747), by Paul Sandby (1725–1809).

figure | 8

The Silver Club was presented to the Edinburgh Golfers in 1744 by the City of Edinburgh.

figure | 9

St. Andrews (artist unknown), between 1680 and 1720.

Women's golf was increasing, as depicted in "A Hazard on the Ladies Course" (1890), by Lucien Davis, RI (1860–1941).

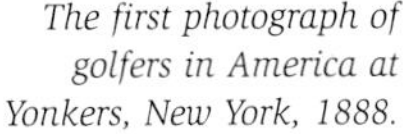

The first photograph of golfers in America at Yonkers, New York, 1888.

figure | 11

with their Scottish roots and adopted the rules of St. Andrews.

New York City (1887):
Robert Lockhart, a linen merchant and golfer from Dunfermline, Scotland, decided to introduce his American friends to the game of golf. The first golf ball hit in the United States was in Central Park by Mr. Lockhart and his sons. They were testing newly arrived clubs from Scotland. These new clubs and balls were then sent to a dear friend in Yonkers, New York.

Yonkers, New York (1888):
John Reid, a boyhood friend of Robert Lockhart from Dunfermline, was the recipient of the New York City Clubs. He and a group of six friends met on President George Washington's birthday in a cow pasture to give golf a try. Immediately they took to the game and soon developed a three-hole golf course. Within a few years the membership grew and prompted the occasion to find a new course. The New York golfers soon found themselves playing in an apple orchard and became known as the Apple Tree Gang. For some members, golf just wasn't golf if not played in an apple orchard. Perhaps Yonkers was the first golf club devoted to playing the game for exercise and eating healthy during the game. During the right season, apples were no doubt readily available (Fig. 11).

St. Andrew's of Yonkers (New York):
John Reid and his friends established the first golf club in the United States. On November 14, 1888, golf officially began in the United States. The St. Andrew's Club is the oldest continuously functioning golf club in the United States (Fig. 12).

First Amateur Golf Championship in America (1894):
John Reid's St. Andrew's Club hosted a match-play tournament to determine the true amateur champion. The outcome of the play was not without some controversy. It was evident that an official body for tournaments would be greatly needed. From the tournament of 1894 developed the setting-up of official golf championships under the United States Golf Association (USGA) Pipe in hand on the left is John Reid, often referred to as the "Father of American Golf" (Fig. 13).

Alan B. Shepard and the Apollo 14 Lunar Mission (January 31, 1971 to February 9, 1971):
Golf was a game that had been played only on this planet until the Apollo 14 Lunar Mission of 1971. Alan B. Shepard, the first American in space, commanded the Apollo 14 during the 1971 mission. He was 47 years old. He placed a 6-iron onto a special shaft. To prepare for the "Lunar Course," he would go to the suit room and put on a full suit including oxygen tanks. Wearing the suit he would practice his golf swing. On January 31, 1971, the Apollo 14 left the launch pad. During the second day of the mission, Shepard dropped the first golf ball onto the surface of the moon. His first attempted shot was not a success. It rolled into a crater about 40 yards away. The suit was so clumsy that he could not place both hands comfortably around the shaft. Another ball was dropped. This was truly the first golf ball to travel through the lunar atmosphere. Shepard hit the ball soundly and it soared some 200 yards. Golf had now traveled to another planet. Its history and migration to other lands continues (Fig. 14).

figure | 12

John Reid (Father of American Golf), circa 1900, by Frank Flower.

figure | 13

First amateur golf championship in America in 1894, by Everett Henry (1893–1961). John Reid is shown with pipe in hand.

figure | 14

First golf ball to travel through the lunar atmosphere. Alan B. Shepard and the Apollo 14 Lunar Mission (January 31, 1971 to February 9, 1971).

AFTERTHOUGHTS TO GOLF FOREVER

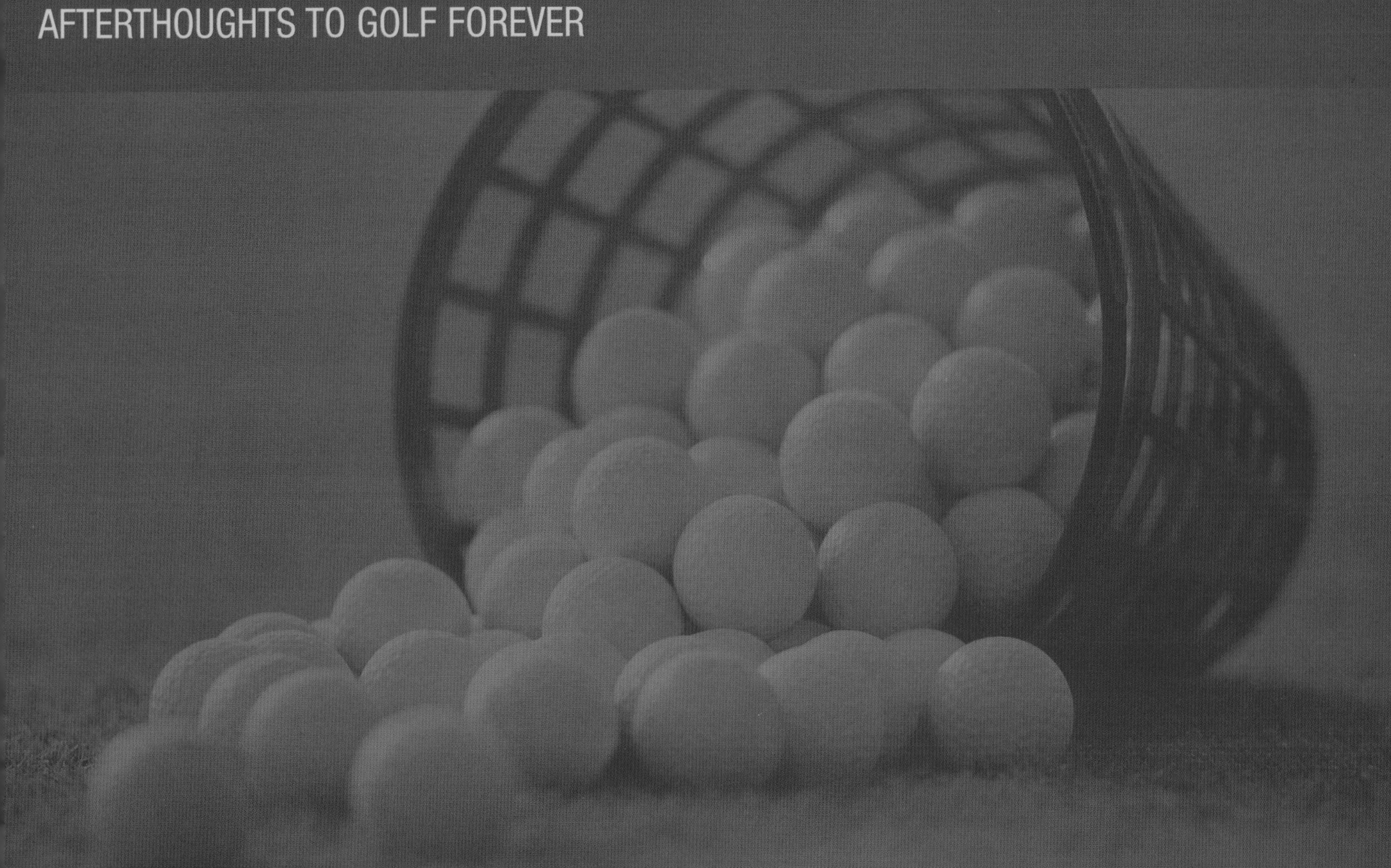

Every sense of purpose is driven by moments of inspiration. And the inspiration to put in book form a wealth of information about keeping the human body fit and flexible enough to play our wonderful game of golf for a lifetime came from my many friends who love golf as much as I do.

Once a man reaches a mature age as a golfer, the daily greetings he shares with his contemporaries take on additional meaning and substance. When we ask each other, "How are you?" we are not just throwing out a cursory salutation. We really want to know how the other fellow or woman is feeling healthwise, emotionally, and spiritually. But underlying all of that is the real question: "Are you well enough to play golf these days, and if so, how's your game?"

Too many of my dear friends in recent years have answered, "Oh, I'm doing all right, all things considered, but because of my (back, shoulder, hip, sore neck, arthritis, knee, tendonitis in the joints, *etc.* . . . fill in any or all of the above), I haven't been able to play golf in months." And it is as though a bright candle has been extinguished from their eyes when they report the news, because true golfers who have had their clubs taken away by infirmity are missing an enormously important aspect of their lives.

After meeting and undergoing spinal surgeries from Dr. T. Glenn Pait, I recognized that this was a man of enormous talents who loved the game of golf with the same passion that I did. Our conversations eventually turned to the idea that ultimately resulted in this book: what could we do as a gift for our golfing friends that would help them play golf better and longer and without the aches and pains so often associated with the act of striking a golf ball? Thus was the inspiration for *Golf Forever.*

When we lost our good friend Sam Snead not long ago (fortunately, he was able to contribute an anecdote for this book shortly before he passed), it occurred to me that Sam had always been able to keep a great sense of humor and zest for living because he was able to swing a golf club—perhaps better than anyone who ever lived—for the full nine decades of his life. It is the hope of Dr. Pait and myself that this book will provide information to keep all our golfing friends healthy and fit enough to keep playing this game for their respective lifetimes.

I'd like first of all to thank Dr. Pait for his tireless devotion to this project. He worked long hours into the night on *Golf Forever,* many times after performing surgery on seriously ill patients at the University of Arkansas Medical Center.

I'd like also to thank Craig Campbell for his organizational efforts on the book, making certain every step of the way that the manuscript and printing was in keeping with our original vision.

I'd also like to thank our friend Jack Sheehan, out in the desert air of Las Vegas, for his editorial assistance and golfing knowledge as we put this work together.

Here's wishing all the wonderful friends I've made in my lifetime of golf a full measure of good health, good companionship, and good golfing.

Sincerely,
Jack Stephens

Abnormal plasma cells: The abnormal blood cells in multiple myeloma that may destroy bone tissue.

Abscess: A collection of pus caused by bacterial or fungal infections.

Acetaminophen: Effective for pain relief, but not inflammation. It is gentler on the stomach than aspirin or ibuprofen. It does not significantly prolong bleeding time. Individuals with known ulcers, frequent nosebleeds or other bleeding problems may be able to take acetaminophen for pain. It is a safer alternative for children because it is not associated with Reye's syndrome.

Achilles' tendon: Largest tendon in the body. Important for walking, jumping, running, and golf. Attaches calf muscles to heel bone.

Achilles' tendonitis: Inflammation of the Achilles' tendon, common among athletes, primarily due to overuse.

Acute annulus fissure (tear): Common cause of acute sudden onset of low back pain produced by a fissure or tear in the annulus (outer covering of the disc).

Aerobic exercise: A variety of sustained exercises that strengthen the heart and lungs and therefore improves the body's utilization of oxygen. Exercises that increase the flow of blood through the soft tissues of the body. Should be performed 3-5 times a week for 20-60 minutes at each session. Examples include: bicycling; running; using a stair-stepping machine; and swimming.

Aging: Universal human experience. An extremely broad range of phenomena, affecting biological systems. Progressive biological changes that tend to reduce an individual's viability with gradual changes in the structure of any organism.

Analgesic: A pain relief medication.

Anemia: A deficiency or an abnormality of hemoglobin, the component of red blood cells that binds with oxygen from the lungs and carries it through the circulatory system to the tissues of the body.

Aneurysmal bone cyst: Benign primary bone tumor composed of blood vessel tissues.

Angina pectoris: Chest pain that is a common symptom of heart disease. It is produced when the amount of blood flowing to the heart is insufficient to accomplish the work demanded of the heart.

Angiogram: An x-ray picture of a blood vessel made after injecting a dye substance through a catheter into a blood vessel to make it visible on x-ray films.

Angiography: A radiological test that uses x-rays combined with special dye injections into the heart or blood vessels to determine blood flow to the heart or other organs. A blockage will be demonstrated by a poor visualization of the dye.

Angioplasty: (also called balloon angioplasty or percutaneous transluminal coronary angioplasty or PTCA). A procedure in which a special catheter is inserted into a narrowed artery and a balloon at the tip of the catheter is inflated to push aside any blockage. Angioplasty is very effective in certain situations; however, the blockage may return.

Angular motion: Sense by the semicircular canals in the inner ear.

Ankylosing spondylitis (AS): Special class of arthritis that causes inflammation of the spine, causes spine to become stiff and rigid. A chronic multi-system inflammatory disease; may involve the sacroiliac joints (SI) and the spine. Four times more common in men than in women.

Annular fissure (also called annular tears): Separations between annular fibers, evulsion of fibers from their vertebral body insertions or breaks through the fibers that extend radially, transversely, or concentrically. May involve one or many layers of the annulus fibrosus. Often causes back pain.

Annulus fibrosus: The tough outer fibrous portion of the intervertebral disc. It surrounds the nucleus pulposus of the disc. It is made up of concentric layers of collagen and elastin fibers that contain proteoglycans and water.

Anterior arch: The anterior (front) portion of the vertebra. It consists of the vertebral body and the anterior third of the pedicles.

Anterior bone fusion (bone graft): After an anterior cervical discectomy, a bone graft is placed at the discectomy site to bring about long-term spinal stability. The bone graft is an arthrodesis, which is the surgical fixation to promote fusion of bones.

Anterior cervical discectomy: Operation of the cervical spine from anteriorly (front) in which part or all of the intervertebral disc is removed.

Anterior interbody fusion: An operation performed in front of the spine, either open or with a laparoscope to remove a disc. Once the disc is removed, a bone graft is then placed at the discectomy site to achieve a solid union between the bone graft and the bone to which it is attached. It is a coupling of the two bones so that they become united. It is performed to reduce motion and eliminate spinal pain.

Anterior longitudinal ligament (ALL): A thick strong bundle of fibers connecting the anterior (front) surfaces of the vertebral bodies from C2 (cervical) to the sacrum.

Anterior spine surgery: Surgery performed either in front of the spine or along the side of the spine to address spinal deformities, instability, infections, fractures, tumors, or other disorders of the spine.

Anterior to Posterior (A/P) **x-ray:** X-ray obtained from the front to the back. Radiation is passed from the front of the patient to the back of the patient.

Anterior: In human anatomy, the front surface of the body, or the position of one structure relative to another. The opposite of anterior is posterior.

Antibody: A substance made by the immune system to neutralize a foreign or invading substance in the body.

Antigen: A foreign or an invading substance within the body that triggers an immune system reaction.

Arches of the foot: A series of arches formed by bones and strengthened by ligaments and tendons of the foot in order to support the weight of the body in an upright posture. Arches are evident by a gap between the inner side of the foot and the ground when an individual is standing.

Arteriosclerosis: Hardening of the arteries caused by deposits (plaques) of fats (cholesterol) in blood vessel walls that restrict the flow of blood and facilitate the forming of blood clots.

Arthritis: The inflammation of one or more joints. More than 100 types exist.

Aspirin: Medication which contains a salt called salicylates. An anti-inflammatory medication and analgesic (pain) medication. Is effective for relief of mild to moderate pain and reduces inflammation, but only at maximum daily doses. It reduces the clotting capacity of blood, therefore, it prolongs bleeding time. It prolongs bleeding time more than ibuprofen or acetaminophen. Aspirin can cause or worsen ulcers. It can also trigger asthma attacks in 5-10% of people with asthma. Heartburn and stomach upset may be caused by aspirin. Taking aspirin after a meal and following with a glass of milk or water may help to lessen the irritation. Enteric-coated or buffered aspirin tablets are less upsetting. Aspirin should never be given to a child under the age of 12 years because of a possible rare but dangerous illness called Reye's syndrome (characterized by liver changes, acute brain swelling, disturbances of consciousness, seizures, and even death).

Atherosclerosis: A condition in which the inner layers of the walls of arteries become thick and irregular due to deposits of fat, cholesterol and other substances.

Athlete's foot: Tinea pedis, a fungal infection of the foot.

Atlas: The first cervical vertebra, C1. It is named after the mythological Greek figure, Atlas, who holds up the world just as C1 holds up the head.

Autogenous graft: Bone graft originating from the patient themselves.

Autograft: A bone graft derived from another site in or on the body of the patient receiving it.

Autonomic nervous system (ANS): A specialized part of the nervous system that regulates heart (cardiac), glandular (hormone) functions and muscles in the digestive tract.

Avascular: A structure not supplied with blood vessels, or a lack of blood.

Axial load: A force that creates pressure and increases the weight on bony and soft tissue elements of the spine. Axial loads influence the vertebrae, ligaments, tendons and discs of the spine.

Axial rotation: Twisting of the spine around the long axis of the body.

Axis: The second cervical vertebra, C2. It connects to the atlas, C1, and provides rotation of the head.

Babinski's reflex: A neurological test in which the bottom of the foot is gently stroked along the lateral side of the sole. A positive test is evident when the big toe dorsiflexes (moves toward the face), may indicate an underlying disease process of the nervous system .

Balance: Complex interaction between the inner ear, input from the eye, proprioception, and the ability to feel position of joints in space.

Barometric pain: Pain in joints and bones often associated with changes in weather.

Benign paroxysmal positional vertigo (BPPV): A condition in which otoliths become detached from the otolith organ and become lodged in the portion of the inner ear called the posterior semicircular canal, which senses angular motion. Movement such as rolling onto the affected ear while lying prone will bring about vertigo.

Benign: Not cancerous.

Biologic response-modifiers (BRMs): Medications intended to reduce pain and inflammation in arthritic patients.

Biological aging: One type of aging. With increasing biological aging, an individual will have an increased liability to various kinds of illnesses and trauma with a lack of recuperative power. Often influenced by an individual's family history, occupation, social habits such as diet, tobacco and alcohol use.

Biophosphonates: A group of drugs that are anti-reabsorptive. Involved in the treatment and prevention of osteoporosis in certain patients; inhibits breakdown of bone and slows down bone removal.

Biopsy: The removal of a portion of body tissue for analysis under a microscope. Often used to
determine the status of an abnormal growth that may be cancerous.

Bone cage: A special surgical bone cage made of metal or carbon. A bone cage is intended to replace removed bone such as after a corpectomy, or placed between bones such as an interbody fusion.

Bone densitometry: A test using low doses of x-rays to measure bone mass or bone density in the body.

Bone fusion (bone graft): A surgical technique in which a bone graft, either from the patient or from a bone bank (another human being) is selected, processed and preserved, and then placed at the operation site in and about the bone of a patient to achieve a solid union between the bone graft and the bone to which it is attached. The consequence of a successful bone fusion is reduced mobility. Bone fusion is often done to reduce motion and eliminate pain. A bone graft is like grafting a limb onto a tree.

Bone metastases: Cancerous bone tumors or lesions that have traveled or spread from a cancer originating elsewhere in the body.

Bone mineral density (BMD): The amount of bone unit of skeletal tissue.

Bone screws: Special surgical screws, usually made of a metal called titanium, placed into the spine, either anteriorly (front) or posteriorly (back) and attached to bone plates or bone rods. Bone screws provide fixation to bony structures to provide stabilization of the spine.

Brittle bone disease: Osteoporosis; porous bone disease.

Bulging disc (also called a prolapse of the disc): Occurs when the ruptured nucleus pulposus distorts the fibers of the annulus causing a discrete bulge, but no nuclear material escapes through the annular fibers.

Bunions: An enlargement or swelling of the large toe joint on the inner side of the foot. Tends to run in families.

Calcaneus: The quadrangular-shaped bone at the back of the tarsus, referred to as the heel bone.

Calcitonin: Hormone produced in thyroid gland.

Callus: A thickened layer of skin or the epidermis (outer layer of skin) due to repeated, excessive friction or pressure. Happens on the bottom of the foot.

When it occurs on the top of the foot, it is called a corn.

Calorie: A unit used to measure energy. Energy for the body is supplied by food. When a golfer expends the same number of calories that they take in, their weight stays the same. If a golfer eats more than he or she burns off, the calories are stored away in fat cells in the body for future use. If a golfer plays more and burns off more than he or she eats, the fat cells release some of their stored energy and the golfer may lose weight. The average adult man or woman needs between 1800 and 2200 calories per day to maintain a healthy weight.

Canal mouse: A sequestered herniated disc of the extruded nuclear substance that may float around the spinal canal and is totally remote from the site from which it originally extruded. It is like a mouse traveling in the canal.

Carbohydrates: Energy source for the body. Two main types: 1) simple and 2) complex. Simple carbohydrates are sugars. They provide the body with quick energy boosts. Food groups such as cookies, candies and cakes contain large quantities of simple carbohydrates. Complex carbohydrates have more complicated structures. They are made of starches and dietary fibers. Starches are digested slowly and provide sustained energy. Foods such as pasta, bread, vegetables, potatoes and rice contain high levels of starch. Eating more carbohydrates than the body needs, will be stored as fat.

Cardiopulmonary system: Systems of the body pertaining to the heart and lungs.

Cartilage: Often known as gristle. A special tissue characterized by a lack of blood vessels. Found in joints, ribs and tubular structures such as the larynx (voice box), air passages and ears. It is firm tissue. The three kinds of cartilage include: hyaline, elastic, and fibrocartilage.

Cauda equina: A bundle of spinal nerves extending from the conus medullaris (end of the spinal cord) into the spinal canal below the L1 (lumbar spine).

Cauda equina syndrome: Lesions of the end of the spinal cord that interrupt multiple motor and sensory nerve roots to the legs. Often produces bilateral lower extremity atrophy and weakness, loss of reflexes. Also involves bowel and urinary bladder with retention, incontinence and a weak anal sphincter.

Caudal: In anatomy, relates to the lower portion of a structure. It pertains to the tail or near the tail. The opposite of caudal is cranial.

Central nervous system (CNS): Comprised of the brain and spinal cord. It is the primary part of the nervous system.

Cerebrospinal fluid (CSF): The clear colorless fluid surrounding the central nervous system (brain and spinal cord). It is formed by cells in the brain and circulates throughout the central nervous system. It has both a protective function as a shock absorber, as well as providing nutrients to the brain and spinal cord.

Cervical bone fixation device: A metal bone plate or rods placed into the cervical spine, either anteriorly (front) or posteriorly (back) to provide stabilization of the cervical spine.

Cervical bone plate: A plate made of metal, usually titanium, which is placed either anteriorly (front) or posteriorly (back) to provide stabilization of the cervical spine.

Cervical spine: The bones of the spine located in the neck. It is comprised of seven (7) vertebra.

Cervical spondylosis: Degeneration of bones and cartilage in the neck, which may cause pain and stiffness of the neck. Also called osteoarthritis of the cervical spine.

Cervicalgia: Neck pain.

Chemotherapy: A therapy that uses anticancer drugs to kill cancer cells. These drugs can be administered orally (by mouth) or through an injection into the bloodstream. The chemotherapeutic agents are designed to try to limit and kill only the cancer cells; however, chemotherapeutic agents will also affect normal cells. Thus, chemotherapy is given in cycles of a treatment, then followed by a recovery period and then another treatment and so on. A special physician called an oncologist is involved with chemotherapy.

Cholecystitis: Inflammation of the gallbladder.

Cholelithiasis: Presence or formation of gall stones.

Cholesterol: A soft, waxy, fat-like substance found in the body's cells. Cholesterol doesn't dissolve in water or blood and is carried through the bloodstream by a special protein called lipoprotein.

Chondritis: Inflammation of cartilage.

Chondrosarcoma: Slow-growing malignant bone tumor; originates in cartilage.

Chordoma: A very invasive spine tumor that destroys surrounding healthy bones. May metastasize or spread.

Chronological aging: One type of aging. It is the number of birthdays that an individual has celebrated. Often the type of aging that society imposes on people as they reach a certain chronological age. Chronological age often has nothing to do with an individual's employability, intelligence, activity level, and ability to contribute to society.

Claw toe: Toe that is contracted at one of the joints of the lesser toes. May occur in any toe, except the big toe.

Clonus: Alternate muscular contractions and relaxations in rapid succession. May indicate an abnormal underlying neurological disorder.

Coccydynia (also called coccygodynia): Sharp pain in the coccyx, the small triangular bone located at the end of the spinal column.

Coccygectomy: Surgical excision of the coccyx.

Coccyx: The bony structure at the very tip of the spine. Often referred to as the tailbone. It is the small bone connected to the sacrum, formed by the union of four (sometimes three or five) rudimentary vertebra. It is the distal or caudal extremity of the vertebral column.

Cold massage: The use of ice during a massage. Care must be taken not to leave the ice directly on the skin for any length of time due to possible tissue or skin damage.

Cold therapy: The use of ice to help reduce inflammation and pain. A cold pack (a commercial preparation), bag of frozen peas, or ice cubes in a plastic bag, used for 15-20 minutes at a time. Ice should never be placed directly on the skin due to possible cold-induced damage to the underlying skin.

Collagen: The protein substance of the white fibers of the skin, tendon, bone, cartilage and other connective tissues.

Complete blood count (CBC): An examination of blood samples to obtain a count of the number of red cells, white cells, and hemoglobin in the blood, and to determine the percentage of red cells in the blood. Used to check and screen for blood disorders and infections.

Complete spinal cord injury: An injury to the spinal cord in which nerve impulses are not able to travel below the site of injury.

Computerized axial tomography (CAT or CT scan): A machine that produces and detects X-rays in conjunction with a computer. X-rays produced by a CAT scanner show different layers of density in bone tissues. A radiological diagnostic procedure that uses x-rays to create cross-sectional images of internal body parts. Bone is better visualized with a CAT scan than an MRI.

Concordant pain: During a discogram, the pain response to an injection of the contrast dye will elicit pain that is very similar to the pain which prompted the patient to see a physician in the first pace. Concordant pain may help to determine that a specific disc is indeed the problem disc.

Congenital abnormalities: Defects existing at or usually before birth. Often refers to conditions that are present at birth.

Contraindication: A condition or a disease that makes or renders a particular type of treatment, either surgical or medical, not possible or recommended due to increased risks and complications.

Corns: Develops from accumulation of dead skin on the foot, forms thick hardened areas. A thickening of the outer layer of the skin (epidermis) due to excessive friction or pressure; occurs on top of the foot. When it occurs on the bottom of the foot, it is called a callus.

Coronary artery bypass graft (CABG): A surgical procedure in which the blocked artery of the heart is bypassed by using a graft taken from a patient's leg or thigh. The procedure is to return blood supply to the heart.

Coronary Artery Disease (CAD): Also called coronary heart disease (CHD) or coronary vascular heart disease (CVHD), caused by a build-up of fatty deposits referred to as plaques on the walls of the arteries of the heart. Such build-ups will lead to a degeneration of the artery and will eventually obstruct the flow of oxygen and nutrient-rich blood throughout the body, including the heart. If the heart does not receive sufficient oxygen-rich blood, the heart muscles can be damaged. A minor blockage can cause chest pain called angina. If muscles are damaged, it is referred to as a myocardial infarction of the heart. Symptoms of a heart attack include: constant pressure, fullness or a squeezing pain in the chest that lasts for a few minutes, resolves or goes away and then returns. Other symptoms include: dizziness; fainting; sweating; nausea, unusual shortness of breath or breathing difficulties, pain that radiates into the shoulders, neck or jaw and travels down the arms or into the back; discomfort with any activity that often subsides during a period of rest; and finally, indigestion that antacids or other medications fail to relieve. If a heart attack is suspected, emergency medical care is needed.

Corpectomy: Removal of a vertebral body due to trauma, tumor or other pathological processes.

Corticosteroid: Related to corticosteroid hormones produced by the body. Often given to relieve inflammation by blocking production of natural substances that promote inflammation such as prostaglandins. Corticosteroids may also suppress the immune system by decreasing the production and effectiveness of certain white blood cells, which are important in the body's defense mechanism. Corticosteroids may also be given as replacement therapy if the body is unable to produce sufficient natural corticosteroid hormones.

Costochondritis: An inflammation of the ribs or the cartilage where the ribs attach to the sternum (breast bone).

Costotransversectomy: A surgical approach to the thoracic spine in which the transverse process of the vertebra and the costal process, rib, is removed to gain access to abnormalities of the thoracic disc or bony elements. The operation is performed with the patient in the prone position (face down); an incision is made in the posterior or back portion of the spine.

Costovertebral pain syndrome: Pain originating from the articulation of the rib to the vertebral body.

Cranial: Relates to the skull or cranium. In anatomy, the direction towards the head. The opposite of cranial is caudal.

C-reactive protein measurements: During inflammation, the level of a C-reactive protein in the blood rises and falls. The C-reactive protein is a useful test for assessing a response to treatment for an infection. The levels of C-reactive protein may fall following effective treatment before symptoms of inflammation have started to resolve or subside.

Cuboid bone: One of the seven tarsal bones of the foot. It is located on the side of the foot (lateral side) and forms part of the mid-foot.

Cuneiform bones: Small, wedge-shaped bones that articulate with the navicular bone and with the first three metatarsal bones. The wedge shape of these bones contributes greatly to the formation and the maintenance of the transverse arch of the foot.

Curvature of the Spine: A description of the anatomical curvature of the spine described as lordosis or kyphosis. The spinal curvature may deviate from its normal position or direction.

Degeneration: A change of tissue from one form and function to another. A process of maturing or aging.

Degenerative changes: A change in the makeup of body tissues from one form and function to another. Often a consequence of maturing or aging. Includes biomechanical and chemical changes of tissue. When there is a chemical change in the tissue itself, this is referred to as a true degeneration. When the degenerative change consists of deposits of abnormal material into tissues, it is called infiltration. Often used to describe changes in the intervertebral disc. May or may not be symptomatic.

Denis Classification of Spine Fractures: A classification system for cervical (neck) and thoracolumbar fractures in which the spine is divided into anterior (front), middle, and posterior (back) columns. The middle column's integrity is important for spinal stability.

Dens: The dens is the same anatomical structure as the odontoid. Dens is the

Latin word for tooth, and odontoid is a Greek word for tooth.

Diabetes Mellitus: A chronic disease caused by the body's inability to handle the breakdown of carbohydrates into sugars. Caused by low levels of insulin, a hormone produced in the pancreas. Insulin enables cells to remove sugar from the blood stream and produce energy within the cells. Diabetic patients have either a pancreas that does not produce enough insulin, or insulin that does not function properly. Two types of diabetes: Type I can occur at any age; it is most commonly found in patients under the age of 30. It is sometimes called insulin-dependent diabetes or Juvenile Diabetes. Type II diabetes is referred to as non-insulin dependent diabetes, usually found in individuals older than 40 years of age, but can occur at any age. Type II accounts for approximately 80-90% of all cases of diabetes. Some women will develop diabetes during pregnancy; this is referred to as Gestational Diabetes. Common symptoms for diabetes include: sudden, unexplained weight loss; need to frequently urinate; excessive thirst; increased hunger or appetite; visual problems; circulation problems with tingling and numbness in the arms, hands, legs or feet; skin itching; slow healing after cuts or bruises; and frequent infections. A positive diagnosis for diabetes can be made by using blood tests to measure the sugar levels (glucose) in the blood. Maintaining a normal blood glucose (sugar) level can help reduce complications of diabetes. Golfers with diabetes are able to play, but should inform their physician that they are golfers. Adjustments to their medications, nutritional demands, and golf wear (gloves and shoes) may need to be re-evaluated.

Diagnosis: The identification of a disease or a condition.

Diagnostic Radiology: A branch of medical radiology that involves the imaging of body organs and tissues and their functions. Ionizing radiation provides a window to view normal and abnormal anatomy.

Differential diagnosis: A list of different diagnoses that may be possible causes of pain and disorders.

Disc extrusion: The nucleus pulposus central disc material is present in the spinal canal and has migrated through disrupted fibers of the annulus. The disc material, however, remains connected or attached to the nucleus inside the disc.

Disc protrusion: Synonymous with a bulging or prolapsed disc.

Discectomy: The removal of all or part of the intervertebral disc.

Discogram: A radiographic technique in which a contrast dye is injected into the intervertebral disc under a special x-ray machine called fluoroscopy. The radio-opaque dye is injected into the center of the disc, nucleus pulposus, for the purpose of identifying the disc configuration.
Discordant pain: If the dye injection during the discogram does not reproduce a patient's presenting pain, it is referred to as discordant pain. It is therefore assumed that this disc is not the source of the patient's pain.

Disease-modifying anti-rheumatic drugs (DMARDs): Drugs for altering the course of certain arthritic diseases, or a second line of defense against rheumatoid arthritis after less potent drugs are ineffective. Also used for other types of related conditions.

Disk: Another spelling for disc.

Dix-Hallpike examination: A test to confirm the diagnosis of benign paroxysmal positional vertigo (BPPV).

Dizziness: Sensation of being off balance.

Doppler ultrasound scan: Produces sound waves used to produce an image of blood flow. Often used to detect abnormal blood flow through blood vessels in the neck.

Drug – Drug interactions: Drugs or botanical medicines that can affect each other's activities. The activity of one particular drug may be decreased or increased when the second drug is taken. The combination of two drugs or botanical medications may cause an undesirable and totally different effect than initially intended.

Dual energy x-ray absorptiometry (DEXA): A commonly used method for bone densitometry.

Dura mater: The tough fibrous membrane making up the outer covering of the central nervous system (brain and spinal cord). In anatomy, it is called the dura mater (hard mother).

Dynamic abnormal bracing: Strengthening exercises for the abdominal muscles.

Electrolytes: Elements that carry electrical currents in body fluids. They work to maintain fluid balance and pressure in cells of the body. Sodium, potassium and chloride act as electrolytes. They help regulate blood pressure, heart rate, muscle contraction, nerve transmission and acidity. Sodium and chloride are prime ingredients of table salt. Eating too much sodium chloride can cause high blood pressure. Potassium is found in fruits, potato skins, whole grains and milk. Supplements of these electrolytes should only be done with a doctor's permission.

Electrolytes: Sodium, potassium and chloride. Found in body fluids; work to maintain fluid balance, blood pressure, and pressure in cells. Regulate blood pressure, heart rate, muscle contraction, nerve transmission, and acidity.

Electromyography (EMG): A special test using electrode needles to help distinguish between nerve and muscle disorders. During the examination, a recording needle is placed into the muscle.

Endoscopy: The use of a surgical tube containing a light source and a viewing lens to examine interior parts of the body. Small surgical instruments can be threaded through the working channel in the scope to perform or facilitate surgical procedures.

End-plate: A thin plate of tissue that is attached to the cortical rim of the vertebral body. It is composed of an outer layer of cartilage and an inner layer of bone. It is well-vascularized (many blood vessels) and provides nutrients to the intervertebral discs.

Enthesopathy: An inflammatory process that causes new bone formation at the attachments of tendons and ligaments to the bone.

Epidural abscess: A collection of pus caused by bacterial or fungal infections on the outside of the dura (covering of the brain and spinal cord).

Epilepsy: Seizures. First onset in an adult may indicate a brain tumor. A symptom of over-active brain impulses and excitability of the brain.

Erythrocyte sedimentation rate (ESR): The body responds to inflammation caused by damage or infection by producing higher than normal amounts of particular proteins, the inflammatory proteins. Common tests for inflammation are based on assessment of the levels of certain proteins in the blood. ESR measures the rate at which red blood cells settle to the bottom of a sample of blood, leaving the liquid part of the blood at the top. The red blood cells clump together in the presence of inflammation and settle more rapidly than usual. The speed or rate at which the red blood cells settle to the bottom is called the erythrocyte sedimentation rate. This test is related to the severity of the inflammation.

Ewing's sarcoma: A highly malignant bone tumor.

Extension: In the spine, it is straightening or backward bending.

Extensor muscles of the hand: Muscles that straighten the fingers and the thumb and bend the wrist backwards away from the palm.

Extrinsic: Outside; in anatomy, having a relationship to parts outside of a structure.

Extrinsic foot muscles: Muscles located outside of the foot whose tendons cross the ankle to insert onto bones of the feet.

Facet arthropathy: Refers to a painful degenerative spine joint. May occur in the cervical, thoracic and lumbar spines.

Facet joint (a zygapophyseal joint): Located behind the vertebral bodies of the spine. These paired joints connect the posterior bony elements of the vertebra. They have a slick, lubricating surface and are covered by a synovial capsule.

Facet rhizotomy: Denervation of a facet joint (zygaphophyseal) by destruction of the joint capsule and surrounding tissue.

Facetectomy: Excision of the articular process that contains the facets of the facet joint.

Fats: Energy source in the body. Essential for the absorption of some vitamins. Fats may be saturated or unsaturated. Dietary fat provides energy, insulation from cold, protection for internal organs, and helps in the absorption of certain vitamins. Saturated fats found in dairy products, meat, and coconut oil contribute to raised cholesterol levels. Hydrogenated fats are artificially produced and have properties similar to saturated fats. Unsaturated fats have a greater protective effect than monounsaturates. Monounsaturated fats are found in olive, peanut, and canola oils. Polyunsaturated fats are found in corn, cotton seed, safflower, soy and sunflower oils.

Fat-soluble vitamins: A, D, E and K. Fat-soluble vitamins can be retained in the body and can be toxic in high amounts. Other vitamins are water-soluble and are most unlikely to be toxic, excess amounts are excreted in the urine.

Fiber: Indigestible portion of plant foods. High fiber diet reduces risk of various gastrointestinal problems and disease, and promotes good cardiovascular health.

Fibrous tissue: Tissue composed of and containing fibers. Fibrosis is the formation of fibrous tissue. It can be found in many organ systems throughout the body. Fibrositis is the inflammation of tissue in the body; in certain situations an overgrowth of fibrous tissue, particularly in the muscles, may cause pain and stiffness. Formation may be due to a traumatic event.

Fibula: The slender needle-shaped lateral (outside) bone of the leg.

Flatfoot: Also called fallen arches. Feet that have a low arch or no arch.

Flexion: The act of bending. In regards to the spine, it is forward bending.

Flexor muscles of the hand: Muscles that bend the fingers into a fist and bend the wrist forward towards the palm.

Fluoroscopic microsurgical procedure: A closed surgical technique that employs the use of an endoscope.

Fluoroscopy: Radiological studies in which anatomical structures may be viewed on a screen as live X-ray images.

Foot blisters: Due to shearing forces rapidly applied to the skin. Blood or fluid accumulates between the outer (epidermal) layer of the foot and above the dermal (second) layer of the skin. Frequently due to ill-fitting shoes.

Foramen (plural = foramina): A natural opening or passage in bone or soft (membranous) tissues and structures. In the spine, it is a hole formed by the superior (top) and inferior (bottom) bony elements of the spine that allows the passage of a spinal nerve and blood vessels.

Foramen magnum: The large opening at the base of the skull through which the brain connects to the spinal cord. It is through this opening that the spinal cord and important blood vessels pass.

Forefoot: Made up of five metatarsal bones and phalanges.

Gadolinium: An X-ray dye used for special radiological procedures to better appreciate underlying abnormal structures, i.e., tumors.

Gastric ulcer: An open sore or lesion in the lining of the stomach, esophagus or duodenum (intestines). Symptoms include a burning or gnawing pain in the abdomen between the breastbone and the navel. Often occurs early in the morning and between meals.

Gastroesophageal reflux disease (GERD): A chronic heartburn.

Genetics: The study of genes and heredity. Genetic material is made up of deoxyribonucleic acid (DNA). Every cell contains 46 chromosomes arranged in 23 pairs. Half of the chromosomes are inherited from the mother and half from the father. Bits of genetic information can be defective resulting in a health disorder. Some genetic traits can cause serious disease. Understanding your family's disease history is important for your health and the health of your loved ones. A family's disease history is started with an individual's parents and siblings and then other relatives.

Giant cell tumor: Benign primary bone tumor; may be locally aggressive.

Glucose: It is the chief source of energy for living organisms. Found in certain foods, especially fruits. It is the end product of carbohydrate metabolism. Its utilization is controlled by insulin. Excess glucose is converted to glycogen and stored in the liver and muscles for use as needed. When glucose builds up in the bloodstream, the result can be serious. Glucose appears in the urine of patients with diabetes mellitus.

Golfer's elbow: A form of tendonitis. Occurs when the tendon attachment of the bone to the muscle of the elbow becomes damaged.

Hallus rigidus: Arthritis of the great toe joint.

Hamate: A small bone of the wrist located in the palm in line with the little and ring fingers.

Hammertoes: A rigid or flexible contraction of the toe caused by shortening of the tendons that control toe movements. The toe knuckle is enlarged, drawing the toe back. Over time, balance is affected.

Hard corns: Forms at the top of toes due to friction and pressure. Contains a cone-shaped core; often due to poor-fitting shoes.

Hard disc: Formation of a hard calcified ligament, annulus or other soft tissue that can compromise nervous tissue such as a nerve root.

Heartburn: A burning in the chest that radiates upward towards the neck. It is caused by acid reflux from the stomach. The pain is produced by the presence of stomach acid in the esophagus.

Heat exhaustion: The accumulation of large amounts of blood near the skin in an attempt to cool the body, producing a simultaneous deprivation of blood to the body's organs.

Heat stroke: An emergency condition caused by the blockage of the sweat glands that causes a dangerously high body temperature.

Heat therapy: The use of heat for the reduction of inflammation and pain. Often rotated with cold pack therapy. Heat may be applied by using hot packs, heating pads, or warm showers. Heat should never be used longer than 20 minutes at a time. Users should never fall asleep on a heating pad for fear of burning their skin.

Hemangioma: Common benign primary bone tumor composed of blood vessels (vascular lesion).

Hematoma: Blood clot.

Hemoglobin: The oxygen carrying pigment found in red blood cells.

Herniation: A localized displacement of disc material (beyond the normal limits of the intervertebral disc space). The disc material may include the nucleus pulposus, cartilage, fragmented bone, annular tissue, or any combination thereof. Often commonly referred to as a herniated nucleus pulposus (HNP). May compromise or pinch an exiting nerve or spinal cord. Pain is often a presenting symptom for patients.

Herpes zoster: An infection caused by the varicella zoster virus. The virus initially causes Chicken Pox, then remains dormant in nerve cells. When the virus is reactivated later in life, it causes herpes zoster, also known as shingles. The infection is characterized by a painful rash of blisters along the path of a nerve.

Herpes: A group of recurring viral illnesses caused by outbreaks of blisters in the genitals, cornea, mouth, anus and brain. Herpes virus can be transmitted sexually.

High density lipoprotein (HDL): Responsible for transferring cholesterol to the liver where it is removed from the body. It rids the body of excess cholesterol. It is the good cholesterol. A good way to remember that high density lipoprotein is the good one is that the "H" stands for healthy.

High sprain foot injury: Injury to ligaments connecting tibia and fibula bones.

High-arched foot: Also called a cavus foot. Characterized by an unusually high arch. The front part of the foot is drawn downward more than normal.

Hind-foot: Contains the two tarsal bones (talus and calcaneus).

Hip replacement: Commonly replaced joint. . During the operation, both the pelvic socket and the head of the femur (thigh bone), which fits into the socket, are replaced. Minimally invasive procedures are now developing.

Hoffman's sign: A sudden nipping of the nail of the index finger produces flexion of the thumb. This may indicate an abnormal underlying neurological process or spinal cord disorder.

Hormone: A substance produced by a gland in the body that influences the activity, metabolism and function of the body.

Hormone replacement therapy (HRT): Use of hormone therapy for treatment and management of brittle bone disease, osteoporosis. May increase the occurrence of certain cancers, particularly cancer of the lining of the uterus.

Hypertension (High Blood Pressure): A chronic condition that puts the heart and blood vessels under great strain. Blood pressure is the force that the blood exerts on the walls of blood vessels as it courses through the body. Narrow or constricted blood vessels can cause an increase in blood pressure. High blood pressure can lead to strokes, heart attacks, kidney failures and injury to other organs. The cause of hypertension is unknown in some 90-95% of cases. Hypertension may be caused due to kidney (renal) disease or congenital heart defects. Hypertension is a silent killer because it often has no symptoms. Symptoms of high blood pressure include: headaches, heart palpitations, blurry vision, flushed face, frequent nosebleeds, breathing difficulties after exercising or golfing, fatigue, dizziness, ringing in the ears, and increased frequency of urination.

Immune system: Cells, glands and vessels that function in preventing and defending the body against bacterial, viral and other types of infections.

Incomplete spinal cord injury: Preservation of some functioning of the spinal cord after injury.

Incontinence: The inability to control urination or defecation.

Inferior: Located beneath or below a point of reference. The opposite is superior.

Ingrown toenail (Onychocryptosis): The toenail pierces the lateral (side) nail fold and enters the skin where it acts as a foreign body. Causes pain and swelling. May become infected. Often caused by pressure or poorly-fitting shoes, and improper or excessive trimming of toenails.

Interventional radiology: A branch of radiology that provides a non-surgical treatment of certain diseases using imaging techniques to navigate small catheters, balloons, filters, needles and micro-instruments through blood vessels and into organs.

Intervertebral disc (IVD): A shock absorber or cushion-like structure located between the concave articular surfaces of the vertebral body endplates. Allows slight motion at each vertebral level. Situated between two contiguous vertebra. Composed of an outer tough lining called the annulus and an inner gel-like material called the nucleus pulposus.

Intradiscal electrothermy therapy (IDET): Also called intradiscal electrothermal annuloplasty (IDEA). A minimally invasive procedure for patients with fissures or tears in the annulus of a disc. A flexible electrothermal catheter is placed into the diseased disc under x-ray guidance. Heating coils of the catheter delivers an electric current to the disc. The electric current heats the disc in an attempt to ablate the pain receptors of the disc.

Intrinsic: Inside or belonging to a particular body part.

Intrinsic foot muscles: Muscles inside the foot, responsible for toe movement.

Ischemia: Lack of blood flow, especially to the heart or brain.

Joint Replacement: Replacement of joints that have been severely damaged by disorders such as arthritis, trauma, infections or other injuries. May be surgically replaced with artificial joints made of metal, ceramic or plastic materials.

Joint: An articulation or union between two or bones of the skeleton. A junction that allows more or less motion of one or more bones.

Kyphoplasty: Treatment for osteoporosis and other bone diseases causing fractures of vertebral bodies. Involves placement of a bone needle into the vertebral body, insertion of a bone balloon for restoration of vertebral body height and then placement of polymethylmethacrylate (PMMA) bone cement. Kyphoplasty may restore the lost height of the fractured vertebral body, return spinal stability and reduce bony pain.

Lamina: (plural = laminae) The rooftops of the posterior bony elements of the spine. Two flat plates of bone that extend from the pedicles and comprise the posterior arches of the spine.

Laminectomy: Surgical removal of part or all of the posterior vertebral elements, such as the lamina (rooftop) to allow room for underlying neural structures such as nerve roots.

Laminoplasty: Surgical reconstruction of the posterior vertebral elements to increase space and room for the underlying neural structures. It is an opening up of the posterior arch to allow more space for neural structures, i.e., spinal cord and nerves.

Laminotomy: A surgical procedure which creates an opening in one or more lamina.

Lateral: Pertains to the side. Denotes a position farther from the midline of the body or structure.

Lateral epicondyle: Bony prominence on the outside of the elbow. Site of attachment of the extensor muscles.

Lateral X-ray: X-rays are passed through the patient's side from one side to the other side.

Lhermitte's sign: The development of sudden transient electric-like shocks spreading down the body when a patient flexes the head forward. May be seen in conditions such as multiple sclerosis, but also in compression and other disorders of the cervical spinal cord.

Ligament injuries: Damage or injury to ligaments, the fibrous bands of tissue that hold bone together at a joint.

Ligamentum flavum: The yellow ligament of the spine. A strong longitudinal ligament connecting the lamina of each vertebra extending from C2 (cervical spine) to the sacrum. I is referred to as the yellow ligament of the body because it is made up of elastic tissue that is yellow in color.

Lineal motion: Sense by the otolithic organs.

Low density lipoprotein (LDL): A lipoprotein that carries cholesterol to cells within the body. Too much low-density lipoprotein in an individual's system will eventually cause sticking of the cholesterol to the walls of arteries and can contribute to heart disease. Low density lipoprotein is the bad cholesterol.

Lumbar Spine: Commonly referred to as the low back area. It is the section of the back inferior (below) the thoracic spine and between the ribs and the pelvis. It is made up of five (5) vertebra.

Lumbosacral sprain: A ligamentous injury of the lumbosacral region. Often used to describe localized pain following a specific moderately traumatic injury.

Lumbosacral strain: A muscular injury in the lumbosacral region. An imprecise term used in a similar fashion to a lumbosacral sprain when associated with localized pain following a specific moderately traumatic injury.

Lymphoma: A group of diseases that arise from the lymphatic system.

Magnetic resonance imaging (MRI or MR): An imaging procedure that does not use ionizing radiation to produce pictures of the body. Uses strong electromagnets and special radio waves to visualize anatomical structures.

Malignant primary bone tumor: Bone tumors that arise from the bone itself and have a tendency to spread elsewhere.

Mallet toe: Occurs when the joint at the end of the toe cannot straighten. Caused by bone and muscle imbalances. Often found in individuals who are constantly on their feet, such as in golf or athletic activities.

Marie Stumpell disease: Ankylosing spondylitis.

Massage: Any kind of systematic manipulation of the soft tissues of the body, *i.e.*, muscle and connective tissue. Manipulation can mean any combination of rubbing, kneading, slapping, tapping, rolling, pressing or jostling of the soft tissues.

Medial: Pertaining to the middle. Closer to the midline of the body or structure.

Medial epicondyle: Bony prominence on the inner side of the elbow. Better known as the "funny bone." Site of attachment of the flexor muscles.

Metastasis: The migration of cancerous cells from a primary site of origin to a secondary site.

Metastasize: To spread to distant organs or tissue. Metastatic disease originates in one organ and spreads to others.

Metastatic bone tumor: Most common tumor of spine; tumors that originate at one site and travel to another, i.e., lung cancer that travels to the spine.

Meyerding Grading System: A method of grading spondylolisthesis or slippage by determining the percentage of translation or movement of the slipped vertebra over the adjacent inferior (below) vertebra.

Mid-foot: Comprised of five of the seven tarsal bones of the foot.

Minerals: Twenty-two (22) minerals are needed for good health; classified as major or minor. Minerals include calcium, magnesium, phosphorus; chromium; copper; iron; selenium; zinc; sulfur; iodine; molybdenum; manganese; boron; fluoride; cobalt; silicone; vanadium; nickel, tin, sodium, potassium, and chloride.

Minimally invasive lumbar disc surgery: Involves a small incision in the skin through which a small probe is inserted and directed to the herniated disc. Small microsurgical instruments are used to remove the herniated disc material.

Morton's neuroma: A neuroma due to thickening of a nerve in the foot located between two metatarsal heads. The nerve is compressed, pinched or bruised.

Motion segment: The functional unit of the spine. It consists of two adjacent vertebra, the intervertebral disc, facets joints, and ligamentous tissues.

Multiple myeloma: Disease of plasma or white blood cells that undergo changes and become cancerous.

Muscle spasms: Involuntarily contracted, intensely painful muscles.

Musculoskeletal System: All of the skeletal muscles, tendons, ligaments and their bony attachments.

Myelogram: A radiology technique in which a contrast material or dye is injected into the subarachnoid space, usually in the patient's lower lumbar spine. After the dye has been injected, x-rays or CAT scans or MRIs are obtained. The contrast dye in the spinal canal allows visualization of neurological structures such as nerves and spinal cord. A water-soluble myelogram is often done; this involves use of a contrast medium that is absorbed by the body.

Myelopathy: A disease of the spinal cord.

Myocarditis: Inflammation of muscle of heart.

Navicular bone: A concave bone of the human foot, it is located between the talus and the metatarsals. Located in front of the ankle bone on the instep of the foot. Sometimes called the scaphoid.

Neoplasm: An abnormal growth of tissue. Tissue growth is uncontrolled and progressive. May be malignant or benign.

Nerve: A collection of nerve fibers which convey impulses from the part of the central nervous system (brain and spinal cord) to other regions of the body.

Nerve Conduction Study (NCS): A study to determine that nerves are conducting electrical impulses in a normal manner.

Nerve entrapment: Pressure placed on a nerve by soft tissue or bony elements causing pain.

Nerve root: The portion of the nerve as it goes through the foramen (spine bone window) and just beyond the vertebra. It combines with other nerve roots to form larger nerves that travel to distant sites.

Neurogenic claudication: Occurs in patients with lumbar spinal stenosis. It is caused by an individual walking and standing upright. May be caused by narrowing of the spinal canal, which causes pressure on the nerves and blood vessel elements in the area that is narrowed. Individuals often report that when they walk, they have pain; when they stop or lie down, the pain may be relieved. Neurogenic claudication usually causes pain the low back area, which is followed by pain traveling into the legs.

Neurologic deficit: Loss of a reflex, loss of normal motor or extremity strength, or loss of the ability to feel touch or pinprick.

Neuroma: A growth or tumor largely made up of nerve cells.

Non-steroidal anti-inflammatory drugs (NSAIDs): NSAIDs are non-opioid analgesics that are used to reduce inflammation and pain. Includes medications such as aspirin and ibuprofen. Commonly prescribed medications to relieve pain and inflammation, particularly in muscles, ligaments and joints. Limit the release of prostaglandins thereby reducing the inflammation. May be bought over the counter; others require a physician's prescription.

Nucleus pulposus: The soft gelatinous central portion of the intervertebral disc.

Obese: Weighing 20% or more over a healthy weight.

Oblique plain x-rays: Radiographic tests in which x-rays are passed anterolaterally (front to side) or posterolaterally (back to side).

Occipitocervical joint: The joint where the occipital condyles of the skull articulate to the superior joint surfaces of the atlas (C1). Also called the occipitoatlantal joint.

Odontoid (also called the Dens): It is a tooth-like process projecting from the body of C2. It provides a pivot joint for rotation of the atlas and axis.

Onychomycosis: Fungal toenails.

Open lumbar discectomy surgery: A surgical procedure in which an incision is made at the site of the abnormal disc herniation. The skin and the deeper tissues are exposed to reveal the underlying bony elements. Through the opened procedure, the abnormal disc is removed.

Orthostatic hypotension: Blood pressure that is too low, which can be a side-effect of some high blood pressure medications. Due to not enough blood getting to the brain when positional changes of the head are made, i.e., changing from a down to an upright position.

Osteoarthritis: Common form of arthritis, a chronic disease, causes breakdown of cushioning, cartilage and joints and formation of new bones at the margins of the joints. Frequently called degenerative joint disease (DJD). Can affect any joint in the body. Hips, knees, fingers and spine are most frequently affected.

Osteoblast: Bone cells responsible for moving and rebuilding bone.

Osteoclast: Large bone cells involved in breaking down and re-absorption of bone.

Osteoma: Benign bone tumor.

Osteomalacia: A reduction in the physical strength of bone due to decreased mineralization.

Osteomyelitis: Infection of bone, usually caused by bacteria. More common in young children, elderly individuals at risk, and people with reduced immunity. Causes damage to surrounding tissues and bone. Patients often have severe spinal pain.

Osteopenia: Loss of bone mass; any state in which bone mass is reduced below normal.

Osteophyte: Bone spur.

Osteoporosis: A condition in which the bone loses its strength and the various minerals of which it is composed. It is a loss of both the mineral and matrix components of bone. Common signs of osteoporosis: pain in the lower back, bone fractures, poor posture, bad gums, and gradual loss of height.

Otolithic organs: Part of the inner ear that contains little flecks of calcium called otoliths.

Over-the-counter medication: Non-prescription medication. Medications that can be bought without a doctor's prescription.

Overuse fracture: Stress fracture.

Overuse Syndrome: Injury to soft tissues, such as muscles, ligaments and tendons, due to repeated motions. Overexertion of tissues through strenuous exercise or as a result of repetitive physical activity. Such injuries are brought about by poor conditioning. Best prevented by a proper conditioning program with strength training of muscles and opposing muscle groups.

Paresthesia: Abnormal sensations such as burning or prickling in the extremities.

Pars: A short expression for pars interarticularis.

Pars interarticularis: A bony element of the spine between the superior and inferior articulating processes (joints).

Pathological reflexes: Abnormal findings during a neurological examination that may indicate a pathological or abnormal underlying disease process.

Pedicle: Two short rounded bony processes that connect the vertebral body to the posterior (back) elements.

Pericarditis: Inflammation of the pericardium (tissue surrounding the heart).

Peripheral nervous system (PNS): The nerves located outside of the central nervous system (brain and spinal cord). Includes the spinal nerves, cranial nerves, sympathetic and parasympathetic nerves.

PET fusion imaging: A hybrid machine that combines positron emission tomography (PET) with a CAT (CT) scanner or MRI. The results of the two types of scanners are fused together. The CAT scanner and the MRI provide the anatomical details, while the PET scanner demonstrates the functional activities of tissues and organs.

Phalanges: Bones in the toes. Each toe has three phalanges, except the big toe that has two.

Pinched nerve: A compromised or squeezed nerve as it exits the spinal cord and travels through the bony foramen of the spine. It may be pinched, squeezed, or compressed anywhere along its course.

Plain X-rays: (See X-rays)

Plane: A real or imaginary flat surface made by cutting through the human body. The cut part is then turned to view the flat surface of the cut. This cut is made either vertically or horizontally through the body.

Plantar fascia: Strong tissue structure that runs from the front of the heel bone (calcaneus) to the ball of the foot.

Plantar fasciitis: Often called heel spur. Causes heel pain during weight-bearing.

Plantar heel pain: Develops as a response to repetitive stress on the heel, an overuse syndrome. Heel pain localized over plantar fascia.

Plantar warts: Located on the sole of the foot. Easily identified by tiny hemorrhages within the core of the wart. Characterized by the appearance of a small black, red or brown spot signifying blood. Well-circumscribed (well-defined) surrounding area of skin, which may appear as a light ring around the central darkened area.

Plaque: A fatty buildup on the linings of a blood vessel. In dental terms, it may mean a mucus that contains bacteria and sugar that collects on the teeth above the gums.

Plasmacytoma: A solitary region of myeloma; usually carries better prognosis than multiple myeloma.

Platelet: The smallest blood cells, helps stop bleeding by plugging the site of the injury in the blood vessel wall and releasing chemicals that promote clotting.

Pleurisy: Inflammation of the pleura (membrane investing the lungs and lining of the thoracic cavity).

Pneumonia: An infection of the lungs caused by bacteria or a virus.

Polymethylmethacrylate (PMMA): Bone cement used for placement into the vertebral body during Vertebroplasty or Kyphoplasty.

Positive straight leg raising test: A test to evaluate irritation of the nerve in the low back area. A healthcare provider raises a patient's leg; if the raising leg produces pain in the low back and radiates into the leg, the test is considered to be positive.

Positron Emission Tomography (PET scan): A special type of radionuclide scanning. PET scan measures the way cells use glucose. Able to detect increase in metabolic activities by using radioactive tracers injected into a patient's bloodstream.

Posterior arch: The posterior (back) section of a vertebra, which is made up of the posterior two-thirds of the pedicles, lamina, and the spinous processes.

Posterior elements: The bony structures located behind the spinal canal and connecting to the vertebral bodies. Posterior elements include the pedicles, lamina, spinous processes, and transverse processes.

Posterior interbody fusion: A surgical operation performed posteriorly (back of the spine). The interbody disc is removed and a bone graft, either from the patient or bone bank, or a bone cage with bone is then placed into the discectomy site between the vertebra. The interbody bone graft is placed in a manner to achieve a solid union between the bone graft and the bone to which it is attached. The posterior interbody fusion is often augmented by bone screws, bone plates and bone rods.

Posterior Longitudinal Ligament (PLL): Strong thick ligament connecting the posterior (back) surfaces of the vertebral bodies from C2 (cervical spine) to the sacrum.

Posterior spinal surgery: Surgery performed from in back of the spine. The patient is placed either in a prone position (face down) or laterally (on their side). Surgery is intended to address spinal instability, tumors, infections, disc disease, degenerative disease, or other abnormalities of the spine.

Posterior to Anterior (P/A) X-ray: A

plain X-ray in which the radiation is passed from the back of the patient to the front of the patient.

Posterior: In human anatomy, the back surface of the body. It is used to describe the position of one structure relative to another. The opposite of posterior is anterior.

Prednisone: A corticosteroid.

Primary bone cancer: Cancerous tumors or lesions that originate within bone tissue.

Primary bone tumor: Tumors that occur and originate from within bone.

Prognosis: The forecast of a possible or probable outcome of a given disease or medical condition.

Prolapsed disc: Synonymous with bulging disc.

Proprioceptors: A type of internal sensory receptor that monitors the degree of stretch of muscles and tendons in the body. Gives information concerning sense of balance and awareness of position of various body parts in relationship to each other.

Prostaglandin: A group of hormone-like substances that cause a wide range of effects on body tissues. Such effects include: inflammation and stimulating uterine contractions.

Prostate-specific antigen (PSA): A chemical substance produced exclusively by the prostate cells. An increased level often indicates the presence of prostate cancer.

Protein: Any group of complex organic compounds that contain carbon, hydrogen, oxygen, nitrogen, and usually sulfur. Proteins are the principal constituents of the protoplasm of all cells. Proteins serve as enzymes, structural elements, hormones, and are involved in a multitude of activities in the body. Proteins are essential for the growth, maintenance and repair of tissue. Proteins should provide about 20% of a golfer's calories. Proteins are a vital part of all body systems; therefore, protein is not used as an energy source unless an individual's carbohydrate and fat intakes are extremely low.

Protein: Essential for building and repairing cells in the human body. Excess protein intake is converted into fat in the body. Support tissue growth and repair; helps produce antibodies, hormones and enzymes which are essential for all chemical reactions in the body. Dietary protein sources include fish, dairy products, poultry, meet, dried nuts, eggs and nuts.

Proteoglycans (PGS): Any group of substances found primarily in the matrix of connected tissues and synovial fluid. Proteoglycans solutions are highly viscous lubricants.

Provocative discogram: A radiological procedure in which a contrast dye or saline is injected into an intervertebral disc. Placement of the needle is performed under fluoroscopy. The saline is injected in an attempt to produce the patient's discogenic pain.

Pseudococcydynia: False coccyx or tailbone pain. Pain felt in the coccyx area but located elsewhere and referred to the coccyx.

Radiation therapy: Also called radiotherapy. It involves the use of high-energy rays to destroy the reproductive material of cancer cells in the hopes of destroying them and preventing them from multiplying. It may be given as an initial therapy or can be given as an adjuvant or supplemental therapy after surgery.

Radicular pain: Pain that radiates from a spinal nerve and travels into the arms or the legs.

Radiculopathy: Disease of a nerve resulting in deterioration and weakness of the muscles supplied by the nerve.

Radioisotope: Radioactive isotope used as a tracer in certain radiographic studies for diagnostic purposes.

Radiology: A branch of medicine and health sciences involved with radioactive substances and radiant energy. This branch of medicine deals with the diagnosis and treatment of disease by using ionizing (i.e. x-rays, CAT scans) and non-ionized (ultrasound) radiation ,magnetic frequencies (MRI), positron emission tomography (PET), and others.

Radionuclide scan: A radiographic procedure in which a radioisotope is injected into a patient's blood system. The radionuclide will be taken up by various tissues. The images will be provided from radiation sources admitted from the substances in the body. A special radiation Geiger counter is positioned outside the body to detect the radiation emitted from the radionuclide. An excellent examination to evaluate the image and functions of certain structures. Hot spots often indicate potential areas of inflammation or tumor.

Radius: A bone of the forearm. When turning the forearm over, the radius rotates around another forearm bone called the ulna.

Red blood cells: Pigmented cells in blood that give blood its color. Red blood cells are manufactured in the bone marrow and circulate throughout the blood stream. They have a large surface area to absorb oxygen from the lungs. These cells are flexible enough to squeeze through very small blood vessels. Their lifetime is approximately 120 days before they are broken down in the spleen.

Referred pain: Pain originating in one site and perceived as originating in a more distant site. It is felt in one part of the body, which is at a distance from its area of origin.

Retinaculum: Strap of firm tissue that holds down the tendons of the extensor muscles to the bone at the level of the wrist.

Reye's Syndrome: A childhood degenerative condition of the liver and brain that often follows a viral disease such as influenza or Chicken pox. Because of the possible link of aspirin to Reye's Syndrome, non-aspirin medications, such as acetaminophen or ibuprofen are often used to control fever during infections in children under the age of 12 years. Parents should always check with a physician before giving such medications.

Rheumatoid arthritis (RA): A chronic disorder that causes joints to become painful, stiff, swollen and deformed. An inflammation of the lining of the joints as well as other internal organs. It occurs when the synovial membranes of joints become inflamed. Joint movements become painful. Rheumatoid arthritis can also cause fatigue, weight loss, and fever.

Rheumatoid arthritis: Typically affects many different joints.

Rheumatoid factor: A blood test to measure abnormal antibodies (immunoglobulin, IgG). Abnormal IgG antibodies are produced by the lymphocytes in the synovial membranes. They act as antigens. Other antibodies react with these abnormal antigens and produce immune complexes. In patients with rheumatoid arthritis, the immune system dysfunctions and creates abnormal antibodies. Approximately 80% of people with rheumatoid arthritis have a positive rheumatoid factor blood test.

Rheumatoid nodules: Affects approximately 20% of patients with rheumatoid arthritis. Painless, hard, oval or round tissue masses that appear under the skin. Found at pressure points such as fingers, elbows, feet, and over the spine.

Rostral: May mean superior (in relationship to areas of the spinal cord) or anterior (in relationship to brain areas),

Rotator cuff tear: Partial or complete tearing of the rotator cuff resulting in shoulder pain, weakness and loss of normal movement. Wear and strain on the rotator cuff can cause weak areas that eventually produce tears. Patients may feel or hear a cracking or popping sound in the shoulder.

Rotator cuff: A group of three powerful muscles and connecting tendons. These muscles and tendons attach the upper arm to the shoulder blade. The rotator cuff is involved with movement of the arm for reaching, throwing, pushing, pulling, lifting, and golfing. The rotator cuff provides shoulder strength, flexibility and control.

Ruptured tendon or tendon injury: A tear in one of the tough and fibrous bands that attach muscle to bone.

Sacroiliac joint: The connection of the sacrum to the pelvis on each side. Contains synovial fluid and is surrounded by strong ligaments and fibrous tissues.

Sacroiliac joint syndrome: Pain originating from the sacroiliac joint.

Sacroiliac ligaments: Paired ligaments with attachments at the sacrum and the ilium.

Sacrum: The triangular shaped bone attached to the lumbar spine. It is made up of five fused vertebra.

Sagittal plane: A plane of the body dividing the body into left and right halves.

Sarcoma: Tumors that arise in bone, muscle, and cartilage.

Sciatica: A pain usually located in the buttocks or posterior thigh region and radiates along the outside or lateral aspect of the leg and/or foot. The name given is due to the patient's complaints of pain in the region of the body that is supplied by the sciatic nerve.

Semicircular canal: Three fluid filled canals of the ear that are concerned with balance.

Sequestered disc: Nucleus pulposus material escapes into the spinal canal as a free fragment. It is no longer attached to the material remaining inside the disc. This type of disc herniation may be referred to as a canal mouse.

Shopping Cart Syndrome: Related to lumbar spinal stenosis. Activities such as pushing a shopping cart will allow an individual to assume a flexion of the lumbar spine, which may relieve the symptoms brought about by the narrowed spinal canal. Individuals may report that using a cart allows them to more effectively complete their task of shopping.

Signs: Physical findings that a physician or healthcare provider is able to elicit during a physical examination.

Slipped disc: Herniated nucleus pulposus. The herniation of the central gelatinous substance of a disc of the cervical, thoracic or lumbar spines.

Soft corns: Soft corns are like calluses that develop due to accumulation of thickened, dead skin between the toes. Result of bony prominences. Are soft due to perspiration between the toes.

Soft disc: Referred to as a herniated nucleus pulposus, it is made up of soft tissue elements such as the nucleus pulposus, annulus and ligament.

Somatosensory Evoked Potentials (SSEP): Diagnostic and monitoring test to assess the speed of electrical conduction across the spinal cord. May be used during certain operations.

Spasticity: Increased tone or rigid state of a muscle. Indicates an abnormal underlying neurological (brain, spinal cord) disorder.

SPECT Scan: A form of radionuclide scanning, produces images that show the function of cells.

Spinal canal: The canal or passageway formed by articulated bones of the spine. It is the foramen through which the spinal cord passes.

Spinal cord: Part of the central nervous system. It is delicate gray and white nervous tissue. It extends from a part of the brain called the medulla oblongata and passes through the spinal canal and terminates as the conus medullaris. Nerves exit the spinal cord and travel to various organs of the body.

Spinal fluid: See cerebrospinal fluid.

Spinal instability: Loss of general support structures in the spine; may be due to disc degeneration, ligament laxity, or bony destruction (traumatic or pathological). Spine unable to maintain normal alignment; may cause slip or movement of bony elements causing pain and injury to nearby nerves and/or spinal cord. May require surgical intervention.

Spinal stenosis: The reduction of the size of the spinal canal or nearby bony elements. May compromise nerves within the canal or exiting the canal. Three types: A). Congenital stenosis: Malformation at birth; B) Developmental stenosis: Malformation of genetic origin; and C) Acquired stenosis: Bony changes after birth and with aging, often leading to entrapment of nerves.

Spinal tap: A sampling of cerebrospinal fluid removed from the spinal canal by use of a long spinal needle. The spinal fluid is used to diagnose certain diseases of the brain and spinal cord.

Spine: The backbone. The vertebral column. The head sits on one end and the individual sits on the other end. It is divided into the cervical, thoracic, lumbar, sacrum and coccyx. It is the entire group of articulated bones that connect to the skull and end with the coccyx.

Spinous process: A projection of bony tissue located on the posterior (back) elements of the spine. It is in the middle of the posterior bony elements at the junction of the lamina (rooftop). It serves as an insertion site for ligaments. It is the spinous process that is often palpated along the middle of an individual's back.

Spondylogenic pain: Pain originating from bony elements.

Spondylolisthesis: An anterior slippage or movement of one vertebra in relationship to the inferior adjacent vertebra.

Spondylolisthesis: The anterior (front) displacement of a vertebra on the adjacent vertebra below. May occur due to several causes: A) Isthmic: Defect of the pars interarticularis. Often a birth defect. B) Degenerative: Anterior displacement of a vertebra due to degenerative changes of the facet joints. This type commonly occurs in the more mature individual, the elderly, and is often associated with spinal stenosis. C) Traumatic: Anterior displacement of vertebra due to traumatic injury. The type seen in an athlete.

Spondylolysis: A defect of the pars interarticularis; however, the vertebral body does not significantly move and the normal alignment of the spine is maintained.

Spondyloptosis: A spondylolisthesis or slippage of L5 in which the vertebral body has entirely slipped off the top of the sacrum and is located in the pelvic cavity.

Spondylosis: Degenerative changes that occur in the spine, vertebra, at articulation points.

Sprain: An injury in which some of the fibers of a supporting ligament are ruptured, but the continuity of the ligament remains intact.

Spur: Calcium growth that develops on bone. May be an abnormal process of bone. In the spine, it may subject nearby nerves to pressure or compression, thus producing pain.

Starch: Complex carbohydrate. Provides sustained energy. Foods such as pasta, bread, potatoes, and rice contain high levels of starch.

Strain: An overstretching or overexertion of some part of the musculature.

Stress fracture: Non-displaced fracture through a bone, caused by repeated episodes of recurrent stress. Bones are broken, yet remain in normal position.

Stroke: A leading cause of death, disability and enormous healthcare costs. A brain attack that occurs when blood supply to the brain is suddenly reduced or cut off. An ischemic stroke occurs when blood flow through vessels in the neck, head or brain are blocked. If the blood vessel ruptures in the vein, it is called a hemorrhagic stroke. A temporary blockage of blood flow to the brain is called transient ischemic attack (TIA). The faster a stroke is diagnosed and treated, the better the outcome with fewer brain cells damaged. Symptoms include: sudden weakness or numbness of the face, arm or leg; sudden loss of vision; sudden difficulty speaking or understanding the spoken word; sudden severe headaches with no cause; unexplained dizziness, unsteadiness or sudden falls. Urgent emergency treatment is needed if a stroke is suspected.

Subarachnoid space: It is the space between the layers of tissue covering the brain and spine. The subarachnoid space is filled with spinal fluid. It is often the site into which an aneurysm (blood blister) of the brain or spinal cord ruptures.

Subaxial: The part of the spine below the axis.

Subluxation: A partial dislocation. May be due to a pathological process in which there is not a normal juxtaposition of the articular surfaces of a joint.

Subtalar joint: The posterior (back) joint between the talus and the calcaneum.

Subtarsal joint: Joint located below the tarsus, the region of the articulation (joint) between the foot and the leg.

Subungual hematoma: Blood accumulation beneath the toenail.

Sugar: Simple carbohydrate. Provides body with quick energy boost.

Superior: An anatomical structure located above a point of reference. The opposite is inferior.

Symptom: A complaint from a patient regarding something that is wrong or something that is perceived as not right. One of the most common symptoms reported by a patient is pain. Other bodily functions that a patient may perceive as abnormal may relate to weakness, burning or numbness throughout the body or an extremity.

Synovial joint: A joint with articulating surfaces that are covered by a layer of hyaline cartilage. The entire joint is contained within a fibrous capsule lined with a membrane and containing synovial fluid. The synovial fluid is a lubricant between the articulating bony surfaces.

Talus: The tarsal bone that joins with the tibia and the fibula bones of the leg to form the ankle bone. Also called the ankle bone.

Tarsal bones: Bones of the foot. The tarsal bones are the calcaneum, the talus, the navicular, the cuboid, and the three cuneiform. The talus bones lie below the ankle joint and form the instep.

Tarsal tunnel: A space on the inner side of the hind-foot, just below the bony prominence at the end of the tibia.

Tendonitis: Inflammation of a tendon, a fibrous cord that attaches muscle to bone.

Tennis elbow: A form of tendonitis. Occurs when the tendon attachment of a muscle to the bone at the elbow becomes damaged.

Tensile band: Commonly referred to as the posterior (back) spinal muscle groups, which work collectively like a rubber band to maintain upright posture.

Therapeutic radiology: Better known as radiation oncology. It is a branch of radiology that uses ionizing radiation in the treatment of cancer, certain abnormal tissues and tumors.

Thoracic disc disease: Abnormalities of the intervertebral discs of the thoracic spine.

Thoracic spine: Relates to the thorax of the body. It is the mid-spine, composed of twelve (12) vertebra located between the cervical spine above and the lumbar spine below.

Thoracic T4 syndrome: Refers to the fourth thoracic vertebra and pain radiating from between the shoulders. Usually occurs in the upper thoracic spine from the first thoracic level to the seventh thoracic level.

Thoracotomy: A surgical incision into the wall of the chest.

Tibia: The shinbone. A large medial (inside) bone of the leg. Supports the greater part of the weight on the leg.

Tietze syndrome: A painful swelling of one or more cartilages, especially the ribs. Causes anterior chest pain, which may mimic pain of coronary artery disease.

Tinea pedis: Athlete's foot, a very common fungal infection of the feet in golfers and athletes.

Transverse process: Located on the right and left side of the vertebral bodies and extends along the side (laterally) of each pedicle.

Triangular fibrocartilage: Tough triangular piece of cartilage, which holds the radius and ulna forearm bones in place.

True coccydynia: Most common cause is trauma. A fracture of the coccyx bone.

Tumor necrosis factor-Alpha (TNF-Alpha): A substance made by cells that promotes inflammation in the body.
Tumor: An uncontrolled growth of cells that can cause an excess of tissue.

Ulna: A bone of the forearm.

Ultrasound: Gentle sound waves used to warm deep tissues in muscles. May improve blood flow and alleviate sore muscles. Cortisone (steroid) cream may be worked into muscles when using ultrasound.

Urinalysis: The physical, chemical and microscopic analysis of urine for abnormalities.

Vascular claudication: Caused by narrowing of major arteries supplying blood to the legs. Worsened by walking. Standing may relieve the symptoms, lying down may aggravate or make the symptoms worse. Vascular claudication usually starts in the lower legs and extends up the legs to the lower back.

Vasculitis: Inflammation of blood vessels.

Vertebra (plural: vertebrae): Any of the 33 bones of the spinal column comprising the seven (7) cervical, twelve (12) thoracic, five (5) lumbar, five (5) sacrum, and the four (4) coccygeal vertebra.

Vertebral body: A large cylindrical portion of a vertebra of the spine. It is the weight-bearing portion of the vertebra. It is located anterior (front) to the spinal cord and nerves.

Vertebral-basilar artery insufficiency: The vertebral artery and basilar artery are blood vessels that carry blood and oxygen to the brain that provides balance.

Vertebroplasty: Fixing the vertebral body. A treatment for vertebral body fractures caused by osteoporosis in which a bone needle is passed into the vertebral body and a bone cement containing polymethylmethacrylate (PMMA) is injected to help restore bone strength and reduce pain.

Vertigo: Sensation of spinning with dizziness, commonly associated with nausea, vomiting and blurred vision. A false sensation of moving or spinning often associated with nausea and vomiting.

Vertigo: The sensation of loss of balance in an irregular and whirling motion of oneself or of nearby object.

Virus: An infectious organism that is cable of growing and reproducing within a living cell. Some viruses produce human disease, difficult to irradicate and may remain in the body indefinitely.

Viscerogenic pain: Pain originating from viscera or organs within the body.

Vitamins and minerals: Vitamins and minerals play vital roles in growth, metabolism and health. All vitamins and minerals must come from an individual's diet, except Vitamin K, which is formed by intestinal bacteria, and Vitamin D, which is produced in the skin by the action of sunlight. Certain vitamins such as A, D, E, and K are harmful if consumed in excess. Always consult a physician, nutritionist, or healthcare provider before using large amounts of any vitamin or mineral.

Warts: Skin growths caused by viruses. Often mistaken for corns or calluses on the sole of the foot.

Water: A nutrient. Water needed more than any other nutrient. Regulates almost every physical process in the body. Accounts for 55-75% of the body's weight. Essential for regulating body temperature, carrying nutrients and vitamins to body cells, removing waste products, and maintaining life. Most individuals do not drink enough water during activities of daily living or playing golf. A minimum of eight 8oz. glasses of water a day are recommended.

White blood cells: Five main types of white blood cells: 1) neutrophils; 2) ephenophils; 3) lymphocytes; 4) basophils; and 5) monocytes. Some of these cells help to destroy foreign organisms.

X-ray: Also called roentgenograms. Commonly generated by passing a high-voltage current through a special tube (Coolidge). Able to penetrate many substances of the body, thus revealing certain body structures, foreign objects, or radio-opaque substances. Used for fluoroscopy and CAT (CT) scans. Due to their high energy, they are used in treating various pathological conditions (radiation treatment).

Randip R. Bindra, M.D.
Associate Professor
Orthopaedic Surgery
College of Medicine
University of Arkansas for
Medical Sciences
Little Rock, Arkansas

Thomas A. Boers, P.T., M.T.
Human Performance &
Rehabilitation Center
Rehabilitation Services of Columbus
Columbus, Georgia

John L. Dornhoffer, M.D.
Associate Professor
Otolaryngology-Head and Neck Surgery
College of Medicine
University of Arkansas for
Medical Sciences
Little Rock, Arkansas

Bill J. Gurley, B.S., Ph.D.
Associate Professor
Pharmaceutical Services
College of Pharmacy
University of Arkansas for
Medical Sciences
Little Rock, Arkansas

Randy Henry, PGA Professional Founder
President
Henry-Griffitts, Inc.
Hayden Lake, Idaho

Carolyn E. Kennedy, M.S., R.D.
Program Coordinator
Center for Weight Control
University of Arkansas for
Medical Sciences
Little Rock, Arkansas

Richard E. McCarthy, M.D.
Arkansas Spine Center, P.A.
Arkansas Children's Hospital
Little Rock, Arkansas

Bruce Mendelson, B.A., P.T., Ph.D.
Assistant Professor
Department of Anatomy
and Neurobiology
College of Medicine
University of Arkansas for
Medical Sciences
Little Rock, Arkansas

T. Glenn Pait, M.D., F.A.C.S.
Associate Professor
Neurosurgery and Orthopaedic Surgery
College of Medicine
University of Arkansas for
Medical Sciences
Little Rock, Arkansas

Jack Sheehan
Author
Las Vegas, Nevada

Jackson T. Stephens
President
Stephens, Inc.
Little Rock, Arkansas

Ruth L. Thomas, M.D.
Associate Professor
Orthopaedic Surgery
College of Medicine
University of Arkansas for
Medical Sciences
Little Rock, Arkansas

John L. VanderSchilden, M.D.
Professor
Orthopaedic Surgery
College of Medicine
University of Arkansas for
Medical Sciences
Little Rock, Arkansas

DePuy AcroMed, Johnson & Johnson and Marks Creative.com

Chapter 2:
Body Changes that Occur with Aging:
Figures 1, 2.
Chapter 3:
Some Thoughts about Spine and Spinal Cord Anatomy:
Figure 6.
Chapter 6:
The Cervical Spine (Neck):
Figure 24a.
Chapter 8:
The Lumbar Spine (Low Back):
Figures 31, 32, 33.
Chapter 10:
Spinal Deformities and Their Effect Upon Golf:
Figures 2a, 6.
Chapter 15:
Osteoporosis:
Figures 18, 19a.
Chapter 18:
Traumatic Fractures of the Spine:
Figures 14a, 15, 18a-d.

Medtronic Sofamor Danek

Chapter 2:
Body Changes that Occur with Aging:
Figures 4, 5, 6, 10, 13, 14.
Chapter 3:
Some Thoughts about Spine and Spinal Cord Anatomy:
Figures 2a, 2b, 3, 4, 5, 7, 8, 9, 10, 11, 13, 18, 19, 20, 22.
Chapter 5:
Medical Radiology:
Figures 1, 5, 6, 7, 14.
Chapter 6:
The Cervical Spine (Neck):
Figures 1a, 1b, 3, 8, 9, 11, 21, 23, 31, 33, 36.
Chapter 7:
The Thoracic Spine (Mid-Spine):
Figures 1, 2, 3, 4, 7, 8.
Chapter 8:
The Lumbar Spine (Low Back):
Figures 1a, 1b, 4, 6, 7, 10, 12, 14, 15, 20, 24, 25, 26, 27a, 27b, 28, 29a-f, 36, 40.
Chapter 9:
Sacroiliac Joint Syndrome and Coccydynia:
Figures 3, 4.
Chapter 10:
Spinal Deformities and Their Effect Upon Golf:
Figures 1, 3, 9, 12a-c, 13, 14a-c.
Chapter 14:
Arthritis:
Figures 1, 2, 3, 9.
Chapter 15:
Osteoporosis:
Figures 2, 4, 5.
Chapter 16:
Tumors of the Spine (Neoplasms):
Figures 1, 3, 6, 7, 8, 9, 10, 11, 12a, 13, 14a, 15, 16, 17.
Chapter 17:
Infections of the Spine:
Figure 4.
Chapter 18:
Traumatic Fractures of the Spine:
Figures 2a, 2b, 3, 4, 5a, 6, 13a, 13b, 21.

SpineUniverse.com

Chapter 2:
Body Changes that Occur with Aging:
Figures 3, 7, 8, 9, 11, 12.
Chapter 3:
Some Thoughts about Spine and Spinal Cord Anatomy:
Figures 1, 12, 14, 15, 16, 17, 21.
Chapter 6:
The Cervical Spine (Neck):
Figures 2, 7, 10.
Chapter 7:
The Thoracic Spine (Mid-Spine):
Figure 5.
Chapter 8:
The Lumbar Spine (Low Back):
Figures 2a, 2b, 3, 8, 9, 13.
Chapter 10:
Spinal Deformities and Their Effect Upon Golf:
Figures 4, 5, 8a.
Chapter 18:
Traumatic Fractures of the Spine:
Figure 1.

Hitachi Medical Systems America, Inc.

Chapter 5:
Medical Radiology:
Figures 11a, 11b.

Fager, Charles A: *Atlas of Spinal Surgery*, Lea & Febiger: Philadelphia, 1989

Chapter 8:
The Lumbar Spine (Low Back):
Figures 21a, 21b.

Kyphon, Inc.

Chapter 15:
Osteoporosis:
Figures 1a, 1b, 13, 14, 15a, 16.

Amy Theriac, Medical Photographer, University of Arkansas for Medical Sciences

Chapter 11:
Maladies of the Upper and Lower Extremity in Golf:
Figures 1-13.

University of Arkansas for Medical Sciences

Chapter 18:
Traumatic Fractures of the Spine:
Figure 7.

Golf "Friends" Forever

Who served, admired, and loved the sport of golf.

Jack Stephens and Bob Jones

Jack Stephens and Clifford Roberts

Hootie Johnson and Jack Stephens